Audiometric Interpretation

AUDIOMETRIC INTERPRETATION
Second Edition

A Manual of Basic Audiometry

Harriet Kaplan
Vic S. Gladstone
Lyle L. Lloyd

Allyn and Bacon
Boston   London   Toronto   Sydney   Tokyo   Singapore

Series Editor: Mylan Jaixen
Editorial Assistant: Sue Hutchinson
Cover Administrator: Linda Dickinson
Manufacturing Buyer: Megan Cochran
Editorial-Production Service: Technical Texts
Cover Designer: Suzanne Harbison

Library of Congress Cataloging-in-Publication Data
Kaplan, Harriet.
    Audiometric interpretation / Harriet Kaplan, Vic S. Gladstone, Lyle L. Lloyd. — 2nd ed.
        p.   cm.
    Includes bibliographical references and index.
    ISBN 0-205-14753-4
    1. Audiometry.   I. Gladstone, Vic.   II. Lloyd, Lyle L.   III. Title.
RF294.K372   1993
617.8'075—dc20
                                                                92-46331
                                                                CIP

Printed in the United States of America
10 9 8 7 6   98 97 96 95

Contents

Preface

This book is designed as a clinical training device for students in audiology, speech–language pathology, and special education, and for others concerned with the problems of deaf and hard-of-hearing people. It is intended as a supplementary text/workbook to be used in conjunction with class lectures and audiology texts, such as *Hearing and Deafness* (Davis and Silverman, 1978), *Audiology* (Newby and Popelka, 1985), *Hearing Assessment* (Rintelman, 1991), *Basic Principles of Auditory Assessment* (Hannley, 1986), and *Introduction to Audiology* (Martin, 1991). Optimal utilization of this book assumes an elementary knowledge of aural anatomy, physiology, and pathology such as would be covered in an introductory course in audiology. An acquaintance with the administration of the basic audiometric tests (air conduction, bone conduction, immittance, and speech audiometry) and the appropriate use of masking are also recommended.

This book is also intended to serve as a basic text in audiometric interpretation. Therefore, it focuses on the interpretation of basic pure tone, immittance, and speech audiometric tests. Such tests as Threshold Tone Decay, SISI, Bekesy, Auditory Evoked Potentials, ENG, and Central Auditory procedures are not discussed in this book although their importance as diagnostic tools is recognized by all authorities.

The interpretation of the audiologic assessment is important to all nonmedical professionals who serve deaf and hard-of-hearing people, as well as to qualified physicians. The nonmedical professional can provide valuable assistance to the physician in the diagnosis of ear pathology by providing information found in the audiogram. Audiometric interpretation is of equal importance for purposes of habilitation and rehabilitation, since the audiologic assessment provides a considerable amount of significant nonmedical information.

Because this book is primarily designed as a programmed introduction to audiometric interpretation, it begins with a general overview of audiometry in Chapter 1. Subsequent chapters (Chapters 2 to 7) confront the student with audiograms and other significant information programmed to provide a progression of experiences in the interpretation of audiometric information. Each of these chapters is internally sequenced from easy to progressively more difficult problems in audiometric interpretation. The chapters are also arranged for increasingly more involved problems of audiometric interpretation, with each chapter utilizing and often reviewing information from earlier chapters. The areas covered in these chapters are as follows:

Chapter 2—Reading the Pure Tone Audiogram

This chapter seeks to train the student to recognize and read basic pure tone air and bone conduction audiometric information upon which interpretation can be based. This chapter applies the principles reviewed in Chapter 1.

Chapter 3—Acoustic Immittance

This chapter deals with tympanometry, static compliance, and acoustic reflex procedures. Its goal is to train the student to use results of the immittance battery in conjunction with pure tone information to identify possible middle ear disorders and to distinguish between conductive, cochlear, and retrocochlear problems.

Chapter 4—Interpreting Speech Audiometry

In this chapter speech recognition thresholds, word recognition, and tolerance tests, as well as the significance of the most comfortable listening level (MCL) are discussed. The student is exposed to various procedures and types of materials. In addition, on the basis of pure tone, immittance, and speech audiometric information presented, the student is asked to make judgments on agreement between results of these procedures. Presence, degree, and type of hearing impairment are also considered. Medical significance is discussed in terms of probable outer or middle ear involvement on the one hand, as opposed to inner ear or central auditory involvement on the other. The consideration of type of impairment in this chapter does not include the more advanced tests of differential diagnosis, such as Auditory Evoked Potentials, ENG, and the tests designed to distinguish between cochlear, retrocochlear, and central auditory sites of dysfunction (except for acoustic reflex measurements).

Chapter 5—Use of Masking

In this chapter the student learns the appropriate use of masking for pure tone and speech audiometry. The student is trained to judge when masking is needed and how much masking is appropriate. Types of maskers, undermasking, overmasking, effective level calibration, and the plateau are discussed. Cases are presented to illustrate these concepts, as well as various types of masking problems.

Chapter 6—Interpreting the Basic Battery

In this chapter the concepts and procedures discussed in the previous chapters are integrated to allow the student to use information present in the entire test battery. This chapter builds upon all the information presented in previous chapters. Here the student learns to evaluate the complete audiometric assessment for its response consistency and inter-test agreement.

Chapter 7—Educational and Communicative Implications of the Hearing Loss

This chapter considers the general educational, medical, and communicative significance of different types and degrees of hearing loss. It also considers ways in which reduced auditory reception and word recognition affect an individual's educational style. Amplification needs associated with various types of hearing problems are discussed, as are the speech and language issues related to hearing impairment. Cases are presented to illustrate how hearing loss disrupts the normal development of speech and language and how they affect the servo mechanism.

Throughout the book, frequent references are made to other texts, didactic articles, and secondary sources, as well as to original and research sources. These references are provided to encourage further investigation and review of specific problems in audiologic assessment. The book departs from conventional form by not only citing authors(s) and date but by also giving the page when reference is made to a basic audiology text. The page reference is provided to facilitate further investigation of a subject by students in training. Page numbers are omitted in references that the authors feel do not require review of the original material.

Each chapter concludes with several review and search projects. These projects consist of questions, discussion topics, and assigned experiences designed to review certain basic audiologic principles covered to that point in the text. The projects are also planned to expand upon material covered in this book. Some of the projects include bibliographical references, while others are less structured and allow students to use their own resources, including references cited elsewhere in this text.

Acknowledgments

This book was partially funded by a faculty development grant from Gallaudet University.

We would like to thank the following reviewers for their helpful suggestions: Carol Messerly, coordinator of the Secondary Hearing Impaired Program, Mayfield City Schools, Mayfield Heights, OH, and instructor at Case Western Reserve University, Cleveland; John Hawks, Kent State University, Kent, OH; and David Shepherd, University of South Florida, Tampa.

Audiometric Interpretation

AUDIOLOGIC ASSESSMENT FORM

There is considerable variation in the audiogram forms used in various clinical settings, but this book consistently uses the Audiologic Assessment Form shown in Figure 1-1. In addition to the pure tone audiogram and general information about it, the Audiologic Assessment Form provides space for recording the results of speech and immittance audiometry. On the audiogram itself is space for recording the levels of masking used to obtain masked thresholds. Figures 1-2 through 1-8 show portions of the Audiologic Assessment Form in the sections in which specific procedures are described. Pure tone audiometry is discussed in this chapter to allow the reader to understand the cases presented in Chapter 2. Speech audiometry, immittance testing, and masking levels are discussed briefly in this chapter and in greater detail in subsequent chapters.

General Information About the Audiogram

Almost all audiogram forms contain space for recording certain basic client identification data, testing conditions (including response consistency), and other information relevant to the audiometric assessment. Identification information is recorded on the top section of the Audiologic Assessment Form shown in Figure 1-1. Some audiogram forms used in various clinics include space for information such as address, phone referral source, otologic report, and other specific case history information. Such information has been eliminated from the Audiologic Assessment Form used in this manual in an attempt to organize all of the basic audiometric information on one page. The general information on the Audiologic Assessment Form includes: (1) identification information, (2) symbols used in recording pure tone responses, (3) response consistency, and (4) space for remarks.

Identifying Information The Audiologic Assessment Form includes the basic information of a given audiologic assessment but avoids unnecessary duplication of information that should be contained elsewhere in the client's case folder. The exclusion of case history information by no means is intended as an indication that such information is not essential in the assessment, diagnosis, and subsequent (re)habilitation of a particular client. In fact, the exclusion of case history information on the Audiologic Assessment Form reflects the philosophy that the audiologic assessment is only one part of a complete audiologic workup. Complete assessment, diagnosis, and planning usually require a considerable amount of non-audiometric but equally significant information. It is important that the basic information requested on the Audiologic Assessment Form be completed for each evaluation.

The age of the client always is considered in evaluating audiometric findings. It should also be noted that the age and date recorded on the audiogram are very important in considering a series of successive audiometric tests. Certain normal changes in audiometric findings may occur with time and may be considered within normal limits, but other changes may be clinically significant. If the age and date information is lacking from a series of audiograms, it may be impossible to establish a progres-

Name: Fig 1-1   Date: XX/XX/XX   Age: 15   Sex: M   Audiologist: H K

AUDIOMETER: GSI-10   ANSI 1969

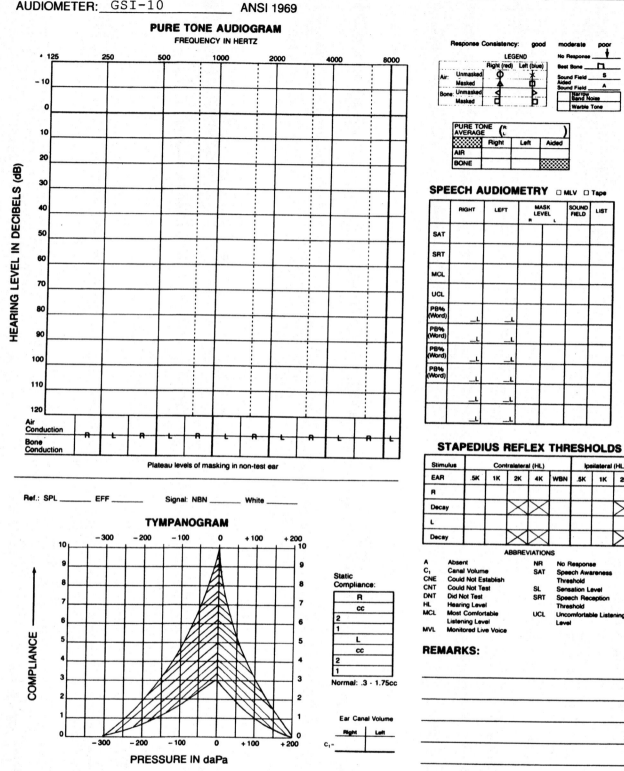

Figure 1-1. Audiologic Assessment Form.

sive history of hearing loss for a particular client. The age and date information on a series of audiograms may account for reasonable changes of hearing for a particular client as being age dependent. The early pure tone results of young children may sometimes be suprathreshold. The elderly client may show a "normal" decrease in hearing acuity with age (Rintelmann, 1991:526–528).

The name of the examiner should always appear on each audiologic assessment. The name of the examiner may be important in scheduling subsequent examinations, in obtaining follow-up information (including observations made during the examination), and for possible inclusion in subsequent staffings of the client. In a training situation, if the testing is done by a student in training (regardless of the level of training), the audiogram should include the name of the supervising audiologist in addition to the student clinician's name.

Inclusion of the names of the audiometers used in the evaluation may also be of practical significance. If a routine calibration check of the audiometers in the clinic reveals that an audiometer is out of calibration, only those audiograms done with that particular instrument need be questioned and possibly retested because of the calibration error.

Response Consistency The clinician should also record judgments concerning the consistency of the client's responses. Good response consistency means that the client responded to the presence of tone whenever a stimulus was presented above the client's threshold and approximately 50% of the time when it was presented at the client's threshold. The client did not respond when stimuli were not presented (a response in the absence of a stimulus is called a false positive) and did not fail to respond to stimuli presented at known suprathreshold levels (false negative response). When there are many false positive or false negative responses, response consistency must be judged poor; when there is a moderate number of false responses, response consistency is judged moderate. Poor response consistency may occur in speech audiometry as well as in pure tone audiometry, although false negative responses are more common than false positive responses when speech is the stimulus. An example of false negative responding in speech audiometry is the client who repeats 100% of the

words presented to a particular level and none of the words presented at a level 5 dB less intense. Since we define threshold as that level at which the client responds to 50% of the stimuli presented, we know that the 100% level is above threshold, and we can assume that we are observing false negative responses.

Judgment of response consistency is used by the clinician to make some judgment about the predicted temporal reliability of audiometric findings or what should be obtained from subsequent tests. If response consistency is judged good or moderate, subsequent test results should vary no more than ±5 dB. If response consistency is judged to be either good or moderate, no further comment is necessary. However, if response consistency is judged to be poor, some remarks about the reasons for the questionable test results should be made.

Symbols Used in Recording Pure Tone Responses
The symbols used to indicate pure tone findings by both air conduction (AC) and bone conduction (BC) with and without masking should be printed on any standard audiometric form. Although most audiologists use the symbols recommended by the ASHA Committee on Audiological Evaluation (ASHA, 1990, Supplement 2:25–30), symbol standardization is not universal. Therefore, a key or legend for the symbols used in a given audiogram is necessary.

The Audiologic Assessment Form (Figure 1-1) uses most of the symbols for reporting pure tone threshold results recommended by the ASHA Committee on Audiological Evaluation (ASHA, 1990, Supplement 2:25–30). The key for symbols used in the Audiologic Assessment Form has been reproduced in Figure 1-2. The unmasked air conduction thresholds are indicated by a blue "X" for the left ear and a red "O" for the right ear. (Students often use the phrase "red round right" to remember these symbols.) Although color coding is helpful in differentiating between ears, ASHA recommendations do not specify color coding and suggest it only as a personal option for clarity. The masked air conduction thresholds are indicated by a blue square for the left ear and a red triangle for the right ear. Color coding is not used in this book because clinicians are frequently required to interpret duplicates of

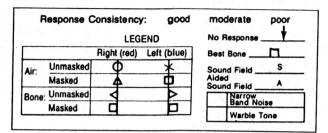

Figure 1-2. Symbols for recording pure tone thresholds on the Audiologic Assessment Form.

audiograms. Color is not preserved in the duplicating process. Nevertheless, the audiologist is encouraged to use the color coding on audiograms whenever possible.

The unmasked bone conduction thresholds are indicated by a blue arrow opening to left for the left ear and a red arrow opening to the right for the right ear. Masked bone conduction thresholds are indicated by rectangles open on one side. A blue rectangle opening to the left represents masked bone conduction for the left ear and a red rectangle opening to the right represents masked bone conduction for the right ear. The symbols always represent the ear receiving the stimulus. The inverted bracket (see Legend) represents "best bone conduction" or "unspecified bone response" [ASHA suggests using the inverted V (Λ)]. Unless bone conduction thresholds are obtained with masking noise in the opposite ear, it is unclear which ear is actually hearing the sound. In some test situations, however, it is not necessary to know which ear is actually hearing the bone-conducted stimulus. We then record the client's response as "best bone conduction." This concept is further discussed in Chapter 5 of this book.

The symbol for sound field air conduction is an "S" centered on the appropriate frequency axis. When sound field responses are obtained with the client using a hearing aid, an "A" centered on the appropriate frequency is used. It is always necessary to indicate on the Audiologic Assessment Form whether the sound field air conduction stimulus was warble tone or narrow band noise. "No response" symbols consist of the appropriate air or bone conduction symbol with an arrow pointing vertically downward.

The air conduction thresholds for the various frequencies are connected with a blue line for the left ear and a red line for the right ear, forming air con-

duction "curves" for the left and right ears, respectively. Some audiologists use appropriately colored broken lines to form bone condition threshold "curves," but this procedure has not been used in this book. For further discussion of the recording of thresholds on the audiogram, see audiology texts such as Martin (1991:70–82), Newby and Popelka (1985:145–150) and Hannley (1986:129–131).

Abbreviations A number of abbreviations are commonly used in recording speech and audiometric results and masking levels. Although not all audiometric forms include an explanatory key, the Audiological Assessment Form used in this book does contain one. The abbreviations CNE (could not establish) or CNT (could not test) are used when a particular measure is attempted but not obtained. For example, if a speech recognition threshold could not be measured, the abbreviation CNE or CNT would be inserted in the appropriate box. If a test was not attempted, the abbreviation DNT (did not test) is used. The terms SL (sensation level) and HL (hearing level) signify reference levels. When a sound level is reported in dB SL, it means that the level is referenced to the listener's threshold for that sound; when a sound level is reported in dB HL, it is referenced to audiometric zero, which is discussed later in this chapter. It is necessary to record the appropriate reference level when indicating the decibel level at which word recognition material is presented. It is also necessary to note whether the masking noise was calibrated in SPL (sound pressure level) or in effective level. The subject of masking is discussed in detail in Chapter 5.

Remarks A small space is provided in the lower righthand side of the Audiologic Assessment Form for the brief notions the audiologist may wish to make. This space is quite small, and many times the audiologist will continue remarks on the back of the audiogram so that they can be a permanent part of the audiogram. In this space the audiologist may comment on client response behavior, on deviations from standard test procedure, or on anything else considered diagnostically important.

The preceding paragraphs briefly discuss the basic information that should be included on every audiogram. The omission of any of this information implies an incomplete assessment and in some cases may seriously limit the usefulness of a particular audiometric test.

Pure Tone Information

Most audiologic assessment forms contain pure tone audiograms, which are graphs on which the pure tone information is recorded. In addition, all forms provide space for recording of masking levels used in air and bone conduction testing, type of masking noise used, and calibration of the masking noise. On the Audiologic Assessment Form used in this manual the masking information is recorded directly under the pure tone audiogram.

Pure Tone Audiogram The results of the pure tone audiometric examination are recorded on the audiogram. An audiogram is a graph showing the hearing level on the ordinate lines and the frequency of the stimulus tone on the abscissa. A basic audiogram is shown in Figure 1-3. There is considerable variation in the audiograms used in clinical practice, but common to most pure tone audiogram forms is the basic graph shown in Figure 1-3.

The ordinate of the audiogram indicates the hearing level in decibels (dB HL). The horizontal line marked "0" on the ordinate represents the average threshold of a large number of non-pathologic ears tested in the United States and abroad. This average of "normal" ears is commonly referred to as "audiometric zero." As the ordinate scale descends, the decibel figures increase. This tells us that the intensity of the stimulus tone is increased above the zero audiometric reference point for "normal" hearing. Above the zero line of the graph the decibel figures are given a minus value. This indicates that the stimulus was even less loud than that represented by the audiometric zero. In

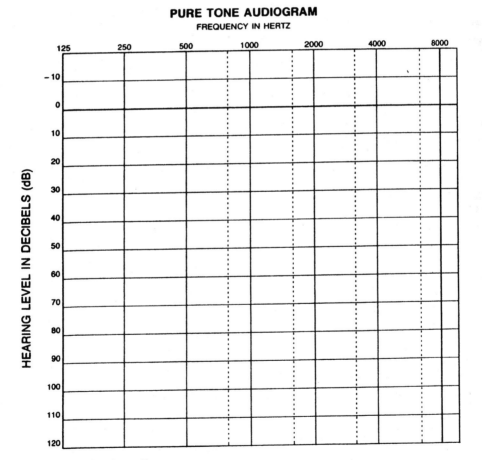

Figure 1-3. Basic audiogram.

summary, the lower a particular client's threshold is marked on the audiogram, the poorer the hearing sensitivity relative to the average "normal" ear, or the more the signal had to be increased in intensity to elicit a response from the client. The poorer a client's hearing, the higher his or her threshold (in decibels HL) is relative to audiometric zero.

It is important to understand that the decibel readings on the ordinate of the audiogram are not in sound pressure level (SPL) and therefore do not have the common physical reference of 0.0002 dynes/cm2, 0.0002 microbars, or 20 micropascals; instead they have as their reference audiometric zero (sometimes referred to as clinical zero) or average normal hearing. The SPL values which constitute audiometric zero are different at different frequencies and are normative values based on 15 separate studies. These normative values were accepted by the American National Standards Institute in 1969 and are known as ANSI S3.6-69 audiometric standards. Although ANSI S3.6-69 recently was replaced by ANSI S3.6-89, the reference thresholds for the Western Electric 705A earphone remain the same in both standards. The relationship between the audiometric scale of intensity and the threshold of audibility in reference to 0.0002 dyne/cm2 is discussed in several audiology texts (Davis and Silverman, 1978:25–27, 194–200; Martin, 1991:33–34; Newby and Popelka, 1985: 137–142; Melnick, 1971:203–206; Hannley, 1986: 90–94; Rintelmann, 1991:817–819).

Listed below are the SPL values that correspond to audiometric zero at each frequency according to ANSI S3.6-69 and ANSI S3.6-89 standards.

Hz	dB SPL
125	45.5
250	24.5
500	11.0
1000	6.5
1500	6.5
2000	8.5
3000	7.5
4000	9.0
6000	8.0
8000	9.5

Note that the SPL values vary slightly depending on the earphone used for calibration. The values

in the table were obtained with the Western Electric 705A earphone. Reference levels for other earphones have been specified in the body of the ANSI S3.6-89 standard. Discussion of the ANSI S3.6-89 standard and the threshold values for various commonly used earphones can be found in Rintelmann (1991:818, 841–842).

The abscissa indicates the frequency of the signal in cycles per second (cps) or Hertz (Hz), which is the more commonly used term. Most audiogram blanks are marked with vertical lines or coordinates which are labeled 125, 250, 500, 1000, 2000, 4000, and 8000 Hz. (Most audiologists do not test at 125 Hz.) In addition to these seven rather standard octave test frequencies, some audiograms indicate interoctave steps such as 750, 1500, 3000, and 6000 Hz. Audiologists tend to test at the interoctave frequencies when there are large differences in threshold between standard octave test frequencies (e.g., threshold would be evaluated at 750 Hz if thresholds of 20 dB HL at 500 Hz and 60 dB HL at 1000 Hz were measured). In the past, standard practice has been to test at 8000 Hz as the upper frequency, but more recently some audiologists have tended to favor testing at 6000 Hz rather than at 8000 Hz because of the possibility of standing waves in the external auditory meatus at 8000 Hz. The presence of standing waves can result in attenuation of the signal reaching the ear and consequent raised thresholds that are purely artifactual. (For a more comprehensive discussion of this discrepancy in the somewhat standard frequencies, see Newby and Popelka (1985:123–124).

Masking Levels Immediately below the audiogram on the Audiologic Assessment Form shown in Figure 1-1 is a space for recording the levels of masking used to obtain masked pure tone thresholds. This space for recording masking levels used has also been reproduced in Figure 1-4. Although there are some differences, most audiogram forms provide a space for recording information about the level of masking used. However, many of the audiogram forms used in various facilities do not provide sufficient space to record different levels used at different frequencies, and when space is provided it is difficult to indicate what levels were used for what specific frequencies. It is the opinion of the authors that if there is a need to provide any information about the masking level used, there is an equal need to provide frequency-dependent information since the level of masking required may vary from frequency to frequency.

It is not appropriate to use a single level of masking for air conduction or bone conduction. Although authorities differ in their masking methods (see Newby and Popelka, 1985:128–129; Martin, 1991: 91–99; and Hannley, 1986:113–120), almost all agree on the need for obtaining a plateau at each frequency masked. A plateau consists of at least two masking levels 10 dB apart at which pure tone thresholds remain constant. When a plateau is obtained, one can have a certain degree of assurance, although by no means complete assurance, that the actual threshold of the ear under test has been found. The proper use of masking is discussed in greater detail in Chapter 5.

When a plateau is obtained, the threshold value is recorded on the pure tone audiogram and the masking levels defining the plateau are recorded in the appropriate box in Figure 1-4. For example, if 500 Hz was being tested by air conduction in the right ear with masking noise introduced into the left ear, and a plateau was obtained using masking levels of 60 and 70 dB, we would record "60–70" in the box labeled "Air Conduction L" under 500 Hz on the audiogram. An alternative procedure recommended by ASHA (1990) is to record only the maximum effective masking level used to obtain threshold (e.g., in the above example, only "70" dB would be recorded).

Although narrow band noise is the most desirable masker for pure tone signals (Hannley, 1986:109–

113), not all audiometers provide this type of noise. In some evaluation situations, white noise is used for masking. Therefore, it is important to note on the Audiologic Assessment Form the type of masking used. The form used in this manual provides a space labeled "Signal: NBN _____ (meaning narrow band noise) White _____," in which the type of noise used should be recorded. The calibration of the masking noise, effective level or SPL, should also be recorded. Types of masking noise and calibration are discussed in Chapter 5.

For a discussion of the need for masking and its appropriate use, the student is again referred to any number of audiology texts (Martin, 1986:88–89, 123–127; Newby, 1985:124–129, 183–184; Hannley, 1986:107–127).

Pure Tone Average (PTA) In the section of the Audiologic Assessment Form above the "Speech Audiometry" section is a place to record the pure tone average. Pure tone average (three frequency) refers to the average hearing level of the three "speech frequencies" included in standard audiometric testing (500, 1000, and 2000 Hz). It is sometimes referred to as the "average pure tone loss," the so-called "speech frequency average," or the "predicted loss for speech."

The "speech frequency average" refers to the average of the thresholds at 500, 1000, and 2000 Hz because supposedly these three frequencies carry most of the information necessary for the understanding of speech. Many studies have shown there is a high correlation between the average hearing level at these frequencies and the loss for speech

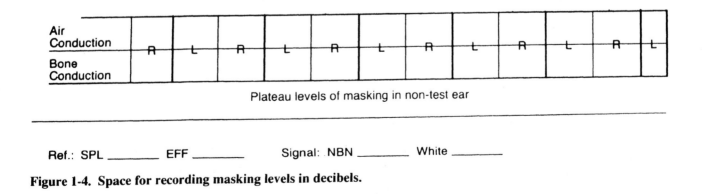

Ref.: SPL _____ EFF _____   Signal: NBN _____ White _____

Figure 1-4. Space for recording masking levels in decibels.

measured by a speech audiometer (Newby and Popelka, 1985:155–156).

Sometimes when the pure tone configuration falls sharply in the high frequencies the three-frequency pure tone average overestimates the threshold level for hearing speech. In that situation it is more valid to compute a two-frequency pure tone average that is the average hearing level of the best two of three speech frequencies. The two-frequency average is also referred to as the Fletcher Average (Fletcher, 1950). If the pure tone averages are based on two frequencies, a comment should be included in the "Remarks" section.

There is also space for bone conduction and aided sound field pure tone averages. Comparison of air and bone conduction pure tone averages provides information about type of hearing loss. An aided sound field average can be compared to an unaided sound field average to provide information about one benefit of amplification. It is also possible to compute high-frequency pure tone averages based on the average of thresholds at 1000, 2000, and 4000 Hz. This PTA in comparison with the three-frequency PTA can provide additional information when high-frequency hearing loss is significantly greater than low-frequency hearing loss (Hannley, 1986:133).

The relationship between the pure tone average and speech audiometry is discussed more fully later, but the pure tone average should be in general agreement with the speech reception threshold (Martin, 1991:73, 75; Newby and Popelka, 1985:155–156; Rintelmann, 1991:48–49).

Speech Audiometry

The middle righthand portion of the Audiologic Assessment Form (Figure 1-1) is used to record the results of speech audiometry. The space for recording speech audiometry results has been reproduced in Figure 1-5. In Figure 1-5, "right" and "left" indicate that the stimulus material was presented to the client's right and left ears, respectively. The column marked "sound field" is used to record the speech audiometry results when the materials are presented to the client in a sound field situation utilizing a loudspeaker rather than earphones.

The client's speech awareness threshold (SAT), speech reception threshold (SRT), most comfortable

loudness level (MCL), uncomfortable loudness level (UCL), and word recognition scores in quiet or in noise are recorded. There are also spaces to record masking levels when appropriate, as well as descriptive information about stimuli used and mode of presentation of stimuli.

Each of the above speech audiometry measures is discussed in greater detail in Chapter 4. For a discussion of speech audiometry in general, the reader is referred to Martin (1991:113–160), Newby and Popelka (1985:163–186), Hannley (1986:147–172), and Rintelmann (1991:39–140).

IMMITTANCE MEASUREMENT

The immittance battery has become an integral part of the basic audiologic assessment. The three parts of the battery, static compliance, tympanometry, and acoustic reflex measurement, can differentiate between conductive and sensorineural loss, cochlear

SPEECH AUDIOMETRY ☐ MLV ☐ Tape

	RIGHT	LEFT	MASK LEVEL R	L	SOUND FIELD	LIST
SAT						
SRT						
MCL						
UCL						
PB% (Word)	_L	_L				
PB% (Word)	_L	_L				
PB% (Word)	_L	_L				
PB% (Word)	_L	_L				
	_L	_L				
	_L	_L				

Figure 1-5. Space for recording speech audiometry results.

and retrocochlear sites of auditory dysfunction, and different types of middle ear disorders. Immittance measurement can also provide information about the integrity of the facial nerve and Eustachian tube function. In addition, immittance has become useful for auditory screening in the schools. The immittance battery and its applications will be discussed in detail in Chapter 3 of this manual.

The term "immittance" is used in this book to include both "impedance" and "admittance." It is defined as "the total opposition offered by the system to the flow of energy" (Lilly, 1973:353). Precise definitions of these terms may be found in Chapter 3 of this text. Unlike pure tone and speech audiometry, immittance does not rely on behavioral responses of the client; it is an electrophysiological procedure. Therefore, it can be used with clients of all ages and degrees of cooperativeness.

Static Compliance When a sound enters the normal ear canal, most of it is transmitted to the inner ear by the tympanic membrane (eardrum) and middle ear. Some of the sound energy, however, is reflected back from the tympanic membrane because of the normal impedance (immittance) of the middle ear system. Norms for the reflected (or admitted) sound have been developed and expressed in terms of cubic centimeters (cc) of "static compliance." Any condition of the middle ear negatively affecting the mobility of the tympanic membrane will affect the amount of static compliance. In the lower middle section of the Audiologic Assessment Form is a box with spaces for recording static compliance of each ear. The space for recording static compliance has been reproduced in Figure 1-6.

Static compliance of the middle ear is measured by delivering a low-frequency pure tone, usually 220 Hz, to the ear and measuring the amount of reflected energy in cubic centimeters (cc). Since it is not possible to measure the compliance of the middle ear directly, it is done as a two-step procedure. The first step involves measuring static compliance with the eardrum stressed so that it does not vibrate (the method for doing this is described in Chapter 3 of this text). This value, representing the compliance of the ear canal only, is entered into the space on the Audiologic Assessment Form labeled C1. That same value also represents ear canal volume and is there-

fore entered into the space labeled "Ear Canal Volume" (Figures 1-1 and 1-6). Abnormally high ear canal volume suggests an eardrum that is not intact (Northern and Downs, 1984:189–190).

The second part of the static compliance procedure involves measurement of compliance with the tympanic membrane at its point of maximum mobility (with a normal middle ear this occurs at ambient pressure). This value, which represents the compliance of the middle ear and ear canal together, is entered into the space on the Audiologic Assessment Form labeled C2 (Figures 1-1 and 1-6). C1 is then subtracted from C2 to obtain the compliance of the middle ear system.

Tympanometry Tympanometry can be conceptualized as a succession of measurements of compliance in the presence of systematically changing air pressure in the ear canal. In the lower lefthand portion of the Audiologic Assessment Form is a graph labeled "Tympanogram." The tympanogram is reproduced

Static Compliance:

R
ml
2
1
L
ml
2
1

Normal: .3–1.75 ml

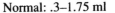

Ear Canal Volume

	Right	Left
C1 =		

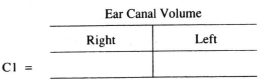

Figure 1-6. Space for recording static compliance and ear canal volume.

in Figure 1-7. Relative compliance is shown on the ordinate (0 represents minimum compliance or mobility of the tympanic membrane and 10 represents maximum compliance or mobility). Relative air pressure in decaPascals (daPa) is shown on the abscissa. 0 daPa means that the air pressure in the ear is the same as ambient pressure, +100 is 100 daPa greater than ambient pressure, and −100 is 100 daPa less. For further discussion of this type of calibration, see Hannley (1986:53).

The immittance meter or bridge prints out a tympanogram, which is then compared to the normal tympanogram (triangular shape) shown on the Audiologic Assessment Form (Figures 1-1 and 1-7). There are a variety of immittance tympanograms which suggest either normal middle ear function or different types of middle ear disorders. Interpretation of tympanogram types and their significance will be discussed in Chapter 3 of this manual.

Acoustic (Stapedius) Reflex Measurement of the threshold of the acoustic reflex is the third part of the immittance battery. The acoustic reflex is a contraction of the middle ear muscles, primarily the stapedius, in response to intense sound. The lowest-level sound (threshold) that will elicit a reflex is measured, using 500, 1000, 2000, and 4000 Hz, and sometimes wide band noise (WBN) as stimuli. These thresholds are entered into the Audiologic Assessment Form in the appropriate spaces of the box labeled "Stapedius Reflex Thresholds." This portion of the Audiologic Assessment Form is reproduced in Figure 1-8. Comparison of a client's acoustic reflex thresholds to the norms in conjunction with other audiometric data (e.g., tympanometry, pure tone thresholds, and speech audiometry) can provide information about site of auditory dysfunction.

Acoustic reflex thresholds can be measured with the stimulating sound in the ear opposite to the ear receiving the probe tone of the immittance meter or with both stimuli in the same ear. When the two signals are in opposite ears, the thresholds are considered contralateral and are entered into the spaces on the Audiologic Assessment Form labeled "contralateral"; when both the probe and stimulus tones are in the same ear, the thresholds are considered ipsilateral and

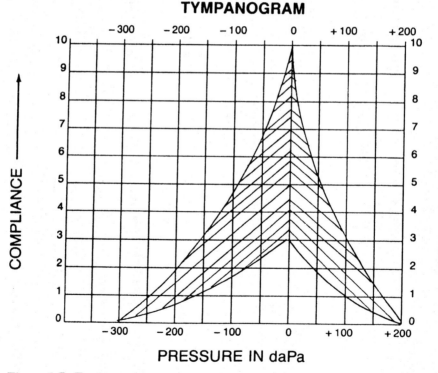

Figure 1-7. Tympanogram.

STAPEDIUS REFLEX THRESHOLDS

Stimulus	Contralateral (HL)					Ipsilateral (HL)		
EAR	.5K	1K	2K	4K	WBN	.5K	1K	2K
R								
Decay			X	X				X
L								
Decay			X	X				X

Figure 1-8. Space for recording acoustic reflex results.

are entered into the spaces labeled "ipsilateral" (Figures 1-1 and 1-8). Comparison of contralateral and ipsilateral reflex thresholds can help distinguish between cochlear and retrocochlear sites of dysfunction.

Still another acoustic reflex procedure routinely performed at 500 and 1000 Hz is called "reflex decay." It can be measured contralaterally or ipsilaterally. The stimulating frequency is presented 10 dB above the acoustic reflex threshold for 10 seconds. If the magnitude of the reflex decreases by 50% within 5 seconds or less, the rate of decay is considered abnormal and suggests the possibility of eighth nerve disorder. The time in seconds in which the reflex decays to 50% magnitude is entered into the Audiologic Assessment Form (Figures 1-1 and 1-8).

The immittance battery is discussed in depth in Chapter 3 of this book. Additional references include Hannley (1986:29–88), Northern and Downs (1984:180–205, 261–266), Martin (1991:175–192), Rintelmann (1991:179–319), and others included in Chapter 3.

CLASSIFICATION

Type of Hearing Loss

Although the diagnosis of the type of hearing loss a particular client presents is a medical decision to be made by a qualified physician based on more than the audiometric test results, audiometric interpretation involves considerable understanding of the various types of hearing loss. Although there is no universally accepted terminology for the various types of hearing loss, most audiology texts use similar classification systems. The terminology used in this book as related to the location of the disorder is shown in Figure 1-9.

As presented in Figure 1-9, organic hearing loss is described as conductive, sensorineural, or mixed. If there is an air–bone gap of 10 dB or greater and bone conduction is within normal limits, the hearing loss is considered conductive. A conductive hearing loss is caused by a problem anywhere in the outer or middle ear. If both air and bone conduction thresholds are within 10 dB of each other and are poorer than normal, the hearing loss is considered sensorineural. The site of dysfunction may be in the inner ear, eighth nerve, or central auditory pathways. Some audiologists (Jacobson and Northern, 1991:8) find it useful to differentiate between cochlear site of dysfunction on the one hand and auditory nerve or central auditory pathways disorder on the other. According to this classification system, the term "sensory" hearing loss is used to describe cochlear impairment and the term "neural" for problems in the eighth nerve and brain. The term "sensorineural" indicates that both cochlear and neural dysfunction contribute to the hearing disorder. This differentiation between sensory and neural is not used in this text.

A mixed hearing loss involves both conductive and sensorineural components. Audiometric manifestations involve an air–bone gap of 10 dB or greater, with bone conduction thresholds poorer than normal. The poorer the bone conduction thresholds, the greater the sensorineural component of the hearing loss. The audiometric correlates of conductive, sensorineural, and mixed hearing losses are illustrated in subsequent chapters.

The following anatomical terms used in this book are shown in Figure 1-9. Hearing disorders that occur within the central nervous system are called "central." They include brain stem and temporal lobe pathologies. Disorders occurring outside the central auditory system, including the eighth nerve, are called "peripheral." The term "retrocochlear" refers to sensorineural hearing loss rostral to the cochlea (eighth nerve and central auditory pathway disorders). An eighth nerve problem is peripheral and retrocochlear; a central auditory problem is central and retrocochlear.

Hearing losses are also classified by authors as organic or non-organic. The terms "functional," "psychogenic," "malingering," "pseudohypacusis,"

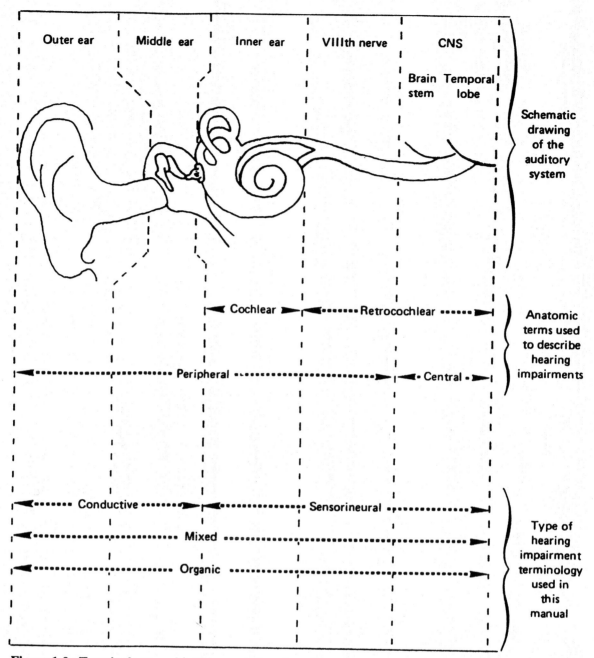

Figure 1-9. Terminology used in this manual to describe the types of organic hearing impairment related to the site of lesion.

and "hysterical deafness" are also used to refer to losses which are not organic in nature. For further discussion of this topic, see Newby and Popelka (1985:248–259), Hannley (1986:156, 194, 198–201), Martin (1991:341–360), Northern and Downs (1984: 164–168), and Rintelmann (1991:603–652).

Degree of Hearing Loss In addition to classification based on site of dysfunction, hearing losses may be classified in terms of degree of loss. Classification can be based on sensitivity at a single frequency of interest, the SRT, or most commonly the pure tone average. Although there is not a standard way of

Table 1-1. General classification system used in this book to describe the severity (degree) of hearing loss.

Hearing level (dB)	Classification
–10 to 15	Normal hearing
16 to 25	Slight hearing loss
26 to 40	Mild hearing loss
41 to 55	Moderate hearing loss
56 to 70	Moderately severe hearing loss
71 to 90	Severe hearing loss
91 plus	Profound hearing loss

Note: The left column gives the range of hearing levels (losses) in dB based on the mean of the three speech frequencies (500, 1000, and 2000 Hz) for pure tone results or for the SRT for speech results. In reporting results that fall near the cutoff point, +3 dB, both classifications adjacent to the cutoff may be used, e.g., a mean of 55 dB may be reported as "moderate" or "moderately severe."

classifying degree of loss, most audiologists use a system based on that of Goodman (1965:262–263).

This text uses the classification system shown in Table 1-1. This severity system represents Clark's (Katz, 1985:164) modification of the Goodman Severity Scale. It should be noted that the system in Table 1-1 applies to both pure tone and speech thresholds. Although this system attempts to describe the communicative effect of a hearing impairment, it should be remembered that the communicative effect of a hearing impairment on a given person is subject to considerable individual variation. Because of this individual variation, the present (or any other) terminology should not be interpreted too literally. The mean of the three speech frequencies (500, 1000, and 2000 Hz) for the better ear is utilized to estimate the communicative effect from information provided by a pure tone audiogram, except in those cases (sharply falling configuration) where it is more appropriate to use the best two of the three speech frequencies. For a detailed discussion of the "two-frequency method," see Fletcher (1950:1–5), Newby and Popelka (1985:156), and Rintelmann (1991:48–49).

The classification system usually refers to the communicative effect of a hearing loss based on the speech frequencies, but it may also be used to describe various frequency ranges—for example, "The client has a moderate hearing loss in the lower fre-

quencies (250 to 1000 Hz)." The system may also apply to either ear if so specified—for example, "The client has a severe hearing loss in the right ear." The varied applications of this system of classification are considered in subsequent chapters. Although a severity classification system such as the one used in this book lacks precision, it is frequently of value in describing audiometric results to consumers.

Although it is customary to use the terminology found in Table 1-1 to describe degree of hearing loss, the clinician must realize that an individual's communication difficulty (or degree of impairment) depends upon a number of factors in addition to auditory sensitivity. These factors have been previously summarized as follows:

> The degree of hearing impairment is the result of the degree of deviation in hearing (sensitivity and/or other auditory abilities) interacting with a number of other factors, e.g., age of onset, age of detection and intervention, duration, type of pathology and related factors, use of amplification, habilitative programming, family factors, and resilience of compensatory (or adaptive) abilities. [Lloyd, 1973:47]

Table 1-2. Classification system (modified from Carhart, 1945) used in this book to describe audiometric configuration.

Term	Description
Flat	Less than 5 dB rise or fall per octave
Gradually falling	5–12 dB decrease per octave
Sharply falling	13 dB or more decrease per octave
Abruptly falling	Flat or gradually falling, then sharply falling
Rising	5 dB or more increase per octave
Trough	20 dB or greater loss at 1000 Hz and/or 2000 Hz than at 500 and 4000 Hz
Miscellaneous	Does not fit any of the above

Note: The primary frequencies considered in describing the audiometric configuration are 500 through 4000 Hz.

Audiometric Configuration

In addition to classifying (or describing) pure tone results in terms of degree (severity) and type of hearing loss (site of dysfunction), pure tone thresholds may be categorized according to audiometric configuration. In subsequent chapters the interpretation of audiometric results is considered according to all three types of classification. The audiometric configuration classification system used in this text is shown in Table 1-2. This configuration scheme is a modification of the system originally described by Carhart in 1945.

REVIEW AND SEARCH PROJECTS

1. Briefly discuss the purposes of audiometric testing (Katz, 1985; Martin, 1991; Newby and Popelka, 1985; Hannley, 1986; Rintelmann, 1991).

2. Briefly discuss the purposes of speech audiometry (Katz, 1985; Martin 1991; Newby and Popelka, 1985; Hannley, 1986; Rintelmann, 1991).

3. How does speech audiometry relate to pure tone audiometry?

4. Briefly discuss tuning fork tests:

   a. As forerunners of modern pure tone audiometry.
   b. As they are currently used as an adjunct to the complete pure tone audiometric examination.
   c. Their limitations.

5. Write an explanation of the audiogram that you could present to an in-service training session of elementary school teachers or vocational rehabilitation counselors who have not had any courses in the area of hearing.

6. Briefly describe what is meant by the reliability of an audiogram.

7. Discuss the value of using a severity classification system such as that presented in Table 1-1.

8. Discuss the problems involved in using a severity classification system such as that presented in Table 1-1.

9. Review other methods (e.g., percentage of hearing loss) describing the severity of a client's hearing loss.

10. Discuss the similarities and the differences in methods used for pure tone testing of young children and adults.

11. Review several articles or books on methods and materials for speech audiometry with children.

12. Discuss the concept of audiometric zero and the history leading up to the development of the present ANSI S3.6-89 standard.

REFERENCES

American National Standard Psychoacoustic Terminology, ANSI S3.20–1973 (p. 45). New York: American National Standards Institute.

ASHA Committee on Audiometric Evaluation. Guidelines for Audiometric Symbols. 1990. *ASHA* 32 (Suppl. 2): 25–30.

Carhart, R. 1945. Classifying audiograms: an improved method for classifying audiograms. *Laryngoscope* 55.

Davis, H., and Silverman, S. R. 1978. *Hearing and Deafness.* New York: Holt, Rinehart and Winston.

Fletcher, H. 1950. A Method of calculating hearing loss for speech from an audiogram. *JASA* 22: 1–5.

Fulton, R. T., and Lloyd, L. L. 1975. *Auditory Assessment of the Difficult-to-Test.* Baltimore: Williams & Wilkins.

Goodman, A. 1965. Reference zero levels for pure tone audiometer. *ASHA* 7: 262–263.

Hannley, M. 1986. *Basic Principles of Auditory Assessment.* San Diego: College-Hill Press.

Jacobson, J. T., and Northern, J. L. 1991. *Diagnostic Audiology.* Austin: Pro-Ed.

Jerger, J., and Jerger, S. 1971. Diagnostic speech audiometry. *Archives of Otolaryngology* 93: 573–580.

Katz, J. 1985. *Handbook of Clinical Audiology.* Baltimore: Williams & Wilkins.

Lilly, D. 1973. Measurement of acoustic impedance at the tympanic membrane. In J. Jerger (Ed.), *Modern Developments in Audiology* (pp. 345–406). New York: Academic Press.

Lloyd, L. 1973. Mental retardation and hearing impairment. In A. G. Norris (Ed.), *PRWAD Deafness Annual* (Vol. 1). Washington D. C.: Professional Rehabilitation Workers with the Adult Deaf.

Martin, F. N. 1991. *Introduction to Audiology,* 4th ed. Englewood Cliffs, N.J.: Prentice-Hall.

Melnick, W. 1971. American National Standard Specification for Audiometers. *ASHA* 13: 203–206.

Newby, H., and Popelka, G. R. 1985. *Audiology,* 5th ed. Englewood Cliffs, N.J.: Prentice-Hall.

Northern, J. L., and Downs, M. P. 1984. *Hearing in Children,* 3rd ed. Baltimore: Williams & Wilkins.

Rintelmann, W. F. (Editor). 1991. *Hearing Assessment,* 2nd ed. Austin: Pro-Ed.

Reading the Pure Tone Audiogram

This chapter contains Audiologic Assessment Forms programmed to develop the ability to recognize basic air conduction and bone conduction information. The ability to skillfully read audiograms is a prerequisite of audiometric interpretation.

In this chapter the reader will learn to:

1. Interpret air conduction and bone conduction symbols.
2. Compute the pure tone average for each ear individually and the better ear average.
3. Interpret sound field pure tone results.
4. Evaluate consistency of response and intertest agreement.
5. Interpret degree of loss based on audiometric information.
6. Describe pure tone configurations.
7. Describe the type of loss based on relationships between pure tone measures and understand their medical significance.

Preceding each audiogram are several questions designed to lead the reader to certain information which he/she should be able to read from the audiogram. Read the questions, scan the audiogram, and attempt to answer the questions in the space provided in the workbook. After formulating your answers to each of the questions, check your answers with those on the reverse side of the audiogram. In addition to answering the specific questions asked about the audiogram, the reader should also scan the audiogram for relationships between the various audiometric results. Some of the relationships the reader should observe are as follows:

1. Air conduction and the bone conduction thresholds
2. Reported response consistency and the air and bone conduction thresholds

As discussed in the preceding chapter, the audiograms presented in this and the subsequent chapters are not presented with red and blue markings primarily because clinicians often need to interpret black-and-white duplicate audiograms sent from other facilities. However, for reasons outlined in the first chapter, we encourage the use of color-coded original audiograms. To help you interpret the audiograms, the legend (Figure 1-2) is shown on the next page.

Response Consistency:	good	moderate	poor

LEGEND

		Right (red)	Left (blue)
Air:	Unmasked	Φ	✕
	Masked	▲	☐
Bone:	Unmasked	◁	▷
	Masked	☐	☐

No Response _____↓_____

Best Bone _____⊓_____

Sound Field ____S____

Aided Sound Field ____A____

	Narrow Band Noise
	Warble Tone

Symbols for recording pure tone threshold on the Audiologic Assessment Form.

Questions

QUESTIONS FOR FIGURE 2-1

1. What is the three-frequency pure tone average (sometimes referred to as PT Average) for the right ear?
2. What is the three-frequency PT Average for the left ear?
3. Which ear is the better ear?

Name: Fig 2-1   Date: XX/XX/XX   Age: 15   Sex: M   Audiologist: HK
AUDIOMETER: GSI-10   ANSI 1969

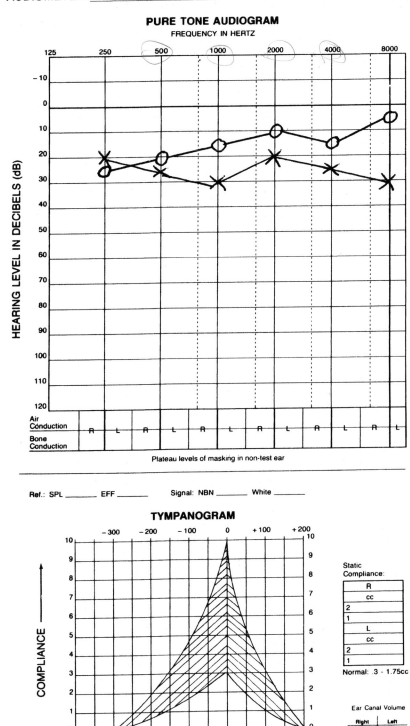

PURE TONE AUDIOGRAM
FREQUENCY IN HERTZ

HEARING LEVEL IN DECIBELS (dB)

Air Conduction

Bone Conduction

Plateau levels of masking in non-test ear

Ref.: SPL _____ EFF _____   Signal: NBN _____ White _____

TYMPANOGRAM

COMPLIANCE

PRESSURE IN daPa

Static Compliance:

	R
	cc
2	
1	
	L
	cc
2	
1	

Normal: .3 - 1.75cc

Ear Canal Volume

Right	Left

$C_1 =$

Response Consistency: (good) moderate poor

No Response

LEGEND

		Right (red)	Left (blue)
Air:	Unmasked	◯	✕
	Masked	△	▢
Bone:	Unmasked	◁	▷
	Masked	▢	▢

Best Bone
Sound Field ___ S
Aided
Sound Field ___ A
Narrow Band Noise
Warble Tone

PURE TONE AVERAGE (R L)			
	Right	Left	Aided
AIR			
BONE			

SPEECH AUDIOMETRY ✕ MLV ☐ Tape

	RIGHT	LEFT	MASK LEVEL R	L	SOUND FIELD	LIST
SAT						
SRT	14	26			16	
MCL						
UCL						
PB% (Word)	_ L	_ L				
PB% (Word)	_ L	_ L				
PB% (Word)	_ L	_ L				
PB% (Word)	_ L	_ L				
	_ L	_ L				
	_ L	_ L				

STAPEDIUS REFLEX THRESHOLDS

Stimulus	Contralateral (HL)					Ipsilateral (HL)		
EAR	.5K	1K	2K	4K	WBN	.5K	1K	2K
R								
Decay		✕	✕					✕
L								
Decay		✕	✕					✕

ABBREVIATIONS

A	Absent	NR	No Response
C₁	Canal Volume	SAT	Speech Awareness
CNE	Could Not Establish		Threshold
CNT	Could Not Test	SL	Sensation Level
DNT	Did Not Test	SRT	Speech Reception
HL	Hearing Level		Threshold
MCL	Most Comfortable	UCL	Uncomfortable Listening
	Listening Level		Level
MVL	Monitored Live Voice		

REMARKS:

_____

_____

_____

_____

Reading the Pure Tone Audiogram

1. The three-frequency PT Average for the right ear is 15 dB HL, which is in good agreement with the SRT obtained for the right ear (14 dB). The thresholds for 500, 1000, and 2000 Hz are 20, 15, and 10 dB HL, respectively, the sum of which is 45 dB; 45 dB divided by three gives a PT Average of 15 dB HL.

2. The PT Average for the left ear is 25 dB HL, which is in good agreement with the 26 dB HL speech reception threshold obtained for the left ear.

3. The right ear is the better ear because the PT Average is 15 dB HL; the PT Average for the left ear is 25 dB HL. Note that the right ear SRT is also better than the left.

QUESTIONS FOR FIGURE 2-2

1. What is the three-frequency PT Average for the right ear?
2. What is the three-frequency PT Average for the left ear?
3. What is the "better ear average?"

Name: Fig 2-2   Date: XX/XX/XX   Age: 11   Sex: M   Audiologist: HK

AUDIOMETER: GSI-10   ANSI 1969

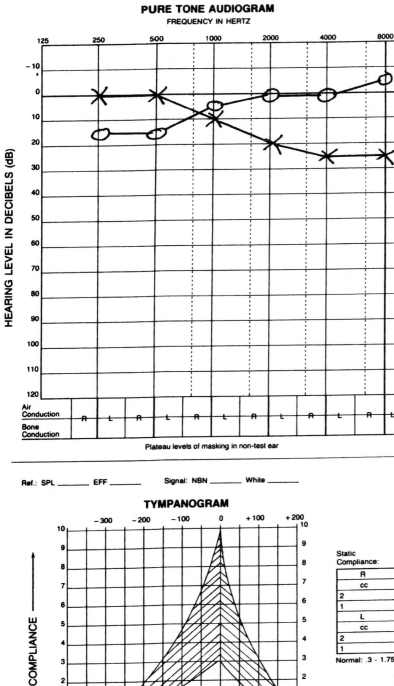

PURE TONE AUDIOGRAM
FREQUENCY IN HERTZ

Response Consistency: good   (moderate)   poor

No Response

LEGEND

		Right (red)	Left (blue)
Air:	Unmasked	○	×
	Masked	△	□
Bone:	Unmasked	◁	▷
	Masked	□	□

Best Bone

Sound Field   S
Aided
Sound Field   A

Narrow Band Noise

Warble Tone

PURE TONE AVERAGE (R L)	Right	Left	Aided
AIR			
BONE			

SPEECH AUDIOMETRY   ☒ MLV   ☐ Tape

	RIGHT	LEFT	MASK LEVEL R L	SOUND FIELD	LIST
SAT					
SRT	6	12		2	
MCL					
UCL					
PB% (Word)	_L	_L			
PB% (Word)	_L	_L			
PB% (Word)	_L	_L			
PB% (Word)	_L	_L			
	_L	_L			
	_L	_L			

STAPEDIUS REFLEX THRESHOLDS

Stimulus	Contralateral (HL)					Ipsilateral (HL)		
EAR	.5K	1K	2K	4K	WBN	.5K	1K	2K
R								
Decay		✕	✕					✕
L								
Decay		✕	✕			✕		✕

ABBREVIATIONS

A	Absent	NR	No Response
C₁	Canal Volume	SAT	Speech Awareness
CNE	Could Not Establish		Threshold
CNT	Could Not Test	SL	Sensation Level
DNT	Did Not Test	SRT	Speech Reception
HL	Hearing Level		Threshold
MCL	Most Comfortable	UCL	Uncomfortable Listenin
	Listening Level		Level
MVL	Monitored Live Voice		

REMARKS:

_____
_____
_____
_____
_____

Ref.: SPL _____ EFF _____   Signal: NBN _____ White _____

TYMPANOGRAM

PRESSURE IN daPa

Static Compliance:

R	
	cc
2	
1	
L	
	cc
2	
1	

Normal: .3 - 1.75cc

Ear Canal Volume

	Right	Left
C₁ =		

Reading the Pure Tone Audiogram

Answers for Figure 2-2

1. The pure tone average for the right ear is 7 dB HL (6.66 dB HL), which is in general agreement with the SRT of 6 dB HL obtained for the right ear. Note that the 6.66 dB HL is rounded to the nearest decibel, i.e., 7 dB HL.

2. The left ear PT Average is 10 dB HL, which is in general agreement with the 12 dB HL SRT obtained for the left ear.

3. The better ear average is 2 dB HL, which is in good agreement with the sound field SRT of 2 dB HL. The better ear average is computed as follows:

The better threshold for 500 Hz is	0 dB	(i.e., the left ear)
The better threshold for 1000 Hz is	5 dB	(i.e., the right ear
The better threshold for 2000 Hz is	0 dB	(i.e., the right ear)
	5 dB	

Considering both ears, the sum of the better threshold at each of the three speech frequencies is 5 dB HL, which when divided by three gives a better ear average of 1.67 or 2 dB HL. Note that the better ear average agrees well with the sound field SRT. For review of these concepts, see Martin (1986:73, 75), Newby (1985:155–156), and Rintelmann (1991:48–49).

QUESTIONS FOR FIGURE 2-3

1. What is the right ear three-frequency pure tone average?
2. What is the left ear three-frequency pure tone average?
3. What is the better ear average?

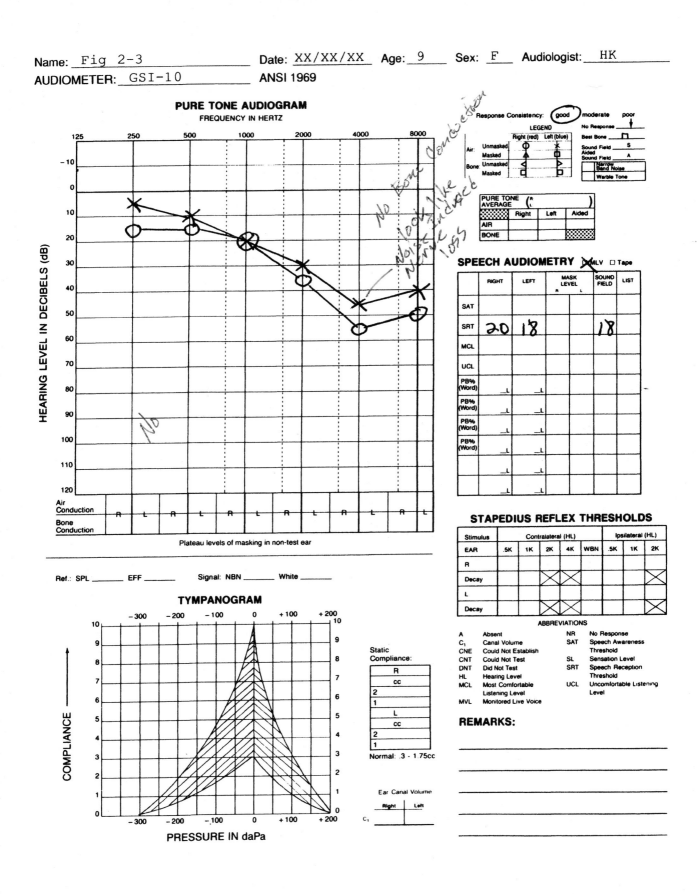

Answers for Figure 2-3

1. The right ear three-frequency PT Average is 23 dB HL. Note that, again, the PT Average has been rounded to the nearest decibel (i.e., 23.33 dB becomes 23 dB). This score is in good agreement with the SRT of 20 dB HL.
2. The left ear PT Average is 20 dB HL, which is in good agreement with the SRT of 18 dB HL.
3. The better ear average is 20 dB HL, which is in general agreement with the sound field SRT of 18 dB HL. It will be noted that in this case the better ear average (20 dB HL) is the same as the left ear three-frequency PT Average (20 dB HL). It should be remembered, however, that the better ear average does not have to equal the PT Average of either the right or left ear.

QUESTIONS FOR FIGURE 2-4

1. What is the right ear three-frequency PT Average? Does it agree with the SRT?
2. What is the right ear two-frequency PT Average? Does it agree with the SRT?
3. What is the left ear three-frequency PT Average?
4. What is the better ear average?

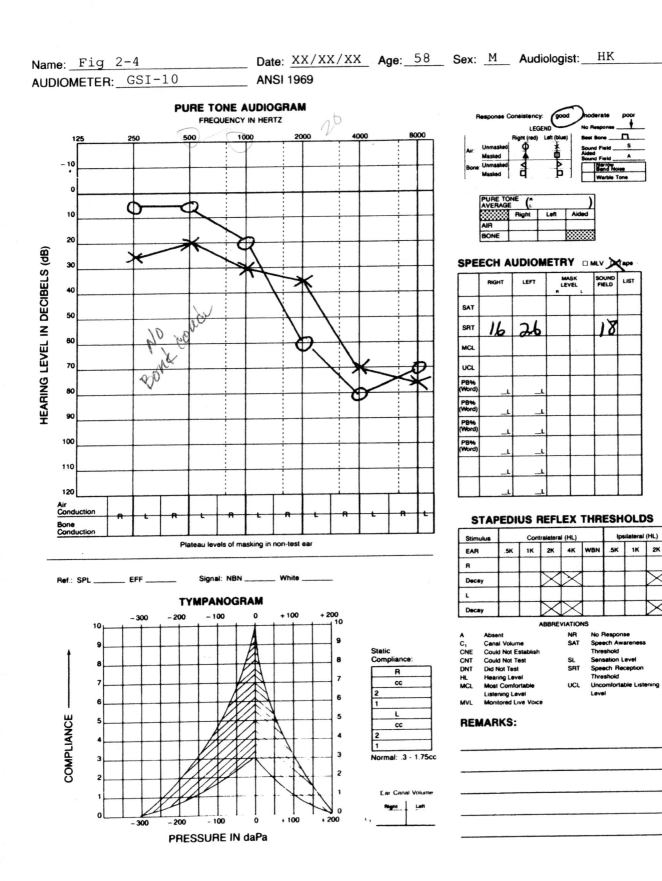

Name: Fig 2-4   Date: XX/XX/XX   Age: 58   Sex: M   Audiologist: HK

AUDIOMETER: GSI-10   ANSI 1969

PURE TONE AUDIOGRAM
FREQUENCY IN HERTZ

Response Consistency: good moderate poor

LEGEND

	Right (red)	Left (blue)
Air: Unmasked		
Masked		
Bone: Unmasked		
Masked		

No Response
Best Bone
Sound Field S
Aided
Sound Field A
Narrow Band Noise
Warble Tone

PURE TONE AVERAGE (R / L)	Right	Left	Aided
AIR			
BONE			

No Bone cond.

SPEECH AUDIOMETRY   ☐ MLV ☒ Tape

	RIGHT	LEFT	MASK LEVEL R / L	SOUND FIELD	LIST
SAT					
SRT	16	26		18	
MCL					
UCL					
PB% (Word)	L	L			
PB% (Word)	L	L			
PB% (Word)	L	L			
PB% (Word)	L	L			
	L	L			
	L	L			

STAPEDIUS REFLEX THRESHOLDS

Stimulus	Contralateral (HL)					Ipsilateral (HL)		
EAR	.5K	1K	2K	4K	WBN	.5K	1K	2K
R								
Decay			X	X				X
L								
Decay			X	X			X	

ABBREVIATIONS

A	Absent	NR	No Response
C₁	Canal Volume	SAT	Speech Awareness Threshold
CNE	Could Not Establish		
CNT	Could Not Test	SL	Sensation Level
DNT	Did Not Test	SRT	Speech Reception Threshold
HL	Hearing Level		
MCL	Most Comfortable Listening Level	UCL	Uncomfortable Listening Level
MVL	Monitored Live Voice		

Ref.: SPL _____ EFF _____   Signal: NBN _____ White _____

TYMPANOGRAM

Static Compliance:

R	
cc	
2	
1	

L	
cc	
2	
1	

Normal: .3 - 1.75cc

Ear Canal Volume
Right   Left

PRESSURE IN daPa

REMARKS:

_____
_____
_____
_____
_____

Plateau levels of masking in non-test ear

Answers for Figure 2-4

1. The right ear three-frequency PT Average is 28 dB HL. It does not agree well with the SRT of 16 dB HL. Sometimes when there are large differences in threshold between the speech frequencies, the SRT is lower than the three-frequency pure tone average. This is particularly true when the large difference in threshold occurs between 1000 and 2000 Hz. In such cases the SRT reflects the better low-frequency thresholds.

2. The right ear two-frequency PT Average is 13 dB HL. It is in general agreement with the SRT of 16 dB HL. When there is a large difference in threshold between 1000 and 2000 Hz and the three-frequency PT Average does not agree well with the SRT, we compute a two-frequency PT Average. We do this by averaging the thresholds of the two best speech frequencies for the given ear (i.e., threshold at 500 Hz is 5 dB; threshold at 1000 Hz is 20 dB; dividing the sum of these two thresholds by two gives us a two-frequency average of 12.5 dB or 13 dB HL). The two-frequency PT Average agrees better with the SRT. For a discussion of the two-frequency average see Newby and Popelka (1985:155–156) and Hannley (1986:133).

3. The left ear three-frequency PT Average is 28 dB HL (actual computation was 28.33 dB). Since this PT Average agrees well with the SRT of 26 dB HL and the pure tone thresholds of the three speech frequencies are fairly close, there is no need to compute a two-frequency PT Average.

4. The better ear average is 20 dB HL. To compute this 20 dB HL better ear average, the thresholds for the right ear at 500 and 1000 Hz, along with the threshold for the left ear at 2000 Hz, were used. Note the good agreement between the better ear PT Average and the sound field SRT.

QUESTIONS FOR FIGURE 2-5

1. What are the bone conduction (BC) thresholds for the right ear?
2. What are the bone conduction thresholds for the left ear?
3. For which thresholds was masking used?
4. What is the left ear three-frequency pure tone average? Does it agree with the SRT?
5. What is the left ear two-frequency pure tone average? Does it agree with the SRT?
6. What is the better ear average?

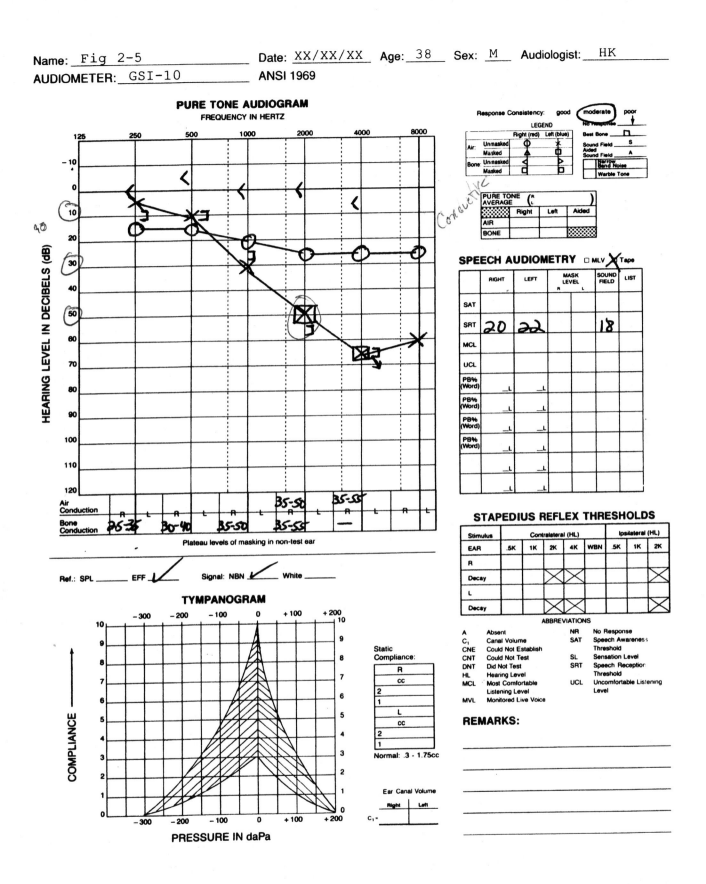

Name: Fig 2-5   Date: XX/XX/XX   Age: 38   Sex: M   Audiologist: HK
AUDIOMETER: GSI-10   ANSI 1969

PURE TONE AUDIOGRAM
FREQUENCY IN HERTZ

Conductive

SPEECH AUDIOMETRY   ☐ MLV ☒ Tape

	RIGHT	LEFT	MASK LEVEL R	MASK LEVEL L	SOUND FIELD	LIST
SAT						
SRT	20	22			18	
MCL						
UCL						
PB% (Word)	_L	_L				
PB% (Word)	_L	_L				
PB% (Word)	_L	_L				
PB% (Word)	_L	_L				
	_L	_L				
	_L	_L				

STAPEDIUS REFLEX THRESHOLDS

Stimulus	Contralateral (HL)					Ipsilateral (HL)		
EAR	.5K	1K	2K	4K	WBN	.5K	1K	2K
R								
Decay		☒	☒					☒
L								
Decay		☒	☒					☒

ABBREVIATIONS

A — Absent
C₁ — Canal Volume
CNE — Could Not Establish
CNT — Could Not Test
DNT — Did Not Test
HL — Hearing Level
MCL — Most Comfortable Listening Level
MVL — Monitored Live Voice
NR — No Response
SAT — Speech Awareness Threshold
SL — Sensation Level
SRT — Speech Reception Threshold
UCL — Uncomfortable Listening Level

REMARKS:

_____
_____
_____
_____
_____

TYMPANOGRAM

Static Compliance:

R	
	cc
2	
1	

L	
	cc
2	
1	

Normal: .3 - 1.75cc

Ear Canal Volume

Right	Left
C₁ =

PRESSURE IN daPa

Ref.: SPL _____ EFF ✓   Signal: NBN ✓ White _____

Reading the Pure Tone Audiogram

Answers for Figure 2-5

1. The BC thresholds for the right ear are as follows:

$$250 \text{ Hz} = 0 \text{ dB HL}$$
$$500 \text{ Hz} = -5 \text{ dB HL}$$
$$1000 \text{ Hz} = 0 \text{ dB HL}$$
$$2000 \text{ Hz} = 0 \text{ dB HL}$$
$$4000 \text{ Hz} = 5 \text{ dB HL}$$

2. The BC thresholds for the left ear are as follows:

$$250 \text{ Hz} = 10 \text{ dB HL}$$
$$500 \text{ Hz} = 10 \text{ dB HL}$$
$$1000 \text{ Hz} = 25 \text{ dB HL}$$
$$2000 \text{ Hz} = 55 \text{ dB HL}$$

At 4000 Hz bone conduction was tested, but there was no response when the signal was presented at the most intense level the audiometer was capable of delivering.

3. Masking was used in the right ear to test all bone conduction thresholds in the left ear. Masking was also used in the right ear when air conduction thresholds at 2000 Hz and 4000 Hz were obtained in the left ear. Note the masking levels listed in the appropriate spaces on the Audiologic Assessment Form, as well as the type of masking noise used (narrow band). Masking is more fully discussed in Chapter 5.

4. The left ear three-frequency pure tone average is 30 dB HL. It does not agree well with the SRT, probably because of the large difference in threshold between 1000 and 2000 Hz.

5. The left ear two-frequency pure tone average is 20 dB HL. It is in good agreement with the SRT of 22 dB HL.

6. The better ear average is 18 dB HL, which is in excellent agreement with the sound field SRT.

QUESTIONS FOR FIGURE 2-6

1. In the bone conduction testing, which ear had the masking presented to it?
2. Which ear had masking presented to it during air conduction testing?
3. What is this client's correct air conduction (AC) threshold for the left ear at 4000 Hz?
4. What is this client's correct AC threshold for the left ear at 8000 Hz?
5. What masking levels were used for bone conduction?
6. What masking levels were used for air conduction?
7. What type of masking noise was used and how was it calibrated?

Name: Fig 2-6   Date: XX/XX/XX Age: 35 Sex: M Audiologist: HK

AUDIOMETER: GSI-10   ANSI 1969

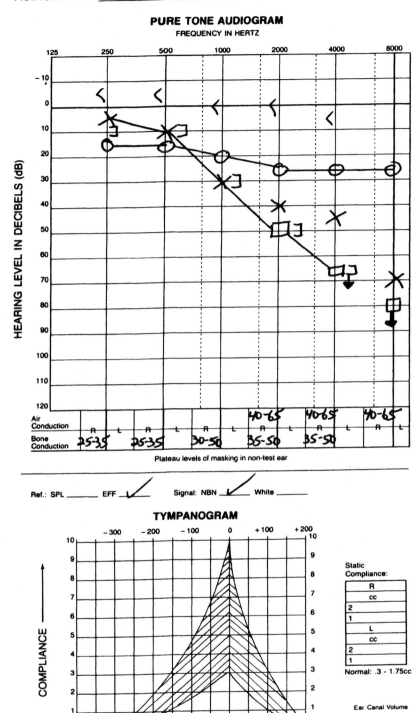

PURE TONE AUDIOGRAM
FREQUENCY IN HERTZ

Air Conduction plateau levels of masking in non-test ear:

	250	500	1000	2000	4000	8000
Air Conduction (R L)			40-65	40-65	40-65	
Bone Conduction (R L)	25-35	25-35	30-50	35-50	35-50	

Plateau levels of masking in non-test ear

Ref.: SPL _____ EFF ✓   Signal: NBN ✓ White _____

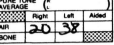

Response Consistency: (good) moderate poor

LEGEND

		Right (red)	Left (blue)
Air:	Unmasked	O	X
	Masked	△	◻
Bone:	Unmasked	◁	▷
	Masked	◻	◻

No Response
Best Bone
Sound Field S
Aided
Sound Field A
Narrow Band Noise
Warble Tone

PURE TONE AVERAGE (R / L)			
	Right	Left	Aided
AIR	20	38	
BONE			

SPEECH AUDIOMETRY ☐ MLV ☐ Tape

	RIGHT	LEFT	MASK LEVEL R / L	SOUND FIELD	LIST
SAT					
SRT					
MCL					
UCL					
PB% (Word)	L	L			
PB% (Word)	L	L			
PB% (Word)	L	L			
PB% (Word)	L	L			
	L	L			
	L	L			

STAPEDIUS REFLEX THRESHOLDS

Stimulus	Contralateral (HL)					Ipsilateral (HL)		
EAR	.5K	1K	2K	4K	WBN	.5K	1K	2K
R								
Decay		✕	✕			✕	✕	
L								
Decay		✕	✕			✕	✕	

ABBREVIATIONS

A	Absent	NR	No Response
C₁	Canal Volume	SAT	Speech Awareness
CNE	Could Not Establish		Threshold
CNT	Could Not Test	SL	Sensation Level
DNT	Did Not Test	SRT	Speech Reception
HL	Hearing Level		Threshold
MCL	Most Comfortable	UCL	Uncomfortable Listening
	Listening Level		Level
MVL	Monitored Live Voice		

REMARKS:

Left ear 2 freq. PT average = 20 dB; best binaural average = 18 dB

TYMPANOGRAM

PRESSURE IN daPa

Static Compliance:

R	
cc	
2	
1	

L	
cc	
2	
1	

Normal: .3 - 1.75cc

Ear Canal Volume

Right	Left
C₁ =	

Answers for Figure 2-6

1. When the bone conduction thresholds were obtained for the left ear, masking was presented to the right ear.

2. When the masked AC thresholds were obtained for the left ear at 2000, 4000, and 8000 Hz, masking was presented to the right ear.

3. This man's air conduction threshold for 4000 Hz is 65 dB HL; it is not 45 dB HL as one might think from looking at the unmasked AC threshold.

4. This man's threshold for 8000 Hz is something greater than 80 dB HL, but we cannot be sure just exactly what it is. The arrow pointing down from the usual marking for a threshold means there was no response at that level. The maximum output level for 8000 Hz on the audiometer used is 80 dB HL. Note that the threshold at this frequency is not 70 dB HL as one might think by looking at the unmasked AC threshold.

5. The following masking levels were used in the right ear when bone conduction thresholds were obtained in the left ear:

   $$250 \text{ Hz} = 25\text{--}35 \text{ dB HL}$$
   $$500 \text{ Hz} = 25\text{--}35 \text{ dB HL}$$
   $$1000 \text{ Hz} = 30\text{--}50 \text{ dB HL}$$
   $$2000 \text{ Hz} = 35\text{--}50 \text{ dB HL}$$
   $$4000 \text{ Hz} = 35\text{--}50 \text{ dB HL}$$

   Note that at all frequencies thresholds were obtained at several masking levels. The proper selection of masking levels is discussed in Chapter 5.

6. The following masking levels were used in the right ear when air conduction thresholds were obtained in the left ear:

   $$2000 \text{ Hz} = 40\text{--}65 \text{ dB HL}$$
   $$4000 \text{ Hz} = 40\text{--}65 \text{ dB HL}$$
   $$8000 \text{ Hz} = 40\text{--}65 \text{ dB HL}$$

   As with bone conduction thresholds, air conduction thresholds were obtained at several masking levels.

7. The type of masking noise used was narrow band noise, which was calibrated in effective level. Types of masking noise and calibration are discussed in Chapter 5.

QUESTIONS FOR FIGURE 2-7

1. In the bone conduction testing, which ear had the masking presented to it?
2. In the AC testing which ear received the masking noise?
3. What are this client's BC thresholds for the right ear?
4. What are this client's BC thresholds for the left ear?
5. What are this client's AC thresholds for the left ear?

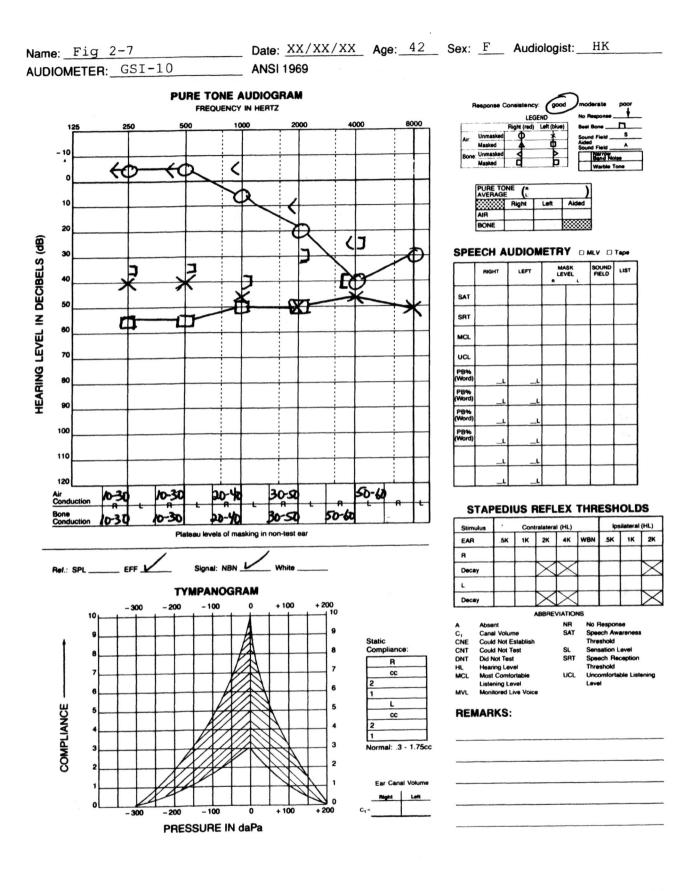

Answers for Figure 2-7

1. When the BC thresholds were obtained for the left ear, the right ear was masked out. Masking was not employed in obtaining the BC thresholds for the right ear.
2. When the masked AC thresholds for the left ear were obtained (250, 500, 1K, and 2K Hz), masking was presented to the right ear.
3. The client's BC thresholds for the right ear are as follows:

$$250 \text{ Hz} = -5 \text{ dB HL}$$
$$500 \text{ Hz} = -5 \text{ dB HL}$$
$$1000 \text{ Hz} = -5 \text{ dB HL}$$
$$2000 \text{ Hz} = 10 \text{ dB HL}$$
$$4000 \text{ Hz} = 40 \text{ dB HL}$$

The BC threshold for the right ear at 4000 Hz is not 25 dB as one would read from the unmasked "threshold" marks. The unmasked BC marks for the right ear at 4000 Hz were actually made possible by the left cochlea.

4. The client's BC thresholds for the left ear are as follows:

$$250 \text{ Hz} = 35 \text{ dB HL}$$
$$500 \text{ Hz} = 35 \text{ dB HL}$$
$$1000 \text{ Hz} = 40 \text{ dB HL}$$
$$2000 \text{ Hz} = 30 \text{ dB HL}$$
$$4000 \text{ Hz} = 25 \text{ dB HL}$$

The BC threshold at 4000 Hz is more sensitive than the corresponding BC threshold for the right ear, despite the fact that the air conduction threshold for the right ear is lower. The unmasked bone conduction threshold at 4000 Hz is actually the response of the left cochlea, although it was obtained with the bone oscillator behind the right ear.

5. The client's AC thresholds for the left ear are as follows:

$$250 \text{ Hz} = 55 \text{ dB HL}$$
$$500 \text{ Hz} = 55 \text{ dB HL}$$
$$1000 \text{ Hz} = 50 \text{ dB HL}$$
$$2000 \text{ Hz} = 50 \text{ dB HL}$$
$$4000 \text{ Hz} = 45 \text{ dB HL}$$
$$8000 \text{ Hz} = 50 \text{ dB HL}$$

It should be noted that the crosses indicate the unmasked thresholds, which at 250, 500, and 1000 Hz do not represent the actual thresholds of the left ear; they are actually a shadow of the right ear. The lines connect the masked thresholds at those frequencies which represent an accurate estimate of threshold.

QUESTIONS FOR FIGURE 2-8

1. What is the pure tone average for the right ear?
2. According to the classification system used in Chapter 1 (see Table 1-1), what is the degree of loss in the right ear?
3. What is the pure tone average for the left ear?
4. According to the classification system described in Chapter 1, what is the degree of loss in the left ear?
5. What is the better ear average?
6. When the two ears are considered together, what degree of loss does this client have?

Name: Fig 2-8 **Date:** XX/XX/XX **Age:** 48 **Sex:** M **Audiologist:** HK
AUDIOMETER: GSI-10 **ANSI 1969**

PURE TONE AUDIOGRAM

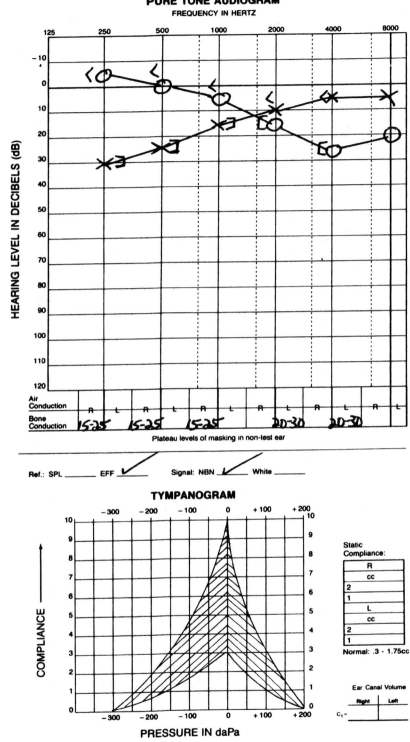

FREQUENCY IN HERTZ

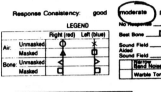

Response Consistency: good (moderate) poor

No Response

LEGEND			
		Right (red)	Left (blue)
Air:	Unmasked	○	✕
	Masked	▲	☐
Bone:	Unmasked	☐	▷
	Masked	☐	☐

Best Bone ☐
Sound Field S
Aided
Sound Field A
Narrow Band Noise
Warble Tone

PURE TONE AVERAGE (R: L:)	Right	Left	Aided
AIR			
BONE			

SPEECH AUDIOMETRY ☐ MLV ☑ Tape

	RIGHT	LEFT	MASK LEVEL R	L	SOUND FIELD	LIST
SAT						
SRT	10	18			4	
MCL						
UCL						
PB% (Word)	L	L				
PB% (Word)	L	L				
PB% (Word)	L	L				
PB% (Word)	L	L				
	L	L				
	L	L				

Plateau levels of masking in non-test ear

Air Conduction — R L R L R L R L R L R L R L R L
Bone Conduction — 15-25 15-25 15-25   20-30   20-30

Ref.: SPL _____ EFF _____   Signal: NBN _____ White _____

STAPEDIUS REFLEX THRESHOLDS

Stimulus	Contralateral (HL)					Ipsilateral (HL)		
EAR	.5K	1K	2K	4K	WBN	.5K	1K	2K
R								
Decay		✕	✕					✕
L								
Decay		✕	✕			✕		✕

ABBREVIATIONS

A	Absent	NR	No Response
C₁	Canal Volume	SAT	Speech Awareness
CNE	Could Not Establish		Threshold
CNT	Could Not Test	SL	Sensation Level
DNT	Did Not Test	SRT	Speech Reception
HL	Hearing Level		Threshold
MCL	Most Comfortable	UCL	Uncomfortable Listening
	Listening Level		Level
MVL	Monitored Live Voice		

REMARKS:

_____
_____
_____
_____
_____

TYMPANOGRAM

PRESSURE IN daPa

Static Compliance:

R	
	cc
2	
1	
L	
	cc
2	
1	

Normal: .3 - 1.75cc

Ear Canal Volume

Right	Left

C₁ = _____

Answers for Figure 2-8

1. The pure tone average for the right ear is 7 dB HL, which agrees well with the SRT of 10 dB HL.
2. According to the classification system used in Chapter 1, the right ear would be classified as having normal hearing. Thresholds at all frequencies except 4000 Hz are within normal limits. However, since threshold at 4000 Hz is 25 dB HL, which is borderline, the audiogram must be described as "normal hearing except for a slight hearing loss at 4000 Hz."
3. The pure tone average for the left ear is 17 dB HL, which agrees well with the SRT of 18 dB HL.
4. According to the classification system used in Chapter 1, the left ear would also be considered within normal limits. However, since thresholds at 250 and 500 Hz are not within normal limits (30 and 25 dB HL, respectively), the audiogram must be described as a mild loss in the low frequencies with normal hearing at 1000 Hz and above. This audiogram illustrates that although classification systems are valuable guides, they cannot be used in a rigid fashion.
5. The better ear average is 5 dB HL (the average of 0 dB at 500 Hz in the right ear, 5 dB HL at 1000 Hz in the right ear, and 10 dB HL at 2000 Hz in the left ear).
6. When the two ears are considered together, this client functions as a normal hearing individual. The right ear contributes normal low-frequency hearing while the left ear contributes normal high-frequency hearing.

QUESTIONS FOR FIGURE 2-9

1. What is the degree of loss in the right ear?
2. What is the degree of loss in the left ear?
3. What are the bone conduction thresholds in the right ear?
4. What are the bone conduction thresholds in the left ear?
5. If a second qualified audiometrist re-administered the pure tone test on this client, how would you expect those results to compare with the ones shown in Figure 2-9?

Name: Fig 2-9   Date: XX/XX/XX   Age: 58   Sex: F   Audiologist: HK
AUDIOMETER: GSI-10   ANSI 1969

PURE TONE AUDIOGRAM

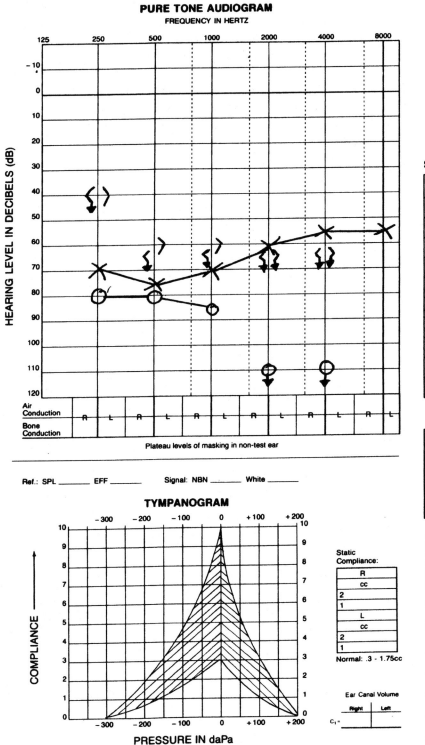

FREQUENCY IN HERTZ

HEARING LEVEL IN DECIBELS (dB)

Air Conduction

Bone Conduction

Plateau levels of masking in non-test ear

Ref.: SPL _____ EFF _____   Signal: NBN _____ White _____

Response Consistency: good moderate poor

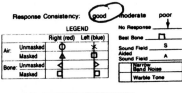

LEGEND		Right (red)	Left (blue)	No Response	
Air:	Unmasked	○	×	Best Bone	□
	Masked	△	□	Sound Field	S
Bone:	Unmasked	<	>	Aided Sound Field	A
	Masked	□	□	Narrow Band Noise	
				Warble Tone	

PURE TONE AVERAGE (R: / L:)				
	Right	Left	Aided	
AIR				
BONE				

SPEECH AUDIOMETRY □ MLV □ Tape

	RIGHT	LEFT	MASK LEVEL R	L	SOUND FIELD	LIST
SAT						
SRT						
MCL						
UCL						
PB% (Word)	_L	_L				
PB% (Word)	_L	_L				
PB% (Word)	_L	_L				
PB% (Word)	_L	_L				
	_L	_L				
	_L	_L				

STAPEDIUS REFLEX THRESHOLDS

Stimulus	Contralateral (HL)					Ipsilateral (HL)		
EAR	.5K	1K	2K	4K	WBN	.5K	1K	2K
R								
Decay			✕	✕			✕	
L								
Decay			✕	✕			✕	

ABBREVIATIONS

A	Absent	NR	No Response
C₁	Canal Volume	SAT	Speech Awareness
CNE	Could Not Establish		Threshold
CNT	Could Not Test	SL	Sensation Level
DNT	Did Not Test	SRT	Speech Reception
HL	Hearing Level		Threshold
MCL	Most Comfortable	UCL	Uncomfortable Listening
	Listening Level		Level
MVL	Monitored Live Voice		

REMARKS:

_____
_____
_____
_____

TYMPANOGRAM

PRESSURE IN daPa

COMPLIANCE

Static Compliance:

R	
	cc
2	
1	
L	
	cc
2	
1	

Normal: .3 - 1.75cc

Ear Canal Volume

	Right	Left
C₁ =		

Answers for Figure 2-9

1. We cannot determine the pure tone average in the right ear because there is no response at 2000 Hz; the degree of loss is usually based on the pure tone average. Therefore, we must describe degree of loss based on the individual thresholds of the speech frequencies. The loss is described as "severe to profound" because the thresholds at 500 and 1000 Hz are 80 and 85 dB HL, respectively, which fall into the severe category (70 to 90 dB HL), and threshold at 2000 Hz is greater than the limit of the severe category.

2. The pure tone average in the left ear is 68 dB HL, which makes the loss moderately severe.

3. The bone conduction thresholds in the right ear were not measurable. The client did not respond to signals presented at the limits of the audiometer at those frequencies (i.e., 40 dB HL at 250 Hz, 65 dB HL at all other frequencies).

4. The bone conduction thresholds in the left ear are as follows:

    250 Hz — 40 dB HL
    500 Hz — 60 dB HL
    1000 Hz — 60 dB HL
    2000 Hz — No response (NR)
    4000 Hz — No response (NR)

5. Since the audiometrist who administered these tests marked the response consistency as "good," it can be expected that the pure tone results of a second audiometrist will agree very closely with the results reported (within ±5 dB).

QUESTIONS FOR FIGURE 2-10

1. According to the scheme presented in Chapter 1, how would you describe the audiometric configurations for this client?

2. What can you conclude from the judgments made about response consistency?

Name: Fig 2-10   Date: XX/XX/XX Age: 23 Sex: M Audiologist: HK
AUDIOMETER: GSI-10   ANSI 1969

PURE TONE AUDIOGRAM
FREQUENCY IN HERTZ

[Audiogram graph with HEARING LEVEL IN DECIBELS (dB) on vertical axis from -10 to 120, and frequencies 125, 250, 500, 1000, 2000, 4000, 8000 on horizontal axis]

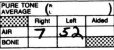

PURE TONE AVERAGE (R: L:)	Right	Left	Aided
AIR	7	52	
BONE			

SPEECH AUDIOMETRY   ☐ MLV ☒ Tape

	RIGHT	LEFT	MASK LEVEL R L	SOUND FIELD	LIST
SAT					
SRT	4	56		6	
MCL					
UCL					
PB% (Word)	L	L			
PB% (Word)	L	L			
PB% (Word)	L	L			
PB% (Word)	L	L			
	L	L			
	L	L			

	Air Conduction						
	10-30	10-30	20-40	30-50			
	R L	R L	R L	R L	R L	R L	R L
Bone Conduction	10-30	10-30	20-40	30-50	50-60		

Plateau levels of masking in non-test ear

Ref.: SPL ___ EFF ✓   Signal: NBN ✓ White ___

TYMPANOGRAM

[Tympanogram graph with COMPLIANCE on vertical axis 0-10, PRESSURE IN daPa on horizontal axis -300 to +200]

Static Compliance:

R	
	cc
2	
1	
L	
	cc
2	
1	

Normal: .3 - 1.75cc

Ear Canal Volume

	Right	Left
C₁ =		

STAPEDIUS REFLEX THRESHOLDS

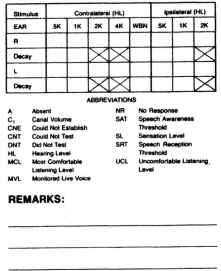

Stimulus	Contralateral (HL)					Ipsilateral (HL)		
EAR	.5K	1K	2K	4K	WBN	.5K	1K	2K
R								
Decay		✗	✗				✗	
L								
Decay		✗	✗					✗

ABBREVIATIONS

A	Absent	NR	No Response
C₁	Canal Volume	SAT	Speech Awareness
CNE	Could Not Establish		Threshold
CNT	Could Not Test	SL	Sensation Level
DNT	Did Not Test	SRT	Speech Reception
HL	Hearing Level		Threshold
MCL	Most Comfortable	UCL	Uncomfortable Listening
	Listening Level		Level
MVL	Monitored Live Voice		

REMARKS:

_____

_____

_____

_____

Answers for Figure 2-10

1. This client presents a sharply falling audiometric configuration for the right ear and essentially a flat audiometric configuration for the left ear.

2. The judgment of "moderate" response consistency suggests that if another qualified audiometrist tested this client the results would differ by no more than ±5 dB HL. We can infer that during the present evaluation the client did not exhibit an undue number of false responses. Intertest agreement was also acceptable. As can be seen from the audiogram, the pure tone averages (7 dB for the right ear and 52 dB for the left) are in general agreement with the SRTs of 4 db HL and 56 dB HL for the right and left ears, respectively. We may infer that these test results are measuring this client's true organic level of hearing.

QUESTIONS FOR FIGURE 2-11

1. How would you describe the audiometric configurations presented by this client?

2. If a second audiometrist re-administered the pure tone test on this client, how would his results compare with those shown?

3. Why are test results considered questionable?

4. Based on the judgments of poor response consistency and questionable intertest agreement, what procedures are necessary?

Name: Fig 2-11   Date: XX/XX/XX Age: 48 Sex: M Audiologist: HK
AUDIOMETER: GSI-10   ANSI 1969

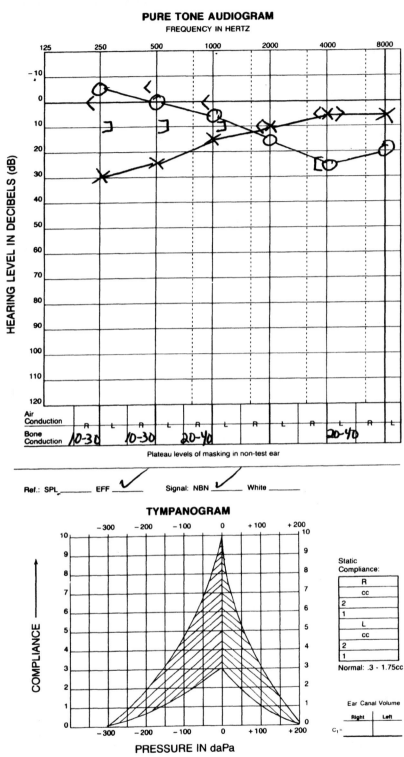

PURE TONE AUDIOGRAM
FREQUENCY IN HERTZ

Air Conduction

	R	L	R	L	R	L	R	L	R	L

Bone Conduction: 10-30 10-30 20-40 20-40

Plateau levels of masking in non-test ear

Ref.: SPL ___ EFF ✓ ___   Signal: NBN ✓ ___ White ___

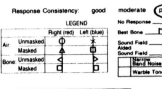

Response Consistency: good moderate (poor)

LEGEND		Right (red)	Left (blue)
Air:	Unmasked	○	✗
	Masked	△	☐
Bone:	Unmasked	◁	▷
	Masked	☐	☐

No Response ___
Best Bone ⊓
Sound Field ___ S
Aided
Sound Field ___ A
Narrow Band Noise
Warble Tone

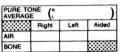

PURE TONE AVERAGE (R L)			
	Right	Left	Aided
AIR			
BONE			

SPEECH AUDIOMETRY   ☐ MLV ☐ Tape

	RIGHT	LEFT	MASK LEVEL R L	SOUND FIELD	LIST
SAT					
SRT	20	5		4	
MCL					
UCL					
PB% (Word)	_L	_L			
PB% (Word)		_L			
PB% (Word)	_L	_L			
PB% (Word)	_L	_L			
	_L	_L			
	_L	_L			

STAPEDIUS REFLEX THRESHOLDS

Stimulus	Contralateral (HL)					Ipsilateral (HL)		
EAR	.5K	1K	2K	4K	WBN	.5K	1K	2K
R								
Decay			✗	✗				✗
L								
Decay		✗				✗		✗

ABBREVIATIONS

A	Absent	NR	No Response
C₁	Canal Volume	SAT	Speech Awareness
CNE	Could Not Establish		Threshold
CNT	Could Not Test	SL	Sensation Level
DNT	Did Not Test	SRT	Speech Reception
HL	Hearing Level		Threshold
MCL	Most Comfortable	UCL	Uncomfortable Listening
	Listening Level		Level
MVL	Monitored Live Voice		

TYMPANOGRAM

PRESSURE IN daPa

Static Compliance:

R	
	cc
2	
1	
L	
	cc
2	
1	

Normal: .3 - 1.75cc

Ear Canal Volume

	Right	Left
C₁ =		

REMARKS:

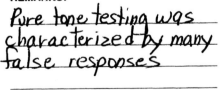

Pure tone testing was characterized by many false responses

Answers for Figure 2-11

1. This client presents a gradually falling configuration for the right ear and a rising audiometric configuration for the left ear.

2. If a second qualified audiometrist re-administered the pure tone test, the results would not necessarily be in good agreement with the results shown in Figure 2-11. The judgment of poor response consistency and the report of many false responses indicate that the reliability of these results cannot be trusted.

3. Test results are considered questionable because the response consistency is judged poor and the agreement between the pure tone averages and the SRTs is poor. Note that there is a difference of 13 dB between the PT Average and the SRT in the right ear and a difference of 12 dB in the left ear.

4. Since response consistency and intertest agreement are judged to be poor, pure tone and speech reception testing need to be redone to resolve the inconsistencies.

QUESTIONS FOR FIGURE 2-12

1. How would you describe the audiometric configurations presented by this client?
2. How do the AC and BC results agree with each other?
3. What type of hearing loss does this indicate?

PURE TONE AUDIOGRAM
FREQUENCY IN HERTZ

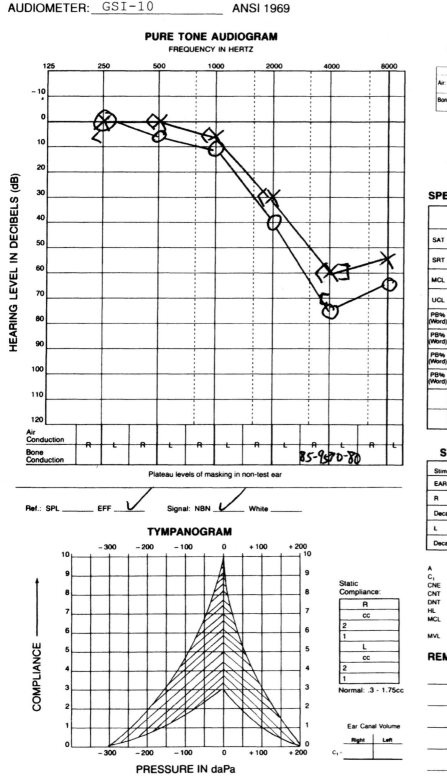

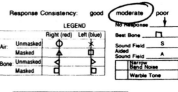

Response Consistency: good   moderate   poor

		Right (red)	Left (blue)
Air:	Unmasked	◯	✕
	Masked	△	☐
Bone:	Unmasked	◁	▷
	Masked	☐	☐

No Response
Best Bone
Sound Field   S
Aided
Sound Field   A
Narrow Band Noise
Warble Tone

PURE TONE AVERAGE (R: / L:)	Right	Left	Aided
AIR			
BONE			

SPEECH AUDIOMETRY ✕ MLV ☐ Tape

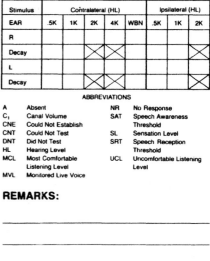

	RIGHT	LEFT	MASK LEVEL R L	SOUND FIELD	LIST
SAT					
SRT	12	8		10	
MCL					
UCL					
PB% (Word)	_L	_L			
PB% (Word)	_L	_L			
PB% (Word)	_L	_L			
PB% (Word)	_L	_L			
	_L	_L			
	_L	_L			

Plateau levels of masking in non-test ear

Ref.: SPL _____ EFF ✓____ Signal: NBN ✓____ White _____

85-9090-80

STAPEDIUS REFLEX THRESHOLDS

Stimulus	Contralateral (HL)					Ipsilateral (HL)		
EAR	.5K	1K	2K	4K	WBN	.5K	1K	2K
R								
Decay		✕	✕					✕
L								
Decay		✕	✕					✕

ABBREVIATIONS

A	Absent	NR	No Response
C_1	Canal Volume	SAT	Speech Awareness
CNE	Could Not Establish		Threshold
CNT	Could Not Test	SL	Sensation Level
DNT	Did Not Test	SRT	Speech Reception
HL	Hearing Level		Threshold
MCL	Most Comfortable	UCL	Uncomfortable Listening
	Listening Level		Level
MVL	Monitored Live Voice		

TYMPANOGRAM

Static Compliance:

R	
	cc
2	
1	
L	
	cc
2	
1	

Normal: .3 - 1.75cc

Ear Canal Volume

	Right	Left
C_1 -		

PRESSURE IN daPa

REMARKS:

_____
_____
_____
_____
_____

Answers for Figure 2-12

1. This client presents abruptly falling audiometric configurations for both ears.
2. There is no significant air–bone gap. The AC and BC thresholds are essentially the same. The slight (5 dB) difference between the AC and BC thresholds at 1K and 2K is not clinically significant.
3. Since the air conduction and bone conduction thresholds are in agreement, the loss is sensorineural in both ears.

QUESTIONS FOR FIGURE 2-13

Case History Information This child has had a history of middle ear infections requiring medical treatment. At age 8 she had a tonsillectomy and adenoidectomy to remove infected tissue and eliminate blockage of the Eustachian tube. At present, she complains that her ears frequently pop. She consistently turns the television volume louder than is comfortable for her family.

1. What type of hearing impairment does this client have?
2. What audiometric and case history information support your answer to the above question?
3. What is the prognosis for medical restoration of this client's hearing?

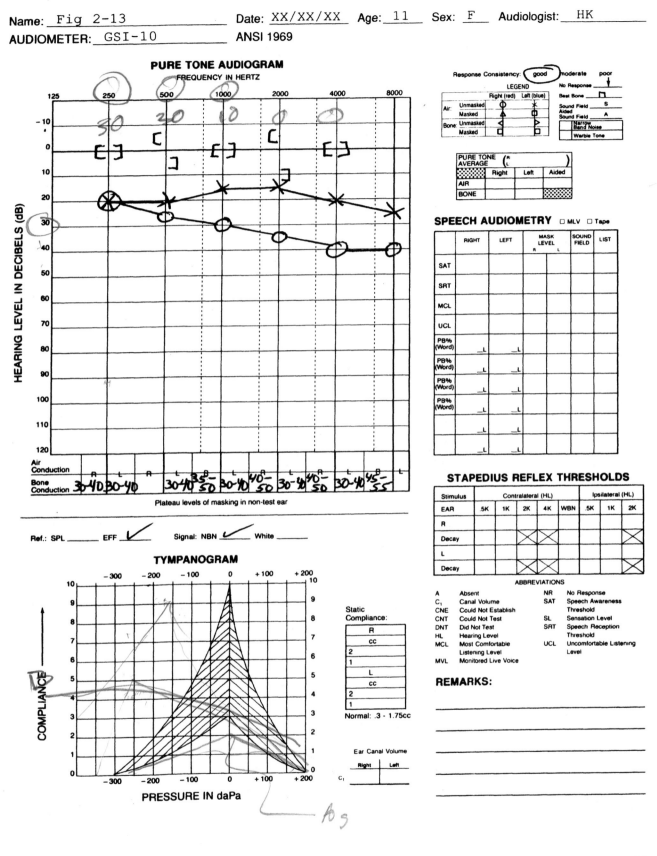

Answers for Figure 2-13

1. This client has a mild bilateral hearing impairment. Otologic examination and the audiometric examination reveal that this is a conductive-type impairment.
2. The air–bone gaps (the significant difference between the air and bone conduction thresholds) are consistent with a diagnosis of a conductive-type hearing impairment. Speech audiometry and immittance audiometry should be performed. Immittance audiometry can provide information about the physiologic nature of the conductive problem. The diagnosis of a conductive-type impairment is corroborated by the history of middle ear problems, the report of frequently popping ears, and the need for increased sound volume to listen comfortably.
3. There is considerable individual variation, but in general the prognosis for medical restoration is good.

QUESTIONS FOR FIGURE 2-14

1. Does this client have a hearing impairment?
2. What type of hearing impairment does this client have?

Name: Fig 2-14   Date: XX/XX/XX   Age: 52   Sex: M   Audiologist: HK
AUDIOMETER: GSI-10   ANSI 1969

PURE TONE AUDIOGRAM
FREQUENCY IN HERTZ

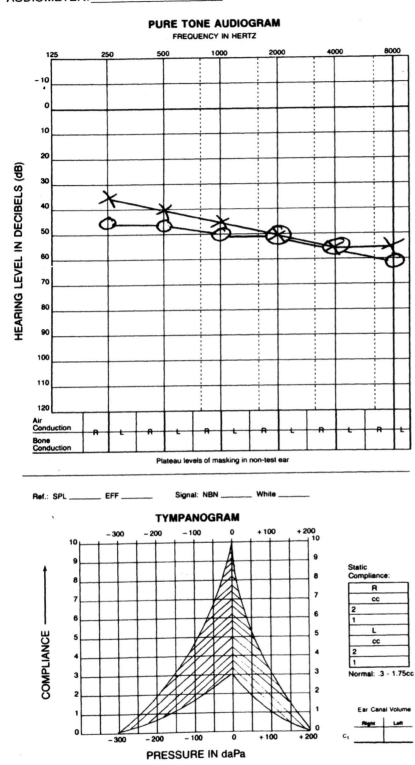

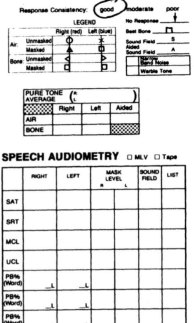

PURE TONE AVERAGE (R: L:)	Right	Left	Aided
AIR			
BONE			

SPEECH AUDIOMETRY ☐ MLV ☐ Tape

	RIGHT	LEFT	MASK LEVEL R L	SOUND FIELD	LIST
SAT					
SRT					
MCL					
UCL					
PB% (Word)	_L_	_L_			
PB% (Word)	_L_	_L_			
PB% (Word)	_L_	_L_			
PB% (Word)	_L_	_L_			
	_L_	_L_			
	_L_	_L_			

Ref.: SPL _____ EFF _____   Signal: NBN _____ White _____

STAPEDIUS REFLEX THRESHOLDS

Stimulus	Contralateral (HL)					Ipsilateral (HL)		
EAR	.5K	1K	2K	4K	WBN	.5K	1K	2K
R								
Decay		X	X					X
L								
Decay		X	X					X

ABBREVIATIONS

A	Absent	NR	No Response
C₁	Canal Volume	SAT	Speech Awareness
CNE	Could Not Establish		Threshold
CNT	Could Not Test	SL	Sensation Level
DNT	Did Not Test	SRT	Speech Reception
HL	Hearing Level		Threshold
MCL	Most Comfortable	UCL	Uncomfortable Listening
	Listening Level		Level
MVL	Monitored Live Voice		

REMARKS:

_____

_____

_____

_____

_____

TYMPANOGRAM

Static Compliance:

R	
cc	
2	
1	
L	
cc	
2	
1	

Normal: .3 - 1.75cc

Ear Canal Volume

	Right	Left
C₁		

Answers for Figure 2-14

1. Yes, this man has a moderate bilateral hearing impairment with gradually falling configurations.
2. There is not sufficient information to determine what type of impairment this man has. The AC results alone are not sufficient to make the judgment. The diagnosis of conductive loss is usually made on the basis of an air–bone gap (see Figure 2-13); the diagnosis of a sensorineural loss is based on the absence of an air–bone gap (see Figure 2-12). Since there are no bone conduction thresholds in this case, the type of loss cannot be determined.

QUESTIONS FOR FIGURE 2-15

Supplementary Information This is the same client as in Figure 2-14.

1. How do the AC and BC results agree with each other?
2. What type of hearing impairment does this man have?

Name: Fig 2-15   Date: XX/XX/XX   Age: 52   Sex: M   Audiologist: HK
AUDIOMETER: GSI-10   ANSI 1969

PURE TONE AUDIOGRAM
FREQUENCY IN HERTZ

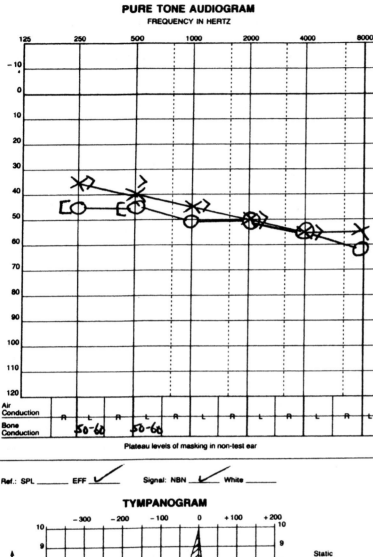

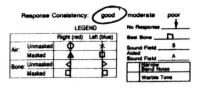

Response Consistency: (good) moderate poor

LEGEND

		Right (red)	Left (blue)
Air:	Unmasked	○	×
	Masked	▲	◻
Bone:	Unmasked	◁	▷
	Masked	◻	◻

No Response ⌐
Best Bone ◻
Sound Field ___ S
Aided
Sound Field ___ A
Narrow Band Noise
Warble Tone

PURE TONE AVERAGE (R L)			
	Right	Left	Aided
AIR			
BONE			

Air Conduction — R L R L R L R L R L R L R L
Bone Conduction — 50-60   50-60

Plateau levels of masking in non-test ear

Ref.: SPL ___ EFF ✓   Signal: NBN ✓   White ___

TYMPANOGRAM

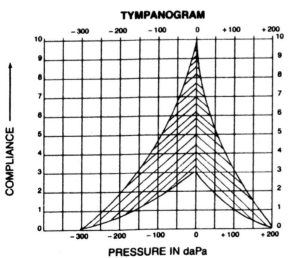

PRESSURE IN daPa

Static Compliance:

R	
	cc
2	
1	
L	
	cc
2	
1	

Normal: .3 - 1.75cc

Ear Canal Volume

	Right	Left
C₁		

SPEECH AUDIOMETRY   ☐ MLV ☐ Tape

	RIGHT	LEFT	MASK LEVEL R L	SOUND FIELD	LIST
SAT					
SRT					
MCL					
UCL					
PB% (Word)	_L_	_L_			
PB% (Word)	_L_	_L_			
PB% (Word)	_L_	_L_			
PB% (Word)	_L_	_L_			
	_L_	_L_			
	_L_	_L_			

STAPEDIUS REFLEX THRESHOLDS

Stimulus	Contralateral (HL)					Ipsilateral (HL)		
EAR	.5K	1K	2K	4K	WBN	.5K	1K	2K
R								
Decay			✕	✕				✕
L								
Decay			✕	✕				✕

ABBREVIATIONS

A   Absent
C₁   Canal Volume
CNE   Could Not Establish
CNT   Could Not Test
DNT   Did Not Test
HL   Hearing Level
MCL   Most Comfortable
       Listening Level
MVL   Monitored Live Voice

NR   No Response
SAT   Speech Awareness
       Threshold
SL   Sensation Level
SRT   Speech Reception
       Threshold
UCL   Uncomfortable Listening
       Level

REMARKS:

_____
_____
_____
_____
_____

Reading the Pure Tone Audiogram

Answers for Figure 2-15

1. There is no significant air–bone gap. The BC thresholds are in good agreement with the AC thresholds.

2. The lack of a significant air–bone gap would suggest this man has a bilateral sensorineural hearing impairment.

QUESTIONS FOR FIGURE 2-16

Case History Information This 69-year-old woman reported first noticing a hearing problem 5 years ago. It is becoming gradually worse. She experiences no tinnitus, vertigo, or cranial nerve symptoms. There is no history of family hearing problems, noise exposure, or taking of ototoxic drugs. She reports no earaches, ear infections, nor drainage at present or in the past. She has no difficulty understanding speech in a quiet situation, but she does have difficulty understanding conversation when there is competing noise or when several people are talking at once.

1. What type of hearing impairment does this client have?
2. Does the audiometric configuration provide any information about the type of hearing loss?
3. Does the case history provide information about the type of hearing loss?
4. What is the prognosis for medical restoration of this client's hearing?

Name: Fig 2-16   Date: XX/XX/XX   Age: 69   Sex: F   Audiologist: HK

AUDIOMETER: GSI-10   ANSI 1969

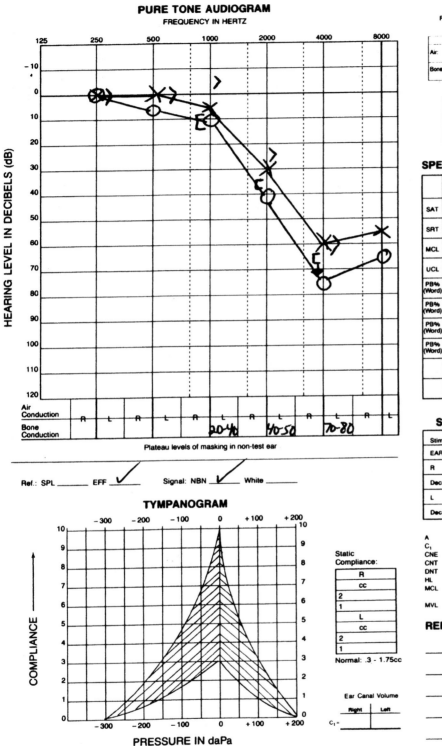

PURE TONE AUDIOGRAM
FREQUENCY IN HERTZ

HEARING LEVEL IN DECIBELS (dB)

Air Conduction — R L R L R L R L R L R L R L

Bone Conduction — 20-40   40-50   70-80

Plateau levels of masking in non-test ear

Ref.: SPL _____ EFF ✓   Signal: NBN ✓   White _____

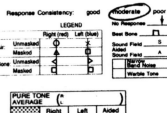

Response Consistency: good (moderate) poor

LEGEND

		Right (red)	Left (blue)
Air:	Unmasked	O	X
	Masked	▲	◻
Bone:	Unmasked	◁	▷
	Masked	◻	◻

No Response
Best Bone ◻
Sound Field S
Aided Sound Field A
Narrow Band Noise
Warble Tone

PURE TONE AVERAGE (R L		Right	Left	Aided
AIR				
BONE				

SPEECH AUDIOMETRY ☐ MLV ☐ Tape

	RIGHT	LEFT	MASK LEVEL R L	SOUND FIELD	LIST
SAT					
SRT					
MCL					
UCL					
PB% (Word)	L	L			
PB% (Word)	L	L			
PB% (Word)	L	L			
PB% (Word)	L	L			
	L	L			
	L	L			

STAPEDIUS REFLEX THRESHOLDS

Stimulus	Contralateral (HL)					Ipsilateral (HL)		
EAR	.5K	1K	2K	4K	WBN	.5K	1K	2K
R			✕					✕
Decay			✕	✕				
L			✕					✕
Decay			✕	✕				

ABBREVIATIONS

A   Absent   NR   No Response
C_1 Canal Volume   SAT   Speech Awareness
CNE   Could Not Establish   Threshold
CNT   Could Not Test   SL   Sensation Level
DNT   Did Not Test   SRT   Speech Reception
HL   Hearing Level   Threshold
MCL   Most Comfortable   UCL   Uncomfortable Listening
   Listening Level   Level
MVL   Monitored Live Voice

REMARKS:

_____

_____

_____

_____

TYMPANOGRAM

PRESSURE IN daPa

COMPLIANCE

Static Compliance:

R
cc
2
1

L
cc
2
1

Normal: .3 - 1.75cc

Ear Canal Volume

	Right	Left
C_1 =		

1. Although the actual medical diagnosis must be made by an otologist, the lack of a significant air–bone gap would suggest this client has a sensorineural hearing impairment.
2. The abruptly falling audiometric configurations would suggest some sensorineural loss, although it is possible to have a conductive problem which shows poorer sensitivity by air conduction in the high frequencies than in the low frequencies. Again, the final diagnosis depends upon otologic evaluation.
3. The absence of reported middle ear symptoms (earaches, ear infections, or drainage) tends to reduce the probability of conductive loss. Her age plus her report of word recognition difficulty in different listening situations suggests possible presbycusis, which usually includes a sensorineural component.
4. The otologist does have some medical assistance in his armentarium for people with certain sensorineural hearing impairments. However, in most cases of sensorineural hearing impairment, medical treatment is not indicated. Nevertheless, if the client has not had a medical evaluation of her ears and hearing, she should receive the benefit of an otologic examination whenever a hearing impairment is observed.

QUESTIONS FOR FIGURE 2-17

Case History Information This 25-year-old man reports extreme difficulty understanding speech when the speaker is on his right side, even when there is no competing noise. He has been aware of this problem for approximately 5 years and the problem seems to be getting worse. In addition, he experiences constant tinnitus in his right ear which seems to be getting more intense. During the past year he reported two attacks of vertigo which lasted 5 to 10 minutes each.

1. What type of hearing impairment does this client have?
2. What recommendations would you have for:
    a. An otologic examination?
    b. An audiometic re-evaluation?
3. What audiometric information suggests a sensorineural impairment for the right ear?

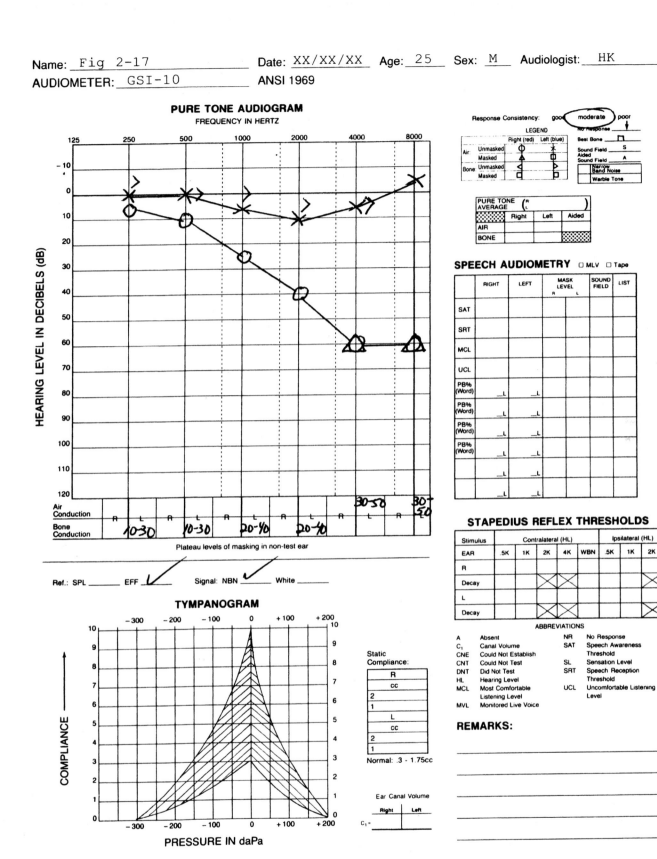

51

Answers for Figure 2-17

1. Although the actual diagnosis would depend upon an otologic examination, this man appears to have a mild to moderate unilateral sensorineural hearing impairment of the right ear with essentially normal hearing sensitivity in the left ear. The report of extreme word recognition difficulty only on the right side corroborates this diagnosis.

2. (a) If this man has not had the benefit of a medical examination of his ears, he should be referred for an otologic examination. The symptoms of unilateral loss, severe word recognition difficulty in the presence of a mild to moderate hearing loss, tinnitus, and vertigo make it mandatory for the client to be evaluated by a physician.

   (b) Any person with a unilateral hearing impairment should have a hearing re-evaluation approximately every year because eighth nerve lesions are frequently unilateral. In addition, possible progression of hearing loss, whatever the cause, can thus be monitored.

3. The lack of a significant air–bone gap and the sharply falling audiometric configuration are consistent with a diagnosis of a sensorineural hearing impairment. Further audiometric testing including speech audiometry, particularly speech recognition, and site of lesion tests should be performed to further define the nature of the loss. Speech audiometry is discussed in Chapter 4; site of lesion testing is beyond the scope of this book.

QUESTIONS FOR FIGURE 2-18

1. What type of hearing impairment does this client have?
2. What audiometric information supports your answer to the above question?

Name: Fig 2-18   Date: XX/XX/XX   Age: 8   Sex: F   Audiologist: HK

AUDIOMETER: GSI-10   ANSI 1969

PURE TONE AUDIOGRAM
FREQUENCY IN HERTZ

HEARING LEVEL IN DECIBELS (dB)

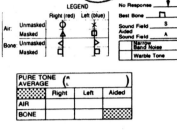

Response Consistency: (good) moderate poor

LEGEND

		Right (red)	Left (blue)	No Response	
Air:	Unmasked	O	X	Best Bone	
	Masked	△	☐	Sound Field	S
Bone:	Unmasked	<	>	Aided Sound Field	A
	Masked	☐	☐	Narrow Band Noise	
				Warble Tone	

PURE TONE AVERAGE (R / L)			
	Right	Left	Aided
AIR			
BONE			

SPEECH AUDIOMETRY ☐ MLV ☐ Tape

	RIGHT	LEFT	MASK LEVEL R / L	SOUND FIELD	LIST
SAT					
SRT					
MCL					
UCL					
PB% (Word)	_L_	_L_			
PB% (Word)	_L_	_L_			
PB% (Word)	_L_	_L_			
PB% (Word)	_L_	_L_			
	_L_	_L_			
	_L_	_L_			

	125	250	500	1000	2000	4000	8000		
Air Conduction		R30/40	35/40	R30/40	25/55	R30/40	35/50	R55/65	35/50	53/65	40/50	R	L
Bone Conduction						40/30			

Plateau levels of masking in non-test ear

Ref.: SPL _____ EFF ✓ _____ Signal: NBN ✓ White _____

TYMPANOGRAM
PRESSURE IN daPa

COMPLIANCE

Static Compliance:	
R	
cc	
2	
1	
L	
cc	
2	
1	

Normal: .3 - 1.75cc

Ear Canal Volume

	Right	Left
C₁ =		

STAPEDIUS REFLEX THRESHOLDS

Stimulus	Contralateral (HL)					Ipsilateral (HL)		
EAR	.5K	1K	2K	4K	WBN	.5K	1K	2K
R								
Decay			✕	✕				✕
L								
Decay		✕	✕			✕		✕

ABBREVIATIONS

A	Absent	NR	No Response
C₁	Canal Volume	SAT	Speech Awareness Threshold
CNE	Could Not Establish		
CNT	Could Not Test	SL	Sensation Level
DNT	Did Not Test	SRT	Speech Reception Threshold
HL	Hearing Level		
MCL	Most Comfortable Listening Level	UCL	Uncomfortable Listening Level
MVL	Monitored Live Voice		

REMARKS:

_____

_____

_____

_____

Answers for Figure 2-18

1. This client has a mild bilateral hearing impairment which is greater in the right ear than in the left. Based on audiometric and otologic examination, this client has been diagnosed as having a conductive hearing impairment.

2. The air–bone gap with essentially normal hearing acuity by bone conduction supports a diagnosis of a conductive impairment. Speech audiometry and immittance testing are indicated to further define the nature of the loss.

QUESTIONS FOR FIGURE 2-19

Case History Information This child suffered several respiratory infections accompanied by high fevers during his first year of life. During one illness he experienced a grand mal seizure. He has also had a history of recurrent ear infections in the right ear that required medical treatment.

1. What type of hearing impairment does this client have?
2. What audiometric and case history information support your answer to the above question?
3. What is the prognosis for medical restoration of this client's hearing?

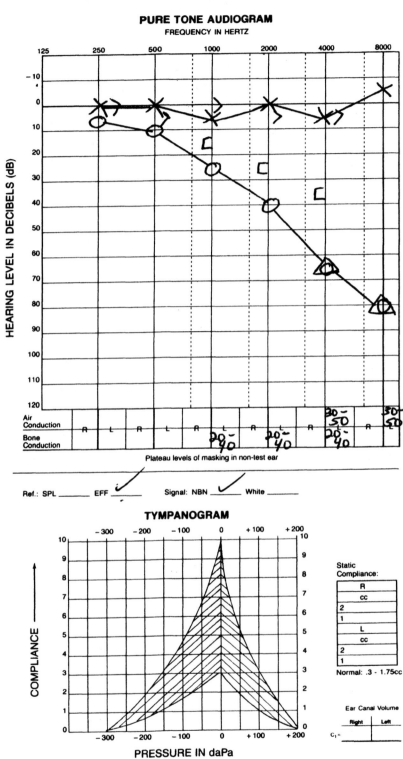

PURE TONE AUDIOGRAM
FREQUENCY IN HERTZ

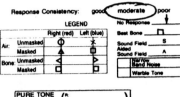

Response Consistency: good (moderate) poor

SPEECH AUDIOMETRY ☐ MLV ☐ Tape

	RIGHT	LEFT	MASK LEVEL R	L	SOUND FIELD	LIST
SAT						
SRT						
MCL						
UCL						
PB% (Word)	_L_	_L_				
PB% (Word)	_L_	_L_				
PB% (Word)	_L_	_L_				
PB% (Word)	_L_	_L_				
	_L_	_L_				
	_L_	_L_				

STAPEDIUS REFLEX THRESHOLDS

Stimulus	Contralateral (HL)					Ipsilateral (HL)		
EAR	.5K	1K	2K	4K	WBN	.5K	1K	2K
R								
Decay			X	X				
L								
Decay			X	X			X	X

ABBREVIATIONS

A	Absent	NR	No Response
C₁	Canal Volume	SAT	Speech Awareness
CNE	Could Not Establish		Threshold
CNT	Could Not Test	SL	Sensation Level
DNT	Did Not Test	SRT	Speech Reception
HL	Hearing Level		Threshold
MCL	Most Comfortable	UCL	Uncomfortable Listening
	Listening Level		Level
MVL	Monitored Live Voice		

Ref.: SPL _____ EFF _____   Signal: NBN _____ White _____

TYMPANOGRAM

REMARKS:

Static Compliance:

R	
cc	
2	
1	

L	
cc	
2	
1	

Normal: .3 - 1.75cc

Ear Canal Volume

Right	Left
C₁ =	

1. This child has a mild unilateral mixed-type hearing impairment of the right ear.
2. The significant air–bone gap (difference) with a significant loss by bone conduction is consistent with a mixed impairment diagnosis. A mixed loss is characterized by bone conduction thresholds which are not normal, but are more sensitive than the air conduction thresholds by at least 10 dB. The sharply falling audiometric configuration supports the sensorineural component of this mixed-type impairment. However, compare this audiogram with that in Figure 2-16, where the air conduction configuration is essentially the same but the type of loss is different. Audiometric configuration may provide some corroborative information, but it does not predict the type of loss.

   The case history contains possible etiologic factors to explain both the conductive and sensorineural components of the loss in the right ear (recurrent ear infections and high fevers).
3. In general, the prognosis for medical restoration to the level of the bone conduction curve is favorable, depending upon other medical considerations. The prognosis for medical restoration to normal is poor.

QUESTION FOR FIGURE 2-20

Case History Information This boy has had recurrent attacks of tonsillitis, during which he has complained that his right ear felt stuffed. He also suffers from allergies which produce respiratory symptoms. There have been no communicative difficulties.

1. Does this boy have a hearing impairment?

Name: Fig 2-20   Date: XX/XX/XX   Age: 9   Sex: M   Audiologist: HK
AUDIOMETER: GSI-10   ANSI 1969

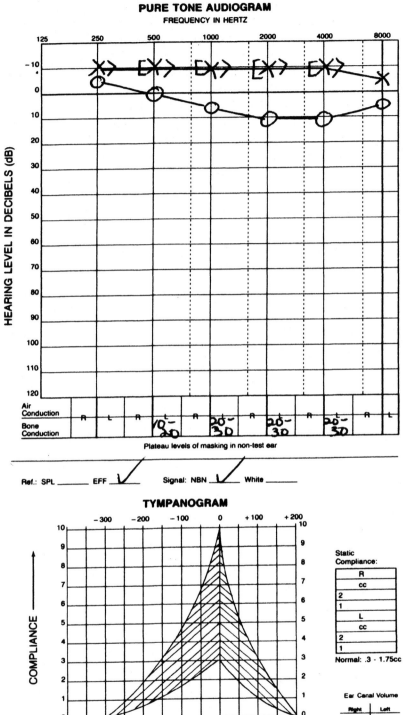

PURE TONE AUDIOGRAM
FREQUENCY IN HERTZ

HEARING LEVEL IN DECIBELS (dB)

Air Conduction
Bone Conduction

| | | 10–20 | 20–30 | 20–30 | 20–30 | | |

Plateau levels of masking in non-test ear

Ref.: SPL _____ EFF _____   Signal: NBN _____ White _____

TYMPANOGRAM
PRESSURE IN daPa
COMPLIANCE

Static Compliance:

R	
cc	
2	
1	
L	
cc	
2	
1	

Normal: .3 - 1.75cc

Ear Canal Volume

	Right	Left
C₁ =		

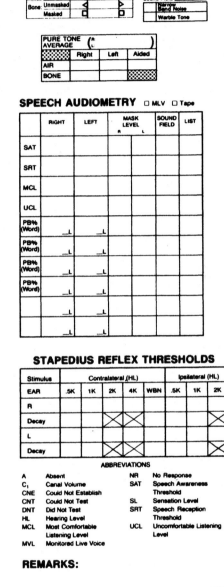

Response Consistency: good moderate poor

LEGEND

		Right (red)	Left (blue)
Air:	Unmasked	O	X
	Masked	▲	▣
Bone:	Unmasked	◁	▷
	Masked	▢	▣

No Response
Best Bone
Sound Field — S
Aided Sound Field — A
Narrow Band Noise
Warble Tone

PURE TONE AVERAGE	(R L)		
	Right	Left	Aided
AIR			
BONE			

SPEECH AUDIOMETRY   ☐ MLV ☐ Tape

	RIGHT	LEFT	MASK LEVEL R L	SOUND FIELD	LIST
SAT					
SRT					
MCL					
UCL					
PB% (Word)	L	L			
PB% (Word)	L	L			
PB% (Word)	L	L			
PB% (Word)	L	L			
	L	L			
	L	L			

STAPEDIUS REFLEX THRESHOLDS

Stimulus	Contralateral (HL)					Ipsilateral (HL)		
EAR	.5K	1K	2K	4K	WBN	.5K	1K	2K
R								
Decay			✕					✕
L								
Decay			✕					✕

ABBREVIATIONS

A	Absent	NR	No Response
C₁	Canal Volume	SAT	Speech Awareness
CNE	Could Not Establish		Threshold
CNT	Could Not Test	SL	Sensation Level
DNT	Did Not Test	SRT	Speech Reception
HL	Hearing Level		Threshold
MCL	Most Comfortable	UCL	Uncomfortable Listening
	Listening Level		Level
MVL	Monitored Live Voice		

REMARKS:

_____
_____
_____
_____
_____

Answer for Figure 2-20

1. This boy's hearing sensitivity appears to be essentially within normal limits as usually defined (e.g., Figure 1-9, Table 1-1), but based on careful evaluation of these results, this boy may have a mild unilateral ear pathology and should have the benefit of an otologic evaluation and possible treatment. Immittance audiometry should be performed to further define the nature of the conductive problem.

   Based on the AC results this boy would have passed most conventional screening tests even at a level as low as 10 dB HL. It may further be noted that based on the AC results, this looks like essentially normal hearing. However, the air–bone gap for the right ear and the difference between the AC results of the right and the left ear would indicate there is some pathology in the right ear. The history of recurrent tonsillitis and allergies further corroborates the suspicion of pathology. The air–bone gap would suggest a slight unilateral conductive type of hearing loss. This mild impairment is of minor educational significance but may be of considerable medical significance.

QUESTION FOR FIGURE 2-21

1. What type of hearing impairment does this woman have?

Name: Fig 2-21   Date: XX/XX/XX   Age: 47   Sex: F   Audiologist: HK

AUDIOMETER: GSI-10   ANSI 1969

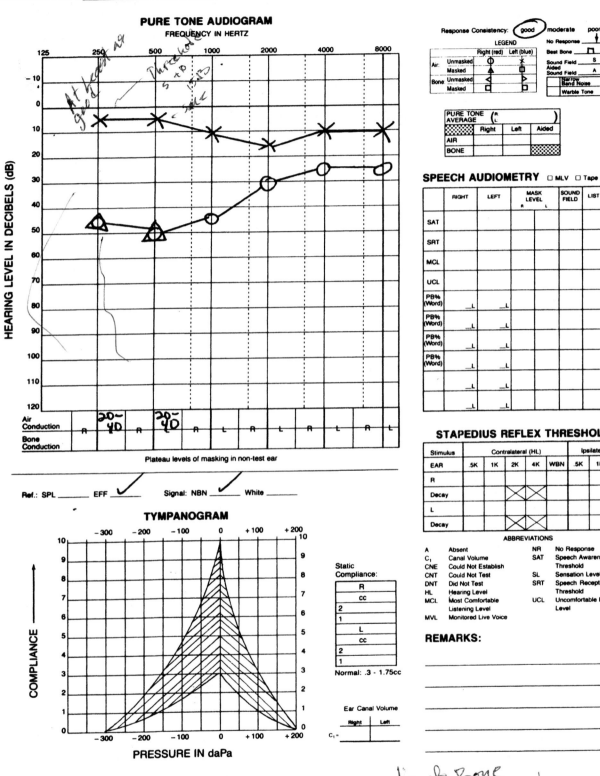

PURE TONE AUDIOGRAM
FREQUENCY IN HERTZ

HEARING LEVEL IN DECIBELS (dB)

Response Consistency: (good) moderate poor

LEGEND

	Right (red)	Left (blue)
Air: Unmasked	O	X
Masked	▲	▢
Bone: Unmasked	□	▷
Masked	◁	▷

No Response
Best Bone
Sound Field — S
Aided
Sound Field — A
Narrow Band Noise
Warble Tone

PURE TONE AVERAGE (R / L)	Right	Left	Aided
AIR			
BONE			

Air Conduction	R	20~40	R	20~40	R	L	R	L	R	L	R	L	R	L
Bone Conduction														

Plateau levels of masking in non-test ear

Ref.: SPL _____ EFF _____   Signal: NBN _____ White _____

TYMPANOGRAM

COMPLIANCE

PRESSURE IN daPa

Static Compliance:

R	
cc	
2	
1	
L	
cc	
2	
1	

Normal: .3 - 1.75cc

Ear Canal Volume

	Right	Left
C₁ =		

SPEECH AUDIOMETRY   ☐ MLV ☐ Tape

	RIGHT	LEFT	MASK LEVEL R L	SOUND FIELD	LIST
SAT					
SRT					
MCL					
UCL					
PB% (Word)	L	L			
PB% (Word)	L	L			
PB% (Word)	L	L			
PB% (Word)	L	L			
	L	L			
	L	L			

STAPEDIUS REFLEX THRESHOLDS

Stimulus	Contralateral (HL)					Ipsilateral (HL)		
EAR	.5K	1K	2K	4K	WBN	.5K	1K	2K
R								
Decay		X	X					X
L								
Decay		X	X			X		X

ABBREVIATIONS

A — Absent
C₁ — Canal Volume
CNE — Could Not Establish
CNT — Could Not Test
DNT — Did Not Test
HL — Hearing Level
MCL — Most Comfortable Listening Level
MVL — Monitored Live Voice
NR — No Response
SAT — Speech Awareness Threshold
SL — Sensation Level
SRT — Speech Reception Threshold
UCL — Uncomfortable Listening Level

REMARKS:

_____
_____
_____
_____

In Absence of Bone make assumption is equal to air Conduction

Reading the Pure Tone Audiogram

59

Answer for Figure 2-21

1. This woman has a moderate hearing impairment with a rising configuration in the right ear and normal hearing in the left ear. There is insufficient information to suggest the type of hearing impairment. The rising audiometric configuration would possibly suggest a conductive type of hearing impairment. However, in many cases the audiometric configuration is a poor index of the type of impairment.

QUESTIONS FOR FIGURE 2-22

Supplementary Information This client is the same as in Figure 2-21.

Case History Information This woman reports a history of fluctuating hearing loss in the right ear. Each episode of hearing loss is accompanied by an increase in tinnitus that is always present to some degree in the right ear, severe vertigo, and extreme sensitivity to loud sound. After the vertigo subsides, the hearing in the right ear improves somewhat but does not return to normal.

1. What type of hearing impairment does this woman have?
2. What audiometric and case history information support your answer to the above question?

Name: Fig 2-22   Date: XX/XX/XX   Age: 47   Sex: F   Audiologist: HK
AUDIOMETER: GSI-10   ANSI 1969

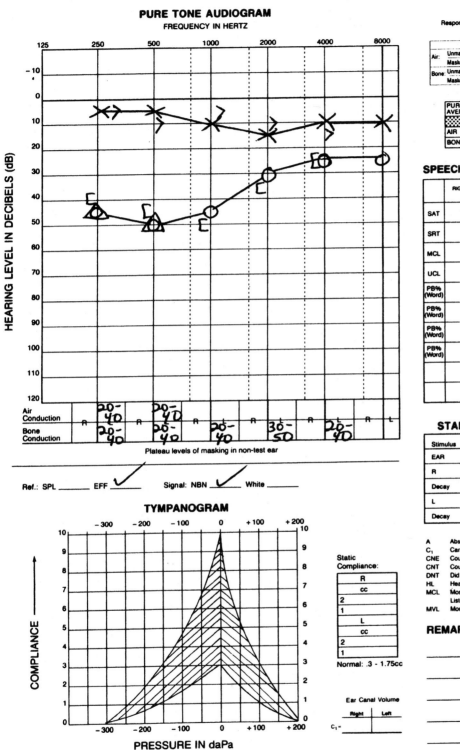

PURE TONE AUDIOGRAM
FREQUENCY IN HERTZ

Air Conduction	R	20-40	R	20-40	R		R		R		R	L
Bone Conduction		20-40		20-40		20-40		30-50		20-40		

Plateau levels of masking in non-test ear

Ref.: SPL _____ EFF ✓   Signal: NBN ✓   White _____

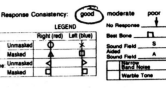

Response Consistency: (good) moderate poor

LEGEND			No Response
	Right (red)	Left (blue)	Best Bone
Air: Unmasked			Sound Field S
Masked			Aided
Bone: Unmasked			Sound Field A
Masked			Narrow Band Noise / Warble Tone

PURE TONE AVERAGE (R: L:)			
	Right	Left	Aided
AIR			
BONE			

SPEECH AUDIOMETRY ☐ MLV ☐ Tape

	RIGHT	LEFT	MASK LEVEL R	L	SOUND FIELD	LIST
SAT						
SRT						
MCL						
UCL						
PB% (Word)	_L_	_L_				
PB% (Word)	_L_	_L_				
PB% (Word)	_L_	_L_				
PB% (Word)	_L_	_L_				
	_L_	_L_				
		_L_				

STAPEDIUS REFLEX THRESHOLDS

Stimulus	Contralateral (HL)					Ipsilateral (HL)		
EAR	.5K	1K	2K	4K	WBN	.5K	1K	2K
R								
Decay			✕	✕				✕
L								
Decay			✕	✕		✕		✕

ABBREVIATIONS

A	Absent	NR	No Response
C₁	Canal Volume	SAT	Speech Awareness
CNE	Could Not Establish		Threshold
CNT	Could Not Test	SL	Sensation Level
DNT	Did Not Test	SRT	Speech Reception
HL	Hearing Level		Threshold
MCL	Most Comfortable	UCL	Uncomfortable Listening
	Listening Level		Level
MVL	Monitored Live Voice		

REMARKS:

_____

_____

_____

_____

_____

TYMPANOGRAM

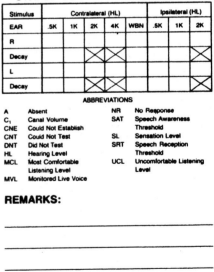

PRESSURE IN daPa

Static Compliance:

R	
	cc
2	
1	
L	
	cc
2	
1	

Normal: .3 - 1.75cc

Ear Canal Volume

	Right	Left
C₁ =		

Answers for Figure 2-22

1. This woman has a moderate sensorineural loss with a rising configuration in her right ear and normal hearing in her left. Note that the rising configuration of the audiogram can exist with sensorineural loss as well as with conductive loss.

2. Based on the otologic examination—a case history of vertigo, tinnitus, fluctuating hearing, and recruitment—and audiological tests, this woman's impairment has been diagnosed as Ménière's disease. The lack of a significant air–bone gap is consistent with the diagnosis of a sensorineural type of hearing impairment. Speech audiometry is needed here to provide further corroborative information, as are site of lesion tests to differentiate between cochlear and retrocochlear sites of lesions. Speech audiometry is discussed in Chapter 4, and site of lesion testing is beyond the scope of this book.

QUESTIONS FOR FIGURE 2-23

1. What type of hearing impairment does this man have?
2. Based on the audiometric configuration alone, would this most likely be a sensorineural or a conductive type of hearing impairment?

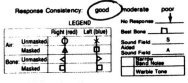

PURE TONE AUDIOGRAM
FREQUENCY IN HERTZ

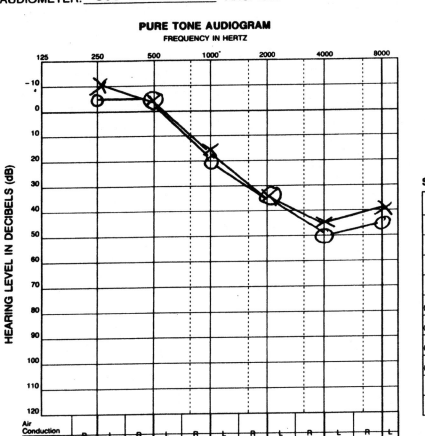

Air Conduction: R L R L R L R L R L R L R L R L
Bone Conduction:

Plateau levels of masking in non-test ear

Ref.: SPL _____ EFF _____   Signal: NBN _____ White _____

TYMPANOGRAM

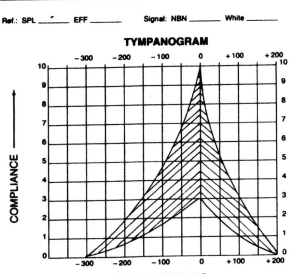

PRESSURE IN daPa

SPEECH AUDIOMETRY   □ MLV □ Tape

	RIGHT	LEFT	MASK LEVEL R / L	SOUND FIELD	LIST
SAT					
SRT					
MCL					
UCL					
PB% (Word)	_L_	_L_			
PB% (Word)	_L_	_L_			
PB% (Word)	_L_	_L_			
PB% (Word)	_L_	_L_			
	_L_	_L_			
	_L_	_L_			

STAPEDIUS REFLEX THRESHOLDS

Stimulus	Contralateral (HL)					Ipsilateral (HL)		
EAR	.5K	1K	2K	4K	WBN	.5K	1K	2K
R								
Decay			✗	✗		✗		
L								
Decay			✗	✗		✗		✗

ABBREVIATIONS

A	Absent	NR	No Response
C₁	Canal Volume	SAT	Speech Awareness
CNE	Could Not Establish		Threshold
CNT	Could Not Test	SL	Sensation Level
DNT	Did Not Test	SRT	Speech Reception
HL	Hearing Level		Threshold
MCL	Most Comfortable	UCL	Uncomfortable Listening
	Listening Level		Level
MVL	Monitored Live Voice		

A = Absent, C₁ = Canal Volume, CNE = Could Not Establish, CNT = Could Not Test, DNT = Did Not Test, HL = Hearing Level, MCL = Most Comfortable Listening Level, MVL = Monitored Live Voice, NR = No Response, SAT = Speech Awareness Threshold, SL = Sensation Level, SRT = Speech Reception Threshold, UCL = Uncomfortable Listening Level

REMARKS:

_____

_____

_____

_____

_____

Static Compliance:

R	
cc	
2	
1	
L	
cc	
2	
1	

Normal: .3 - 1.75cc

Ear Canal Volume

Right	Left

C₁ =

Reading the Pure Tone Audiogram

Answers for Figure 2-23

1. This client has a mild bilateral hearing impairment. There is insufficient audiometric information to suggest a type of impairment.

2. A sharply falling audiometric configuration such as this one suggests a possible sensorineural component, but the audiometric configuration may be misleading.

   It should also be noted that some texts (Newby and Popelka, 1985) suggest that high-frequency losses are indicative of sensorineural-type impairment. However, a review of Figures 2-7, 2-17, 2-18, and 2-19 indicates that certain conductive impairments affect the high frequencies more than the low frequencies. The fallacy of determining the type of pathology on the basis of the audiometric configuration is further confirmed by Downs and Doster (1959), who reported 50% of the group tested with sensorineural impairments had flat or rising audiometric configurations. In summary, to answer this question, the sharply falling audiometric configuration shown in Figure 2-23 suggests a sensorineural impairment, but the reader should be cognizant of the fallacies of determining the type of impairment on the basis of the pure tone audiometric pattern.

QUESTIONS FOR FIGURE 2-24

Supplementary Information This is the same client as in Figure 2-23.

1. What type of hearing impairment does this man have?
2. What is the prognosis for medical restoration of this client's hearing?

Name: Fig 2-24   Date: XX/XX/XX   Age: 29   Sex: M   Audiologist: HK

AUDIOMETER: GSI-10   ANSI 1969

PURE TONE AUDIOGRAM
FREQUENCY IN HERTZ

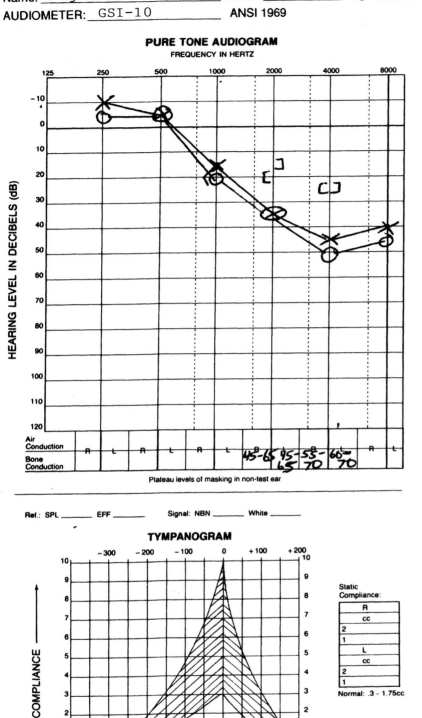

Air Conduction | R | L | R | L | R | L | R | L | R | L
Bone Conduction | | | | | | 45-65 | 45-55 | 60-70 | R | L

45-65   45-55   60-70
65   70   70

Plateau levels of masking in non-test ear

Ref.: SPL _____ EFF _____   Signal: NBN _____ White _____

TYMPANOGRAM

PRESSURE IN daPa

COMPLIANCE

Static Compliance:

R	
cc	
2	
1	
L	
cc	
2	
1	

Normal: .3 - 1.75cc

Ear Canal Volume

	Right	Left
$C_1 =$		

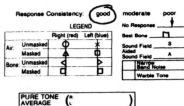

Response Consistency: (good) moderate poor

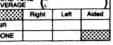

		Right (red)	Left (blue)
Air:	Unmasked	◯	✕
	Masked	△	◻
Bone:	Unmasked	◁	▷
	Masked	◻	◻

No Response
Best Bone
Sound Field ____ S
Aided Sound Field ____ A
Narrow Band Noise
Warble Tone

PURE TONE AVERAGE (R L)			
	Right	Left	Aided
AIR			
BONE			

SPEECH AUDIOMETRY   ☐ MLV ☐ Tape

	RIGHT	LEFT	MASK LEVEL R L	SOUND FIELD	LIST
SAT					
SRT					
MCL					
UCL					
PB% (Word)	_L	_L			
PB% (Word)	_L	_L			
PB% (Word)	_L	_L			
PB% (Word)	_L	_L			
	_L	_L			
	_L	_L			

STAPEDIUS REFLEX THRESHOLDS

Stimulus	Contralateral (HL)					Ipsilateral (HL)		
EAR	.5K	1K	2K	4K	WBN	.5K	1K	2K
R								
Decay			✕	✕				✕
L								
Decay			✕					✕

ABBREVIATIONS

A	Absent	NR	No Response
C₁	Canal Volume	SAT	Speech Awareness
CNE	Could Not Establish		Threshold
CNT	Could Not Test	SL	Sensation Level
DNT	Did Not Test	SRT	Speech Reception
HL	Hearing Level		Threshold
MCL	Most Comfortable	UCL	Uncomfortable Listening
	Listening Level		Level
MVL	Monitored Live Voice		

REMARKS:

_____

_____

_____

_____

_____

Answers for Figure 2-24

1. This man's hearing impairment has been otologically diagnosed as a mixed type of hearing impairment containing both a sensorineural and a conductive component. The BC results reveal a significant air–bone gap with the BC results significantly deviant from audiometric zero. The air–bone relationship is consistent with a mixed type of impairment diagnosis.

2. There is considerable individual variation, but in general the prognosis for partial medical restoration to the level of the bone conduction thresholds for a mixed type of impairment is good. However, the prognosis for complete restoration is poor.

QUESTIONS FOR FIGURE 2-25

1. What type of hearing impairment does this woman have?
2. Based on the audiologic information, what is the prognosis for medical restoration?

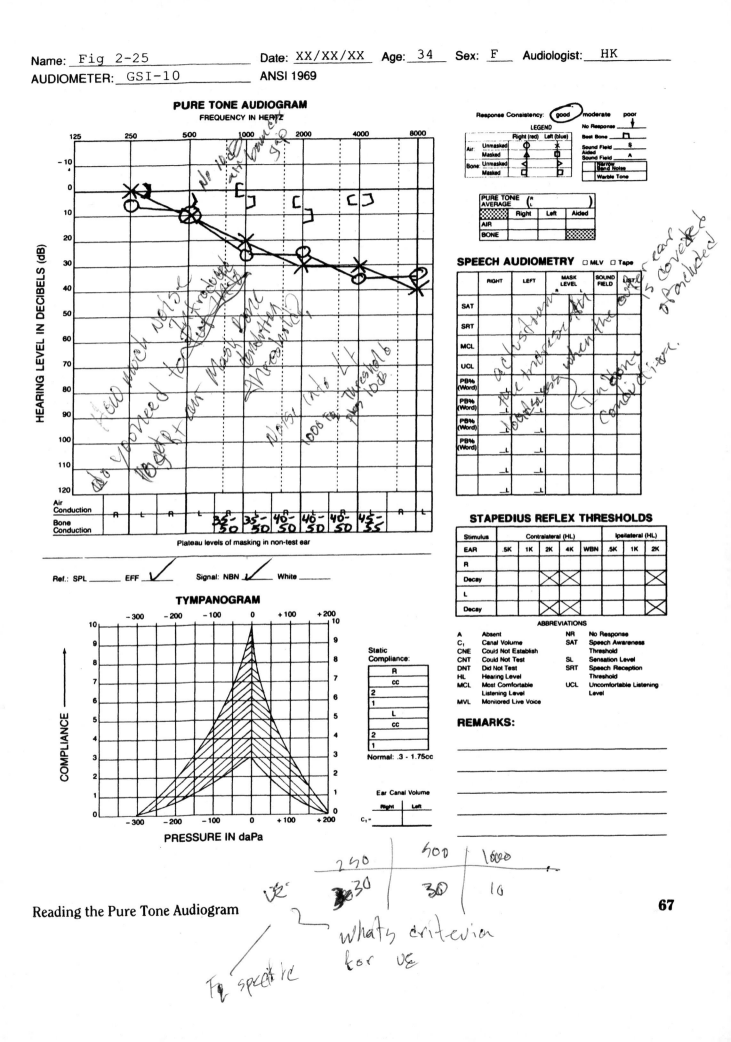

PURE TONE AUDIOGRAM

Name: Fig 2-25   **Date:** XX/XX/XX   **Age:** 34   **Sex:** F   **Audiologist:** HK

AUDIOMETER: GSI-10   **ANSI 1969**

PURE TONE AUDIOGRAM
FREQUENCY IN HERTZ

	Right	Left	Aided
AIR			
BONE			

Air Conduction	R	L	R	L	R	L	R	L	R	L	R	L	R	L
Bone Conduction					35-50	35-50	40-50	40-50	40-50	45-35				

Plateau levels of masking in non-test ear

Ref.: SPL _____ EFF ✓   Signal: NBN ✓   White _____

TYMPANOGRAM
PRESSURE IN daPa

Static Compliance:

R	
cc	
2	
1	
L	
cc	
2	
1	

Normal: .3 - 1.75cc

Ear Canal Volume

Right	Left

$C_1 =$

LEGEND

Response Consistency: (good) moderate poor

	Right (red)	Left (blue)
Air: Unmasked	O	X
Masked		
Bone: Unmasked	<	>
Masked		

No Response ↓
Best Bone
Sound Field   S
Aided Sound Field   A
Narrow Band Noise
Warble Tone

SPEECH AUDIOMETRY   ☐ MLV ☐ Tape

	RIGHT	LEFT	MASK LEVEL R L	SOUND FIELD	LIST
SAT					
SRT					
MCL					
UCL					
PB% (Word)					
PB% (Word)					
PB% (Word)					
PB% (Word)					

STAPEDIUS REFLEX THRESHOLDS

Stimulus	Contralateral (HL)					Ipsilateral (HL)		
EAR	.5K	1K	2K	4K	WBN	.5K	1K	2K
R								
Decay			X	X				X
L								
Decay								X

ABBREVIATIONS

A	Absent	NR	No Response
C₁	Canal Volume	SAT	Speech Awareness
CNE	Could Not Establish		Threshold
CNT	Could Not Test	SL	Sensation Level
DNT	Did Not Test	SRT	Speech Reception
HL	Hearing Level		Threshold
MCL	Most Comfortable	UCL	Uncomfortable Listening
	Listening Level		Level
MVL	Monitored Live Voice		

REMARKS:

_____

_____

_____

_____

_____

Answers for Figure 2-25

1. Both otologic diagnosis and audiometric results indicate a pure conductive hearing loss bilaterally. In both ears there are significant air–bone gaps (more than 10 dB) with bone conduction thresholds normal. Despite the sloping configurations, the hearing losses are conductive in nature.
2. Based on the audiologic information, the prognosis for complete restoration of hearing is good. However, the final decision as to prognosis must be made by the physician.

QUESTION FOR FIGURE 2-26

Case History Information This girl is experiencing no communicative difficulties, nor does she report any symptoms suggestive of ear pathology. There is extensive history of hearing impairment in her family; her mother, aunt, one brother, and one female cousin all developed hearing problems in their late teens or early twenties.

1. Does this girl have a significant hearing impairment?

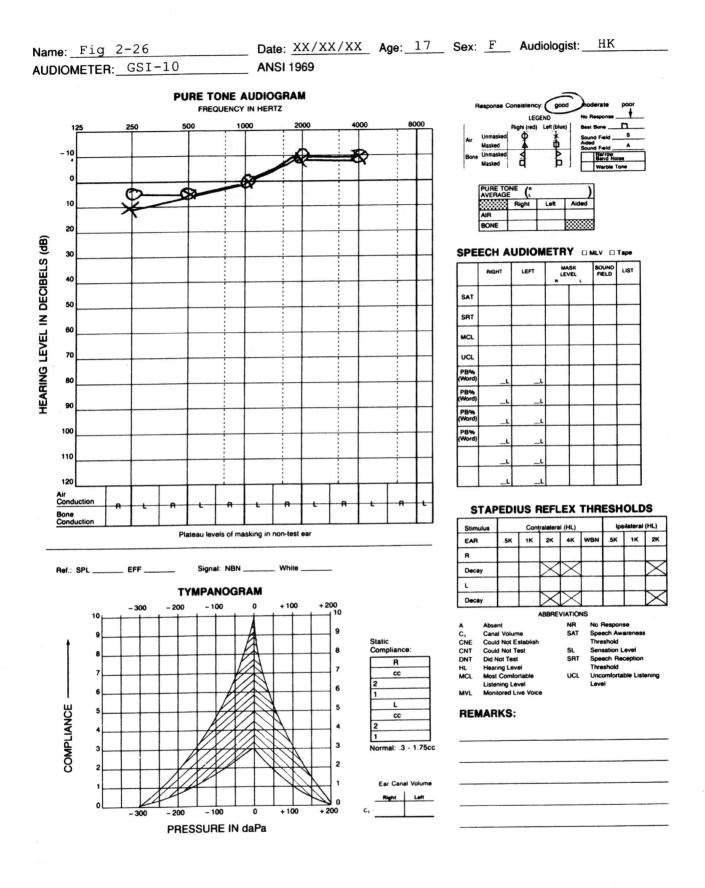

Answer for Figure 2-26

1. This girl does not have a hearing impairment of clinically noticeable magnitude. Although she appears to have essentially normal hearing sensitivity, the audiometric configuration suggests increased stiffness in the transmission (or conductive) system. This particular configuration has been suggested as a preclinical sign of otosclerosis (Carhart, 1958). The family history of hearing problems starting in young adulthood increases the possibility of early otosclerosis in this client.

QUESTIONS FOR FIGURE 2-27

Case History Information This woman first became aware of a hearing problem, accompanied by constant tinnitus, in her early twenties. It has gradually worsened. Her grandmother, mother, sister, and a male cousin developed similar hearing problems in late adolescence or early twenties.

1. What type of hearing impairment does this woman have?
2. What audiometric and case history information support your answer to the above question?
3. What is this woman's better ear average?

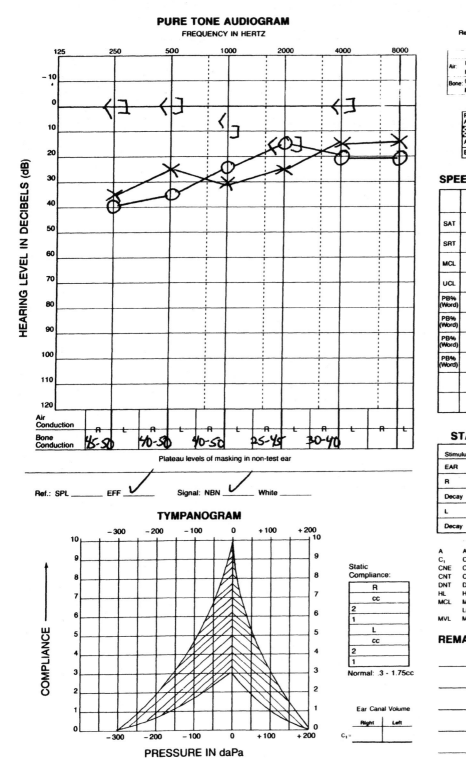

PURE TONE AUDIOGRAM
FREQUENCY IN HERTZ

Air Conduction: R L / L R (across frequencies)

Bone Conduction: 45-50 40-50 40-50 25-45 30-40

Plateau levels of masking in non-test ear

Ref.: SPL _____ EFF ✓   Signal: NBN ✓ White _____

TYMPANOGRAM

PRESSURE IN daPa

Static Compliance:

R	
cc	
2	
1	

L	
cc	
2	
1	

Normal: .3 - 1.75cc

Ear Canal Volume

	Right	Left
C₁ =		

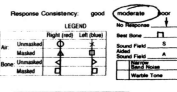

Response Consistency: good (moderate) poor

LEGEND

		Right (red)	Left (blue)
Air	Unmasked	◯	X
	Masked	△	▢
Bone	Unmasked	<	>
	Masked	▢	▢

No Response
Best Bone ▢
Sound Field S
Aided
Sound Field A
Narrow Band Noise
Warble Tone

PURE TONE AVERAGE (R L)	Right	Left	Aided
AIR			
BONE			

SPEECH AUDIOMETRY   ☐ MLV ☒ Tape

	RIGHT	LEFT	MASK LEVEL R L	SOUND FIELD	LIST
SAT					
SRT	26	26		20	
MCL					
UCL					
PB% (Word)	_ L	_ L			
PB% (Word)	_ L	_ L			
PB% (Word)	_ L	_ L			
PB% (Word)	_ L	_ L			
	_ L	_ L			
	_ L	_ L			

STAPEDIUS REFLEX THRESHOLDS

Stimulus	Contralateral (HL)					Ipsilateral (	
EAR	.5K	1K	2K	4K	WBN	.5K	1K
R							
Decay			✗	✗			
L							
Decay			✗	✗			

ABBREVIATIONS

A	Absent	NR	No Response
C₁	Canal Volume	SAT	Speech Awareness
CNE	Could Not Establish		Threshold
CNT	Could Not Test	SL	Sensation Level
DNT	Did Not Test	SRT	Speech Reception
HL	Hearing Level		Threshold
MCL	Most Comfortable	UCL	Uncomfortable Listen
	Listening Level		Level
MVL	Monitored Live Voice		

REMARKS:

_____

_____

_____

_____

Answers for Figure 2-27

1. This woman has a mild bilateral conductive-type hearing impairment. The audiometric symptoms are consistent with the diagnosis of otosclerosis made by her otologist.

2. The age of onset of the problem and family history suggest otosclerosis. This problem usually becomes evident in late adolescence or young adulthood, is familial, and is more prevalent in females than in males.

   Conductive-type impairments with rising audiometric configurations are frequently caused by stiffness problems, such as restricted movement of the ossicular chain, which is consistent with a diagnosis of otosclerosis. The significant air–bone gap is consistent with a conductive diagnosis. Frequently with otosclerosis the bone conduction configuration takes a characteristic shape: the conductive component produces an apparent depression of 5 dB HL at 500 and 4000 Hz, 10 dB HL at 1000 Hz, and 15 dB HL at 2000 Hz, on the average. Note that bone conduction thresholds at 1000 Hz are 5 dB HL for the right ear and 10 dB HL for the left, and 15 dB HL at 4000 Hz for both ears. This characteristic configuration is known as the Carhart Notch (Carhart, 1958; also see Newby and Popelka 1985:245). Although the presence of the Carhart Notch is an audiometric sign suggesting otosclerosis, it does not always appear with otosclerosis. Furthermore, what appears to be a Carhart Notch may actually indicate a sensorineural hearing loss. Therefore, the Carhart Notch must be interpreted with caution.

3. This woman's better ear average is 22 dB HL, which is in good agreement with the sound field SRT of 20 dB HL.

QUESTIONS FOR FIGURE 2-28

1. What type of hearing impairment does this man have?
2. What is the prognosis for medical restoration of this man's hearing?

Name: Fig 2-28   Date: XX/XX/XX   Age: 42   Sex: M   Audiologist: HK
AUDIOMETER: GSI-10   ANSI 1969

PURE TONE AUDIOGRAM
FREQUENCY IN HERTZ

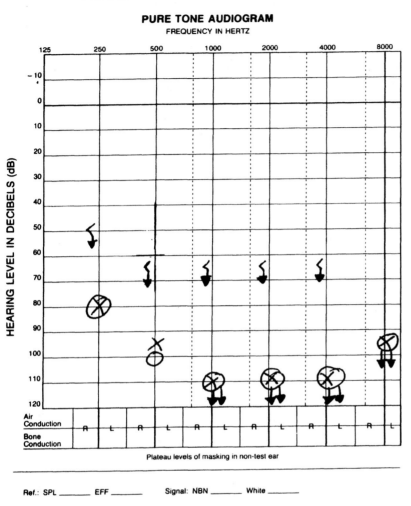

Air
Conduction
Bone
Conduction

Plateau levels of masking in non-test ear

Ref.: SPL _____ EFF _____   Signal: NBN _____ White _____

TYMPANOGRAM

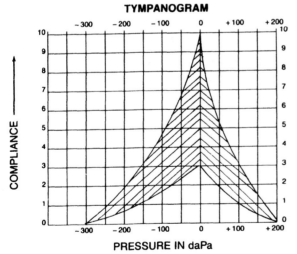

PRESSURE IN daPa

Static
Compliance:

R	
	cc
2	
1	
L	
	cc
2	
1	

Normal: .3 - 1.75cc

Ear Canal Volume

	Right	Left
C₁ =		

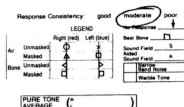

Response Consistency: good (moderate) poor

LEGEND

		Right (red)	Left (blue)	
Air	Unmasked	O	X	
	Masked	△	☐	
Bone	Unmasked	◁	▷	
	Masked	☐	☐	

No Response
Best Bone
Sound Field _____ S
Aided
Sound Field _____ A
Narrow Band Noise
Warble Tone

PURE TONE AVERAGE (R L)			
	Right	Left	Aided
AIR			
BONE			

SPEECH AUDIOMETRY   ☐ MLV ☐ Tape

	RIGHT	LEFT	MASK LEVEL R	L	SOUND FIELD	LIST
SAT						
SRT						
MCL						
UCL						
PB% (Word)	_L	_L				
PB% (Word)	_L	_L				
PB% (Word)	_L	_L				
PB% (Word)	_L	_L				
	_L	_L				
	_L	_L				

STAPEDIUS REFLEX THRESHOLDS

Stimulus	Contralateral (HL)					Ipsilateral (HL)		
EAR	.5K	1K	2K	4K	WBN	.5K	1K	2K
R								
Decay			✕	✕			✕	✕
L								
Decay			✕	✕			✕	✕

ABBREVIATIONS

A	Absent	NR	No Response
C₁	Canal Volume	SAT	Speech Awareness
CNE	Could Not Establish		Threshold
CNT	Could Not Test	SL	Sensation Level
DNT	Did Not Test	SRT	Speech Reception
HL	Hearing Level		Threshold
MCL	Most Comfortable	UCL	Uncomfortable Listening
	Listening Level		Level
MVL	Monitored Live Voice		

REMARKS:

_____
_____
_____
_____

Reading the Pure Tone Audiogram

1. This man has a profound bilateral sensorineural impairment. The maximum bone conduction output levels of the audiometer used in this evaluation do not permit us to obtain BC thresholds greater than the no-response levels shown (↓). The degree of the hearing impairment necessitates a sensorineural component—that is, this cannot be a purely conductive impairment because the maximum limit of a conductive hearing loss is considered to be around 60 dB HL. Therefore, even if we did not have the bone conduction thresholds, we would know that there must be a sensorineural component. Since there is no measurable bone conduction, we know that the hearing loss is either entirely or primarily sensorineural in nature. This could be a mixed-type loss, but if it is mixed, the conductive component is small in relation to the sensorineural component.

2. In general, the prognosis for medical restoration of this man's hearing is extremely poor. If BC thresholds had suggested a significant air–bone gap, there would be a possibility of partial medical restoration.

QUESTIONS FOR FIGURE 2-29

1. What type of impairment does this boy have?
2. What is the prognosis for medical restoration of this boy's hearing?

Name: Fig 2-29   **Date:** XX/XX/XX   **Age:** 11   **Sex:** M   **Audiologist:** HK

AUDIOMETER: GSI-10   **ANSI 1969**

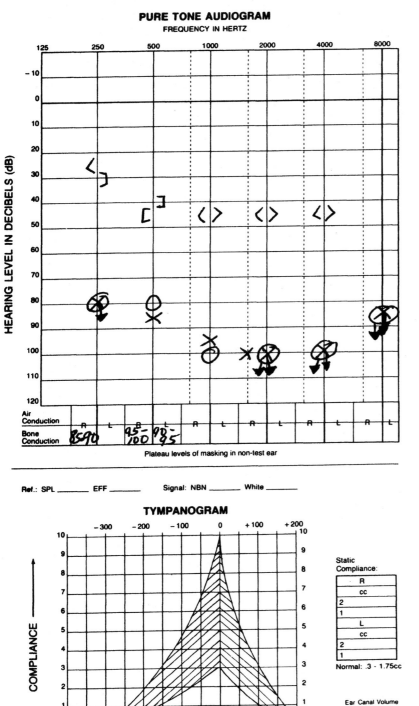

PURE TONE AUDIOGRAM
FREQUENCY IN HERTZ

HEARING LEVEL IN DECIBELS (dB)

Air Conduction	R	L	95	L	R	L	R	L	R	L	R	L
Bone Conduction	85	90	100	90 85								

Plateau levels of masking in non-test ear

Ref.: SPL _____ EFF _____   Signal: NBN _____ White _____

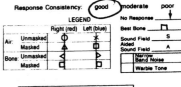

Response Consistency: (good) moderate poor

LEGEND

		Right (red)	Left (blue)
Air:	Unmasked	O	X
	Masked	△	◻
Bone:	Unmasked	◁	▷
	Masked	◻	◻

No Response

Best Bone

Sound Field   S

Aided Sound Field   A

Narrow Band Noise

Warble Tone

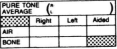

PURE TONE AVERAGE (R: L:)	Right	Left	Aided
AIR			
BONE			

SPEECH AUDIOMETRY   ☐ MLV ☐ Tape

	RIGHT	LEFT	MASK LEVEL R L	SOUND FIELD	LIST
SAT					
SRT					
MCL					
UCL					
PB% (Word)	_L_	_L_			
PB% (Word)	_L_	_L_			
PB% (Word)	_L_	_L_			
PB% (Word)	_L_	_L_			
	_L_	_L_			
	_L_	_L_			

STAPEDIUS REFLEX THRESHOLDS

Stimulus	Contralateral (HL)					Ipsilateral (HL)		
EAR	.5K	1K	2K	4K	WBN	.5K	1K	2K
R								
Decay			☒	☒				☒
L								
Decay			☒	☒			☒	

ABBREVIATIONS

A	Absent	NR	No Response
C₁	Canal Volume	SAT	Speech Awareness
CNE	Could Not Establish		Threshold
CNT	Could Not Test	SL	Sensation Level
DNT	Did Not Test	SRT	Speech Reception
HL	Hearing Level		Threshold
MCL	Most Comfortable	UCL	Uncomfortable Listening
	Listening Level		Level
MVL	Monitored Live Voice		

TYMPANOGRAM

COMPLIANCE

PRESSURE IN daPa

Static Compliance:

R	
cc	
2	
1	
L	
cc	
2	
1	

Normal: .3 - 1.75cc

Ear Canal Volume

	Right	Left
C₁ =		

REMARKS:

_____

_____

_____

_____

Reading the Pure Tone Audiogram

Answers for Figure 2-29

1. This boy has a profound bilateral mixed impairment as suggested by the significant air–bone gap with bone conduction thresholds that are significantly poorer than audiometric zero.

2. Based on the audiometric finding alone, the prognosis for *partial* medical restoration of this boy's hearing is favorable. Audiologically, the prognosis for complete medical restoration seems extremely poor because the BC results suggest a considerable sensorineural component in this mixed type of impairment. The best that can be expected is to restore the hearing to the level of the bone conduction thresholds, which would leave the boy with a moderate hearing loss.

   Note: Although audiologically the prognosis for partial medical restoration is favorable, otologic treatment may be contraindicated for medical reasons.

QUESTIONS FOR FIGURE 2-30

Case History Information This man is a veteran who saw active duty. He reports no communicative difficulties but does experience constant tinnitus in both ears. The tinnitus is a high-frequency sound comparable to a 4000-Hz audiometric tone.

1. Describe this man's hearing. What type of impairment does he have?
2. What type of etiology is suggested by the audiometric configuration and the case history information?

Congenital atresia ____
Serous otitis media ____
Otosclerosis ____
Noise-induced loss ____
Ménière's disease (or endolymphatic hydrops) ____

Name: Fig 2-30   Date: XX/XX/XX   Age: 48   Sex: M   Audiologist: HK

AUDIOMETER: GSI-10   ANSI 1969

PURE TONE AUDIOGRAM
FREQUENCY IN HERTZ

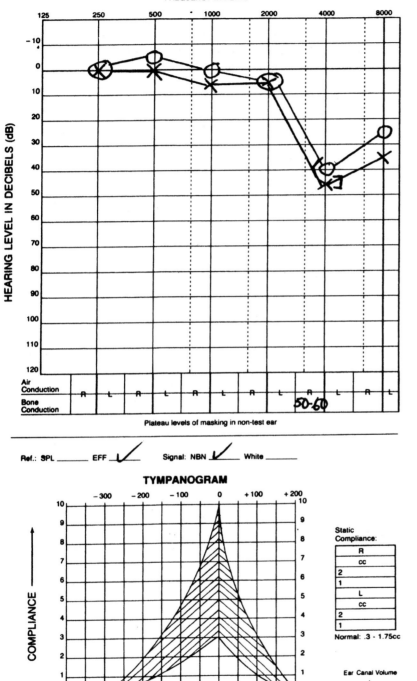

Air
Conduction
Bone
Conduction

50-60

Plateau levels of masking in non-test ear

Ref.: SPL _____ EFF ✓   Signal: NBN ✓   White _____

Response Consistency: (good) moderate poor   No Response ↓

LEGEND

		Right (red)	Left (blue)
Air:	Unmasked	○	X
	Masked	▲	◻
Bone:	Unmasked	◁	▷
	Masked	◻	◻

Best Bone ___◻___
Sound Field ___S___
Aided
Sound Field ___A___
Narrow Band Noise
Warble Tone

PURE TONE AVERAGE (R: ___ L: ___)

	Right	Left	Aided
AIR			
BONE			▨

SPEECH AUDIOMETRY ☐ MLV ☐ Tape

	RIGHT	LEFT	MASK LEVEL R / L	SOUND FIELD	LIST
SAT					
SRT					
MCL					
UCL					
PB% (Word)	_L_	_L_			
PB% (Word)	_L_	_L_			
PB% (Word)	_L_	_L_			
PB% (Word)	_L_	_L_			
	_L_	_L_			
	_L_	_L_			

STAPEDIUS REFLEX THRESHOLDS

Stimulus	Contralateral (HL)					Ipsilateral (HL)		
EAR	.5K	1K	2K	4K	WBN	.5K	1K	2K
R								
Decay			☒	☒				☒
L								
Decay			☒	☒				☒

ABBREVIATIONS

A	Absent	NR	No Response
C₁	Canal Volume	SAT	Speech Awareness
CNE	Could Not Establish		Threshold
CNT	Could Not Test	SL	Sensation Level
DNT	Did Not Test	SRT	Speech Reception
HL	Hearing Level		Threshold
MCL	Most Comfortable	UCL	Uncomfortable Listening
	Listening Level		Level
MVL	Monitored Live Voice		

REMARKS:

_____
_____
_____
_____
_____

TYMPANOGRAM

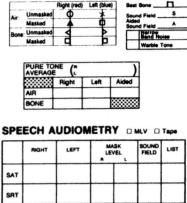

Static Compliance:

R	
cc	
2	
1	
L	
cc	
2	
1	

Normal: .3 - 1.75cc

Ear Canal Volume

Right	Left
C₁=	

PRESSURE IN daPa

Answers for Figure 2-30

1. This man appears to have essentially normal hearing sensitivity for the middle and lower frequencies, with a moderate sensorineural impairment of the higher frequencies bilaterally.

2. This audiometric configuration is typical of the loss from noise exposure. The sensorineural nature of the loss, the maximum loss at 4000 Hz, and the partial recovery at 8000 Hz are all indications of this etiology. This man's history of noise exposure makes this diagnosis more probable. However, diagnosis should not be made on the basis of audiometric pattern alone. Other etiologic factors can produce similar patterns, although it is highly unlikely that any of the other etiologic factors listed would produce this audiometric pattern.

QUESTIONS FOR FIGURE 2-31

Case History Information This man has been aware of a hearing problem for the past 8 years and reports that his hearing has been gradually getting worse. There is no history of ear pathology, familial hearing problems, noise exposure, or ototoxic drugs. The client reports mild intermittent tinnitus and occasional dizziness upon quick change of position.

1. What type of hearing impairment does this man have?
2. What type of etiology does this audiometric pattern and the case history information suggest?

Name: Fig 2-31   **Date:** XX/XX/XX   **Age:** 68   **Sex:** M   **Audiologist:** HK

AUDIOMETER: GSI-10   **ANSI 1969**

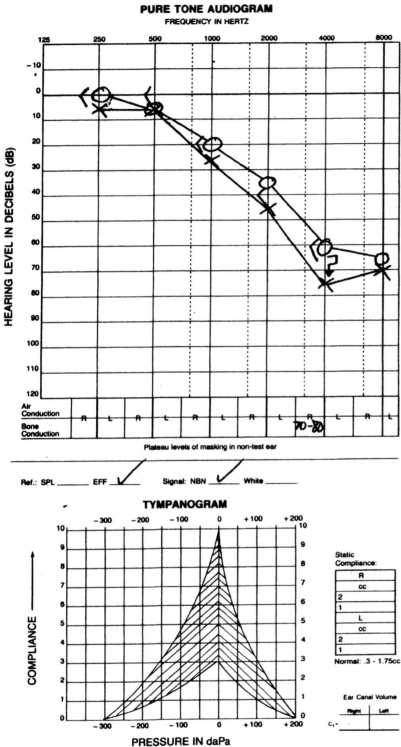

PURE TONE AUDIOGRAM
FREQUENCY IN HERTZ

HEARING LEVEL IN DECIBELS (dB)

Air Conduction / Bone Conduction

Plateau levels of masking in non-test ear

Ref.: SPL _____ EFF _____   Signal: NBN _____ White _____

TYMPANOGRAM

PRESSURE IN daPa

COMPLIANCE

Static Compliance:

R	
cc	
2	
1	

L	
cc	
2	
1	

Normal: .3 - 1.75cc

Ear Canal Volume

	Right	Left
C₁ =		

$C_1 =$

Response Consistency: (good) moderate poor

LEGEND

		Right (red)	Left (blue)
Air:	Unmasked	O	X
	Masked	▲	▢
Bone:	Unmasked	◁	▷
	Masked	◻	◻

No Response ↓
Best Bone ▢
Sound Field S
Aided Sound Field A
Narrow Band Noise
Warble Tone

PURE TONE AVERAGE	R: L:	

	Right	Left	Aided
AIR			
BONE			

SPEECH AUDIOMETRY ☐ MLV ☐ Tape

	RIGHT	LEFT	MASK LEVEL R L	SOUND FIELD	LIST
SAT					
SRT					
MCL					
UCL					
PB% (Word)	L	L			
PB% (Word)	L	L			
PB% (Word)	L	L			
PB% (Word)	L	L			
	L	L			
	L	L			

STAPEDIUS REFLEX THRESHOLDS

Stimulus	Contralateral (HL)					Ipsilateral (HL)		
EAR	.5K	1K	2K	4K	WBN	.5K	1K	2K
R								
Decay			✕	✕			✕	
L								
Decay			✕	✕			✕	

ABBREVIATIONS

A	Absent	NR	No Response
C₁	Canal Volume	SAT	Speech Awareness
CNE	Could Not Establish		Threshold
CNT	Could Not Test	SL	Sensation Level
DNT	Did Not Test	SRT	Speech Reception
HL	Hearing Level		Threshold
MCL	Most Comfortable	UCL	Uncomfortable Listening
	Listening Level		Level
MVL	Monitored Live Voice		

REMARKS:

_____

_____

_____

_____

_____

Reading the Pure Tone Audiogram

Answers for Figure 2-31

1. This man has a mild to moderate bilateral sensorineural hearing impairment.
2. This audiometric configuration is typical of presbycusis (hearing loss associated with aging), but a diagnosis should not be made on the basis of audiometric pattern alone. This pattern can be associated with other etiologies, and other audiometric patterns can be associated with presbycusis. The diagnosis should be made by a qualified physician based on both audiologic and otologic information. Note, however, that the case history information indicating late onset of loss and no other apparent etiologic indications supports the diagnosis of presbycusis.

QUESTIONS FOR FIGURE 2-32

Case History Information This little girl was brought to the clinic for hearing evaluation because she exhibits delayed speech and language. Her mother reports the need for much gesturing and pointing in order to communicate with her. Her understanding of speech seems much improved when she is able to see the speaker. She enjoys watching television but insists on turning the volume to a level uncomfortable for other members of the family.

The child was somewhat frightened of the testing situation and refused to wear earphones. However, she conditioned easily to the task of placing a peg in a hole in response to sound.

1. Describe this child's hearing.
2. Which ear do the thresholds represent?
3. How were these thresholds obtained? What kind of signal was used?

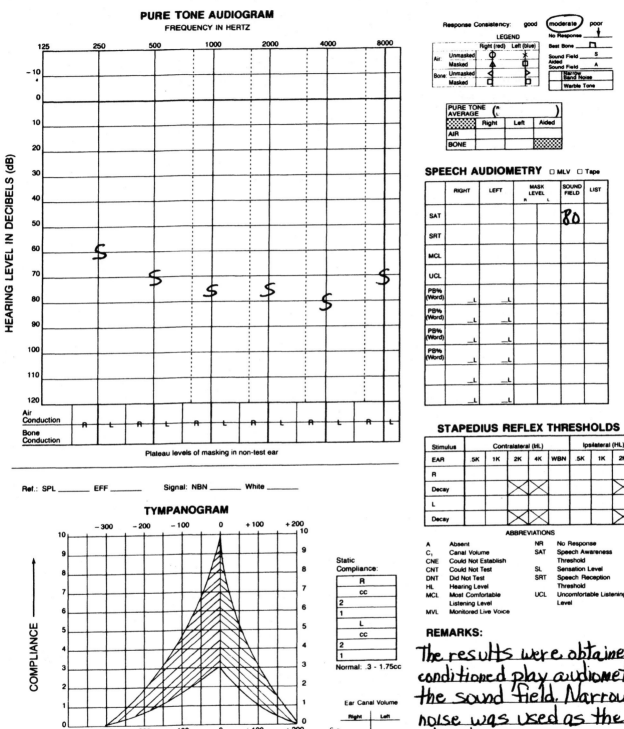

PURE TONE AUDIOGRAM
FREQUENCY IN HERTZ

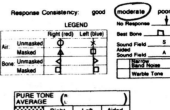

Response Consistency: good   (moderate)   poor

LEGEND

		Right (red)	Left (blue)
Air:	Unmasked	○	✕
	Masked	△	□
Bone:	Unmasked	◁	▷
	Masked	□	□

No Response
Best Bone
Sound Field   S
Aided Sound Field   A
Narrow Band Noise
Warble Tone

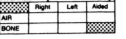

PURE TONE AVERAGE (R L)			
	Right	Left	Aided
AIR			
BONE			

SPEECH AUDIOMETRY   ☐ MLV ☐ Tape

	RIGHT	LEFT	MASK LEVEL R	L	SOUND FIELD	LIST
SAT					80	
SRT						
MCL						
UCL						
PB% (Word)	_L_	_L_				
PB% (Word)	_L_	_L_				
PB% (Word)	_L_	_L_				
PB% (Word)	_L_	_L_				
	_L_	_L_				
	_L_	_L_				

STAPEDIUS REFLEX THRESHOLDS

Stimulus	Contralateral (HL)					Ipsilateral (HL)		
EAR	.5K	1K	2K	4K	WBN	.5K	1K	2K
R								
Decay			✕	✕			✕	✕
L								
Decay			✕	✕			✕	✕

ABBREVIATIONS

A	Absent	NR	No Response
C₁	Canal Volume	SAT	Speech Awareness
CNE	Could Not Establish		Threshold
CNT	Could Not Test	SL	Sensation Level
DNT	Did Not Test	SRT	Speech Reception
HL	Hearing Level		Threshold
MCL	Most Comfortable	UCL	Uncomfortable Listening
	Listening Level		Level
MVL	Monitored Live Voice		

Air Conduction
Bone Conduction

Plateau levels of masking in non-test ear

Ref.: SPL _____ EFF _____   Signal: NBN _____ White _____

TYMPANOGRAM

Static Compliance:

R	
	cc
2	
1	

L	
	cc
2	
1	

Normal: .3 - 1.75cc

Ear Canal Volume

	Right	Left
C₁		

COMPLIANCE
PRESSURE IN daPa

REMARKS:

The results were obtained using conditioned play audiometry in the sound field. Narrow band noise was used as the stimulus.

Answers for Figure 2-32

1. This child has a severe bilateral hearing loss, flat in configuration. Both ears may have essentially the same loss, or one ear may have an even greater loss. We have insufficient information to determine the type of loss since bone conduction thresholds could not be obtained.

2. These thresholds represent the sensitivity of the better ear, but we do not know which ear that may be. To determine the thresholds of the individual ears, earphones must be used.

3. These thresholds were obtained using conditioned play audiometry with the signals presented through a loudspeaker. They are known as "sound field" thresholds. Narrow band noise centering around various frequencies was used as the stimulus. For sound field audiometry, continuous pure tones are not used because of possible interference patterns that may be set up. Instead, warble tones (fluctuating slightly in frequency) or narrow band noise are used. Sound field audiometry is used when an individual cannot initially be tested with earphones.

   Sound field thresholds should be considered initial information in an ongoing audiologic evaluation. In most cases, young or difficult-to-test clients can be induced to accept earphones after several test sessions have occurred. Operant procedures can be very useful in obtaining thresholds through earphones. For a more complete discussion of operant procedures see Lloyd (in Fulton and Lloyd, 1975:Ch. 1) and Northern (1984:148–155).

REVIEW AND SEARCH PROJECTS

1. Draw and label, according to Table 1-2, five different hypothetical audiograms showing five different audiometric configurations.

2. Draw and label five different hypothetical audiograms illustrating conductive, mixed, and sensorineural loss.

3. Write a short paper comparing the advantages and disadvantages of forehead and mastoid placement of the bone oscillator.

4. Develop a one-page pre-examination questionnaire that a parent can complete without your assistance. Include items to elicit the most important case history information about a child with a suspected hearing impairment.

5. Develop a comprehensive list of questions you might ask the parent of the child you have examined and found to have a moderate bilateral hearing impairment.

6. List the symptoms (both audiometric and non-audiometric) of conductive hearing impairment.

7. List the symptoms (both audiometric and non-audiometric) of sensorineural hearing impairment.

8. Cite a verbatim account of how you would explain a client's hearing impairment to him or her, following a pure tone audiometric test. Attach the client's hypothetical audiogram to your explanation.

9. Briefly describe your reason(s) as a speech-language pathologist or audiologist for not providing any nonmedical rehabilitative services for a hearing-impaired individual until he or she has had the benefit of an otologic examination.

10. You are an audiologist in a community hearing and speech center, and a pediatrician refers a 4-year-old child to you for a hearing test. On examination you find the child has a mild bilateral hearing impairment. The mother asks you what she should do about getting adequate treatment. Write your answer to this mother's question.

11. Describe several medical treatments for conductive and sensorineural hearing impairments.

12. Make a list of causes of hearing impairment. Briefly discuss the implications of each etiologic factor.

13. Discuss symptoms and treatments for otosclerosis.

14. Explain how tonsils and adenoids can affect the hearing of an individual.

15. Write a brief statement describing the air–bone relationships for each of the three types of hearing impairment (conductive, sensorineural, and mixed).

REFERENCES

Carhart, R. 1958. Audiometry in diagnosis. *Laryngoscope* (special issue of the International Conference on Audiology) 68.

Downs, M., and Doster, M.E. 1959. A hearing testing program for preschool children. *Rocky Mountain Medical Journal*, September.

Fulton, R.T., and Lloyd, L.L. 1975. *Auditory Assessment of the Difficult-to-Test*. Baltimore: Williams & Wilkins.

Hannley, M. 1986. *Basic Principles of Auditory Assessment*. San Diego: College-Hill Press.

Martin, F.N. 1991. *Introduction to Audiology*, 4th ed. Englewood Cliffs, N.J.: Prentice-Hall.

Newby, H., and Popelka, G.R. 1985. *Audiology*, 5th ed. Englewood Cliffs, N.J.: Prentice-Hall.

Northern, J.L., and Downs, M.P. 1984. *Hearing in Children*, 3rd ed. Baltimore: Williams & Wilkins.

Rintelmann, W.F. (Editor). 1991. *Hearing Assessment*, 2nd ed. Austin: Pro-Ed.

Acoustic Immittance

ACOUSTIC IMMITTANCE MEASUREMENTS

Acoustic immittance measurements are an integral part of basic audiologic assessment. The three parts of the battery—static immittance/compliance, dynamic immittance/tympanometry, and dynamic immittance/acoustic reflex measures—can differentiate between conductive and sensorineural hearing loss, cochlear and retrocochlear sites of auditory dysfunction, and different types of middle ear disorders. Acoustic immittance measures can also provide information about the integrity of the facial nerve and Eustachian tube function. In addition, acoustic immittance has become useful as an adjunct to auditory screening in school populations. Under certain circumstances, acoustic immittance procedures may be the only measures that are able to be undertaken. Together with diagnostic audiologic procedures, acoustic immittance measurements give the audiologist a very powerful tool with which to determine the locus of the dysfunction within the auditory system. The acoustic immittance battery and its applications will be presented in this chapter.

This initial section introduces the reader to the physical and biomechanical principles underlying acoustic immittance measurements. The term immittance is used throughout this section as it implies both admittance and impedance. A discussion of nomenclature—that is, differences between admittance and impedance measures—is included, as well as a description of current instrumentation. Although this section may be utilized in conjunction with more comprehensive discussions of the principles of acoustic immittance (see Silman and Silverman,

1991), the reader need not fully comprehend the material to understand the procedures and applications discussed later. This section provides a basic knowledge of the underlying concepts of acoustic immittance for the serious student of audiology. However, readers may start this chapter with the second section, the Acoustic Immittance Test Battery, which begins on p. 90.

Principles of Acoustic Immittance

It is important to understand the physical and biomechanical principles of acoustic immittance to appreciate the impact certain pathologies have on the transformer or transfer function of the middle ear system.

It should be remembered that the middle ear system serves as an impedance matching transformer to effectively match the relatively low impedance offered to acoustic energy by the air in the external auditory canal to the high impedance offered by the fluid medium of the inner ear (Dallos, 1973). Impedance is the opposition to the flow of energy through a medium and is determined by characteristics inherent to that medium. If it were not for the impedance-matching characteristics of the middle ear system there would be a transmission loss of approximately 35 dB between the airborne acoustic signal and its hydraulic analog in the cochlea due to significant reflection of sound energy at the entrance to the cochlea. Only 0.1% of the acoustic energy would then enter the cochlea (Lipscomb, 1976).

Dallos (1973) noted two middle ear mechanisms of the impedance matching transformer that result in a

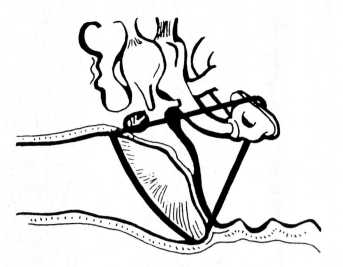

Figure 3-1. Pressure amplification across middle ear. (After Glover's rendition in Berlin and Cullen, 1975; special appreciation to Phyllis Randal.)

force amplification of the acoustic signal: the lever action of the malleus excursion compared to that of the incus and the pressure amplification due to the difference in the surface areas of the tympanic membrane and the footplate of the stapes. Because the latter is considerably smaller than the former, the force per unit is greater at the footplate (Figure 3-1.). The pressure amplification provided by these two mechanisms serves to counteract what would otherwise be a loss of sound energy due to impedance mismatch.

The vibratory characteristics of the middle ear system are dependent on the resistance, stiffness/admittance, and mass of the components of the middle ear system, as well as the external canal and the cochlea. Impedance is an interaction of these factors of resistance, stiffness/admittance, and mass. Depending on the characteristics of these factors operating within a particular vibratory system, some amount of energy directed toward the system will be reflected back toward the source (Feldman, 1975).

Actually, much acoustic energy is lost due to friction created by the vibration and interaction of the middle ear structures. This is the resistive component of impedance. Acoustic resistance has been described as independent of frequency, thus providing equal opposition to all frequencies in impeding transmission through a system. Acoustic mass, resulting from the mass of the structures within the auditory system, offers inertial opposition to a change from silence to

sound and back again, posing an additional barrier to efficient transmission of acoustic energy. The effect of mass is more significant for high frequencies. Reduced transmission of high frequencies occurs when there is increased acoustic mass.

Acoustic admittance (the stiffness factor) is the ability of components within a vibratory system to comply with the driving force. Stiff structures will offer opposition to inertial changes additional to that offered by mass. However, these admittance effects are maximized for the transmission of *low* frequencies through the system, thus reducing their transmission (Lipscomb, 1976).

Table 3-1 presents the sources and factors related to the flow of acoustic energy through the auditory system. Also included are the conventional symbols and units for each component. One can see from the table that there are biologic sources for the various acoustic immittance components. Also, there are similar concepts that are applicable to mechanical and electrical systems as well as acoustic systems.

The reciprocal relationship between impedance and admittance components is also depicted in the table. It is evident, then, that admittance or springiness of an acoustic system can be expressed as negative reactance (noted as $-X_a$ ohms) or the admittance reciprocal of positive susceptance (noted as B_a mmhos). The mass of a system can be expressed in impedance terms as positive reactance (X_a ohms) or, in admittance terms, negative susceptance ($-B_a$ mmhos). The resistance of a system can be expressed as resistance (R_a ohms) in impedance terminology or as conductance (G_a mmhos) in admittance terminology. The subscript "a" in each of the above notations depicts an acoustic system. Additionally, the reciprocal relationship between impedance (Z) and admittance (Y) is depicted by the unit notation of mho (actually millimho) being the reciprocal or opposite of ohm.

In normal ears, resistance and mass contribute minimally at low frequencies. Impedance is determined by the interaction of the admittances. For frequencies above 500 Hz, however, mass and resistance begin to contribute to the impedance.

Berlin and Cullen (1975) described the principle of component interaction in impedance:

If the mass of a given unit is "1" and the frequency of stimulation is 100 Hz we might say that the mass

Table 3-1. Sources and factors related to the flow of acoustic energy through the auditory system.

Biologic	Mechanical	Electrical	Acoustic	
			Impedance	Admittance
Membranes, ME air cushion, ossicular attachments	Stiffness/ admittance (springiness)	Capacitance (C) ohms	Negative reactance $(-X_a)$ ohms	Positive susceptance (B_a) mmhos
Ossicles, tympanic membrane	Mass (inertia)	Inductance (L) ohms	Positive reactance (X_a) ohms	Negative susceptance $(-B_a)$ mmhos
Cochlear fluids, ME airflow	Resistance (friction)	Resistance (R) ohms	Resistance (R_a) ohms	Conductance (G_a) mmhos

Adapted from Newman and Fanger (1973).

reactance of this system is "628 mass reactance units." Now, there are two ways of increasing this mass reactance factor. One way is to increase the mass itself. In this case, if the frequency is held at 100 Hz and the mass doubled, the mass reactance will now go up to 1256 mass reactance units. However, if the mass remains the same and the frequency is doubled to 200 Hz, we will still have 1256 units of mass reactance. Thus mass reactance increases in direct proportion to frequency.

If we look at the elastic reactance (the expression related to stiffness) we see that if we have a stiffness value of 1 and a frequency of 100, we have an elastic reactance of 1/628 units. If the stiffness increases, the value of that fraction increases and therefore the elastic reactance increases. However, if we hold the stiffness constant and increase the frequency of stimulation, we find that the elastic reactance decreases as frequency goes up. (p. 6)

Thus, component assessment provides a more complete description of the acoustic immittance properties of the auditory system as measured at the plane of the tympanic membrane. (For additional discussion see Gladstone, 1977; Gladstone et al., 1980; Van Camp and Creten, 1976; Wiley and Block, 1979.)

Principles of Operation

Electroacoustic immittance instruments are classified as either bridges or meters. Their performance characteristics and calibration are specified by a 1987 ANSI standard, *Specifications for Instruments to Measure Aural Acoustic Impedance and Admittance (Aural Acoustic Immittance)* (ANSI, 1987). Electroacoustic immittance meters automatically and continuously maintain a constant ear canal sound pressure level, providing an absolute measurement of impedance or admittance in ohms or millimhos. Electroacoustic immittance bridges, however, must be manipulated by the examiner to maintain or balance the ear canal sound pressure level as ear canal volume is changed. This external balancing yields relative rather than absolute values of impedance or admittance. The tympanometric shape in each case will be quantitatively different, yet qualitatively similar.

In Figure 3-2 tympanogram #1 was produced by a bridge with relative, uncalibrated units, whereas tympanogram #2 was produced by a meter with absolute, calibrated units. The difference between these two tympanograms is merely one of shape; both depict the same general characteristics of normal middle ear pressure and mobility.

With tympanogram #2, the absolute values obtained with a meter enable a direct determination of static values from the tympanogram. In contrast, two distinct steps are required for the computation of static immittance values with the use of an impedance bridge. We will learn how to determine these characteristics in the next section.

The principles of operation of an electroacoustic immittance instrument are similar whether a bridge or meter. There are three major sections to each: (1)

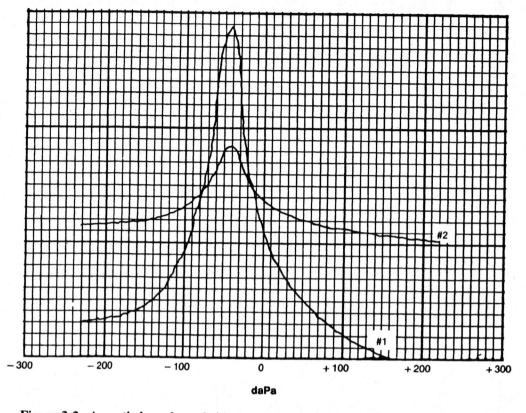

daPa

Figure 3-2. Acoustic impedance bridge tympanogram (larger, #1) and admittance meter tympanogram (shallower, #2).

a sound generating source or probe tone; (2) a receiver which accepts and conveys the reflected sound from the tympanic membrane for analysis; and (3) a pressure system which manipulates the tension of the tympanic membrane and attached ossicular chain. Specifically, the probe tone, which is typically low in frequency (approximately 220 or 660 Hz) relative to the resonance of the middle ear system, is generated by a pure tone oscillator, amplified, and fed to a small speaker or microphone which projects the probe tone into the ear canal.

The acoustic signal is reflected from the tympanic membrane, received by a miniature microphone, amplified, and fed to an analysis system. The characteristics of the reflected acoustic signal are dependent upon the transmission qualities of the tympanic membrane and the middle ear system. Thus, the analysis of the reflected signal in the ear canal provides information regarding the acoustic immittance properties of the middle ear system as measured at the plane of the tympanic membrane.

The air pressure system is independently operated, usually over a pressure range of between +200 and −300 decaPascals (daPa). A tympanogram is a graphic representation of the effects of pressure variation on the immittance characteristics of the auditory system. In order to be able to observe the effect of such pressure variation, the probe assembly, which serves as the termination for the probe tone speaker, pickup microphone, and pressure systems, must be comfortably yet hermetically (airtight) sealed in the ear canal. If the seal is not complete, pressure variations are not possible and a tympanogram cannot be generated.

The air pressure system provides for a way of effectively decoupling or removing from participation the middle ear system by tensing the tympanic membrane under significant positive or negative pressure. This creates a situation in which the acoustic impedance parameters are a function of the ear canal volume only because the tensed tympanic membrane reflects most of the incident acoustic energy from the probe. When the air pressure system

Chapter 3

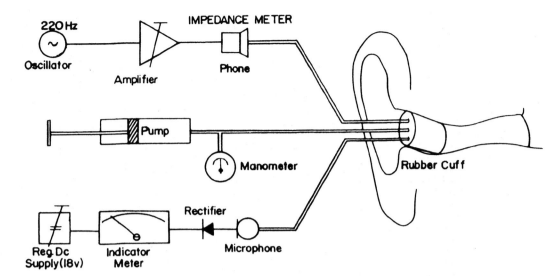

Figure 3-3. Electroacoustic impedance bridge. Reprinted by permission from B.T. Newman and D.M. Fanger, *Otoadmittance Handbook 2* (Bolton, MA: Grason-Stadler Co., 1973).

produces a pressure equal to ambient (normal atmospheric) pressure, however, the acoustic signal received by the microphone in the probe assembly is dependent on not only the immittance characteristics of the ear canal but also the immittance characteristics of the middle ear system. Under this condition the ear canal volume is coupled to the middle ear volume via the optimally mobile tympanic membrane. At ambient pressure, the flow of acoustic energy through the middle ear is maximal due to the normal immittance of the system. The amount of reflected acoustic energy is minimal. Thus, one need only examine the difference between the immittance values at ambient pressure and under conditions of maximum stress to determine the middle ear immittance characteristics.

When the tympanic membrane is stressed by either ±200 daPa the ear canal is acoustically decoupled from the middle ear. The increased immittance is measured by an increase in the sound pressure level of the probe tone due to the relatively small volume of the ear canal. When the air pressure in the ear canal equals the middle ear pressure the ear canal is acoustically coupled to the middle ear, allowing sound to be transferred efficiently via the maximally mobile tympanic membrane and middle ear system. The decreased immittance is measured by a decrease in the sound pressure level of the probe tone due to the

larger volume of the ear canal volume acoustically coupled to the middle ear volume.

This concept of equivalent volume (EV) represents the immittance value identical to a volume of the ear canal alone and an immittance value identical to a volume of the ear canal acoustically coupled to the middle ear and is expressed in milliliters (ml). To determine the immittance of the middle ear, one subtracts the volume equivalent to the ear canal coupled to the middle ear from the volume equivalent to the ear canal alone. The result represents the volume equivalent to the middle ear. This procedure will be discussed shortly in the Static Immittance/Compliance section.

Figure 3-3 illustrates a typical electroacoustic impedance bridge (note the three sections discussed above). Such a bridge provides a measure of the magnitude of the impedance value.

Figure 3-4 illustrates an electroacoustic admittance meter which can measure the two components of admittance separately. Note the separation between conductance (G) and susceptance (B) in the analysis section. This separation enables determination of a mass- versus stiffness-dominated middle ear system. (For additional discussion of the value of component assessment, see Gladstone, 1977; Gladstone et al., 1980; Newman and Fanger, 1973; Van Camp and Creten, 1976; and Wiley and Block, 1979.)

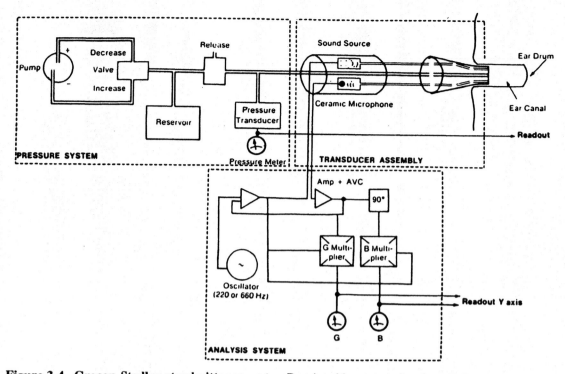

Figure 3-4. Grason-Stadler otoadmittance meter. Reprinted by permission from B.T. Newman and D.M. Fanger, *Otoadmittance Handbook 2* (Bolton, MA: Grason-Stadler Co., 1973).

This section has presented a basic introduction to the foundation of acoustic immittance measurements and a discussion of impedance and admittance sources, symbols, and nomenclature. Principles of operation of electroacoustic immittance instruments have been described, including the differences between impedance bridges and meters.

ACOUSTIC IMMITTANCE TEST BATTERY

This section is designed to provide an understanding of the techniques and procedures of the acoustic immittance test battery. A description of dynamic immittance/tympanometry, static immittance/compliance procedures, and methods for determining the dynamic immittance/acoustic reflex threshold, as well as relationships between these measures, is included. Prior to insertion of the probe assembly, an otoscopic examination should be administered to ensure against excessive cerumen, tympanic membrane perforation, or any other condition that might adversely affect acoustic immittance measurements.

Dynamic Immittance/Tympanometry

The term tympanometry was coined by Terkildsen in 1962. It is defined as a technique by which the acoustic immittance characteristics of the middle ear system are assessed. The measurement, which is made at the plane of the tympanic membrane, is influenced by systematic changes in examiner-controlled air pressure in the external ear canal. Because tympanic measurements of middle ear immittance are made with changing air pressure, this measure has been referred to as dynamic immittance.

Tympanometry can be conceptualized as a succession of measurements of acoustic immittance under the influence of systematically changing air pressure in the ear canal. In the lower left-hand portion of the Audiologic Assessment Form is a graph labeled "Tympanogram." The tympanogram is reproduced in Figure 1-7. Relative immittance or compliance is shown on the ordinate [0 represents minimum immittance (compliance) or tympanic membrane mobility, and 10 represents maximum immittance (compliance) or tympanic membrane mobility]. Relative air pressure in decaPascals (daPa) is shown on the abscissa. Zero (0) daPa indicates air pressure in the ear canal equal to atmospheric pressure or ambient, +100 is 100 daPa greater than ambient pressure, and −100 is 100 daPa less than ambient pressure. For further discussion of this type of calibration, see Hannley (1986).

The acoustic immittance instrument prints out a tympanogram which is then compared to the normal tympanogram (triangular shape) shown on the Audiologic Assessment Form (Figures 1-1 and 1-7). There are a variety of acoustic immittance tympanograms which suggest either normal middle ear function or middle ear disorder. Interpretation of tympanogram types and their significance will be discussed at the end of this chapter.

Procedure Once the probe assembly has been hermetically sealed in the ear canal, air pressure is increased to +200 daPa. This places the tympanic membrane under stress by tightening it toward the middle ear cavity, decoupling or removing from participation the middle ear system. Under this condition the immittance is raised. This is because the external ear is acting as a hard-walled cavity. The immittance characteristic under this condition is noted and then the air pressure in the external canal is systematically reduced from +200 daPa through 0 daPa to at least −200 daPa. One should be careful to observe that at approximately 0 daPa (±50 daPa for the normal ear) the immittance characteristically lowers. This is to be expected because at ambient pressure the tympanic membrane becomes maximally mobile, restoring the middle ear system's mobility. As the pressure is further reduced in the ear canal from 0 daPa to −200 daPa one notes that the immittance rises once again because the tympanic membrane is placed under stress once more. This time it is tensed by being pulled toward the probe assembly by the negative pressure in the ear canal.

Thus, by manually or automatically recording the immittance characteristics of the middle ear system for various positive and negative air pressure values (usually ±200, ±100, 0 daPa, and the point of maximum mobility for manual recording) a tympanogram can be obtained. Simply stated, the tympanogram is merely a recording or plot of middle ear mobility versus ear canal pressure.

Lilly (1973) summarized the relationship between air pressure in the external auditory canal and acoustic impedance at the plane of the tympanic membrane:

Acoustic impedance at the tympanic membrane of a normal middle ear will increase if air pressure in the external auditory meatus is made higher or lower than ambient (atmospheric) air pressure. This predictable relation between changes in air pressure and changes in acoustic impedance is modified by middle-ear disease, by perforations of the tympanic membrane, by abnormal air pressures in the middle ear, or by scars on the tympanic membrane. The general term tympanometry refers to methods and techniques for measuring, for recording, and for evaluating changes in acoustic impedance with systematic changes in air pressure. [p. 350]

The value of tympanometry is that the relationship between the impedance and air pressure changes can be expressed in a diagnostically useful manner (Alberti and Kristensen, 1970; Feldman, 1974, 1976; Jerger, 1970; Liden et al., 1970; Lilly, 1970; and Wilber et al., 1970).

Figure 3-5 shows typical impedance tympanograms for various middle ear pathologies in addition to normal middle ear function. The tympanometric characteristics are similar for admittance measurements (made with a 220-Hz probe tone) of the same pathologies, although the tympanogram may appear different due to scale value differences, as depicted in Figure 3-2. Actually, when a properly calibrated acoustic immittance instrument employing a probe tone frequency of 220 Hz is used, cubic centimeters, millimhos, and milliliters are equivalent units. Of particular clinical value is that when component admittance measurements are made, the susceptance (B) trace at 220 Hz can be compared to the complex impedance trace for the same 220-Hz probe tone. Thus, when data from an impedance instrument and an admittance instrument are used to evaluate the same middle ear system, the B220 tympanogram can be compared directly to the impedance tympanogram obtained with a 220-Hz probe tone. This point is discussed further in the section on static immittance.

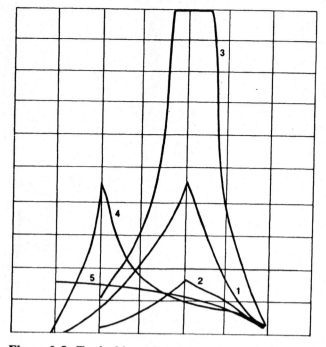

Figure 3-5. Typical impedance tympanograms for normal middle ear function and various middle ear pathologies.

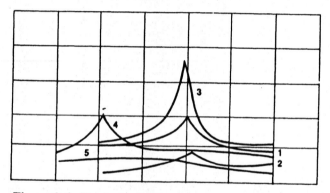

Figure 3-6. Typical admittance tympanograms (susceptance with 220-Hz probe tone) for normal middle ear function and various middle ear pathologies.

As can be seen from Figures 3-5 and 3-6, several characteristics of the tympanogram can be affected by changes in the condition of the middle ear. Certain middle ear conditions alter tympanometric amplitude but have no effect on middle ear pressure because transmission/ immittance characteristics reflecting mobility have been affected. Other condi-

tions significantly alter middle ear pressure (i.e., make it more negative than −150 daPa) but may have little influence upon tympanometric amplitude. Therefore, the tympanogram can be described according to the pressure value at which the middle ear is maximally mobile and by the amplitude of the tympanogram at that point of maximum mobility.

In addition, tympanometric width (TW) can be used to further describe the tympanogram. Tympanometric width is a measure of tympanometric gradient which can be used to describe the shape of the tympanogram in the region of the point of maximum amplitude. These measures have been valuable indicators for middle ear effusion (Fiellau-Nikolajsen, 1983). The procedure described by Liden et al. (1970, 1974) requires the clinician to calculate the pressure interval (in daPa) which corresponds to a 50% reduction in peak (static) admittance or tympanometric amplitude. Gradient measures of tympanometric peak shape appear sensitive to mechanical changes in the middle ear. As such they are valuable in the detection of middle ear effusion and applicable in screening protocol, which will be discussed in the next section.

For example, in Figures 3-5 and 3-6, traces 1 depict normal middle ear pressure and normal middle ear mobility. Traces 2 depict normal middle ear pressure and reduced middle ear mobility as is typically seen in stiffening pathologies such as otosclerosis, tympanosclerosis, adhesive otitis media, and congenital ossicular fixation. Traces 3 reveal normal middle ear pressure and excessive middle ear mobility as seen in ossicular chain discontinuity, tympanic membrane perforations, monomeric tympanic membranes, and atalectasis. Traces 4 reveal negative or reduced middle ear pressure but generally normal middle ear mobility as is seen with Eustachian tube deficiency. Traces 5 exhibit no discernible point of maximum middle ear mobility or middle ear pressure as seen with middle ear effusion or fluid in cases of otitis media. Specific cases are presented later in this chapter that illustrate the tympanometric characteristics of these various middle ear conditions.

Interpretation of tympanograms has generally taken one of two approaches. Jerger (1970) advocated categorizing tympanograms according to various patterns. Type A curves have normal mobility and pressure and typify normal hearing and sensorineural hearing loss with normally functioning middle ear systems. Type B curves have little or no point of maximum mobility and reduced admittance—that is, a relatively flat tympanometric trace. This curve is typical of a very stiff middle ear system as is seen in otitis media. Type C curves have normal mobility and negative pressure at the point of maximum mobility. This is seen in cases of Eustachian tube obstruction. Variations on these curves enable one to categorize such pathologies as otosclerosis, which reveals normal middle ear pressure but reduced mobility (Type A_s). Ossicular discontinuity is characterized by normal pressure and hypermobility and is depicted by a Type A_d curve.

Feldman (1975) has taken a descriptive approach to tympanogram interpretation. He describes the following features: (1) middle ear pressure in daPa as normal, positive, or negative; (2) amplitude, which is an indication of mobility of the middle ear system, in acoustic ohms, mmhos, or cubic centimeters; and (3) shape of the tympanogram, which can provide information about the condition of the tympanic membrane and the resonance properties of the middle ear system. Such a descriptive system is advocated because it provides the flexibility to convey the essence of the performance characteristics of the middle ear system to those unfamiliar with the curve-typing system.

Certain immittance instruments provide for measurements that can be obtained with a 660-Hz probe tone. As discussed in the first section, although the middle ear system is stiffness/compliance dominated, the use of a higher probe tone frequency increases the sensitivity of the measurement to changes in the mass of the middle ear system. Thus, conditions in the middle ear system altering the mass will be more readily observed with the use of a high (660 Hz) probe tone versus a low (220 Hz) probe tone frequency. Conditions that influence the mass of the middle ear system are ossicular discontinuity, tympanic membrane perforations undergoing healing, and middle ear effusions. These effects are summarized in Figure 3-7.

As can be seen from this figure, the 660-Hz probe tone provides additional tympanometric information. For example, tympanogram #1 demonstrates the wide, deep notching of the 660-Hz trace that is usually characteristic of ossicular chain disarticulation. There is no indication of this in the 220-Hz trace. Tympanogram #2 reveals a narrow, constricted inversion or notching of the 660-Hz trace seen in cases of healed tympanic membrane perforations. The 220-Hz trace may only show a hint of notching in the W-pattern at the point of maximum amplitude or mobility—and this is not always evident. Tympanogram #3 shows the converging of the B220- and B660-Hz traces seen in cases of middle ear fluid. These differences in the 660-Hz traces are due to conditions that have altered the mass within the middle ear. Specific cases are presented below that depict these differences.

In summary, tympanometry provides an objective means of evaluating the mobility of the middle ear system and thus its transmission/immittance characteristics. The resulting tympanograms can be

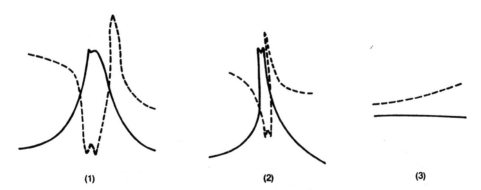

(1)   (2)   (3)

Figure 3-7. Mass changes in the middle ear system demonstrated via use of 660-Hz (dashed) versus 220-Hz (solid) probe tones.

readily classified and described according to the parameters of middle ear mobility and pressure characteristic of various middle ear conditions.

Static Immittance/Compliance

When sound enters the normal ear canal, most of it is transmitted through the middle ear to the inner ear. However, some of the sound energy is reflected back from the tympanic membrane because of the immittance characteristics of the normal middle ear system. Norms for this reflected acoustic energy have been developed and are expressed in terms of cubic centimeters (cc) or, more currently, milliliters (ml) of "static immittance/compliance." Any condition adversely affecting the immittance of the middle ear system will affect the static immittance/compliance measurement. In the lower middle section of the Audiologic Assessment Form is a box with spaces for recording static immittance/compliance of each ear.

The immittance characteristics of the middle ear system in its resting or static state are assessed by determining the volume of air that has immittance characteristics equivalent to those of the middle ear system. Static admittance or compliance is a measure of the amplitude of the tympanogram relative to its minimum or tail value. This determination requires testing under two conditions: the tympanic membrane stressed, and the tympanic membrane at the point of maximum mobility.

Some debate exists as to whether or not the second condition should be assessed at atmospheric pressure or at that pressure providing maximum mobility (Wiley and Block, 1979). In the normal middle ear and in some pathologic conditions these two pressures are essentially the same. When there is negative pressure in the middle ear, however, point of maximum mobility often occurs at a pressure significantly different than atmospheric or ambient pressure. Assessment at ambient pressure depicts the immittance of the middle ear system under everyday conditions. Assessment at maximum mobility provides a better value for determining the immittance characteristics of the middle ear for diagnostic purposes.

Procedure With bridges such as the Madsen-type instruments, two measures are made for the purpose of computing the static immittance/compliance.

First, the impedance in acoustic ohms or equivalent volume in cubic centimeters is obtained with the eardrum stressed, usually at +200 daPa. This measure, which essentially represents the impedance and equivalent volume of the ear canal (V_{ec}) because the stressed tympanic membrane restricts acoustic flow through the middle ear system, is the C1 measure. It is also the basis of the Physical Volume Test (PVT) described by Northern and Downs (1978). Normal ear canal volumes for adults are 1.0–1.75 ml and for children are 0.3–1.0 ml. If the tympanic membrane is not intact, abnormally high PVT values will occur. Next, the impedance in ohms or equivalent volume in cubic centimeters is obtained with the tympanic membrane at the point of maximum mobility (or ambient pressure). This condition, which provides for maximum acoustic flow through the middle ear system and thus represents the impedance or equivalent volume of the middle ear system plus that of the ear canal, is referred to as the C2 measure.

By subtracting the impedance of the ear canal (the measure obtained with the tympanic membrane stressed), C1, from that of the ear canal plus the middle ear system (obtained with the tympanic membrane mobile), C2, one is left with the impedance in acoustic ohms or equivalent volume in cubic centimeters of the middle ear system. For instruments like the Grason-Stadler-type otoadmittance meter, the admittance values, which are expressed in millimhos, for the tympanic membrane stressed and maximally mobile can be obtained directly from the tympanogram with its absolute scale values. Impedance meters such as the Amplaid provide the same convenience. The MAX/MIN method (Margolis and Popelka, 1975; Wiley and Block, 1979), with MAX representing the tympanic membrane mobile condition (point of maximum amplitude) and MIN the tympanic membrane stressed condition (point of least amplitude), is a simple yet statistically sound computational procedure for determining the middle ear immittance. One merely subtracts the MIN value from the MAX value for each trace on the tympanogram.

Figure 3-8a, which is from the acoustic immittance section of the Audiogram Report form that is used to present clinical cases later in this section, depicts how one represents static compliance/admittance values based upon the C2–C1 computation. Figure 3-8b depicts how one displays the ear canal

Static Compliance:

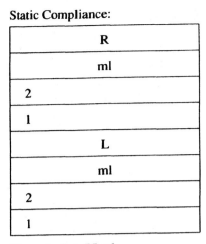

R	
ml	
2	
1	
L	
ml	
2	
1	

Normal: .3–1.75 ml

Figure 3-8a. Static immittance/compliance.

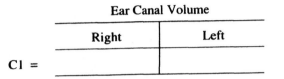

Ear Canal Volume

	Right	Left
C1 =		

Figure 3-8b. Ear canal volume.

volume, the C1 value which is the basis for the Physical Volume Test noted above.

As previously discussed, where only the B220 trace is available, or used, the static admittance value is directly comparable to static impedance values obtained with a 220-Hz probe tone. When both conductance (G) and susceptance (B) are used, the static admittance value (Y) is obtained by using the following expression:

$$Z = \sqrt{G^2 + B^2}$$

The admittance value can be converted to impedance values by the following expression:

$$Z = \frac{1}{Y} \times 1000$$

This expression demonstrates the reciprocal relationship between acoustic admittance and impedance. That is, as admittance increases, impedance decreases and vice versa.

One must remember that the ear canal volume contributes to the immittance characteristics of the auditory system, and these techniques do not completely eliminate its contributions. Thus, the derived middle ear immittance is an estimated value and not an absolute value.

The resultant static immittance values, acoustic ohms or milliliters of equivalent volume for impedance measures and millimhos for admittance measures, can be compared to normative data (Table 3-2) to aid in determining the middle ear condition. One should note that, as described in the section on tympanometry, the immittance values obtained with the B220 trace are comparable to the impedance values obtained with a 220-Hz probe tone. Thus, the similarity in static immittance values when one observes the B220 values compared to the values computed from 220-Hz probe tone impedance data is readily noted in Table 3-2. For example, the 50th percentile data from Jerger et al. (1972) and Brooks (1971) using a 220-Hz probe tone are 0.67 and 0.70 ml, respectively, whereas the data from Feldman (1974) and Porter (1972) using a B220-Hz probe tone are 0.50 and 0.71 mmhos of susceptance, respectively.

Dynamic Immittance/Acoustic Reflex

Measurement of the threshold of the acoustic reflex is the third part of the acoustic immittance battery. The acoustic reflex is a contraction of the middle ear muscles, primarily the stapedius in man, in response to an intense acoustic stimulus. Although middle ear muscle contraction can be elicited by pneumatic, electrical, and tactile stimulation, acoustic stimulation is of primary interest to the audiologist. With sufficient intensity, the reflex will occur bilaterally, regardless of the side of stimulation. That is, sound in either ear causes both stapedius muscles to contract. This contraction of the stapedius muscle moves the stapes away from the oval window, stiffening the ossicular chain and resulting in a flexing of the tympanic membrane. This stiffening of the ossicular chain and resultant tympanic membrane movement can be observed as an immittance change when the probe assembly of the immittance instrument is hermetically sealed in the ear canal. The middle ear immittance change, deflecting the tympanic membrane, changes the ear canal volume, which is being monitored by the microphone in the probe assembly. It is observed as a deflection on the immittance meter or

Acoustic Immittance

Table 3-2. Normative values for static immittance.

		Values		
		Percentile		
Study	Probe tone	10th	50th	90th
Jerger et al. (1972)	ml @ 220 Hz	0.39	0.67	1.30
Brooks (1971)	ml @ 220 Hz	0.42	0.70	1.05
Jerger (1970)	acoustic ohms @ 220 Hz	1750	2050	2750
Wilber et al. (1969)	acoustic ohms @ 220 Hz	880	1395	1890
Lilly (1972)	acoustic ohms @ 220 Hz	1075	1530	2060
Feldman (1974)	acoustic ohms @ 220 Hz	1124	1856	3048
Lilly (1972)	acoustic ohms @ 660 Hz	329	521	798
Feldman (1974)	acoustic ohms @ 660 Hz	220	409	715
Feldman (1974)	millimhos @ 220 Hz: G	0.05	0.15	0.35
	millimhos @ 220 Hz: B	0.30	0.50	0.75
	millimhos @ 660 Hz: G	1.00	1.95	4.20
	millimhos @ 660 Hz: B	0.90	1.30	2.45
	millimhos @ 220 Hz: G		0.35	
Porter (1972)[a]	millimhos @ 220 Hz: B		0.71	
	millimhos @ 660 Hz: G		2.75	
	millimhos @ 660 Hz: B		1.01	

[a]These are mean values.

is recorded on a strip-chart or X-Y recorder (see Figure 3-9).

If the reflex activating signal is presented to one ear and the immittance change (reflex) is recorded in the opposite ear, this mode is referred to as contralateral stimulation. Ipsilateral reflex testing occurs when both the reflex activating signal and the recording of the immittance change occur in the same ear. One must be cautioned against recording false reflexes due to the interaction of the reflex activating frequency and the probe tone.

The acoustic reflex is typically elicited by pure tone stimuli ranging in frequency from 500–4000 Hz and in intensity from 70–100 dB hearing level (HL). Elevated or absent acoustic reflexes at 4000 Hz have been observed in normal-hearing subjects. Thus, this frequency may be omitted. The lowest stimulus intensity that elicits a reflex is recorded as threshold and is recorded in appropriate spaces of the box labeled "Stapedius Reflex Thresholds" on the Audiologic Assessment Form. The mean acoustic reflex threshold for pure tones in adults is approximately 85 dB and is approximately 90 dB for children below the age of 6 years.

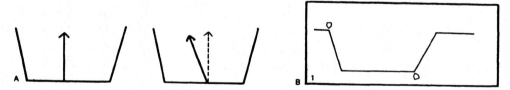

Figure 3-9. Acoustic reflex monitoring. (A) Compliance or mmho meter deflection. (B) X-Y or strip chart recorder.

Procedure Whether obtaining the acoustic reflex to ipsilateral (same ear) stimulation and recording or contralateral (opposite ear) stimulation and recording, the probe assembly must first be hermetically sealed in the ear canal. In some cases, it is possible to measure the presence of the acoustic reflex without a hermetic seal (Kaplan et al., 1980; Surr and Schuchman, 1976). First, the air pressure pump must be adjusted to the middle ear pressure value corresponding to the point of maximum tympanic membrane mobility. Next, the sensitivity of the immittance instrument must be increased so that the slight ear canal volume changes created by tympanic membrane movement can be more easily monitored. The intensity of the reflex activating signal is then increased in 5-dB steps from an initial presentation level of approximately 70–75 dB HL. A threshold bracketing technique is used similar to that used in pure tone auditory threshold determination. The acoustic reflex threshold is the lowest intensity at which a systematic deflection on either the balance or millimho meter is observed. To avoid interpretation errors, reflex thresholds should be reported according to the ear that is *stimulated.*

Interpretation Generally speaking, with a bilateral conductive hearing loss, the acoustic reflex will be absent bilaterally to either ipsilateral or contralateral stimulation. In the presence of a unilateral conductive hearing loss the reflex will be absent bilaterally with contralateral stimulation. If the ear with the hearing loss is stimulated and the probe placed in the normal ear, there will be insufficient intensity to elicit the reflex. If the probe is placed in the ear with the hearing loss, the conductive pathology generally will prevent the contraction of the stapedius muscle from altering the condition of the tympanic membrane, precluding the observation of the reflex. With ipsilateral stimulation, if the stimulus and probe are in the impaired ear the reflex will be absent for the reasons outlined above. However, if the stimulus and probe systems are in the normal ear, reflexes will be present. The case presentations that follow demonstrate these principles as well as some of the exceptions.

In the case of a unilateral sensorineural hearing loss of cochlear origin, the acoustic reflex will be present with either ipsilateral or contralateral stimulation of the normal ear and may be present with either ipsilateral or contralateral stimulation of the impaired ear if there is sufficient residual hearing in that ear. In fact, Metz (1952) described a reduction of the acoustic reflex threshold relative to the pure tone threshold with stimulation of the impaired ear in cases of cochlear loss demonstrating recruitment. In the normal ear, reflex thresholds are expected at 70–100 dB above the threshold of pure tone sensitivity. In the recruiting ear, thresholds of less than 60 dB sensation level (SL) have been noted. Jerger et al. (1972) reported that as the hearing loss increases, the likelihood of a reflex decreases. It was demonstrated that the chance of obtaining a reflex is 90% with a hearing loss up to 60 dB HL, but only 50% with a loss up to 85 dB HL, and 5–10% with a 100-dB hearing loss. With a bilateral cochlear loss, reflexes can be expected in both ears unless the loss of sensitivity is too great.

In cases of unilateral sensorineural hearing loss of neural origin, the acoustic reflex will be present with both ipsilateral and contralateral stimulation of the normal ear. With stimulation in the impaired ear the reflex may be absent, present but at an elevated acoustic reflex threshold sensation level, or present but with acoustic reflex decay (see next section). For cases with central auditory lesions below the level of the superior olivary complex, stimulation in the ear contralateral to the lesion will usually result in an absent reflex.

Although these findings are the generally expected outcomes to acoustic reflex threshold determination in various auditory conditions, there are exceptions. For further information, the reader is referred to Feldman and Wilber (1976) and other current literature in acoustic immittance.

Acoustic Reflex Decay

Another acoustic reflex procedure routinely performed at 500 and 1000 Hz is called "reflex decay." It can be measured with contralateral or ipsilateral stimulation and provides an assessment of the integrity of the sensory or afferent portion of the auditory nervous system (eighth nerve) as well as the motor or efferent portion of the reflex arc (seventh nerve) which enervates the stapedius muscle.

Anderson et al. (1970) reported that in patients with eighth nerve tumors there was abnormal decay of the acoustic reflex. This was measured by presenting a stimulating frequency of 500 or 1000 Hz at a level 10 dB above the acoustic reflex threshold for 10 seconds. Higher frequencies were not used because it has been shown that a certain percentage of the normal population does not present reflexes at frequencies above 1000 Hz. Abnormal decay was defined as a reduction in reflex magnitude to 50% within 5 seconds (see Figure 3-10). The time in seconds in which the reflex decays to 50% magnitude is entered into the Audiologic Assessment Form.

The clinician needs to be aware, however, that in patients with cochlear hearing loss there is a high false-positive rate associated with the reflex decay procedure. For example, Olsen et al. (1981) reported that as many as 27% of the patients with Ménière's disease studied exhibited positive acoustic reflex decay findings.

Thus, this technique is sensitive to deficiencies of the ability of the eighth nerve to maintain continuous firing. After an initial response, there is rapid decay as the eighth nerve on the affected side adapts. This procedure, however, is also sensitive to deficiencies of the seventh nerve, which innervates the stapedius muscle. Pathologies such as Bell's palsy or other facial nerve involvement can affect the seventh or facial nerve, which can be monitored using the acoustic reflex decay procedure. For example, a Bell's palsy patient may initially have absent lacri-

mal (tearing) function in conjunction with abnormal acoustic reflex decay function. With restoration of peripheral seventh nerve function, the reflex decay pattern may return to normal before the lacrimal function. Measurement of reflex decay as well as reflex thresholds is useful to monitor seventh nerve function.

Eustachian Tube Assessment

The acoustic immittance measurement technique is extremely valuable in assessing competency of the Eustachian tube in the presence of either a perforated or an intact tympanic membrane. In fact, the negative pressure tympanogram (less than −150 daPa of middle ear pressure) is indicative of inadequate ventilation of the middle ear.

However, the clinician is frequently faced with the necessity of evaluating the dynamic function of the Eustachian tube. In the case of an open or perforated tympanic membrane, tubal function can be assessed using an inflation–deflation technique. This procedure requires the hermetic placement of the probe assembly in the ear canal. The air pressure is increased to the point just below which the Eustachian tube is forced open—noted by a sudden pressure drop. The client is asked to swallow several times (a cup of water is sometimes helpful and appreciated). By swallowing, the client activates the tensor and levator veli palatini muscles which open the Eustachian tube under normal conditions. After several swallows the residual air pressure is noted by observing the manometer on the immittance instrument. The amount of residual air pressure is representative of Eustachian tube performance. For example, normal Eustachian tube function would allow for equilibration of air pressure and the manometer would read approximately 0 daPa. With obstructed Eustachian tubes, successive swallows may not open the tube adequately and the residual air pressure may remain close to the originally observed opening pressure. It is not wise to perform this procedure by applying negative pressure to the ear canal instead of positive pressure because the Eustachian tube may "lock" rather than open. The lock prevents equilibration of pressure upon successive swallows and may lead to misinterpretation of the results.

For intact tympanic membranes, a Pressure

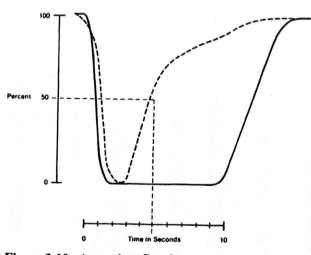

Figure 3-10. Acoustic reflex decay. Solid trace reveals normal function. Dashed trace reveals abnormal (>50% decay within 5 seconds) function.

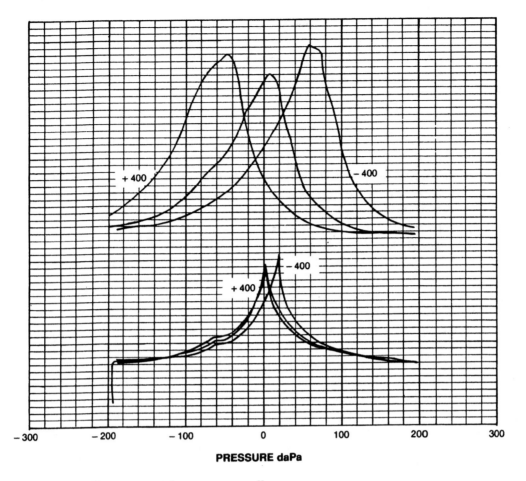

Figure 3-11. Tympanometric pressure swallow.

Swallow (PSW) technique (Williams, 1975) is appropriate. This technique is a version of the inflation–deflation procedure just described. The procedure requires obtaining a tympanogram after a normalization swallow at ambient pressure. Next, a tympanogram is run on the same chart after the client is instructed to swallow 3 to 4 times with +400 daPa pressure in the external canal. Following a normalization swallow at ambient pressure, –400 daPa pressure is created in the external canal, the patient swallows 3 to 4 times and a third tympanogram is obtained. A comparison is made between the normalization tympanogram and the positive and negative pressure swallow tympanograms. Normal Eustachian tube function, as illustrated in Figure 3-11, is defined as at least a 15–20 daPa pressure difference. With Eustachian tube dysfunction there would be little (5 daPa) or no pressure difference between positive and negative swallow traces and the normalization trace. This is because the Eustachian tube is unable to equalize air pressure.

The upper portion of Figure 3-11 demonstrates an excellent example of good Eustachian tube function. A greater than 20 daPa pressure difference between the normal middle ear pressure trace and the +400 daPa positive, as well as –400 daPa negative, pressure swallow traces is seen. The lower portion of this figure reveals adequate ventilation of the middle ear by the Eustachian tube. This is evident by the approximately 15 daPa difference between the normal pressure and the –400 daPa pressure swallow. Poor ventilation is revealed, however, in the comparison between the normal middle ear pressure trace and the +400 daPa pressure swallow.

The information obtained regarding the dynamic functioning of the Eustachian tube is extremely valu-

Acoustic Immittance

able, particularly in cases of prospective middle ear reconstructive surgery. It has been reported that adequate Eustachian tube function is a prerequisite to successful reconstruction efforts (Bluestone, 1975; Holmquist, 1970). Thus the audiologist will want to be familiar with this technique.

Screening

Acoustic immittance measurement procedures, being rapid and objective, are applicable to screening programs. It is of primary importance to recognize that immittance procedures screen for middle ear disorders, whereas the traditional individual pure tone screen is designed to identify educationally significant hearing loss (American Speech and Hearing Association, 1975; American Speech-Language-Hearing Association, 1985). Ideally, the two procedures should be used together (American Speech-Language-Hearing Association, 1990).

Various populations have been identified as being at risk for middle ear disorders, particularly developmentally delayed, cleft palate, deaf, native American, preschool, and early-school-age children (American Speech-Language-Hearing Association, 1979; Harford et al., 1978). Therefore, guidelines for acoustic immittance screening have been developed.

The current ASHA guideline, *Guidelines for Screening for Hearing Impairment and Middle-Ear Disorders*, was published in 1990 (American Speech-Language-Hearing Association, 1990). The ASHA Committee on Audiologic Evaluation revised the 1979 guidelines based upon review of clinical data pertaining to screening protocols. Specific concern had been expressed regarding overreferral for medical intervention based upon tympanometric findings from screening data. As a result, the acous-

tic immittance measurements utilized in the 1990 guidelines are: static admittance (Peak Y expressed in mmho, ml or cm^3), which provides information regarding the tympanometric height and shape; equivalent ear canal volume (V_{ec} expressed in ml or cm^3), which is an estimate of the volume of air in front of the probe assembly and provides information regarding the integrity of the tympanic membrane; and tympanometric width (TW expressed in daPa), which, as a measure of tympanometric gradient, describes the shape of the tympanogram in the region of the peak and provides information related to mechanical changes in the middle ear associated with disease.

The acoustic immittance procedures recommended for screening for middle ear disorders are as follows: (1) Low static admittance (Peak Y) in the presence of equivalent ear canal volume (V_{ec}) in excess of the 90% range in Table 3-3 below is suggestive of tympanic membrane perforation and necessitates referral. (2) Low static admittance (Peak Y) below the 90% range in Table 3-3 and in the absence of any other positive finding should be observed and re-evaluated prior to medical referral. Medical referral should be made following two successive abnormal findings over a 4–6 week interval. (3) Abnormally wide tympanometric width (TW) in the absence of any other positive finding should, likewise, be observed and re-evaluated prior to medical referral. Referral on the basis of this finding alone should be made following two successive abnormal findings over a 4–6 week interval.

It is important to recognize that the acoustic immittance screening protocol is to be incorporated with procedures including case history, visual inspection of the ear, and pure tone audiometry. The reader who wishes to develop an acoustic immittance

Table 3-3. Interim norms for 1990 ASHA acoustic immittance screening.

	Peak Y (mmho, ml or cm^3)		V_{ec} (ml or cm^3)		TW (daPa)	
	Mean	90% Range	Mean	90% Range	Mean	90% Range
Children	0.5	0.2–0.9	0.7	0.4–1.0	100	60–150
Adults	0.8	0.3–1.4	1.1	0.6–1.5	80	50–110

screening program with any population is referred to both the Nashville Symposium references (Harford et al., 1978) and the ASHA references (American Speech and Hearing Association, 1978; American Speech-Language-Hearing Association, 1979; 1990).

For further information and additional clinical applications the reader is referred to Stach and Jerger (1991) and Lew and Jerger (1991), as well as other current advanced acoustic immittance literature. A comprehensive bibliography on acoustic immittance measures has been prepared by Dr. Terry L. Wiley of the University of Wisconsin in conjunction with the American Speech-Language-Hearing Association's Committee on Audiologic Evaluation (American Speech-Language-Hearing Association, 1991).

Questions

1. Describe the middle ear pressure for the right ear.
2. Describe the middle ear pressure for the left ear.
3. Describe the middle ear mobility for the right ear.
4. Describe the middle ear mobility for the left ear.

Name: Fig 3-12   Date: XX/XX/XX   Age: 31   Sex: M   Audiologist: VSG

AUDIOMETER: _____   ANSI 1969

PURE TONE AUDIOGRAM
FREQUENCY IN HERTZ

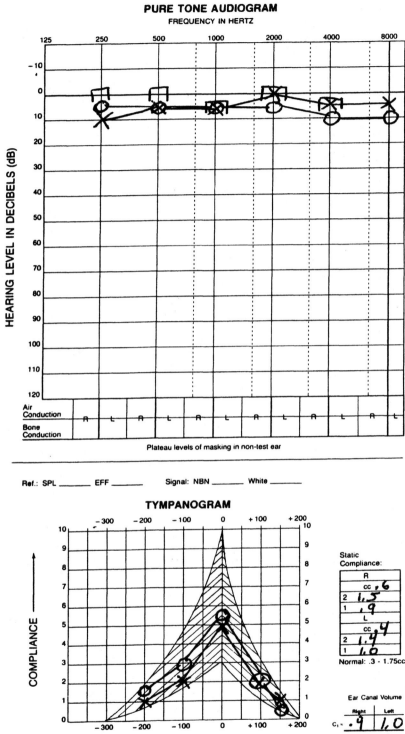

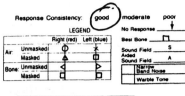

Response Consistency:	good	moderate	poor

LEGEND

No Response

		Right (red)	Left (blue)
Air	Unmasked	○	×
	Masked	△	▢
Bone	Unmasked	◁	▷
	Masked	◁	▷

Best Bone
Sound Field ___ S
Aided
Sound Field ___ A

Narrow Band Noise

Warble Tone

PURE TONE AVERAGE (R) (L)			
	Right	Left	Aided
AIR	5	3	
BONE			

SPEECH AUDIOMETRY ☒ MLV ☐ Tape

	RIGHT	LEFT	MASK LEVEL R	L	SOUND FIELD	LIST
SAT						
SRT	5	0				W-1
MCL						
UCL						
PB% (Word)	100 35SL	100 35SL				NU-6
PB% (Word)	L	L				
PB% (Word)	L	L				
PB% (Word)	L	L				
	L	L				
	L	L				

STAPEDIUS REFLEX THRESHOLDS

Stimulus	Contralateral (HL)					Ipsilateral (HL)		
EAR	.5K	1K	2K	4K	WBN	.5K	1K	2K
R			✕	✕				✕
Decay			✕	✕				✕
L			✕	✕				✕
Decay		✕	✕					✕

ABBREVIATIONS

A	Absent	NR	No Response
C₁	Canal Volume	SAT	Speech Awareness
CNE	Could Not Establish		Threshold
CNT	Could Not Test	SL	Sensation Level
DNT	Did Not Test	SRT	Speech Reception
HL	Hearing Level		Threshold
MCL	Most Comfortable	UCL	Uncomfortable Listening
	Listening Level		Level
MVL	Monitored Live Voice		

C_1 — Canal Volume

REMARKS:

_____

_____

_____

_____

_____

Air Conduction: R L R L R L R L R L R L R L

Bone Conduction:

Plateau levels of masking in non-test ear

Ref.: SPL _____ EFF _____   Signal: NBN _____ White _____

TYMPANOGRAM

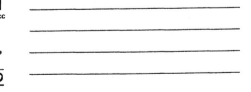

Static Compliance:

R	
cc	.6
2	1.5
1	.9
L	
cc	.4
2	1.4
1	1.0

Normal: .3 - 1.75cc

Ear Canal Volume

	Right	Left
C_1 =	.9	1.0

PRESSURE IN daPa

Acoustic Immittance

1. Normal middle ear pressure of 0 daPa for the right ear.
2. Normal middle ear pressure of 0 daPa for the left ear.
3. Normal middle ear mobility of 0.60 cc for the right ear.
4. Normal middle ear mobility of 0.40 cc for the left ear.

These data can be summarized by stating normal middle ear pressure and mobility bilaterally. This is consistent with the normal hearing bilaterally that is shown on the pure tone and speech audiograms.

QUESTIONS FOR FIGURE 3-13

1. Describe the middle ear pressure for the right and left ears.
2. Describe the middle ear mobility for the right and left ears.

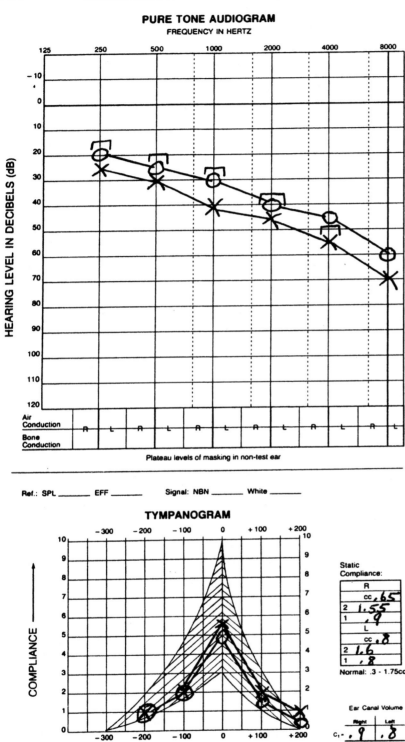

Name: Fig 3-13   **Date:** XX/XX/XX   **Age:** 67   **Sex:** M   **Audiologist:** VSG

AUDIOMETER: _____   ANSI 1969

PURE TONE AUDIOGRAM
FREQUENCY IN HERTZ

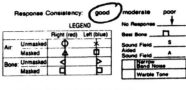

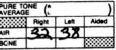

PURE TONE AVERAGE (R, L)			
	Right	Left	Aided
AIR	32	38	
BONE			

SPEECH AUDIOMETRY   ☒MLV ☐ Tape

	RIGHT	LEFT	MASK LEVEL R	MASK LEVEL L	SOUND FIELD	LIST
SAT						
SRT	25	35				W-1
MCL						
UCL						
PB% (Word)	88 35SL	84 35SL				NU-6
PB% (Word)	_L	_L				
PB% (Word)	_L	_L				
PB% (Word)	_L	_L				
	_L	_L				
	_L	_L				

Plateau levels of masking in non-test ear

Ref.: SPL _____ EFF _____   Signal: NBN _____ White _____

STAPEDIUS REFLEX THRESHOLDS

Stimulus	Contralateral (HL)					Ipsilateral (HL)		
EAR	.5K	1K	2K	4K	WBN	.5K	1K	2K
R								
Decay		☒	☒					☒
L								
Decay		☒	☒			☒		☒

ABBREVIATIONS

A	Absent	NR	No Response
C₁	Canal Volume	SAT	Speech Awareness
CNE	Could Not Establish		Threshold
CNT	Could Not Test	SL	Sensation Level
DNT	Did Not Test	SRT	Speech Reception
HL	Hearing Level		Threshold
MCL	Most Comfortable	UCL	Uncomfortable Listening
	Listening Level		Level
MVL	Monitored Live Voice		

TYMPANOGRAM

Static Compliance:

R	
cc	.65
2	1.55
1	.9

L	
cc	.8
2	1.6
1	.8

Normal: .3 - 1.75cc

Ear Canal Volume

	Right	Left
C₁ =	.9	.8

REMARKS:

_____
_____
_____
_____
_____

Answers for Figure 3-13

1. Normal middle ear pressure of 0 daPa for both ears.
2. Normal middle ear mobility of 0.65 cc for the right ear and .80 cc for the left ear.

These data are consistent with normal middle ear function. The presence of a mild bilateral hearing loss by both air and bone conduction and slightly reduced word recognition suggest a mild bilateral sensorineural hearing loss.

QUESTIONS FOR FIGURE 3-14

1. Describe the middle ear pressure for each ear.
2. Describe the middle ear mobility for each ear.

Name: Fig 3-14   Date: XX/XX/XX   Age: 1.5   Sex: F   Audiologist: VSG

AUDIOMETER: _____   ANSI 1969

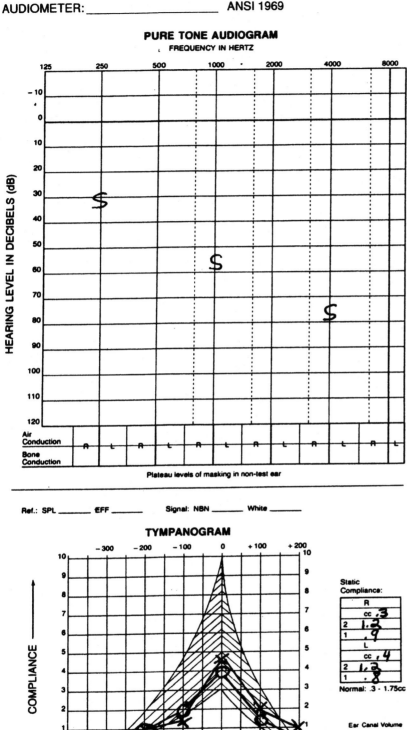

PURE TONE AUDIOGRAM
FREQUENCY IN HERTZ

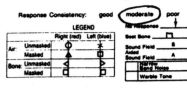

Response Consistency: good   (moderate)   poor

PURE TONE AVERAGE (R L)	Right	Left	Aided
AIR			
BONE			

SPEECH AUDIOMETRY   ☐ MLV ☐ Tape

	RIGHT	LEFT	MASK LEVEL R L	SOUND FIELD	LIST
SAT				30	
SRT					
MCL					
UCL					
PB% (Word)	_L_	_L_			
PB% (Word)	_L_	_L_			
PB% (Word)	_L_	_L_			
PB% (Word)	_L_	_L_			
	_L_	_L_			
	_L_	_L_			

Plateau levels of masking in non-test ear

Ref.: SPL _____ EFF _____   Signal: NBN _____ White _____

STAPEDIUS REFLEX THRESHOLDS

Stimulus	Contralateral (HL)					Ipsilateral (HL)		
EAR	.5K	1K	2K	4K	WBN	.5K	1K	2K
R								
Decay			X	X				X
L								
Decay			X	X				X

TYMPANOGRAM

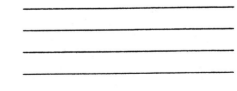

Static Compliance:

R	
cc	.3
2	1.3
1	.9
L	
cc	.4
2	1.3
1	.8

Normal: .3 - 1.75cc

Ear Canal Volume

	Right	Left
c_1 =	.9	.8

ABBREVIATIONS

A	Absent	NR	No Response
C_1	Canal Volume	SAT	Speech Awareness
CNE	Could Not Establish		Threshold
CNT	Could Not Test	SL	Sensation Level
DNT	Did Not Test	SRT	Speech Reception
HL	Hearing Level		Threshold
MCL	Most Comfortable	UCL	Uncomfortable Listening
	Listening Level		Level
MVL	Monitored Live Voice		

REMARKS:

_____

_____

_____

_____

_____

Acoustic Immittance

109

Answers for Figure 3-14

1. Normal middle ear pressure bilaterally. The point of maximum admittance occurs at 0 daPa for both ears, which is within normal limits.
2. Normal middle ear mobility bilaterally. The static admittance values of 0.3 cc for the right ear and 0.4 mmhos for the left ear are within normal limits.

These findings are consistent with normal middle ear function bilaterally. The sound field data, in conjunction with the immittance data, suggest the possibility of a sensorineural hearing loss for this youngster.

QUESTION FOR FIGURE 3-15

Case History Information This 39-year-old female has noticed a gradual decrease in her hearing for about 7 years since the birth of her third child. Her mother and maternal aunt have hearing losses; one has had successful middle ear surgery, the other benefits from amplification.

1. Describe the middle ear pressure and mobility for each ear.

Name: Fig 3-15   Date: XX/XX/XX   Age: 39   Sex: F   Audiologist: VSG
AUDIOMETER:_____ ANSI 1969

PURE TONE AUDIOGRAM
FREQUENCY IN HERTZ

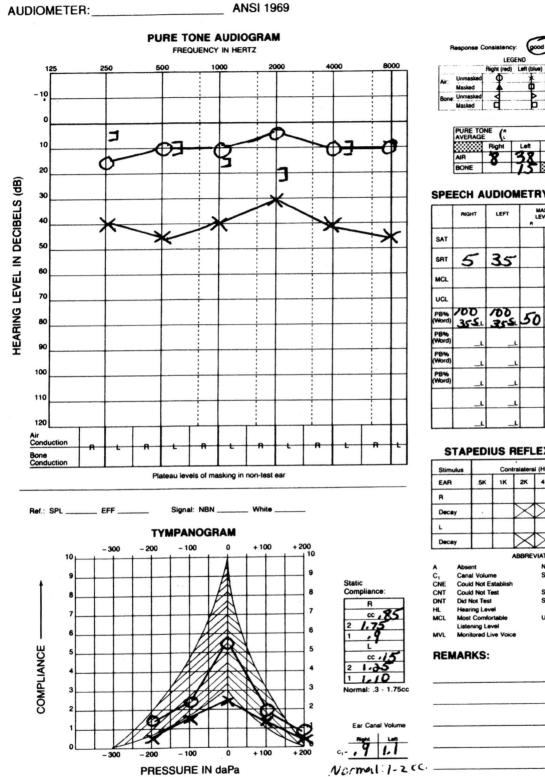

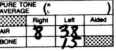

Response Consistency: (good) moderate poor

LEGEND

		Right (red)	Left (blue)	No Response	
Air:	Unmasked	O	X	Best Bone	☐
	Masked	△	☐	Sound Field	S
Bone:	Unmasked	<	>	Aided Sound Field	A
	Masked	☐	☐	Narrow Band Noise	
				Warble Tone	

PURE TONE AVERAGE (R L)			
	Right	Left	Aided
AIR	8	38	
BONE		15	

SPEECH AUDIOMETRY ☒MLV ☐ Tape

	RIGHT	LEFT	MASK LEVEL R L	SOUND FIELD	LIST
SAT					
SRT	5	35			W-1
MCL					
UCL					
PB% (Word)	100 35SL	100 35SL	50		NU-6
PB% (Word)	_L	_L			
PB% (Word)	_L	_L			
	_L	_L			
	_L	_L			

STAPEDIUS REFLEX THRESHOLDS

Stimulus	Contralateral (HL)					Ipsilateral (HL)		
EAR	.5K	1K	2K	4K	WBN	.5K	1K	2K
R								
Decay	·		☒	☒				☒
L							·	
Decay			☒	☒		☒		☒

ABBREVIATIONS

A	Absent	NR	No Response
C₁	Canal Volume	SAT	Speech Awareness
CNE	Could Not Establish		Threshold
CNT	Could Not Test	SL	Sensation Level
DNT	Did Not Test	SRT	Speech Reception
HL	Hearing Level		Threshold
MCL	Most Comfortable	UCL	Uncomfortable Listening
	Listening Level		Level
MVL	Monitored Live Voice		

Note: C_1 = Canal Volume

REMARKS:
_____
_____
_____
_____

Ref.: SPL _____ EFF _____   Signal: NBN _____ White _____

TYMPANOGRAM

PRESSURE IN daPa

Static Compliance:

R	
cc	.85
2	1.75
1	.9
L	
cc	.15
2	1.25
1	1.10

Normal: .3 - 1.75cc

Ear Canal Volume

	Right	Left
C₁	.9	1.1

Normal: 1-2 cc

1. There is: (a) normal middle ear pressure of 0 daPa bilaterally; (b) normal middle ear mobility of 0.85 cc in the right ear; (c) reduced middle ear mobility of 0.15 cc for the left ear.

    These results are consistent with normal hearing in the right ear and a mild to moderate conductive hearing loss in the left ear not inconsistent with the possibility of otosclerosis. The reduced left middle ear mobility agrees with the presence of the air–bone gap in that ear.

QUESTION FOR FIGURE 3-16

1. Describe the middle ear pressure and mobility for both ears.

Name: Fig 3-16   Date: XX/XX/XX Age: 3.4 Sex: F   Audiologist: VSG
AUDIOMETER: _____ ANSI 1969

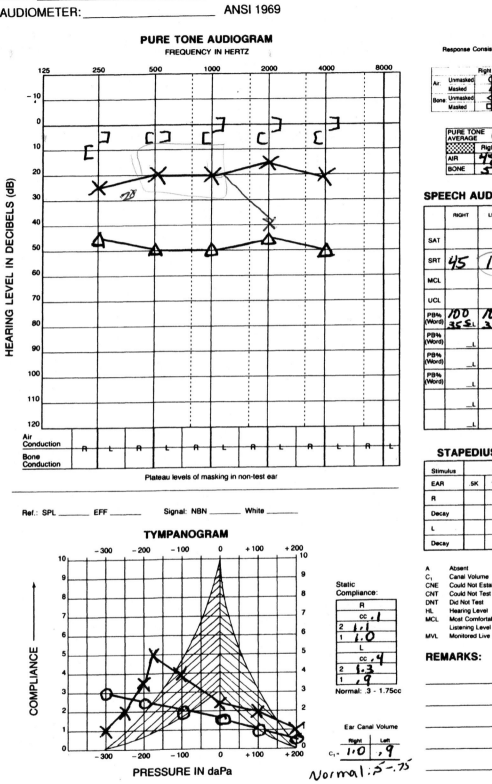

PURE TONE AUDIOGRAM
FREQUENCY IN HERTZ

Response Consistency: good moderate poor

LEGEND

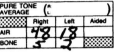

		Right (red)	Left (blue)
Air.	Unmasked	O	X
	Masked	▲	☐
Bone.	Unmasked	<	>
	Masked	☐	☐

No Response: ⊓
Best Bone: ⊓
Sound Field: S
Aided Sound Field: A
Narrow Band Noise
Warble Tone

PURE TONE AVERAGE (R L)	Right	Left	Aided
AIR	78	18	
BONE	5	2	

SPEECH AUDIOMETRY MLV ☐ Tape

	RIGHT	LEFT	MASK LEVEL R L	SOUND FIELD	LIST
SAT					
SRT	45	15			W-1
MCL					
UCL					
PB% (Word)	100 35SL	100 35SL	60		PBK
PB% (Word)	L	L			
PB% (Word)	L	L			
PB% (Word)	L	L			
	L	L			
	L	L			

STAPEDIUS REFLEX THRESHOLDS

Stimulus	Contralateral (HL)					Ipsilateral (HL)		
EAR	.5K	1K	2K	4K	WBN	.5K	1K	2K
R				✕				✕
Decay	✕							
L								
Decay		✕	✕					✕

ABBREVIATIONS

A	Absent	NR	No Response
C₁	Canal Volume	SAT	Speech Awareness
CNE	Could Not Establish		Threshold
CNT	Could Not Test	SL	Sensation Level
DNT	Did Not Test	SRT	Speech Reception
HL	Hearing Level		Threshold
MCL	Most Comfortable	UCL	Uncomfortable Listening
	Listening Level		Level
MVL	Monitored Live Voice		

REMARKS:

_____
_____
_____
_____
_____

Ref.: SPL _____ EFF _____   Signal: NBN _____ White _____

TYMPANOGRAM

PRESSURE IN daPa

Static Compliance:

R	
cc	.1
2	1.1
1	1.0
L	
cc	.4
2	1.3
1	.9

Normal: .3 - 1.75cc

Ear Canal Volume

	Right	Left
C₁	1.0	.9

Normal: .5 - .75

Answer for Figure 3-16

1. The right tympanogram is essentially flat (0.1 cc static admittance) with no discernible point of maximum admittance depicting middle ear pressure. This middle ear system is immobile. The configuration is indicative of middle ear effusion and consistent with a conductive hearing loss. The left tympanogram depicts significant negative middle ear pressure of –175 daPa. The mobility of this middle ear system is normal with 0.4 cc static admittance. These results are consistent with Eustachian tube dysfunction and are frequently accompanied by a conductive component to the hearing loss. There may or may not be middle ear effusion (fluid) present. With a shallower and more rounded area of maximum mobility there would be a likelihood of middle ear effusion.

QUESTION FOR FIGURE 3-17

1. Describe the middle ear mobility and pressure for both ears.

Name: Fig 3-17   Date: XX/XX/XX Age: 34 Sex: F Audiologist: VSG
AUDIOMETER: _____   ANSI 1969

PURE TONE AUDIOGRAM
FREQUENCY IN HERTZ

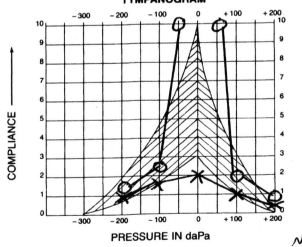

HEARING LEVEL IN DECIBELS (dB)

Plateau levels of masking in non-test ear

Ref.: SPL _____ EFF _____   Signal: NBN _____ White _____

TYMPANOGRAM

COMPLIANCE

PRESSURE IN daPa

Static Compliance:

R	
cc →	2.2
2	3.2
1	1.0
L	
cc →	.2
2	1.3
1	1.1

Normal: .3 - 1.75cc

Ear Canal Volume

	Right	Left
$c_1 =$	1.0	1.1

Normal 1-2cc

Response Consistency: (good) moderate poor

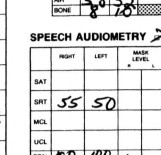

PURE TONE AVERAGE

	Right	Left	Aided
AIR	58	52	
BONE	8	10	

SPEECH AUDIOMETRY ☑ MLV ☐ Tape

	RIGHT	LEFT	MASK LEVEL R	L	SOUND FIELD	LIST
SAT						
SRT	55	50				W-1
MCL						
UCL						
PB% (Word)	100 35SL	100 35SL	65	70		NU-6
PB% (Word)	_L	_L				
PB% (Word)	_L	_L				
	_L	_L				
	_L	_L				

STAPEDIUS REFLEX THRESHOLDS

Stimulus	Contralateral (HL)					Ipsilateral (HL)		
EAR	.5K	1K	2K	4K	WBN	.5K	1K	2K
R								
Decay			✕	✕		✕		
L								
Decay			✕	✕		✕		✕

ABBREVIATIONS

A   Absent
C_1 Canal Volume
CNE   Could Not Establish
CNT   Could Not Test
DNT   Did Not Test
HL   Hearing Level
MCL   Most Comfortable Listening Level
MVL   Monitored Live Voice
NR   No Response
SAT   Speech Awareness Threshold
SL   Sensation Level
SRT   Speech Reception Threshold
UCL   Uncomfortable Listening Level

REMARKS:

_____
_____
_____
_____
_____

1. The right tympanogram depicts normal middle ear pressure and excessive or greater than normal mobility (2.2 cc static admittance). Excessive mobility can be caused by a healed tympanic membrane perforation or ossicular disarticulation and can be accompanied by a conductive hearing loss. Note the large air–bone gaps.

   The left tympanogram shows normal middle ear pressure and reduced mobility (0.2 cc static admittance) as is seen in otosclerosis or tympanosclerosis. These conditions are typically accompanied by a conductive hearing loss. Large air–bone gaps are present in this ear as well as in the right.

   It is important to recognize that it may be difficult to differentiate tympanic membrane perforations from disarticulation of the ossicular chain tympanometrically using an impedance bridge with only a low-frequency probe tone. However, differences between these etiologies may become evident by the use of an admittance meter, the addition of a 660-Hz probe tone, and the use of component tympanometry (see Figure 3-18).

   The present case also underscores the clinical value of immittance measures. If one were to observe only the audiometric data, it would be difficult to differentiate a hypermobile middle ear system from a stiff system. These differences are readily observed via immittance measures.

QUESTION FOR FIGURE 3-18

1. Describe the tympanograms.

Name: Fig 3-18   Date: XX/XX/XX   Age: 34   Sex: F   Audiologist: VSG

AUDIOMETER: _____   ANSI 1969

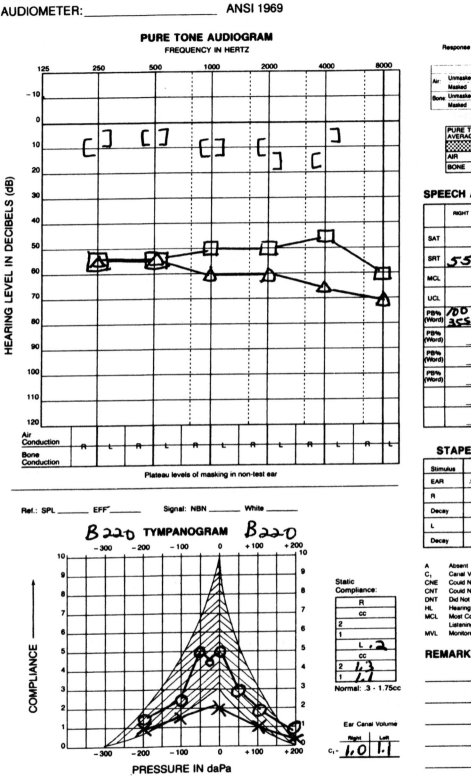

PURE TONE AUDIOGRAM
FREQUENCY IN HERTZ

HEARING LEVEL IN DECIBELS (dB)

Air Conduction

Bone Conduction

Plateau levels of masking in non-test ear

Ref.: SPL _____ EFF _____   Signal: NBN _____ White _____

B 220 TYMPANOGRAM B 220

PRESSURE IN daPa

COMPLIANCE

Static Compliance:

R	
cc	
2	
1	
L .2	
cc	
2	1.3
1	1.1

Normal: .3 - 1.75cc

Ear Canal Volume

	Right	Left
C_1 -	1.0	1.1

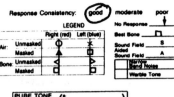

Response Consistency: (good) moderate poor

No Response

LEGEND

	Right (red)	Left (blue)
Air: Unmasked	O	X
Masked	△	□
Bone: Unmasked	◁	▷
Masked	□	□

Best Bone, Sound Field S, Aided Sound Field A, Narrow Band Noise, Warble Tone

PURE TONE AVERAGE (R/L)			
	Right	Left	Aided
AIR	58	52	
BONE	8	10	

SPEECH AUDIOMETRY ☒MLV ☐ Tape

	RIGHT	LEFT	MASK LEVEL R	L	SOUND FIELD	LIST
SAT						
SRT	55	50				W-1
MCL						
UCL						
PB% (Word)	100 35SL	100 35SL	65	70		W-6
PB% (Word)	_L	_L				
PB% (Word)	_L	_L				
PB% (Word)	_L	_L				
	_L	_L				
	_L	_L				

STAPEDIUS REFLEX THRESHOLDS

Stimulus	Contralateral (HL)					Ipsilateral (HL)		
EAR	.5K	1K	2K	4K	WBN	.5K	1K	2K
R								
Decay			☒	☒				☒
L								
Decay			☒	☒				☒

ABBREVIATIONS

A — Absent
C_1 — Canal Volume
CNE — Could Not Establish
CNT — Could Not Test
DNT — Did Not Test
HL — Hearing Level
MCL — Most Comfortable Listening Level
MVL — Monitored Live Voice
NR — No Response
SAT — Speech Awareness Threshold
SL — Sensation Level
SRT — Speech Reception Threshold
UCL — Uncomfortable Listening Level

REMARKS:

_____

_____

_____

_____

_____

Acoustic Immittance

117

Answer for Figure 3-18

1. The right tympanogram depicts normal middle ear pressure. There is a wide and broad area of peaking and **notching** of the tympanometric trace. The B220 trace demonstrates hypermobility and notching at the point of maximum mobility. If available, the B660 trace would show the broad, characteristic inversion and notching of a mass-controlled middle ear system. These characteristics are frequently seen with ossicular discontinuity or post-stapedectomy.

   The left tympanogram shows normal middle ear pressure and reduced mobility. Note that the tympanometric trace is smooth and not notched, suggesting the absence of a mass-controlled middle ear system. This pattern is consistent with a stiff middle ear system such as that seen in otosclerosis or tympanosclerosis or congenital fixation of the ossicular chain.

   Keep in mind that static admittance values are computed from both conductance (G) and susceptance (B) values at 220 Hz by using the formula:

$$Y = \sqrt{G^2 + B^2}$$

QUESTIONS FOR FIGURE 3-19

1. Why are the acoustic reflex thresholds absent for bilateral contralateral stimulation?
2. Why are the acoustic reflex thresholds present with ipsilateral stimulation in the right ear but absent with ipsilateral stimulation in the left ear?
3. What type of hearing loss does this (and the other acoustic immittance and audiometric) information suggest?

Name: Fig 3-19   Date: XX/XX/XX   Age: 39   Sex: F   Audiologist: VSG
AUDIOMETER: _____ ANSI 1969

PURE TONE AUDIOGRAM

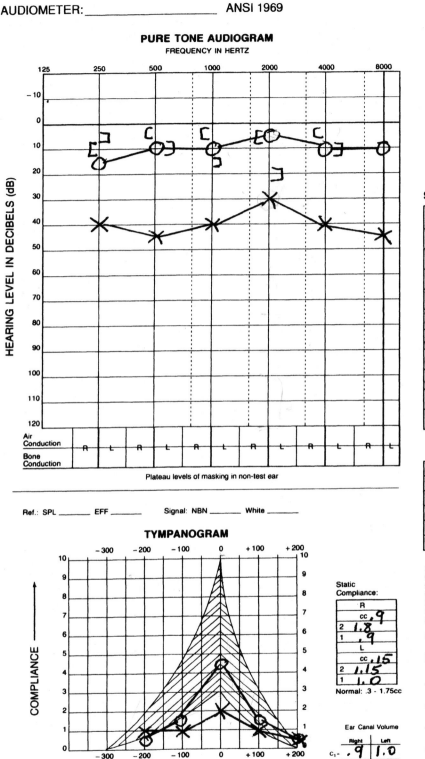

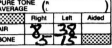

PURE TONE AVERAGE (R L)			
	Right	Left	Aided
AIR	8	38	
BONE	5	15	

SPEECH AUDIOMETRY   ☒ MLV ☐ Tape

	RIGHT	LEFT	MASK LEVEL R	L	SOUND FIELD	LIST
SAT						
SRT	5	35				W-1
MCL						
UCL						
PB% (Word)	100 35 SL	100 35 SL				NU-6
PB% (Word)	L	L				
PB% (Word)	L	L				
	L	L				
	L	L				

STAPEDIUS REFLEX THRESHOLDS

Stimulus	Contralateral (HL)					Ipsilateral (HL)		
EAR	.5K	1K	2K	4K	WBN	.5K	1K	2K
R	NR	NR	NR	NR		85	90	90
Decay								
L	NR	NR	NR	NR		NR	NR	NR
Decay								

ABBREVIATIONS

A   Absent
C₁   Canal Volume
CNE   Could Not Establish
CNT   Could Not Test
DNT   Did Not Test
HL   Hearing Level
MCL   Most Comfortable
       Listening Level
MVL   Monitored Live Voice

NR   No Response
SAT   Speech Awareness
       Threshold
SL   Sensation Level
SRT   Speech Reception
       Threshold
UCL   Uncomfortable Listening
       Level

REMARKS:

_____
_____
_____
_____

Ref.: SPL _____ EFF _____   Signal: NBN _____ White _____

TYMPANOGRAM

Static Compliance:	
R	
cc	.9
2	1.8
1	.9
L	
cc	.15
2	1.15
1	1.0

Normal: .3 - 1.75cc

Ear Canal Volume	
Right	Left
C_1 .9	1.0

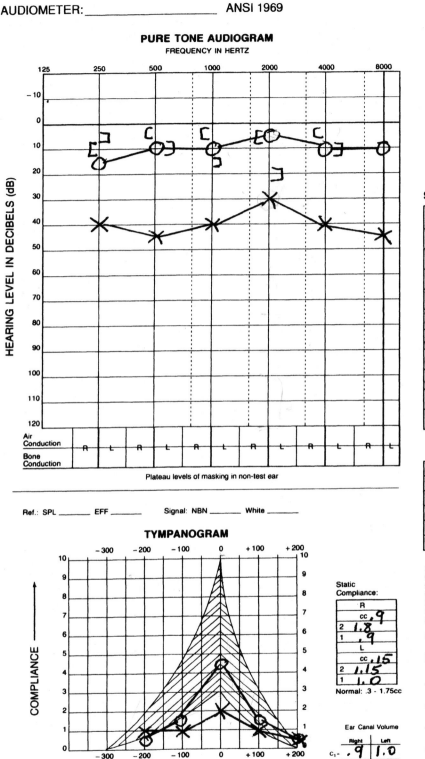

Answers for Figure 3-19

1. With even a mild conductive hearing loss in one ear, the acoustic reflex thresholds will be absent with contralateral stimulation. This is because with stimulation in the impaired ear, the hearing loss will be sufficient to prevent the signal from becoming intense enough to elicit the reflex. (Remember, the reflex is intensity controlled.) With stimulus in the normal ear and the monitor or probe in the impaired ear, the acoustic reflex will not be observed because of the inability of that ear to respond due to pathology.

2. Ipsilateral stimulation of the right ear will produce normal responses since both stimulation and recording are taking place in a normal ear. Since the left ear has the pathology, stimulating and recording in that ear will yield absent reflexes.

3. Conductive hearing loss in the left ear characterized by reduced mobility. This pattern is typical of otosclerosis.

QUESTIONS FOR FIGURE 3-20

1. Explain why acoustic reflexes are absent (NR) bilaterally with contralateral stimulation.

2. Why are the acoustic reflexes present but at elevated threshold levels with ipsilateral stimulation in the left ear but absent with ipsilateral stimulation in the right ear?

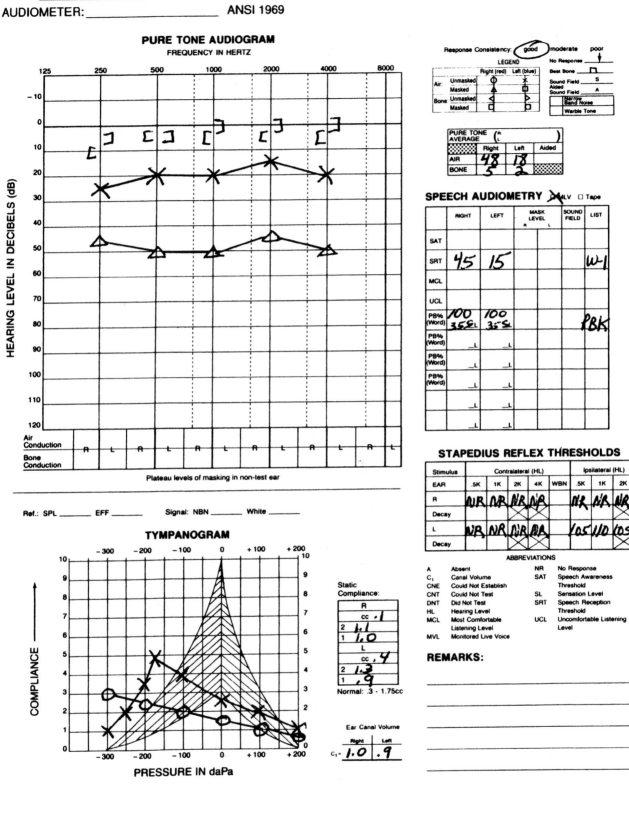

PURE TONE AUDIOGRAM
FREQUENCY IN HERTZ

Name: Fig 3-20   Date: XX/XX/XX   Age: 3.4   Sex: F   Audiologist: VSG

AUDIOMETER: _____   ANSI 1969

Response Consistency: (good) moderate poor

LEGEND

	Right (red)	Left (blue)
Air: Unmasked	○	×
Air: Masked	△	□
Bone: Unmasked	◁	▷
Bone: Masked	□	□

No Response

Best Bone

Sound Field — S
Aided
Sound Field — A

Narrow Band Noise

Warble Tone

PURE TONE AVERAGE (R/L)

	Right	Left	Aided
AIR	48	18	
BONE	5	2	

SPEECH AUDIOMETRY ☒ MLV ☐ Tape

	RIGHT	LEFT	MASK LEVEL R	L	SOUND FIELD	LIST
SAT						
SRT	45	15				W-1
MCL						
UCL						
PB% (Word)	100 35SL	100 35SL				PBK
PB% (Word)	L	L				
PB% (Word)	L	L				
PB% (Word)	L	L				
	L	L				
	L	L				

STAPEDIUS REFLEX THRESHOLDS

Stimulus	Contralateral (HL)					Ipsilateral (HL)		
EAR	.5K	1K	2K	4K	WBN	.5K	1K	2K
R	NR	NR	NR	NR		NR	NR	NR
Decay								
L	NR	NR	NR	NR		105	110	105
Decay								

ABBREVIATIONS

A	Absent	NR	No Response
C₁	Canal Volume	SAT	Speech Awareness Threshold
CNE	Could Not Establish		
CNT	Could Not Test	SL	Sensation Level
DNT	Did Not Test	SRT	Speech Reception Threshold
HL	Hearing Level		
MCL	Most Comfortable Listening Level	UCL	Uncomfortable Listening Level
MVL	Monitored Live Voice		

REMARKS:

_____
_____
_____
_____

Ref.: SPL ____ EFF ____   Signal: NBN ____ White ____

TYMPANOGRAM

PRESSURE IN daPa

Static Compliance:

R	
cc	.1
2	1.1
1	1.0
L	
cc	.4
2	1.3
1	.9

Normal: .3 - 1.75cc

Ear Canal Volume

	Right	Left
C₁	1.0	.9

Acoustic Immittance

Answers for Figure 3-20

1. Refer to Figure 3-19, answer 1 for explanation.
2. With hearing levels less than approximately 30 dB, acoustic reflex thresholds may be obtained, but at elevated levels. This is because the output of the audiometer section is sufficient to elicit the reflex—provided the pathology is not severe enough to preclude observation of the reflex. Thus, in this case we observe elevated acoustic reflex thresholds in the left ear but with sensation levels within normal limits. In the right ear there is too much hearing loss for a measurable reflex.

QUESTIONS FOR FIGURE 3-21

Case History Information Numerous ear aches and ear infections involving both ears since infancy. Failed school hearing screening. Receiving resource help in math and reading and speech intervention in school. Ear, nose, and throat (ENT) exam reveals a left patent tympanostomy (PE) tube and a right tympanic membrane perforation.

1. Describe the immittance data, particularly as they relate to the ENT findings. What recommendations would you make?
2. Would the tympanometric information be different if it were obtained from an otoadmittance meter rather than an impedance bridge?

Name: Fig 3-21   Date: XX/XX/XX   Age: 8   Sex: M   Audiologist: VSG
AUDIOMETER: _____   ANSI 1969

PURE TONE AUDIOGRAM
FREQUENCY IN HERTZ

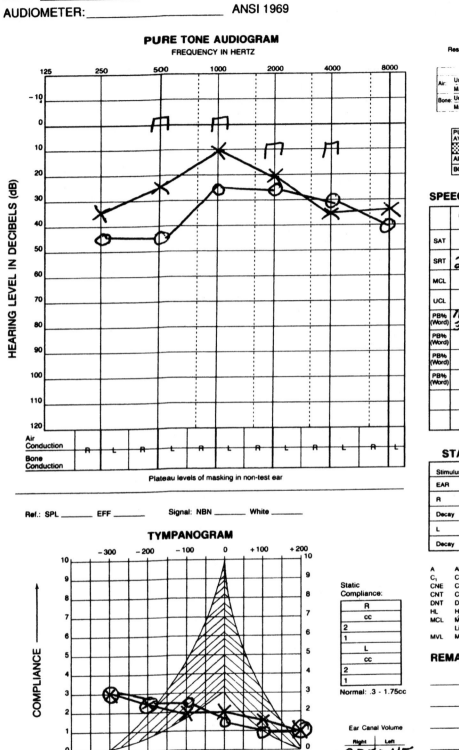

Air Conduction — R L R L R L R L R L R L R L
Bone Conduction

Plateau levels of masking in non-test ear

Ref.: SPL _____ EFF _____   Signal: NBN _____ White _____

TYMPANOGRAM

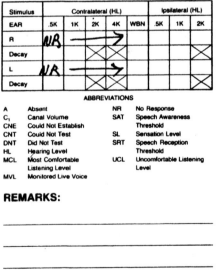

COMPLIANCE ⟶

PRESSURE IN daPa

Static Compliance:

R	
	cc
2	
1	
L	
	cc
2	
1	

Normal: .3 - 1.75cc

Ear Canal Volume

Right	Left
C_1= 2.85	2.45

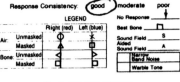

Response Consistency: (good) moderate poor

LEGEND

		Right (red)	Left (blue)
Air:	Unmasked	○	×
	Masked	△	□
Bone:	Unmasked		>
	Masked	□	□

No Response
Best Bone ⊓
Sound Field S
Aided
Sound Field A
Narrow Band Noise
Warble Tone

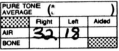

PURE TONE AVERAGE (R L)			
	Right	Left	Aided
AIR	32	18	
BONE			

SPEECH AUDIOMETRY ☑ MVL ☐ Tape

	RIGHT	LEFT	MASK LEVEL R L	SOUND FIELD	LIST
SAT					
SRT	25	25			W-1
MCL					
UCL					
PB% (Word)	100 35SL	100 35SL			W-22
PB% (Word)	_L	_L			
PB% (Word)	_L	_L			
PB% (Word)	_L	_L			
	_L	_L			
	_L	_L			

STAPEDIUS REFLEX THRESHOLDS

Stimulus	Contralateral (HL)					Ipsilateral (HL)		
EAR	.5K	1K	2K	4K	WBN	.5K	1K	2K
R	NR →							
Decay		✗	✗	✗				
L	NR →							
Decay		✗	✗	✗				✗

ABBREVIATIONS

A	Absent	NR	No Response
C_1	Canal Volume	SAT	Speech Awareness
CNE	Could Not Establish		Threshold
CNT	Could Not Test	SL	Sensation Level
DNT	Did Not Test	SRT	Speech Reception
HL	Hearing Level		Threshold
MCL	Most Comfortable	UCL	Uncomfortable Listening
	Listening Level		Level
MVL	Monitored Live Voice		

REMARKS:

_____

_____

_____

_____

_____

Answers for Figure 3-21

1. Both tympanograms are flat (and low) but the Physical Volume Test (PVT) is high. Static admittance values are significantly above normal limits. This suggests an immobile system with a volume larger than normal. This can occur if there is an opening between the outer and middle ears, creating a large volume, as occurs with a patent (open) tympanostomy tube (left ear) or a perforated tympanic membrane (right ear). The absent acoustic reflexes are consistent with these findings, as the tympanic membranes are not affected by ossicular chain movement. Thus, immittance measures confirm the presence of a right tympanic membrane perforation and a left patent tympanostomy tube.

   This youngster should remain under frequent ENT and audiologic care. He should receive preferential classroom seating and continue with speech and language remediation, along with resource help in math and reading.

2. Qualitatively, the tympanometric information obtained with an otoadmittance meter would not be different, but quantitatively it would be. The otoadmittance meter automatically compensates for ear canal volume (which in this case includes middle ear volume) while the impedance bridge does not. Thus, the otoadmittance meter would show flat tympanograms, but they would be higher on the graph to indicate the large volume. The static admittance information would be the same.

QUESTIONS FOR FIGURE 3-22

Case History Information There is a history of recurrent ear infections involving both ears dating back to infancy. ENT examination revealed atrophic tympanic membranes with missing incus bilaterally. The bilateral stapediomyringopexy is evidenced by the tympanic membrane being draped over the malleus and stapes head.

1. Describe the immittance data.
2. How does this relate to the audiometric data?

Name: Fig 3-22   Date: XX/XX/XX Age: 16 Sex: F Audiologist: VSG
AUDIOMETER:_____   ANSI 1969

PURE TONE AUDIOGRAM
FREQUENCY IN HERTZ

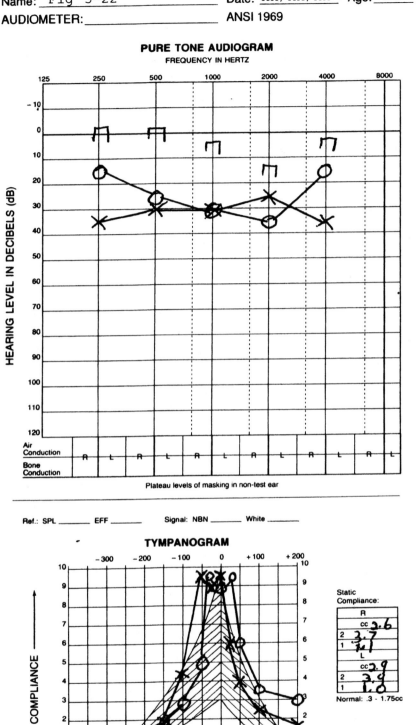

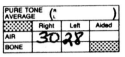

Response Consistency: (good) moderate poor

	PURE TONE AVERAGE (R / L)		
	Right	Left	Aided
AIR	30	28	
BONE			

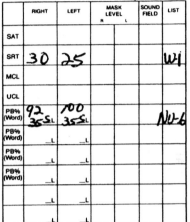

SPEECH AUDIOMETRY ☒MLV ☐ Tape

	RIGHT	LEFT	MASK LEVEL R	L	SOUND FIELD	LIST
SAT						
SRT	30	25				W1
MCL						
UCL						
PB% (Word)	92 35SL	100 35SL				NU-6
PB% (Word)	L	L				
PB% (Word)	L	L				
PB% (Word)	L	L				
	L	L				
	L	L				

STAPEDIUS REFLEX THRESHOLDS

Stimulus	Contralateral (HL)					Ipsilateral (HL)		
EAR	.5K	1K	2K	4K	WBN	.5K	1K	2K
R	NR			→		NR		→
Decay								
L	NR			→		NR		→
Decay								

ABBREVIATIONS

A	Absent	NR	No Response
C₁	Canal Volume	SAT	Speech Awareness
CNE	Could Not Establish		Threshold
CNT	Could Not Test	SL	Sensation Level
DNT	Did Not Test	SRT	Speech Reception
HL	Hearing Level		Threshold
MCL	Most Comfortable	UCL	Uncomfortable Listening
	Listening Level		Level
MVL	Monitored Live Voice		

REMARKS:
_____
_____
_____
_____
_____

Ref.: SPL _____ EFF _____   Signal: NBN _____ White _____

TYMPANOGRAM

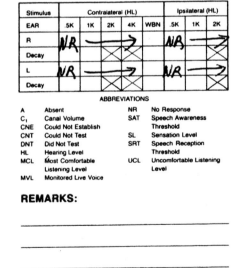

Static Compliance:

R	
cc	2.6
2	3.7
1	4.1

L	
cc	2.9
2	3.9
1	4.0

Normal: .3 - 1.75cc

Ear Canal Volume

	Right	Left
C₁=	1.1	1.0

Answers for Figure 3-22

1. Normal middle ear pressure bilaterally with above normal static admittance bilaterally. Absent acoustic reflexes bilaterally. The very steep, broadly notched tympanograms are consistent with ossicular discontinuity. The elevated admittance values convert to very low impedance values, suggesting hypermobile middle ear systems, yet the ear canal volumes are normal. The absent acoustic reflexes are also consistent with conductive pathology.

Conversion Formulas:

$$Y = \sqrt{G^2 + B^2}$$

$$Z = \frac{1}{Y} \times 1000$$

2. Audiometry suggests mild bilateral hearing loss of apparent conductive origin with normal unmasked bone conduction thresholds and excellent word recognition bilaterally. Although the unmasked bone conduction thresholds indicate a conductive component in at least one ear, the immittance data support a bilateral conductive impairment. Thus, in some cases masking during bone conduction testing may not be required.

QUESTIONS FOR FIGURE 3-23

Case History Information Nine-year-old with congenital renal abnormality which necessitated surgery and treatment with kanamycin. There is also a history of ear infections and a left ear hearing loss. Prior audiologic evaluation at a major center suggested an essentially sensorineural hearing loss in the left ear. Recent ENT examination was within normal limits.

1. Describe the tympanograms with regard to mobility and middle ear pressure. Please note static admittance data.
2. Discuss the acoustic reflex thresholds and how they relate to the case.
3. Do the audiometric and immittance data support a sensorineural or conductive hearing loss in the left ear? Why?

Name: Fig 3-23   Date: XX/XX/XX   Age: 9   Sex: M   Audiologist: VSG
AUDIOMETER: _____   ANSI 1969

PURE TONE AUDIOGRAM
FREQUENCY IN HERTZ

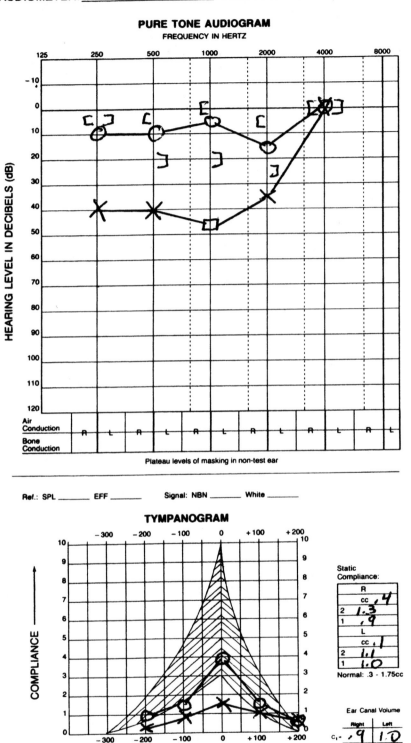

Plateau levels of masking in non-test ear

Ref.: SPL _____ EFF _____   Signal: NBN _____ White _____

TYMPANOGRAM

COMPLIANCE

PRESSURE IN daPa

Static Compliance:

R	
cc	.4
2	1.3
1	.9
L	
cc	.1
2	1.1
1	1.0

Normal: .3 - 1.75cc

Ear Canal Volume

	Right	Left
$c_1 =$	.9	1.0

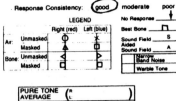

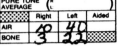

PURE TONE AVERAGE (R / L)			
	Right	Left	Aided
AIR	10	40	
BONE	3	21	

SPEECH AUDIOMETRY ☒ MLV ☐ Tape

	RIGHT	LEFT	MASK LEVEL R	MASK LEVEL L	SOUND FIELD	LIST
SAT						
SRT	10	40				W-1
MCL						
UCL						
PB% (Word)	100 / 35SL	100 / 35SL				W-22
PB% (Word)	_L	_L				
PB% (Word)	_L	_L				
PB% (Word)	_L	_L				
	_L	_L				
	_L	_L				

STAPEDIUS REFLEX THRESHOLDS

Stimulus	Contralateral (HL)					Ipsilateral (HL)		
EAR	.5K	1K	2K	4K	WBN	.5K	1K	2K
R	115	110	110	NR		95	90	90
Decay								
L	110	105	95	90		NR	→	
Decay								

ABBREVIATIONS

A	Absent	NR	No Response
C_1	Canal Volume	SAT	Speech Awareness
CNE	Could Not Establish		Threshold
CNT	Could Not Test	SL	Sensation Level
DNT	Did Not Test	SRT	Speech Reception
HL	Hearing Level		Threshold
MCL	Most Comfortable	UCL	Uncomfortable Listening
	Listening Level		Level
MVL	Monitored Live Voice		

REMARKS:

_____
_____
_____
_____
_____

1. Normal middle ear pressure bilaterally; normal admittance and mobility in the right ear; reduced admittance and mobility in the left ear.

2. Normal acoustic reflex thresholds with stimulus in the left ear at 2000 and 4000 Hz where hearing is normal or nearly normal; elevated acoustic reflex thresholds where hearing loss is mild. With right ear stimulation, acoustic reflex thresholds are elevated or absent. These results are consistent with a mild conductive pathology in the left ear.

3. All data (air–bone gap, excellent word recognition, and the acoustic immittance results) suggest a conductive hearing loss in the left ear, probably congenital fixation in origin (later confirmed by otolaryngologist). This would account for the reduced bone conduction thresholds frequently seen in conductive pathology due to the reduced influence of the ossicular inertial component of bone conduction. Unfortunately, this is occasionally overlooked and a sensorineural component is suspected. Reduced static admittance and middle ear mobility coupled with normal middle ear pressure and elevated or absent acoustic reflex thresholds all suggest fixation of the ossicular chain.

QUESTION FOR FIGURE 3-24

Case History Information "Dead" right ear since age 5 following high fever. Followed in audiology and ENT clinics routinely. Good school performance with preferential seating (left ear was toward the class and teacher). Latest ENT exam (new clinician) suggested the possibility of "malingering" based upon tuning fork tests.

1. Describe the acoustic immittance data, particularly as they relate to the audiometric and ENT results.

Name: Fig 3-24   Date: XX/XX/XX Age: 7 Sex: F Audiologist: VSG
AUDIOMETER: _____   ANSI 1969

PURE TONE AUDIOGRAM
FREQUENCY IN HERTZ

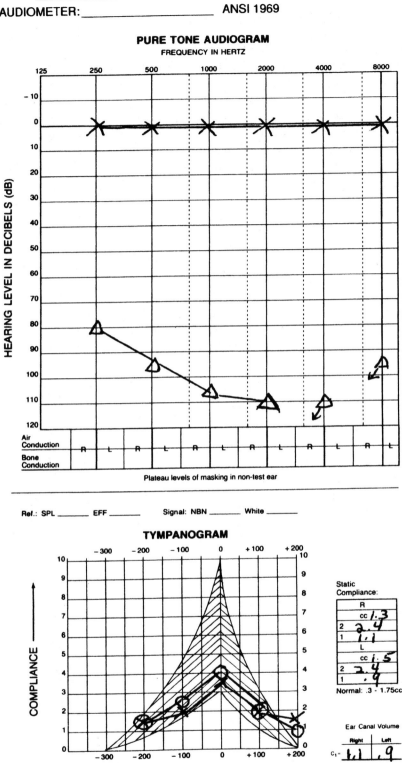

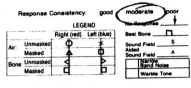

PURE TONE AVERAGE (R / L)

	Right	Left	Aided
AIR	103	0	
BONE			

SPEECH AUDIOMETRY   ☒ MLV ☐ Tape

	RIGHT	LEFT	MASK LEVEL R	MASK LEVEL L	SOUND FIELD	LIST
SAT						
SRT	100	0		60		W-1
MCL						
UCL						
PB% (Word)	0 / 105L	100 / 35SL		60		W-22
PB% (Word)	_L	_L				
PB% (Word)	_L	_L				
PB% (Word)	_L	_L				
	_L	_L				
	_L	_L				

STAPEDIUS REFLEX THRESHOLDS

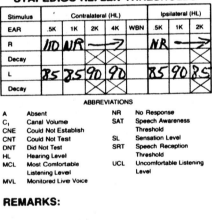

Stimulus	Contralateral (HL)					Ipsilateral (HL)		
EAR	.5K	1K	2K	4K	WBN	.5K	1K	2K
R	110	NR	→			NR	→	
Decay								
L	85	85	90	90		85	90	85
Decay								

ABBREVIATIONS

A	Absent	NR	No Response
C₁	Canal Volume	SAT	Speech Awareness Threshold
CNE	Could Not Establish		
CNT	Could Not Test	SL	Sensation Level
DNT	Did Not Test	SRT	Speech Reception Threshold
HL	Hearing Level		
MCL	Most Comfortable Listening Level	UCL	Uncomfortable Listening Level
MVL	Monitored Live Voice		

Ref.: SPL _____ EFF _____   Signal: NBN _____ White _____

TYMPANOGRAM

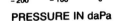

Static Compliance:

R	
cc	1.3
2	2.4
1	1.1
L	
cc	1.5
2	2.4
1	.9

Normal: .3 - 1.75cc

Ear Canal Volume

	Right	Left
C₁	1.1	.9

REMARKS:

_____

_____

_____

_____

_____

1. The tympanograms reveal normal middle ear pressure and mobility bilaterally. The contralateral acoustic reflex thresholds are present and within normal limits with stimulus in the left ear. With right ear stimulation the reflex thresholds are elevated (at 500 Hz) or absent. These results are consistent with a severe to profound unilateral sensorineural hearing loss and are borne out by the audiometric findings. The supposition of malingering implies better hearing in the right ear than admitted. However, the elevated and absent reflexes in that ear do not support this, as reflexes would be present with significantly better hearing in that ear. Additionally, the reduced acoustic reflex threshold sensation level at 500 Hz is consistent with cochlear site of lesion in the right ear.

   Thus, the acoustic immittance and audiometric data support a severe to profound unilateral sensorineural hearing loss in the right ear. One is cautioned that without a Barany noise box or other masking device, tuning fork data are tenuous at best in the case of a unilateral hearing loss. The presence, or absence, of a nonorganic hearing loss should be determined by careful immittance and audiometric measurements.

QUESTIONS FOR FIGURE 3-25

Case History Information Struck on left side of the head above the ear with a baseball bat and admitted to the hospital for 3 days with a probable concussion as well as a left hemotympanum. Subsequent ENT clinic visits revealed bilateral serous otitis media and suggested a left-sided ossicular chain discontinuity. A bilateral adenoidectomy and tympanostomy tube procedure was undertaken for the bilateral serous otitis media. An exploratory tympanostomy and possible ossicular chain reconstruction was recommended.

1. Describe the acoustic immittance battery results.
2. Discuss the relationship between the immittance data and the audiometric data.

Name: Fig 3-25 **Date:** XX/XX/XX **Age:** 7 **Sex:** F **Audiologist:** VSG

AUDIOMETER: _____ **ANSI 1969**

PURE TONE AUDIOGRAM

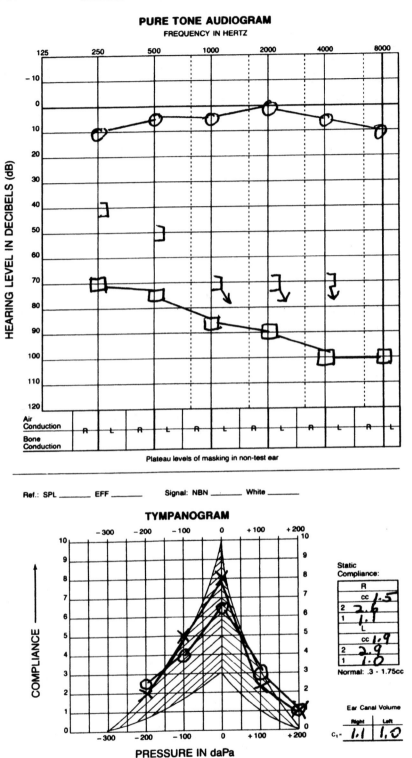

FREQUENCY IN HERTZ

HEARING LEVEL IN DECIBELS (dB)

Ref.: SPL _____ EFF _____ Signal: NBN _____ White _____

TYMPANOGRAM

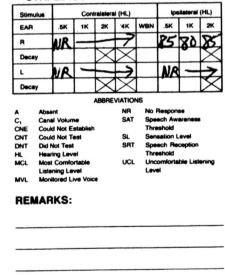

PRESSURE IN daPa

COMPLIANCE

Static Compliance:

R	
cc	1.5
2	2.6
1	1.1
L	
cc	1.9
2	2.9
1	1.0

Normal: .3 - 1.75cc

Ear Canal Volume

	Right	Left
c_1 -	1.1	1.0

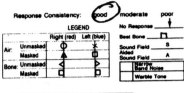

Response Consistency: good moderate poor

LEGEND

		Right (red)	Left (blue)
Air:	Unmasked	O	X
	Masked		
Bone:	Unmasked	<	>
	Masked		

No Response
Best Bone
Sound Field — S
Aided
Sound Field — A
Narrow Band Noise
Warble Tone

PURE TONE AVERAGE (R L)

	Right	Left	Aided
AIR	3	93	
BONE		63	

SPEECH AUDIOMETRY ☑ MLV ☐ Tape

	RIGHT	LEFT	MASK LEVEL R	L	SOUND FIELD	LIST
SAT						
SRT	5	80	60			W-1
MCL						
UCL						
PB% (Word)	96 35SL	0 25SL	60			W-22
PB% (Word)	L	L				
PB% (Word)	L	L				
PB% (Word)	L	L				
	L	L				
	L	L				

STAPEDIUS REFLEX THRESHOLDS

Stimulus	Contralateral (HL)					Ipsilateral (HL)		
EAR	.5K	1K	2K	4K	WBN	.5K	1K	2K
R	NR	→				85	80	85
Decay								
L	NR	→				NR	→	
Decay								

ABBREVIATIONS

A	Absent	NR	No Response
C_1	Canal Volume	SAT	Speech Awareness
CNE	Could Not Establish		Threshold
CNT	Could Not Test	SL	Sensation Level
DNT	Did Not Test	SRT	Speech Reception
HL	Hearing Level		Threshold
MCL	Most Comfortable	UCL	Uncomfortable Listening
	Listening Level		Level
MVL	Monitored Live Voice		

REMARKS:

_____
_____
_____
_____
_____

Acoustic Immittance

131

Answers for Figure 3-25

1. Normal middle ear pressure bilaterally. Normal static admittance in the right ear, slightly elevated static admittance in the left ear. Absent acoustic reflex thresholds bilaterally with contralateral stimulation.

2. Audiometric results suggest an essentially sensorineural hearing loss in the left ear. (With the bone conduction thresholds for 250 and 500 Hz obtained at the limits of the audiometer, the responses may have been vibrotactile.) The acoustic immittance data are suggestive of a hypermobile left middle ear system which could be indicative of ossicular chain discontinuity, which is consistent with the reported history. With a recent tympanostomy tube insertion and removal, however, the hypermobility of the left middle ear system may be related to the healing tympanic membrane. The bilaterally absent acoustic reflexes are consistent with some conductive component on the left side. Thus, there is a strong possibility that there is both an ossicular discontinuity and sensorineural hearing loss on the left side. Due to the extent of the sensorineural component, however, reconstructive surgery would be ruled out. Preferential classroom seating and an audiologic re-evaluation were recommended prior to any surgical intervention.

QUESTION FOR FIGURE 3-26

Case History Information Sensorineural hearing loss in the right ear for 6 years following a bicycle/truck accident resulting in a fractured skull, spinal fluid drainage from the right ear, and subsequent meningitis. There is a history of allergies and noise exposure to power tools, lawn mower, and band music.

1. Describe the acoustic immittance and audiometric data. What does the notched tympanogram for the right ear suggest? How do the absent acoustic reflexes relate to the data?

Name: Fig 3-26   Date: XX/XX/XX   Age: 17   Sex: M   Audiologist: VSG

AUDIOMETER: _____   ANSI 1969

PURE TONE AUDIOGRAM
FREQUENCY IN HERTZ

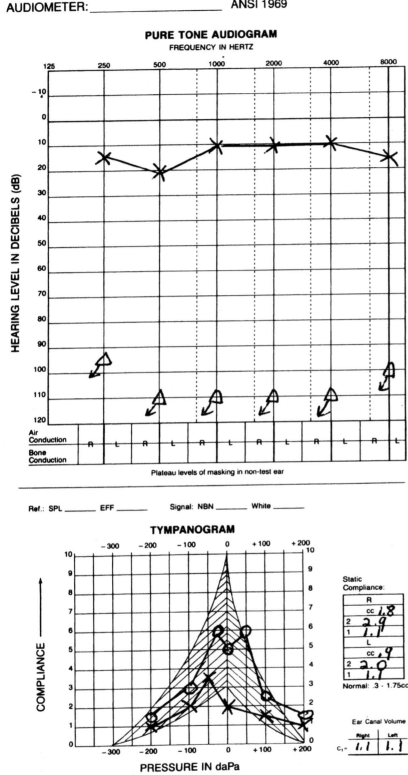

Plateau levels of masking in non-test ear

Ref.: SPL _____ EFF _____   Signal: NBN _____ White _____

TYMPANOGRAM

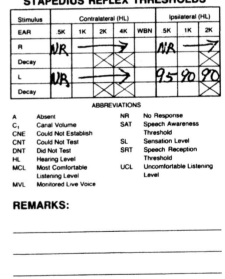

PRESSURE IN daPa

Static Compliance:

R	
cc	1.8
2	2.9
1	1.1

L	
cc	.9
2	2.0
1	1.1

Normal: .3 - 1.75cc

Ear Canal Volume

	Right	Left
C₁ =	1.1	1.1

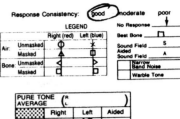

Response Consistency: (good) moderate poor

LEGEND

		Right (red)	Left (blue)
Air:	Unmasked	O	X
	Masked	△	◻
Bone:	Unmasked		▷
	Masked	◻	◻

No Response

Best Bone ⊓

Sound Field ____ S
Aided
Sound Field ____ A

Narrow Band Noise

Warble Tone

PURE TONE AVERAGE (R L)			
	Right	Left	Aided
AIR	CNE	13	
BONE			

SPEECH AUDIOMETRY   ☒ MLV   ☐ Tape

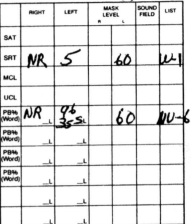

	RIGHT	LEFT	MASK LEVEL R L	SOUND FIELD	LIST
SAT					
SRT	NR	5	60		W-1
MCL					
UCL					
PB% (Word)	NR	96 35 SL	60		NU-6
PB% (Word)	_L_	_L_			
PB% (Word)	_L_	_L_			
PB% (Word)	_L_	_L_			
	_L_	_L_			
	_L_	_L_			

STAPEDIUS REFLEX THRESHOLDS

Stimulus	Contralateral (HL)					Ipsilateral (HL)		
EAR	.5K	1K	2K	4K	WBN	.5K	1K	2K
R	NR →			7		NR →		7
Decay								
L	NR →			7		95	90	90
Decay								

ABBREVIATIONS

A	Absent	NR	No Response
C₁	Canal Volume	SAT	Speech Awareness
CNE	Could Not Establish		Threshold
CNT	Could Not Test	SL	Sensation Level
DNT	Did Not Test	SRT	Speech Reception
HL	Hearing Level		Threshold
MCL	Most Comfortable	UCL	Uncomfortable Listening
	Listening Level		Level
MVL	Monitored Live Voice		

REMARKS:

_____
_____
_____
_____

Acoustic Immittance

Answer for Figure 3-26

1. Pure tone audiometrics reveal normal hearing in the left ear and a profound sensorineural hearing loss in the right ear not inconsistent with the history of skull fracture. Acoustic immittance results reveal normal middle ear pressure bilaterally. Left ear static admittance values are within normal limits, suggesting normal mobility of the middle ear system. The right ear tympanogram is notched with a broad, undulating trace suggestive of a mass-controlled middle ear system. This finding indicates the possibility of ossicular discontinuity, which is consistent with the history of skull fracture. The absent acoustic reflexes with right ear stimulation are consistent with a profound sensorineural hearing loss. The absent acoustic reflexes with left ear stimulation support the suggestion of a conductive pathology in the right ear in addition, for if the conductive mechanism were intact the acoustic reflex with left ear stimulation would be monitored (observed) in the right ear.

QUESTION FOR FIGURE 3-27

Case History Information Congenital kidney abnormality surgically repaired. Urinary tract infection treated with kanamycin. Followed in ENT clinic initially for suspected serous otitis media in the left ear, determined by tuning fork tests, which suggested a left-sided conductive loss. An antihistamine-decongestant medication regime was recommended, along with retesting prior to adenoidectomy and possible myringotomy. Subsequent ENT visits noted facial anomalies, notably low-set ears and slanting eyes, along with essentially negative ENT findings except for a persistent left-sided conductive hearing loss.

1. Describe the acoustic immittance data and relate those data to the audiometric results. Pay particular attention to the reflex data. How does this relate to ENT findings and the recommendations?

Name: Fig 3-27 Date: XX/XX/XX Age: 10 Sex: M Audiologist: VSG
AUDIOMETER: _____ ANSI 1969

PURE TONE AUDIOGRAM
FREQUENCY IN HERTZ

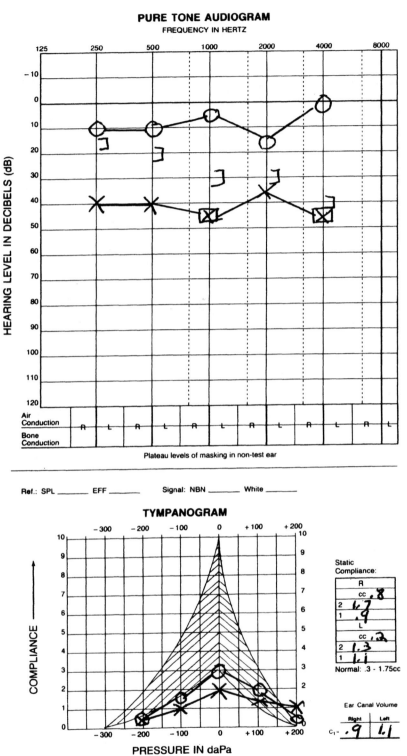

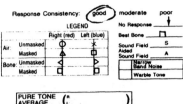

Response Consistency: good moderate poor

No Response

LEGEND

		Right (red)	Left (blue)
Air:	Unmasked	◯	✕
	Masked	△	☐
Bone:	Unmasked	<	>
	Masked	☐	☐

Best Bone ☐
Sound Field ___ S
Aided
Sound Field ___ A
Narrow Band Noise
Warble Tone

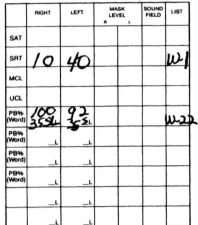

PURE TONE AVERAGE (R L)	Right	Left	Aided
AIR	10	40	
BONE		27	

SPEECH AUDIOMETRY ✕ MLV ☐ Tape

	RIGHT	LEFT	MASK LEVEL R	L	SOUND FIELD	LIST
SAT						
SRT	10	40				W1
MCL						
UCL						
PB% (Word)	100 35SL	92 25SL				W22
PB% (Word)	_L	_L				
PB% (Word)	_L	_L				
PB% (Word)	_L	_L				
	_L	_L				
	_L	_L				

STAPEDIUS REFLEX THRESHOLDS

Stimulus	Contralateral (HL)					Ipsilateral (HL)		
EAR	.5K	1K	2K	4K	WBN	.5K	1K	2K
R	NR	→		→		95	95	90
Decay								
L	NR		→			NR	→	
Decay								

ABBREVIATIONS

A	Absent	NR	No Response
C₁	Canal Volume	SAT	Speech Awareness
CNE	Could Not Establish		Threshold
CNT	Could Not Test	SL	Sensation Level
DNT	Did Not Test	SRT	Speech Reception
HL	Hearing Level		Threshold
MCL	Most Comfortable	UCL	Uncomfortable Listening
	Listening Level		Level
MVL	Monitored Live Voice		

A = Absent, C_1 = Canal Volume

REMARKS:

_____

_____

_____

_____

_____

Ref.: SPL _____ EFF _____ Signal: NBN _____ White _____

TYMPANOGRAM

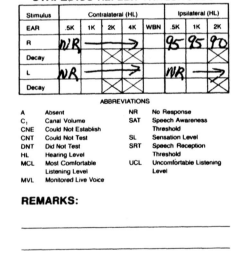

COMPLIANCE

PRESSURE IN daPa

Static Compliance:

R		
	cc	.8
2	1.7	
1	.9	
L		
	cc	.2
2	1.3	
1	1.1	

Normal: .3 - 1.75cc

Ear Canal Volume

	Right	Left
C₁ =	.9	1.1

Answer for Figure 3-27

1. Initial ENT findings and recommendations were directed toward possible effusion and surgery was considered. Subsequent audiologic and acoustic immittance measures revealed normal hearing in the right ear and a normal right middle ear system. The left ear results revealed a mild mixed conductive and sensorineural hearing loss with a hypomobile middle ear system. Acoustic reflexes were absent bilaterally with contralateral stimulation and absent with left ear but present with right ear ipsilateral stimulation. These results confirm a conductive component in the left ear consistent with the possibility of congenital fixation of the ossicular chain. This is further supported by the subsequent ENT observations of facial anomaly suggestive of Treacher-Collins syndrome. The sensorineural component in the left ear may have been present at birth or related to the kanamycin therapy. As a result of these acoustic immittance findings, surgery was canceled. Preferential classroom seating was recommended.

QUESTION FOR FIGURE 3-28

Case History Information Nine-year-old youngster who failed the school hearing screening and was referred to ENT clinic and audiology clinic. He was treated for cerumen impaction and left ear serous otitis media, which resolved. No family concern regarding hearing.

1. Describe the acoustic immittance data, paying particular attention to the reflex results. What does this suggest?

Name: Fig 3-28   Date: XX/XX/XX   Age: 9   Sex: M   Audiologist: VSG

AUDIOMETER: _____   ANSI 1969

PURE TONE AUDIOGRAM
FREQUENCY IN HERTZ

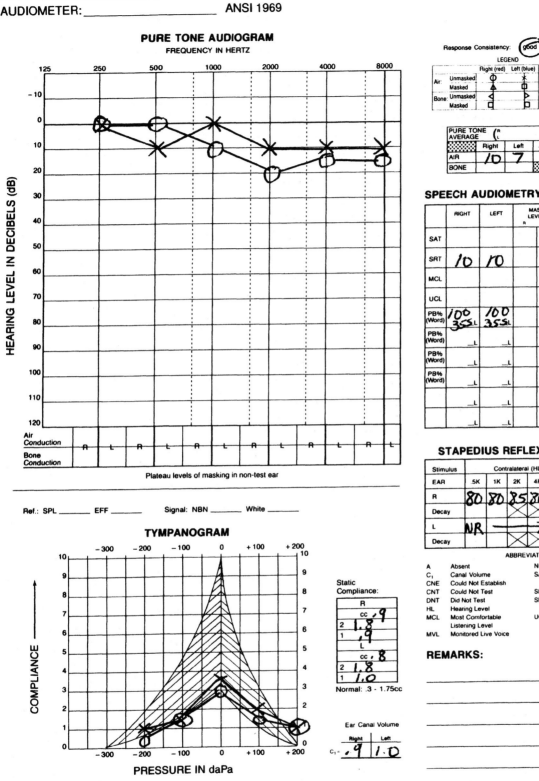

Ref.: SPL _____ EFF _____   Signal: NBN _____ White _____

TYMPANOGRAM

COMPLIANCE →

PRESSURE IN daPa

Static Compliance:

R	
cc	.9
2	1.8
1	.9

L	
cc	.8
2	1.8
1	1.0

Normal: .3 - 1.75cc

Ear Canal Volume

	Right	Left
C₁	.9	1.0

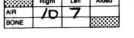

Response Consistency: good moderate poor

LEGEND

		Right (red)	Left (blue)
Air:	Unmasked	O	X
	Masked	△	☐
Bone:	Unmasked		▷
	Masked	☐	☐

No Response ⊓
Best Bone ⊓
Sound Field ___ S
Aided Sound Field ___ A
Narrow Band Noise
Warble Tone

PURE TONE AVERAGE (R / L)

	Right	Left	Aided
AIR	10	7	
BONE			

SPEECH AUDIOMETRY   ☑ MLV ☐ Tape

	RIGHT	LEFT	MASK LEVEL R	L	SOUND FIELD	LIST
SAT						
SRT	10	10				W-1
MCL						
UCL						
PB% (Word)	100 35SL	100 35SL				W-22
PB% (Word)	L	L				
PB% (Word)	L	L				
PB% (Word)	L	L				
	L	L				
	L	L				

STAPEDIUS REFLEX THRESHOLDS

Stimulus	Contralateral (HL)					Ipsilateral (HL)		
EAR	.5K	1K	2K	4K	WBN	.5K	1K	2K
R		80	80	85	80	NR →		
Decay								
L	NR →					75	75	80
Decay								

ABBREVIATIONS

A	Absent	NR	No Response
C₁	Canal Volume	SAT	Speech Awareness
CNE	Could Not Establish		Threshold
CNT	Could Not Test	SL	Sensation Level
DNT	Did Not Test	SRT	Speech Reception
HL	Hearing Level		Threshold
MCL	Most Comfortable	UCL	Uncomfortable Listening
	Listening Level		Level
MVL	Monitored Live Voice		

REMARKS:

_____
_____
_____
_____
_____

Acoustic Immittance

Answer for Figure 3-28

1. Normal middle ear pressure and mobility bilaterally. Normal audiometrics bilaterally. Reflexes are present and within normal limits with contralateral stimulation in the right ear and with ipsilateral stimulation in the left ear. However, reflexes are absent with contralateral stimulation in the left ear and with ipsilateral stimulation in the right ear. Thus, with the probe assembly in the left ear, reflexes are recorded (observed), but with the probe assembly in the right ear, reflexes are absent.

    These results suggest an intact reflex arc when auditory information is presented to both ears and the reflex is monitored in the left ear. The reflex arc is not complete when the reflex is monitored in the right ear. The interruption appears to be in the right middle ear system, which would preclude the observation of the reflex. However, with normal hearing and a normal tympanogram on the right side, there is a strong suggestion of an absent right stapedial tendon. One must also consider the remote possibility of a central lesion in the efferent reflex arc for the right ear.

QUESTION FOR FIGURE 3-29

Case History Information Question of decreased hearing during recent winter at the time of a viral infection. Hearing subsequently improved. Recent hospitalization for virus and ear infection.

1. Describe the audiometric and immittance data. What inconsistencies exist and what results are suggested?

Name: Fig 3-29   **Date:** XX/XX/XX **Age:** 7 **Sex:** M **Audiologist:** VSG
AUDIOMETER: _____ **ANSI 1969**

PURE TONE AUDIOGRAM
FREQUENCY IN HERTZ

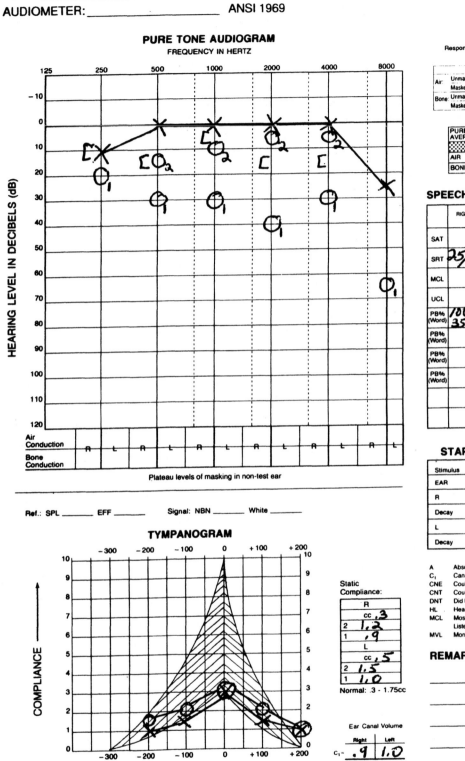

HEARING LEVEL IN DECIBELS (dB)

Plateau levels of masking in non-test ear

Ref.: SPL _____ EFF _____   Signal: NBN _____ White _____

TYMPANOGRAM

PRESSURE IN daPa

COMPLIANCE

Static Compliance:

R	
cc	.3
2	1.2
1	.9
L	
cc	.5
2	1.5
1	1.0

Normal: .3 - 1.75cc

Ear Canal Volume

	Right	Left
C_1 =	.9	1.0

Response Consistency: (good) moderate poor

LEGEND
No Response

		Right (red)	Left (blue)
Air	Unmasked	○	X
	Masked	△	□
Bone	Unmasked	<	>
	Masked	□	□

Best Bone
Sound Field ___ S
Aided
Sound Field ___ A
Narrow Band Noise
Warble Tone

PURE TONE AVERAGE (R: / L:)

	Right	Left	Aided
AIR	33/10	0	
BONE	15		

SPEECH AUDIOMETRY ☒MLV ☐ Tape

	RIGHT	LEFT	MASK LEVEL R	L	SOUND FIELD	LIST
SAT						
SRT	25/5	0				W-1
MCL						
UCL						
PB% (Word)	100 35SL	100 35SL				W-22
PB% (Word)	_L	_L				
PB% (Word)	_L	_L				
PB% (Word)	_L	_L				
	_L	_L				
	_L	_L				

STAPEDIUS REFLEX THRESHOLDS

Stimulus	Contralateral (HL)					Ipsilateral (HL)		
EAR	.5K	1K	2K	4K	WBN	.5K	1K	2K
R	105	110	115	NR		85	85	90
Decay								
L	85	85	90	95		90	90	90
Decay								

ABBREVIATIONS

A	Absent	NR	No Response
C_1	Canal Volume	SAT	Speech Awareness
CNE	Could Not Establish		Threshold
CNT	Could Not Test	SL	Sensation Level
DNT	Did Not Test	SRT	Speech Reception
HL	Hearing Level		Threshold
MCL	Most Comfortable	UCL	Uncomfortable Listening
	Listening Level		Level
MVL	Monitored Live Voice		

REMARKS:

_____
_____
_____
_____
_____

Answer for Figure 3-29

1. The initial audiometric data suggest a conductive hearing loss in the right ear (air–bone gaps; excellent word recognition). However, the normal tympanograms are not consistent with this, although a stiffening pathology such as otosclerosis or adhesive otitis media cannot be dismissed.

   The acoustic reflex data are inconsistent. That is, for a mild unilateral conductive hearing loss to exist, the contralateral reflexes would be expected to be elevated with stimulus in the impaired ear and absent with stimulus in the normal ear. The ipsilateral reflexes would be expected to be normal in the normal ear and absent in the impaired ear. Otoscopic examination revealed a very narrow right external ear canal, suggesting a collapsed condition under earphones. Audiometric re-examination using an otoscope speculum placed in the right ear canal resulted in normal thresholds, confirming a collapsed canal. This also explained the right ear stimulus contralateral reflex thresholds: the placement of the earphone collapsed the canal.

QUESTION FOR FIGURE 3-30

Case History Information This 15-year-old youngster recently failed the school hearing screening test for the first time. Positive family history of hearing loss with use of amplification on the father's side of the family. Youngster has been diagnosed as having Von Recklinghausen's disease. Otoscopic exam revealed impacted cerumen in the right ear canal.

1. Describe the acoustic immittance data and relate them to the audiometric findings and the history.

Name: Fig 3-30   Date: XX/XX/XX   Age: 15   Sex: M   Audiologist: VSG
AUDIOMETER: _____   ANSI 1969

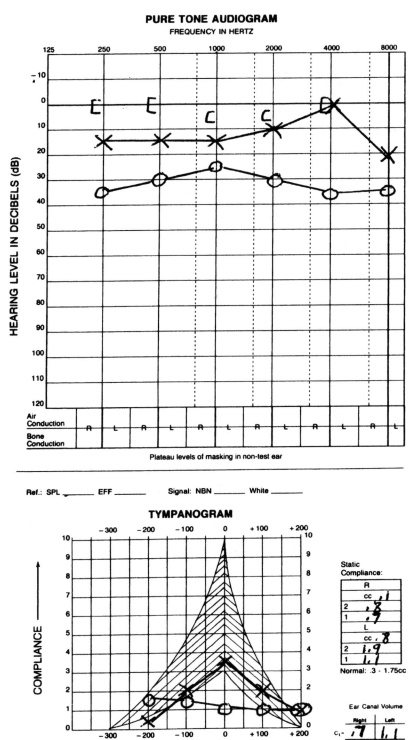

PURE TONE AUDIOGRAM
FREQUENCY IN HERTZ

HEARING LEVEL IN DECIBELS (dB)

Frequencies: 125, 250, 500, 1000, 2000, 4000, 8000

Air Conduction: R L R L R L R L R L R L R L

Bone Conduction

Plateau levels of masking in non-test ear

Ref.: SPL _____ EFF _____   Signal: NBN _____ White _____

TYMPANOGRAM

PRESSURE IN daPa

COMPLIANCE

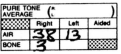

Response Consistency: (good) moderate poor

LEGEND

		Right (red)	Left (blue)
Air:	Unmasked	O	x
	Masked	Δ	▯
Bone:	Unmasked	<	>
	Masked	▯	▯

No Response ↓
Best Bone ▯
Sound Field S
Aided Sound Field A
Narrow Band Noise
Warble Tone

PURE TONE AVERAGE (R / L)

	Right	Left	Aided
AIR	38	13	
BONE	3		

SPEECH AUDIOMETRY ☑ MLV ☐ Tape

	RIGHT	LEFT	MASK LEVEL R L	SOUND FIELD	LIST
SAT					
SRT	25	10			W-1
MCL					
UCL					
PB% (Word)	100 35 SL	100 35 SL			W-6
PB% (Word)	_L	_L			
PB% (Word)	_L	_L			
	_L	_L			
	_L	_L			

STAPEDIUS REFLEX THRESHOLDS

Stimulus	Contralateral (HL)					Ipsilateral (HL)		
EAR	.5K	1K	2K	4K	WBN	.5K	1K	2K
R		110	105	105	105	NR	NR	NR
Decay	CNT	POS						
L	NR	→				100	95	45
Decay								

ABBREVIATIONS

A	Absent	NR	No Response
C₁	Canal Volume	SAT	Speech Awareness
CNE	Could Not Establish		Threshold
CNT	Could Not Test	SL	Sensation Level
DNT	Did Not Test	SRT	Speech Reception
HL	Hearing Level		Threshold
MCL	Most Comfortable	UCL	Uncomfortable Listening
	Listening Level		Level
MVL	Monitored Live Voice		

REMARKS:

Static Compliance:

R	
cc	.1
2	.8
1	.9
L	
cc	.8
2	.9
1	1.1

Normal: .3 - 1.75cc

Ear Canal Volume

	Right	Left
C₁ =	.7	1.1

Answer for Figure 3-30

1. Normal middle ear pressure and mobility in the left middle ear system consistent with normal hearing in that ear. The right tympanogram exhibited no point of maximum admittance, and the static admittance value of 0.1 ml indicates a hypomobile system consistent with cerumen impaction.

    The absent contralateral acoustic reflex thresholds with left ear stimulation and the elevated and absent thresholds with right stimulation are consistent with a mild conductive hearing loss in the right ear. Moreover, the significant acoustic reflex decay with right ear stimulation warrants concern due to the diagnosis of Von Recklinghausen's disease. Refer to ENT clinic for removal of cerumen and return for an audiologic and acoustic immittance re-evaluation.

QUESTION FOR FIGURE 3-31

Case History Information Refer to Figure 3-30. The results of this case, however, follow removal of impacted cerumen from the right ear canal.

1. Discuss the differences in the test results compared to Figure 3-30.

Name: Fig 3-31   Date: XX/XX/XX   Age: 15   Sex: M   Audiologist: VSG
AUDIOMETER: _____   ANSI 1969

PURE TONE AUDIOGRAM

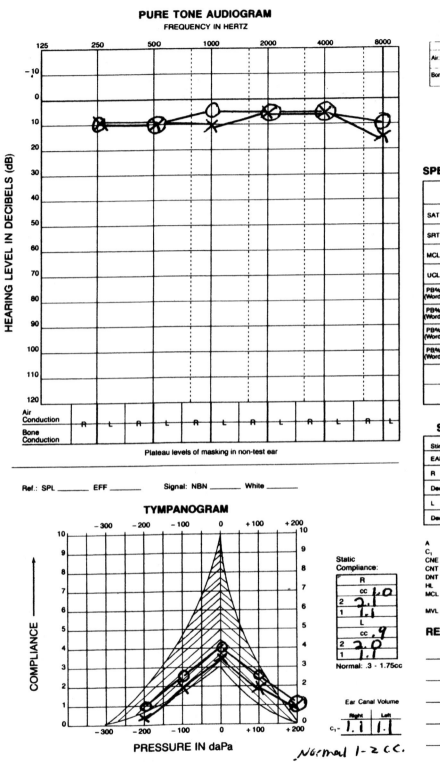

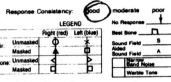

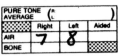

PURE TONE AVERAGE	(R)		
	Right	Left	Aided
AIR	7	8	
BONE			

SPEECH AUDIOMETRY   □ MLV   □ Tape

	RIGHT	LEFT	MASK LEVEL R / L	SOUND FIELD	LIST
SAT					
SRT	5	10			W-1
MCL					
UCL					
PB% (Word)					
PB% (Word)	100 35 SL	100 35 SL			NU-1
PB% (Word)					
PB% (Word)					

STAPEDIUS REFLEX THRESHOLDS

Stimulus	Contralateral (HL)					Ipsilateral (HL)		
EAR	.5K	1K	2K	4K	WBN	.5K	1K	2K
R	110	100	100	95		NR	105	105
Decay	POS	POS				CNT	POS	
L	100	95	90	90		95	90	95
Decay								

ABBREVIATIONS

A	Absent	NR	No Response
C₁	Canal Volume	SAT	Speech Awareness
CNE	Could Not Establish		Threshold
CNT	Could Not Test	SL	Sensation Level
DNT	Did Not Test	SRT	Speech Reception
HL	Hearing Level		Threshold
MCL	Most Comfortable	UCL	Uncomfortable Listening
	Listening Level		Level
MVL	Monitored Live Voice		

C_1 Canal Volume

REMARKS:

_____
_____
_____
_____

Ref.: SPL _____ EFF _____   Signal: NBN _____ White _____

TYMPANOGRAM

Static Compliance:

R	
cc	1.0
2	2.1
1	1.1
L	
cc	.9
2	2.0
1	1.1

Normal: .3 - 1.75cc

Ear Canal Volume

Right	Left
C₁ - 1.1	1.1

Normal 1-2 CC.

PRESSURE IN daPa

Acoustic Immittance

Answer for Figure 3-31

1. Now there is normal hearing as well as normal middle ear function bilaterally. The contralateral acoustic reflex thresholds reveal normal responses with left ear stimulation and elevated or normal thresholds with right ear stimulation. There is slight elevation of the acoustic reflex threshold sensation level in the right ear compared to the left, but not significantly so. The acoustic reflex decay, however, is significant.

   Ipsilateral acoustic reflex thresholds are normal in the left ear and elevated or absent in the right ear with significant acoustic reflex decay.

   These results suggest the possibility of early involvement of the eighth nerve on the right side, which is consistent with the medical diagnosis of Von Recklinghausen's disease.

QUESTION FOR FIGURE 3-32

Case History Information Child failed hearing screening in school; poor academic performance recently. Complaints of left ear pain. Normal ENT exam.

1. Describe the audiometric and acoustic immittance results.

Name: Fig 3-32   Date: XX/XX/XX Age: 11 Sex: F Audiologist: VSG
AUDIOMETER: _____   ANSI 1969

PURE TONE AUDIOGRAM
FREQUENCY IN HERTZ

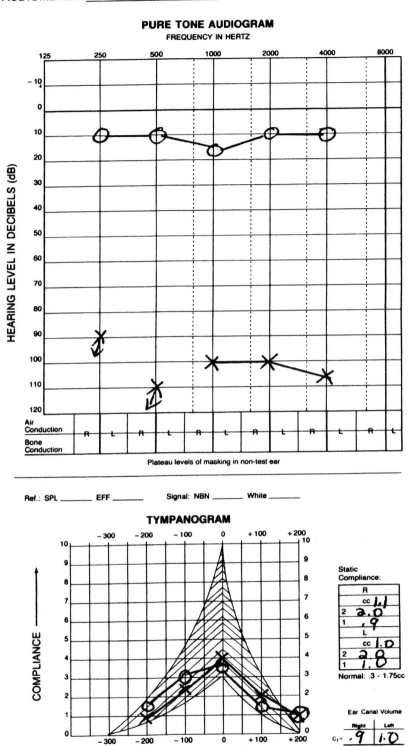

Air
Conduction
Bone
Conduction

Plateau levels of masking in non-test ear

Ref.: SPL _____ EFF _____   Signal: NBN _____ White _____

TYMPANOGRAM

PRESSURE IN daPa

COMPLIANCE

Response Consistency: good moderate (poor)
No Response

	LEGEND		
		Right (red)	Left (blue)
Air:	Unmasked	◯	✕
	Masked	△	☐
Bone:	Unmasked	◁	▷
	Masked		

Best Bone
Sound Field S
Aided
Sound Field A

Narrow
Band Noise
Warble Tone

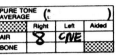

PURE TONE AVERAGE (R: L:)			
	Right	Left	Aided
AIR	8	CNE	
BONE			

SPEECH AUDIOMETRY ☒ MLV ☐ Tape

	RIGHT	LEFT	MASK LEVEL R L	SOUND FIELD	LIST
SAT					
SRT	10	40			W-1
MCL					
UCL					
PB% (Word)	100 35SL	96 10SL			NU-6
PB% (Word)	___ L	___ L			
PB% (Word)	___ L	___ L			
PB% (Word)	___ L	___ L			
	___ L	___ L			
	___ L	___ L			

STAPEDIUS REFLEX THRESHOLDS

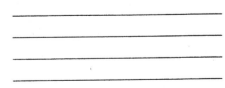

Stimulus	Contralateral (HL)					Ipsilateral (HL)		
EAR	.5K	1K	2K	4K	WBN	.5K	1K	2K
R	75	80	70	85				✕
Decay			✕					
L		80	80	85	80			✕
Decay			✕	✕				✕

ABBREVIATIONS

A — Absent
C_1 — Canal Volume
CNE — Could Not Establish
CNT — Could Not Test
DNT — Did Not Test
HL — Hearing Level
MCL — Most Comfortable Listening Level
MVL — Monitored Live Voice

NR — No Response
SAT — Speech Awareness Threshold
SL — Sensation Level
SRT — Speech Reception Threshold
UCL — Uncomfortable Listening Level

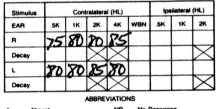

Static Compliance:

R	
cc	1.1
2	2.0
1	.9
L	
cc	1.0
2	2.8
1	1.8

Normal: .3 - 1.75cc

Ear Canal Volume

	Right	Left
C_1	.9	1.0

REMARKS:

_____
_____
_____
_____

Acoustic Immittance

Answer for Figure 3-32

1. Normal results for the right ear; discrepant results for the left ear. Pure tone and speech audiometrics do not agree. Tympanograms reveal normal middle ear function. Acoustic reflex thresholds are normal with contralateral stimulation bilaterally. However, the reflex thresholds with left ear stimulation are better than the admitted behavioral pure tone thresholds in the left ear.

    These results suggest a nonorganic hearing loss in the left ear. In fact, this youngster ultimately was found to have normal hearing bilaterally. She was extremely upset that her "favorite" teacher was leaving. With family and new teacher support, hearing dramatically improved.

QUESTION FOR FIGURE 3-33

Case History Information Refer to Figure 3-22.

1. Describe the Eustachian tube test and the results.

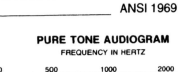

Name: Fig 3-33　　　　　　Date: XX/XX/XX　Age: 16　Sex: F　Audiologist: VSG
AUDIOMETER:　　　　　　　　　ANSI 1969

PURE TONE AUDIOGRAM

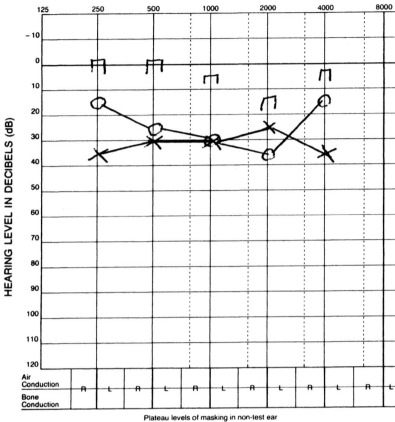

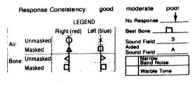

PURE TONE AVERAGE (R / L)			
	Right	Left	Aided
AIR	30	28	
BONE			

SPEECH AUDIOMETRY ☒ MLV ☐ Tape

	RIGHT	LEFT	MASK LEVEL R	MASK LEVEL L	SOUND FIELD	LIST
SAT						
SRT	30	25				W-1
MCL						
UCL						
PB% (Word)	92 35≤SL	100 35≤SL				W-6
PB% (Word)	_L	_L				
PB% (Word)	_L	_L				
PB% (Word)	_L	_L				
	_L	_L				
	_L	_L				

STAPEDIUS REFLEX THRESHOLDS

Stimulus	Contralateral (HL)					Ipsilateral (HL)		
EAR	.5K	1K	2K	4K	WBN	.5K	1K	2K
R	N/R	→	↗			N/R	→	↗
Decay		✕	✕				✕	✕
L	N/R	→	↗			N/R	→	↗
Decay		✕	✕				✕	✕

ABBREVIATIONS

A　Absent　　　　　　　　　NR　No Response
C₁　Canal Volume　　　　　　SAT　Speech Awareness
CNE　Could Not Establish　　　　　Threshold
CNT　Could Not Test　　　　　SL　Sensation Level
DNT　Did Not Test　　　　　SRT　Speech Reception
HL　Hearing Level　　　　　　　Threshold
MCL　Most Comfortable　　　　UCL　Uncomfortable Listening
　　　Listening Level　　　　　　　Level
MVL　Monitored Live Voice

REMARKS:

Ref.: SPL ＿＿＿　EFF ＿＿＿　　Signal: NBN ＿＿＿　White ＿＿＿

Right TYMPANOGRAM PSW)

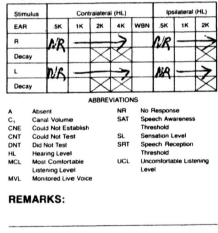

Static Compliance:

R	
cc	2.6
2	3.7
1	1.7
L	
cc	2.9
2	3.9
1	1.0

Normal: .3 - 1.75cc

Ear Canal Volume

	Right	Left
C₁	1.1	1.0

PRESSURE IN daPa

Acoustic Immittance

147

Answer for Figure 3-33

1. The right tympanograms show poor Eustachian tube function via the Pressure Swallow (PSW) test as there is negligible shift following successive swallows under pressure. Tympanograms depicting normal Eustachian tube function via the PSW test would reveal shifts of between 50 and 75 daPa after successive swallows under extreme positive and then negative pressure (see text).

REVIEW AND SEARCH PROJECTS

1. Describe the mechanism of the middle ear impedance matching transformer (Dallos, 1973).

2. Discuss why a middle ear is necessary.

3. Discuss the differences between acoustic impedance and admittance.

4. List and label the unit notations for the impedance and admittance factors or components.

5. What is the relationship between mass and stiffness in an acoustic system?

6. Describe the similarities between electroacoustic immittance measurement instruments.

7. Discuss the differences between an impedance bridge and an otoadmittance meter.

8. Discuss the value of component analysis.

9. Describe the process of tympanometry (Lilly, 1973).

10. Discuss the tympanometric patterns for various middle ear pathologies.

11. Compare impedance and admittance patterns for various middle ear pathologies.

12. What is the relationship between a 660-Hz and a 220-Hz probe tone?

13. What is the value in describing a tympanogram (Feldman, 1975)?

14. Discuss the concept of equivalent volume in static immittance determination.

15. Describe contralateral and ipsilateral acoustic reflex stimulation and recording.

16. Why are acoustic reflexes usually absent bilaterally with contralateral stimulation in the presence of a unilateral conductive hearing loss? Would ipsilateral stimulation provide different information? Discuss.

17. Discuss the diagnostic significance of reduced acoustic reflex threshold sensation levels.

18. Compare and contrast the acoustic immittance and audiometric characteristics of a client with a 50-dB hearing loss in the right ear due to otosclerosis versus a client with a 50-dB hearing loss in the left ear due to Ménière's disease.

19. Discuss the diagnostic significance of acoustic reflex decay (Anderson et al., 1970).

20. Discuss what you feel is the major advantage of being able to predict hearing loss from the acoustic reflex threshold.

21. Describe some procedures using immittance measuring techniques to assess Eustachian tube function that are available to the audiologist.

22. Discuss how you would implement a hearing aid and immittance screening program.

23. Describe the audiometric and acoustic immittance characteristics of a patient believed to have an eighth nerve tumor on the right side.

REFERENCES

Alberti, P., and Kristensen, R. 1970. The clinical application of impedance audiometry. *Laryngoscope* 80:735.

American National Standards Institute. 1987. Specifications for instruments to measure aural acoustic impedance and admittance (Aural Acoustic Immittance) (ANSI S3.39–1987). New York.

American Speech and Hearing Association. 1975. Guidelines for identification audiometry. *ASHA* 17:94.

American Speech and Hearing Association. 1978. Guidelines for acoustic immittance screening of middle-ear function. *ASHA* 20:550.

American Speech-Language-Hearing Association. 1979. Guidelines for acoustic immittance screening of middle-ear function. *ASHA* 21:283.

American Speech-Language-Hearing Association. 1985. Guidelines for identification audiometry. *ASHA* 27:49.

American Speech-Language-Hearing Association. 1990. Guidelines for screening for hearing impairment and middle-ear disorders. *ASHA* 32 (Suppl. 2):17.

Anderson, H., Barr, B., and Wedenberg, E. 1970. Early diagnosis of VIIIth nerve tumors by acoustic reflex tests. *Acta Otolaryngologica* (Suppl. 263).

Baker, S., and Lilly, D. 1976. Prediction of hearing level from acoustic reflex data. Paper presented at the American Speech-Language-Hearing Association Convention, Houston, TX.

Berlin, C., and Cullen, J. 1975. The physical basis of impedance measurement. In: J. Jerger (Ed.), *Handbook of Clinical Impedance Audiometry*. Dobbs Ferry, NY: Cahill and Company.

Bluestone, C. 1975. Assessment of Eustachian tube function. In: J. Jerger (Ed.), *Handbook of Clinical Impedance Audiometry*. Dobbs Ferry, NY: Cahill and Company.

Brooks, D. N. 1971. Electroacoustic impedance bridge

studies on normal ears of children. *Journal of Speech and Hearing Research* 14:247.

Dallos, P. 1973. *The Auditory Periphery.* New York: Academic Press.

Feldman, A. 1974. Ear drum abnormality and the measurement of middle ear function. *Archives of Otolaryngology* 99:211.

Feldman, A. 1975. Acoustic impedance-admittance measurements. In: L. Bradford (Ed.), *Physiological Measures of the Audio-Vestibular System.* New York: Academic Press.

Feldman, A. 1976. Tympanometry—procedures, interpretations and variables. In: A. Feldman and L. Wilber (Eds.), *Acoustic Impedance and Admittance.* Baltimore: Williams & Wilkins.

Feldman, A., and Wilber, L. (Eds.). 1976. *Acoustic Impedance and Admittance.* Baltimore: Williams & Wilkins.

Fiellau-Nikolajsen, M. 1983. Tympanometry and secretory otitis media. Observations on diagnosis, epidemiology, treatment and prevention in prospective cohort studies of three-year-old children. *Acta Otolaryngologica* (Suppl. 394):1.

Flottorp, G., Djupesland, G., and Winther, F. 1971. The acoustic stapedius reflex in relation to critical bandwidth. *Journal of the Acoustical Society of America* 49:457.

Gladstone, V. S. 1977. A comparison of the effects of middle ear grafting material on acoustic impedance measurements and audiometry. Doctoral dissertation, University of Maryland.

Gladstone, V. S., Lee, S., and Wenger, A. P. 1980. Homograft tympanoplasty: Graft material effects on otoadmittance and audiometric measurements. *Ear and Hearing* 1:102.

Hall, J. W. 1978. Predicting hearing level from the acoustic reflex. *Archives of Otolaryngology* 104:601.

Hannley, M. 1986. Clinical applications of acoustic immittance. In: *Basic Principles of Auditory Assessment.* San Diego: College-Hill Press.

Harford, E., Bess, F., Bluestone, C., and Klein, J. 1978. *Impedance Screening for Middle Ear Disease in Children.* New York: Grune & Stratton.

Holmquist, J. 1970. Middle ear ventilation in chronic otitis media. *Archives of Otolaryngology* 92:617

Jerger, J. 1970. Clinical experience with impedance audiometry. *Archives of Otolaryngology* 92:311.

Jerger, J., Burney, P., Mauldin, L., and Crump, B. 1974. Predicting hearing loss from the acoustic reflex. *Journal of Speech and Hearing Disorders* 39:11.

Jerger, J., Jerger, S., and Maudlin, L. 1972. Studies in impedance audiometry: Normal and sensorineural ears. *Archives of Otolaryngology* 95:513.

Johnson, C., Bordenick, R., and Suter, C. 1979. Audiologic assessment of the developmentally disabled: A test battery approach. Paper presented at the Maryland Speech and Hearing Convention, Fall.

Kaplan, H., Babecki, S., and Thomas, C. 1980. The acoustic reflex in children without an hermetic seal. *Ear and Hearing* 1:83.

Lew, H. and Jerger, J. 1991. Diagnostic applications of supra-threshold acoustic reflex morphology. *Hearing Instruments* 42:21.

Liden, G., Harford, E.R., and Hallen, O. 1974. Tympanometry for the diagnosis of ossicular disruption. *Archives of Otolaryngology* 99:23.

Liden, G., Peterson, J., and Bjorkman, G. 1970. Tympanometry. *Archives of Otolaryngology* 92:248.

Lilly, D. 1970. A comparison of acoustic impedance data obtained with Madsen and Zwislocki instruments. *ASHA* 12:441.

Lilly, D. 1972. A comparison of acoustic impedance tympanic membrane, a review of basic concepts. Proceedings of Impedance Symposium, Mayo Clinic, Rochester, MN.

Lilly, D. 1973. Measurements of acoustic impedance at the tympanic membrane. In J. Jerger (Ed.), *Modern Developments in Audiology.* New York: Academic Press.

Lipscomb, D. 1976. Mechanisms of the middle ear. In: J. Northern (Ed.), *Hearing Disorders.* Boston: Little Brown.

Margolis, R., and Popelka, G. 1975. Static and dynamic acoustic impedance measurements in infant ears. *Journal of Speech and Hearing Research* 18:435.

Margolis, R., and Fox, C. 1977. A comparison of three methods for predicting hearing loss from acoustic reflex thresholds. *Journal of Speech and Hearing Research* 20:241.

Metz, O. 1952. Studies on the contraction of the tympanic muscles as indicated by changes in the impedance of the ear. *Archives of Otolaryngology* 55:536.

Newman, B. T., and Fanger, D. M. 1973. *Otoadmittance Handbook 2.* Bolton, MA: Grason-Stadler.

Niemeyer, W., and Sesterhenn, G. 1974. Calculating the teaching threshold from the stapedius reflex threshold for different sound stimuli. *Audiology* 13:421.

Northern, J., and Downs, M. 1978. *Hearing in Children,* 2nd ed. Baltimore: Williams & Wilkins.

Olsen, W.O., Stach, B.A., and Kurdziel, S.A. 1981. Acoustic reflex decay in 10 seconds and in 5 seconds for Meniere's disease patients and for VIIIth nerve patients. *Ear and Hearing* 2:180.

Popelka, G., Karlovich, R., and Wiley, T. 1974. Acoustic

reflex and critical bandwidth. *Journal of the Acoustical Society of America* 55:883.

Porter, T. 1972. Normative otoadmittance values for three populations. *Journal of Audiology Research* 12:53.

Silman, S., and Silverman, C. A. 1991. Acoustic Immittance Assessment. In: *Auditory Diagnosis. Principles and Applications.* New York: Academic Press.

Stach, B.A., and Jerger, J.F. 1991. Immittance measures in auditory disorders. In J.T. Jacobson and J.L. Northern (Eds.), *Diagnostic Audiology.* Austin, TX: Pro-Ed.

Surr, R., and Schuchman, G. 1976. Measurement of the acoustic reflex without a pressure seal. *Archives of Otolaryngology* 102:160.

Van Camp, K. J., and Creten, W. L. 1976. Principles of acoustic impedance and admittance. In: A. Feldman and L. Wilber (Eds.), *Acoustic Impedance and Admittance.* Baltimore: Williams & Wilkins.

Wilber, L., Goodhill, V., and Hogue, A. 1969. Diagnostic implication of acoustic impedance measurements. Paper presented at the Convention of the American Speech-Language-Hearing Association, Chicago, IL.

Wilber, L., Goodhill, V., and Hogue, A. 1970. Comparative acoustic impedance measurements. *ASHA* 2:417.

Wiley, T., and Block, M. 1979. Static acoustic immittance measurements. *Journal of Speech and Hearing Research* 22:677.

Williams, P. 1975. A tympanic swallow test for assessment of Eustachian tube function. *Annals of Otology, Rhinology and Laryngology* 84:339.

Interpreting Speech Audiometry

This chapter contains Audiologic Assessment Forms programmed to develop the ability to interpret speech audiometric measures and relate them to the pure tone and immittance information available. Some of the audiograms discussed in Chapter 2 are presented again, complete with immittance and speech audiometric scores to help the reader become aware of the increased diagnostic and rehabilitative information available.

In this chapter the reader will learn to:

1. Identify speech recognition thresholds (SRT) and relate them to pure tone and immittance information.
2. Identify speech detection thresholds (SDT) and understand their diagnostic and rehabilitative significance and limitations.
3. Interpret the most comfortable listening level (MCL) and relate it to differential diagnosis and rehabilitation.
4. Interpret the uncomfortable listening level (UCL) and relate it to differential diagnosis and rehabilitation.
5. Understand the concept of dynamic range.
6. Understand the concept of PB Max and how it is obtained.
7. Interpret word recognition scores in quiet and noise at average conversational level and at PB Max.
8. Understand how the use of different types of stimulus material for the various speech audiometric tests affects scores and their interpretation.

The various speech audiometric measures are briefly discussed before case histories and programmed audiograms are presented.

SPEECH DETECTION THRESHOLD (SDT)

The SDT is an index of the lowest level of speech the client can hear and make some observable response. This is sometimes referred to as the "speech awareness threshold" (SAT). The SAT or SDT is usually not recorded in the audiologic evaluation of most clients because in most cases it would not provide additional information. However, in the evaluation of some profoundly deaf and some profoundly mentally retarded clients the SAT may contribute information. Also the SAT is often used in the evaluation of very young children. An alternative measure to the SAT is the use of sound field pure tone responses (actually, warble tones or narrow bands of noise are used in place of pure tones). Although relatively little has been written about the SAT or sound field pure tone audiometry, the utilization of these measures is illustrated in this chapter.

The SAT or SDT is usually obtained when it is not possible to obtain an SRT, which is discussed in the following section. For example, sometimes a deaf or hard-of-hearing child might be able to hear a word but either not have the speech to repeat it or not know what the word means and thus not be able to point to the appropriate picture. In such a situation, an SRT cannot be measured. Although it does provide an indication of the level at which speech awareness first occurs, the significance of this measure is questionable. Many audiologists feel that the same information can be obtained by using noise or warbled pure tones as stimuli.

The speech awareness threshold (SAT), or speech detection threshold (SDT), is defined as the lowest level at which the listener detects the presence of speech 50% of the time. For this measure the client does not need to identify stimuli but simply to indicate awareness of their presence. Continuous discourse or spondee words may be used as the stimulus; the type of stimulus used should be recorded on the Audiologic Assessment Form. The SDT often relates most closely to the best single pure tone threshold in the 250–4000 Hz range (Rintelmann, 1991:50, 53). Although average SDT is approximately 8–9 dB lower than average SRT, there is considerable variation (Beattie, Svihovec, and Edgerton, 1975; Chaiklin, 1959). Chaiklin (1959) found that several normal-hearing subjects had SAT and SRT scores within 2 dB of each other, while others showed thresholds that were 12–16 dB apart. For a more complete discussion of SRT–SAT relationships, consult Chaiklin (1959), Martin (1986:123), Rintelmann (1991:49–50), and Hannley (1986:153–154).

SPEECH RECOGNITION THRESHOLD (SRT)

The SRT is an index of the lowest level of speech a client can hear and understand. The speech recognition threshold (SRT) is defined as the lowest hearing level (dB re: audiometric zero) at which the client can repeat or otherwise identify 50% of a message. Recently the Committee on Audiologic Evaluation of the American Speech-Language-Hearing Association (1988) recommended that SRT be used to mean speech recognition threshold, rather than the older term "speech reception threshold." "Speech reception threshold," however, is still being used by some audiologists and means the same thing as "speech recognition threshold."

Newby and Popelka (1985:175–177) clearly describe the usual method used to obtain the SRT. Although spondaic words (W-1 lists) are the usual stimulus material for obtaining the SRT, other materials are used at times for special purposes. For example, when testing clients with limited receptive language, it is often necessary to use a restricted list

of spondee words to ensure that the stimuli are within the language competence of the client. In such cases, it is recommended that the term "restricted spondee list" be entered in the space on the Audiologic Assessment Form labeled "Remarks."

Since spondee words are usually the preferred stimulus, the term "spondee threshold" (ST) is sometimes used in place of SRT. With most adults and older children, the 36 words of Auditory Test W-1 developed at the Central Institute for the Deaf are used with live voice or recorded presentation (Newby and Popelka, 1985:168–169; Rintelmann, 1991:42–46; and Martin, 1991:118–119). However, for very young children, or for developmentally delayed, deaf, or otherwise difficult-to-test clients, the standard procedure must frequently be modified. Where English language deficiency exists, it may not be possible to use the entire spondee list; only those words known by the client should be used. In such a situation the SRT is being measured by a restricted list of words; since the alternatives the client can choose from in identifying a stimulus item are more limited, the probability of correct identification by chance may be increased. Therefore, the SRT tends to be lower than if the entire spondee list were used. In interpreting the significance of the SRT, the clinician must be cognizant of whether a restricted list was used. If any deviation from the standard SRT procedure was necessary in obtaining the test, it should be noted on the Audiologic Assessment Form.

Sometimes the SRT is obtained using a closed message set. Instead of repeating or writing the perceived word, the client points to one of a group of pictures or one of a group of printed words. This procedure is used when, because of age or disability, the stimulus words cannot be repeated intelligibly. The closed message set serves to reduce the number of alternatives and tends to lower the SRT in much the same manner as the restricted word list. If a closed message set is used, it should be noted in the "Remarks" section of the Audiological Assessment Form and be noted by the clinician when interpreting the scores.

Other test variables which can affect the SRT are familiarity with the test words and whether a descending, ascending, or bracketing approach is used. For further discussion of test procedures and their effect on scores, see Newby and Popelka (1985:169, 175–

179), Martin (1986:118–121), Hannley (1986:160–162), and Rintelmann (1991:46–48, 82–83, 89–92).

The typical mode of response in obtaining the SRT is repetition of the stimulus word by the client. In some cases verbal repetition is not possible and other modes of response (picture pointing, signing, fingerspelling) are used. The response mode of the client should be entered in the space labeled "Remarks." For discussions of special methods and materials for speech audiometry with children and with difficult-to-test clients, see Fulton and Lloyd (1975:37–70), Newby and Popelka (1985:259–272), Northern and Downs (1984:145–155), and Rintelmann (1991:51–56, 108–115).

SRTs are generally obtained monaurally and in the sound field. There are two purposes for obtaining the SRT. First, it serves as a check on the pure tone thresholds. It is commonly accepted that with a flat configuration, the pure tone average should agree with the SRT within ±6–8 dB. With a sharply sloping configuration, the Fletcher two-frequency pure tone average should be used [Martin (1991:123), Rintelmann (1991:48–49), Newby and Popelka (1985:156) and Hannley (1986:156)]. Lack of agreement between the two measures suggests a problem with equipment calibration, test procedures, patient cooperation, and/or a severe word recognition problem. The significance of such discrepancies is discussed later in this chapter and again in Chapter 6.

MOST COMFORTABLE LISTENING LEVEL (MCL)

The most comfortable listening level (MCL) is a measure of the hearing level (dB re: audiometric zero) at which the client finds listening most comfortable. It is a suprathreshold measure and is obtained by using running speech. As the examiner varies the intensity of the signal, the client indicates when he or she considers the speech "just right."

Although MCL in normal-hearing individuals covers a range, it generally falls around 40–55 dB SL (above SRT). In a hard-of-hearing individual, particularly when there is conductive or mixed hearing loss, one would expect an elevated MCL in terms of hearing level but still approximately 40–55 dB above threshold. A low MCL compared to SRT suggests a tolerance problem, which in turn suggests a

cochlear site of lesion. For further discussion, see Newby and Popelka (1985:180–183).

In addition to diagnostic information, the MCL is an important measure for rehabilitation. In selecting a hearing aid the gain or amount of amplification chosen depends on the MCL. We wish to provide enough gain so that the client can hear average conversational speech, which is considered to be 50 dB HL, at the client's most comfortable listening level.

It is important to keep in mind that the MCL is a subjective measure, requiring a judgment by the client. Since it tends to be more variable than some other measures, such as pure tone thresholds, it must be obtained in a systematic and careful manner. A bracketing procedure with speech presented above and below the judged MCL level is recommended. The MCL is further discussed by Martin (1991:128–129) and Newby and Popelka (1985:116–119).

UNCOMFORTABLE LISTENING LEVEL (UCL)

The uncomfortable listening level (UCL) defines the upper limit of the client's usable hearing. The decibel level in HL (re: audiometric zero) which the client reports as uncomfortably loud is recorded as the uncomfortable loudness level (UCL) on the Audiologic Assessment Form. The UCL is sometimes referred to as the threshold of discomfort (TD).

The normal ear should be able to tolerate speech at hearing levels of 90–100 dB HL without experiencing discomfort (Martin, 1991:129–130; Newby and Popelka, 1985:169–170). It is expected that a deaf or hard-of-hearing person can tolerate speech at similar or higher hearing levels. If a person cannot, a tolerance problem is indicated, suggesting cochlear site of lesion. The UCL also sets the limit for hearing aid output. The maximum power output of a properly selected aid should not exceed the user's UCL.

The difference in decibels between the client's SRT and UCL is known as the dynamic range (DR) (i.e., UCL – SRT = DR). It represents the range between the lower and upper limits of useful hearing. If an SRT is not obtainable for a client, the SAT may be substituted for the SRT in the above formula. The dynamic range is helpful in diagnosis and in selecting a hearing aid. For further discussion of the significance of the dynamic range, see Newby and Popelka (1985:170, 180–185) and Martin (1991:129–130).

WORD RECOGNITION SCORE

Speech audiometry consists of two types of tests. One type involves detection or identification of levels but does not involve the ability to understand speech at suprathreshold levels. This test category includes the SAT (SDT), the MCL, and the UCL. Although the latter two measures involve suprathreshold judgments, the intelligibility of the speech signal is not involved.

For the second type of test, the client must understand enough of the speech signal to repeat or otherwise identify it. The SRT (ST) is a measure of the client's ability to understand 50% of a sample of speech and provides a threshold measure; we are interested in the lowest hearing level at which the client can perform this task. Although this involves some understanding of speech, the audiologist uses the word recognition score rather than the SRT to evaluate the client's ability to understand speech at some specified level above threshold. While the SRT is a level measurement stated in dB, word recognition is expressed as a percentage correct score. The purpose of testing speech understanding is to obtain an indication of how well the individual understands speech when it is intense enough to be heard easily or when it is at some other specified level (e.g., the conversational speech level).

The client's word recognition score [PB% (Word) on the Audiologic Assessment Form] is the percentage of those words presented at a given suprathreshold level that the client can perceive and respond to correctly. Martin (1991:130–140) and Newby and Popelka (1985:170–175) clearly describe the procedure used to obtain the word recognition score. On the Audiologic Assessment Form there is a series of boxes for recording the word recognition score in quiet for each ear and for the sound field.

Definitions

In the past, speech understanding procedures have been called "speech discrimination" tests. In the field of psychology, however, the term "discrimination"

refers to whether stimuli are the same or different. Therefore, most audiologists now use the terms "speech recognition" or "speech identification" to refer to measures of speech understanding at suprathresholds levels. Some audiologists make a distinction between these two terms, depending on whether open or closed set procedures are used. Unfortunately, there is no standardization as to which term refers to closed set and which to open set. Hannley (1986:151–152) uses the term "speech recognition" to refer to closed set procedures, but Olsen and Matkin (Rintelmann,1991:64) use "speech identification" for closed set measurements. Therefore, the terms "speech recognition" and "speech identification" will be used interchangeably in this text. Sometimes the terms "phoneme," "nonsense syllable," "word," or "sentence" precede the label to indicate the type of material used to measure speech understanding.

One important word recognition measure is the "PB Max." The PB Max is defined as the maximum recognition score the client can obtain when speech is presented at a sufficiently "loud" level. The sensation level (SL) at which PB Max is obtained is not the same for all clients. The American National Standards Institute's (1973) definition of SL is used in this manual. (SL is defined as the number of decibels above the threshold of audibility of a given individual at which a signal is presented). Most audiologists use the client's SRT as the threshold of audibility for word recognition evaluation.

For the "normal" ear the PB Max may be obtained at 30–40 dB SL. In other cases, particularly with certain types of hearing loss, this presentation level does not yield the best word recognition score. The optimum presentation level may be at MCL, at a sensation level smaller than 30 dB or greater than 40 dB. It is sometimes necessary to present several word recognition lists at different sensation levels in order to find PB Max. When multiple lists are used in the evaluation of a given ear, each word recognition score is recorded in one of the boxes reserved for that ear. For each score, the list used and the presentation level at which the words were delivered should be noted.

It is important to know the client's PB Max because it provides an index of the client's maximum speech recognition ability when the hearing sensitivity problem is not a factor. This index of the client's maximum speech recognition ability provides information about the client's ability to understand speech when it is sufficiently amplified by an auditory training unit or a personal hearing aid. In addition, the relationship between the PB Max and other audiometric measures provides important diagnostic information about site of lesion. Both the diagnostic and (re)habilitative significance of the word recognition score are discussed further in this chapter and in Chapter 7. Additional information about the concept of PB Max may be obtained from Martin (1991:132, 326), Newby and Popelka (1985:234), Hannley (1986:159–160), Rintelmann (1991:107–108), and Jerger and Jerger (1971:573–580).

In addition to the PB Max, it is important to have an index of the client's word recognition ability when speech is presented at normal conversational level (approximately 50 dB re: audiometric zero). The normal conversational level word recognition score is particularly useful in evaluating a client's performance with a hearing aid. Word recognition score at average conversational level is usually obtained in the sound field and should be recorded in one of the slots labeled "PB% (Word) Sound Field." The presentation level may be recorded either as 50 dB HL (decibels above audiometric zero, or hearing level) or as the appropriate sensation level. The former recording method (in terms of HL) is more commonly used.

Materials

Speech identification is usually measured by presenting a list of words at a single suprathreshold level and determining the percentage correct. This is a person's word recognition or word identification score. Although sentences can be used to obtain speech understanding information, word lists are more commonly used. The most widely used word lists are the CID-W22 lists, developed by Hirsh et al. (1952) and the Northwestern University (NU-6) lists, developed by Tillman and Carhart (1966). These are open set materials which require repetition of each presented item. There are also a number of closed set monosyllabic word lists, such as the Modified Rhyme Test (House et al., 1965) and the California Consonant Test (Owens

and Schubert, 1977). Also available are closed set word tests for children, which require picture pointing responses. Open set sentence tests include the CID Everyday Sentences (Silverman and Hirsh, 1955) and the Speech Perception in Noise (Kalikow et al., 1977; Bilger et al., 1984). A well-known closed set sentence test is the Synthetic Sentence Identification (SSI) test developed by Speaks and Jerger in 1965. This procedure consists of ten third-order approximations to English sentences. Each sentence follows specified rules of syntax and preserves intonation patterns found in conversational speech, but does not make sense. They are presented against a competing message. The individual is presented with a list of ten sentences and identifies the appropriate one as an item is spoken. The SSI test has been used diagnostically for central auditory evaluation and to indicate the presence of retrocochlear dysfunction (Jerger and Jerger, 1971). Further information about speech understanding test materials can be found in Rintelmann (1991:65–82), Hannley (1986:157–170), Newby and Popelka (1985: 170–175), Martin (1991:130–136), and Northern and Downs (1974:152–156).

The materials used with a client, including the number of words (e.g., 25 or 50), should be recorded in the spaces marked "List" or "Remarks." The mode of presentation of the stimuli (live voice or tape) should be recorded in the appropriate space; the type of client response (talkback, written response, selection of a word or sentence from a multiple choice format, signing, picture pointing, etc.) should be recorded in the space marked "Remarks."

The percentage correct, or speech recognition score, obtained with any test will vary depending on the ease or difficulty of the material, the intelligibility of the speaker, whether presentation was via live voice or recording, whether the message set was closed as in a picture pointing task or open as in a task where the client repeats the words, and on the presentation level of the material. Therefore, it is important to be aware of this information, which should be included on the Audiologic Assessment Form.

Often, contralateral masking is needed in order to obtain a valid speech reception threshold, speech awareness threshold, or speech recognition score. The appropriate use of masking is discussed in Chapter 5. When contralateral masking is used, the levels should be recorded in the appropriate spaces on the Audiologic Assessment Form. In addition, the type of masker should also be noted.

Procedures

The various types of speech identification tests have been standardized on normal-hearing individuals, and group data have been plotted in the form of performance-intensity functions. Performance-intensity functions are generated by obtaining a speech recognition score for a list of words at a succession of intensity levels and then plotting a curve. As can be seen in Figure 4-1, different materials generate different curves. The steeper the curve, the easier the speech identification task and the lower the intensity level at which a maximum score is obtained.

It can be seen in Figure 4-1 that as level of presentation increases with both types of material, the speech recognition score increases until it reaches a maximum. Increasing intensity beyond this maximum does not increase identification score further. When we have reached the peak of the performance-intensity curve or the highest speech recognition score possible, we have obtained PB Max. The easier the speech recognition material, the lower the intensity level necessary to achieve PB Max.

The performance-intensity function plotted for a particular set of stimulus words or sentences is based on test results obtained on a large group of listeners. A performance-intensity function can be plotted for a single individual, normal hearing, deaf, or hard of hearing, in the same way. Lists of words are presented at increasing intensity levels, and percentage scores as a function of intensity are plotted on a curve. PB Max can be read directly from the curve; in addition (see Figure 4-2), the clinician can readily find the speech identification score obtained at a particular level of interest, such as average conversational level (70 dB SPL or 50 dB HL).

Inspection of the performance-intensity function can also reveal the presence or absence of the "rollover phenomenon," which provides important diagnostic information in differentiating between cochlear and retrocochlear sites of lesion. With a normal ear, a conductively impaired ear, and a non-recruiting ear with cochlear impairment, once PB Max has been reached, further increase in presentation level neither increases nor decreases the recognition score. (A recruiting ear is one which shows an abnormal increase in loudness perception as the intensity of the signal increases. In a non-recruiting ear, as intensity levels increase in a linear fashion, the perception of loudness also increases linearly. For example, the difference in

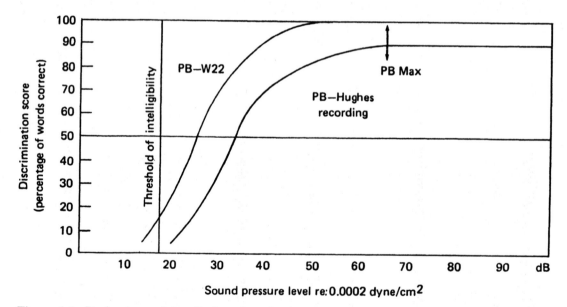

Figure 4-1. Performance-intensity functions for Rush-Hughes and W-22 tests (modified from Davis and Silverman, 1970).

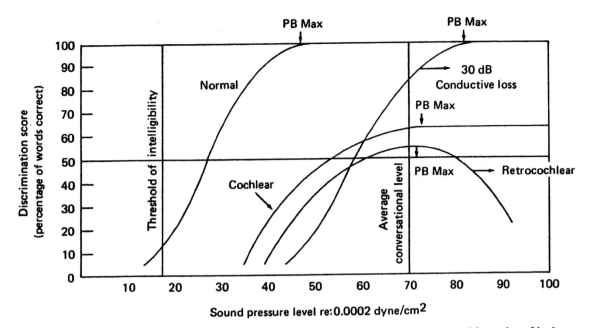

Figure 4-2. Performance-intensity functions for normal ear, conductive loss, cochlear site of lesion, and retrocochlear site of lesion.

perceived loudness between tones presented at 20 and 30 dB SL is the same as the difference in perceived loudness between tones presented at 30 and 40 dB SL. In contrast, the recruiting ear may perceive a much greater loudness difference between the second pair of tones than between the first. Although recruitment is usually found with cochlear site of lesion, it is possible to have a cochlear site of lesion without recruitment.) With a retrocochlear problem, further intensity increases often result in a decreased identification score. The reader must clearly understand that the rollover phenomenon can occur in some cases of cochlear impairment but is generally suggestive of retrocochlear impairment. Further information on the diagnostic significance of the performance-intensity function can be found in Jerger (1973:80, 89–90, 94–111), Hannley (1986:159–160), and Rintelmann (1991: 106–108).

Generally, the performance-intensity function of a given individual can provide the following insights relative to site of lesion:

1. With a pure conductive loss, PB Max is comparable to that of a normal ear, except that the intensity level necessary to achieve it is elevated by the amount of the hearing loss. The individual is able to understand speech well if the presentation level is sufficiently intense.

2. With a sensorineural loss located in the cochlea, PB Max is usually reduced but the rollover phenomenon is not usually evident. The individual is unable to understand speech equally well at increasingly high presentation levels once the plateau has been found.

3. With a sensorineural loss located in the eighth nerve, PB Max is frequently severely reduced and a pronounced rollover may be evident. There may be a marked discrepancy between the amount of word recognition difficulty and the degree of pure tone loss. A mild pure tone hearing loss in conjunction with very poor word identification should alert the clinician to the possibility of retrocochlear impairment. It has been found, however, that the rollover phenomenon is not seen in all eighth nerve patients; it is closely linked to the presence or absence of the acoustic reflex (Hannley and Jerger, 1981; Hannley, 1984:160). Hannley points out that some patients with other diagnoses, such as facial nerve disorders and postapedectomy, have demonstrated rollover; in most of these cases, rollover was associated with the absence of the acoustic reflex.

Interpreting Speech Audiometry

4. With hearing losses in the central auditory pathways, the performance-intensity function may be similar to that found with eighth nerve dysfunction. However, in other cases, this measure does not function as a satisfactory detector and more difficult tasks are needed.

In our routine audiometric testing we generally do not plot a performance-intensity function for an individual because the procedure is too time consuming. Instead, we try to estimate the level at which we are likely to obtain PB Max and obtain a word recognition score at that level. With many clients, PB Max can be obtained at 40 dB SL; but with others, word lists must be presented at several different intensity levels until the best word recognition score is found.

According to Goetzinger (see Katz, 1978:155), the following guide may be used in evaluating word identification ability:

90–100%	Normal word identification
76–88%	Slight difficulty, comparable to listening over a telephone
62–74%	Moderate difficulty
50–60%	Poor understanding; difficulty following conversation
Below 50%	Very poor understanding; great difficulty following running speech

It is important to have some idea of when percentage difference between word recognition scores may be considered significant. In the past, differences of ±6–8 dB have been considered significant and smaller differences between scores have been attributed to chance. However, Raffin and Thornton (1980) and Thornton and Raffin (1978) have demonstrated statistically that the significant difference score depends on the performance of the listener and the length of the list. Given 50-item lists, a 10–12% difference between scores could reasonably be considered significant if the listener's PB Max fell between 80 and 100% or below 20%. If, however, PB Max fell more into the mid-range (e.g., 50–70%), the difference score would have to be closer to 20% to be considered significant. Shortening lists to 25 items, which is done in many clinics, increases the probability that small differences are occurring by chance. Given a PB Max score of 80% and lists of 25 items, a difference score would have to approach 25% to be considered significant. Tables showing statistically significant difference scores as a function of PB Max and length of list can be found in the Thornton and Raffin (1980) and Raffin and Thornton (1978) articles. Whenever the magnitude of a difference between two word recognition scores is greater than 10%, some real difference may exist, especially if PB Max is relatively high or low. The clinician must be more cautious, however, in interpreting the significance of such a difference score if PB Max is less than 80% or greater than 20%. In addition, the practice of shortening lists to save testing time must be questioned, unless it is obvious that word recognition is very high or very low. Additional discussion of this issue can be found in Rintelmann (1991:85–89).

The word identification score at average conversational level, 50 dB HL or 70 dB SPL, provides important information for rehabilitation. In most clinics, the individual's word recognition scores at average conversational level with and without a hearing aid are compared to provide one measure of the benefit of the hearing aid. Although the procedure has become controversial, some audiologists continue to compare word recognition at 50 dB HL using several hearing aids being considered for the client. First, unaided speech identification is evaluated at 50 dB HL in the sound field; then, each hearing aid to be tried is evaluated with a comparable list of speech recognition material presented in the same way, usually with recorded voice. For further information, see Rintelmann (1991:104–106), Martin (1991:408–411), and Newby and Popelka (1985:377–378).

SPEECH UNDERSTANDING IN NOISE OR COMPETING MESSAGE

In increasing numbers of clinics, speech understanding is being evaluated in the presence of competing noise or speech in addition to quiet or in place of it. Most hard-of-hearing individuals, particularly those with sensorineural losses, experience communication difficulties primarily in noisy situations. Measuring speech recognition in quiet in a sound-treated room does not provide a valid indication of the degree of difficulty the client experiences in daily life.

Therefore, noise is added to the signal, and the intensity of the signal relative to the noise is known as the signal-to-noise ratio (S/N). When both signals are the same intensity, the S/N is zero; when the speech is 10 dB more intense, the S/N is 10; when the signal is 10 dB less intense, the S/N is −10 (Martin, 1991:139). Although listening to a list of words in the sound-treated room in the presence of filtered white noise, cafeteria noise, or voice babble is far from an accurate duplication of an actual communication situation, it is a closer approximation of real life than the speech-recognition-in-quiet task. There is considerable evidence in the literature that presentation of test materials against a background of speech or noise enhances the sensitivity of the test in revealing a client's communication difficulties (Rintelmann, 1991:96–97).

The addition of noise to the listening task also serves to make the speech material more difficult and may help to differentiate between hearing aids whose performance otherwise appears to be the same, despite real differences between instruments. A number of researchers (e.g., Jerger and Hayes, 1976; Beattie and Edgerton, 1976; and Orchik and Roddy, 1980) have suggested that performance with hearing aids should be tested against a background of noise or speech competition. For further discussion, see Rintelmann (1991:104–106).

During a hearing aid evaluation, speech and competing noise may be presented through the same loudspeaker or through different loudspeakers and with the noise on the side of the aided ear with the speech on the other side or the reverse. Each of these conditions produces different degrees of communicative difficulty. For example, when the speech signal is delivered through the loudspeaker closest to the aided ear and the noise signal through the loudspeaker on the opposite side of the ear, the intensity level of the noise relative to the speech will be attenuated because of the head shadow effect. When the signals are reversed, the intensity level of the speech will be attenuated relative to the noise, resulting in a far more difficult receptive task. The clinician must choose the manner of presentation that most closely approximates the communicative situations the client experiences in daily life. The most common procedure is to present the speech signal to the ear with the hearing aid microphone and the noise to the opposite ear.

Word recognition scores obtained in noise should be recorded in the "Remarks" section. For each score recorded, the presentation level, signal-to-noise ratio, and list used should also be recorded.

There is a dearth of information in the literature concerning the type of competing noise to use and the optimal level of noise relative to the speech signal. Types of noise used include speech noise (white noise filtered to approximate the long time average spectrum of the speech signal), cafeteria noise, voice babble, and competing speech. However, the relative value of these competing signals has not been evaluated. Similarly, there is little in the literature to indicate the appropriate signal-to-noise ratio to use; since there is a lack of standardized normative data, we do not know what to expect of the average normal ear at the various signal-to-noise ratios, nor do we know which signal-to-noise ratio can provide the greatest amount of diagnostic information for various types of hearing loss.

Several researchers (e.g., Dirks, Morgan, and Dubno, 1982; and Levitt and Resnick, 1978) have used an adaptive procedure to determine the signal-to-noise ratios necessary to reach a predetermined performance level for an individual (e.g., 50%). Usually test stimuli are maintained at a constant level, while the level of the competing noise is varied. Noise level is increased each time several correct responses occur and decreased when several incorrect responses are made, until the desired performance level is reached (e.g., 50% correct). Once the appropriate signal-to-noise ratio is found, it is held constant for all speech recognition testing for that individual.

Questions

QUESTIONS FOR FIGURE 4-3

1. What is the SRT for the right ear?
2. What is the SRT for the left ear?
3. What is the sound field SRT?
4. How do the SRTs compare with the pure tone thresholds?
5. What kind of presentation mode was used?

Name: Fig 4-3   Date: XX/XX/XX Age: 22   Sex: M   Audiologist: HK

AUDIOMETER: GSI-10   ANSI 1969

PURE TONE AUDIOGRAM
FREQUENCY IN HERTZ

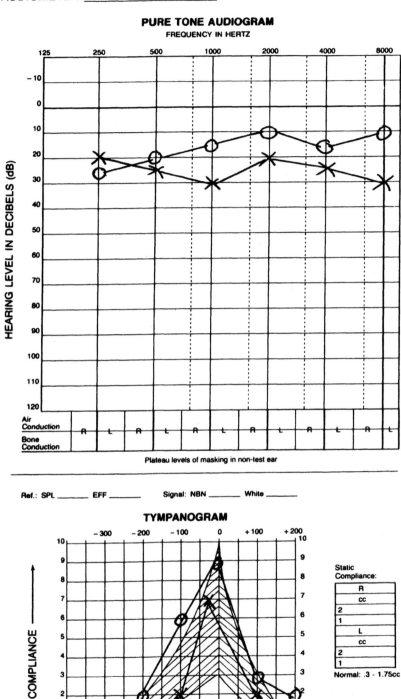

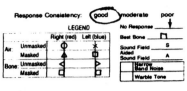

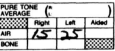

Response Consistency: (good) moderate poor

PURE TONE AVERAGE (R: / L:)

	Right	Left	Aided
AIR	15	25	
BONE			

SPEECH AUDIOMETRY ☒MLV ☐ Tape

	RIGHT	LEFT	MASK LEVEL R / L	SOUND FIELD	LIST
SAT					
SRT	14	26		16	
MCL					
UCL					
PB% (Word)	_L	_L			
PB% (Word)	_L	_L			
PB% (Word)	_L	_L			
PB% (Word)	_L	_L			
	_L	_L			
	_L	_L			

STAPEDIUS REFLEX THRESHOLDS

Stimulus	Contralateral (HL)					Ipsilateral (HL)		
EAR	.5K	1K	2K	4K	WBN	.5K	1K	2K
R								
Decay		⊠	⊠					⊠
L								
Decay			⊠	⊠				⊠

ABBREVIATIONS

A	Absent	NR	No Response
C₁	Canal Volume	SAT	Speech Awareness
CNE	Could Not Establish		Threshold
CNT	Could Not Test	SL	Sensation Level
DNT	Did Not Test	SRT	Speech Reception
HL	Hearing Level		Threshold
MCL	Most Comfortable	UCL	Uncomfortable Listening
	Listening Level		Level
MVL	Monitored Live Voice		

Ref.: SPL _____ EFF _____   Signal: NBN _____ White _____

TYMPANOGRAM

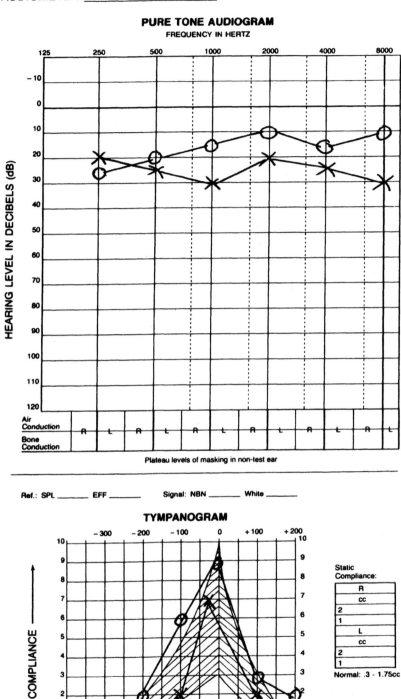

PRESSURE IN daPa

Static Compliance:

R	
cc	
2	
1	
L	
cc	
2	
1	

Normal: .3 - 1.75cc

Ear Canal Volume

	Right	Left
C₁ =		

REMARKS:

_____

_____

_____

_____

_____

Answers for Figure 4-3

1. The SRT for the right ear is 14 dB HL.
2. The SRT for the left ear is 26 dB HL.
3. The sound field SRT is 16 dB HL.
4. All the SRTs agree well with the pure tone thresholds. The three-frequency pure tone averages are 15 dB HL for the right ear and 25 dB HL for the left ear. These scores are very close to the respective SRTs. Both pure tone average and SRT indicate that the right ear is the better ear.
5. The words were presented live voice.

QUESTIONS FOR FIGURE 4-4

Case History Information This 5-year-old child had been diagnosed as moderately retarded. Test results indicate that his receptive vocabulary is approximately at a 2-year age level.

1. What is the SRT for the right ear?
2. What is the SRT for the left ear?
3. Do the SRTs compare favorably with the pure tone averages?
4. Why was it necessary to use a restricted spondee list?
5. Does this child show any indication of middle ear dysfunction?

Name: Fig 4-4   Date: XX/XX/XX   Age: 5   Sex: M   Audiologist: HK

AUDIOMETER: GSI-10   ANSI 1969

PURE TONE AUDIOGRAM
FREQUENCY IN HERTZ

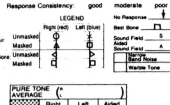

Response Consistency: good   moderate   poor

No Response _____

LEGEND

	Right (red)	Left (blue)
Air: Unmasked	O	X
Masked	△	□
Bone: Unmasked	◁	▷
Masked	◻	□

Best Bone _____
Sound Field ___ S
Aided
Sound Field ___ A
Narrow Band Noise
Warble Tone

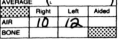

PURE TONE AVERAGE (R L)			
	Right	Left	Aided
AIR	10	12	
BONE			

SPEECH AUDIOMETRY ☐ MLV ☐ Tape

	RIGHT	LEFT	MASK LEVEL R	MASK LEVEL L	SOUND FIELD	LIST
SAT						
SRT	-2	8				
MCL						
UCL						
PB% (Word)	_L	_L				
PB% (Word)	_L	_L				
PB% (Word)	_L	_L				
PB% (Word)	_L	_L				
	_L	_L				
	_L	_L				

STAPEDIUS REFLEX THRESHOLDS

Stimulus	Contralateral (HL)					Ipsilateral (HL)		
EAR	.5K	1K	2K	4K	WBN	.5K	1K	2K
R	100	105	105	NR	✕			✕
Decay					✕			✕
L	NR	NR	NR	NR	✕			✕
Decay					✕			✕

ABBREVIATIONS

A	Absent	NR	No Response
C$_1$	Canal Volume	SAT	Speech Awareness
CNE	Could Not Establish		Threshold
CNT	Could Not Test	SL	Sensation Level
DNT	Did Not Test	SRT	Speech Reception
HL	Hearing Level		Threshold
MCL	Most Comfortable	UCL	Uncomfortable Listening
	Listening Level		Level
MVL	Monitored Live Voice		

Ref.: SPL _____ EFF _____   Signal: NBN _____ White _____

Plateau levels of masking in non-test ear

TYMPANOGRAM

Static Compliance:

R	
	cc
2	
1	

L	
	cc
2	
1	

Normal: .3 - 1.75cc

Ear Canal Volume

Right	Left

C$_1$ = _____

REMARKS:

Because of limited receptive language, only five spondee words were used. A picture pointing response was used

1. The SRT for the right ear is –2 dB HL.
2. The SRT for the left ear is 8 dB HL.
3. Pure tone average–SRT agreement is not good. The right ear SRT is 12 dB better than the pure tone average; the left ear SRT is 10 dB better than the pure tone average. The discrepancies may be explained by the fact that it was necessary to use a list of only five spondee words to obtain SRT. When a restricted list of stimulus words is used, the alternatives a client can choose from in identifying a stimulus item are limited and we can expect a lower score than if the entire list of spondee words is used.
4. It was necessary to use a restricted spondee list because of the child's language limitations. Note that this fact is stated in the "Remarks" section of the Audiologic Assessment Form.
5. There is a Type C tympanogram in the left ear (note the compliance peak occurs at –150 daPA), suggesting negative middle ear pressure. The absence of acoustic reflexes when the left ear is stimulated by pure tone corroborates the probability of a middle ear problem. The right ear tympanogram is Type A, suggesting normal middle ear function.

QUESTIONS FOR FIGURE 4-5

1. What are the SRTs in the right and left ears?
2. What is the sound field SRT?
3. Why is the sound field SRT more sensitive than either ear?
4. Is there evidence of middle ear dysfunction?

Name: Fig 4-5   Date: XX/XX/XX   Age: 9   Sex: M   Audiologist: HK

AUDIOMETER: GSI-10   ANSI 1969

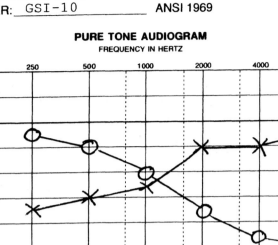

PURE TONE AUDIOGRAM
FREQUENCY IN HERTZ

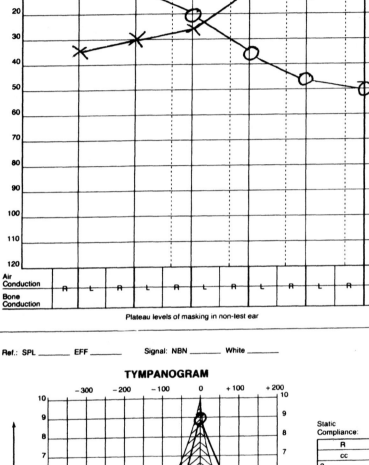

Ref.: SPL _____ EFF _____   Signal: NBN _____ White _____

TYMPANOGRAM

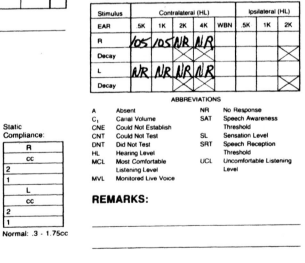

PRESSURE IN daPa

Static Compliance:

R	
	cc
2	
1	
L	
	cc
2	
1	

Normal: .3 - 1.75cc

Ear Canal Volume

Right	Left
c_1 .65	.55

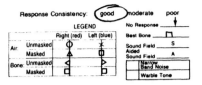

Response Consistency: (good) moderate poor

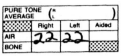

PURE TONE AVERAGE (R L)	Right	Left	Aided
AIR	22	22	
BONE			

SPEECH AUDIOMETRY ☒ MLV ☐ Tape

	RIGHT	LEFT	MASK LEVEL R L	SOUND FIELD	LIST
SAT					
SRT	20	18		10	
MCL					
UCL					
PB% (Word)	_ L	_ L			
PB% (Word)	_ L	_ L			
PB% (Word)	_ L	_ L			
PB% (Word)	_ L	_ L			
	_ L	_ L			
	_ L	_ L			

STAPEDIUS REFLEX THRESHOLDS

Stimulus	Contralateral (HL)					Ipsilateral (HL)		
EAR	.5K	1K	2K	4K	WBN	.5K	1K	2K
R	105	105	NR	NR				☒
Decay			☒	☒				
L	NR	NR	NR	NR				☒
Decay			☒	☒				

ABBREVIATIONS

A	Absent	NR	No Response
C_1	Canal Volume	SAT	Speech Awareness
CNE	Could Not Establish		Threshold
CNT	Could Not Test	SL	Sensation Level
DNT	Did Not Test	SRT	Speech Reception
HL	Hearing Level		Threshold
MCL	Most Comfortable	UCL	Uncomfortable Listening
	Listening Level		Level
MVL	Monitored Live Voice		

REMARKS:

_____
_____
_____
_____
_____

Interpreting Speech Audiometry

169

Answers for Figure 4-5

1. The SRTs in the right and left ears are 20 dB HL and 18 dB HL, respectively. Note that they agree well with the pure tone averages in the right and left ears.
2. The sound field SRT is 10 dB HL.
3. The sound field SRT is more sensitive than either the right or left SRTs because it reflects the functioning of both ears together. Note that the SRT of 10 dB HL agrees well with the best binaural average of 13 dB HL, which also reflects the functioning of both ears working together. The best binaural average is based on the right ear thresholds at 500 and 1000 Hz and the left ear threshold at 2000 Hz. In this case, the best sensitivity for low frequencies is found in the right ear and the best sensitivity for high frequencies is found in the left. In the sound field situation, the left ear can compensate for the poorer right ear sensitivity in the high frequencies and the right ear can compensate for the poorer left ear sensitivity in the low frequencies. Therefore, both ears working together provide a degree of hearing sensitivity that neither can provide alone. In situations where one ear is more sensitive than the other at all frequencies, the sound field SRT reflects the functioning of the better ear.
4. The Type A tympanogram in the right ear suggests normal middle ear function. The absent and elevated acoustic reflex thresholds in that ear are probably caused by a middle ear problem in the left ear. The Type C tympanogram in the left ear strongly suggests the presence of fluid in the left middle ear. This is corroborated by the absence of left ear reflex thresholds.

QUESTIONS FOR FIGURE 4-6

1. How do the SRTs compare with the three-frequency pure tone averages?
2. How do the SRTs compare with the two-frequency pure tone averages?
3. How can the discrepancy be explained?
4. How does the sound field SRT compare to the SRTs obtained under earphones?
5. Is there any evidence of middle ear dysfunction?

Name: Fig 4-6   Date: XX/XX/XX Age: 48 Sex: M Audiologist: HK
AUDIOMETER: GSI-10   ANSI 1969

PURE TONE AUDIOGRAM

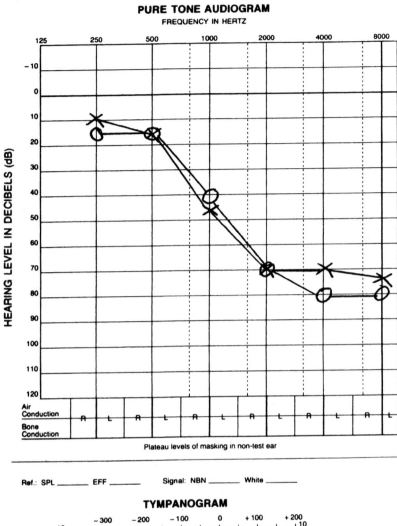

FREQUENCY IN HERTZ

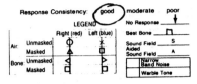

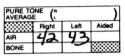

PURE TONE AVERAGE (R, L)			
	Right	Left	Aided
AIR	42	43	
BONE			

SPEECH AUDIOMETRY ☒ MLV ☐ Tape

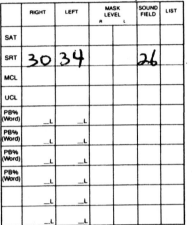

	RIGHT	LEFT	MASK LEVEL R / L	SOUND FIELD	LIST
SAT					
SRT	30	34		26	
MCL					
UCL					
PB% (Word)	_L	_L			
PB% (Word)	_L	_L			
PB% (Word)	_L	_L			
PB% (Word)	_L	_L			
	_L	_L			
	_L	_L			

Plateau levels of masking in non-test ear

Ref.: SPL _____ EFF _____   Signal: NBN _____ White _____

STAPEDIUS REFLEX THRESHOLDS

Stimulus	Contralateral (HL)					Ipsilateral (HL)		
EAR	.5K	1K	2K	4K	WBN	.5K	1K	2K
R	70	80	110	110				
Decay								☒
L	70	85	105	110				
Decay								☒

TYMPANOGRAM

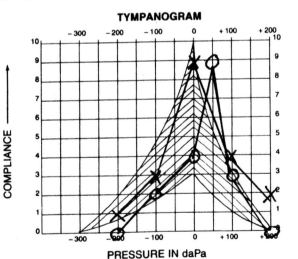

Static Compliance:

R	cc
2	
1	

L	cc
2	
1	

Normal: .3 - 1.75cc

Ear Canal Volume

	Right	Left
C₁ =		

ABBREVIATIONS

A   Absent
C₁   Canal Volume
CNE   Could Not Establish
CNT   Could Not Test
DNT   Did Not Test
HL   Hearing Level
MCL   Most Comfortable
        Listening Level
MVL   Monitored Live Voice

NR   No Response
SAT   Speech Awareness
        Threshold
SL   Sensation Level
SRT   Speech Reception
        Threshold
UCL   Uncomfortable Listening
        Level

REMARKS:

Two frequency pure tone
averages are: right=27dB,
left=30 dB

Answers for Figure 4-6

1. The SRTs for both ears and for the sound field are significantly more sensitive than the three-frequency pure tone averages. For the right ear there is a difference of 12 dB HL; for the left ear there is a difference of 9 dB HL; for the sound field the difference between SRT and best binaural average is 16 dB HL.

2. The SRTs and two-frequency pure tone averages are in good agreement (30 dB and 27 dB for the right ear; 34 dB and 30 dB for the left ear; 26 dB and 27 dB for the sound field). The difference is 4 dB or less in each case.

3. The two-frequency average is the proper score to use in this case to compare SRT with pure tone thresholds. Since the pure tone configurations are sharply sloping, the SRTs reflect the better low-frequency thresholds. When the two-frequency averages are used, SRT and pure tone averages agree very well.

4. The sound field SRT is 4 dB more sensitive than the most sensitive SRT obtained under earphones (right ear SRT). Sometimes an individual can hear slightly better when using both ears together than when using only one ear. In the clinical testing situation, we frequently find that individuals obtain SRTs in the sound field that are approximately 3 dB more sensitive than the SRT of the better ear. This phenomenon is referred to as binaural summation.

5. Tympanograms for both ears are Type A, suggesting normal middle ear function. Acoustic reflex thresholds are consistent with normal middle ear function.

QUESTIONS FOR FIGURE 4-7

Case History Information This 42-year-old man was being evaluated for a job-related injury to his ears for which he was seeking monetary compensation. During the case history interview, he appeared to be watching the speaker very closely, but when the interviewer casually covered her mouth, communication was not affected.

1. What is a reasonable hypothesis for the lack of SRT–pure tone average agreement?
2. What other possible explanations would have to be ruled out?
3. How do immittance results relate to the hypothesis of non-organicity?

Name: Fig 4-7　　　　　　Date: XX/XX/XX　Age: 42　Sex: M　Audiologist: HK

AUDIOMETER: GSI-10　　　ANSI 1969

PURE TONE AUDIOGRAM
FREQUENCY IN HERTZ

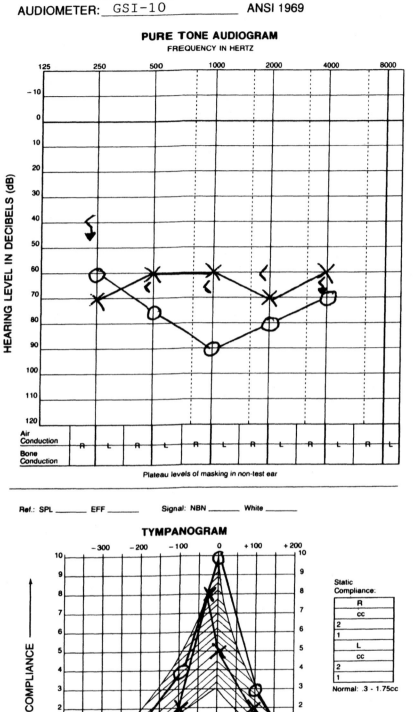

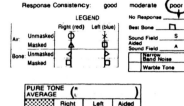

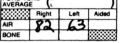

PURE TONE AVERAGE (R, L)	Right	Left	Aided
AIR	82	63	
BONE			

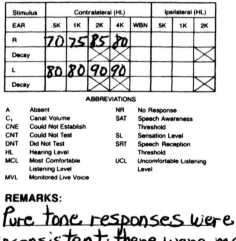

SPEECH AUDIOMETRY ☒MLV ☐ Tape

	RIGHT	LEFT	MASK LEVEL R	L	SOUND FIELD	LIST
SAT						
SRT	32	40			28	
MCL						
UCL						
PB% (Word)	_L	_L				
PB% (Word)	_L	_L				
PB% (Word)	_L	_L				
PB% (Word)	_L	_L				
	_L	_L				
	_L	_L				

STAPEDIUS REFLEX THRESHOLDS

Stimulus	Contralateral (HL)					Ipsilateral (HL)		
EAR	.5K	1K	2K	4K	WBN	.5K	1K	2K
R	70	75	85	80				
Decay								
L	80	80	90	90				
Decay								

ABBREVIATIONS

A	Absent	NR	No Response
C₁	Canal Volume	SAT	Speech Awareness
CNE	Could Not Establish		Threshold
CNT	Could Not Test	SL	Sensation Level
DNT	Did Not Test	SRT	Speech Reception
HL	Hearing Level		Threshold
MCL	Most Comfortable	UCL	Uncomfortable Listening
	Listening Level		Level
MVL	Monitored Live Voice		

REMARKS:

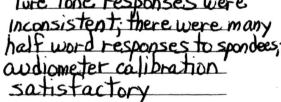

Pure tone responses were inconsistent; there were many half word responses to spondees; audiometer calibration satisfactory

Ref.: SPL _____ EFF _____　Signal: NBN _____ White _____

TYMPANOGRAM

Static Compliance:

R	
	cc
2	
1	

L	
	cc
2	
1	

Normal: .3 - 1.75cc

Ear Canal Volume

	Right	Left
C₁=		

Answers for Figure 4-7

1. Whenever the SRTs are significantly more sensitive than the pure tone averages, non-organicity may be suspected. In this case, this hypothesis may be corroborated by the client's inconsistent response behavior, his half word responses, and his apparent ease in understanding the examiner when visual clues were removed.

2. Other explanations for the SRT–pure tone discrepancy may include: (a) audiometer out of calibration—this must be evaluated whenever inconsistent test results are seen; (b) client misunderstands what he/she is expected to do—client should be reinstructed and retested; and (c) presence of sloping pure tone configuration—this was not the case with this client.

3. Acoustic reflex thresholds are not consistent with pure tone thresholds; when pure tone thresholds are in the severe range, elevated or absent reflexes are expected. The normal reflex thresholds seen on this audiogram are consistent with mild to moderate pure tone loss.

QUESTIONS FOR FIGURE 4-8

Case History Information This severely deaf girl has sufficient receptive language to use a full list of spondee words for the measurement of SRT. However, her speech is unintelligible.

1. What was the response mode used in the measurement of SRT?
2. What stimuli were used to obtain word recognition? Why?
3. What factor might explain the discrepancies between the pure tone averages and the SRTs?

Name: Fig 4-8   Date: XX/XX/XX   Age: 18   Sex: F   Audiologist: HK
AUDIOMETER: GSI-10   ANSI 1969

PURE TONE AUDIOGRAM
FREQUENCY IN HERTZ

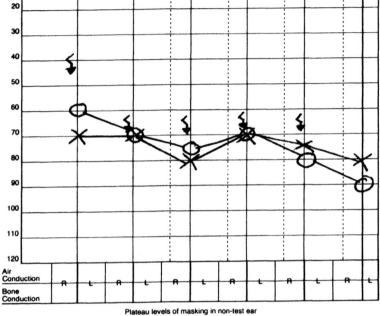

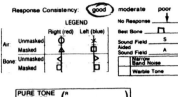

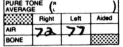

PURE TONE AVERAGE (R / L)			
	Right	Left	Aided
AIR	72	77	
BONE			

SPEECH AUDIOMETRY X MLV [] Tape

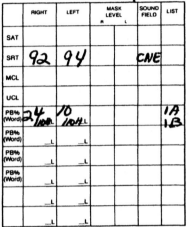

	RIGHT	LEFT	MASK LEVEL R / L	SOUND FIELD	LIST
SAT					
SRT	92	94	CNE		
MCL					
UCL					
PB% (Word)	24 /100	10 /104 L			1A 1B
PB% (Word)	_L	_L			
PB% (Word)	_L	_L			
PB% (Word)	_L	_L			
	_L	_L			
	_L	_L			

STAPEDIUS REFLEX THRESHOLDS

Stimulus	Contralateral (HL)					Ipsilateral (HL)		
EAR	.5K	1K	2K	4K	WBN	5K	1K	2K
R	105	105	110	110				X
Decay			X	X				X
L	110	110	110	NR				X
Decay			X	X				X

ABBREVIATIONS

A	Absent	NR	No Response
C₁	Canal Volume	SAT	Speech Awareness
CNE	Could Not Establish		Threshold
CNT	Could Not Test	SL	Sensation Level
DNT	Did Not Test	SRT	Speech Reception
HL	Hearing Level		Threshold
MCL	Most Comfortable	UCL	Uncomfortable Listening
	Listening Level		Level
MVL	Monitored Live Voice		

REMARKS: Client fingerspelled responses to spondees; written responses to the Modified Rhyme test were used for word recognition

Ref.: SPL _____ EFF _____   Signal: NBN _____ White _____

TYMPANOGRAM

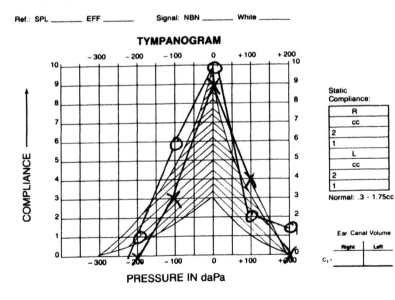

PRESSURE IN daPa

Static Compliance:

R	
cc	
2	
1	

L	
cc	
2	
1	

Normal: .3 - 1.75cc

Ear Canal Volume

Right	Left
C₁ = _____	_____

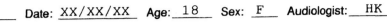

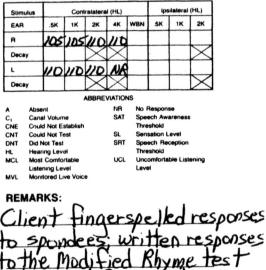

Interpreting Speech Audiometry

Answers for Figure 4-8

1. Fingerspelling was the response mode used to obtain SRT. The client's speech was not intelligible enough to permit a talkback response.
2. Word recognition was measured using the multiple-choice format of a rhyme test. Since the client was unable to intelligibly repeat test words, she was required to circle one of the possible responses for each item on the rhyme test.
3. There is a 20-dB difference between SRT and pure tone average in the right ear and a 17-dB difference in the left ear. Although recognition of spondee words is a relatively simple task, some speech understanding ability is necessary. For example, "hotdog" must be differentiated from "hothouse." When a client's speech understanding is very poor, the SRT may be significantly elevated. Note that this girl's word recognition scores are 24% in the right ear and 10% in the left.

QUESTIONS FOR FIGURE 4-9

Supplementary Information This audiogram is the same as that in Figure 4-8.

1. What are the SATs for the right and left ears?
2. Why were they obtained?
3. How do they agree with the pure tone averages?

Name: <u>Fig 4-9</u> Date: <u>XX/XX/XX</u> Age: <u>18</u> Sex: <u>F</u> Audiologist: <u>HK</u>
AUDIOMETER: <u>GSI-10</u> ANSI 1969

PURE TONE AUDIOGRAM
FREQUENCY IN HERTZ

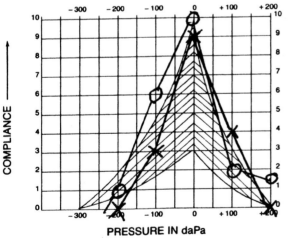

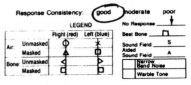

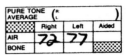

PURE TONE AVERAGE

	Right	Left	Aided
AIR	72	77	
BONE			

SPEECH AUDIOMETRY ☒ MLV ☐ Tape

	RIGHT	LEFT	MASK LEVEL R	MASK LEVEL L	SOUND FIELD	LIST
SAT	70	72				
SRT	92	94		CNE		
MCL						
UCL						
PB% (Word)	24 110H	10 110H				
PB% (Word)	_L_	_L_				
PB% (Word)	_L_	_L_				
PB% (Word)	_L_	_L_				
	_L_	_L_				
	_L_	_L_				

STAPEDIUS REFLEX THRESHOLDS

Stimulus	Contralateral (HL)					Ipsilateral (HL)		
EAR	.5K	1K	2K	4K	WBN	.5K	1K	2K
R	105	105	110	110				
Decay			✕	✕				✕
L	110	110	110	NR				
Decay			✕	✕				✕

ABBREVIATIONS

A	Absent	NR	No Response
C₁	Canal Volume	SAT	Speech Awareness
CNE	Could Not Establish		Threshold
CNT	Could Not Test	SL	Sensation Level
DNT	Did Not Test	SRT	Speech Reception
HL	Hearing Level		Threshold
MCL	Most Comfortable	UCL	Uncomfortable Listening
	Listening Level		Level
MVL	Monitored Live Voice		

REMARKS:

Client fingerspelled responses
to spondees. written responses
to the Modified Rhyme test
were used for word
recognition

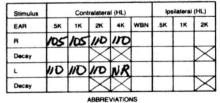

Ref.: SPL _____ EFF _____   Signal: NBN _____ White _____

TYMPANOGRAM

PRESSURE IN daPa

Static Compliance:

R	
	cc
2	
1	
L	
	cc
2	
1	

Normal: .3 - 1.75cc

Ear Canal Volume

Right	Left
C₁	

Answers for Figure 4-9

1. The SAT for the right ear is 70 dB HL; the SAT for the left ear is 72 dB HL.
2. The SATs were obtained because there was poor agreement between SRTs and pure tone averages, and it was hypothesized that the significantly poorer SRTs were due to very poor word recognition. If this hypothesis is correct, the SAT scores should be considerably lower because the SAT measure does not involve speech recognition.
3. The SAT scores agree well with the lowest pure tone thresholds of the speech frequencies (70 dB HL versus 70 dB HL at 500 Hz in the right ear; 72 dB HL versus 70 dB HL at 500 Hz in the left ear). This good agreement supports the hypothesis that the poor SRT–pure tone average agreement is due to poor word recognition (as discussed for Figure 4-7). The measurement of the SAT requires only that the client signal when she is aware that she is hearing something; it is not necessary for her to identify or repeat words.

QUESTIONS FOR FIGURE 4-10

Case History Information This child has been profoundly deaf since birth. His receptive vocabulary is at a 2 year, 8 month level as measured with the Peabody Picture Vocabulary Test, administered using auditory–visual input.

1. Why were SATs obtained?
2. What were the stimuli used to obtain SATs?
3. What was the response mode used?
4. How do the SAT scores compare to the pure tone thresholds?

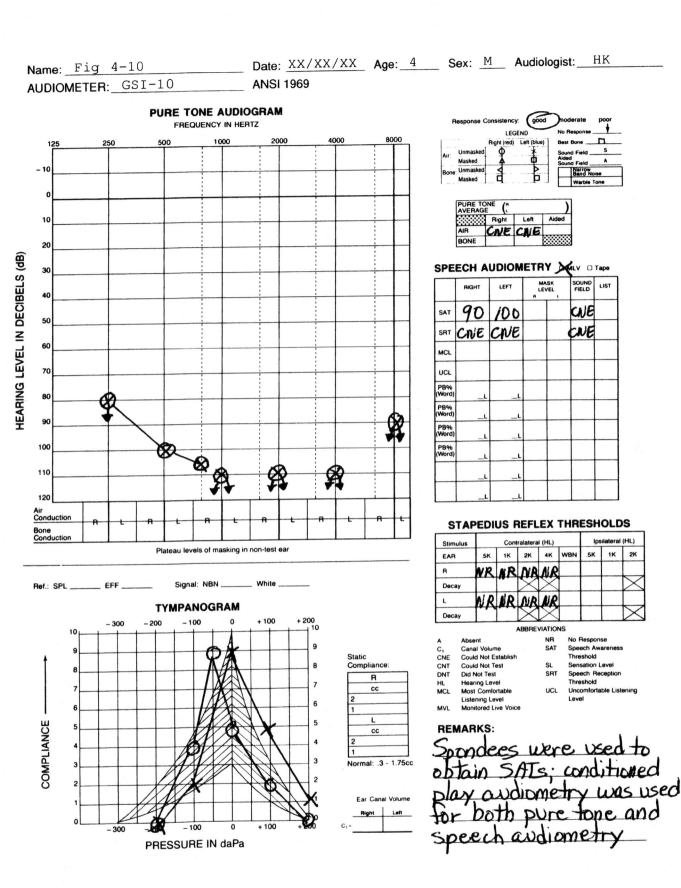

PURE TONE AUDIOGRAM
FREQUENCY IN HERTZ

Response Consistency: (good) moderate poor

LEGEND

		Right (red)	Left (blue)
Air:	Unmasked	◯	☐
	Masked	△	⨯
Bone:	Unmasked	◁	▷
	Masked	☐	☐

No Response
Best Bone
Sound Field ___ S
Aided
Sound Field ___ A
Narrow Band Noise
Warble Tone

PURE TONE AVERAGE (R L)	Right	Left	Aided
AIR	CNE	CNE	
BONE			

SPEECH AUDIOMETRY ⨯ MLV ☐ Tape

	RIGHT	LEFT	MASK LEVEL R L	SOUND FIELD	LIST
SAT	90	100		CNE	
SRT	CNE	CNE		CNE	
MCL					
UCL					
PB% (Word)	_L	_L			
PB% (Word)	_L	_L			
PB% (Word)	_L	_L			
PB% (Word)	_L	_L			
	_L	_L			
	_L	_L			

STAPEDIUS REFLEX THRESHOLDS

Stimulus	Contralateral (HL)					Ipsilateral (HL)		
EAR	.5K	1K	2K	4K	WBN	.5K	1K	2K
R	NR	NR	NR	NR				⨯
Decay			⨯	⨯				⨯
L	NR	NR	NR	NR				⨯
Decay			⨯	⨯				⨯

ABBREVIATIONS

A	Absent	NR	No Response
C₁	Canal Volume	SAT	Speech Awareness
CNE	Could Not Establish		Threshold
CNT	Could Not Test	SL	Sensation Level
DNT	Did Not Test	SRT	Speech Reception
HL	Hearing Level		Threshold
MCL	Most Comfortable	UCL	Uncomfortable Listening
	Listening Level		Level
MVL	Monitored Live Voice		

REMARKS:

Spondees were used to obtain SATs; conditioned play audiometry was used for both pure tone and speech audiometry

Air Conduction   R L R L R L R L R L R L R L
Bone Conduction

Plateau levels of masking in non-test ear

Ref.: SPL _____ EFF _____   Signal: NBN _____ White _____

TYMPANOGRAM

PRESSURE IN daPa

Static Compliance:

R	cc
2	
1	
L	cc
2	
1	

Normal: .3 - 1.75cc

Ear Canal Volume

Right	Left

C₁ =

Answers for Figure 4-10

1. SAT scores were obtained because SRT scores could not be established. With hearing losses of this nature, it is not unusual to be unable to measure SRT. Although it was not attempted, it may be possible to establish SRT using auditory–visual input if the vocabulary is controlled to be within the receptive level of the child.

2. Spondees were used to obtain SATs. Remember that understanding of these words is not necessary for this measure.

3. The response mode was conditioned play audiometry. This technique involves some motor act in response to sound that is part of a play activity (e.g., putting a ring on a peg each time a stimulus is heard). Conditioned play audiometry is generally more motivating to a child than the conventional hand-raising response.

4. The SAT scores agree well with the pure tone thresholds. Since there was no response to tone at 1000 Hz or 2000 Hz, pure tone averages could not be computed. However, the SAT score of 90 dB HL in the right ear is in general agreement with the pure tone thresholds of 80 dB HL at 250 Hz and 100 dB HL at 500 Hz, and the SAT score of 100 dB HL in the left ear is in general agreement with the pure tone threshold of 100 dB HL at 500 Hz.

QUESTIONS FOR FIGURE 4-11

Case History Information Mrs. K has ben aware of a bilateral hearing loss for 10 years. It has been diagnosed as otosclerosis. Although surgery has been suggested, she prefers to use binaural hearing aids instead.

1. What are the MCLs?
2. What are the UCLs?
3. How do these scores relate to the SRTs?
4. Is there any evidence of a tolerance problem?

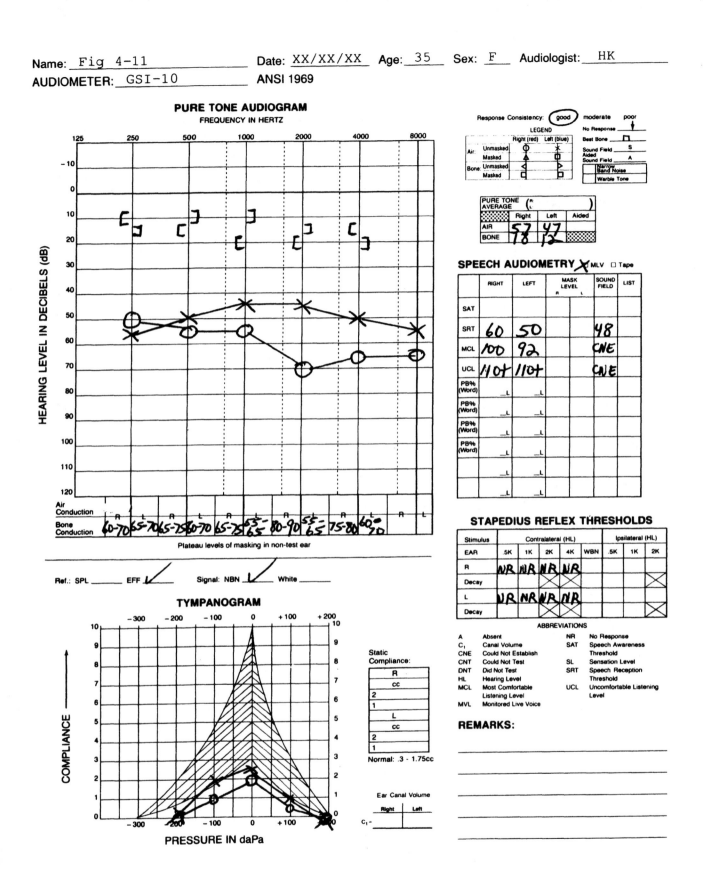

Name: Fig 4-11   Date: XX/XX/XX   Age: 35   Sex: F   Audiologist: HK

AUDIOMETER: GSI-10   ANSI 1969

PURE TONE AUDIOGRAM
FREQUENCY IN HERTZ

Response Consistency: (good) moderate poor

No Response

LEGEND

		Right (red)	Left (blue)
Air:	Unmasked	O	X
	Masked	△	☐
Bone:	Unmasked	⊏	⊐
	Masked	☐	▷

Best Bone
Sound Field: S
Aided
Sound Field: A
Narrow Band Noise
Warble Tone

PURE TONE AVERAGE	Right	Left	Aided
AIR	57	47	
BONE	78	72	

SPEECH AUDIOMETRY ☒ MLV ☐ Tape

	RIGHT	LEFT	MASK LEVEL R	MASK LEVEL L	SOUND FIELD	LIST
SAT						
SRT	60	50			48	
MCL	100	92			CNE	
UCL	110+	110+			CNE	
PB% (Word)	_L	_L				
PB% (Word)	_L	_L				
PB% (Word)	_L	_L				
PB% (Word)	_L	_L				
	_L	_L				
	_L	_L				

Air Conduction: R L R L R L R L R L R L R L R L
Bone Conduction: 60-70 65-70 65-75 60-70 65-75 65 55-65 80-90 55-65 75-80 60-70

Plateau levels of masking in non-test ear

Ref.: SPL _____ EFF ✓ Signal: NBN ✓ White _____

TYMPANOGRAM

PRESSURE IN daPa

Static Compliance:

R	
	cc
2	
1	
L	
	cc
2	
1	

Normal: .3 - 1.75cc

Ear Canal Volume

Right	Left

$C_1 =$

STAPEDIUS REFLEX THRESHOLDS

Stimulus	Contralateral (HL)					Ipsilateral (HL)		
EAR	.5K	1K	2K	4K	WBN	.5K	1K	2K
R	NR	NR	NR	NR				
Decay								
L	NR	NR	NR	NR				
Decay								

ABBREVIATIONS

A	Absent	NR	No Response
C₁	Canal Volume	SAT	Speech Awareness
CNE	Could Not Establish		Threshold
CNT	Could Not Test	SL	Sensation Level
DNT	Did Not Test	SRT	Speech Reception
HL	Hearing Level		Threshold
MCL	Most Comfortable	UCL	Uncomfortable Listening
	Listening Level		Level
MVL	Monitored Live Voice		

REMARKS:

_____

_____

_____

_____

Interpreting Speech Audiometry

Answers for Figure 4-11

1. The MCL for the right ear is 100 dB HL; the MCL for the left ear is 92 dB HL.
2. The UCLs for both ears exceed the limits of the audiometer.
3. Both MCLs are at least 40 dB more intense than the SRTs. Although the actual hearing levels are considerably higher than what one would expect for normal ears, the sensation levels are similar. This pattern is consistent with conductive loss. The high UCLs are also consistent with conductive loss. This client shows a large dynamic range.
4. The normal range between SRTs and MCLs and the high UCLs indicates that there are no tolerance problems in either ear.

QUESTIONS FOR FIGURE 4-12

Case History Information This 52-year-old man has worked on an automobile production line for 25 years. He reports gradual onset of hearing loss with gradually increasing communication difficulty. He has had difficulty adjusting to amplification and uses his hearing aid on a part-time basis.

1. What are the MCLs of the two ears?
2. What are the UCLs of the two ears?
3. What are the dynamic ranges of the two ears?
4. Is there any evidence of tolerance problems?
5. Do any of the test results suggest why this man might be having difficulty adjusting to amplification?

Name: Fig 4-12   Date: XX/XX/XX   Age: 52   Sex: M   Audiologist: HK
AUDIOMETER: GSI-10   ANSI 1969

PURE TONE AUDIOGRAM
FREQUENCY IN HERTZ

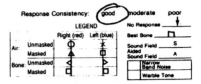

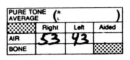

PURE TONE AVERAGE (R L)	Right	Left	Aided
AIR	53	43	
BONE			

SPEECH AUDIOMETRY ☑ MLV ☐ Tape

	RIGHT	LEFT	MASK LEVEL R	MASK LEVEL L	SOUND FIELD	LIST
SAT						
SRT	40	28			24	
MCL	56	50			44	
UCL	82	80			CNE	
PB% (Word)	_L_	_L_				
PB% (Word)	_L_	_L_				
PB% (Word)	_L_	_L_				
PB% (Word)	_L_	_L_				
	_L_	_L_				
	_L_	_L_				

Air Conduction: R L R L R L R L R L R L
Bone Conduction: 80 90 40-60

Plateau levels of masking in non-test ear

Ref.: SPL ___ EFF ✓   Signal: NBN ✓   White ___

STAPEDIUS REFLEX THRESHOLDS

Stimulus	Contralateral (HL)					Ipsilateral (HL)		
EAR	.5K	1K	2K	4K	WBN	.5K	1K	2K
R	80	105	110	NR				
Decay			X	X				X
L	80	85	NR	NR				
Decay			X	X				X

ABBREVIATIONS

A	Absent	NR	No Response
C₁	Canal Volume	SAT	Speech Awareness
CNE	Could Not Establish		Threshold
CNT	Could Not Test	SL	Sensation Level
DNT	Did Not Test	SRT	Speech Reception
HL	Hearing Level		Threshold
MCL	Most Comfortable	UCL	Uncomfortable Listening
	Listening Level		Level
MVL	Monitored Live Voice		

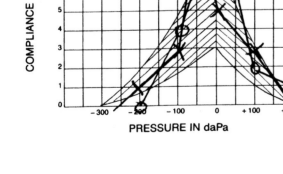

TYMPANOGRAM

Static Compliance:

R	
cc	
2	
1	

L	
cc	
2	
1	

Normal: .3 - 1.75cc

Ear Canal Volume

Right	Left
C₁ =	

REMARKS:
Two-frequency pure tone averages are: right-43dB, left-25dB

Answers for Figure 4-12

1. The MCLs are 56 dB HL in the right ear and 50 dB HL in the left ear.
2. The UCLs are 82 dB HL in the right ear and 80 dB HL in the left ear.
3. The dynamic range in the right ear is 42 dB HL; the dynamic range in the left ear is 52 dB HL.
4. Tolerance problems exist in both ears. In the right ear, there is only a 16-dB difference between SRT and MCL, with a UCL that is below the 90–100 dB expected of ears without tolerance problems. In the left ear, the difference between SRT and MCL is only 22 dB, and the UCL is even lower than that in the right ear. Both ears show restricted dynamic ranges.
5. The difficulty adjusting to amplification may be attributable to the low MCLs and UCLs, which make it difficult for the client to listen to amplified sound.

QUESTIONS FOR FIGURE 4-13

Supplementary Information This audiogram is the same as that in Figure 4-11.

1. What are the word recognition scores for the right ear? the left ear? sound field?
2. What kinds of materials were used?
3. At what sensation levels were the stimuli presented?
4. Do these word recognition scores represent PB Max? How do you know?

Name: Fig 4-13 **Date:** XX/XX/XX **Age:** 35 **Sex:** F **Audiologist:** HK

AUDIOMETER: GSI-10 **ANSI** 1969

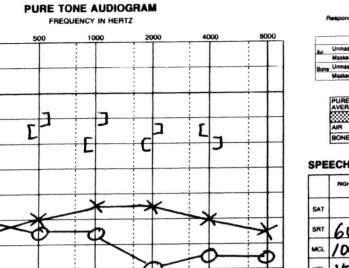

PURE TONE AUDIOGRAM
FREQUENCY IN HERTZ

Air Conduction (R / L):
60-70 / 65-70 / 65-75 / 60-70 / 65-75 / 55-65 / 80-90 / 55-65 / 75-80 / 60-70

Plateau levels of masking in non-test ear

Ref.: SPL _____ EFF ✓ Signal: NBN ✓ White _____

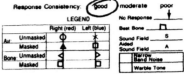

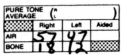

PURE TONE AVERAGE (R / L)

	Right	Left	Aided
AIR	57	47	
BONE	18	12	

SPEECH AUDIOMETRY □ MLV ✗ Tape

	RIGHT	LEFT	MASK LEVEL (R / L)	SOUND FIELD	LIST
SAT					CID-W22
SRT	60	50		48	
MCL	100	92		CNE	
UCL	110+	110+		CNE	
PB% (Word)	100 (40dB)	100 (90dB)		100 (1A, 1B, 2A)	
PB% (Word)	L	L			
PB% (Word)	L	L			
	L	L			
	L	L			

STAPEDIUS REFLEX THRESHOLDS

Stimulus	Contralateral (HL)					Ipsilateral (HL)		
EAR	.5K	1K	2K	4K	WBN	.5K	1K	2K
R	NR	NR	NR	NR				
Decay								
L	NR	NR	NR	NR				
Decay								

ABBREVIATIONS

A — Absent
C₁ — Canal Volume
CNE — Could Not Establish
CNT — Could Not Test
DNT — Did Not Test
HL — Hearing Level
MCL — Most Comfortable Listening Level
MVL — Monitored Live Voice

NR — No Response
SAT — Speech Awareness Threshold
SL — Sensation Level
SRT — Speech Reception Threshold
UCL — Uncomfortable Listening Level

TYMPANOGRAM

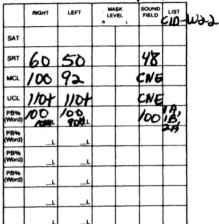

PRESSURE IN daPa

Static Compliance:

R	
	cc
2	
1	

L	
	cc
2	
1	

Normal: .3 - 1.75cc

Ear Canal Volume

Right	Left
C₁	

REMARKS: Recorded CID-22 word lists were used for word recognition, speech noise was used as the masker

Answers for Figure 4-13

1. The word recognition score for the right ear is 100%; the word recognition scores for the left ear and for the sound field condition are also 100%.
2. CID W-22 words were used to obtain word recognition scores. These are monosyllables frequently referred to as PB words.
3. These words were presented at 40 dB SL in each ear. Note that the 40-dB SL presentation levels correspond to or are very close to MCL. That, plus the fact that there is no evidence of a tolerance problem, makes these presentation levels good choices.
4. These word recognition scores definitely represent PB Max. Remember that PB Max is the best score the client is capable of giving, and 100% is the best score possible on the test. In normal clinical practice, if the client gives a score of 90% or better at the first word recognition presentation level, we may assume that score represents PB Max since it is normal speech understanding.

QUESTIONS FOR FIGURE 4-14

Supplementary Information This audiogram is the same as that in Figure 4-12.

1. Which word recognition score would you accept for the right ear? for the left ear? for sound field?
2. Why was a 40-dB sensation level not used for presentation of words to the right ear?
3. Do we have PB Max for the right ear? the left ear? sound field?

Name: Fig 4-14   **Date:** XX/XX/XX   **Age:** 52   **Sex:** M   **Audiologist:** HK

AUDIOMETER: GSI-10   **ANSI 1969**

PURE TONE AUDIOGRAM
FREQUENCY IN HERTZ

Response Consistency: (good) moderate poor

LEGEND

		Right (red)	Left (blue)	
Air:	Unmasked			No Response
	Masked			Best Bone
Bone:	Unmasked			Sound Field S
	Masked			Aided Sound Field A

Narrow Band Noise
Warble Tone

PURE TONE AVERAGE (R L)			
	Right	Left	Aided
AIR	53	43	
BONE			

SPEECH AUDIOMETRY MLV Tape

	RIGHT	LEFT	MASK LEVEL R	MASK LEVEL L	SOUND FIELD	LIST
SAT						CID-W22
SRT	40	28			24	
MCL	56	50			44	
UCL	82	80			CNE	
PB% (Word)	56 30SL	72 30SL			76 30SL	2A 3A, 4B
PB% (Word)	52 34SL	70 40SL			76 20SL	1A 3B, 3B
PB% (Word)	46 20SL	L				1B
PB% (Word)	L	L				
	L	L				
	L	L				

STAPEDIUS REFLEX THRESHOLDS

Stimulus	Contralateral (HL)					Ipsilateral (HL)		
EAR	.5K	1K	2K	4K	WBN	.5K	1K	2K
R	80	105	110	NR				
Decay								
L	80	85	NR	NR				
Decay								

ABBREVIATIONS

A	Absent	NR	No Response
C₁	Canal Volume	SAT	Speech Awareness
CNE	Could Not Establish		Threshold
CNT	Could Not Test	SL	Sensation Level
DNT	Did Not Test	SRT	Speech Reception
HL	Hearing Level		Threshold
MCL	Most Comfortable	UCL	Uncomfortable Listening
	Listening Level		Level
MVL	Monitored Live Voice		

Air Conduction — Bone Conduction

80- 40-
90 60

Plateau levels of masking in non-test ear

Ref.: SPL _____ EFF _____   Signal: NBN _____ White _____

TYMPANOGRAM

PRESSURE IN daPa

Static Compliance:

R	
cc	
2	
1	
L	
cc	
2	
1	

Normal: .3 - 1.75cc

Ear Canal Volume

Right	Left

C₁ =

REMARKS:

_____

_____

_____

_____

_____

Interpreting Speech Audiometry

Answers for Figure 4-14

1. The most acceptable word recognition score for the right ear is 56%; for the left ear the word recognition score is 72%; for the sound field the score is 76%. When we obtain multiple scores for an ear, we accept the highest one.

2. A 40-dB sensation level was not used for presentation of words to the right ear because the words would then be presented at 80 dB HL, which is close to the UCL of 82 dB HL. We try to avoid a presentation level that might prove uncomfortable. Before giving a full list, it is best to present a few words to the client at a desired presentation level to find out if it is tolerable.

3. We can feel confident that PB Max has been obtained in each ear and also in the sound field. In the right ear, word recognition scores of 56% and 52% were obtained at two different sensation levels; these scores are not significantly different from each other. At a sensation level of 20 dB, a significantly poorer score was obtained, suggesting that the presentation level was not intense enough for maximum performance. Note that the presentation level giving poorest word recognition was closest to MCL. In many cases, MCL is not a good guide for the best presentation level for word recognition. If possible, presentation levels of less than 26 dB SL should not be used with CID W-22 words because the normal performance-intensity function does not plateau until that level is reached.

QUESTIONS FOR FIGURE 4-15

Case History Information This 14-year-old boy is developmentally delayed as well as hearing impaired and has semi-intelligible speech. He has been using binaural hearing aids consistently since early childhood.

1. Do the unaided word recognition scores represent PB Max? How do you know?
2. Do the aided word recognition scores represent PB Max? How do you know?
3. What can you conclude about aided versus unaided performance?
4. What kind of stimulus material was used to obtain word recognition scores? Why do you think that type of material was used?

Name: Fig 4-15   Date: XX/XX/XX   Age: 14   Sex: M   Audiologist: HK

AUDIOMETER: _____   ANSI 1969

PURE TONE AUDIOGRAM

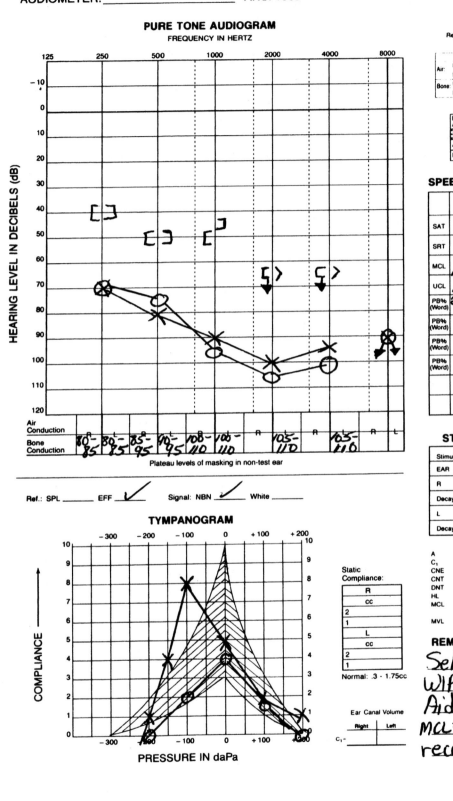

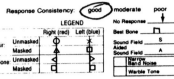

PURE TONE AVERAGE (R L)			
	Right	Left	Aided
AIR	92	90	
BONE	CNE	53	

SPEECH AUDIOMETRY ☒MLV ☐ Tape

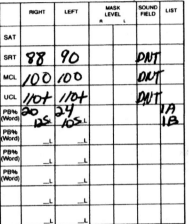

	RIGHT	LEFT	MASK LEVEL R L	SOUND FIELD	LIST
SAT					
SRT	88	90		DNT	
MCL	100	100		DNT	
UCL	110+	110+		DNT	
PB% (Word)	20 125 L	24 105 L			1A 1B
PB% (Word)	_L	_L			
PB% (Word)	_L	_L			
PB% (Word)	_L	_L			
	_L	_L			
	_L	_L			

STAPEDIUS REFLEX THRESHOLDS

Stimulus	Contralateral (HL)					Ipsilateral (HL)		
EAR	.5K	1K	2K	4K	WBN	.5K	1K	2K
R	NR	NR	NR	NR		✕		
Decay	✕					✕		
L	NR	NR	NR	NR		✕		
Decay	✕					✕		

ABBREVIATIONS

A	Absent	NR	No Response
C₁	Canal Volume	SAT	Speech Awareness
CNE	Could Not Establish		Threshold
CNT	Could Not Test	SL	Sensation Level
DNT	Did Not Test	SRT	Speech Reception
HL	Hearing Level		Threshold
MCL	Most Comfortable	UCL	Uncomfortable Listening
	Listening Level		Level
MVL	Monitored Live Voice		

REMARKS:

Selected spondees for SRT;
WIPI for word recognition
Aided scores, binaural: SRT=34dB,
MCL=66dB, UCL=80+dB. Word
recognition=68% at 40dB SL
72% at 30dB SL

TYMPANOGRAM

Static Compliance:

R	
	cc
2	
1	

L	
	cc
2	
1	

Normal: .3 - 1.75cc

Ear Canal Volume

	Right	Left
C₁		

Ref.: SPL _____ EFF ✓   Signal: NBN ✓   White _____

Answers for Figure 4-15

1. The unaided word recognition scores do not represent PB Max for this young man. It is probable that if the output limits of the audiometer were higher, we could obtain higher scores. Note that we were forced to use sensation levels of 12 dB in the right ear and 10 dB in the left because those levels were at audiometric limits. However, when the words were delivered at a higher level via the gain from the hearing aid a higher word recognition score was obtained.

2. The aided word recognition scores do represent PB Max because the scores at two different presentation levels, 40 dB SL and 30 dB SL, are not significantly different.

3. The hearing aid significantly improves understanding of speech. Not only can this client hear speech at a much lower level (34 dB as compared to 88 dB unaided), but he can also understand speech presented at a comfortable listening level significantly better (72% as compared to 24% unaided).

4. The WIPI test was used to obtain all word recognition scores. This is a commercial test consisting of pictures of minimally paired words. The client is shown a group of pictures for each test item, and the task is to point to the picture spoken by the examiner. This type of material was used for two reasons. First, the language used in the test is at a young child's level, and controlled language is necessary for this client because of his retardation. Second, a picture pointing response is necessary because of the client's semi-intelligible speech. Keep in mind, however, that scores obtained with this test cannot be compared to scores obtained with other types of word recognition material.

QUESTIONS FOR FIGURE 4-16

Case History Information This 8-year-old girl has had a history of recurrent middle ear infections. The present evaluation was performed because she failed a hearing screening test in school.

1. What degree of word recognition difficulty exists in the right ear? in the left ear? in the sound field?
2. Are the differences between word recognition scores in the right and left ears significant?
3. Are the differences between the two word recognition scores obtained in the left ear significant?
4. How do the word recognition scores relate to the other information on the audiogram?

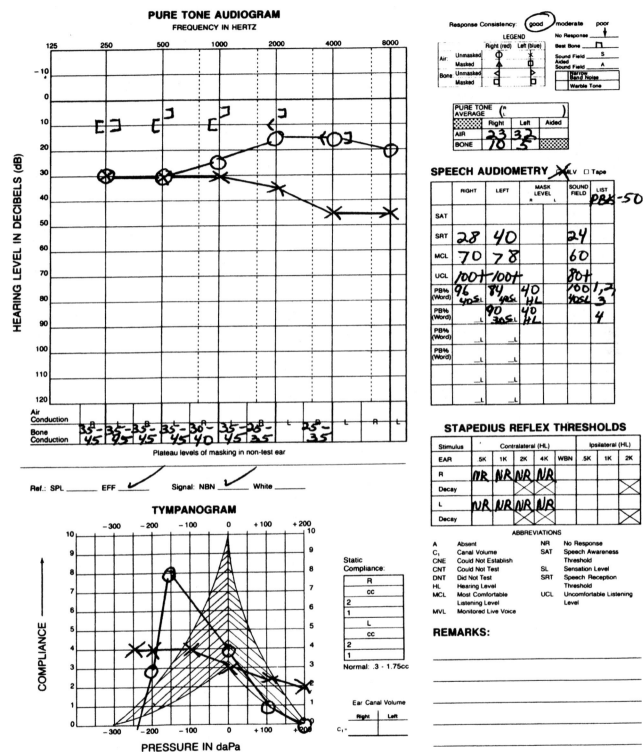

PURE TONE AUDIOGRAM
FREQUENCY IN HERTZ

Name: Fig 4-16   Date: XX/XX/XX   Age: 8   Sex: F   Audiologist: HK

AUDIOMETER: GSI-10   ANSI 1969

Response Consistency: (good) moderate poor

PURE TONE AVERAGE (R / L)	Right	Left	Aided
AIR	23	32	
BONE	10	5	

SPEECH AUDIOMETRY ☒ MLV ☐ Tape

	RIGHT	LEFT	MASK LEVEL R	MASK LEVEL L	SOUND FIELD	LIST PB-50
SAT						
SRT	28	40			24	
MCL	70	78			60	
UCL	100+	100+			80+	
PB% (Word)	96 40SL	84 40SL	40 HL		100 40SL	1,2 3
PB% (Word)		90 30SL	40 HL			4
PB% (Word)	L	L				
PB% (Word)	L	L				
	L	L				
	L	L				

STAPEDIUS REFLEX THRESHOLDS

Stimulus	Contralateral (HL) .5K	1K	2K	4K	WBN	Ipsilateral (HL) .5K	1K	2K
EAR R	NR	NR	NR	NR				
Decay			X	X				X
L	NR	NR	NR	NR				
Decay			X	X				X

ABBREVIATIONS

A	Absent	NR	No Response
C₁	Canal Volume	SAT	Speech Awareness
CNE	Could Not Establish		Threshold
CNT	Could Not Test	SL	Sensation Level
DNT	Did Not Test	SRT	Speech Reception
HL	Hearing Level		Threshold
MCL	Most Comfortable	UCL	Uncomfortable Listening
	Listening Level		Level
MVL	Monitored Live Voice		

REMARKS:

Air Conduction / Bone Conduction plateau levels of masking in non-test ear:
35 35 35 35 30 35 25 25
45 45 45 45 40 45 35 35

Plateau levels of masking in non-test ear

Ref.: SPL _____ EFF _____ Signal: NBN _____ White _____

TYMPANOGRAM
PRESSURE IN daPa

Static Compliance:

R	
cc	
2	
1	
L	
cc	
2	
1	

Normal: .3 - 1.75cc

Ear Canal Volume

Right	Left
C₁ =	

Interpreting Speech Audiometry

Answers for Figure 4-16

1. The word recognition scores in both ears and in the sound field are within normal limits.
2. The differences between the word recognition scores obtained for the right and left ears are not significant. A difference of 6% is not considered significant, even when PB Max is 90% or higher.
3. The two word recognition scores obtained in the left ear are not significantly different since they vary by only 6%.
4. The normal word recognition scores in the right and left ears are consistent with the large air–bone gaps and essentially normal bone conduction seen on the audiogram. The abnormal tympanograms (Type C in the right ear and Type B in the left) and the absence of acoustic reflexes suggest conductive problems in both ears; this is consistent with normal word recognition scores. Also consistent with the conductive losses are the high UCLs (100+) and large dynamic ranges.

QUESTIONS FOR FIGURE 4-17

Case History Information This man is a veteran whose hearing was damaged on the battlefield. He uses a hearing aid in the left ear with partial success because he finds listening to amplified conversation in the presence of competing noise very difficult.

1. What degree of word recognition difficulty exists in the right ear? in the left ear?
2. Are the word recognition scores obtained in the right ear significantly different from each other?
3. Do we have PB Max in the right ear?
4. Why was a higher presentation level not used in the right ear?
5. Are the word recognition scores in the right ear significantly different from those in the left ear?
6. How do the word recognition scores relate to the other information on the audiogram?

Name: Fig 4-17   **Date:** XX/XX/XX   **Age:** 42   **Sex:** M   **Audiologist:** HK
AUDIOMETER: GSI-10   **ANSI 1969**

PURE TONE AUDIOGRAM
FREQUENCY IN HERTZ

Response Consistency: (good) moderate poor

LEGEND

		Right (red)	Left (blue)	
Air:	Unmasked	○	×	
	Masked	▲	▢	
Bone:	Unmasked		▷	
	Masked	▢	▢	

No Response ↓
Best Bone ▢
Sound Field ___ S
Aided
Sound Field ___ A
Narrow Band Noise
Warble Tone

PURE TONE AVERAGE (R / L)

	Right	Left	Aided
AIR	68	47	
BONE			

SPEECH AUDIOMETRY ✗ MLV ☐ Tape

	RIGHT	LEFT	MASK LEVEL R	L	SOUND FIELD	LIST
SAT						CID W22
SRT	56					
MCL	70					
UCL	80					
PB% (Word)	40 / 20 SL	70 / 30 SL				1A / 1B
PB% (Word)	32 / 16 SL	66 / 36 SL				2A / 2B
PB% (Word)	_L_	_L_				
PB% (Word)	_L_	_L_				
	_L_	_L_				
	_L_	_L_				

Air Conduction / Bone Conduction

Air Conduction	R	L	R	L	R	R	R	R	L
Bone Conduction					60-70	65-75	60-70		

Plateau levels of masking in non-test ear

Ref.: SPL _____ EFF _____   Signal: NBN ✓ White _____

TYMPANOGRAM

PRESSURE IN daPa

Static Compliance:

R	cc
2	
1	

L	cc
2	
1	

Normal: .3 - 1.75cc

Ear Canal Volume

Right	Left

C₁ =

STAPEDIUS REFLEX THRESHOLDS

Stimulus	Contralateral (HL)					Ipsilateral (HL)		
EAR	.5K	1K	2K	4K	WBN	.5K	1K	2K
R	75	105	NR	NR				
Decay								
L	80	90	100	95				
Decay								

ABBREVIATIONS

A	Absent	NR	No Response
C₁	Canal Volume	SAT	Speech Awareness Threshold
CNE	Could Not Establish		
CNT	Could Not Test	SL	Sensation Level
DNT	Did Not Test	SRT	Speech Reception Threshold
HL	Hearing Level		
MCL	Most Comfortable Listening Level	UCL	Uncomfortable Listening Level
MVL	Monitored Live Voice		

REMARKS:

_____
_____
_____
_____
_____

Interpreting Speech Audiometry

193

Answers for Figure 4-17

1. This man has very poor word recognition in the right ear. It is unlikely that he could follow a conversation if he had to rely only on the auditory ability of that ear. A moderate word recognition problem exists in the left ear.

2. The word recognition scores obtained in the right ear are not significantly different from each other since the difference is only 8%.

3. We do not know whether we have PB Max in the right ear since increasing the presentation level improves word recognition. A sensation level higher than 20 dB SL may yield a higher score.

4. A higher presentation level was not used in the right ear because a level exceeding 20 dB SL would be very close to the UCL.

5. The very poor word recognition scores in the right ear are consistent with the sharply falling configuration and the restricted dynamic range. The less severe problem in the left ear is consistent with the flatter pure tone configuration and the wider dynamic range. Note that the hearing aid was fitted to the left ear primarily because of the better word recognition, but secondarily because of the higher UCL and flatter configuration.

QUESTIONS FOR FIGURE 4-18

Case History Information During the past year this man has become aware of having to ask some people to raise the level of their voices in some situations. There is a history of otosclerosis in his family.

1. What is PB Max in the right ear? in the left? in the sound field?
2. Is there any evidence of rollover in either ear or in the sound field?
3. From the history and the pure tone test results, would you expect to find rollover?

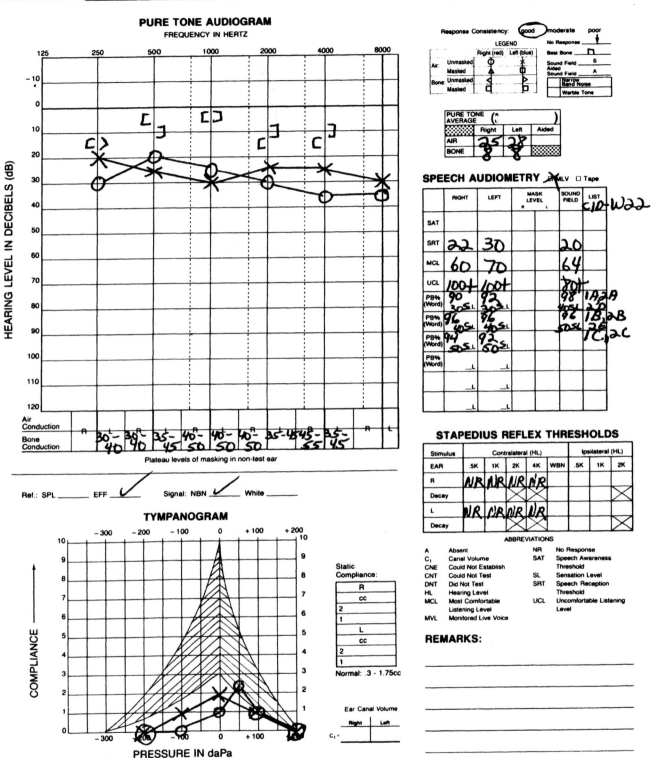

PURE TONE AUDIOGRAM

FREQUENCY IN HERTZ

Name: Fig 4-18   Date: XX/XX/XX   Age: 28   Sex: M   Audiologist: HK
AUDIOMETER: GSI-10   ANSI 1969

Air Conduction / Bone Conduction (plateau levels of masking in non-test ear):

	250	500	1000	2000	4000	8000
Bone R	30	35	40	40	35	35
Bone L	40/70	45	50/50	50	45/55	45

Ref.: SPL ___ EFF ✓ Signal: NBN ✓ White ___

TYMPANOGRAM

PRESSURE IN daPa

Static Compliance:
R: ___ cc
L: ___ cc
Normal: .3 - 1.75cc

Ear Canal Volume

SPEECH AUDIOMETRY ☑ MLV ☐ Tape

LIST: C10 W22

	RIGHT	LEFT	MASK LEVEL R L	SOUND FIELD	LIST
SAT					
SRT	22	30		20	
MCL	60	70		64	
UCL	100+	100+		80+	
PB% (Word)	90 30SL	92 30SL		98 40SL	1A,2A
PB% (Word)	96 40SL	96 40SL		92 50SL	1B,2B 2G
PB% (Word)	94 50SL	92 50SL			1C,2C
PB% (Word)					

STAPEDIUS REFLEX THRESHOLDS

Stimulus	Contralateral (HL)					Ipsilateral (HL)		
EAR	.5K	1K	2K	4K	WBN	.5K	1K	2K
R	NR	NR	NR	NR				
Decay								
L	NR	NR	NR	NR				
Decay								

ABBREVIATIONS

A	Absent	NR	No Response
C₁	Canal Volume	SAT	Speech Awareness Threshold
CNE	Could Not Establish		
CNT	Could Not Test	SL	Sensation Level
DNT	Did Not Test	SRT	Speech Reception Threshold
HL	Hearing Level		
MCL	Most Comfortable Listening Level	UCL	Uncomfortable Listening Level
MVL	Monitored Live Voice		

REMARKS:

_____

_____

_____

_____

_____

Interpreting Speech Audiometry

195

Answers for Figure 4-18

1. PB Max is 96% in the right ear, 96% in the left ear, and 98% in the sound field.
2. There is no evidence of rollover in either ear or in the sound field. The slight decreases in word recognition score with increasing level of presentation are not significant differences.
3. Since both the history and pure tone information suggest a middle ear problem, rollover would not be expected. Remember, rollover suggests a retrocochlear problem, or it may occur in a recruiting ear.

QUESTIONS FOR FIGURE 4-19

Case History Information For the past two years this woman has been aware that speech sounds distorted. The situation has gradually been getting worse. She reports continuous tinnitus in her right ear.

1. Is there evidence of rollover in either ear or in the sound field?
2. Are word recognition scores consistent with the rest of the audiogram?
3. Do the word recognition scores in the right ear suggest a particular site of lesion?

Name: Fig 4-19   **Date:** XX/XX/XX   **Age:** 32   **Sex:** F   **Audiologist:** HK
AUDIOMETER: GSI-10   **ANSI 1969**

PURE TONE AUDIOGRAM
FREQUENCY IN HERTZ

HEARING LEVEL IN DECIBELS (dB)

Frequencies: 125, 250, 500, 1000, 2000, 4000, 8000

Plateau levels of masking in non-test ear

Air Conduction: R L R L R L R L R L R L R L
Bone Conduction

Ref.: SPL _____ EFF _____   Signal: NBN _____ White _____

Response Consistency: (good) moderate poor

LEGEND
		Right (red)	Left (blue)
Air	Unmasked	O	X
	Masked	△	☐
Bone	Unmasked	<	>
	Masked	☐	☐

No Response
Best Bone ☐
Sound Field S
Aided Sound Field A
Narrow Band Noise
Warble Tone

PURE TONE AVERAGE (R L)
	Right	Left	Aided
AIR	20	18	
BONE			

SPEECH AUDIOMETRY ☑ MLV ☐ Tape

	RIGHT	LEFT	MASK LEVEL R L	SOUND FIELD	LIST C1DW22
SAT	22	16		14	
SRT	40	22		18	
MCL	64	48		50	
UCL	100+	100		80+	
PB% (Word)	40 30SL	68 30SL		72 30SL	1A,2B, 2C
PB% (Word)	32 40SL	66 40SL		70 36SL	2D,2E, 1B
PB% (Word)	20 50SL	64 50SL			2B 2C
PB% (Word)	_	_			
PB% (Word)	_	_			

STAPEDIUS REFLEX THRESHOLDS

Stimulus	Contralateral (HL)					Ipsilateral (HL)		
EAR	.5K	1K	2K	4K	WBN	.5K	1K	2K
R	NR	NR	NR	NR		NR	NR	NR
Decay			☒	☒				
L	NR	NR	NR	NR		85	90	90
Decay			☒	☒				☒

ABBREVIATIONS

A	Absent	NR	No Response
C₁	Canal Volume	SAT	Speech Awareness
CNE	Could Not Establish		Threshold
CNT	Could Not Test	SL	Sensation Level
DNT	Did Not Test	SRT	Speech Reception
HL	Hearing Level		Threshold
MCL	Most Comfortable	UCL	Uncomfortable Listening
	Listening Level		Level
MVL	Monitored Live Voice		

REMARKS:

_____

_____

_____

_____

_____

TYMPANOGRAM

PRESSURE IN daPa

COMPLIANCE

Pressure: -300, -200, -100, 0, +100, +200

Static Compliance:
R
cc
2
1

L
cc
2
1

Normal: .3 - 1.75cc

Ear Canal Volume
Right	Left

C₁

Answers for Figure 4-19

1. Rollover is present in the right ear. PB Max of 40% was obtained at a presentation level of 30 dB SL; subsequent increases in presentation level resulted in decreased word recognition scores to a maximum of 20%. Although scores in the left ear and in the sound field decreased slightly with increasing presentation levels, these decreases were not large enough to be significant. There is no evidence of rollover in the left ear or in the sound field.

2. Word recognition scores are consistent with other test results. In the right ear the poor agreement between pure tone average and SRT suggests extremely poor speech understanding. Moreover, the very poor word recognition in the presence of a mild pure tone loss is consistent with a rollover phenomenon.

   In the left ear the SRT agrees well with the pure tone average, and the word recognition scores reveal moderate difficulty understanding speech when it is comfortably loud. There is no evidence of rollover. The sound field test results reflect the better ear.

3. The extremely poor word recognition in the right ear in the presence of a mild pure tone loss is suggestive of a retrocochlear problem. The presence of rollover and the absence of contralateral and ipsilateral acoustic reflexes are additional support for this hypothesis. In contrast, the better word recognition, lack of rollover, and presence of ipsilateral reflexes suggest cochlear site of lesion in the left ear. It must be stressed, however, that other site-of-lesion tests must be performed before diagnosis can be made.

QUESTIONS FOR FIGURE 4-20

Case History Information This woman has been aware of a mild hearing loss in her left ear for about five years but did not report appreciable communication difficulty until last year. At that time she suffered severe vertigo, severe tinnitus in her right ear, and a drop in her hearing in that ear. Although the right ear symptoms subsided with some recovery of hearing, attacks have been recurrent. At present she is extremely sensitive to loud sound in her right ear.

1. Is there evidence of rollover in either ear or in the sound field?
2. Does the total audiometric pattern suggest a retrocochlear site of lesion in either ear?
3. Why were higher presentation levels not used in the right ear?

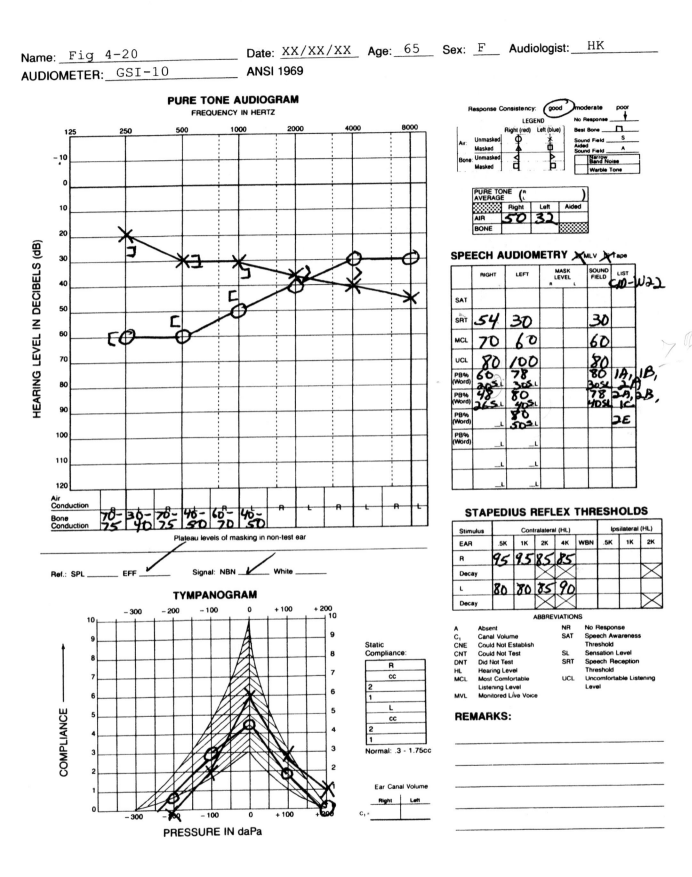

Answers for Figure 4-20

1. There is evidence of rollover in the right ear since the word recognition score decreased by 12% with a 6-dB increase in presentation level. Word recognition scores in the left ear and in the sound field did not change significantly with an increase in presentation level.

2. In the left ear there is nothing to suggest retrocochlear site of lesion. The word recognition scores reveal only slight difficulty, the SRT is consistent with the pure tone average, and there is nothing in the history to suggest such a problem. Although there is rollover in the right ear, all other information suggests a cochlear problem. The case history suggests a Ménière's-like problem; the UCL is reduced with a subsequent narrow dynamic range, suggesting recruitment, which is a strong sign of cochlear site of lesion. Although speech understanding is poor, it is consistent with the degree of pure tone loss and the restricted dynamic range. It is quite likely that the rollover seen in the right ear is due to the fact that the second score was obtained at a level that the client identified as her UCL (26 dB SL = 80 dB HL).

3. Higher presentation levels were not used in the right ear because any level above 26 dB SL would exceed the UCL for that ear.

QUESTIONS FOR FIGURE 4-21

Case History Information This woman is being evaluated for a hearing aid in her left ear. She experiences difficulty hearing at business meetings and in other situations where the speaker has a soft voice.

1. What is the unaided speech understanding at average conversational level in the sound field?
2. Why do you think this score is poorer than the word recognition score for the better ear?
3. How does the aided sound field word recognition at average conversational level compare with the unaided score?
4. Do you feel the hearing aid is helping? Justify your answer by citing test scores.

Name: Fig 4-21　　　Date: XX/XX/XX　Age: 35　Sex: F　Audiologist: HK
AUDIOMETER: GSI-10　　　ANSI 1969

PURE TONE AUDIOGRAM
FREQUENCY IN HERTZ

Response Consistency:　good　moderate　poor

	LEGEND			No Response	↓
		Right (red)	Left (blue)	Best Bone	⊓
Air:	Unmasked	○	×	Sound Field	S
	Masked	△	▢	Aided Sound Field	A
Bone:	Unmasked	<	>	Narrow Band Noise	
	Masked	▢	▢	Warble Tone	

PURE TONE AVERAGE (R / L)

	Right	Left	Aided
AIR	20	30	12
BONE	25	3	

SPEECH AUDIOMETRY　☐ MLV　☒ Tape

LIST: CID-W22

	RIGHT	LEFT	MASK LEVEL R	MASK LEVEL L	SOUND FIELD
SAT					
SRT	24	32			24
MCL	42	74			
UCL	90	100+			
PB% (Word)	78 / 30SL	90 / 40SL			80 / 30HL 1A,2A,1B
PB% (Word)	L	L			
PB% (Word)	L	L			
PB% (Word)	L	L			
	L	L			
	L	L			

STAPEDIUS REFLEX THRESHOLDS

Stimulus	Contralateral (HL)					Ipsilateral (HL)		
EAR	.5K	1K	2K	4K	WBN	5K	1K	2K
R	105	105	110	NR				×
Decay								
L	NR	NR	NR	NR				×
Decay								

ABBREVIATIONS

A	Absent	NR	No Response
C₁	Canal Volume	SAT	Speech Awareness
CNE	Could Not Establish		Threshold
CNT	Could Not Test	SL	Sensation Level
DNT	Did Not Test	SRT	Speech Reception
HL	Hearing Level		Threshold
MCL	Most Comfortable	UCL	Uncomfortable Listening
	Listening Level		Level
MVL	Monitored Live Voice		

REMARKS:

Hearing aid in left ear;
Word recognition = 94%
at 50 dB HL (CID-W22 list 2B)

TYMPANOGRAM

Static Compliance:

R	
cc	
2	
1	

L	
cc	
2	
1	

Normal: .3 - 1.75cc

Ear Canal Volume

Right	Left
C₁ =	

Air Conduction

Bone Conduction	30-40	40-50	30-40	40-50	30-50	40-50	40-50	35-45	35-45	40-50	35-45	R	L

Plateau levels of masking in non-test ear

Ref.: SPL ____　EFF ✓　Signal: NBN ✓　White ____

Answers for Figure 4-21

1. The unaided sound field word recognition score at average conversational level is 80%. Note that this test was administered at 50 dB HL, which is considered to be average conversational level, and not at PB Max.

2. The unaided sound field word recognition score is poorer than the unaided score for the left ear because the latter score was probably obtained at PB Max, while the sound field score was obtained at only 26 dB above the best threshold (the right ear threshold of 24 dB). The unaided sound field score does not represent PB Max.

3. The aided sound field word recognition score of 94% is significantly better than the unaided sound field score obtained at the same hearing level. Since both tests were administered at the same hearing level, they can be compared directly to assess improvement provided by the hearing aid.

4. The hearing aid is definitely helping the client. Not only does it improve her ability to understand speech presented at average conversational level, but also it allows her to hear sound at softer levels. Unaided, a sound field SRT of 24 dB HL was obtained; with the hearing aid, however, a sound field pure tone average of 12 dB HL was measured.

QUESTIONS FOR FIGURE 4-22

1. What is the unaided sound field word recognition score?
2. Why is it so much poorer than word recognition scores obtained under earphones?
3. What is the aided sound field word recognition score?
4. Is amplification beneficial to this client? How do you know?

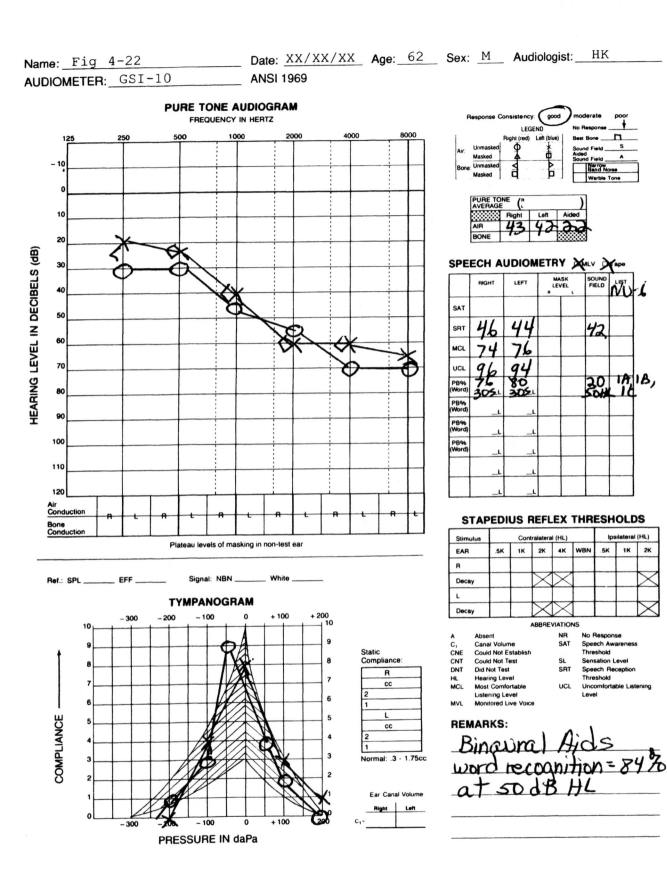

PURE TONE AUDIOGRAM

SPEECH AUDIOMETRY MLV Tape

	RIGHT	LEFT	MASK LEVEL R L	SOUND FIELD	LIST
SAT					MU-6
SRT	46	44		42	
MCL	74	76			
UCL	96	94			
PB% (Word)	76 30SL	80 30SL		20 50SL	1A 1B, 1C
PB% (Word)	L	L			
PB% (Word)	L	L			
PB% (Word)	L	L			
	L	L			
	L	L			

PURE TONE AVERAGE (R / L)

	Right	Left	Aided
AIR	43	42	22
BONE			

STAPEDIUS REFLEX THRESHOLDS

Stimulus	Contralateral (HL)					Ipsilateral (HL)		
EAR	.5K	1K	2K	4K	WBN	.5K	1K	2K
R								
Decay								
L								
Decay								

ABBREVIATIONS

A	Absent	NR	No Response
C₁	Canal Volume	SAT	Speech Awareness
CNE	Could Not Establish		Threshold
CNT	Could Not Test	SL	Sensation Level
DNT	Did Not Test	SRT	Speech Reception
HL	Hearing Level		Threshold
MCL	Most Comfortable	UCL	Uncomfortable Listening
	Listening Level		Level
MVL	Monitored Live Voice		

TYMPANOGRAM

REMARKS:

Binaural Aids
word recognition = 84%
at 50 dB HL

Static Compliance:

R	
	cc
2	
1	

L	
	cc
2	
1	

Normal: .3 - 1.75cc

Ear Canal Volume

Right	Left
C₁ =	

Answers for Figure 4-22

1. The unaided sound field word recognition score is 20%.
2. The word recognition scores obtained under earphones probably represent PB Max. The sound field word recognition score was obtained at average conversational level (50 dB HL), which is only 8 dB HL above the sound field SRT. This definitely does not represent PB Max but gives an estimation of the difficulty this client experiences understanding average conversation unaided.
3. The aided sound field word recognition score is 84%. Note that it was obtained at average conversational level (50 dB HL) so that it can be directly compared to the unaided score.
4. Amplification is definitely beneficial to this client. His ability to understand at average conversational level is improved from 20% to 84%. In addition, the hearing aids allow him to hear sound at a significantly softer level. Note that without the hearing aid, his SRT was 42 dB HL; with the hearing aid, a sound field pure tone average of 22 dB HL was measured.

QUESTIONS FOR FIGURE 4-23

Case History Information Miss F's hearing problem has been medically diagnosed as otosclerosis. She has undergone unsuccessful surgery. Her major complaint is that she cannot hear speech unless the speaker shouts, at which point everything is completely intelligible.

1. What is the word recognition in noise in the sound field?
2. How does word recognition in noise compare to word recognition in quiet?
3. On the basis of the word recognition in noise score, what can you conclude about her ability to understand speech in a noisy environment?

Chapter 4

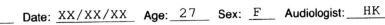

Name: Fig 4-23   Date: XX/XX/XX Age: 27 Sex: F Audiologist: HK
AUDIOMETER: GSI-10   ANSI 1969

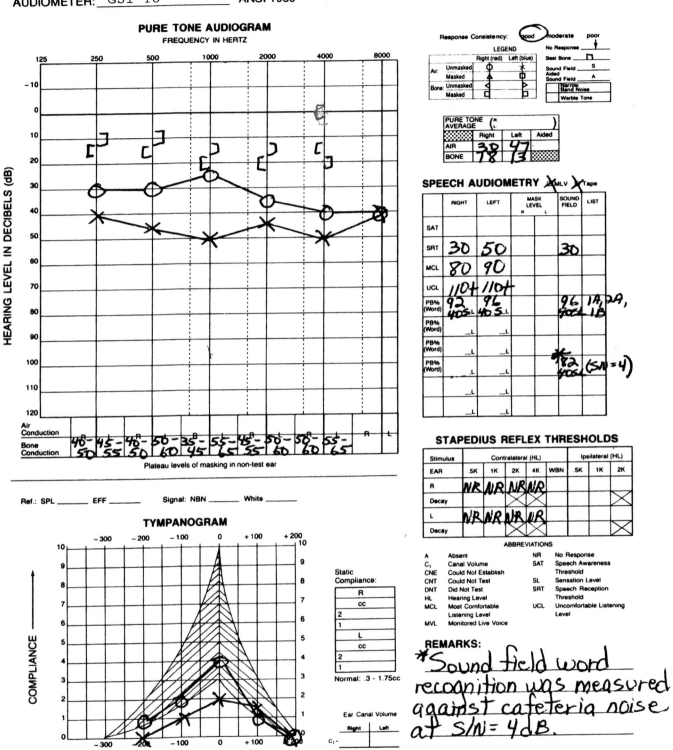

PURE TONE AUDIOGRAM
FREQUENCY IN HERTZ

PURE TONE AVERAGE (R / L)			
	Right	Left	Aided
AIR	30	47	
BONE	78	73	

SPEECH AUDIOMETRY ⊠MLV ✕Tape

	RIGHT	LEFT	MASK LEVEL R / L	SOUND FIELD	LIST
SAT					
SRT	30	50		30	
MCL	80	90			
UCL	110+	110+			
PB% (Word)	92 40S L	96 40S L		96 1A,2A, 40S 1B	
PB% (Word)	_ L	_ L			
PB% (Word)	_ L	_ L		*82 40S L (S/N=4)	
PB% (Word)	_ L	_ L			
	_ L	_ L			
	_ L	_ L			

STAPEDIUS REFLEX THRESHOLDS

Stimulus	Contralateral (HL)					Ipsilateral (HL)		
EAR	.5K	1K	2K	4K	WBN	.5K	1K	2K
R	NR	NR	NR	NR				✕
Decay			✕	✕				
L	NR	NR	NR	NR				✕
Decay			✕	✕				

ABBREVIATIONS

Air Conduction | 40ᴿ 45 40ᴿ 50 35ᴮ 55 45ᴿ 50 50ᴸ 55 | R L
Bone Conduction | 50 55 50 60 45 65 55 60 60 65 |
Plateau levels of masking in non-test ear

Ref.: SPL _____ EFF _____   Signal: NBN _____ White _____

TYMPANOGRAM

Static Compliance:

R	
	cc
2	
1	

L	
	cc
2	
1	

Normal: .3 - 1.75cc

Ear Canal Volume

	Right	Left
C₁ =		

PRESSURE IN daPa

REMARKS:
*Sound field word recognition was measured against cafeteria noise at S/N = 4dB.

Interpreting Speech Audiometry

205

Answers for Figure 4-23

1. Word recognition in the sound field in noise is 82% at a presentation level of 40 dB SL. Note that the level of the speech was 4 dB more intense than the level of the noise.
2. Word recognition in noise is 10 dB poorer than word recognition in quiet in the right ear and 14 dB poorer in the left ear. These are probably significant differences.
3. Miss F's speech understanding in the presence of competing noise is probably comparable to that of a normal-hearing individual, provided the signal is intense enough to be heard easily. Note that the presentation level of the signal is 72 dB HL. This is considerably more intense than the presentation level for a normal-hearing individual, which would be around 50 dB HL, average conversational level. One can conclude that Miss F has little difficulty understanding speech in the presence of competing noise, provided the speech is intense enough to be heard easily.

QUESTIONS FOR FIGURE 4-24

Case History Information This man's major complaint is that speech sounds are blurred unless the speaker speaks very clearly and distinctly and in a somewhat louder than normal voice. However, the presence of any competing noise or speech makes understanding of conversation very difficult. The most difficult communicative situation is group conversation.

1. How does word recognition in noise compare to word recognition in quiet in each ear?
2. What predictions can you make about this man's everyday communication from the audiometric information?
3. On the basis of the audiometric information, which ear would you choose for a hearing aid fitting?

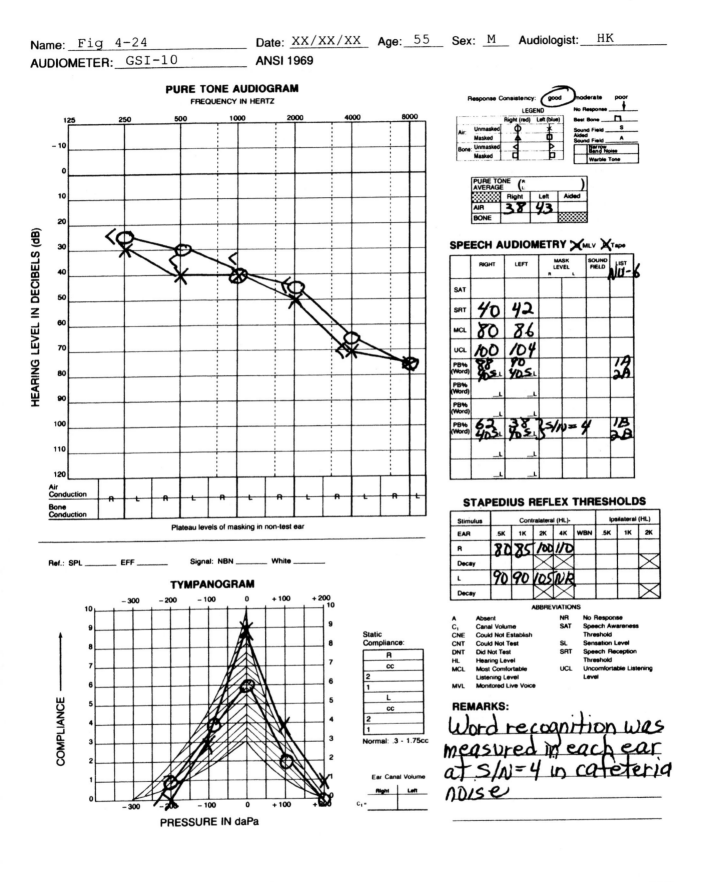

Name: Fig 4-24   **Date:** XX/XX/XX   **Age:** 55   **Sex:** M   **Audiologist:** HK

AUDIOMETER: GSI-10   **ANSI 1969**

PURE TONE AUDIOGRAM
FREQUENCY IN HERTZ

Response Consistency: good (circled) moderate poor

LEGEND

	Right (red)	Left (blue)
Air: Unmasked	O	X
Masked	▲	▣
Bone: Unmasked	<	>
Masked	□	□

No Response
Best Bone
Sound Field — S
Aided Sound Field — A
Narrow Band Noise
Warble Tone

PURE TONE AVERAGE (R / L)

	Right	Left	Aided
AIR	38	43	
BONE			

SPEECH AUDIOMETRY   ☒ MLV   ☒ Tape

	RIGHT	LEFT	MASK LEVEL R	L	SOUND FIELD	LIST NU-6
SAT						
SRT	40	42				
MCL	80	86				
UCL	100	104				
PB% (Word)	88 40SL	90 40SL				1A 2A
PB% (Word)	L	L				
PB% (Word)	L	L				
PB% (Word)	62 40SL	38 40SL	} S/N = 4			1B 2B
	L	L				
	L	L				

STAPEDIUS REFLEX THRESHOLDS

Stimulus	Contralateral (HL)					Ipsilateral (HL)		
EAR	.5K	1K	2K	4K	WBN	.5K	1K	2K
R	80	85	100	110				
Decay			✕	✕				✕
L	90	90	105	NR				
Decay			✕	✕				✕

ABBREVIATIONS

A — Absent
C_1 — Canal Volume
CNE — Could Not Establish
CNT — Could Not Test
DNT — Did Not Test
HL — Hearing Level
MCL — Most Comfortable Listening Level
MVL — Monitored Live Voice
NR — No Response
SAT — Speech Awareness Threshold
SL — Sensation Level
SRT — Speech Reception Threshold
UCL — Uncomfortable Listening Level

TYMPANOGRAM

PRESSURE IN daPa

Static Compliance:

R	
cc	
2	
1	

L	
cc	
2	
1	

Normal: .3 - 1.75cc

Ear Canal Volume

Right	Left
$C_1 =$	

Ref.: SPL _____ EFF _____   Signal: NBN _____ White _____

Plateau levels of masking in non-test ear

REMARKS:

Word recognition was measured in each ear at S/N = 4 in cafeteria noise

Answers for Figure 4-24

1. Word recognition in noise is significantly poorer than word recognition in quiet in both ears, with a difference of 26% in the right ear and 52% in the left. Note that these scores were obtained with both speech and cafeteria noise presented to the same ear; the level of the speech was 4 dB more intense than the noise.

2. From the word recognition information one could predict a great deal of difficulty understanding speech in the presence of any kind of competing signal, regardless of the level of speech. This prediction is borne out by the client's complaints.

3. Since the word recognition in noise is poorer in the left ear than in the right by 24 dB, the right ear would be the preferable ear for the hearing aid. Without the information about word recognition in noise, the ears appear to be identical in their communicative ability. The only distinguishing feature is word recognition in noise.

QUESTIONS FOR FIGURE 4-25

1. What is the word recognition in noise for the right ear? for the left ear?
2. What kind of communication difficulty would you predict?
3. On the basis of audiometric information, which ear would you choose for the hearing aid? Would binaural amplification be a consideration?

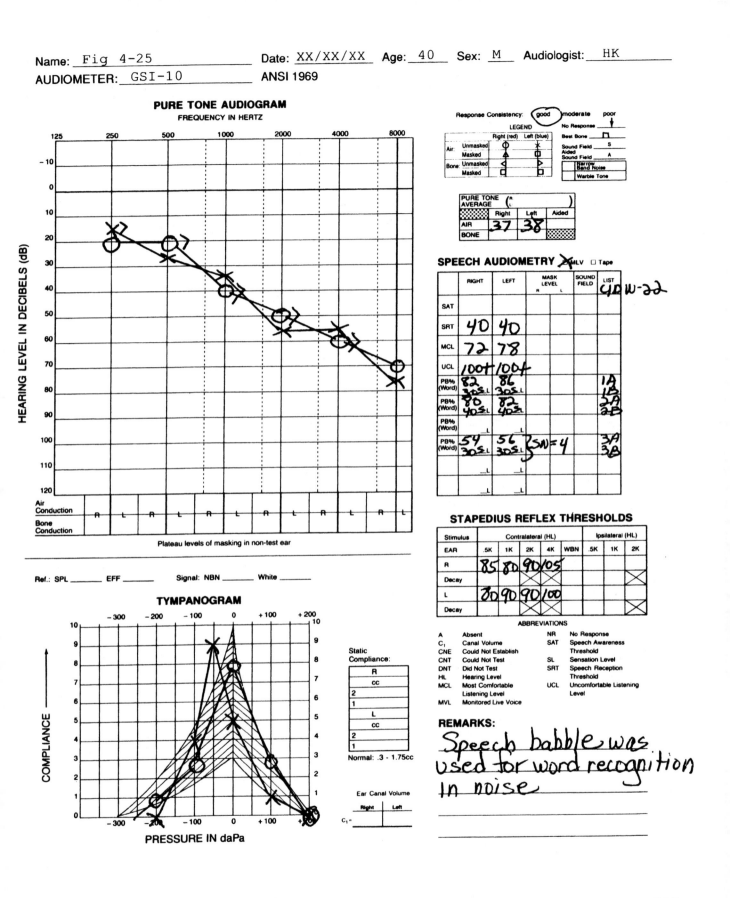

Answers for Figure 4-25

1. In the right ear, the word recognition in noise is 54%; in the left ear it is 56%, not significantly different from the right.

2. On the basis of audiometric information, one could predict great difficulty understanding conversation in the presence of competing noise even when the speech is intense enough to be heard easily. In quiet, the client would have slight difficulty understanding speech when it was intense enough to be heard comfortably.

3. Since all audiometric information (the pure tone averages, the pure tone configurations, the SRTs, UCLs, word recognition in quiet, word recognition in noise) is similar for the two ears, this client probably would be a good candidate for binaural amplification. In contrast, Figure 4-24 shows a client whose ears differed in their ability to understand speech in the presence of noise. That client was not a good candidate for binaural amplification.

QUESTIONS FOR FIGURE 4-26

Case History Information This man was fitted with a hearing aid in his right ear. The hearing aid was evaluated on the client in the sound room with all speech signals sent through the speaker on his right and cafeteria noise sent through the speaker on his left at the same intensity level as the speech, 50 dB HL. The results were compared to previous test results obtained without the hearing aid under identical conditions in the sound field.

The following aided scores were obtained: SRT = 8 dB HL; word recognition in quiet at 50 dB HL = 84%; word recognition in noise at 50 dB HL (S/N = 0) = 70%.

1. What is the unaided sound field SRT?
2. What are the unaided word recognition scores in the sound field in quiet and in noise?
3. What is meant by a signal-to-noise ratio (S/N) of 0 dB?
4. How do the aided and unaided word recognition scores compare?
5. What can you conclude about the performance of the hearing aid?

Name: Fig 4-26   **Date:** XX/XX/XX   **Age:** 48   **Sex:** M   **Audiologist:** HK

AUDIOMETER: GSI-10   **ANSI 1969**

PURE TONE AUDIOGRAM

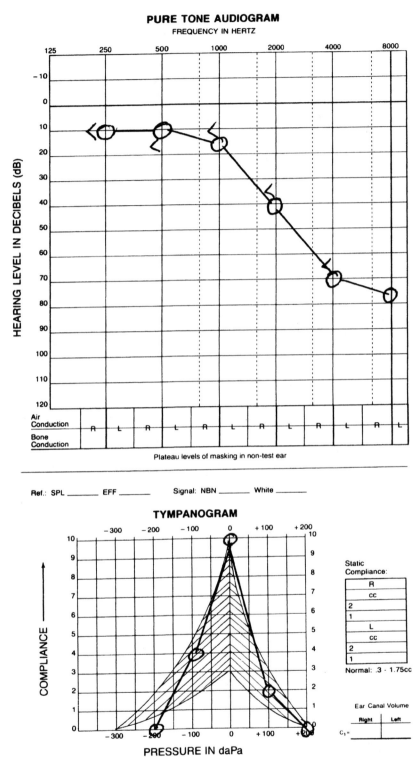

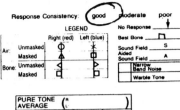

Response Consistency: (good) moderate poor

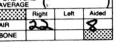

PURE TONE AVERAGE (R / L)			
	Right	Left	Aided
AIR	22	8	
BONE			

SPEECH AUDIOMETRY ☒MLV ☒Tape

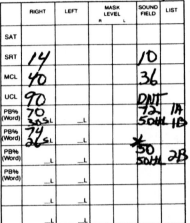

	RIGHT	LEFT	MASK LEVEL R L	SOUND FIELD	LIST
SAT					
SRT	14			10	
MCL	40			36	
UCL	90			DNT	
PB% (Word)	70 30SL	L		72 50HL	1A 1B
PB% (Word)	74 26SL	L		✱50 50HL	2B
PB% (Word)	L	L			
PB% (Word)	L	L			
	L	L			
	L	L			

STAPEDIUS REFLEX THRESHOLDS

Stimulus	Contralateral (HL)					Ipsilateral (HL)		
EAR	.5K	1K	2K	4K	WBN	.5K	1K	2K
R	80	80	90	110				✕
Decay								
L			✕	✕				✕
Decay			✕	✕				✕

ABBREVIATIONS

A — Absent
C₁ — Canal Volume
CNE — Could Not Establish
CNT — Could Not Test
DNT — Did Not Test
HL — Hearing Level
MCL — Most Comfortable Listening Level
MVL — Monitored Live Voice

NR — No Response
SAT — Speech Awareness Threshold
SL — Sensation Level
SRT — Speech Reception Threshold
UCL — Uncomfortable Listening Level

REMARKS:
✱ Word recognition in noise was obtained in the sound field at a S/N=0

Ref.: SPL _____ EFF _____   Signal: NBN _____ White _____

TYMPANOGRAM

Static Compliance:

R	
	cc
2	
1	

L	
	cc
2	
1	

Normal: .3 - 1.75cc

Ear Canal Volume

Right	Left

C₁ =

Interpreting Speech Audiometry

Answers for Figure 4-26

1. The unaided sound field SRT is 10 dB HL.

2. The unaided word recognition score in quiet is 72% and the unaided word recognition score in noise is 50%. Note that the presentation level of the speech was average conversational level (50 dB HL).

3. A signal-to-noise ratio of 0 dB means that the speech and noise are presented at the same intensity level. Note that both unaided and aided word recognition in noise measures were performed with a signal-to-noise ratio of 0 dB. Both speech and noise were presented at 50 dB HL.

4. With the hearing aid, word recognition in quiet and in noise improved significantly. Without the hearing aid, the client showed moderate difficulty understanding speech in quiet and great difficulty understanding speech in noise. With the hearing aid, he showed slight difficulty understanding speech in quiet and moderate difficulty understanding speech in noise.

5. From the audiometric information we can conclude that the hearing aid significantly improves the client's understanding of speech in quiet and in noise at average conversational level. Note that the hearing aid does not significantly change the SRT; with and without the hearing aid, speech can be heard within normal limits.

QUESTIONS FOR FIGURE 4-27

Case History Information This client was evaluated with several hearing aids in his left ear. Aid X was found to perform best. The following scores were obtained with hearing aid X: SRT = 32 dB HL; word recognition in quiet at 50 dB HL = 56%; word recognition in noise at 50 dB HL (S/N = 0) = 20%.

1. What is the unaided sound field SRT?
2. How does it compare to the aided SRT?
3. What are the sound field unaided word recognition scores in quiet and in noise?
4. How do the aided and unaided word recognition scores compare?
5. What can you conclude about the performance of the hearing aid?

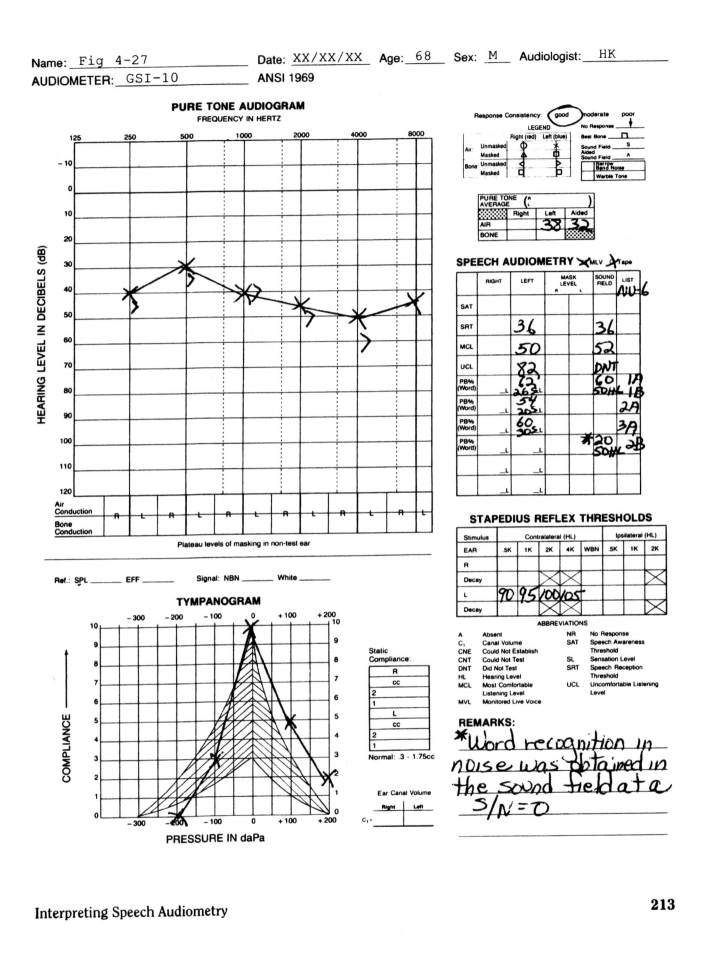

Answers for Figure 4-27

1. The unaided sound field SRT is 36 dB HL.
2. The unaided sound field SRT is only 4 dB poorer than the aided score. This difference is not significant. The hearing aid is not allowing the client to hear speech at a significantly softer level than he can hear without amplification.
3. The unaided sound field word recognition score in quiet is 60% and the score in noise is 20%.
4. The aided scores are not significantly different form the unaided scores. No improvement in understanding of speech is apparent, either in quiet or in noise.
5. From the audiometric information we may conclude that the hearing aid is not improving the client's communication. Unless strong contradictory evidence based on the client's subjective trial of the instrument exists, the hearing aid should not be recommended. In some cases, a hearing aid may not show improvement during audiometric testing but subsequent home trial use of the instrument indicates that it is helpful to the client. This is not a usual situation; but if it should occur, the hearing aid may be recommended after an extended period of home trial under audiologic supervision.

REVIEW AND SEARCH PROJECTS

1. Discuss the development of open set materials used for SRT and word recognition with adults.

2. Discuss the development of current speech audiometric materials used with young children and difficult-to-test clients.

3. Compare open set and closed set word recognition materials.

4. Review the literature on Jerger's Synthetic Sentences.

5. Describe how the MCL and UCL are used to select appropriate hearing aids.

6. Draw and compare performance-intensity functions for different speech recognition materials (CID-W22 words, NU-6 words, Rush Hughes recordings, Modified Rhyme Test, Synthetic Sentences, California Consonant Test, etc.)

7. Discuss the use of open and closed set sentence speech identification materials, such as CID Everyday Sentences (CHABA), Speech Perception in Noise (SPIN), and Synthetic Sentences (SSI).

8. Discuss test batteries for severe to profound hearing losses, such as the Minimal Auditory Capabilities (MAC) battery.

9. Review the literature on the rollover phenomenon and its diagnostic significance.

10. Make up audiograms illustrating a conductive loss, a sensorineural loss of cochlear origin, and a sensorineural loss of retrocochlear origin. Include performance-intensity functions for each type.

11. Make a list of causes of hearing impairments. Briefly describe the pure tone and speech audiometric results you might expect to find.

12. Discuss the validity of traditional hearing aid procedures. Include information from at least one article for and one article against traditional procedures.

13. Review several articles concerned with speech identification in noise.

REFERENCES

ASHA Committee on Audiologic Evaluation 1988. Guidelines for determining threshold level for speech. *ASHA* 30: 85–89.

Beattie, R. C., and Edgerton, C. 1976. Reliability of monosyllabic discrimination tests in white noise for differentiating among hearing aids. *Journal of Speech and Hearing Disorders* 41: 464–476.

Beattie, R. C., Svihovec, D. A., and Edgerton, B. J. 1975. Relative intelligibility of the CID spondees as presented via monitored live voice. *Journal of Speech and Hearing Disorders* 40: 84–91.

Bilger, R. C., Neutzel, J. M., Rabinowitz, W. M., and Rzeczowski, C. 1984. Standardization of a test of speech perception in noise. *Journal of Speech and Hearing Research* 27: 32–48.

Chaiklin, J. B. 1959. The relation among three selected auditory speech thresholds. *Journal of Speech and Hearing Research* 2: 237–243.

Davis, H., and Silverman, S. R. 1970. *Hearing and Deafness*. New York: Holt, Rinehart and Winston.

Dirks, D. D., Morgan, D. E., and Dubno, J. R. 1982. A procedure for quantifying the effects of noise in speech recognition. *Journal of Speech and Hearing Disorders* 47: 114–123.

Hannley, M. 1986. *Basic Principles of Auditory Assessment*. San Diego: College-Hill Press.

Hannley, M., and Jerger, J. 1981. PB rollover and the acoustic reflex. *Audiology* 20: 251–258.

Hirsh, I. J., Davis, H., Silverman, S. R., Reynolds, E. G., Eldert, E., and Benson, R. W. 1952. Development of materials for speech audiometry. *Journal of Speech and Hearing Disorders* 17: 321–337.

House, A. S., Williams, C. E., Hecker, M. H. L., and Kryter, K. D. 1965. Articulation testing methods. Consonantal differentiation in a closed-response set. *Journal of the Acoustical Society of America* 36: 158–166.

Jacobson, J. T., and Northern, J. L. 1991. *Diagnostic Audiology*. Austin: Pro-Ed.

Jerger, J. 1973. *Modern Developments in Audiology*. New York: Academic Press.

Jerger, J., and Hayes, D. 1976. Hearing aid evaluation: Clinician experience with a new philosophy. *Archives of Otolaryngology* 102: 214–225.

Jerger, J., and Jerger, S. 1971. Diagnostic significance of PB word functions. *Archives of Otolaryngology* 93: 573–580.

Kalikow, D. N., Stevens, K. N., and Elliot, L. L. 1977. Development of a test of speech intelligibility in noise using sentence materials with controlled word predictability. *Journal of the Acoustical Society of America* 61: 1337–1351.

Levitt, H., and Resnick, S. B. 1978. Speech reception by the hearing-impaired: Methods of testing and the development of new tests. *Scandinavian Audiology* (Suppl. 6): 107–130.

Martin, F. N. 1991. *Introduction to Audiology*, 4th ed. Englewood Cliffs, N. J.: Prentice-Hall.

Newby, H., and Popelka, G. R. 1985. *Audiology*, 5th ed. Englewood Cliffs, N. J.: Prentice-Hall.

Northern, J. L., and Downs, M. P. 1974. *Hearing in Children*, 3rd ed. Baltimore: Williams & Wilkins.

Orchick, D. J., and Roddy, N. 1980. The SSI and NU6 in clinical hearing aid evaluation. *Journal of Speech and Hearing Disorders* 45: 401–407.

Owens, E., and Schubert, E. D. 1977. Development of the California consonant test. *Journal of Speech and Hearing Research* 20: 463–474.

Raffin, M. J. M., and Thornton, A. R. 1980. Confidence levels for differences between speech discrimination scores. *Journal of Speech and Hearing Research* 23: 5–18.

Rintelmann, W. F. (Editor). 1991. *Hearing Assessment*, 2nd ed. Austin: Pro-Ed.

Silverman, S. R., and Hirsh, I. J. 1955. Problems related to the use of speech in clinical audiometry. *Annals of Otology, Rhinology and Laryngology* 64: 1234–1244.

Speaks, C., and Jerger, J. 1965, Performance-intensity characteristics of synthetic sentences. *Journal of Speech and Hearing Research* 9: 305–312.

Speaks, C., and Jerger, J. 1966. Method for measurement of speech identification. *Journal of Speech and Hearing Research* 10: 344–353.

Thornton, A., and Raffin, M. J. M. 1978. Speech discrimination scores modeled as a binomial variable. *Journal of Speech and Hearing Research* 21: 507–518.

Tillman, T. W., and Carhart, R. 1966. *An expanded test for speech discrimination utilizing CNC monosyllabic words. Northwestern University Auditory Test No. 6.* Brooks Air Force Base, TX: USAF School of Aerospace Medicine Technical Report.

Use of Masking

In this chapter the student will learn to appropriately use masking for pure tone and speech audiometry. Whenever a client has one good ear and one bad ear, it is important to ensure that the good ear does not hear the tone presented to the poor ear. If such precautions are not taken, misdiagnoses can easily be made, leading to inappropriate hearing aid fitting, unnecessary ear surgery, and so on. To eliminate the non-test ear from participation in the evaluation, a noise called a masker must be introduced into the good ear.

This chapter contains Audiologic Assessment Forms programmed to help the student develop the ability to:

1. Determine when masking is needed.
2. Determine how much masking is needed.
3. Understand the concepts of undermasking, overmasking, and plateau.

WHEN IS MASKING NEEDED?

Air Conduction

When a pure tone is introduced into one ear by air conduction it may be heard by the opposite ear, but at a level approximately 40–60 dB less intense. As a sound travels from one ear to the other, primarily by vibrating the bones of the skull, it loses energy. This loss of energy is known as interaural attenuation. Coles and Priede (1968) have shown that the amount of interaural attenuation varies with individuals, showing a considerable range. They have also shown that different frequencies show different amounts of interaural attenuation. Table 5-1 shows mean interaural attenuation for pure tones used in audiometric testing and the range for each frequency.

Table 5-1. Interaural attenuation (IA) for pure tones.

Frequency (Hz)	IA (dB)	
	Mean	Range
250	61	50–80
500	63	45–80
1000	63	40–80
2000	68	45–75
4000	68	50–85
Average	63	51–70

Other investigators (Chaiklin, 1967; Liden et al., 1959a; Zwislocki, 1953) have reported norms which differed from those of Coles and Priede, perhaps because of type of earphone used, type of subject (normal hearing versus hearing impaired), measurement method, or simply inherent intersubject variability. Chaiklin (1967) found that mean interaural attenuation ranged from 38 dB at 125 Hz to 70 dB at 4000 Hz. Generally there tends to be greater interaural attenuation at high frequencies, with somewhat greater variability as well. For further discussion of interaural attenuation of air-conducted signals, see Hannley (1986:108–109), Rintelmann (1991:142–145), and Martin (1991:86–88).

The non-test ear must be masked whenever there is a possibility that it will respond to the tone presented to the test ear. Since we have information about the amounts of interaural attenuation that can be expected at each frequency, we need to subtract the interaural attenuation (IA) from the threshold obtained in the test ear. If the non-test ear is capable of hearing at that level we must retest at that frequency with appropriate masking noise in the non-test ear to rule out its possible participation. In view of the high degree of variability of interaural attenuation normative data, it is well to follow Studebaker's suggestion and accept an extreme value for each frequency (Studebaker, 1964). Studebaker suggests that masking should be used whenever the difference between bone conduction threshold hearing level in the non-test ear and air conduction signal level in the test ear equals or exceeds 35 dB at 250 Hz; 40–45 dB at 500, 1000, or 2000 Hz; or 50 dB at 4000 Hz).

In cross-hearing, the non-test ear is apparently stimulated largely through the mechanism of bone conduction (Zwislocki, 1953). Therefore, when we decide whether masking is needed to obtain an accurate air conduction threshold, we must compare the air conduction threshold of the ear being tested with the bone conduction threshold of the contralateral ear. If the difference exceeds interaural attenuation values for that frequency, the air conduction threshold must be re-established using masking in the non-test ear. This means that there may be times when the need to mask for air conduction is not apparent until bone conduction thresholds have been obtained. Immittance results can also indicate probable need for masking. If the tympanogram and reflex pattern suggest middle ear disorder, it is highly probable that an air–bone gap will be seen; if immittance results are entirely normal, it can be assumed that there is no middle ear disorder.

Let us consider an example. The difference between Mr. Jones' air conduction thresholds at 1000 Hz was only 25 dB, suggesting that the use of masking was not necessary. However, abnormal tympanograms were found in both ears, and the difference between the air conduction threshold of the poorer ear and unmasked bone conduction threshold (which represents the bone conduction threshold of the better ear) was 50 dB. It is quite possible that the air conduction threshold of the poorer ear is less sensitive than it appears to be. The air conduction threshold of the poorer ear should be retested using appropriate levels of masking in the better ear.

Bone Conduction

It is the consensus of opinion that interaural attenuation for a signal presented through bone conduction should be considered zero (Martin, 1986:87; Studebaker, 1964, 1967; Sanders and Rintelmann, 1964). Although slight

amounts of attenuation at the higher frequencies may exist for some clients, the values are extremely variable and cannot be depended upon. Therefore, it is well to expect no interaural attenuation for bone conduction. Since we cannot count on interaural attenuation for sounds presented through bone conduction, the only way to rule out the participation of the contralateral ear is to always use masking when testing bone conduction. Otherwise, regardless of where the bone receiver (vibrator) is placed, there is no way of knowing which ear is being evaluated. However, it is not always necessary to know which ear is being evaluated by bone conduction. The purpose of obtaining bone conduction thresholds is to compare them with air conduction thresholds to determine whether the loss is conductive, sensorineural, or mixed. If an air–bone gap of 10 dB HL or more exists between unmasked bone conduction and the air conduction thresholds of either ear, it signifies a conductive component. It is then necessary to determine in which ear this conductive component exists and where masking is indicated. However, if an air–bone gap does not exist in either ear we may conclude that the hearing loss is sensorineural in both ears and individual bone conduction thresholds for the two ears are not necessary. As was discussed in the section on masking for air conduction, immittance results can determine if masking is needed and in which ear. Normal tympanograms and acoustic reflex patterns indicate normal middle ear function and preclude the presence of air–bone gaps. In such a situation neither masking nor bone conduction testing are needed. Some audiologists, however, prefer to measure bone conduction.

Speech Recognition Thresholds (SRT)

Minimal interaural attenuation for speech is considered to be 40–50 dB (Martin, 1986:123–124; Rintelmann, 1991:172). It is assumed that contralateralization for speech stimuli occurs through bone conduction similar to contralateralization for pure tone stimuli. Therefore, there is a need to use masking in the non-test ear whenever the SRT of the test ear exceeds the lowest bone conduction threshold in the non-test ear by 40 dB or more.

Word Recognition

Since word recognition is tested at suprathreshold levels, the danger of cross-hearing is greater than with threshold testing. Whenever masking is necessary to obtain a valid SRT, it is automatically necessary for word recognition testing. Frequently, masking is need for word recognition, although it is not necessary for obtaining speech recognition thresholds. According to Martin (1991), "whenever the HL of the words, minus the interaural attenuation, is above the bone-conduction threshold of the non-test ear, cross-hearing is a strong probability. As in the case of the ST (spondee threshold), the interaural attenuation is considered to be as little as 40 dB and the bone-conduction threshold is the lowest (i.e., best) one obtained in the non-test ear."

Summary

Masking is needed in the non-test ear when:

1. The air-conducted signal presented to the test ear exceeds the bone conduction threshold of the non-test ear by 40 dB or more at 250, 500, 1000, and 2000 Hz and by 50 dB at 4000 Hz.
2. Tones presented through bone conduction result in an air–bone gap of 10 dB or more at any frequency.
3. There is a 40 dB or greater difference between the SRT of the test ear and the lowest bone conduction threshold of the non-test ear.
4. The presentation level of the speech signal used for word recognition testing exceeds the best bone conduction threshold of the non-test ear by 40 dB or more.

TYPES OF MASKERS

The best and most commonly used type of noise for masking pure tones is narrow band noise. It is possible to generate a noise that has approximately equal energy per cycle and covers a broad range of frequencies. This type of noise is referred to as broad band or white noise. With the use of electronic filters, it is possible to shape the broad band noise into narrow noise bands, each band consisting of frequencies surrounding a center frequency which corresponds to the pure tone to be masked. Surrounding every pure tone is a critical band of frequencies which provides maximum masking for that pure tone with minimum sound pressure. For example, let us assume that a narrow noise band corresponding to the critical band around 1000 Hz provides 40 dB of masking with a sound pressure level of 50 dB. If we add frequencies outside the critical band to the noise band, we do not increase the amount of masking provided by it, but we do increase the overall sound pressure level of the noise. Increases in sound pressure level and loudness increase the likelihood of fatiguing the ear and providing discomfort to the client. Narrow band noise is the most efficient masker we have for pure tone signals and, therefore, is preferred to broad band noise.

Since speech is a broad band signal, narrow band noise is not a suitable masker because some of the frequency components of the speech signal would not be adequately masked. The preferred masker for speech is white noise or speech spectrum noise. Speech spectrum noise is white noise filtered so that it approximates the overall frequency spectrum of speech. It has relatively more energy in the low frequencies, attenuating above 1000 Hz at the rate of about 12 dB per octave. On most speech audiometers, both white and speech spectrum noise are available to be used as speech maskers. For further discussion of maskers, see Hannley (1986:109–113), Martin (1991:88–90, 124–125), Sanders and Rintelmann (1991:145–149, 173), and Studebaker (1967).

CALIBRATION OF MASKING NOISES

Masking noises may be calibrated in SPL to a decibel reference of 0.0002 dynes/cm squared, in HL to a decibel reference of audiometric zero, or in effective level. The use of effective level calibration is preferred, particularly with narrow band noise. When a masking dial is calibrated in effective level, each numerical reading indicates the amount of threshold shift from audiometric zero which that amount of noise will produce when the signal and the noise are in the same ear. A given effective level corresponds to different SPL levels at different frequencies. The advantage of effective level calibration is that it enables us to predict the amount of masking or threshold shift produced by a given amount of noise and thereby specify more precisely the levels of masking noise sufficient to mask the contralateral ear. For example, if a given level of noise is calibrated at 50 dB effective level (EL) at 1000 Hz, that level of noise is just sufficient to make a 50-db HL 1000-Hz tone inaudible.

Although narrow band noise is the masker that is usually calibrated in effective level, other types of maskers may also be calibrated in the same way. For example, to calibrate speech noise in effective level we could use the following procedure:

1. Obtain unmasked SRTs on 10 to 12 normal-hearing individuals.
2. For each subject, present a given level of noise to the same ear in which the unmasked SRT was obtained.
3. Obtain a masked SRT in that ear.
4. The mean masked threshold value represents effective level for that masker attenuator setting.
5. Repeat the procedure for several attenuator settings.

For further discussion of effective level calibration, see Rintelmann (1991:155–165) and Martin (1991:90–91).

HOW MUCH MASKING?

There are a number of masking methods in use for masking of pure tones. However, with all methods one must find a minimum effective masking level, a maximum effective masking level, and a plateau.

Minimum Effective Masking Level

The minimum effective masking level is the minimum amount of noise necessary to mask a pure tone that might appear in the non-test ear because of cross-hearing. When the masking noise is calibrated in effective level, it is possible to compute the minimum masking level for a given client. For an air-conducted signal, minimum effective masking equals the air conduction threshold in the test ear minus interaural attenuation for that frequency plus the air–bone gap in the non-test ear. For example, let us assume that the unmasked air conduction threshold in the test ear is 60 dB HL, the unmasked air conduction threshold in the non-test ear is 40 dB HL, the unmasked bone conduction threshold (which represents the better ear) is 20 dB HL, and the interaural attenuation at that frequency is 40 dB. Using our formula, 60 – 40 + 20 (air–bone gap) = 40 dB. The minimum masking level would be 40 dB effective level.

For a bone-conducted signal, minimum masking equals the unmasked bone conduction threshold (for purposes of computing minimum masking we as-

sume that unmasked bone conduction is the threshold of both ears) plus the air–bone gap in the non-test ear. Since we assume that interaural attenuation for bone-conducted sounds is zero, it is not a factor in our computation. Let us compute minimum effective masking for bone conduction for the same individual described above. Using our formula, 20 (unmasked bone conduction) + 20 (air–bone gap) = 40 dB. The minimum masking level would be 40 dB effective level. For further discussion, see Martin (1991:91–93), Hannley (1986:116–118), and Rintelmann (1991:154–155).

To determine minimum effective masking levels in this fashion, one must compute values for air and bone conduction separately for each frequency. This can be time consuming and impractical in a clinical situation. Therefore, several methods of determining minimum effective masking level have been proposed. Hood (1960) recommends introducing masking noise at 10 dB above the air conduction threshold of the non-test ear. To avoid undermasking, Studebaker (1964) recommends that the first masking level in the non-test ear should be 40 dB above the unmasked bone conduction threshold. Martin (1986:92) suggests that the minimum masking level introduced to the non-test ear should be equal to the air conduction threshold of that ear. To provide additional insurance against undermasking, however, the first level of masking used in the non-test ear should be 15 dB above the air conduction threshold of that ear.

Martin points out that in determining the minimum masking level for bone-conducted sound, the occlusion effect must be taken into account. When an ear is covered during a test, bone conduction thresholds for the low frequencies (250, 500, and 1000 Hz) are improved unless there is a conductive loss in that ear. Norms for the occlusion effect are not available, but the effect may be as great as 25 dB in a normal ear or one with a sensorineural hearing loss (Hannley, 1986:100). During air conduction testing, both ears are covered at all times; therefore, an occlusion effect is not created when masking is introduced into the non-test ear. In contrast, unmasked bone conduction thresholds are obtained with both ears uncovered. If masking is necessary, the non-test ear is then covered by an earphone, and an occlusion effect is created in that ear unless a conductive loss is present. This means that the likeli-

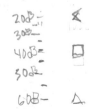

220

Chapter 5

hood of the non-test ear responding to low-frequency tones presented to the test ear is increased. If the occlusion effect is not taken into account, undermasking will occur in a significant number of cases. Martin suggests increasing the minimum effective masking level by the amount of the occlusion effect. The occlusion effect for the individual being tested can be obtained by: (1) obtaining unmasked bone conduction thresholds with both ears uncovered; (2) obtaining unmasked bone conduction thresholds with the non-test ear covered; and (3) subtracting occluded thresholds from unoccluded thresholds at each frequency (250, 500, and 1000 Hz). The difference is the client's own occlusion effect and should be added to the minimum effective masking levels.

Maximum Effective Masking Levels

Just as it is important to determine the minimum effective masking level in order to avoid undermasking, it is equally important to determine what maximum level of masking can be used without overmasking. Whenever the level of masking presented to the non-test ear exceeds the bone conduction threshold of the test ear plus interaural attenuation, there is danger that the masking noise may be heard in the test ear through cross-hearing. Should that occur, the unwanted noise in the test ear will shift the threshold of the pure tone presented to that ear. Therefore, we must find the maximum effective masking level and not exceed that level of noise in the non-test ear. Maximum masking equals the threshold of the test ear by bone conduction plus the interaural attenuation minus 5 dB. If the bone conduction threshold of the test ear is 20 dB and the interaural attenuation for that frequency is 40 dB, the maximum effective masking level is 55 dB. Maximum masking is calculated in the same way for air-conducted and bone-conducted sound delivered to the test ear.

Finding the Plateau

The concept of finding a plateau was introduced by Hood (1960) and is a part of every masking method. When it is believed that a tone presented to the test ear is actually being heard by the non-test ear, a masking noise is introduced into the non-test ear at a minimum level of intensity. Threshold is re-established in the test ear. If a threshold shift is noted in the test ear, it is assumed that the non-test ear is participating in the perception of the tone but to a lesser degree than before the introduction of the masking noise. The level of the masking noise is increased in 5- or 10-dB steps with threshold in the test ear re-established each time there is an increase in masking level. As long as threshold in the test ear continues to shift, it is assumed that the non-test ear is not adequately masked. When the level of the noise can be increased several times (i.e., 20 dB) without shifting the threshold in the test ear, the plateau has been reached. The non-test ear may be assumed to be adequately masked, and the test ear threshold may be recorded on the audiogram using the appropriate symbols. The levels of masking at which the plateau was found are also recorded on the audiogram (e.g., 40–60 dB). If masking levels are increased beyond maximum effective masking level, the threshold in the test will again increase. This threshold shift is not caused by participation of the non-test ear but by the masking effect of the noise which has crossed over into the test ear.

The masking method we recommend involves using noise which is calibrated in effective level. Masking is introduced at or near minimum effective masking level and increased until a 20-dB plateau is found. The test ear threshold at which the plateau occurred and the masking levels are recorded on the Audiologic Assessment Form. Masking levels must not be increased beyond maximum effective masking level. See Figure 5-1 for an illustration of the plateau method. This figure is similar to that used by Martin (1991:94) and Studebaker (1967). Further discussion may be found in Martin (1991:91–97), Hannley (1986:114–116), and Rintelmann (1991:169:172).

MASKING PROBLEMS

Problems of overmasking occur with all masking methods. Whenever large air–bone gaps exist, minimum effective masking level and maximum effective masking level are very close in intensity and the plateau is narrow. Sometimes it may not be possible to find a plateau. Let us assume that the right ear shows an air conduction threshold of 60 dB and a bone conduction threshold of 20 dB and that the left ear shows an air conduction threshold of 50 dB and a bone conduction threshold of 20 dB. Since there is a

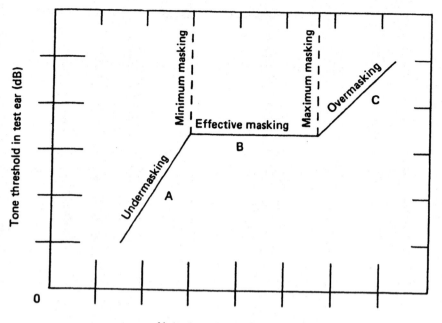

Figure 5-1. The masking function. (A) Undermasking. The tone, despite the presence of the noise, is heard in the masked ear because the level of the noise is not sufficient to mask it out. (B) The plateau. The tone has reached the threshold of the test ear, and the level of noise in the masked ear is sufficient to mask out any tone that might be present there because of cross-hearing. Since the tone is being heard in the test ear, further increments of noise do not produce threshold shift. Minimum masking is found at the lower limit of the plateau, maximum masking at the upper limit. (C) Overmasking. The masking noise is now so intense that it is heard in the test ear along with the tone because of cross-hearing. Since both signals are present in the test ear, the noise causes a threshold shift in that ear.

difference of 40 dB between right ear air conduction and left ear bone conduction, the air conduction threshold must be retested with masking noise in the left ear. Minimum effective masking level in the left ear is 50 dB; maximum effective masking level is 55 dB because 60 dB of noise may be heard in the test ear since interaural attenuation is 40 dB and the bone conduction threshold is 20 dB. In all probability a plateau cannot be found in this situation. Masking is also necessary for bone conduction since potential air–bone gaps exist in both ears. Here the situation is even more problematic because the occlusion effect must be added to the minimum effective masking level, resulting in a starting masking level that is higher in intensity than the maximum level permissi-ble. If it is not possible to obtain valid thresholds because of masking problems, it should be noted on the Audiologic Assessment Form in the "Remarks" section, and other procedures such as immittance audiometry should be used to determine the nature of the hearing loss. For further discussion of masking problems, see Hannley (1986:118–120) and Rintel-mann (1991:168–169).

Some authorities suggest the use of the insert receiver as a way to overcome masking problems. Instead of delivering the masking noise through a standard earphone, the noise is delivered to the non-test ear through a hearing aid type of receiver coupled to a stock earmold which is inserted into the ear canal. In this way the interaural attenuation can be increased about 15–20 dB, reducing the likelihood of overmasking. For further information on insert earphones, see Rose (1971:187–188), Rintelmann (1991:17–18, 825–826), Hannley (1986:118–120), and Martin (1991:89–90).

CENTRAL MASKING

When a low-level masker of insufficient intensity to cross the skull to the opposite ear is introduced into the non-test ear, it tends to produce a small shift in the pure tone or speech reception threshold of the test ear. Although Liden, Nilsson, and Anderson (1959b) observed shifts of up to 15 dB and others (Dirks and Malmquist, 1964; Studebaker, 1962) suggest that the central masking effect increases with the intensity of the masker, Martin (1991:91) states that the threshold shift averages about 5 dB. Central masking is believed to be the result of interaction of the central auditory pathways from the two ears. Martin suggests that whenever contralateral masking must be used for air or bone conduction, 5 dB should be subtracted from threshold values obtained to compensate for central masking. Since it has been demonstrated that central masking also occurs for speech signals, a 5-dB correction should be made whenever an SRT has been obtained with masking in the non-test ear. In selecting a presentation level for speech recognition material, the corrected SRT should be used. If masking is not used in obtaining the SRT but is needed for speech recognition testing, the presentation level of the stimulus should be increased by 5 dB. For further discussion of the role of central masking, see Martin (1991:91, 109, 125–126, 137) and Rintelmann (1991:145).

MASKING METHODS FOR SRT

The following procedure is suggested, based on Martin's discussion of masking (1991:91–97, 126–127):

1. Introduce a minimum level of effective masking equal to the SRT of the non-test ear or use a level 10 dB higher if there is little danger of overmasking.
2. Obtain an SRT. If this SRT shifts by no more than 5 dB from the unmasked threshold, the unmasked threshold was correct.

3. If the threshold has shifted by more than 5 dB, another SRT is obtained with an additional 5 dB of noise in the non-test ear.
4. If the threshold again shifts, the noise level is increased further and SRT is again obtained. This procedure is continued until a plateau is reached—that is, when the level of the noise can be raised or lowered in at least three 5-dB steps without affecting SRT.
5. Five dB are subtracted from this threshold to compensate for central masking. This threshold is recorded on the Audiologic Assessment Form along the maximum level of effective masking required to obtain this value.

As with pure tones, overmasking must be avoided. Maximum effective masking for speech equals the best threshold of the test ear by bone conduction plus the interaural attenuation minus 5 dB.

Some clinical facilities consider the Hood plateau method inappropriate for masking during speech audiometry (Hannley, 1986:170–171). Instead, masking noise is delivered to the non-test ear at a level 20 dB lower than the speech signal.

MASKING METHODS FOR WORD RECOGNITION

According to Martin (1991:136–137), whatever noise was used for obtaining SRT, it should also be used for word recognition and should be calibrated in effective level. A single level of masking is used. That level is determined by subtracting interaural attenuation, which is considered to be 40 dB, from the presentation level of the words to the test ear, and adding the largest air–bone gap of the non-test ear. For example, if the words are to be presented to the test ear at 80 dB HL and there is an air–bone gap in the non-test ear of 30 dB, the effective masking level is 80 − 40 + 30 = 70 dB. As with all other measures, overmasking must be avoided. Maximum effective masking level is the same as that determined for SRT. If the best bone conduction threshold in the test ear of the client described above is 40 dB HL, maximum effective masking level is 40 (bone conduction threshold) + 40 (interaural attenuation) − 5 dB = 75 dB. The larger the air–bone gap in the test ear, the greater the danger of overmasking.

Questions

QUESTIONS FOR FIGURE 5-2

1. Is masking needed for air conduction in either ear?
2. What type and degree of hearing loss are we looking at in each ear?

Name: Fig 5-2   Date: XX/XX/XX Age: 21 Sex: F Audiologist: HK

AUDIOMETER: _____   ANSI 1969

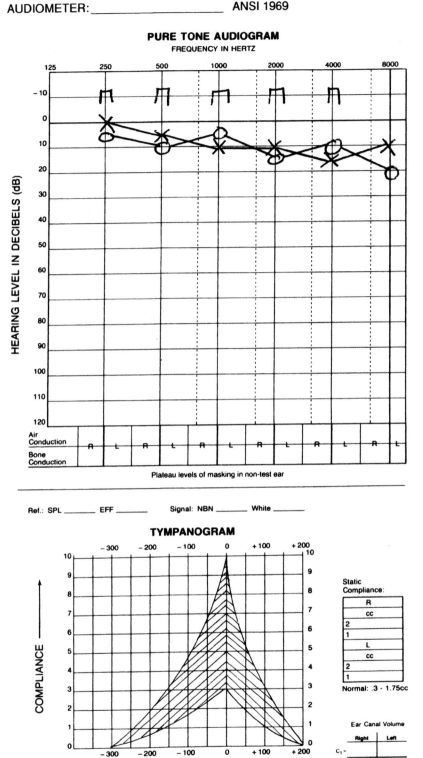

PURE TONE AUDIOGRAM
FREQUENCY IN HERTZ

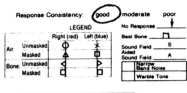

SPEECH AUDIOMETRY □ MLV □ Tape

	RIGHT	LEFT	MASK LEVEL R L	SOUND FIELD	LIST
SAT					
SRT					
MCL					
UCL					
PB% (Word)	_L_	_L_			
PB% (Word)	_L_	_L_			
PB% (Word)	_L_	_L_			
PB% (Word)	_L_	_L_			
	_L_	_L_			
	_L_	_L_			

STAPEDIUS REFLEX THRESHOLDS

Stimulus	Contralateral (HL)					Ipsilateral (HL)		
EAR	.5K	1K	2K	4K	WBN	.5K	1K	2K
R								
Decay		✕	✕					✕
L								
Decay		✕	✕			✕		✕

ABBREVIATIONS

A	Absent	NR	No Response
C₁	Canal Volume	SAT	Speech Awareness
CNE	Could Not Establish		Threshold
CNT	Could Not Test	SL	Sensation Level
DNT	Did Not Test	SRT	Speech Reception
HL	Hearing Level		Threshold
MCL	Most Comfortable	UCL	Uncomfortable Listening
	Listening Level		Level
MVL	Monitored Live Voice		

REMARKS:

_____

_____

_____

_____

_____

Ref.: SPL _____ EFF _____   Signal: NBN _____ White _____

TYMPANOGRAM

Static Compliance:

R	
cc	
2	
1	
L	
cc	
2	
1	

Normal: .3 - 1.75cc

Ear Canal Volume

	Right	Left
C₁ =		

Answers for Figure 5-2

1. Masking for air conduction is not needed at any frequency in either ear. Although air–bone gaps exist at all frequencies, none of the gaps is great enough to make suspect the air conduction thresholds. When an air-conducted signal is delivered to the test ear, we can count on 40–50 dB of interaural attenuation before that reaches the non-test ear. From our bone conduction thresholds we know that neither cochlea can hear better than –10 dB; all signals delivered to the test ear would be attenuated far below –10 dB by the time they reached the non-test ear. Therefore, masking for air conduction is not necessary.

2. Both ears show thresholds which are within normal limits. However, an air–bone gap exists in at least one ear. Without masked bone conduction thresholds, we cannot be sure which ear has the air–bone gap or whether gaps exist in both ears. It is possible that one or both ears have middle ear abnormalities despite the fact that thresholds are within normal limits. Immittance testing is clearly needed.

QUESTIONS FOR FIGURE 5-3

1. Is masking needed for air conduction in either ear?
2. What type of hearing loss are we looking at in each ear?

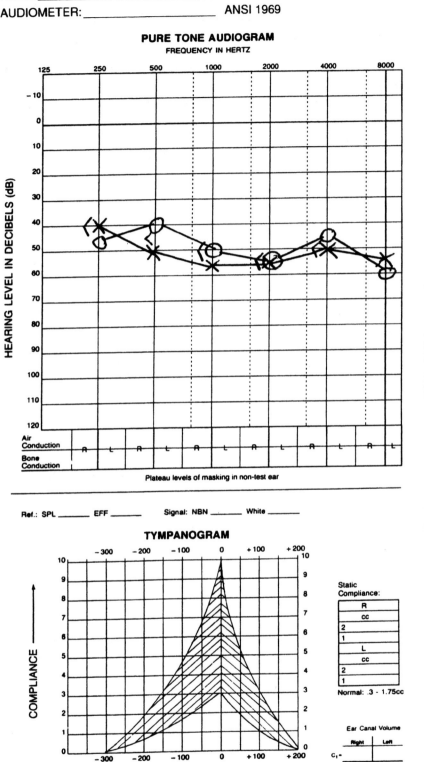

PURE TONE AUDIOGRAM
FREQUENCY IN HERTZ

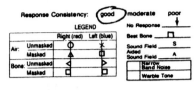

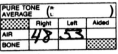

Response Consistency: (good) moderate poor

LEGEND	Right (red)	Left (blue)
Air: Unmasked	○	×
Air: Masked	△	▢
Bone: Unmasked	<	>
Bone: Masked	▢	▢

No Response
Best Bone
Sound Field   S
Aided
Sound Field   A
Narrow Band Noise
Warble Tone

PURE TONE AVERAGE	Right	Left	Aided
AIR	48	53	
BONE			

SPEECH AUDIOMETRY   ☐ MLV ☐ Tape

	RIGHT	LEFT	MASK LEVEL R L	SOUND FIELD	LIST
SAT					
SRT					
MCL					
UCL					
PB% (Word)	_L	_L			
PB% (Word)	_L	_L			
PB% (Word)	_L	_L			
PB% (Word)	_L	_L			
	_L	_L			
	_L	_L			

STAPEDIUS REFLEX THRESHOLDS

Stimulus	Contralateral (HL)					Ipsilateral (HL)		
EAR	.5K	1K	2K	4K	WBN	.5K	1K	2K
R								
Decay		✕	✕					✕
L								
Decay		✕	✕	✕				✕

ABBREVIATIONS

A	Absent	NR	No Response
C₁	Canal Volume	SAT	Speech Awareness
CNE	Could Not Establish		Threshold
CNT	Could Not Test	SL	Sensation Level
DNT	Did Not Test	SRT	Speech Reception
HL	Hearing Level		Threshold
MCL	Most Comfortable	UCL	Uncomfortable Listening
	Listening Level		Level
MVL	Monitored Live Voice		

Ref.: SPL _____ EFF _____   Signal: NBN _____ White _____

TYMPANOGRAM

PRESSURE IN daPa

Static Compliance:

R	
	cc
2	
1	
L	
	cc
2	
1	

Normal: .3 - 1.75cc

Ear Canal Volume

Right	Left

C₁ = _____

REMARKS:

_____
_____
_____
_____
_____

Answers for for Figure 5-3

1. Since air conduction thresholds in both ears and unmasked bone conduction thresholds are essentially the same, it is not necessary to mask at any frequency.
2. Each ear shows a pure sensorineural hearing loss. The unmasked bone conduction scores give us the bone conduction thresholds of the better ear. We know that bone conduction cannot be significantly poorer than air conduction. Therefore, since the two ears show essentially similar air conduction thresholds and there are no air–bone gaps, we can assume that bone conduction is similar in the two ears and comparable to the air conduction thresholds.

QUESTIONS FOR FIGURE 5-4

Case History Information This young lady lost the hearing in her left ear at age 6 because of chicken pox. She has experienced localization problems all her life and some difficulty understanding speech in the presence of noise. She reported that stimulation of the left ear was perceived as noise rather than tones or speech.

1. Do we need to retest the air conduction thresholds of either ear with masking?
2. What type of loss does the right ear have?
3. From the case history information, what type of loss would you suspect in the left ear?

Name: Fig 5-4 _____ Date: XX/XX/XX Age: 18 Sex: F Audiologist: HK
AUDIOMETER: _____ ANSI 1969

PURE TONE AUDIOGRAM
FREQUENCY IN HERTZ

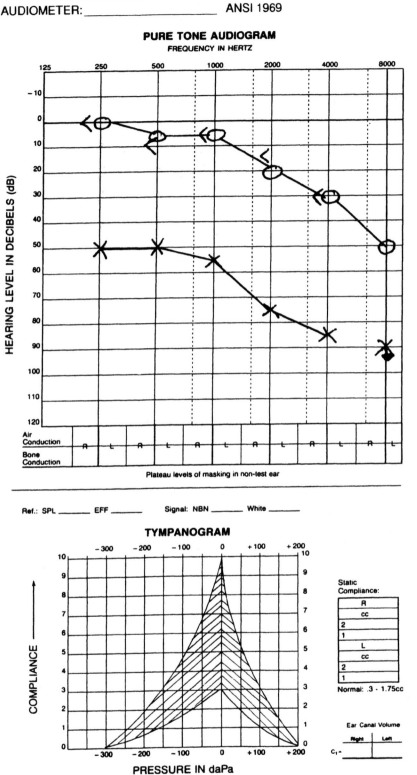

Air Conduction: R L R L R L R L R L R L R L

Bone Conduction

Plateau levels of masking in non-test ear

Ref.: SPL _____ EFF _____ Signal: NBN _____ White _____

TYMPANOGRAM

PRESSURE IN daPa

Static Compliance:

R	
	cc
2	
1	
L	
	cc
2	
1	

Normal: .3 - 1.75cc

Ear Canal Volume

	Right	Left
C₁ =		

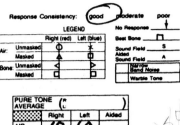

Response Consistency: good moderate poor

LEGEND

		Right (red)	Left (blue)
Air:	Unmasked	○	✗
	Masked	△	◻
Bone:	Unmasked	<	>
	Masked	◻	◻

No Response
Best Bone
Sound Field ___ S
Aided Sound Field ___ A
Narrow Band Noise
Warble Tone

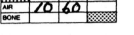

PURE TONE AVERAGE (R L)			
	Right	Left	Aided
AIR	10	60	
BONE			

SPEECH AUDIOMETRY □ MLV □ Tape

	RIGHT	LEFT	MASK LEVEL R L	SOUND FIELD	LIST
SAT					
SRT					
MCL					
UCL					
PB% (Word)	_L_	_L_			
PB% (Word)	_L_	_L_			
PB% (Word)	_L_	_L_			
PB% (Word)	_L_	_L_			
	_L_	_L_			
	_L_	_L_			

STAPEDIUS REFLEX THRESHOLDS

Stimulus	Contralateral (HL)					Ipsilateral (HL)		
EAR	.5K	1K	2K	4K	WBN	.5K	1K	2K
R								
Decay		✗	✗					✗
L								
Decay		✗	✗					✗

ABBREVIATIONS

A	Absent	NR	No Response
C₁	Canal Volume	SAT	Speech Awareness
CNE	Could Not Establish		Threshold
CNT	Could Not Test	SL	Sensation Level
DNT	Did Not Test	SRT	Speech Reception
HL	Hearing Level		Threshold
MCL	Most Comfortable	UCL	Uncomfortable Listening
	Listening Level		Level
MVL	Monitored Live Voice		

REMARKS:

_____

_____

_____

_____

Use of Masking

231

Answers for Figure 5-4

1. The left ear must be retested using appropriate levels of masking in the right ear. There are differences between air conduction thresholds and bone conduction thresholds of at least 40 dB at all frequencies. It is highly possible that the left ear may have thresholds that are considerably poorer than those shown on the audiogram. The unmasked thresholds may reflect the participation of the better ear rather than the actual thresholds of the left ear. We may be looking at a "shadow curve" or the response of the right ear to attenuated signals that reached it after contralateralizing from the left ear.

2. The right ear has a pure sensorineural loss in the high frequencies with normal hearing through 2000 Hz. Note the absence of an air–bone gap.

3. The etiology of chicken pox strongly suggests a sensorineural loss in the left ear. The inability of that ear to perceive tone as tone or speech as speech also suggests sensorineural loss. However, it is not possible to diagnose type of loss with any certainty until masked air and bone conduction thresholds are obtained for the left ear.

QUESTIONS FOR FIGURE 5-5

Supplementary Information This is the same audiogram as that presented in Figure 5-4. Masked air conduction thresholds were obtained for the left ear.

1. How do masked and unmasked air conduction thresholds for the left ear compare to each other? What can you conclude about unmasked thresholds?
2. What type of masking was used and how was it calibrated?
3. What type of loss exists in the left ear?

Name: Fig 5-5   Date: XX/XX/XX   Age: 18   Sex: F   Audiologist: HK

AUDIOMETER: _____   ANSI 1969

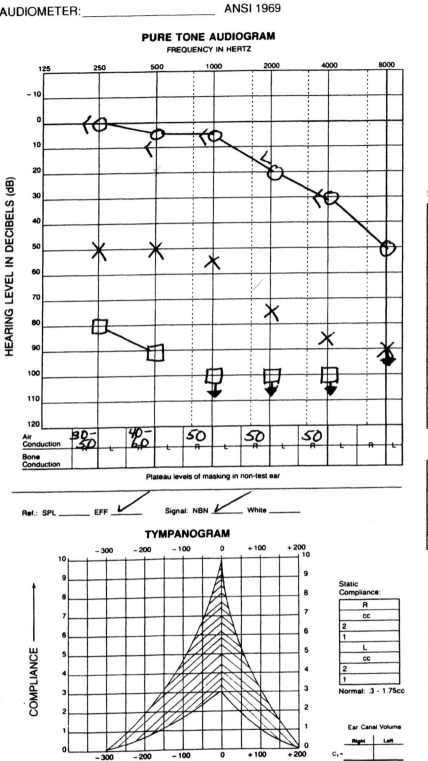

PURE TONE AUDIOGRAM
FREQUENCY IN HERTZ

HEARING LEVEL IN DECIBELS (dB)

| Air Conduction | 30-50 | 40-60 | 50 | 50 | 50 | | |
| Bone Conduction | | | | | | | |

Plateau levels of masking in non-test ear

Ref.: SPL _____ EFF _____   Signal: NBN _____ White _____

TYMPANOGRAM

COMPLIANCE

PRESSURE IN daPa

Static Compliance:

R	
	cc
2	
1	
L	
	cc
2	
1	

Normal: .3 - 1.75cc

Ear Canal Volume

	Right	Left
C₁ =		

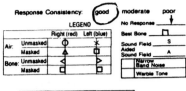

Response Consistency: (good) moderate poor

LEGEND

		Right (red)	Left (blue)
Air:	Unmasked	O	X
	Masked	△	☐
Bone:	Unmasked	<	>
	Masked	☐	☐

No Response
Best Bone ☐
Sound Field ___ S
Aided Sound Field ___ A
Narrow Band Noise
Warble Tone

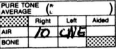

PURE TONE AVERAGE	Right	Left	Aided
AIR	10	CNE	
BONE			

SPEECH AUDIOMETRY   ☐ MLV ☐ Tape

	RIGHT	LEFT	MASK LEVEL R / L	SOUND FIELD	LIST
SAT					
SRT					
MCL					
UCL					
PB% (Word)	_L	_L			
PB% (Word)	_L	_L			
PB% (Word)	_L	_L			
PB% (Word)		_L			
	_L	_L			
	_L	_L			

STAPEDIUS REFLEX THRESHOLDS

Stimulus	Contralateral (HL)					Ipsilateral (HL)		
EAR	.5K	1K	2K	4K	WBN	.5K	1K	2K
R								
Decay			✕	✕				✕
L								
Decay			✕	✕			✕	✕

ABBREVIATIONS

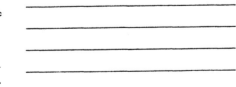

A	Absent	NR	No Response
C₁	Canal Volume	SAT	Speech Awareness Threshold
CNE	Could Not Establish		
CNT	Could Not Test	SL	Sensation Level
DNT	Did Not Test	SRT	Speech Reception Threshold
HL	Hearing Level		
MCL	Most Comfortable Listening Level	UCL	Uncomfortable Listening Level
MVL	Monitored Live Voice		

REMARKS:

_____

_____

_____

_____

Answers for Figure 5-5

1. When masking was used in the right ear, the left ear air conduction thresholds became considerably poorer. At 1000, 2000, 4000, and 8000 Hz, responses could not be obtained. One must conclude that unmasked left ear thresholds represent a shadow curve of the right ear.
2. Narrow band masking calibrated in effective level was used.
3. Since we do not have masked bone conduction thresholds for the left ear, we do not know what type of loss exists in that ear. The loss may be purely sensorineural or it may be mixed, particularly in the low frequencies. We do know that the loss cannot be purely conductive in nature because of its severity. Any hearing loss that exceeds 65 to 70 dB must have a sensorineural component.

QUESTIONS FOR FIGURE 5-6

1. Do we need to retest air conduction thresholds of either ear with masking? Why?
2. Which ear is the better ear?

PURE TONE AUDIOGRAM

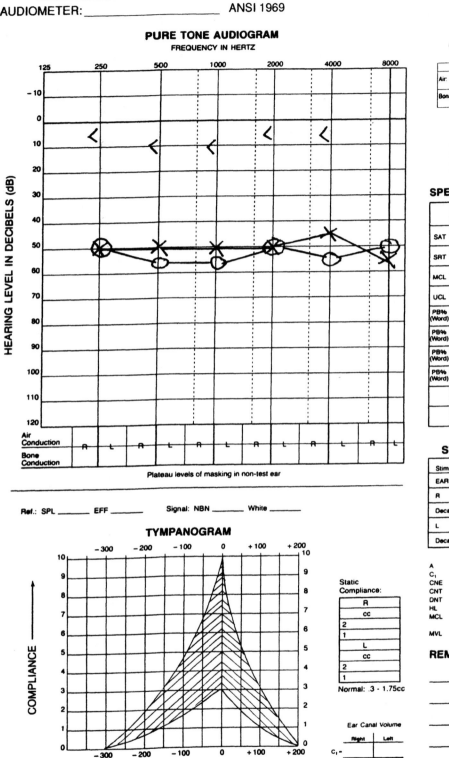

SPEECH AUDIOMETRY □ MLV □ Tape

	RIGHT	LEFT	MASK LEVEL R	L	SOUND FIELD	LIST
SAT						
SRT						
MCL						
UCL						
PB% (Word)	_L	_L				
PB% (Word)	_L	_L				
PB% (Word)	_L	_L				
PB% (Word)	_L	_L				
	_L	_L				
	_L	_L				

STAPEDIUS REFLEX THRESHOLDS

Stimulus	Contralateral (HL)					Ipsilateral (HL)		
EAR	.5K	1K	2K	4K	WBN	.5K	1K	2K
R								
Decay			✕	✕				✕
L								
Decay		✕	✕			✕		✕

ABBREVIATIONS

A	Absent	NR	No Response
C₁	Canal Volume	SAT	Speech Awareness
CNE	Could Not Establish		Threshold
CNT	Could Not Test	SL	Sensation Level
DNT	Did Not Test	SRT	Speech Reception
HL	Hearing Level		Threshold
MCL	Most Comfortable	UCL	Uncomfortable Listening
	Listening Level		Level
MVL	Monitored Live Voice		

REMARKS:

_____

_____

_____

_____

_____

Ref.: SPL _____ EFF _____   Signal: NBN _____ White _____

TYMPANOGRAM

Static Compliance:

R	
	cc
2	
1	
L	
	cc
2	
1	

Normal: .3 - 1.75cc

Ear Canal Volume

	Right	Left
C₁ -		

Answers for Figure 5-6

1. We need to retest both ears at all frequencies with contralateral masking because there are air–bone gaps of at least 40 dB at all frequencies.

2. From the information on this audiogram there is no way to know which ear is better. All we can tell is that the unmasked air and bone conduction thresholds represent one ear, but until masked air conduction thresholds are obtained, we cannot determine which ear that may be. It is possible that both ears have the same air conduction thresholds, but that information will be available to us only when masked thresholds are obtained.

   The same observations are true for bone conduction. Although the symbols for bone conduction indicate that the receiver was placed on the right mastoid, without masking we cannot be sure which ear(s) has thresholds at the levels reported. It should also be noted that if there are conductive losses bilaterally of the magnitude suggested by the unmasked air conduction thresholds, this represents one of the most difficult masking situations for obtaining true bone conduction results for each ear. Masking problems are illustrated later in this chapter.

QUESTIONS FOR FIGURE 5-7

Supplementary Information This is the same client as reported for the unmasked audiogram in Figure 5-6.

1. How do masked air conduction thresholds compare to unmasked thresholds obtained in Figure 5-6?
2. What type of masking was used and how was it calibrated?
3. What did the use of the insert receiver accomplish?

Name: Fig 5-7   Date: XX/XX/XX   Age: 10   Sex: M   Audiologist: HK

AUDIOMETER: _____   ANSI 1969

PURE TONE AUDIOGRAM
FREQUENCY IN HERTZ

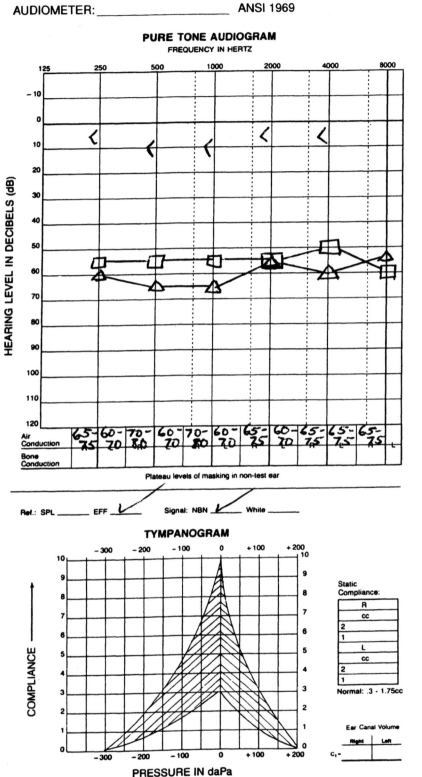

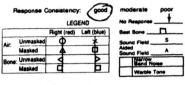

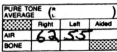

PURE TONE AVERAGE (R / L)

	Right	Left	Aided
AIR	62	55	
BONE			

Air Conduction	65-75	60-70	70-80	60-70	70-80	60-70	65-75	60-70	65-75	65-75	65-75
Bone Conduction											

Plateau levels of masking in non-test ear

Ref.: SPL _____ EFF ✓   Signal: NBN ✓   White _____

SPEECH AUDIOMETRY ☐ MLV ☐ Tape

	RIGHT	LEFT	MASK LEVEL R	L	SOUND FIELD	LIST
SAT						
SRT						
MCL						
UCL						
PB% (Word)	L	L				
PB% (Word)	L	L				
PB% (Word)	L	L				
PB% (Word)	L	L				
	L	L				
	L	L				

STAPEDIUS REFLEX THRESHOLDS

Stimulus	Contralateral (HL)					Ipsilateral (HL)		
EAR	.5K	1K	2K	4K	WBN	.5K	1K	2K
R								
Decay		X	X					X
L								
Decay		X	X					X

ABBREVIATIONS

A — Absent
C₁ — Canal Volume
CNE — Could Not Establish
CNT — Could Not Test
DNT — Did Not Test
HL — Hearing Level
MCL — Most Comfortable Listening Level
MVL — Monitored Live Voice
NR — No Response
SAT — Speech Awareness Threshold
SL — Sensation Level
SRT — Speech Reception Threshold
UCL — Uncomfortable Listening Level

TYMPANOGRAM

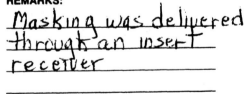

Static Compliance:

R	
	cc
2	
1	
L	
	cc
2	
1	

Normal: .3 - 1.75cc

Ear Canal Volume

	Right	Left
C₁ =		

PRESSURE IN daPa

REMARKS: Masking was delivered through an insert receiver

Use of Masking

Answers for Figure 5-7

1. Masked air conduction thresholds in both ears are 5–10 dB poorer than unmasked thresholds. This threshold shift is probably due to central masking, which is the interaction of the noise and pure tone signals in the central auditory pathways.
2. Narrow band noise calibrated in effective level was used as the masker.
3. The insert receiver was used to increase the amount of interaural attenuation to allow higher levels of masking noise to be used without risk of overmasking. Whenever there are large air–bone gaps, there is an increased risk of overmasking, and insert receivers reduce this risk. The insert increases the amount of interaural attenuation by reducing the amount of occlusion effect. See discussion of the occlusion effect in this chapter.

QUESTIONS FOR FIGURE 5-8

1. How do unmasked air conduction thresholds compare to masked thresholds?
2. What type of hearing loss exists in each ear?
3. What do the tympanograms suggest?

Name: Fig 5-8   Date: XX/XX/XX   Age: 15   Sex: M   Audiologist: HK

AUDIOMETER: _____   ANSI 1969

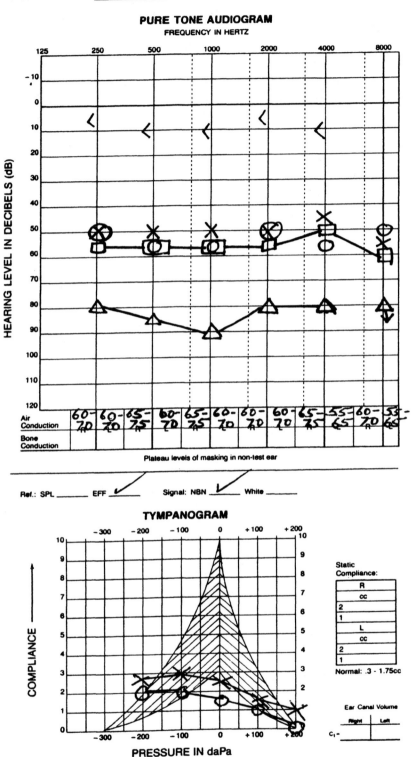

PURE TONE AUDIOGRAM
FREQUENCY IN HERTZ

Air Conduction plateau levels:
125	250	500	1000	2000	4000	8000
60-70	60-70	65-75	60-70	65-75	60-70	60-70	60-70	65-75	55-65	60-70	55-65

Bone Conduction

Plateau levels of masking in non-test ear

Ref.: SPL _____ EFF _____   Signal: NBN _____ White _____

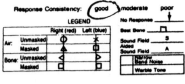

Response Consistency: (good) moderate poor

LEGEND

		Right (red)	Left (blue)
Air:	Unmasked	O	X
	Masked	▲	☐
Bone:	Unmasked	◁	▷
	Masked		

No Response
Best Bone
Sound Field S
Aided Sound Field A
Narrow Band Noise
Warble Tone

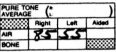

PURE TONE AVERAGE (R: / L:)

	Right	Left	Aided
AIR	85	55	
BONE			

SPEECH AUDIOMETRY ☐ MLV ☐ Tape

	RIGHT	LEFT	MASK LEVEL R	L	SOUND FIELD	LIST
SAT						
SRT						
MCL						
UCL						
PB% (Word)	L	L				
PB% (Word)	L	L				
PB% (Word)	L	L				
PB% (Word)	L	L				
	L	L				
	L	L				

STAPEDIUS REFLEX THRESHOLDS

Stimulus	Contralateral (HL)					Ipsilateral (HL)		
EAR	.5K	1K	2K	4K	WBN	.5K	1K	2K
R								
Decay		X	X				X	X
L								
Decay		X	X			X	X	X

ABBREVIATIONS

A	Absent	NR	No Response
C₁	Canal Volume	SAT	Speech Awareness
CNE	Could Not Establish		Threshold
CNT	Could Not Test	SL	Sensation Level
DNT	Did Not Test	SRT	Speech Reception
HL	Hearing Level		Threshold
MCL	Most Comfortable	UCL	Uncomfortable Listening
	Listening Level		Level
MVL	Monitored Live Voice		

REMARKS:
Masking was delivered through an insert receiver

TYMPANOGRAM

Static Compliance:
R	
	cc
2	
1	
L	
	cc
2	
1	

Normal: .3 - 1.75cc

Ear Canal Volume
Right	Left
C₁ =	

PRESSURE IN daPa

Use of Masking

239

Answers for Figure 5-8

1. In the left ear, masked air conduction thresholds are 5 dB poorer than unmasked thresholds, probably due to central masking. In the right ear, however, there is more of a threshold shift than can be attributed to central masking; the masked thresholds are 25–35 dB poorer than the unmasked thresholds. This indicates that in the unmasked condition, the apparent response of the right ear was actually the response of the left ear, and the right ear is actually significantly poorer than the left. Note that in Figure 5-6 the unmasked thresholds were identical to those in this audiogram, but when appropriate masking was used, the audiograms no longer remained the same.

2. Although we need to obtain masked bone conduction thresholds to completely answer this question, certain conclusions can be drawn from the information we already have. First, the unmasked bone conduction thresholds must represent the left ear. The maximum conductive loss possible is 65 dB; when the air conduction thresholds are in excess of 65–70 dB, there must be a sensorineural component and bone conduction thresholds cannot be normal. This is the situation in the right ear. Therefore, the normal unmasked bone conduction thresholds must represent the better left ear. Second, since the bone conduction thresholds represent the left ear, we know that the loss in that ear is purely conductive. Third, the loss in the right ear cannot be purely conductive because of the extent of the air conduction loss. However, without masked bone conduction thresholds, we cannot tell whether the hearing loss is purely sensorineural or mixed.

3. The tympanograms in both ears are essentially flat, suggesting an immobile middle ear system. They are consistent with conductive hearing loss.

QUESTIONS FOR FIGURE 5-9

Supplementary Information The unmasked data in Figure 5-9 are the same as the unmasked data in Figure 5-2.

1. Why were bone conduction thresholds retested with masking in the non-test ear while air conduction thresholds were not?
2. What type of loss exists in the left ear? What type of loss exists in the right?
3. Are the tympanograms consistent with the pure tone results?

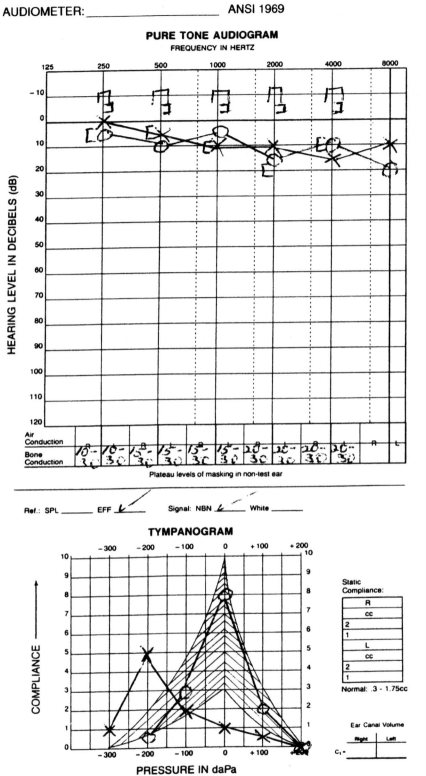

PURE TONE AUDIOGRAM
FREQUENCY IN HERTZ

HEARING LEVEL IN DECIBELS (dB)

Air Conduction										R	L
Bone Conduction	10-30	10-30	15-30	15-30	15-30	20-30	15-30	20-30	20-30		

Plateau levels of masking in non-test ear

Ref.: SPL _____ EFF ↙   Signal: NBN ↙ White _____

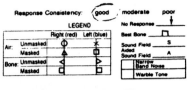

Response Consistency: (good) moderate poor

LEGEND

		Right (red)	Left (blue)
Air:	Unmasked	◯	✗
	Masked	△	☐
Bone:	Unmasked	◁	▷
	Masked	☐	☐

No Response
Best Bone ☐
Sound Field ___ S
Aided
Sound Field ___ A
Narrow Band Noise
Warble Tone

PURE TONE AVERAGE (R / L)			
	Right	Left	Aided
AIR	10	8	
BONE			

SPEECH AUDIOMETRY ☐ MLV ☐ Tape

	RIGHT	LEFT	MASK LEVEL R	MASK LEVEL L	SOUND FIELD	LIST
SAT						
SRT						
MCL						
UCL						
PB% (Word)	_L_	_L_				
PB% (Word)	_L_	_L_				
PB% (Word)	_L_	_L_				
PB% (Word)	_L_	_L_				
	_L_	_L_				
	_L_	_L_				

STAPEDIUS REFLEX THRESHOLDS

Stimulus	Contralateral (HL)					Ipsilateral (HL)		
EAR	.5K	1K	2K	4K	WBN	.5K	1K	2K
R								
Decay		✗	✗					✗
L								
Decay			✗	✗				✗

ABBREVIATIONS

A	Absent	NR	No Response
C₁	Canal Volume	SAT	Speech Awareness
CNE	Could Not Establish		Threshold
CNT	Could Not Test	SL	Sensation Level
DNT	Did Not Test	SRT	Speech Reception
HL	Hearing Level		Threshold
MCL	Most Comfortable	UCL	Uncomfortable Listening
	Listening Level		Level
MVL	Monitored Live Voice		

REMARKS:

_____

_____

_____

_____

TYMPANOGRAM

COMPLIANCE

PRESSURE IN daPa

Static Compliance:

R	
	cc
2	
1	

L	
	cc
2	
1	

Normal: .3 - 1.75cc

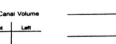

Ear Canal Volume

Right	Left
C₁ =	

Answers for Figure 5-9

1. It was unnecessary to use contralateral masking for air conduction because none of the air–bone gaps were as great as 40 dB; therefore, we could feel confident that right and left ear thresholds represented hearing in the actual ears tested. However, we use a different masking rule for bone conduction. Without masking in the non-test ear, we cannot be sure which ear is responding to the bone-conducted signal. Whenever significant air–bone gaps (bone better than air by at least 10 dB) appear, it is important to obtain accurate estimates of threshold in each ear in order to find out in which ear the conductive loss exists. Since unmasked bone conduction thresholds were at least 10 dB more sensitive than air conduction thresholds in both ears, it was necessary to retest all frequencies in each ear with masking in the non-test ear to find out where a conductive loss existed.

2. Although the left ear has essentially normal hearing by air conduction, there is evidence of middle ear pathology; significant air–bone gaps exist between masked bone conduction and air conduction thresholds. Note the 5-dB threshold shift between unmasked and masked bone conduction caused by central masking.

    The right ear has normal hearing. Air and masked bone conduction thresholds agree well with each other and are within normal limits.

3. The tympanogram for the right ear shows normal middle ear pressure and mobility, consistent with normal hearing. On the other hand, the left ear tympanogram shows significant negative middle ear pressure of –200 daPa. These results are consistent with conductive hearing loss.

QUESTIONS FOR FIGURE 5-10

Supplementary Information The air conduction and the unmasked bone conduction data are the same as in Figures 5-4 and 5-5.

1. Why was left ear bone conduction tested with masking in the non-test ear while right ear bone conduction was not?
2. What type of loss exists in the right ear? What type of loss exists in the left?
3. Are the tympanograms consistent with the air and bone conduction thresholds?

PURE TONE AUDIOGRAM
FREQUENCY IN HERTZ

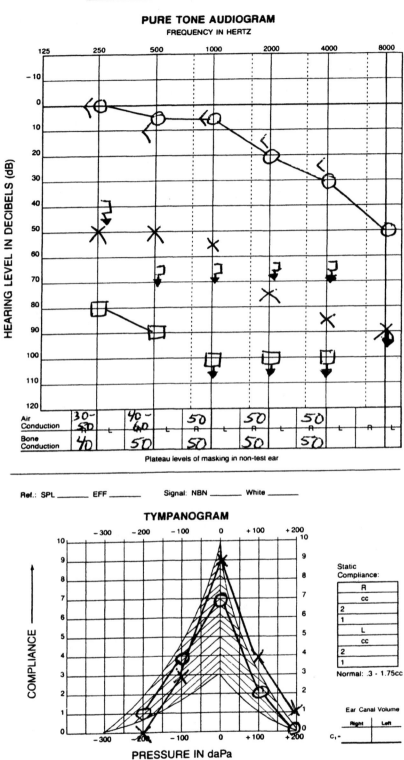

| Air Conduction | 30-50 | | 40-60 | | 50 | | 50 | | 50 | | | |
| Bone Conduction | 40 | | 50 | | 50 | | 50 | | 50 | | | |

Plateau levels of masking in non-test ear

Ref.: SPL _____ EFF _____   Signal: NBN _____ White _____

TYMPANOGRAM

Static Compliance:

R	
	cc
2	
1	
L	
	cc
2	
1	

Normal: .3 - 1.75cc

Ear Canal Volume

	Right	Left
C₁ -		

PRESSURE IN daPa

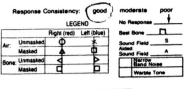

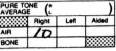

PURE TONE AVERAGE (R / L)			
	Right	Left	Aided
AIR	10		
BONE			

SPEECH AUDIOMETRY   ☐ MLV ☐ Tape

	RIGHT	LEFT	MASK LEVEL R L	SOUND FIELD	LIST
SAT					
SRT					
MCL					
UCL					
PB% (Word)	_L_	_L_			
PB% (Word)		_L_ _L_			
PB% (Word)		_L_ _L_			
PB% (Word)		_L_ _L_			
	_L_	_L_			
	_L_	_L_			

STAPEDIUS REFLEX THRESHOLDS

Stimulus	Contralateral (HL)					Ipsilateral (HL)		
EAR	.5K	1K	2K	4K	WBN	.5K	1K	2K
R								
Decay			✕	✕				✕
L								
Decay			✕	✕				✕

ABBREVIATIONS

A	Absent	NR	No Response
C₁	Canal Volume	SAT	Speech Awareness
CNE	Could Not Establish		Threshold
CNT	Could Not Test	SL	Sensation Level
DNT	Did Not Test	SRT	Speech Reception
HL	Hearing Level		Threshold
MCL	Most Comfortable	UCL	Uncomfortable Listening
	Listening Level		Level
MVL	Monitored Live Voice		

REMARKS:

_____

_____

_____

_____

Answers for Figure 5-10

1. No air–bone gaps existed in the right ear between air conduction and unmasked bone conduction; therefore, we can assume that the unmasked bone conduction thresholds represent the actual thresholds of the right ear. (The bone conduction cannot be significantly poorer than the air conduction.) However, large air–bone gaps exist between air conduction and unmasked bone conduction in the left ear; there is no way to determine the actual bone conduction thresholds of that ear without contralateral masking.

2. The right ear has a pure sensorineural loss in the high frequencies with normal hearing through 1000 Hz. Because of the lack of responses to bone conduction and the history (see Figure 5-4), the left ear also has a pure sensorineural loss. Although there is a chance the loss in the left ear is mixed, if there is a conductive component we would expect that some responses to bone-conducted signals presented with contralateral masking would have been obtained.

3. The tympanograms in both ears indicate normal middle ear pressure and mobility and are consistent with sensorineural hearing loss.

QUESTIONS FOR FIGURE 5-11

Supplementary Information The unmasked data are the same as in Figures 5-6 and 5-7.

1. Why was it necessary to mask both ears for both air and bone conduction?
2. What type of hearing loss exists in the right ear? Why type exists in the left ear?
3. To what do you attribute the threshold shifts that occurred when masking was used in the non-test ear?

Name: Fig 5-11   Date: XX/XX/XX Age: 10   Sex: M   Audiologist: HK

AUDIOMETER: _____   ANSI 1969

PURE TONE AUDIOGRAM
FREQUENCY IN HERTZ

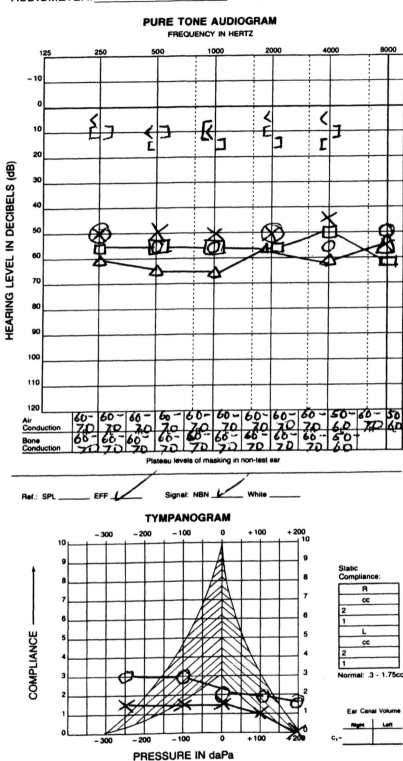

Air Conduction

60- 70	60- 70	60- 70	60- 70	60- 70	60- 70	60- 70	60- 70	60- 70	50- 60	60- 70	50 60

Bone Conduction

60- 70	60- 70	60- 70	60- 70	70 70	60- 70	70 70	70 70	60- 70	50- 60	

Plateau levels of masking in non-test ear

Ref.: SPL _____ EFF ✓   Signal: NBN ✓ White _____

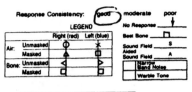

Response Consistency: (good) moderate poor

LEGEND

		Right (red)	Left (blue)
Air	Unmasked	O	X
	Masked	△	☐
Bone	Unmasked	<	>
	Masked	☐	☐

No Response _____
Best Bone _____ ☐
Sound Field _____ S
Aided
Sound Field _____ A
Narrow Band Noise
Warble Tone

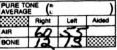

PURE TONE AVERAGE (R: / L:)	Right	Left	Aided
AIR	60 55		
BONE	73 73		

SPEECH AUDIOMETRY   ☐ MLV ☐ Tape

	RIGHT	LEFT	MASK LEVEL R	L	SOUND FIELD	LIST
SAT						
SRT						
MCL						
UCL						
PB% (Word)	_L_	_L_				
PB% (Word)	_L_	_L_				
PB% (Word)	_L_	_L_				
PB% (Word)	_L_	_L_				
	_L_	_L_				
	_L_	_L_				

STAPEDIUS REFLEX THRESHOLDS

Stimulus	Contralateral (HL)					Ipsilateral (HL)		
EAR	.5K	1K	2K	4K	WBN	.5K	1K	2K
R	NR	NR	NR	NR				
Decay			✗	✗				✗
L	NR	NR	NR	NR				
Decay			✗	✗				✗

ABBREVIATIONS

A	Absent	NR	No Response
C₁	Canal Volume	SAT	Speech Awareness
CNE	Could Not Establish		Threshold
CNT	Could Not Test	SL	Sensation Level
DNT	Did Not Test	SRT	Speech Reception
HL	Hearing Level		Threshold
MCL	Most Comfortable	UCL	Uncomfortable Listening
	Listening Level		Level
MVL	Monitored Live Voice		

TYMPANOGRAM

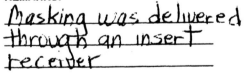

Static Compliance:

R	
	cc
2	
1	

L	
	cc
2	
1	

Normal: .3 - 1.75cc

Ear Canal Volume

Right	Left

C₁ -

REMARKS:

Masking was delivered through an insert receiver

_____
_____

Answers for Figure 5-11

1. It was necessary to retest air conduction in both ears because air–bone gaps of at least 40 dB exist in both ears at all frequencies. Masked bone conduction thresholds had to be obtained to find out whether one or both ears had a conductive loss and which ear it might be. With only unmasked bone conduction, the following situations were possible: (a) a conductive loss in the right ear and a pure sensorineural loss in the left (if that were the case, the unmasked bone conduction thresholds would represent the right ear); (b) the reversed situation, with the unmasked bone conduction thresholds representing the left ear; (c) a bilateral conductive hearing loss with unmasked bone conduction thresholds similar in both ears (this is the actual situation depicted in the audiogram); and (d) a pure conductive loss in one ear and a mixed loss in the other (in this situation, bone conduction thresholds would be poorer in one ear but not as poor as air conduction). Only with appropriate contralateral masking can we determine which of the above possibilities exists.

2. Both ears have pure conductive hearing losses. Note the abnormal tympanograms and absent acoustic reflexes.

3. The threshold shifts that occurred with contralateral masking with air conduction and bone conduction may be attributed to central masking. Note that the threshold shifts are very small, no more than 10 dB at any frequency.

QUESTIONS FOR FIGURE 5-12

1. Which ears were masked for air conduction? Why?
2. Which ears were masked for bone conduction? Why?
3. What type of loss exists in the right ear? What type of loss exists in the left ear?
4. Are immittance results consistent with pure tone test results?

Name: Fig 5-12   Date: XX/XX/XX Age: 30 Sex: F Audiologist: HK
AUDIOMETER: _____   ANSI 1969

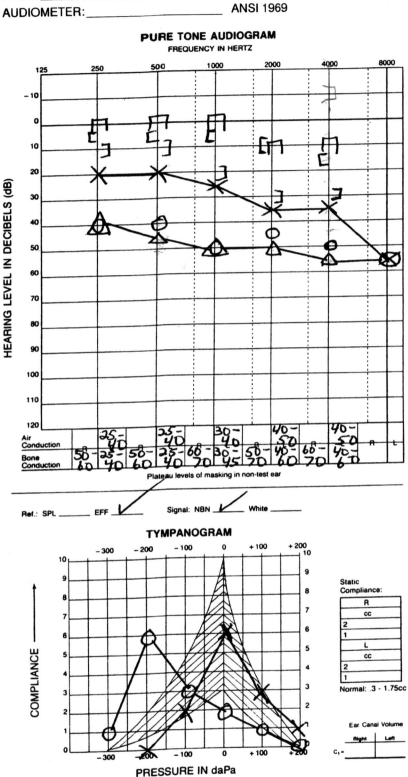

PURE TONE AUDIOGRAM
FREQUENCY IN HERTZ

Air Conduction / Bone Conduction plateau levels table:

	125	250	500	1000	2000	4000	8000	R	L
Air Conduction		25–40	25–40	30–40	40–50	40–50			
Bone Conduction	50–25–60	40	50–25–60	40	60–30–70	45	50–40–60	40	60–70	6–0

Plateau levels of masking in non-test ear

Ref.: SPL _____ EFF ↙   Signal: NBN ↙   White _____

TYMPANOGRAM

PRESSURE IN daPa

COMPLIANCE

Static Compliance:

R	
cc	
2	
1	

L	
cc	
2	
1	

Normal: .3 - 1.75cc

Ear Canal Volume

Right	Left

C₁ =

$C_1 =$

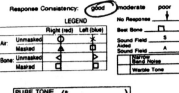

Response Consistency: (good) moderate poor

No Response ↓

LEGEND

		Right (red)	Left (blue)
Air:	Unmasked	○	✕
	Masked	△	□
Bone:	Unmasked	◁	▷
	Masked	□	□

Best Bone	⊓
Sound Field	S
Aided Sound Field	A
Narrow Band Noise	
Warble Tone	

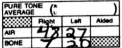

PURE TONE AVERAGE (R L)			
	Right	Left	Aided
AIR	43	27	
BONE	7	20	

SPEECH AUDIOMETRY ☐ MLV ☐ Tape

	RIGHT	LEFT	MASK LEVEL R	L	SOUND FIELD	LIST
SAT						
SRT						
MCL						
UCL						
PB% (Word)	_L_	_L_				
PB% (Word)	_L_	_L_				
PB% (Word)	_L_	_L_				
PB% (Word)	_L_	_L_				
	_L_	_L_				
	_L_	_L_				

STAPEDIUS REFLEX THRESHOLDS

Stimulus	Contralateral (HL)					Ipsilateral (HL)		
EAR	.5K	1K	2K	4K	WBN	.5K	1K	2K
R	NR	NR	NR	NR	✕	✕	✕	✕
Decay					✕			✕
L	NR	NR	NR	NR	✕	✕	✕	✕
Decay					✕			✕

ABBREVIATIONS

A	Absent	NR	No Response
C₁	Canal Volume	SAT	Speech Awareness
CNE	Could Not Establish		Threshold
CNT	Could Not Test	SL	Sensation Level
DNT	Did Not Test	SRT	Speech Reception
HL	Hearing Level		Threshold
MCL	Most Comfortable	UCL	Uncomfortable Listening
	Listening Level		Level
MVL	Monitored Live Voice		

REMARKS:

_____

_____

_____

_____

_____

Use of Masking

Answers for Figure 5-12

1. Only the right ear was masked for air conduction. It was not necessary to test the left ear with contralateral masking because the air–bone gaps were not as great as 40 dB at any frequency. Thus we can assume that unmasked air conduction thresholds in the left ear were not influenced by participation of the right. In the right ear, on the other hand, the air–bone gaps all exceeded 40 dB except for 250, making contralateral masking necessary.

2. It was necessary to obtain masked bone conduction thresholds for both ears because significant air–bone gaps were present. With unmasked bone conduction thresholds only, it was not possible to determine which ear had the conductive loss.

3. The right ear has a pure conductive loss. The left ear shows a mixed loss which is borderline conductive in the low frequencies and purely sensorineural at 1000 Hz and above. Note that the poorer ear by air conduction is the better ear by bone conduction.

4. The right ear tympanogram indicates normal pressure and mobility, consistent with sensorineural hearing loss. The left ear tympanogram shows impaired mobility (–200 daPa), which is consistent with conductive or mixed hearing loss. The absent acoustic reflexes in both ears are to be expected when one ear has a conductive component. Immittance and pure tone test results are in agreement.

QUESTIONS FOR FIGURE 5-13

1. Which ear(s) was masked for air conduction and at which frequencies? Why?
2. Which ear(s) was masked for bone conduction and at which frequencies? Why?
3. Why was it necessary to use masking for right ear SRT?
4. How much and what kind of masking was used?

Name: Fig 5-13   Date: XX/XX/XX   Age: 33   Sex: M   Audiologist: HK
AUDIOMETER: _____   ANSI 1969

PURE TONE AUDIOGRAM
FREQUENCY IN HERTZ

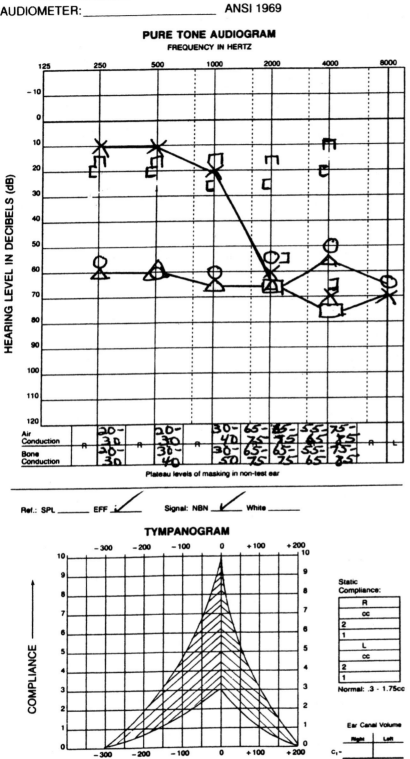

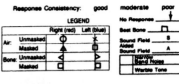

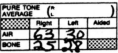

PURE TONE AVERAGE (R L)			
	Right	Left	Aided
AIR	63	30	
BONE	25	28	

Air Conduction	R	20-30	R	20-30	R	30-40	65-75	65-75	55-65	75-75	R	L
Bone Conduction		20-30		30-40		30-50	65-75	65-75	55-65	75-85		

Plateau levels of masking in non-test ear

Ref.: SPL _____ EFF ✓   Signal: NBN ✓   White _____

SPEECH AUDIOMETRY ☑MLV ☐Tape

	RIGHT	LEFT	MASK LEVEL R L	SOUND FIELD	LIST
SAT					
SRT	56	12	20-30		W-1
MCL					
UCL					
PB% (Word)	_L_	_L_			
PB% (Word)	_L_	_L_			
PB% (Word)	_L_	_L_			
PB% (Word)	_L_	_L_			
	_L_	_L_			
	_L_	_L_			

STAPEDIUS REFLEX THRESHOLDS

Stimulus	Contralateral (HL)					Ipsilateral (HL)		
EAR	.5K	1K	2K	4K	WBN	.5K	1K	2K
R								
Decay			X	X				X
L								
Decay			X	X				X

ABBREVIATIONS

A	Absent	NR	No Response
C₁	Canal Volume	SAT	Speech Awareness
CNE	Could Not Establish		Threshold
CNT	Could Not Test	SL	Sensation Level
DNT	Did Not Test	SRT	Speech Reception
HL	Hearing Level		Threshold
MCL	Most Comfortable	UCL	Uncomfortable Listening
	Listening Level		Level
MVL	Monitored Live Voice		

TYMPANOGRAM

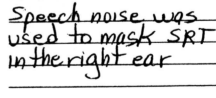

Static Compliance:

R	
cc	
2	
1	

L	
cc	
2	
1	

Normal: .3 - 1.75cc

Ear Canal Volume

	Right	Left
C₁ =		

REMARKS:

Speech noise was used to mask SRT in the right ear

Answers for Figure 5-13

1. It was necessary to mask the left ear for air conduction testing of the right ear at all frequencies because air–bone gaps of 40 dB or more exist between air conduction and unmasked bone conduction thresholds. In the left ear, however, significant air–bone gaps exist only at 2000 and 4000 Hz. Therefore, in testing the left ear, masking was necessary only at those frequencies.

2. The same situation exists for bone conduction as for air conduction. Air–bone gaps of more than 10 dB are present at all frequencies in the right ear but only at 2000 and 4000 Hz in the left. Since air conduction and bone conduction thresholds are within 5 dB of each other at 250, 500, and 1000 Hz in the left ear, we can assume that no middle ear component exists at those frequencies. However, we cannot make that assumption about the other frequencies in the left ear or any of the frequencies in the right ear without obtaining masked bone conduction thresholds.

3. It was necessary to mask the left ear while obtaining SRT in the right ear because the unmasked SRT was 44 dB poorer than the SRT in the left. In addition, unmasked SRT was 41 dB poorer than the most sensitive bone conduction threshold in the left ear. According to the rules for masking for SRT, noise must be used in the non-test ear (a) whenever the SRT exceeds the lowest bone conduction threshold of the non-test ear by 40 dB or more; or (b) whenever there is a difference of 40 dB or more between the two unmasked SRTs. In this case, both rules indicate the need for masking the non-test ear.

4. Three levels of masking were used to obtain masked SRT in the right ear: 20, 25, and 30 dB of speech noise. At all levels of masking noise the SRT remained the same. We can feel confident that 56 dB represents the SRT of the right ear without participation of the left. Note that speech noise was used as the masker instead of narrow band noise, which is used for pure tones. Speech is a broad band signal and requires a broad band masker. In contrast, pure tones are narrow band signals, requiring a narrow band masker.

QUESTIONS FOR FIGURE 5-14

1. Why was masking not presented to the left ear when the SRT was obtained in the right ear?
2. Why was masking used to obtain a word recognition score in the right ear? Why was it not necessary for the left?

Name: Fig 5-14   Date: XX/XX/XX   Age: 62   Sex: M   Audiologist: HK
AUDIOMETER: _____   ANSI 1969

PURE TONE AUDIOGRAM

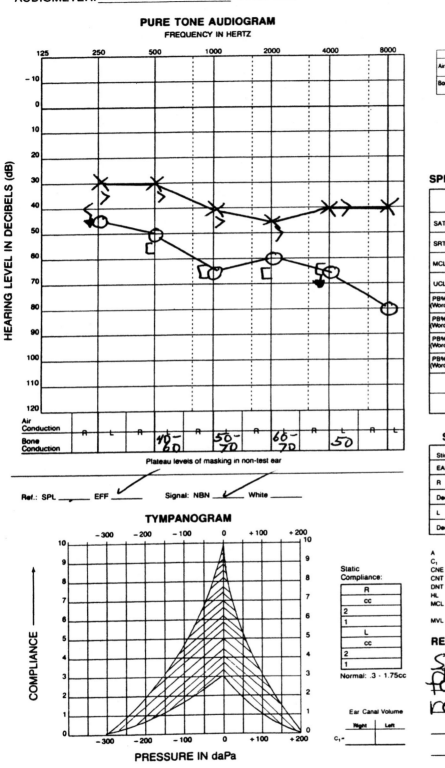

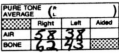

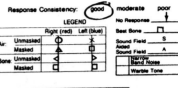

PURE TONE AVERAGE (R / L)

	Right	Left	Aided
AIR	58	38	
BONE	63	43	

SPEECH AUDIOMETRY MLV Tape

	RIGHT	LEFT	MASK LEVEL R / L	SOUND FIELD	LIST
SAT					
SRT	52	36			W-1
MCL					
UCL					
PB% (Word)	90 40SL	100 40SL	50		W-22
PB% (Word)	L	L			
PB% (Word)	L	L			
PB% (Word)	L	L			
	L	L			
	L	L			

STAPEDIUS REFLEX THRESHOLDS

Stimulus	Contralateral (HL)					Ipsilateral (HL)		
EAR	.5K	1K	2K	4K	WBN	.5K	1K	2K
R								
Decay			X	X				X
L								
Decay			X	X				X

ABBREVIATIONS

A	Absent	NR	No Response
C₁	Canal Volume	SAT	Speech Awareness
CNE	Could Not Establish		Threshold
CNT	Could Not Test	SL	Sensation Level
DNT	Did Not Test	SRT	Speech Reception
HL	Hearing Level		Threshold
MCL	Most Comfortable	UCL	Uncomfortable Listening
	Listening Level		Level
MVL	Monitored Live Voice		

REMARKS:

Speech noise was used for masking for word recognition testing

TYMPANOGRAM

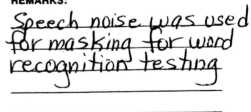

Static Compliance:

R	
	cc
2	
1	

L	
	cc
2	
1	

Normal: .3 - 1.75cc

Ear Canal Volume

	Right	Left
C₁		

Use of Masking

Answers for Figure 5-14

1. It was not necessary to use masking for SRT in the right ear because the difference between the SRTs of the two ears is only 16 dB. The difference between the SRT of the right ear and best bone conduction threshold of the left is 17 dB. Contralateral masking is necessary only when differences of 40 dB or more exist.

2. In word recognition testing, the need for masking must be determined on the basis of the presentation level of the words. In the right ear the words were presented at 40 dB above SRT or 92 dB HL. The difference between 92 dB HL and the SRT of the left ear is 56 dB. Since we can depend on only 40 dB of interaural attenuation, it is possible that without masking, the left ear will participate in the task. In the left ear the presentation level of the words was 76 dB; this is only 24 dB above the SRT in the opposite (right) ear. Therefore, masking is not needed.

QUESTIONS FOR FIGURE 5-15

1. At which frequencies in which ear is masking needed for air conduction?
2. Where is masking needed for bone conduction?
3. Using the formulas discussed in the text, compute minimum masking levels for each frequency at which contralateral masking is necessary.
4. At what levels would Martin (1991) introduce masking at each frequency where masking is necessary?

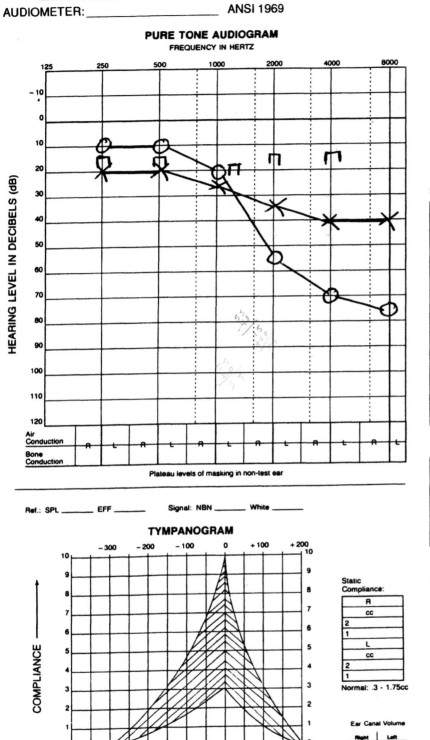

PURE TONE AUDIOGRAM
FREQUENCY IN HERTZ

Name: Fig 5-15   Date: XX/XX/XX   Age: 22   Sex: M   Audiologist: HK
AUDIOMETER: _____   ANSI 1969

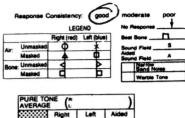

Response Consistency: good moderate poor

LEGEND		Right (red)	Left (blue)
Air:	Unmasked	○	✕
	Masked	▲	▢
Bone:	Unmasked	<	>
	Masked	☐	☐

No Response
Best Bone
Sound Field   S
Aided Sound Field   A
Narrow Band Noise
Warble Tone

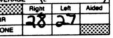

PURE TONE AVERAGE	Right	Left	Aided
AIR	28	27	
BONE			

SPEECH AUDIOMETRY   ☐ MLV ☐ Tape

	RIGHT	LEFT	MASK LEVEL R L	SOUND FIELD	LIST
SAT					
SRT					
MCL					
UCL					
PB% (Word)	_L	_L			
PB% (Word)	_L	_L			
PB% (Word)	_L	_L			
PB% (Word)	_L	_L			
	_L	_L			
	_L	_L			

STAPEDIUS REFLEX THRESHOLDS

Stimulus	Contralateral (HL)					Ipsilateral (HL)		
EAR	.5K	1K	2K	4K	WBN	.5K	1K	2K
R			✕					✕
Decay								
L								
Decay		✕						✕

ABBREVIATIONS

A	Absent	NR	No Response
C₁	Canal Volume	SAT	Speech Awareness
CNE	Could Not Establish		Threshold
CNT	Could Not Test	SL	Sensation Level
DNT	Did Not Test	SRT	Speech Reception
HL	Hearing Level		Threshold
MCL	Most Comfortable	UCL	Uncomfortable Listening
	Listening Level		Level
MVL	Monitored Live Voice		

REMARKS:

_____

_____

_____

_____

_____

Ref.: SPL _____ EFF _____   Signal: NBN _____ White _____

TYMPANOGRAM

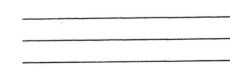

COMPLIANCE

PRESSURE IN daPa

Static Compliance:

R	
cc	
2	
1	
L	
cc	
2	
1	

Normal: .3 - 1.75cc

Ear Canal Volume

Right	Left
C₁ -	

Use of Masking

Answers for Figure 5-15.

1. For air conduction, it is necessary to mask the left ear when 2000 and 4000 Hz are being tested in the right ear. At these two frequencies there are air–bone gaps of 40 dB or more. Although air–bone gaps exist in the left ear at 2000 and 4000 Hz, they are not of sufficient magnitude to necessitate the use of masking. At 250, 500, and 1000 Hz there are no air–bone gaps in either ear.

2. For bone conduction, it is necessary to use masking at 2000 and 4000 Hz in both ears. The criterion for masking with bone conduction is the presence of an air–bone gap of 10 dB or more; in both left and right ears air–bone gaps of 20 dB or greater exist at 2000 and 4000 Hz. Therefore, masking must be used to determine whether the hearing losses at these frequencies are conductive, sensorineural, or mixed.

3. For air conduction, the minimum masking formula is: air conduction in test ear minus interaural attenuation plus air–bone gap in non-test ear.

    Using this formula for 2000 Hz in the right ear we obtain: 55 (AC in right ear) – 40 (IA) + 20 (air–bone gap in left ear) = 35 dB of masking noise in the left ear.

    At 4000 Hz in the right ear, the corresponding figures would be: 70 (AC in right ear) – 50 (IA) + 25 (air–bone gap in left ear) = 45 dB of masking noise in the left ear.

    For bone conduction, the minimum masking formula is: unmasked bone conduction of test ear plus air–bone gap in non-test ear.

    Using this formula for 2000 Hz in the right ear, we obtain: 15 (BC right ear) + 20 (air–bone gap in left ear) = 35 dB of masking noise in the left ear.

    For 4000 Hz in the right ear, the corresponding figures would be: 15 + 25 = 40 dB of masking noise in the left ear.

    For 2000 Hz in the left ear, minimum masking equals: 15 + 40 (air–bone gap in right ear) = 55 dB of masking noise in the right ear.

    For 4000 Hz in the left ear, corresponding figures would be: 15 + 55 = 70 dB of masking noise in the right ear.

4. According to Martin (1986), minimum effective masking level introduced to the non-test ear equals the air conduction threshold of that ear. However, to provide a margin of safety against the possibility of undermasking, he adds 15 dB. Using this logic, the following minimum masking levels in the non-test ear would be used:

	Air conduction		Bone conduction	
	2000 Hz	4000 Hz	2000 Hz	4000 Hz
Left	50 dB	55 dB	50 dB	55 dB
Right	70 dB	85 dB	70 dB	85 dB

    Inspection of these figures reveals the following: First, minimum masking for air conduction and for bone conduction is the same. If we were dealing with low frequencies, the minimum levels might be different for air and bone conduction because the occlusion effect would have to be considered. However, at 2000 and 4000 Hz there is no significant occlusion effect.

    Second, for both air and bone conduction, Martin's starting masker level is generally 10 dB above the minimum masking level determined by the formula. This 10 dB represents his safety margin. The only frequency at which this relationship does not exist is 4000 Hz in the right ear, where Martin's starting level is 5 dB more intense than that determined by the formula.

QUESTIONS FOR FIGURE 5-16

Supplementary Information The occlusion effect for the left ear for bone conduction testing of the right has been found to be: 250 Hz = 20 dB; 500 Hz = 10 dB; 1000 Hz = 5 dB.

1. Where is masking needed for air conduction?
2. Where is masking needed for bone conduction?
3. Using the formulas, compute minimum masking levels at which contralateral masking is necessary.
4. At what levels would Martin introduce masking at each frequency where masking is necessary?

Name: Fig 5-16   Date: XX/XX/XX   Age: 11   Sex: F   Audiologist: HK
AUDIOMETER: _____   ANSI 1969

PURE TONE AUDIOGRAM
FREQUENCY IN HERTZ

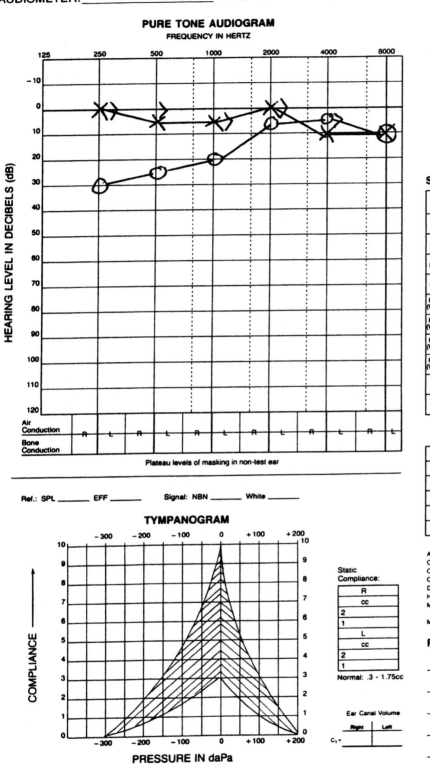

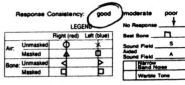

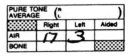

PURE TONE AVERAGE (R / L)			
	Right	Left	Aided
AIR	17	3	
BONE			

Ref.: SPL _____ EFF _____   Signal: NBN _____ White _____

TYMPANOGRAM

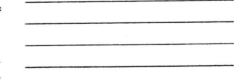

PRESSURE IN daPa

Static Compliance:

R	
	cc
2	
1	
L	
	cc
2	
1	

Normal: .3 - 1.75cc

Ear Canal Volume

	Right	Left
C₁ =		

SPEECH AUDIOMETRY □ MLV □ Tape

	RIGHT	LEFT	MASK LEVEL R L	SOUND FIELD	LIST
SAT					
SRT					
MCL					
UCL					
PB% (Word)	_L_	_L_			
PB% (Word)	_L_	_L_			
PB% (Word)	_L_	_L_			
PB% (Word)	_L_	_L_			
	_L_	_L_			
	_L_	_L_			

STAPEDIUS REFLEX THRESHOLDS

Stimulus	Contralateral (HL)					Ipsilateral (HL)		
EAR	.5K	1K	2K	4K	WBN	.5K	1K	2K
R								
Decay			✕	✕				✕
L								
Decay			✕	✕				✕

ABBREVIATIONS

A	Absent	NR	No Response
C₁	Canal Volume	SAT	Speech Awareness
CNE	Could Not Establish		Threshold
CNT	Could Not Test	SL	Sensation Level
DNT	Did Not Test	SRT	Speech Reception
HL	Hearing Level		Threshold
MCL	Most Comfortable	UCL	Uncomfortable Listening
	Listening Level		Level
MVL	Monitored Live Voice		

REMARKS:

_____

_____

_____

_____

Use of Masking

Answers for Figure 5-16

1. Masking is not needed for air conduction at any frequency in either ear. The left ear shows normal thresholds for both air and bone conduction. In the right ear, air–bone gaps exist at 250, 500, and 1000 Hz, but none of the gaps is as great as 40 dB.

2. Masking is needed for bone conduction in the right ear at 250, 500, and 1000 Hz. At these frequencies air–bone gaps of more than 10 dB exist. It is important to determine whether air–bone gaps continue to exist when the left ear is masked, indicating a conductive loss in the right ear. If the bone conduction shifts when masking is introduced to the left ear, the loss in the right ear is mixed or sensorineural.

3. For bone conduction, the minimum masking formula is: unmasked bone conduction of test ear plus air–bone gap in non-test ear.

   Using this formula for 250 Hz in the right ear, we obtain: 0 (BC test ear) + 0 (air–bone gap in non-test ear) = 0 dB of masking noise in the left ear.

   For 500 Hz in the right ear, the corresponding figures would be: 0 + 5 = 5 dB of masking noise in the left ear.

   At 1000 Hz in the right ear, the corresponding figures would be: 5 + 0 = 5 dB of masking noise in the left ear.

4. According to Martin (1991), the first level of masking introduced into the non-test ear should equal the air conduction threshold of that ear plus 10 dB of margin. In addition, in the low frequencies a possible occlusion effect in the non-test ear must be considered when masked bone conduction is obtained. Therefore, for 250 Hz the initial masking level would be determined by adding: 0 (air conduction threshold of non-test ear) + 10 (safety margin) + 20 (known occlusion effect). The initial masking level in the left ear would be 30 dB. Corresponding figures for 500 Hz would be: 5 + 10 + 10 = 25 dB of masking noise in the left ear. At 1000 Hz, corresponding figures would be: 5 + 10 + 5 = 20 dB of masking noise in the left ear. The difference between Martin's levels and the formula levels is attributable to the occlusion effect, which Martin considers but the formula does not.

QUESTIONS FOR FIGURE 5-17

1. Compute minimum masking levels at those frequencies at which masking is necessary according to the formulas discussed in the text and according to Martin's (1986) approach.
2. Using the appropriate formula, compute maximum masking at appropriate frequencies.
3. How do maximum masking levels compare to minimum masking levels? What range of levels can be safely used without overmasking?

Name: 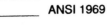 Fig 5-17   Date: XX/XX/XX   Age: 65   Sex: F   Audiologist: HK

AUDIOMETER: _____   ANSI 1969

PURE TONE AUDIOGRAM
FREQUENCY IN HERTZ

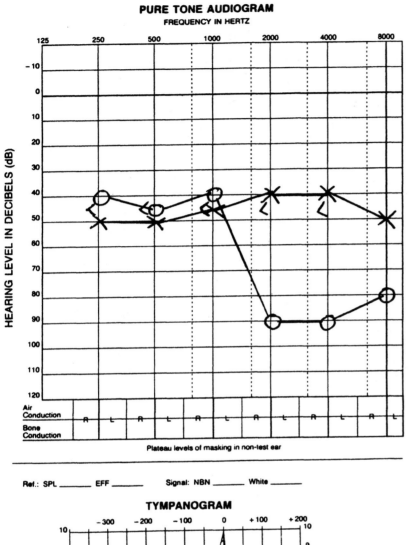

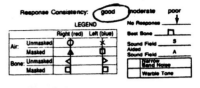

Response Consistency: (good) moderate poor

LEGEND

		Right (red)	Left (blue)
Air:	Unmasked	O	X
	Masked	▲	▢
Bone:	Unmasked	<	>
	Masked	▢	▢

Best Bone ▢
Sound Field S
Aided Sound Field A
Narrow Band Noise
Warble Tone

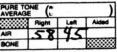

PURE TONE AVERAGE (R / L)	Right	Left	Aided
AIR	58	95	
BONE			

SPEECH AUDIOMETRY   ☐ MLV ☐ Tape

	RIGHT	LEFT	MASK LEVEL (R / L)	SOUND FIELD	LIST
SAT					
SRT					
MCL					
UCL					
PB% (Word)	_L	_L			
PB% (Word)	_L	_L			
PB% (Word)	_L	_L			
PB% (Word)	_L	_L			
	_L	_L			
	_L	_L			

STAPEDIUS REFLEX THRESHOLDS

Stimulus	Contralateral (HL)					Ipsilateral (HL)		
EAR	.5K	1K	2K	4K	WBN	.5K	1K	2K
R								
Decay			X	X			X	
L								
Decay			X	X		X		X

ABBREVIATIONS

A	Absent	NR	No Response
C₁	Canal Volume	SAT	Speech Awareness
CNE	Could Not Establish		Threshold
CNT	Could Not Test	SL	Sensation Level
DNT	Did Not Test	SRT	Speech Reception
HL	Hearing Level		Threshold
MCL	Most Comfortable	UCL	Uncomfortable Listening
	Listening Level		Level
MVL	Monitored Live Voice		

Plateau levels of masking in non-test ear

Ref.: SPL _____ EFF _____   Signal: NBN _____ White _____

TYMPANOGRAM

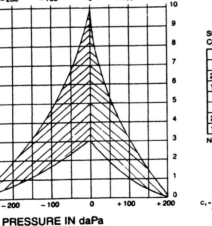

PRESSURE IN daPa

Static Compliance:

R	
	cc
2	
1	
L	
	cc
2	
1	

Normal: .3 - 1.75cc

Ear Canal Volume

	Right	Left
C₁ -		

REMARKS:

_____
_____
_____
_____
_____

Answers for Figure 5-17

1. Masking is needed only at 2000 and 4000 Hz when the right ear is being tested by both air conduction and bone conduction. The formula for minimum masking for air conduction is: air conduction in test ear minus interaural attenuation plus air–bone gap in non-test ear. Using this formula for 2000 Hz in the right ear, we obtain: 90 (AC in right ear) – 40 (IA) + 0 (air–bone gap in left ear) = 50 dB of masking in the left ear. The corresponding figures at 4000 Hz are 90 – 50 + 0 = 40 dB of masking in the left ear.

    According to Martin's approach, minimum masking equals the air conduction threshold of the non-test ear plus a 15 dB margin of safety. At 2000 Hz, minimum masking would be 55 dB; at 4000 Hz, minimum masking would also be 55 dB.

    The formula for minimum masking for bone conduction is: unmasked bone conduction of the test ear plus air–bone gap of the non-test ear. Using this formula for 2000 Hz in the right ear, we obtain: 45 (BC of the right ear) + 0 (air–bone gap of the left) = 45 dB of masking in the left ear. The corresponding figures for 4000 Hz are: 45 + 0 = 45 dB of masking in the left ear.

    Martin's approach uses the same approach as for air conduction. Therefore, minimum masking levels at 2000 and 4000 Hz are 50 dB.

2. The maximum masking formula is: unmasked bone conduction of the test ear plus interaural attenuation minus 5 dB. Using this formula, we obtain at 2000 Hz: 45 + 40 – 5 = 80 dB of masking in the left ear. Corresponding figures for 4000 Hz are: 45 + 50 – 5 = 90 dB masking in the left ear. Maximum masking is the same for air conduction and bone conduction.

3. For air conduction at 2000 Hz, there is a range of 30 dB between minimum masking (50 dB) and maximum masking (80 dB). At 4000 Hz using the formula, there is a range of 50 dB between minimum masking (40 dB) and maximum masking (90 dB). If Martin's approach is used, the range at 4000 Hz is 35 dB (maximum masking of 90 dB minus minimum masking of 55 dB).

    For bone conduction at 2000 Hz, there is a range of 35 dB between minimum masking (45 dB) and maximum masking (80 dB). At 4000 Hz, the range is 45 dB (90 – 45 dB). If Martin's approach is used, the range at 2000 Hz is 25 dB (80 – 55 dB) and at 4000 Hz the range is 35 dB (90 – 55 dB).

    Regardless of whether the formulas or Martin's approach is used, there is a sufficiently wide range of levels between minimum and maximum masking to allow for the accurate determination of masked thresholds in the right ear.

QUESTIONS FOR FIGURE 5-18

Supplementary Information This audiogram is the same as that in Figure 5-16.

1. What are the maximum masking levels for the left ear?
2. How do these maximum masking levels compare to the minimum masking levels obtained in Figure 5-16?
3. Do we have masking problems anywhere?

Name: Fig 5-18   Date: XX/XX/XX   Age: 11   Sex: F   Audiologist: HK

AUDIOMETER: _____   ANSI 1969

PURE TONE AUDIOGRAM

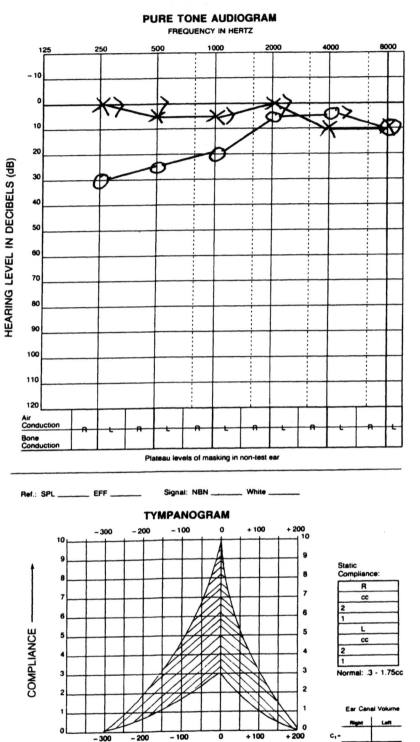

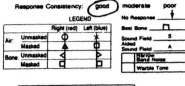

SPEECH AUDIOMETRY ☐ MLV ☐ Tape

	RIGHT	LEFT	MASK LEVEL R	MASK LEVEL L	SOUND FIELD	LIST
SAT						
SRT						
MCL						
UCL						
PB% (Word)	L	L				
PB% (Word)	L	L				
PB% (Word)	L	L				
PB% (Word)	L	L				
	L	L				
	L	L				

STAPEDIUS REFLEX THRESHOLDS

Stimulus	Contralateral (HL)					Ipsilateral (HL)		
EAR	.5K	1K	2K	4K	WBN	.5K	1K	2K
R								
Decay			✕	✕				✕
L								
Decay			✕	✕				✕

ABBREVIATIONS

A	Absent	NR	No Response
C₁	Canal Volume	SAT	Speech Awareness
CNE	Could Not Establish		Threshold
CNT	Could Not Test	SL	Sensation Level
DNT	Did Not Test	SRT	Speech Reception
HL	Hearing Level		Threshold
MCL	Most Comfortable	UCL	Uncomfortable Listening
	Listening Level		Level
MVL	Monitored Live Voice		

REMARKS:

_____

_____

_____

_____

_____

Ref.: SPL _____ EFF _____   Signal: NBN _____ White _____

Use of Masking

259

Answers for Figure 5-18

1. The formula used to obtain maximum masking is: bone conduction threshold of the test ear plus interaural attenuation at that frequency minus 5 dB. Using the formula, we find that the maximum levels permitted in the left ear are: 35 dB at 250 Hz, 35 dB at 500 Hz, and 40 dB at 1000 Hz.

2. Using the formula for minimum masking we find levels of 0 dB at 250 Hz, 5 dB at 500 Hz, and 5 dB at 1000 Hz. Note that masking is needed only for bone conduction. If Martin's (1991) approach, including the occlusion effect, is used, minimum masking levels of 30, 25, and 20 dB at 250, 500, and 1000 Hz, respectively, are found. In either case, masking is possible.

3. We do not have a masking problem with bone-conducted tone in the right ear and noise in the left unless we consider the occlusion effect. If we attempt to set our initial masker level to compensate for the effect of covering the left ear during testing, we restrict our usable range of masker levels, particularly at 250 and 500 Hz, where we are dealing with usable ranges of 5 and 10 dB, respectively. Should it not be possible to obtain a plateau at those masker levels, accurate masked thresholds cannot be obtained unless an insert receiver is used to deliver the masker.

QUESTIONS FOR FIGURE 5-19

Supplementary Information This audiogram is basically the same as that in Figure 5-15.

1. What are the maximum masking levels for the left ear?
2. What are the maximum masking levels for the right ear?
3. How do the maximum masking levels compare to the minimum masking levels obtained in Figure 5-15? For the different frequencies requiring masking, what ranges of masking noise can we use without risking overmasking?
4. Do we have masking problems anywhere?

PURE TONE AUDIOGRAM

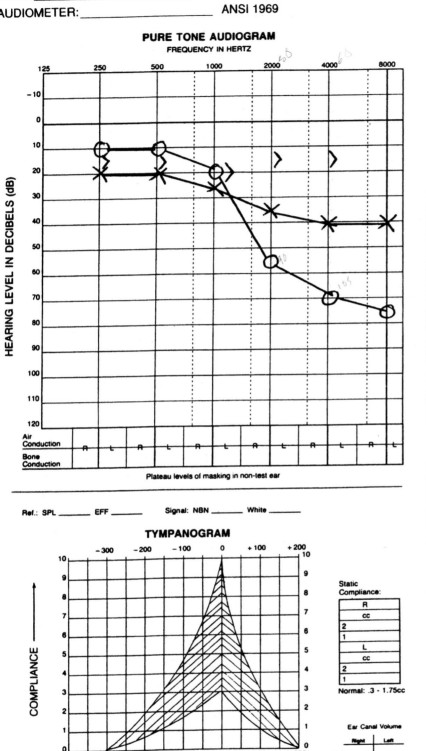

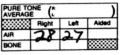

Response Consistency: (good) moderate poor

LEGEND

		Right (red)	Left (blue)
Air:	Unmasked	O	X
	Masked	▲	▣
Bone:	Unmasked	△	▷
	Masked	☐	☐

No Response _____|

Best Bone ☐

Sound Field ___ S

Aided
Sound Field ___ A

Narrow Band Noise

Warble Tone

PURE TONE AVERAGE

	Right	Left	Aided
AIR	28	27	
BONE			

SPEECH AUDIOMETRY   ☐ MLV ☐ Tape

	RIGHT	LEFT	MASK LEVEL R / L	SOUND FIELD	LIST
SAT					
SRT					
MCL					
UCL					
PB% (Word)	_L_	_L_			
PB% (Word)	_L_	_L_			
PB% (Word)	_L_	_L_			
PB% (Word)	_L_	_L_			
	_L_	_L_			
	_L_	_L_			

STAPEDIUS REFLEX THRESHOLDS

Stimulus	Contralateral (HL)					Ipsilateral (HL)		
EAR	.5K	1K	2K	4K	WBN	.5K	1K	2K
R								
Decay		✕	✕					✕
L								
Decay		✕	✕					✕

ABBREVIATIONS

A	Absent	NR	No Response
C₁	Canal Volume	SAT	Speech Awareness
CNE	Could Not Establish		Threshold
CNT	Could Not Test	SL	Sensation Level
DNT	Did Not Test	SRT	Speech Reception
HL	Hearing Level		Threshold
MCL	Most Comfortable	UCL	Uncomfortable Listening
	Listening Level		Level
MVL	Monitored Live Voice		

REMARKS:

_____

_____

_____

_____

Ref.: SPL _____ EFF _____   Signal: NBN _____ White _____

TYMPANOGRAM

Static Compliance:

R
cc
2
1

L
cc
2
1

Normal: .3 - 1.75cc

Ear Canal Volume

	Right	Left
C₁ =		

COMPLIANCE →

PRESSURE IN daPa

Use of Masking

Answers for Figure 5-19

1. The formula for maximum masking is: bone conduction threshold of the test ear plus interaural attenuation at that frequency minus 5 dB. The same formula is used regardless of whether the test ear is stimulated by air- or bone-conducted sound. Using the formula, we find that the maximum masking level permitted in the left ear at 2000 Hz is 15 (BC of test ear) + 40 (IA) − 5 = 50 dB. At 4000 Hz the corresponding figures are: 15 + 50 (IA) − 5 = 60 dB.

2. The maximum masking levels for the right ear are the same as for the left: 50 dB at 2000 Hz and 60 dB at 4000 Hz. Maximum masking levels for the two ears will be the same so long as only one set of unmasked bone conduction thresholds is obtained. In computing maximum masking levels for each ear we assume that the unmasked bone conduction thresholds represent both ears. Although this may not be correct, it represents a conservative approach and minimizes the possibility of overmasking.

3. The minimum masking levels permissible in the left ear for testing the right ear are:

Air conduction		Bone conduction	
2000 Hz	4000 Hz	2000 Hz	4000 Hz
35 dB	45 dB	35 dB	40 dB
45 dB	50 dB	40 dB	50 dB (Martin's approach)

For testing the right ear, maximum masking (50 dB at 2000 Hz and 60 dB at 4000 Hz) does not exceed minimum masking. At 2000 Hz we have a range of 5–15 dB (depending on the system used to determine minimum masking) of masking levels that we can use without undermasking or overmasking. At 4000 Hz, we have a usable range of masking levels of 10 to 20 dB.

For testing the left ear, the minimum permissible masking levels in the right ear are:

Air conduction		Bone conduction	
2000 Hz	4000 Hz	2000 Hz	4000 Hz
(Masking is		55 dB	70 dB
not needed)		70 dB	85 dB (Martin's approach)

Maximum masking levels for this ear are the same as for the left ear: 50 dB at 2000 Hz and 60 dB at 4000 Hz. The minimum levels exceed the maximum levels; there is no usable range of masking levels.

4. There is definitely a masking problem when bone conduction must be tested in the left ear with masking noise in the right. Since minimum masking levels exceed maximum masking levels, masking is not possible unless an insert receiver is used to deliver the noise to the right ear. If contralateral masking were needed to test air conduction in the left ear, the same problem would exist. Fortunately, masking is not needed for air conduction in that ear.

Although there is a usable range of masking levels in the left ear, the range is small. If a plateau cannot be achieved within the range of masking levels between minimum and maximum masking, it is not possible to obtain accurate masked thresholds in the right ear without the use of an insert receiver.

QUESTIONS FOR FIGURE 5-20

Supplementary Information Occlusion effects were not found for either ear.

1. Is masking needed for air conduction?
2. Is masking needed for bone conduction?
3. Compute minimum masking for appropriate frequencies.
4. Compute maximum masking for appropriate frequencies.
5. How does maximum masking agree with minimum masking?

Name: Fig 5-20   Date: XX/XX/XX   Age: 8   Sex: M   Audiologist: HK

AUDIOMETER: _____   ANSI 1969

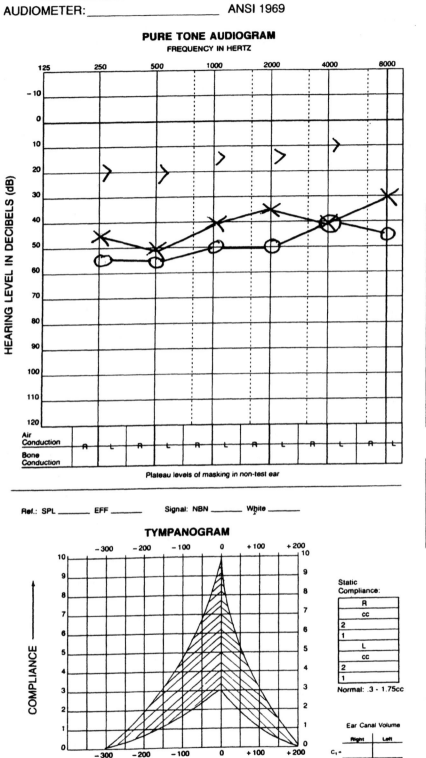

PURE TONE AUDIOGRAM
FREQUENCY IN HERTZ

HEARING LEVEL IN DECIBELS (dB)

Plateau levels of masking in non-test ear

Ref.: SPL _____ EFF _____   Signal: NBN _____ White _____

TYMPANOGRAM

COMPLIANCE

PRESSURE IN daPa

Static Compliance:

R	
cc	
2	
1	
L	
cc	
2	
1	

Normal: .3 - 1.75cc

Ear Canal Volume

	Right	Left
C₁ =		

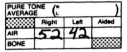

Response Consistency: (good) moderate poor   No Response

LEGEND

		Right (red)	Left (blue)
Air:	Unmasked	○	×
	Masked	△	▢
Bone:	Unmasked	<	>
	Masked	▢	▢

Best Bone ▢
Sound Field ___ S
Aided ___ A
Sound Field
Narrow Band Noise
Warble Tone

PURE TONE AVERAGE (R/L)

	Right	Left	Aided
AIR	52	42	
BONE			

SPEECH AUDIOMETRY ☐ MLV ☐ Tape

	RIGHT	LEFT	MASK LEVEL R L	SOUND FIELD	LIST
SAT					
SRT					
MCL					
UCL					
PB% (Word)	_L_	_L_			
PB% (Word)	_L_	_L_			
PB% (Word)	_L_	_L_			
PB% (Word)	_L_	_L_			
	_L_	_L_			
	_L_	_L_			

STAPEDIUS REFLEX THRESHOLDS

Stimulus	Contralateral (HL)					Ipsilateral (HL)		
EAR	.5K	1K	2K	4K	WBN	.5K	1K	2K
R								
Decay			☒	☒				☒
L								
Decay			☒	☒				☒

ABBREVIATIONS

A	Absent	NR	No Response
C₁	Canal Volume	SAT	Speech Awareness
CNE	Could Not Establish		Threshold
CNT	Could Not Test	SL	Sensation Level
DNT	Did Not Test	SRT	Speech Reception
HL	Hearing Level		Threshold
MCL	Most Comfortable	UCL	Uncomfortable Listening
	Listening Level		Level
MVL	Monitored Live Voice		

REMARKS:

_____
_____
_____
_____
_____

Answers for Figure 5-20

1. Masking is not needed for air conduction because none of the air–bone gaps is as great as 40 dB.
2. Masking is needed for bone conduction at all frequencies in both ears because all air–bone gaps exceed 10 dB.
3. Minimum masking—bone conduction:

	Right					Left				
250 Hz	500 Hz	1000 Hz	2000 Hz	4000 Hz		250 Hz	500 Hz	1000 Hz	2000 Hz	4000 Hz
55 dB	55 dB	50 dB	50 dB	40 dB		45 dB	50 dB	40 dB	35 dB	40 dB
				(Martin's approach):						
65 dB	65 dB	60 dB	60 dB	50 dB		55 dB	60 dB	50 dB	45 dB	50 dB

4. Maximum masking (same for both ears):

250 Hz	500 Hz	1000 Hz	2000 Hz	4000 Hz
55 dB	55 dB	50 dB	50 dB	45 dB

5. At all frequencies in the right ear except for 4000 Hz, minimum masking exceeds or is equal to maximum masking. In this situation accurate masked thresholds are impossible to obtain unless an insert receiver is used to deliver the masking noise. The use of an insert receiver in place of an earphone serves to increase interaural attenuation. In the left ear we have a small range of masking levels we can use without overmasking unless we use Martin's method to compute minimum masking. The use of an insert receiver would be advisable in this ear as well as in the right to extend the useable range of masker levels.

QUESTIONS FOR FIGURE 5-21

Supplementary Information Occlusion effects of 15 dB at 250 Hz, 10 dB at 500 Hz, and 5 dB at 1000 Hz were found in the right ear.

1. For the frequencies at which masking is required, what are the minimum masking levels?
2. What are maximum masking levels?
3. Which masker levels comprise the plateau? How do plateau levels compare to minimum and maximum masking levels at the same frequency?
4. At 250 Hz for air conduction and at 500 and 2000 Hz for bone conduction, the lowest of the plateau levels does not correspond to minimum masking. Why do you think that is true?
5. At 4000 Hz for bone conduction, the highest of the plateau levels does not correspond to maximum masking. Why do you think that is true?
6. What type of loss is present in the left ear?

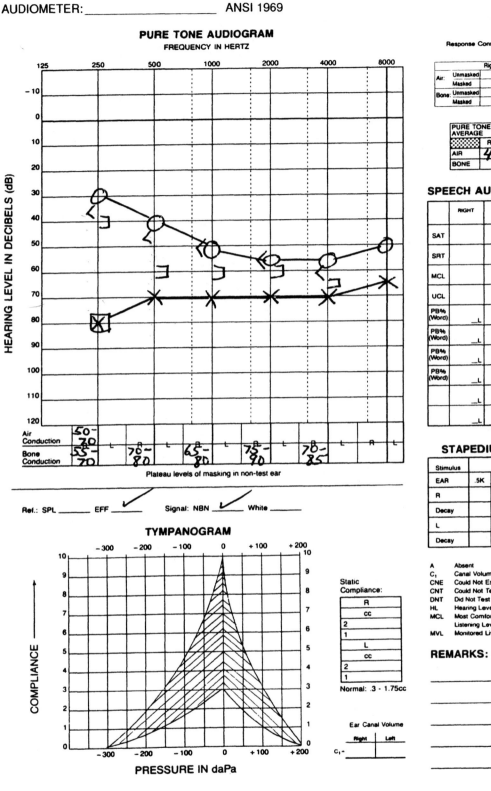

PURE TONE AUDIOGRAM
FREQUENCY IN HERTZ

HEARING LEVEL IN DECIBELS (dB)

Frequencies: 125, 250, 500, 1000, 2000, 4000, 8000

	250	500	1000	2000	4000
Air Conduction	50–70	70–80 (R)	65–80 (R)	75–90 (R)	78–85 (R)
Bone Conduction	55–70				

Plateau levels of masking in non-test ear

Ref.: SPL _____ EFF _____ Signal: NBN ✓ White _____

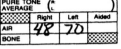

Response Consistency: (good) moderate poor

LEGEND

		Right (red)	Left (blue)
Air:	Unmasked	◯	✕
	Masked	△	☐
Bone:	Unmasked	<	>
	Masked	☐	☐

No Response
Best Bone ☐
Sound Field S
Aided
Sound Field A
Narrow Band Noise
Warble Tone

PURE TONE AVERAGE (R / L)	Right	Left	Aided
AIR	48	70	
BONE			

SPEECH AUDIOMETRY ☐ MLV ☐ Tape

	RIGHT	LEFT	MASK LEVEL R	MASK LEVEL L	SOUND FIELD	LIST
SAT						
SRT						
MCL						
UCL						
PB% (Word)	L	L				
PB% (Word)	L	L				
PB% (Word)	L	L				
PB% (Word)	L	L				
	L	L				
	L	L				

STAPEDIUS REFLEX THRESHOLDS

Stimulus	Contralateral (HL)					Ipsilateral (HL)		
EAR	.5K	1K	2K	4K	WBN	.5K	1K	2K
R								✕
Decay			✕	✕				
L								✕
Decay			✕	✕				✕

ABBREVIATIONS

A	Absent	NR	No Response
C_1	Canal Volume	SAT	Speech Awareness Threshold
CNE	Could Not Establish		
CNT	Could Not Test	SL	Sensation Level
DNT	Did Not Test	SRT	Speech Reception Threshold
HL	Hearing Level		
MCL	Most Comfortable Listening Level	UCL	Uncomfortable Listening Level
MVL	Monitored Live Voice		

REMARKS:

_____
_____
_____
_____
_____

TYMPANOGRAM

PRESSURE IN daPa

COMPLIANCE

Static Compliance:

R	
cc	
2	
1	

L	
cc	
2	
1	

Normal: .3 - 1.75cc

Ear Canal Volume

	Right	Left
C_1		

1. Minimum masking levels (right ear):

Air conduction	Bone conduction				
250 Hz	250 Hz	500 Hz	1000 Hz	2000 Hz	4000 Hz
40 dB	35 dB	45 dB	50 dB	55 dB	60 dB
40 dB	55 dB	60 dB	65 dB	65 dB	65 dB (Martin's approach)

Note that Martin's approach includes the 10-dB safety margin and occlusion effects of 15 dB, 10 dB, and 5 dB at 250, 500, and 1000 Hz, respectively.

2. Maximum masking levels (right ear):

250 Hz	500 Hz	1000 Hz	2000 Hz	4000 Hz
70 dB	80 dB	85 dB	90 dB	105 dB

3. The plateau consists of those masker levels at which threshold remains constant. When there is insufficient masking in the contralateral ear, threshold in the test ear will shift as masking levels are increased because the signal is being perceived by the non-test ear. When the non-test ear has received sufficient masking to eliminate its participation in the perception of the signal delivered to the test ear, threshold will no longer shift as masking levels are increased until maximum masking has been reached. If masking levels are increased beyond that point and further threshold shift occurs, that shift may be attributed to overmasking. For further discussion of the plateau concept, review the section "Finding the Plateau," found earlier in this chapter.

    Clinically, the following plateau levels were obtained:

Air conduction	Bone conduction				
250 Hz	250 Hz	500 Hz	1000 Hz	2000 Hz	4000 Hz
50–70 dB	55–70 dB	70–80 dB	65–80 dB	75–90 dB	70–85 dB

At 250 Hz for air conduction and at 500, 2000, and 4000 Hz for bone conduction, plateau levels do not correspond to minimum masking. At 4000 Hz, plateau levels do not correspond to maximum masking.

4. The lowest of the plateau levels at 250 Hz for air conduction and at 500 and 2000 Hz for bone conduction are higher than minimum masking levels at those frequencies. This is probably the case because threshold shifts occurred when masking levels were increased from minimum levels to the lowest plateau levels. At the plateau levels, threshold shifts did not occur.

5. The highest plateau level at 2000 Hz does not correspond to maximum masking at that frequency. This is probably true because after obtaining a 25-dB plateau (75–90 dB), it was not considered necessary to increase the masking further. It is highly probable that if masking levels were increased to maximum masking (105 dB), further threshold shifts would not occur. However, a 15-dB plateau is considered sufficient, and it is unnecessary to expose the ear to higher levels of noise.

6. The left ear shows a mixed hearing loss with a small conductive component at all frequencies above 250 Hz.

QUESTIONS FOR FIGURE 5-22

1. What are the minimum masking levels?
2. What are the maximum masking levels?
3. What are the plateau levels?
4. For bone conduction testing, the lowest plateau levels exceed minimum masking. Why do you think this is so?
5. For bone conduction at 1000 and 2000 Hz, the highest plateau levels exceed maximum masking. Has overmasking occurred?
6. What type of loss exists in the right ear?

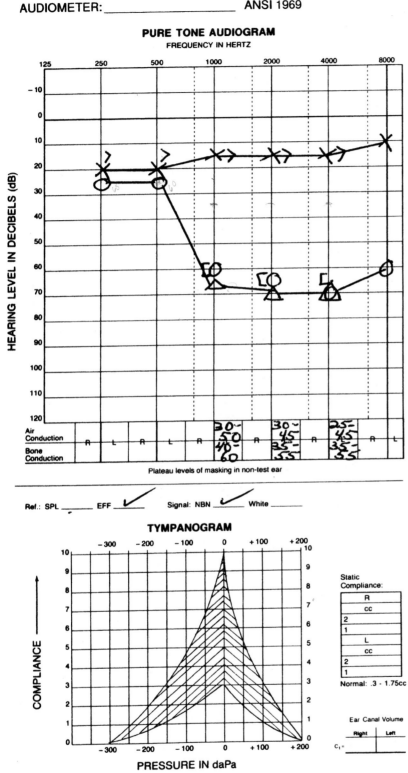

PURE TONE AUDIOGRAM
FREQUENCY IN HERTZ

Response Consistency: good moderate poor

PURE TONE AVERAGE	Right	Left	Aided
AIR	53	17	
BONE			

SPEECH AUDIOMETRY ☐ MLV ☐ Tape

	RIGHT	LEFT	MASK LEVEL R	MASK LEVEL L	SOUND FIELD	LIST
SAT						
SRT						
MCL						
UCL						
PB% (Word)	_L	_L				
PB% (Word)	_L	_L				
PB% (Word)	_L	_L				
PB% (Word)	_L	_L				
	_L	_L				
	_L	_L				

Air Conduction: 30~50 / 40~60 (1000) 30~45 / 35~55 (2000) 25~45 / 35~55 (4000)

Plateau levels of masking in non-test ear

Ref.: SPL ____ EFF ✓   Signal: NBN ✓ White ____

STAPEDIUS REFLEX THRESHOLDS

Stimulus	Contralateral (HL) .5K	1K	2K	4K	WBN	Ipsilateral (HL) .5K	1K	2K
EAR R								
Decay			✕	✕				✕
L								
Decay			✕	✕				✕

ABBREVIATIONS

A	Absent	NR	No Response
C₁	Canal Volume	SAT	Speech Awareness
CNE	Could Not Establish		Threshold
CNT	Could Not Test	SL	Sensation Level
DNT	Did Not Test	SRT	Speech Reception
HL	Hearing Level		Threshold
MCL	Most Comfortable	UCL	Uncomfortable Listening
	Listening Level		Level
MVL	Monitored Live Voice		

TYMPANOGRAM

PRESSURE IN daPa

Static Compliance:

R	
cc	
2	
1	

L	
cc	
2	
1	

Normal: .3 - 1.75cc

Ear Canal Volume

	Right	Left
C₁ =		

REMARKS:
Two frequency average for right ear = 45dB

1. Minimum masking levels (left ear):

Air conduction			Bone conduction		
1000 Hz	2000 Hz	4000 Hz	1000 Hz	2000 Hz	4000 Hz
20 dB	25 dB	30 dB	15 dB	15 dB	15 dB
25 dB	25 dB	25 dB	25 dB	25 dB	25 dB (Martin's approach)

2. Maximum masking levels (left ear):

1000 Hz	2000 Hz	4000 Hz
50 dB	50 dB	50 dB

3. Plateau levels (left ear):

Air conduction			Bone conduction		
1000 Hz	2000 Hz	4000 Hz	1000 Hz	2000 Hz	4000 Hz
30–50 dB	30–45 dB	25–45 dB	40–60 dB	35–55 dB	35–55 dB

4. For bone conduction testing at 1000, 2000, and 4000 Hz, the lowest plateau levels are higher than minimum masking levels by 10–20 dB. This suggests that threshold shifts occurred between minimum masking levels and the lowest plateau levels, indicating undermasking.

5. For bone conduction testing at 1000 Hz, the plateau levels are 40–60 dB while the maximum masking level is 50 dB. At 2000 Hz the plateau levels are 35 to 55 dB while the maximum masking level is 50 dB. At 4000 Hz the plateau levels are 35–55 dB while maximum masking is 50 dB. Although the highest plateau level exceeds minimum masking, we can be fairly certain that overmasking is not taking place. The plateau represents several masking levels at which threshold remains stable; the lack of threshold shift indicates that the test ear is perceiving the signal and that overmasking is not occurring. If masking levels exceeding maximum masking were producing overmasking, we would expect to see a threshold shift; we would then be in the "overmasking" portion of the masking function shown on page 222. If it is necessary to exceed maximum masking level in order to obtain a plateau it is permissible to do so. However, if threshold shifts occur as a result of exceeding maximum masking, they must be considered evidence of overmasking.

6. The masked bone conduction thresholds in the right ear indicate a pure sensorineural loss in that ear.

QUESTIONS FOR FIGURE 5-23

Supplementary Information This audiogram is basically the same as that in Figure 5-17.

1. What are the minimum masking levels at 2000 and 4000 Hz?
2. What are the maximum masking levels at 2000 and 4000 Hz?
3. What are the plateau levels?
4. Why were plateaus not established for bone conduction at 2000 and 4000 Hz?
5. What are the bone conduction thresholds in the right ear at 2000 and 4000 Hz? What type of loss exists in the right ear?

Name: Fig 5-23   Date: XX/XX/XX   Age: 65   Sex: F   Audiologist: HK
AUDIOMETER: _____   ANSI 1969

PURE TONE AUDIOGRAM
FREQUENCY IN HERTZ

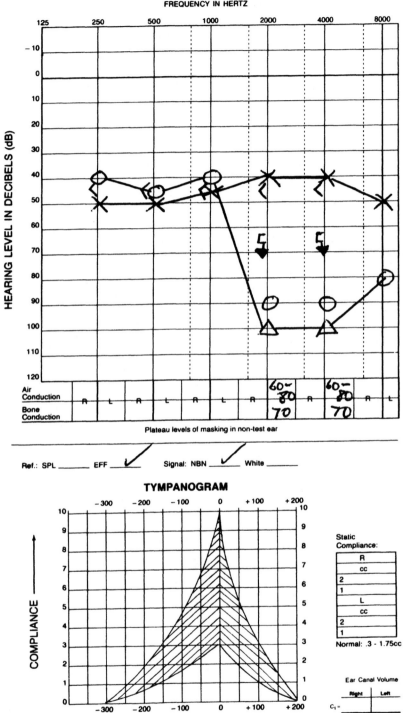

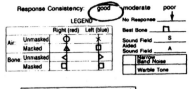

PURE TONE AVERAGE (R L)			
	Right	Left	Aided
AIR	62	45	
BONE			

SPEECH AUDIOMETRY   □ MLV   □ Tape

	RIGHT	LEFT	MASK LEVEL R L	SOUND FIELD	LIST
SAT					
SRT					
MCL					
UCL					
PB% (Word)	_L	_L			
PB% (Word)	_L	_L			
PB% (Word)	_L	_L			
PB% (Word)	_L	_L			
	_L	_L			
	_L	_L			

STAPEDIUS REFLEX THRESHOLDS

Stimulus	Contralateral (HL)					Ipsilateral (HL)		
EAR	.5K	1K	2K	4K	WBN	.5K	1K	2K
R								
Decay		X	X					X
L								
Decay		X	X					X

ABBREVIATIONS

A	Absent	NR	No Response
C₁	Canal Volume	SAT	Speech Awareness
CNE	Could Not Establish		Threshold
CNT	Could Not Test	SL	Sensation Level
DNT	Did Not Test	SRT	Speech Reception
HL	Hearing Level		Threshold
MCL	Most Comfortable	UCL	Uncomfortable Listening
	Listening Level		Level
MVL	Monitored Live Voice		

REMARKS:

_____

_____

_____

_____

_____

TYMPANOGRAM

Static Compliance:

R
cc
2
1

L
cc
2
1

Normal: .3 - 1.75cc

Ear Canal Volume

	Right	Left
C₁ =		

Plateau levels of masking in non-test ear

Ref.: SPL _____ EFF _____   Signal: NBN _____ White _____

Answers for Figure 5-23

1. Minimum masking levels (left ear):

Air conduction		Bone conduction	
2000 Hz	4000 Hz	2000 Hz	4000 Hz
50 dB	50 dB	45 dB	45 dB

2. Maximum masking (left ear):

2000 Hz	4000 Hz
30–45 dB	25–45 dB

3. Plateau levels (left ear):

Air conduction		Bone conduction	
2000 Hz	4000 Hz	2000 Hz	4000 Hz
60–80 dB	60–80 dB	70 dB	70 dB

4. Plateaus were not established at 2000 and 4000 Hz for bone conduction because with 70 dB of masking in the left ear, the right ear did not respond to bone-conducted tones at the limits of the audiometer. With lesser amounts of masking, 55 and 65 dB, the threshold shifted (became poorer) with each increment of masking, indicating that the responses were actually those of the left ear.

5. Bone conduction thresholds at 2000 and 4000 Hz could not be measured. Therefore, we must conclude that the right ear cannot respond to bone-conducted signals at these frequencies at the limits of the audiometer. The unmasked bone conduction responses must be discounted and considered to be the responses of the left ear. The right ear has a pure sensorineural loss because no air–bone gaps exist at any frequency.

QUESTIONS FOR FIGURE 5-24

1. Why is masking needed for the SRT in the left ear?
2. According to Martin's (1986) approach, what is the minimum effective masking level for SRT?
3. What is the maximum effective masking level for SRT?
4. What are the plateau levels for SRT? How do they compare to minimum and maximum masking levels?

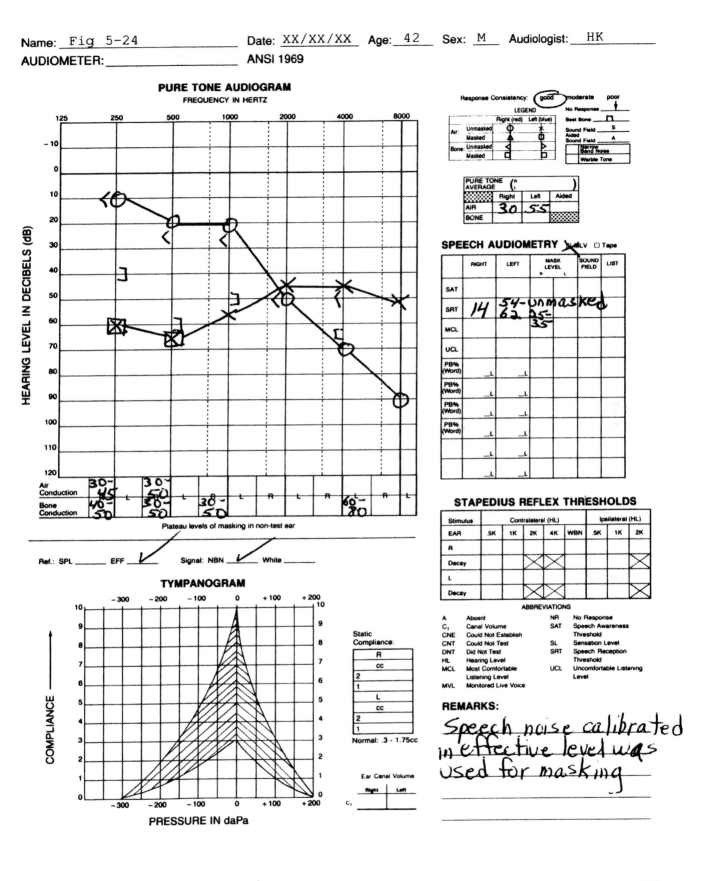

Answers for Figure 5-24

1. Masking is needed for the SRT because the unmasked SRT of the left ear is 40 dB more intense than the SRT of the left ear (54 dB as compared to 14 dB). The rule for using masking for SRT is that contralateral masking is needed whenever unmasked SRT is 40 dB or more greater than the SRT of the non-test ear or the best bone conduction thresholds at 500, 1000, or 2000 Hz.

2. Minimum effective masking for SRT is defined as the SRT of the non-test ear, according to Martin (1986). Since masking noise is calibrated in 5-dB steps, the minimum level may be considered to be 15 dB effective level.

3. Maximum effective masking for SRT equals the best threshold of the test ear by bone conduction plus interaural attenuation minus 5 dB. The best bone conduction threshold of the test ear (the left ear) is 50 dB (we consider only the speech frequencies). Interaural attenuation is considered to be 40 dB. Therefore 50 + 40 − 5 = a maximum masking level of 85 dB in the right ear.

4. The plateau levels used are 25–35 dB. The lowest masking level used is 10 dB higher than minimum masking because it is considered desirable to use a level slightly higher than minimum masking as a margin of safety. The highest of the plateau levels is considerably lower than maximum masking. Since the threshold remained stable over a 15-dB range of masking levels, there is no need to increase masking further. The actual threshold of the left ear may be considered to be 62 dB.

QUESTIONS FOR FIGURE 5-25

1. Can minimum and maximum effective levels be determined for the SRT for this audiogram as they were in Figure 5-24?
2. What level of masking would you use as a starting level?
3. Why is the unmasked SRT not considered the true SRT of the right ear?
4. Why could a masked SRT not be obtained in the right ear?

Name: Fig 5-25   Date: XX/XX/XX Age: 18 Sex: M Audiologist: HK

AUDIOMETER: _____   ANSI 1969

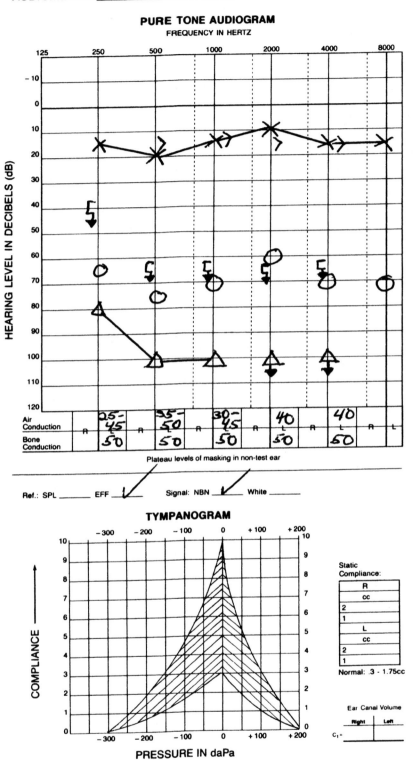

PURE TONE AUDIOGRAM
FREQUENCY IN HERTZ

Air Conduction / Bone Conduction (Plateau levels of masking in non-test ear):

	250	500	1000	2000	4000
Air Conduction	25-45	35-50	30-45	40	40
Bone Conduction	50	50	50	50	50

Ref.: SPL _____ EFF _____   Signal: NBN _____ White _____

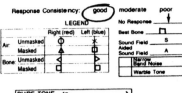

Response Consistency: (good) moderate poor

LEGEND

		Right (red)	Left (blue)
Air:	Unmasked	○	✕
	Masked	△	☐
Bone:	Unmasked	<	>
	Masked	☐	☐

No Response
Best Bone
Sound Field _____ S
Aided
Sound Field _____ A
Narrow Band Noise
Warble Tone

PURE TONE AVERAGE

	Right	Left	Aided
AIR	CNE	15	
BONE		15	

SPEECH AUDIOMETRY ☐ MLV ☐ Tape

	RIGHT	LEFT	MASK LEVEL R L	SOUND FIELD	LIST
SAT					
SRT	70* CNE	18	50 HL		
MCL					
UCL					
PB% (Word)	_L_	_L_			
PB% (Word)	_L_	_L_			
PB% (Word)	_L_	_L_			
PB% (Word)	_L_	_L_			
	_L_	_L_			
	_L_	_L_			

STAPEDIUS REFLEX THRESHOLDS

Stimulus	Contralateral (HL)					Ipsilateral (HL)		
EAR	5K	1K	2K	4K	WBN	.5K	1K	2K
R								
Decay			✕	✕				✕
L								
Decay			✕	✕				✕

ABBREVIATIONS

A	Absent	NR	No Response
C_1	Canal Volume	SAT	Speech Awareness
CNE	Could Not Establish		Threshold
CNT	Could Not Test	SL	Sensation Level
DNT	Did Not Test	SRT	Speech Reception
HL	Hearing Level		Threshold
MCL	Most Comfortable	UCL	Uncomfortable Listening
	Listening Level		Level
MVL	Monitored Live Voice		

TYMPANOGRAM

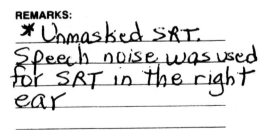

PRESSURE IN daPa

Static Compliance:

R	
	cc
2	
1	

L	
	cc
2	
1	

Normal: .3 - 1.75cc

Ear Canal Volume

	Right	Left
C_1 =		

REMARKS:

* Unmasked SRT. Speech noise was used for SRT in the right ear

Answers for Figure 5-25

1. The speech noise used to mask for SRT is not calibrated in effective level. Therefore, we cannot with precision predict the amount of masking produced by a given level of noise. For this reason, we cannot accurately determine minimum and maximum effective levels as we can do for Figure 5-24, where the noise is calibrated in effective level.

2. It is recommended that the starting level be no less than 40 dB HL. After obtaining an SRT at that level of contralateral masking, a 20-dB plateau should be obtained.

3. The unmasked SRT of 70 dB must be rechecked with contralateral masking because it is more than 40 dB greater than both the left ear SRT of 18 dB and the best bone conduction threshold of the left ear (15 dB). An additional reason to suspect that the unmasked SRT represents the participation of the left ear is the fact that pure tone thresholds in the right ear became considerably poorer when masking was introduced into the left ear.

4. With the introduction of 40 dB of masking noise into the left ear, the SRT of the right ear probably shifted from the unmasked threshold. Increasing the masking level by 10 dB to 50 dB HL produced an additional threshold shift which exceeded the limits of the audiometer. Therefore, a plateau could not be established and a masked SRT could not be obtained.

QUESTIONS FOR FIGURE 5-26

Supplementary Information This audiogram is basically the same as that in Figure 5-13.

1. Why was contralateral masking needed for word recognition in the right ear?
2. What is the appropriate level of masking to use in the left ear for word recognition testing?
3. What is the maximum masking level for word recognition testing in the right ear?

Name: Fig 5-26   Date: XX/XX/XX   Age: 33   Sex: M   Audiologist: HK

AUDIOMETER: _____   ANSI 1969

PURE TONE AUDIOGRAM

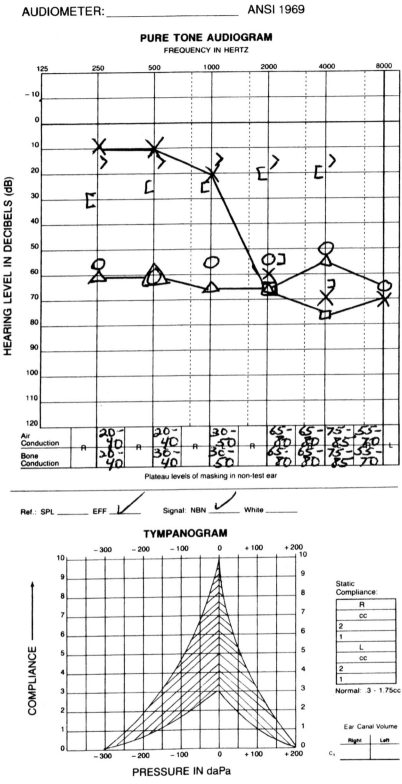

FREQUENCY IN HERTZ

HEARING LEVEL IN DECIBELS (dB)

		125	250	500	1000	2000	4000	8000	
Air Conduction	R		20-40	20-40	30-50	65-80	65-80	75-85	55-70	L
Bone Conduction	R		20-40	30-40	30-50	65-80	65-80	75-85	55-70	L

Plateau levels of masking in non-test ear

Ref.: SPL _____ EFF ✓   Signal: NBN ✓   White _____

TYMPANOGRAM

PRESSURE IN daPa

COMPLIANCE

Static Compliance:

R	
	cc
2	
1	
L	
	cc
2	
1	

Normal: .3 - 1.75cc

Ear Canal Volume

	Right	Left
C₁		

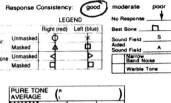

Response Consistency: (good) moderate poor

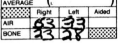

PURE TONE AVERAGE (R / L)

	Right	Left	Aided
AIR	63	33	
BONE	33	28	

SPEECH AUDIOMETRY X MLV ✓ Tape

	RIGHT	LEFT	MASK LEVEL R	L	SOUND FIELD	LIST
SAT						
SRT	56	12	20-30			
MCL						
UCL						
PB% (Word)	98 30SL	72 45SL	30-50			1A 2A
PB% (Word)	L	78 35SL				1B
PB% (Word)	L	L				
PB% (Word)	L	L				
	L	L				
	L	L				

STAPEDIUS REFLEX THRESHOLDS

Stimulus	Contralateral (HL)					Ipsilateral (HL)		
EAR	.5K	1K	2K	4K	WBN	5K	1K	2K
R								
Decay								
L								
Decay								

ABBREVIATIONS

A	Absent	NR	No Response
C₁	Canal Volume	SAT	Speech Awareness
CNE	Could Not Establish		Threshold
CNT	Could Not Test	SL	Sensation Level
DNT	Did Not Test	SRT	Speech Reception
HL	Hearing Level		Threshold
MCL	Most Comfortable	UCL	Uncomfortable Listening
	Listening Level		Level
MVL	Monitored Live Voice		

REMARKS:

Masking was delivered through an insert receiver Speech noise calibrated in effective level was used for masking in speech audiometry. Unmasked SRT = 56 dB

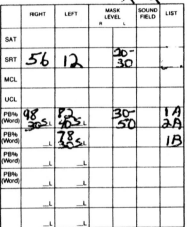

Use of Masking

Answers for Figure 5-26

1. In word recognition testing, contralateral masking is needed whenever the presentation level of the words to the test ear is (a) 40 dB or more above the best bone conduction threshold of the opposite ear, or (b) 40 dB or more above the SRT of the opposite ear. In this case the presentation level of the PB words to the right ear is 86 dB HL, which is 71 dB above the bone conduction threshold of 15 dB at 500 and 1000 Hz in the left ear and also 74 dB above left ear SRT.

2. According to Martin (1986) the appropriate level of masking to use for word recognition testing is determined by subtracting interaural attenuation (40 dB) from the presentation level of the words (86 dB) and adding the largest air–bone gap of the non-test ear (5 dB at 1000 and 2000 Hz). The appropriate level in this case is 50 dB effective level.

3. The maximum masking level is determined in the same manner as for SRT. See Figure 5-24 for a more complete discussion of this point. Maximum masking in this case equals the best bone conduction threshold of the test ear (25 dB) plus interaural attenuation (40 dB) minus 5 dB. We arrive at a figure of 60 dB, which is 10 dB greater than the 50-dB level we consider most appropriate.

QUESTIONS FOR FIGURE 5-27

Supplementary Information This audiogram is basically the same as that in Figure 5-12.

1. Is masking needed for the SRT in either ear?
2. Is masking needed for word recognition testing in either ear?
3. In the ears where masking is needed, what are appropriate levels?
4. In the ears where masking is needed, what are maximum masking levels?
5. Are there any masking problems with either SRTs or word recognition?

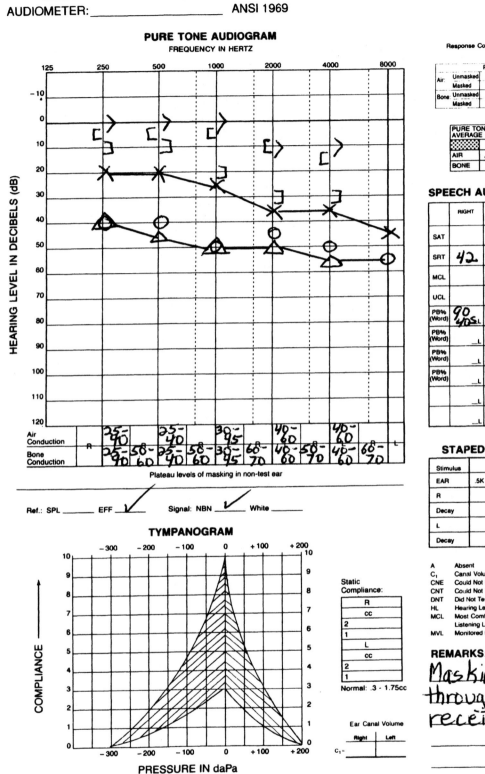

Name: Fig 5-27 Date: XX/XX/XX Age: 30 Sex: F Audiologist: HK
AUDIOMETER: ANSI 1969

PURE TONE AUDIOGRAM
FREQUENCY IN HERTZ

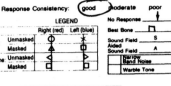

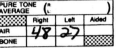

PURE TONE AVERAGE (R / L)

	Right	Left	Aided
AIR	48	27	
BONE			

SPEECH AUDIOMETRY MLV Tape

	RIGHT	LEFT	MASK LEVEL R L	SOUND FIELD	LIST
SAT					
SRT	42	30			
MCL					
UCL					
PB% (Word)	90 40SL	94 40SL	75 55		W-22
PB% (Word)	⌐	⌐			
PB% (Word)	⌐	⌐			
PB% (Word)	⌐	⌐			
	⌐	⌐			
	⌐	⌐			

Air Conduction	R	25-40		25-40		30-95		40-60		40-60			L
Bone Conduction		25-70	58-60	25-40	58-60	30-95	60-70	40-60	50-70	40-60	60-70		

Plateau levels of masking in non-test ear

Ref.: SPL _____ EFF ✓ _____ Signal: NBN ✓ _____ White _____

STAPEDIUS REFLEX THRESHOLDS

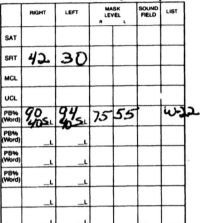

Stimulus	Contralateral (HL)					Ipsilateral (HL)		
EAR	.5K	1K	2K	4K	WBN	.5K	1K	2K
R				✕				
Decay								
L				✕				
Decay			✕					✕

ABBREVIATIONS

A   Absent
C₁   Canal Volume
CNE Could Not Establish
CNT Could Not Test
DNT Did Not Test
HL   Hearing Level
MCL Most Comfortable Listening Level
MVL Monitored Live Voice

NR   No Response
SAT Speech Awareness Threshold
SL   Sensation Level
SRT Speech Reception Threshold
UCL Uncomfortable Listening Level

TYMPANOGRAM

Static Compliance:

R
cc
2
1

L
cc
2
1

Normal: .3 - 1.75cc

Ear Canal Volume

Right	Left
C₁ =	

PRESSURE IN daPa

REMARKS:

Masking was delivered through an insert receiver

Answers for Figure 5-27

1. Masking is not needed for the SRT in either ear. In the right ear the SRT of 42 is less than 40 dB above the SRT of the left ear or the best bone conduction threshold of the left ear (10 dB at 500 Hz). The SRT of the left ear is less than 40 dB above the best bone conduction of the right ear (5 dB at 500 and 1000 Hz) and is less than the SRT of the right ear.

2. For word recognition testing, however, masking is required for both ears. In the right ear the presentation level of the words is 82 dB; this level is 52 dB above the SRT in the left ear and 72 dB above the best bone conduction threshold of the left ear.

   In the left ear the presentation level of the words is 70 dB; although this level is not 40 dB above the SRT of the right ear it is more than 40 dB above the best bone conduction threshold of the right ear (70 − 5 = 65 dB).

   It is entirely possible not to need masking for the SRT but to require it for word recognition since we are dealing with a suprathreshold measure. It is also possible to require masking for word recognition testing in an ear in which the SRT is lower than in the opposite ear. In determining whether masking is needed for word recognition testing, one must pay close attention to the air–bone gaps in both ears.

3. The formula for appropriate level of masking for word recognition is: the presentation level of the words to the test ear minus interaural attenuation plus the air–bone gap of the non-test ear. Using this formula for masking in the left ear, we obtain: 82 − 40 + 10 = 52 dB. Using the formula for masking in the right ear, we obtain: 70 − 40 + 45 = 75 dB.

4. The formula for maximum masking for word recognition is: best bone conduction threshold in the test ear plus interaural attenuation minus 5 dB. Using this formula for masking in the left ear, we obtain: 5 + 40 − 5 = 40 dB. Using this formula for masking in the right ear, we obtain: 10 + 40 − 5 = 45 dB.

5. There are masking problems for word recognition testing in both ears. Appropriate masking levels exceed maximum masking levels because of the air–bone gaps present in both ears. It is absolutely necessary to use insert receivers to deliver the masking noise to increase interaural attenuation.

REVIEW AND SEARCH PROJECTS

1. Compile a glossary of terms relating to masking.

2. Discuss advantages and disadvantages of using insert earphones for masking.

3. Discuss the literature on the occlusion effect and the effects it has on determination of minimum masking.

4. Review the literature on interaural attenuation.

5. Discuss the Schwabach, Rinne, Weber, and Bing tuning fork tests with regard to their use in determining type of hearing loss.

6. Discuss the advantages and disadvantages for different types of masking noise (complex, white, speech, narrow band).

7. Explain what is meant by critical band theory and explain how it is used in masking.

8. Make up three hypothetical audiograms (one conductive, one sensorineural, and one mixed) and discuss where masking is needed for air and/or bone conduction.

9. Using the same audiograms in project 8, determine minimum and maximum masking levels for all frequencies at which masking is needed. Do this for air and bone conduction.

10. Review the literature on central masking.

11. Describe how you would develop an Effective Masking Table for Speech.

12. Compare and contrast the masking methods of Hood, Martin, and Studebaker.

13. Describe the SAL test and discuss its advantages and disadvantages.

REFERENCES

Chaiklin, J. B. 1967. Interaural attenuation and cross-hearing in air conduction audiometry. *Journal of Auditory Research* 7: 413–424.

Coles, R. R. A., and Priede, V. M. 1968. Clinical and subjective acoustics. *Institute of Sound and Vibration Research* 26: ch. 3A.

Dirks, D. D., and Malmquist, C. W. 1967. Changes in bone conduction thresholds produced in masking the nontest ear. *Journal of Speech and Hearing Research* 7: 271–278.

Hannley, M. 1986. *Basic Principles of Auditory Assessment.* San Diego: College-Hill Press.

Hood, J. D. 1960. The principles and practices of bone conduction audiometry. *Laryngoscope* 70: 1211–1288.

Liden, G., Nilsson, G., and Anderson, H. 1959a. Narrow band masking with white noise. *Acta Otolaryngologica* (Stockholm) 50: 116–124.

Liden, G., Nilsson, G., and Anderson, H. 1959b. Masking in clinical audiometry. *Acta Otolaryngologica* (Stockholm) 50: 125–136.

Martin, F. N. 1991. *Introduction to Audiology,* 4th ed. Englewood Cliffs, N. J.: Prentice Hall.

Rintelmann, W. F. 1991. *Hearing Assessment,* 2nd ed. Austin: Pro-Ed.

Rose, D. E. 1971. *Audiological Assessment.* Englewood Cliffs, N. J.: Prentice-Hall.

Sanders, J. W., and Rintelmann, W. F. 1964. Masking in audiometry. *Archives of Otolaryngology* 80: 541–556.

Studebaker, G. A. 1962. On masking in bone conduction testing. *Journal of Speech and Hearing Research* 5: 215–227.

Studebaker, G. A. 1964. Clinical masking of air and bone conducted stimuli. *Journal of Speech and Hearing Disorders* 29: 23–24.

Studebaker, G. A. 1967. Clinical masking of the non-test ear. *Journal of Speech and Hearing Disorders* 32: 360–371.

Zwislocki, J. 1953. Acoustic attenuation between ears. *Journal of the Acoustical Society of America* 25: 752–759.

CHAPTER 6

Interpreting the Basic Battery

For the majority of clients an audiological test battery is used in the diagnosis and remediation of an auditory problem. A battery of tests is needed for several reasons. First, the auditory system includes a number of levels (e.g., the outer or middle ear, the cochlea, the eighth nerve or lower brain stem, and higher order brain centers). Auditory dysfunction can occur at any of these levels or at more than one level at the same time. Audiological abnormalities differ depending on the affected level. For example, the primary symptom of a middle ear disorder is loudness attenuation; in contrast, a brain stem disorder may show minimal loss of sensitivity but severe difficulty in speech understanding in quiet or noise. Therefore, a test battery must include procedures to evaluate possible dysfunction at several levels so that the level or levels contributing to the problem can be identified. In addition, the results of a test battery can identify those auditory processes that are normal.

A second need for a test battery is to verify the results of a single test with at least one other procedure. All tests are subject to some degree of error, which is minimized when results of several procedures lead to the same conclusion. Therefore, test results must be consistent with each other. This concept is called the cross-check principle of the test battery and is discussed thoroughly in Hannley (1986:2–3, 173–209).

A third use of an audiological test battery is to screen a client for the need for a more definitive test that identifies pathology. For example, the definitive test for retrocochlear disease is generally a radiological procedure, usually preceded by ABR. However, it is impractical to use radiological tests on every sus-

pect client, and ABR is not available in all facilities. Therefore, an appropriate audiological battery needs to be used as a screening procedure to identify those clients who need further testing. The concept is developed in Rintelmann (1991:700–702, 725–730).

The components of a test battery vary with the presenting problem and the desired goal of the evaluation. Different procedures are included in a battery designed to identify site of dysfunction for purposes of medical intervention than in a battery designed to develop a rehabilitation program. All test batteries, however, must address the client's primary complaint. For example, if the complaint is difficulty understanding speech under conditions of low redundancy, procedures that evaluate speech recognition in noise or competing message must be included.

Although test batteries may differ depending on the problem, there is usually a great deal of overlap of test procedures. The basic battery, consisting of air conduction, bone conduction, immittance, and speech audiometry, is used for most diagnostic and rehabilitative purposes. In this chapter audiograms and case history information are presented to introduce the student to results of test batteries suggesting conductive, cochlear, retrocochlear, and non-organic problems. In addition, factors other than non-organicity that contribute to audiometric inconsistencies are discussed. These include short attention span, fatigue, poor motivation, tinnitus, collapsed canals, and inappropriate testing materials.

In the ideal situation, problems at specific levels in the auditory system show distinctive results on the various tests in the battery. However, test results are not distinctive because the ideal situation is rare. Nevertheless, it is worth discussing distinctive audiometric patterns characteristic of conductive, cochlear, retrocochlear, and non-organic hearing loss.

CONDUCTIVE PROBLEMS

With a problem in the outer or middle ear, the major complaint tends to be difficulty hearing speech and other sounds. Generally, when speech is loud enough to be easily heard, understanding is adequate; if the hearing loss is severe, however, speech may never be comfortably loud. Speech understanding in noise, given adequate loudness, is not a significant problem. There may or may not be a history of outer or middle ear disease.

Pure tone audiometry can demonstrate a range of hearing losses from mild to severe, with any configuration; masked bone conduction is normal. If the hearing loss is mixed (has a sensorineural component), bone conduction is better than air conduction by at least 10 dB HL but will not be within normal limits. If the mixed hearing loss is severe to profound, however, bone conduction thresholds may not be measurable and the conductive component is revealed through immittance testing.

Tympanograms are Type B, C, AS, or AD; ear canal volume and static compliance may or may not be within the norms, depending on the specific pathology. If the conductive loss is bilateral, acoustic reflexes are absent; if the loss is unilateral, reflexes are absent when the affected ear is stimulated. When the normal ear is stimulated, however, reflexes may be seen if the hearing loss in the probe ear is less than 40 dB HL. If there is a sensorineural loss in one ear and a conductive loss in the other, the degree of conductive loss in the probe ear affects the presence or absence of acoustic reflexes in the stimulated sensorineural ear; if the conductive loss is less than 40 dB in the probe ear, reflexes may occur.

Spondee thresholds agree well with pure tone averages. MCLs occur at normal sensation levels and UCLs will be high, possibly at audiometric limits. PB Max is 90% or better, and no rollover is evident; if the hearing loss is severe, however, it may not be possible to establish PB Max.

COCHLEAR HEARING LOSS

Generally the chief complaint is reduced communication ability because of difficulty understanding speech even when it is comfortably loud. The client may complain of tinnitus, difficulty tolerating loud sound, recruitment, and diplacusis, and in some cases vertigo. Recruitment may be defined as a disproportionate increase in loudness sensation with increase in intensity of sound above the person's threshold of audibility. To quote Newby and Popelka (1985:84):

> . . . once a sound is intense enough to be perceived, an increase in intensity causes a disproportionate increase in the sensation of loudness. Thus, such a patient, with a sensorineural loss of 40 dB, can just barely detect the presence of a sound with an intensity of 40 dB above the normal threshold. However, a sound with an intensity of 5 dB above threshold may be perceived by the patient with a loudness greater than that heard by a normal-hearing person at 5 dB above threshold. Further increases in the intensity of the stimulus would result in more rapid increases in the patient's sensation of loudness, so that a sound of 60 dB intensity above the normal threshold might be perceived with the same loudness as a normal ear would perceive a sound of that intensity. Thus, over a range of 20 dB in intensity of the stimulus, in this example, the patient's loudness perception has increased as much as the normal ear's over a range of 60 dB.

Diplacusis is defined as a distortion in the sensation of pitch. A client's two ears may perceive the same frequency as two different pitches, or one ear may perceive the stimulus as a pure tone and the other ear as noise. Another form of diplacusis occurs when one ear perceives a pure tone as two sensations occurring at the same time (Newby and Popelka, 1985:85). There may or may not be medical history pointing to specific pathology.

Air conduction thresholds can indicate degree of loss ranging from mild to profound. Configurations may be flat, falling or rising. Bone conduction thresholds match air conduction within ±10 dB HL.

Tympanograms are Type A, indicating normal middle ear function. Static compliance and ear canal volume should be within normal limits. If the degree of loss in the stimulated ear is 50 dB or less, acoustic reflexes should occur at normal levels (70–100 dB).

If the degree of loss is between 50 and 80 dB, elevated reflexes (above 100 dB) may occur. With hearing losses greater than 80 dB in the stimulated ear, reflexes will probably be absent. Contralateral and ipsilateral reflex thresholds will be essentially the same. Reflex decay at 500 and 1000 Hz should not be seen because of normal eighth nerve function.

Spondee thresholds should agree well with either the two- or three-frequency pure tone average, depending on configuration of loss. With severe cochlear damage, however, speech understanding may be so poor that spondee thresholds cannot be established. In that situation, speech awareness thresholds should agree well with the best threshold of the speech frequencies. MCLs may occur at reduced sensation levels, sometimes approximating levels at which normal MCLs occur. UCLs are frequently low, indicating difficulty tolerating loud sound. Reduced dynamic range (UCL – SRT) is characteristic of cochlear dysfunction, although large differences exist among clients. PB Max scores are generally below 90%, reflecting the complaint of poor speech understanding. Sometimes word recognition tests performed in quiet do not define the speech understanding problem; it is necessary to test against a background of noise or competing message. Performance-intensity functions for monosyllables generally do not show rollover.

RETROCOCHLEAR HEARING LOSS

Retrocochlear hearing loss may occur anywhere in the auditory system central to the cochlea. This includes the eighth nerve, lower brain stem (below the superior olivary complex), upper brain stem, or temporal lobe. Dysfunction within the central auditory pathways of the brain is generally referred to as central hearing loss. Clients may present with tinnitus, vertigo, or neurological signs, including craniofacial or neuromuscular abnormalities such as facial weakness and gait disturbance. Hearing impairment may be unilateral or bilateral; eighth nerve tumors generally show unilateral symptoms. A primary complaint is severe difficulty understanding speech in quiet and/or noise.

Pure tone thresholds are frequently normal or mild to moderate in degree of loss, although more severe losses may be evident. Air and bone conduction thresholds agree within ±10 dB HL.

Tympanograms are Type A, consistent with normal middle ear function; ear canal volume and static compliance are also within normal limits. Acoustic reflex patterns vary depending on site of retrocochlear dysfunction (assuming no conductive component). With unilateral losses of the eighth nerve, stimulation of the affected ear results in one of three possibilities:

1. Contralateral and ipsilateral reflexes are absent.
2. Contralateral and ipsilateral reflexes are present at elevated threshold levels.
3. Contralateral and ipsilateral reflexes are present but show acoustic reflex decay.

Contralateral and ipsilateral reflexes occur at normal levels in the unimpaired ear.

With bilateral eighth nerve involvement, usually in persons with neurofibromatosis, contralateral and ipsilateral reflexes are absent in both ears. With lower brain stem disorder, stimulation of the ear contralateral to the lesion usually results in absent reflexes, while ipsilateral reflexes remain intact. The abnormality usually affects both contralateral reflexes, although occasionally it is seen on only one side. Occasionally massive brain stem involvement may affect both contralateral and ipsilateral reflexes. Problems above the level of the superior olivary complex are above the level of the reflex arc in the brain and generally do not affect reflex thresholds. See Chapter 3 in this textbook and Hannley (1986: Ch. 5) for discussion of interpretation of immittance results.

With retrocochlear hearing loss, spondee thresholds may be higher than predicted by pure tone sensitivity because of the severe speech understanding problem with this disorder. In contrast to cochlear disorders, MCL and UCL are not unusually low, provided that these scores are measurable. A significant indicator of retrocochlear involvement is the distinctive performance-intensity function using PB words (PI-PB). PB Max may be much poorer than can be explained by the degree of pure tone loss; in addition, the PI-PB function may show rollover (reduced word identification accuracy at intensity levels higher than the level at which PB Max was obtained). According to Hannley and Jerger (1981), not all eighth nerve patients demonstrate rollover; it is linked to the absence of the acoustic reflex. With auditory disorders located higher in the brain, monosyllabic word tests in quiet may not show abnormal patterns. It is necessary to use special tests characterized by reduced speech redundancy to identify the problem. Such procedures are beyond the scope of this book.

A thorough discussion of site-of-lesion tests and central auditory nervous system evaluation can be found in Rintelmann (1991:Chs. 7, 11, and 13) and Jacobson and Northern (1991:Chs. 8, 9, 10, and 11).

NON-ORGANIC LOSS

Whenever audiometric inconsistencies occur that cannot be explained by equipment malfunction, poor acoustic conditions, inappropriate testing materials or procedures, or client artifacts, non-organicity must be considered. Sometimes the person actually has normal hearing, and sometimes there is an organic hearing problem which the client is exaggerating. Motivation varies from desire for monetary compensation to attempts to obtain various types of secondary gain, such as increased parental attention, excuse for poor school performance, or avoidance of situations considered undesirable. When non-organicity is present, regardless of cause, it is the audiologist's responsibility to determine true organic thresholds and speech understanding.

There are a variety of non-organic signs of which the alert clinician must be aware. During the interview, the client may make exaggerated statements of communication difficulty but have little difficulty understanding the examiner, even when the examiner casually covers his or her lips. On the other hand, the individual may make exaggerated attempts to understand the examiner, such as fixating attention on the speaker's lips or cupping a hand behind an ear. Another suspicious sign involves the inconsistency between a client's claim of a long-standing total bilateral hearing loss and perfect articulation and voice quality. These signs are not proof of non-organicity, nor is their absence indication of the organic nature of the problem. Their presence should simply serve to alert the clinician to the possibility of a non-organic problem.

During the test procedures the client with a non-organic problem may give highly variable responses. When the difference between initial sampling of a frequency and subsequent recheck exceeds 10 dB, non-organicity must be considered. The same type of variability can occur with speech stimuli. Poor test–retest reliability, either with pure tones or with speech stimuli, suggests a non-organic problem. Discrepancies of more than 10 dB are suspicious.

False negative responses are frequently seen. The client may respond at one intensity level and then not respond to signal presented above that level. Responses to both tones and words may be extremely slow and deliberate, and responses to spondees may be half words (e.g., baseball may be repeated as base). There is no logical explanation for half word responses because both halves of each word are delivered with equal intensity. The person with a non-organic problem may not respond to spondees at all but may respond to casual conversation at a considerably lower intensity level when momentarily caught off guard.

Inconsistent relationships between air conduction and bone conduction thresholds, given proper equipment function and calibration, are suspicious signs. These inconsistencies include bone conduction thresholds significantly poorer than air conduction (20 dB or greater), or lack of bone conduction thresholds when the air conduction thresholds suggest mild or moderate hearing loss.

Immittance results are based on non-behavioral tests which are not within the client's voluntary control. Inconsistencies between tympanometry and acoustic reflex data on the one hand and pure tone thresholds on the other can be revealing. Air–bone gaps are not consistent with Type A tympanograms. Acoustic reflex thresholds within the normal range (e.g., 70–100 dB) are not consistent with pure tone thresholds in the severe to profound range.

The most common indication of non-organicity is poor agreement between poor tone average and speech reception threshold in the absence of other mitigating conditions. Speech reception thresholds are usually better than pure tone thresholds by more than 10 dB. It is felt that pure tone thresholds are usually higher because the loudness level for a pure tone is easier to mentally set (Hannley 1986:156).

It is possible with an organic problem for the speech reception threshold to be significantly poorer than the pure tone average. In that situation, however, one would expect speech understanding to be so poor that the client is unable to understand the spondee words. In that situation, a speech awareness threshold should agree closely either with the pure tone average or with the best air conduction threshold obtained for the speech frequencies. A speech reception threshold significantly poorer than the pure tone average that is accompanied by good word recognition suggests non-organicity.

From time to time we see clients who show normal pure tone thresholds and normal speech reception thresholds but extremely poor word recognition either in quiet or in noise. This apparent inconsistency is not a sign of non-organicity. Instead it is a strong indicator of retrocochlear difficulty and suggests the need for further special tests.

Inconsistencies in earphone–sound field relationships should alert the clinician to the possibility of a non-organic problem. If the word recognition is poor in both ears we would not expect it to be significantly improved in the sound field. Similarly, it is unlikely that the individual with poor unaided speech understanding would obtain a score of 100% with a hearing aid, assuming that all word recognition scores represented PB Max. The sound field speech reception threshold should agree with the better ear SRT within 6 dB. Differences which are significantly greater (more than 10 dB) in either direction should arouse suspicion.

It is theoretically possible for any type of audiometric configuration to have an organic basis; there is no typical pure tone configuration associated with non-organic hearing loss. However, an extremely irregular or otherwise unusual audiometric configuration may suggest non-organicity. For example, it is uncommon to find a sawtooth configuration where hearing at 500 Hz is poorer than at 250 Hz, but at 1000 Hz the threshold is better than at 500 Hz, only to become poorer again at 2000 Hz.

There are some people with non-organic difficulties who claim to have hearing loss in one ear only. When the poor ear of a person with a unilateral loss which is organic in nature is tested without contralateral masking, a shadow curve results. Even though the signal is presented to the poor ear, the good ear hears it when the presentation level exceeds interaural attenuation. If a person has no hearing for air conduction or bone conduction in one ear and the other ear is normal, the unmasked threshold taken from the dead ear would suggest a moderate conductive loss. The shadow curve is discussed more fully in Chapter 5 of this book. A person who can actually hear the signals in the professed poor ear will deny hearing any signals, not realizing that a shadow curve is expected in cases of unilateral impairment when contralateral masking is not used. This lack of contralateral response is a very clear indication of non-organic hearing loss. For further discussion of non-organic hearing loss, see Rintelmann (1991: Ch. 12), Newby and Popelka (1985:248–251, 290–293), Martin (1991:Ch. 10), Northern and Downs (1984:164–168).

Audiometric inconsistencies can be caused by factors other than non-organicity. These factors must be ruled out before a hypothesis of non-organic hearing loss is considered. Equipment must be functioning properly and calibrated appropriately. Tests must be administered under proper acoustic conditions; the American National Standards Institute (ANSI) has developed standards for maximum allowable noise levels for audiometric testing (ANSI S3.1-1977).

Audiometric inconsistencies can also be caused by client artifacts and inappropriate testing materials or procedures. These factors are discussed below.

CLIENT ARTIFACTS

Variability in threshold measurements can be caused by a number of factors related to the client's ability to cooperate. The young or difficult-to-test child may not attend to the task very long and/or have a low level of interest in the test. After a short period of testing, this individual may either cease responding or respond only when the signal is at a higher intensity level than that which produces responses at the beginning of testing. Sometimes changing the response task or switching to another test may restore the child's interest and improve the reliability of responses.

Many elderly people present testing difficulties for similar reasons. Most geriatric clients are eager to cooperate in a test situation; however, many tire easily and cannot attend to the task for long periods of time. Others are reluctant to respond to signals until they are clearly audible, resulting in artifactual elevation of threshold. In both the geriatric and pediatric difficult-to-test populations, false positive and false negative responses can cause problems.

Tinnitus or head noise is a common symptom among many people who have hearing problems. Tinnitus may occur with all kinds of hearing problems, may be tonal or noise-like in nature, may be constant or episodic, and may vary in severity. The patient who suffers from tinnitus may find it difficult to distinguish between his head noises and the test signals, particularly if there is similarity between the test tone and the tinnitus. Frequently a pulsed or warbled tone is used to make the test tone more distinctive.

Diplacusis or pitch distortion is a symptom present with certain types of sensorineural pathology. In this condition the client perceives tonal stimuli as noise and may have difficulty determining when he or she hears the test signal. Again, false positive responses may occur with great frequency, making accurate determination of pure tone thresholds very difficult. Since speech audiometry tends to be less affected than pure tone testing by either tinnitus or diplacusis, there may be poor agreement between SRT and pure tone average.

Another source of significant inter-test or intra-test disagreement is collapsed ear canals due to earphone pressure during testing. When the earphone compresses the pinna in certain clients, the soft cartilaginous portion of the ear canal is completely or partially closed. This condition can result in test variability because: (1) the canal can be opened by jaw movement—the client may deliberately open the canal periodically during testing to relieve the unpleasant sensation of a blocked canal; therefore, responses to test signals will vary from moment to moment depending on the degree of blockage; and (2) movement of the earphone away from the head restores the patency of the canal—if the earphones are removed from the ears after air conduction testing is completed in order to test bone conduction, and if later they are replaced somewhat differently for speech audiometry, there could be poor agreement between pure tone average and SRT. Obviously, testing at some future date could produce thresholds significantly different from initial test thresholds because of different degrees of closure of the ear canal. If canal closure is complete for all tests performed and is stable, inconsistencies would not be noticed and there would be an unrecognized overestimate of the amount of hearing deficit.

A collapsed canal can be kept opened during testing by using circumaural earphones or inserting an ear insert into the canal. For more complete information on collapsed canals, see Ventry, Chaiklin, and Boyle (1961), Hildyard and Valentine (1962) and Bess (1971).

Studebaker points out that, in a group of persons with normal middle ears, bone conduction should exceed air conduction and should be poorer than air conduction in a predictable number of cases because bone conduction vibrators are calibrated for the "average" mastoid. One must expect variations both above and below the average. According to statistical prediction, between 13% and 14% of such individuals should show bone conduction thresholds which differ from air conduction thresholds by more than +10 dB (Studebaker, 1967).

Still another variable affecting air–bone relationships is the effect of middle ear pathology on bone conduction sensitivity. Tonndorf (1964) with animal experiments and Carhart (1962) with human subjects demonstrated that modification of the middle ear structures in some cases resulted in reduced sensitivity to bone-conducted stimuli. The "Carhart Notch," appearing in some cases of otosclerosis, is an example of this phenomenon. Stapes fixation results in depressed bone conduction thresholds of 5 dB at 500 Hz, 10 dB at 1000 Hz, 15 dB at 2000 Hz, and 5 dB at 4000 Hz. Depression of the bone conduction thresholds can result in underestimation of the air–bone gap or obliteration of the gap if it is small to begin with.

INAPPROPRIATE TESTING MATERIALS OR PROCEDURES

Accuracy of test information can be affected detrimentally by the use of inappropriate procedures. With the young or difficult-to-test individual, vocabulary used in instructions or in the speech audiometric materials must be carefully controlled. If instructions are not understood, responses will be inappropriate. If words used to measure SRT or word recognition are not within the client's receptive vocabulary, errors will be made due to language, not auditory factors. Speech audiometric results will not represent the true auditory potential of the client.

In addition to appropriate language, appropriate test procedures must be used with the difficult-to-test client to maintain motivation. Such clients will frequently respond to play audiometry far better than to a standard hand-raising or button-pushing response task. Sometimes tangible reinforcers will expedite performance. It is important to modify test procedures appropriately to obtain the best possible performance from the client. For a more complete discussion of such procedural problems, see Lloyd (1975:Ch. 1) and Northern and Downs (1984:168–172).

Masking must be used when necessary and in the proper amounts in order to avoid misdiagnosis. This subject is discussed in Chapter 5. If there is a unilateral hearing loss and appropriate masking is not used in the better ear, the poorer ear may appear to hear significantly better by air conduction than is actually the case. A shadow curve will be obtained; that is, signals delivered to the poorer ear will be heard at intensity levels equal to the threshold of the better ear plus interaural attenuation. The signal is actually being heard by the better ear because the presentation level to the poorer ear is intense enough to override the attenuation provided by the head. It is thus possible for a "dead" ear to appear to have only a moderate hearing loss.

If insufficient masking is used, the participation of the better ear may not be completely eliminated. A spuriously low threshold may be obtained for the poor ear. If too much masking is used, overmasking of the poorer ear may occur and the threshold may be spuriously high. In some cases, where there are large air–bone gaps, it is not possible to use appropriate masking levels and true thresholds cannot be obtained in the poorer ear.

As discussed in Chapter 5, there is no, or at best minimal, interaural attenuation for bone-conducted signals. When a signal is presented to the poorer ear without contralateral masking, thresholds obtained may approximate bone conduction thresholds found in the better ear. This is the case even if the poorer ear has a profound sensorineural loss. Therefore, if appropriate masking is not used, a non-functional poor ear may appear to have a moderate to severe conductive loss with a large air–bone gap. Undoubtedly, there has been more than one case in which middle ear surgery has been performed unnecessarily because of inappropriate masking.

TACTILE BONE CONDUCTION THRESHOLD

In cases with severe to profound sensorineural losses, we sometimes see artifactual low-frequency air–bone gaps. These gaps can occur even when air conduction responses do not appear. Such artifactual bone conduction thresholds rarely appear at frequencies above 500 Hz and are considered to be responses to tactile or vibratory sensations. For a more complete discussion of pseudoauditory bone conduction thresholds, see Nober (1970) and Martin (1991:86). One must be careful not to interpret tactile bone conduction responses as evidence of mixed hearing loss.

The following audiograms and case history information are designed to give the student experience interpreting the entire basic battery of audiometric tests for conductive, cochlear, retrocochlear, and nonorganic hearing losses. Some of the audiograms demonstrate the effects of patient and testing variables on test consistency. The audiometric and case history information should be used to answer the questions in the manner prescribed for the previous chapters.

Questions

QUESTIONS FOR FIGURE 6-1

Case History Information This 32-year-old woman presented with a complaint of gradually worsening hearing. She had been aware of a problem for approximately ten years. Both parents have had hearing problems since young adulthood and wear hearing aids successfully. One sister has had successful middle ear surgery. She reported a history of ear infections in her left ear as a child but has not experienced such problems for 20 years. To her surprise, she has experienced little difficulty understanding speech in noise; she attributes this to the fact that most people shout under such communication conditions.

1. What type of hearing loss does this woman have in each ear? How do you know?
2. What do the tympanograms and static compliance data tell you about possible pathologies in each ear?
3. Is ear canal volume within normal limits?
4. Why are there no measurable acoustic reflexes?
5. Are the speech audiometric results consistent with the pure tone and immittance results?
6. What do the word recognition scores tell you about her ability to understand speech?

Name: Fig 6-1   Date: XX/XX/XX   Age: 35   Sex: F   Audiologist: HK

AUDIOMETER: GSI-10   ANSI 1969

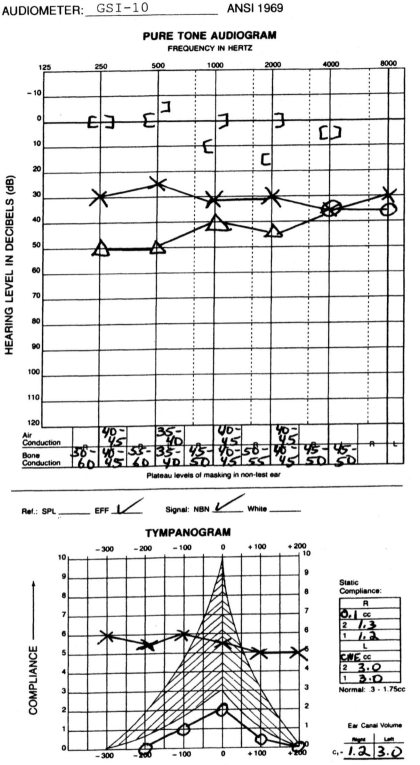

PURE TONE AUDIOGRAM
FREQUENCY IN HERTZ

Air Conduction	40-45	35-40	40-45	40-45	R	L
Bone Conduction	30-60	40-45	55-60	35-35	45-40	40-45	50-55	40-45	45-50	45-50	R	L

Plateau levels of masking in non-test ear

Ref.: SPL _____   EFF ✓   Signal: NBN ✓   White _____

TYMPANOGRAM

PRESSURE IN daPa

Static Compliance:

R	
0.1	cc
2	1.3
1	1.2

L	
CNE	cc
2	3.0
1	3.0

Normal: .3 - 1.75cc

Ear Canal Volume

	Right	Left
c_1 -	1.2	3.0

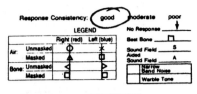

Response Consistency: (good) moderate poor

No Response

LEGEND

		Right (red)	Left (blue)
Air	Unmasked	○	X
	Masked	△	◻
Bone	Unmasked	<	>
	Masked	◻	◻

Best Bone ◻
Sound Field ___ S
Aided Sound Field ___ A
Narrow Band Noise
Warble Tone

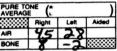

PURE TONE AVERAGE	(R L)		
	Right	Left	Aided
AIR	45	28	
BONE	8	-2	

SPEECH AUDIOMETRY ☒MLV ☒Tape

	RIGHT	LEFT	MASK LEVEL R L	SOUND FIELD	LIST
SAT					
SRT	40	30			
MCL	78	70			
UCL	110	110			
PB% (Word)	98 40SL	100 40SL	60 60		
PB% (Word)	_L	_L			
PB% (Word)	_L	_L			
PB% (Word)	_L	_L			
	_L	_L			
	_L	_L			

STAPEDIUS REFLEX THRESHOLDS

Stimulus	Contralateral (HL)					Ipsilateral (HL)		
EAR	.5K	1K	2K	4K	WBN	.5K	1K	2K
R	NR	NR	NR	NR		NR	NR	NR
Decay			X	X			X	X
L	NR	NR	NR	NR		NR	NR	NR
Decay			X	X			X	X

ABBREVIATIONS

A	Absent	NR	No Response
C_1	Canal Volume	SAT	Speech Awareness
CNE	Could Not Establish		Threshold
CNT	Could Not Test	SL	Sensation Level
DNT	Did Not Test	SRT	Speech Reception
HL	Hearing Level		Threshold
MCL	Most Comfortable	UCL	Uncomfortable Listening
	Listening Level		Level
MVL	Monitored Live Voice		

REMARKS:

_____

_____

_____

_____

_____

Interpreting the Basic Battery

Answers for Figure 6-1

1. This woman has a conductive loss in each ear. There are air–bone gaps greater than 10 dB at all frequencies, with bone conduction thresholds within normal limits. Both tympanograms indicate middle ear problems; static compliance is abnormally low in both ears, and acoustic reflexes are absent.

2. The right ear tympanogram is Type AS and is accompanied by low static compliance; this is consistent with otosclerosis and is supported by her report of adult onset, similar hearing problems in family members, and the possibility of a Carhart Notch in the bone conduction thresholds in the right ear.

   The left ear shows a Type B tympanogram with abnormally high ear canal volume. Static compliance could not be measured. This is consistent with eardrum perforation. The history of childhood ear infection supports this hypothesis.

3. Ear canal volume is within normal limits in the right ear but abnormally high in the left.

4. Acoustic reflexes could not be measured because of the large conductive hearing losses in both ears. See Chapter 3 to review the effects of middle ear disorder on the acoustic reflex.

5. Speech audiometric results are consistent with pure tone and immittance results. SRTs agree well with pure tone averages; MCL and UCL levels indicate wide dynamic range in both ears. These results are consistent with conductive hearing loss.

6. Word recognition scores are excellent in both ears and indicate that when speech is made sufficiently loud for this client, she has little speech understanding difficulty.

QUESTIONS FOR FIGURE 6-2

Case History Information This child was brought to the clinic by his parents because he has been having difficulty in school. The parents have not suspected hearing loss because he seems aware of environmental sound and responds when called; however, he does not always answer questions appropriately, particularly when there is noise in the room. He had several ear infections at age 3 but has had no recent ear problems. There is no family history of hearing loss except that the father developed a hearing problem while in the armed forces.

1. What type of hearing loss is present? How do you know?
2. What is the degree of loss?
3. What do the tympanograms and static compliance data tell you about possible pathologies in each ear?
4. Why are there no contralateral acoustic reflexes? Why are ipsilateral reflexes measurable in the right ear?
5. Are the speech audiometric results consistent with other audiometric data?
6. Can the hearing loss explain the child's difficulties in school?

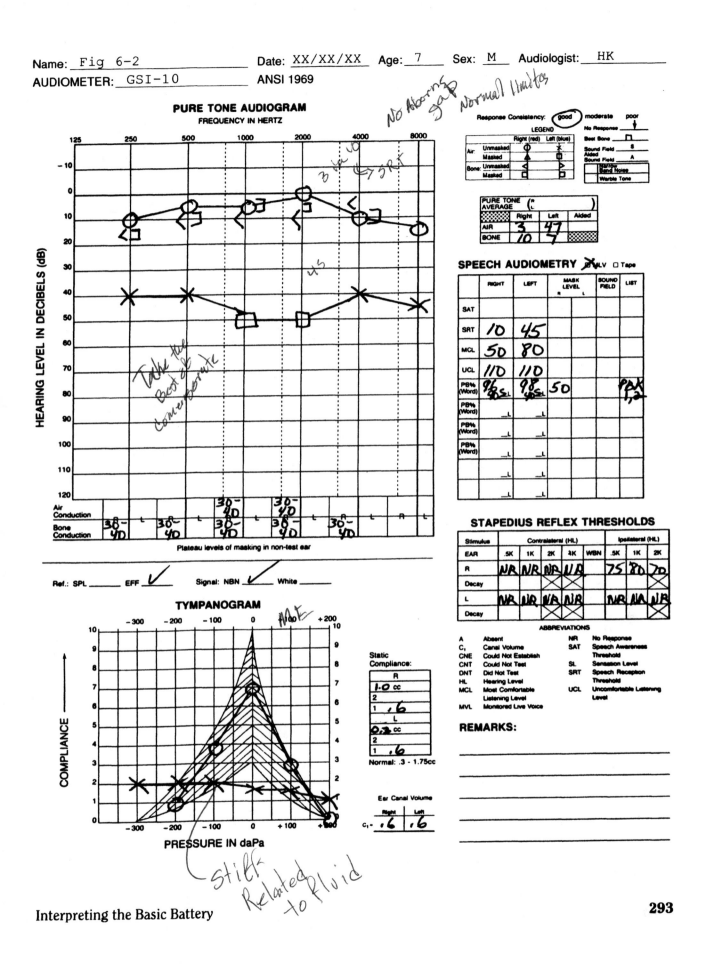

Interpreting the Basic Battery

Answers for Figure 6-2

1. Normal air conduction and bone conduction thresholds, Type A tympanogram, and normal SRT indicate normal hearing in the right ear. The large air–bone gaps at all frequencies, bone conduction thresholds within normal limits, and Type B tympanogram suggest conductive hearing loss in the left ear.

2. The right ear shows normal hearing; the pure tone average and SRT in the left ear indicate a moderate hearing loss.

3. The Type A tympanogram, normal static compliance and normal ear canal volume are consistent with normal middle ear function in the right ear. The Type B tympanogram and low static compliance are consistent with otitis media in the left ear.

4. Contralateral reflexes were not measurable when the left ear was stimulated because of middle ear abnormality in that ear. When the normal right ear was stimulated, contralateral reflexes could not be measured because the probe was in the left ear; the conductive loss in the left ear precluded normal contraction of the stapedius muscle, masking the normal right ear reflex thresholds. However, the normal right ear reflexes were evident with ipsilateral measurement because the right ear served as the probe ear.

5. SRTs are consistent with pure tone averages in both ears. MCLs and UCLs indicate wide dynamic ranges which are consistent with both normal hearing and conductive hearing loss. The high word recognition scores in both ears are also consistent with normal hearing and conductive hearing loss.

6. It is entirely possible that this child's school difficulties are attributable to the unilateral hearing loss. Although a person with one normal ear should be able to function as well as a person with two good ears under optimal, quiet, face-to-face communication conditions, such conditions are not the norm in typical classrooms. Under conditions of noise, reverberation, and distance listening, a unilateral hearing loss can interfere with communication and result in learning problems.

QUESTIONS FOR FIGURE 6-3

Case History Information This client has been hard of hearing since early childhood and has been successfully mainstreamed throughout her school years. She has been an excellent binaural hearing aid user. There is some history of ear infections in early childhood but none in recent years. Her parents brought her to the clinic because she has experienced a sudden increase in hearing loss which has affected her ability to function in school, communicate at home, and use the telephone. Her hearing aid is no longer effective.

1. What type and degree of hearing loss does this girl have? How do you know?
2. What do the tympanograms and acoustic reflex data suggest about middle ear function?
3. What might have caused the sudden drop in hearing?
4. Why is the hearing aid now ineffective?
5. Why are unaided word recognition scores poorer than aided scores?

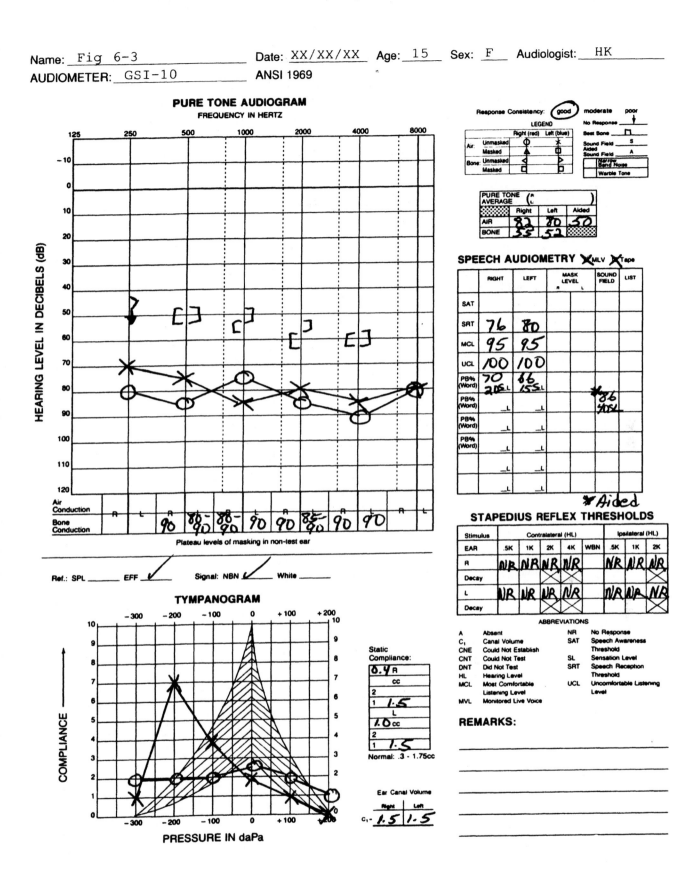

Name: Fig 6-3   Date: XX/XX/XX Age: 15 Sex: F Audiologist: HK
AUDIOMETER: GSI-10   ANSI 1969

PURE TONE AUDIOGRAM
FREQUENCY IN HERTZ

Response Consistency: good moderate poor No Response

LEGEND

		Right (red)	Left (blue)
Air:	Unmasked	O	X
	Masked	▲	◻
Bone:	Unmasked	<	>
	Masked	◻	◻

Best Bone ◻
Sound Field S
Aided
Sound Field A
Narrow Band Noise
Warble Tone

PURE TONE AVERAGE (R / L)

	Right	Left	Aided
AIR	82	70	50
BONE	55	52	

SPEECH AUDIOMETRY MLV Tape

	RIGHT	LEFT	MASK LEVEL R	L	SOUND FIELD	LIST
SAT						
SRT	76	80				
MCL	95	95				
UCL	100	100				
PB% (Word)	70 20SL	66 15SL				
PB% (Word)	_L	_L			*86 40SL	
PB% (Word)	_L	_L				
PB% (Word)	_L	_L				
	_L	_L				
	_L	_L				

*Aided

STAPEDIUS REFLEX THRESHOLDS

Stimulus	Contralateral (HL)					Ipsilateral (HL)		
EAR	.5K	1K	2K	4K	WBN	.5K	1K	2K
R	NR	NR	NR	NR		NR	NR	NR
Decay								
L	NR	NR	NR	NR		NR	NR	NR
Decay								

ABBREVIATIONS

A	Absent	NR	No Response
C₁	Canal Volume	SAT	Speech Awareness Threshold
CNE	Could Not Establish		
CNT	Could Not Test	SL	Sensation Level
DNT	Did Not Test	SRT	Speech Reception Threshold
HL	Hearing Level		
MCL	Most Comfortable Listening Level	UCL	Uncomfortable Listening Level
MVL	Monitored Live Voice		

REMARKS:

Air Conduction / Bone Conduction Plateau levels of masking in non-test ear:
90 80-90 80-90 90 90 85-90 90 90

Ref.: SPL ___ EFF ✓   Signal: NBN ✓ White ___

TYMPANOGRAM

PRESSURE IN daPa

Static Compliance:
0.4 R cc
2
1 1.5 L
1.0 cc
2
1 1.5
Normal: .3 - 1.75cc

Ear Canal Volume
Right | Left
C₁- 1.5 | 1.5

Answers for Figure 6-3

1. This girl is presenting with a mixed severe hearing loss in both ears. Although the air–bone gaps are greater than 10 dB at all frequencies, they are not within normal limits. The hearing loss is primarily sensorineural but shows an approximate 20-dB conductive component. Tympanograms in both ears are abnormal.

2. Tympanograms and absent acoustic reflexes in the presence of air–bone gaps strongly suggest middle ear abnormality. The Type B tympanogram in the right ear is consistent with otitis media, and the Type C tympanogram in the left suggests Eustachian Tube malfunction.

3. It is highly probably that middle ear dysfunction has caused the sudden drop in hearing. Based on the bone conduction thresholds, it is likely that the client was functioning with a moderate to severe sensorineural hearing loss prior to the conductive overlay. Hopefully, after medical treatment, the hearing loss will revert to its former status.

4. The hearing aid is now ineffective because it lacks the power to amplify average conversational speech to a comfortable listening level; note that aided SRT is 50 dB, at which level average conversation is barely audible.

5. Unaided word recognition scores probably do not represent PB Max because they were obtained at low sensation levels. However, increasing the presentation levels would force the client to listen near or above UCL, which is undesirable. The increase in hearing loss has further restricted the client's dynamic range. With amplification, words could be presented at a higher sensation level, resulting in a higher word recognition score.

QUESTIONS FOR FIGURE 6-4

Case History Information This 50-year-old executive has had a hearing problem for 25 years, caused by exposure to gunfire in the army. He has little difficulty understanding conversation in a quiet, face-to-face situation but experiences significant speech understanding problems in groups and in any situation where there is competing noise.

1. Describe the type and degree of hearing loss in each ear.
2. What do the immittance data tell you about site of dysfunction?
3. How might you explain the 12-dB difference between SRT and pure tone average in the right ear?
4. Is there a tolerance problem in either ear?
5. What do the word recognition scores tell you about his ability to understand speech?
6. Which ear do you consider the better ear? Why?

Name: Fig 6-4   Date: XX/XX/XX   Age: 50   Sex: M   Audiologist: HK
AUDIOMETER: GSI-10   ANSI 1969

PURE TONE AUDIOGRAM
FREQUENCY IN HERTZ

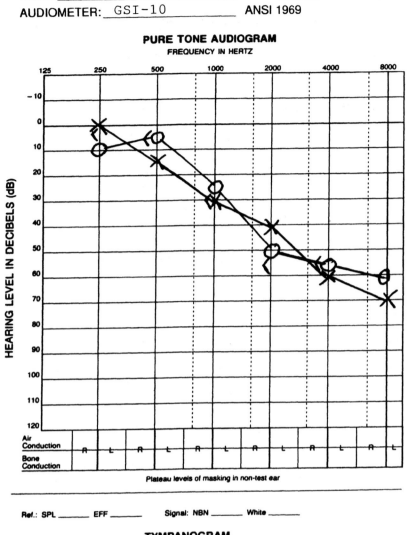

Air Conduction: R L R L R L R L R L R L R L
Bone Conduction:

Plateau levels of masking in non-test ear

TYMPANOGRAM

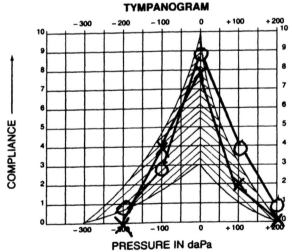

PRESSURE IN daPa

COMPLIANCE

Static Compliance:

R
1.0 cc
2
1

L
1.2 cc
2
1

Normal: .3 - 1.75cc

Ear Canal Volume

	Right	Left
C_1	1.3	1.2

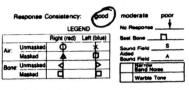

Response Consistency: (good) moderate poor

LEGEND

		Right (red)	Left (blue)
Air:	Unmasked	O	X
	Masked	▲	☐
Bone:	Unmasked	<	>
	Masked	☐	☐

No Response
Best Bone ☐
Sound Field __S__
Aided Sound Field __A__
Narrow Band Noise
Warble Tone

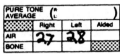

PURE TONE AVERAGE (R: / L:)

	Right	Left	Aided
AIR	27	28	
BONE			

SPEECH AUDIOMETRY ✗MLV ✗Tape

	RIGHT	LEFT	MASK LEVEL R L	SOUND FIELD	LIST
SAT					
SRT	15	25			
MCL	55	50			
UCL	92	80			
PB% (Word)	50 30SL	50 30SL			
PB% (Word)	54 40SL	56 40SL			
PB% (Word)	52 50SL	___ L			
PB% (Word)	___ L	___ L		60% 50HL 32% 50HL (S/N = 10)	
	___ L	___ L			
	___ L	___ L			

STAPEDIUS REFLEX THRESHOLDS

Stimulus	Contralateral (HL)					Ipsilateral (HL)		
EAR	.5K	1K	2K	4K	WBN	.5K	1K	2K
R	80	85	95	105				
Decay		✗	✗					✗
L	80	85	75	110				
Decay		✗	✗					✗

ABBREVIATIONS

A — Absent
C_1 — Canal Volume
CNE — Could Not Establish
CNT — Could Not Test
DNT — Did Not Test
HL — Hearing Level
MCL — Most Comfortable Listening Level
MVL — Monitored Live Voice

NR — No Response
SAT — Speech Awareness Threshold
SL — Sensation Level
SRT — Speech Reception Threshold
UCL — Uncomfortable Listening Level

REMARKS:

_____
_____
_____
_____
_____

Interpreting the Basic Battery

Answers for Figure 6-4

1. Both ears have mild sensorineural hearing losses. However, high-frequency pure tone thresholds are in the moderate to severe range.
2. The Type A tympanograms, normal static compliance, and normal ear canal volume in both ears indicate normal middle ear function. The presence of acoustic reflex thresholds at normal levels suggest cochlear site of dysfunction.
3. The SRT in the right ear agrees better with the two-frequency average (500 and 1000 Hz) of 15 dB than with the three-frequency average of 27 dB. This is typical of falling pure tone configurations.
4. The UCL of 80 dB in the left ear indicates a tolerance problem.
5. The PB Max scores of 54% and 56% in each ear and the 60% sound field score suggest the client has difficulty following conversation when he must rely on auditory information only. His report of having little difficulty in quiet, face-to-face communication situations probably reflects good speechreading skills which supplement what he is able to hear. The 32% word recognition score in noise is consistent with his complaint of significant speech understanding difficulty in groups and in competing noise.
6. Although the two ears look very similar in pure tone configuration, immittance data, and speech audiometric scores, the right ear must be considered better because of the higher UCL in that ear.

QUESTIONS FOR FIGURE 6-5

Case History Information This client is a prelingually deaf child who attends a mainstream school program. His parents brought him to the clinic for a routine evaluation.

1. Describe the hearing loss, using all available audiometric data.
2. Why are there no measurable acoustic reflex thresholds?
3. Why were word recognition scores probably not measured?
4. Which ear do you consider better? Why?

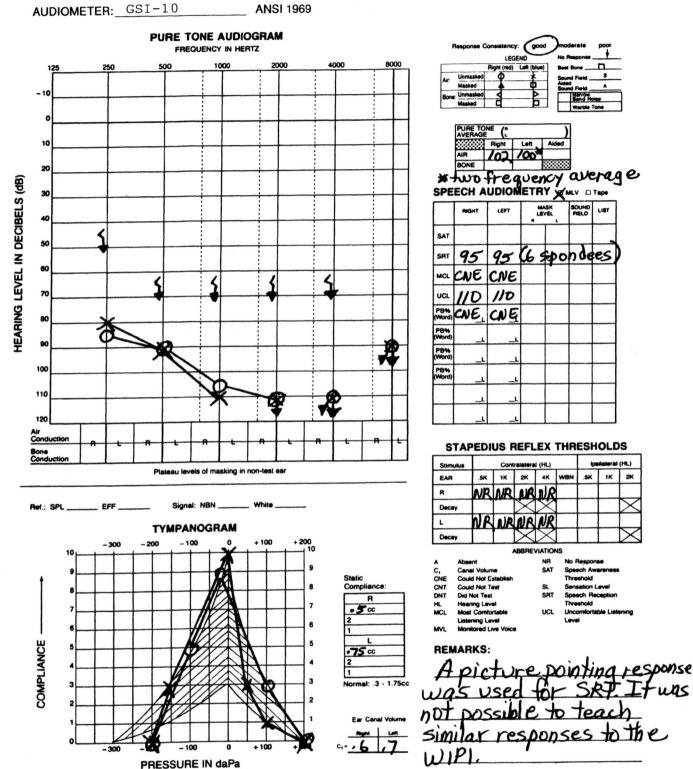

PURE TONE AUDIOGRAM

Name: Fig 6-5   Date: XX/XX/XX   Age: 6   Sex: M   Audiologist: HK

AUDIOMETER: GSI-10   ANSI 1969

FREQUENCY IN HERTZ

Response Consistency: (good) moderate poor

LEGEND

		Right (red)	Left (blue)
Air:	Unmasked	O	X
	Masked	▲	⊠
Bone:	Unmasked	<	>
	Masked	□	□

No Response ↓
Best Bone ⊐
Sound Field S
Aided
Sound Field A
Narrow Band Noise
Warble Tone

PURE TONE AVERAGE (R/L)			
	Right	Left	Aided
AIR	102	100*	
BONE			

✱ two frequency average

SPEECH AUDIOMETRY ✓MLV ☐Tape

	RIGHT	LEFT	MASK LEVEL R L	SOUND FIELD	LIST
SAT					
SRT	95	95 (6 spondees)			
MCL	CNE	CNE			
UCL	110	110			
PB% (Word)	CNE_L	CNE_L			
PB% (Word)	_L	_L			
PB% (Word)	_L	_L			
PB% (Word)	_L	_L			
	_L	_L			

Plateau levels of masking in non-test ear

Ref.: SPL _____ EFF _____   Signal: NBN _____ White _____

TYMPANOGRAM

PRESSURE IN daPa

Static Compliance:

R	
.5 cc	
2	
1	

L	
.75 cc	
2	
1	

Normal: .3 - 1.75cc

Ear Canal Volume

	Right	Left
C₁ =	.6	.7

STAPEDIUS REFLEX THRESHOLDS

Stimulus	Contralateral (HL)					Ipsilateral (HL)		
EAR	.5K	1K	2K	4K	WBN	.5K	1K	2K
R	NR	NR	NR	NR				
Decay			✕		✕			✕
L	NR	NR	NR	NR				
Decay			✕		✕			✕

ABBREVIATIONS

A	Absent	NR	No Response
C,	Canal Volume	SAT	Speech Awareness
CNE	Could Not Establish		Threshold
CNT	Could Not Test	SL	Sensation Level
DNT	Did Not Test	SRT	Speech Reception
HL	Hearing Level		Threshold
MCL	Most Comfortable	UCL	Uncomfortable Listening
	Listening Level		Level
MVL	Monitored Live Voice		

REMARKS:

A picture pointing response was used for SRT. It was not possible to teach similar responses to the WIPI.

Interpreting the Basic Battery

299

Answers for Figure 6-5

1. This child has a profound sensorineural hearing loss in both ears. The Type A tympanograms, normal static compliance, and normal ear canal volume are consistent with normal middle ear function. SRTs agree with pure tone data.
2. Acoustic reflex thresholds could not be measured because the degree of hearing loss in each ear is too great to elicit reflexes.
3. Word recognition scores could not be established because the child was unable to respond to the WIPI, which is a word recognition test designed for young children. It is unclear whether the lack of response is attributable to language difficulties or extremely poor word recognition.
4. The right ear is the better ear because the child was able to respond to pure tone at 2000 Hz; he was unable to do so in the left ear.

QUESTIONS FOR FIGURE 6-6

Case History Information This client presented with a complaint of difficulty understanding speech in his right ear. The hearing loss was accompanied by tinnitus and a tingling sensation on the right side of the face.

1. What type of loss does this client have in each ear? How do you know?
2. Are PB Max scores consistent with pure tone sensitivity?
3. Is the site of dysfunction more likely to be cochlear or retrocochlear? How do you know?
4. If site of lesion is retrocochlear, is it more likely to be located in the eighth nerve or higher brain-stem?

Name: Fig 6-6   Date: XX/XX/XX Age: 45 Sex: M Audiologist: HK
AUDIOMETER: GSI-10   ANSI 1969

PURE TONE AUDIOGRAM

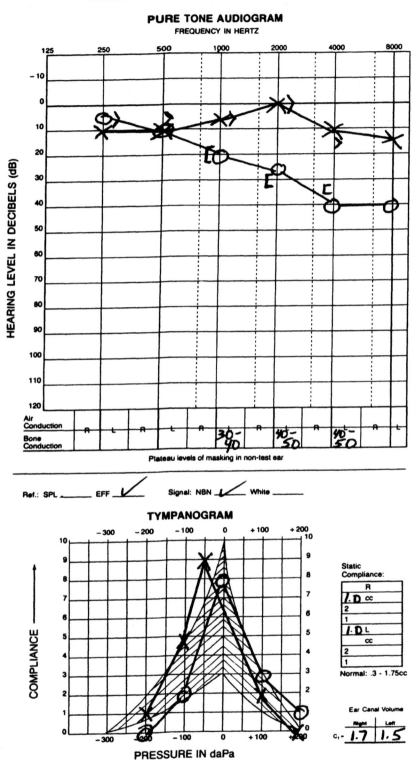

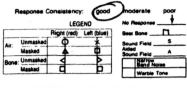

Response Consistency: (good) moderate poor

		Right (red)	Left (blue)	No Response
Air:	Unmasked	○	×	
	Masked	△	▢	
Bone:	Unmasked	<	>	
	Masked	▢	▢	

LEGEND — Best Bone, Sound Field S, Aided Sound Field A, Narrow Band Noise, Warble Tone

PURE TONE AVERAGE (R / L)	Right	Left	Aided
AIR	18	5	
BONE	18	3	

SPEECH AUDIOMETRY MLV Tape

	RIGHT	LEFT	MASK LEVEL R L	SOUND FIELD	LIST
SAT					
SRT	22	5			
MCL	50	50			
UCL	105	110			
PB% (Word)	65 30SL	96 40SL			
PB% (Word)	40 40SL	L			
PB% (Word)	70 50SL	L			
PB% (Word)	L	L			
	L	L			
	L	L			

Air Conduction — R L R L R L R L R L
Bone Conduction — 30-40 (1000), 40-50 (2000), 40-50 (4000)

Plateau levels of masking in non-test ear

Ref.: SPL _____ EFF ✓   Signal: NBN ✓ White _____

TYMPANOGRAM

Static Compliance:

R
1.0 cc
2
1

L
1.0 cc
2
1

Normal: .3 - 1.75cc

Ear Canal Volume

	Right	Left
C₁	1.7	1.5

STAPEDIUS REFLEX THRESHOLDS

Stimulus	Contralateral (HL)					Ipsilateral (HL)		
EAR	.5K	1K	2K	4K	WBN	.5K	1K	2K
R	NR	105	110	NR		NR	NR	NR
Decay								
L	75	80	75	75				
Decay								

ABBREVIATIONS

A	Absent	NR	No Response
C₁	Canal Volume	SAT	Speech Awareness
CNE	Could Not Establish		Threshold
CNT	Could Not Test	SL	Sensation Level
DNT	Did Not Test	SRT	Speech Reception
HL	Hearing Level		Threshold
MCL	Most Comfortable	UCL	Uncomfortable Listening
	Listening Level		Level
MVL	Monitored Live Voice		

REMARKS:

_____

_____

_____

_____

Interpreting the Basic Battery

301

Answers for Figure 6-6

1. Normal air and bone conduction thresholds, tympanograms, acoustic reflex thresholds, and speech audiometric data in the left ear all indicate normal hearing. The mild high-frequency hearing loss in the right ear is sensorineural because of the lack of air–bone gaps, Type A tympanogram, normal static compliance, and normal ear canal volume.

2. The PB Max score of 96% in the left ear is consistent with normal hearing. The PB Max score of 65% in the right ear, however, is poorer than what would be expected of a mild hearing loss with normal low-frequency hearing.

3. It is probable that the hearing loss in the right ear is retrocochlear because of the rollover in the PB scores and the absent or elevated acoustic reflex thresholds. This hypothesis is supported by the client's report of right ear tinnitus and a tingling sensation on the right side of the face.

4. It is probable that the retrocochlear dysfunction is located on the eighth nerve rather than upper brain stem because both contralateral and ipsilateral reflexes are abnormal on the right side and left contralateral reflexes are normal. It is likely that the problem is located below the first crossover point in the brain stem.

QUESTIONS FOR FIGURE 6-7

Case History Information This client complained of difficulty understanding speech in noise or poor listening conditions. He also complained of frequent headaches.

1. Is there any peripheral hearing loss?
2. Is there any evidence of central hearing loss?

PURE TONE AUDIOGRAM
FREQUENCY IN HERTZ

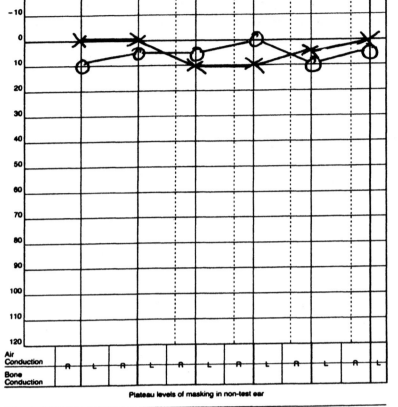

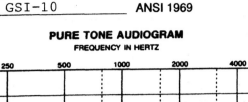

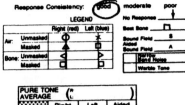

| Response Consistency: | good (circled) | moderate | poor |

LEGEND

		Right (red)	Left (blue)
Air:	Unmasked	O	X
	Masked	△	□
Bone:	Unmasked	<	>
	Masked	⊏	⊐

No Response	↓
Best Bone	□
Sound Field	S
Aided	
Sound Field Aided	A
Narrow Band Noise	
Warble Tone	

PURE TONE AVERAGE (R, L)

	Right	Left	Aided
AIR	2	7	
BONE			

SPEECH AUDIOMETRY MLV / Tape

	RIGHT	LEFT	MASK LEVEL R L	SOUND FIELD	LIST
SAT					
SRT	5	10			
MCL	45	50			
UCL	100	105			
PB% (Word)	90 40SL	100 40SL			
PB% (Word)	_L	_L			
PB% (Word)	_L	_L			
PB% (Word)	_L	_L			
	_L	_L			
	_L	_L			

STAPEDIUS REFLEX THRESHOLDS

Stimulus	Contralateral (HL)					Ipsilateral (HL)		
EAR	.5K	1K	2K	4K	WBN	.5K	1K	2K
R	NR	NR	NR	NR		85	90	90
Decay			✕	✕				✕
L	NR	NR	NR	NR		80	85	80
Decay			✕	✕				✕

ABBREVIATIONS

A	Absent	NR	No Response
C₁	Canal Volume	SAT	Speech Awareness Threshold
CNE	Could Not Establish		
CNT	Could Not Test	SL	Sensation Level
DNT	Did Not Test	SRT	Speech Reception Threshold
HL	Hearing Level		
MCL	Most Comfortable Listening Level	UCL	Uncomfortable Listening Level
MVL	Monitored Live Voice		

REMARKS:

Ref.: SPL _____ EFF _____　　Signal: NBN _____　White _____

TYMPANOGRAM

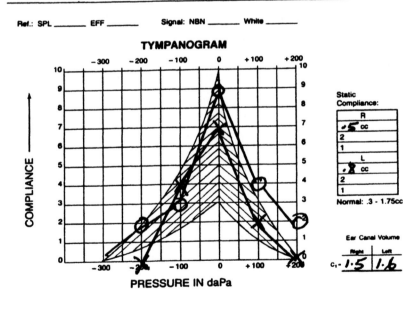

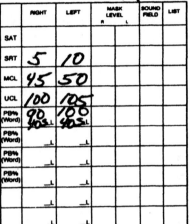

Static Compliance:

R
.5 cc
2
1

L
.8 cc
2
1

Normal: .3 - 1.75cc

Ear Canal Volume

	Right	Left
C₁ -	1.5	1.6

PRESSURE IN daPa

Answers for Figure 6-7

1. Pure tone thresholds, SRTs, word recognition scores, Type A tympanograms, normal static compliance, and normal ear canal volume indicate normal hearing. There is no evidence of a peripheral hearing loss in either ear.

2. The acoustic reflex data suggest the possibility of central auditory pathway disorder above the level of the first crossover in the brain stem for the following reasons: (1) acoustic reflex thresholds should not be absent in the presence of normal hearing; (2) normal ipsilateral reflexes are consistent with normal middle ear and cochlear function, as well as intact eighth nerve pathways up to the crossover point in the brain. Absent contralateral reflexes suggest dysfunction in the crossed central auditory pathways.

QUESTIONS FOR FIGURE 6-8

Case History Information This woman's hearing loss has existed in its present form since early childhood. Otologic examination has revealed no evidence of middle ear abnormalities.

1. What type of hearing loss does this woman have?
2. What can you conclude from the comparison of air and bone conduction thresholds?

Name: Fig 6-8   Date: XX/XX/XX   Age: 28   Sex: F   Audiologist: HK
AUDIOMETER: GSI-10   ANSI 1969

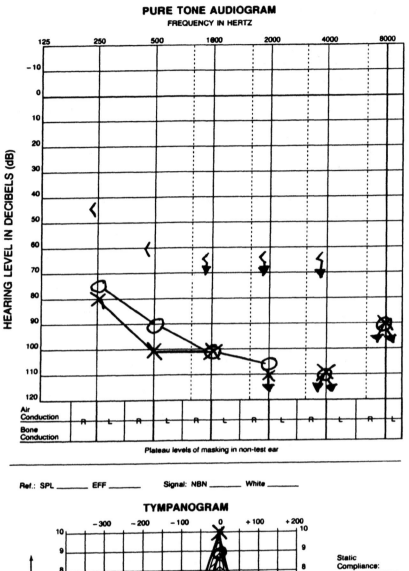

PURE TONE AUDIOGRAM
FREQUENCY IN HERTZ

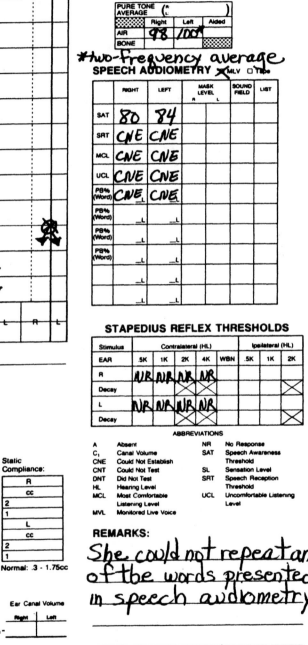

Response Consistency: (good) moderate poor

LEGEND

	Right (red)	Left (blue)
Air: Unmasked	O	X
Masked	△	◻
Bone: Unmasked	<	>
Masked	◻	◻

No Response: ↓
Best Bone: ◻
Sound Field: S
Aided Sound Field: A
Narrow Band Noise
Warble Tone

PURE TONE AVERAGE (R / L)

	Right	Left	Aided
AIR	98	/100*	
BONE			

*two-frequency average

SPEECH AUDIOMETRY ☒ MLV ☐ Tape

	RIGHT	LEFT	MASK LEVEL R	L	SOUND FIELD	LIST
SAT	80	84				
SRT	CNE	CNE				
MCL	CNE	CNE				
UCL	CNE	CNE				
PB% (Word)	CNE _L	CNE _L				
PB% (Word)	_L	_L				
PB% (Word)	_L	_L				
PB% (Word)	_L	_L				
	_L	_L				
	_L	_L				

Air Conduction — R L R L R L R L R L R L R L
Bone Conduction

Plateau levels of masking in non-test ear

Ref.: SPL _____ EFF _____   Signal: NBN _____ White _____

TYMPANOGRAM

PRESSURE IN daPa

Static Compliance:

R	
cc	
2	
1	

L	
cc	
2	
1	

Normal: .3 - 1.75cc

Ear Canal Volume

Right	Left

C₁ -

STAPEDIUS REFLEX THRESHOLDS

Stimulus EAR	Contralateral (HL) .5K	1K	2K	4K	WBN	Ipsilateral (HL) .5K	1K	2K
R	NR	NR	NR	NR				
Decay								
L	NR	NR	NR	NR				
Decay								

ABBREVIATIONS

A	Absent	NR	No Response
C₁	Canal Volume	SAT	Speech Awareness
CNE	Could Not Establish		Threshold
CNT	Could Not Test	SL	Sensation Level
DNT	Did Not Test	SRT	Speech Reception
HL	Hearing Level		Threshold
MCL	Most Comfortable	UCL	Uncomfortable Listening
	Listening Level		Level
MVL	Monitored Live Voice		

REMARKS:

She could not repeat any of the words presented in speech audiometry

1. This woman has a profound bilateral sensorineural hearing loss.
2. Although an air–bone gap seems to be present at 250 and 500 Hz, it is highly unlikely that it represents a conductive component. If the loss were mixed, we would expect to see bone conduction responses above 500 Hz and some responses either to spondee words or to word recognition tests even if the responses were limited. We would also expect abnormal tympanograms. The bone conduction thresholds probably represent responses to tactile stimulation.

QUESTIONS FOR FIGURE 6-9

Case History Information This boy's IQ scores suggest he has mental abilities slightly above average, but his school performance has been poor. He has failed three subjects in high school and is currently doing inferior work in three of his four academic classes. He has had a past history of an otologically confirmed conductive impairment which was corrected medically two years ago. During the interview the boy showed no difficulty understanding the clinician even when her mouth was covered. During the test procedures, the client showed much variability in his responses to pure tones and was extremely slow in responding to words. Equipment was checked prior to testing and was found to be working adequately.

1. What type of hearing impairment does this boy have?
2. What specific audiologic information supports the above impression?

Name: Fig 6-9   Date: XX/XX/XX   Age: 15   Sex: M   Audiologist: HK

AUDIOMETER: GSI-10   ANSI 1969

PURE TONE AUDIOGRAM
FREQUENCY IN HERTZ

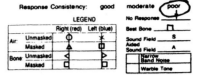

Response Consistency: good   moderate   (poor)

LEGEND

		Right (red)	Left (blue)
Air	Unmasked	O	X
	Masked	△	☐
Bone	Unmasked	<	>
	Masked	☐	☐

No Response
Best Bone ___ ☐
Sound Field ___ S
Aided
Sound Field ___ A
Narrow Band Noise
Warble Tone

PURE TONE AVERAGE (R   L   )

	Right	Left	Aided
AIR	43	45	-5
BONE			

SPEECH AUDIOMETRY   ☒MLV ☒Tape

	RIGHT	LEFT	MASK LEVEL R	L	SOUND FIELD	LIST
SAT						
SRT	26	28			28	
MCL	DNT	DNT				
UCL	DNT	DNT				
PB% (Word)	24 40SL	28 40SL			30 40SL	
PB% (Word)	_L	_L				
PB% (Word)	_L	_L				
PB% (Word)	_L	_L				
	_L	_L				
	_L	_L				

STAPEDIUS REFLEX THRESHOLDS

Stimulus	Contralateral (HL)					Ipsilateral (HL)		
EAR	.5K	1K	2K	4K	WBN	.5K	1K	2K
R	70	75	80	80				
Decay			☒	☒				☒
L	75	80	85	85				
Decay			☒	☒				☒

ABBREVIATIONS

A	Absent	NR	No Response
C₁	Canal Volume	SAT	Speech Awareness Threshold
CNE	Could Not Establish		
CNT	Could Not Test	SL	Sensation Level
DNT	Did Not Test	SRT	Speech Reception Threshold
HL	Hearing Level		
MCL	Most Comfortable Listening Level	UCL	Uncomfortable Listening Level
MVL	Monitored Live Voice		

Ref.: SPL _____ EFF _____   Signal: NBN _____ White _____

TYMPANOGRAM

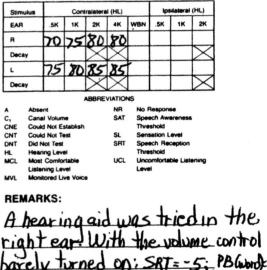

PRESSURE IN daPa

Static Compliance:

	R
	cc
2	
1	

	L
	cc
2	
1	

Normal: .3 - 1.75cc

Ear Canal Volume

Right	Left

C₁ -

REMARKS:

A hearing aid was tried in the right ear. With the volume control barely turned on: SRT=-5; PB(word) 100% at 40dBSL (35dBHL)

Answers for Figure 6-9

1. The audiologic inconsistencies suggest this boy has non-organic hearing impairment. The information presented in the partial history is also consistent with a non-organic impairment. Poor scholastic performance and a previous organic hearing problem are often found in children demonstrating non-organic signs (Rintelmann, 1991:610).

2. The specific audiologic inconsistencies suggesting a possible non-organic impairment are as follows: (a) the lack of any bone conduction response in light of the purported air conduction thresholds; (b) the significant difference between the SRT and pure tone average for monaural and sound field conditions; (c) the poor word recognition scores in light of the SRTs being significantly better than the pure tone results; (d) the poor word recognition scores in light of the lack of communicative difficulty during the interview even when visual cues were not available; (e) the 100% correct aided word recognition score in light of the poor unaided word recognition scores (it is highly unusual for any hearing aid to improve word recognition scores from 30% to 100%); and (f) the poor reliability, the variability of response, and the slow responses to speech audiometry.

QUESTION FOR FIGURE 6-10

Case History Information   This client complained that she had incurred her hearing problem three weeks before her audiologic evaluation as a result of an automobile accident. All equipment was found to be working adequately.

1. What seems to be wrong with the audiologic information presented?

Name: Fig 6-10   Date: XX/XX/XX   Age: 48   Sex: F   Audiologist: HK

AUDIOMETER: GSI-10   ANSI 1969

PURE TONE AUDIOGRAM
FREQUENCY IN HERTZ

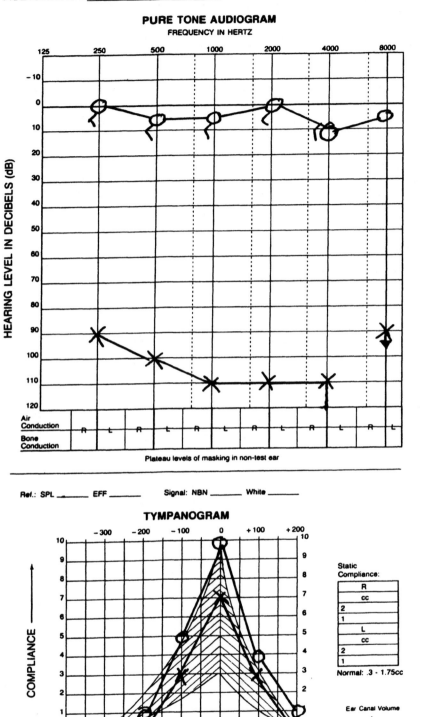

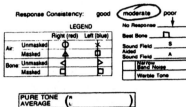

Response Consistency: good   (moderate)   poor

PURE TONE AVERAGE	(R)		
	Right	Left	Aided
AIR	3	107	
BONE			

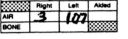

SPEECH AUDIOMETRY ✗MLV ✗Tape

	RIGHT	LEFT	MASK LEVEL R L	SOUND FIELD	LIST
SAT					
SRT	O	NR		30	
MCL					
UCL					
PB% (Word)	100 YDS	DNT		60 YDSL	
PB% (Word)					
PB% (Word)					
PB% (Word)					

STAPEDIUS REFLEX THRESHOLDS

Stimulus	Contralateral (HL)					Ipsilateral (HL)		
EAR	.5K	1K	2K	4K	WBN	.5K	1K	2K
R	70	80	80	90				
Decay								
L	90	95	95	100				
Decay								

ABBREVIATIONS

A — Absent
C₁ — Canal Volume
CNE — Could Not Establish
CNT — Could Not Test
DNT — Did Not Test
HL — Hearing Level
MCL — Most Comfortable Listening Level
MVL — Monitored Live Voice
NR — No Response
SAT — Speech Awareness Threshold
SL — Sensation Level
SRT — Speech Reception Threshold
UCL — Uncomfortable Listening Level

REMARKS:

Ref.: SPL _____ EFF _____   Signal: NBN _____ White _____

TYMPANOGRAM

PRESSURE IN daPa

Static Compliance:

R	
cc	
2	
1	
L	
cc	
2	
1	

Normal: .3 - 1.75cc

Ear Canal Volume

| | Right | Left |
| C₁ = | | |

Answer for Figure 6-10

1. The purported thresholds for the left ear are significantly poorer than one would expect. Without masking of the opposite ear, one would expect to obtain a shadow curve for the left ear within approximately 60 dB of the right ear. Similarly, without contralateral masking one would expect to obtain an SRT or at least an SAT within approximately 60 dB of the right ear.

    The sound field SRT is significantly poorer than the better ear pure tone average and speech reception threshold. In a unilateral loss the sound field SRT should agree well with the scores obtained on the better ear.

    The word recognition score obtained in the sound field is considerably poorer than one would expect, considering the right ear is normal in its performance. As with SRT, sound field word recognition should agree with scores obtained on the better ear.

    Acoustic reflex thresholds are present in the left ear at levels better than purported pure tone thresholds. The reflexes are consistent with pure tone sensitivity of 50 dB HL or better. These discrepancies suggest a non-organic hearing impairment.

QUESTIONS FOR FIGURE 6-11

1. What audiologic inconsistencies are presented in these results?
2. What possible explanations for these inconsistencies exist?

AUDIOMETER: GSI-10   ANSI 1969

PURE TONE AUDIOGRAM
FREQUENCY IN HERTZ

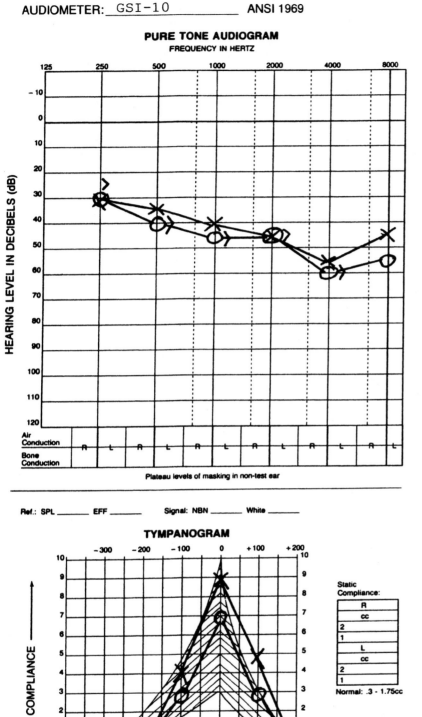

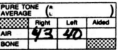

Response Consistency: good moderate (poor)

LEGEND	Right (red)	Left (blue)
Air: Unmasked	O	X
Masked	▲	☐
Bone: Unmasked	<	>
Masked	☐	☐

No Response
Best Bone ☐
Sound Field S
Aided
Sound Field A
Narrow Band Noise
Warble Tone

PURE TONE AVERAGE (R: L:)	Right	Left	Aided
AIR	43	40	
BONE			

SPEECH AUDIOMETRY X MLV X Tape

	RIGHT	LEFT	MASK LEVEL R	MASK LEVEL L	SOUND FIELD	LIST
SAT						
SRT	20	20			26	
MCL	50	50				
UCL	90	95				
PB% (Word)	_L	_L				
PB% (Word)	_L	_L				
PB% (Word)	_L	_L				
PB% (Word)	_L	_L				
	_L	_L				
	_L	_L				

Air Conduction R L R L R L R L R L R L
Bone Conduction

Plateau levels of masking in non-test ear

Ref.: SPL _____ EFF _____   Signal: NBN _____ White _____

TYMPANOGRAM

COMPLIANCE

PRESSURE IN daPa

Static Compliance:

R	
cc	
2	
1	

L	
cc	
2	
1	

Normal: .3 - 1.75cc

Ear Canal Volume

	Right	Left
C₁ -		

STAPEDIUS REFLEX THRESHOLDS

Stimulus	Contralateral (HL)					Ipsilateral (HL)		
EAR	.5K	1K	2K	4K	WBN	.5K	1K	2K
R	80	90	100	NR				
Decay								
L	85	95	100	105				
Decay								

ABBREVIATIONS

A	Absent	NR	No Response
C₁	Canal Volume	SAT	Speech Awareness
CNE	Could Not Establish		Threshold
CNT	Could Not Test	SL	Sensation Level
DNT	Did Not Test	SRT	Speech Reception
HL	Hearing Level		Threshold
MCL	Most Comfortable	UCL	Uncomfortable Listening
	Listening Level		Level
MVL	Monitored Live Voice		

REMARKS:

Complained of constant tinnitus; gave many false positive responses

Answers for Figure 6-11

1. The speech recognition thresholds are significantly lower (better) than one would normally expect with pure tone thresholds presented.

2. There are several possible causes for these discrepancies. First, equipment malfunction must always be considered. If calibration of any of the signals is in error, lack of pure tone–SRT agreement can occur. Pure tone thresholds may be underestimated or speech reception thresholds may be overestimated, depending on the error. Noise in the transducers may affect pure tone thresholds more than the SRT because linguistic factors play a role in the perception of speech.

   Second, patient artifacts may account for the discrepancy. Factors such as poor motivation, short attention span, tinnitus, or diplacusis may result in audiometric inconsistency. In this case, the client complained of constant tinnitus which she said interfered with her ability to determine when the pure tones were being presented. She also gave many false responses which impaired the reliability and validity of the test results. Collapsed canals due to earphone pressure may cause poor agreement between pure tone average and SRT if the occlusion of the canals is greater during pure tone testing than during speech audiometry.

   Third, it is also possible that the client did not understand instructions for the pure tone testing. It is very important that the client understands that she is to respond when she barely hears the tone and not wait until the signal is clearly audible. The client should be instructed to respond even if not completely sure. If poorly understood instructions are the problem in this case, reinstruction followed by retesting of pure tone thresholds should resolve the inconsistencies.

   Finally, the possibility of non-organicity must be considered. The most common indication of non-organicity is poor agreement between pure tone average and speech recognition threshold with SRT better by 10 dB or more. However, people with non-organic problems tend not to show false positive responses; they give false negative responses instead. Still, non-organicity cannot be ruled out as a factor in explaining the audiometric inconsistencies.

REVIEW AND SEARCH PROJECTS

1. Describe what is meant by the Carhart Notch.

2. Support or refute the statement, "Bone conduction testing measures cochlear reserves."

3. Describe audiologic tests used to detect non-organic hearing loss.

4. Describe behavioral tests designed to differentiate between cochlear and retrocochlear hearing loss.

5. Describe electrophysiological tests designed to differentiate between cochlear and retrocochlear hearing loss.

6. Describe a central auditory nervous system (CANS) test battery.

7. Describe a battery of audiologic tests designed to differentiate between conductive and sensorineural hearing loss.

8. What behaviors of the client being seen for an audiologic assessment suggest the possibility of a non-organic component?

9. What conditions might cause poor agreement between speech reception threshold and pure tone average?

10. What is a shadow curve? What is its diagnostic significance?

11. Review the literature on normal speech understanding in noise.

12. Why would you expect a person presenting a non-organic problem to give a large number of false negative responses but relatively few false positive responses?

13. Discuss procedures you would use in checking audiometer calibration.

14. Discuss modifications in test procedures you would need to test a pediatric/difficult-to-test client.

15. Discuss modifications in test procedures needed to test geriatric clients.

16. Discuss the effects of collapsed ear canals on audiometric testing.

17. Prepare a talk to present to a group of teachers explaining why some children who fail screening tests should not be given preferential seating or other special treatment.

REFERENCES

American National Standards Institute 1977. American National Standard criteria for permissible ambient noise during Audiometric testing (ANSI S3.1-1977). New York.

Bess, J. C. 1971. Ear canal collapse. *Archives of Otolaryngology* 93:408-412.

Carhart, R. 1962. Effects of stapes fixation on bone conduction response. *Otosclerosis* (pp. 175–197). Boston: Little, Brown.

Hannley, M. 1986. *Basic Principles of Auditory Assessment.* San Diego: College-Hill Press.

Hannley, M., and Jerger, J. 1981. PB rollover and the acoustic reflex. *Audiology* 20: 251–258.

Hildyard, V. H., and Valentine, M. A. 1962. Collapse of the ear canal during audiometry. *Archives of Otolaryngology* 75:422–423.

Jacobson, J. T., and Northern, J. L. 1991. *Diagnostic Audiology.* Austin: Pro-Ed.

Lloyd, L. L. 1975. Pure tone audiometry. In R. T. Fulton and L. L. Lloyd (Eds.), *Auditory Assessment of the Difficult-to-Test.* Baltimore: Williams & Wilkins.

Martin, F. N. 1991. *Introduction to Audiology,* 4th ed. Englewood Cliffs, N. J.: Prentice-Hall.

Newby, H. A., and Popelka, G. R. 1985. *Audiology,* 5th ed. Englewood Cliffs, N. J.: Prentice-Hall.

Nober, E. H. 1970. Cutile air and bone conduction thresholds of the deaf. *Exceptional Children* 36:571–579.

Northern, J. L., and Downs, M. P. 1984. *Hearing in Children,* 3rd ed. Baltimore: Williams & Wilkins.

Rintelmann, W. F. 1991. *Hearing Assessment,* 2nd ed. Austin: Pro-Ed.

Studebaker, G. A. 1967. Interest variability and the air-bone gap. *Journal of Speech and Hearing Disorders* 32:82–86.

Tonndorf, J. 1964. Animal experiments in bone conduction: clinical conclusions. *Annals of Otology, Rhinology and Laryngology* 73:659–678.

Ventry, I. M., Chaiklin, J. B., and Boyle, W. F. 1961. Collapse of the ear canal during audiometry. *Archives of Otolaryngology* 73:727–731.

Educational and Communicative Implications of Hearing Loss

It is extremely important to realize that inferences made about communication skills and educational and rehabilitative needs from inspection of the audiogram are only generalizations. Large individual differences occur because speech and language abilities and educational achievement depend not only on the audiogram but also on age of onset, age of intervention, intelligence, motivation, quality of communication in the home, quality of education, and problems coexisting with hearing loss. Nevertheless, it is useful to develop an understanding of the verbal receptive and expressive communication difficulties that generally accompany the various types and degrees of hearing loss.

In this chapter, audiograms and case history information are presented to illustrate the relationships between different audiometric patterns, including speech understanding and verbal receptive and expressive communication difficulties. By answering the questions and checking them in the manner prescribed for the previous chapters, the reader will become aware of the communicative, educational and rehabilitative significance of various types of hearing problems. Receptive and expressive communication discussed in this chapter refers to spoken and written English; issues related to manual communication and educational options for deaf children are beyond the scope of this book.

In this chapter the reader will learn to:

1. Understand the relationship between degree of hearing loss and ability to hear and understand speech.

2. Understand the relationship between degree of hearing loss and speech and language problems.
3. Understand the relationship between type of hearing loss and ability to understand speech.
4. Understand the effect of a unilateral hearing loss on receptive and expressive communication.
5. Recognize when amplification is indicated.
6. Determine which ear is preferable for amplification.
7. Understand the relationship between type of hearing loss, speech understanding ability, and speech and language performance.
8. Understand the effect of degree of hearing loss, type of hearing loss, and age of onset on educational needs of deaf and hard-of-hearing children.

DEGREE OF HEARING LOSS

Terminology

In 1975, The Conference of Executives of American Schools for the Deaf adopted the following definitions:

Hearing impaired is a generic term including people with all degrees of hearing loss from mild to profound. Although many people continue to use this term in this way, others find it objectionable or consider it to be synonymous with **hard of hearing**. Because the term **hearing impaired** is controversial, it will not be used in this chapter.

A **deaf** person is one whose hearing loss is so great that successful processing of auditory information is not possible, with or without a hearing aid. This individual uses vision as the primary channel for communication. Generally, when pure tone or speech reception thresholds are poorer than 90 dB HL, a person is considered to be **audiometrically deaf**. However, it is impossible to predict how that person functions based on the audiogram alone. Therefore, it is more accurate to use the functional definition of the terms **deaf** and **hard of hearing**.

There is also a cultural definition of **deafness**; anyone, regardless of degree of loss, who identifies with deaf culture and uses American Sign Language as the primary mode of communication is considered **culturally deaf**. Since cultural deafness is not related to the audiogram, the term will not be used in this chapter.

A **hard-of-hearing** person is one who has sufficient residual hearing for successful processing of linguistic information through audition. Audiometric thresholds can vary from slight to severe and sometimes profound. Most hard-of-hearing individuals use hearing aids; sometimes a deaf person is able to function as hard of hearing with the aid of amplification.

A **deafened** person is usually an adult who has had normal hearing or has been hard of hearing for most of his or her life, and then has become deaf. The onset of deafness may be sudden or gradual, but the degree of loss is always profound. There are usually severe receptive problems and often adjustment difficulties. Language is usually normal but speech may deteriorate over a period of time.

In order to better understand how various degrees of hearing loss affect speech understanding, some information about speech itself is necessary. The level of average conversational speech is approximately 50 dB HL. Soft speech occurs at approximately 35 dB HL and loud speech at 65 dB HL. Speech sounds range in power about 28 dB from the weakest sound (voiceless **th** as in **thin**) to the strongest sound (vowel **aw** as in **law**). A person with average normal hearing should be able to hear all the sounds of conversational-level speech comfortably, but to someone with an SRT of 30 dB HL, average conversational speech would just barely be audible.

Although it is not possible to draw firm boundaries between the deaf and hard-of-hearing person based on the audiogram, it is possible to use a degree-of-loss classification system as a general guide to severity of handicap. The classification of degree of loss used in this chapter is based on Clark's modification of Goodman's system (Clark, 1981), which is described in Chapter 1 (Table 1-1). It is possible to express degree of hearing loss as the average of pure tone thresholds at 500, 1000, and 2000 Hz or the spondee threshold level (SRT) of the better ear; the SRT is used in this chapter.

Hearing Levels of –10 to 25 dB

SRTs of –10 to 15 dB HL are considered normal hearing. There is usually no difficulty understanding speech in reasonably quiet environments, normal speech and language, and no need for a hearing aid. Thresholds between 16 and 25 dB may be considered slight or borderline hearing loss. In most situations, adults with these thresholds will have minimal difficulty, but may demonstrate more speech understanding problems than people with normal hearing in noise, group situations, or in situations with poor acoustics. Minimal levels of hearing loss are more problematic for children than adults because children must use their hearing to learn speech and language rather than simply recognize what they already know; therefore, losses from 16 to 25 dB HL can have negative effects educationally. The handicapping effect of this degree of loss, particularly for children, is increased if there is hearing loss at higher frequencies, such as 3000 and 4000 Hz, because recognition of many consonant sounds and a few vowels is influenced by ability to hear at these frequencies.

Hearing Levels of 26 to 40 dB

This is considered mild hearing loss. There may be difficulty understanding faint or distant speech or conversation in the presence of competing noise. Although there are individual differences in degree of handicap imposed by such a hearing loss, prelingually hard-of-hearing children or those with recurrent otitis media may show language deficits, articulation problems, and some educational difficulties. Many children with mild losses are not diagnosed early or are misdiagnosed as mildly retarded or learning disabled. Even when correctly diagnosed, such children tend to receive low priority for intervention. More attention needs to be paid to obtaining special speech, hearing, language, and educational services for children with mild hearing losses. For both adults and children amplification may be needed on a full- or part-time basis, depending on the communicative demands made of the individual. Amplification, in the form of a hearing aid or an assistive listening device, should be considered for the classroom.

Hearing Levels of 41 to 55 dB

This is considered moderate hearing loss. Usually there is great difficulty hearing speech at average conversational level (50 dB HL), particularly when the speaker and listener are more than 3 to 5 feet apart. Speech and language problems are often present, particularly with prelingual etiology, and amplification is almost always needed. Children with prelingually acquired losses of this magnitude may have difficulty with appropriate English syntax, vocabulary, and idiomatic expressions; there is almost always a problem expressing subtleties of meaning. Reading, writing and other academic skills may be delayed. Articulation may be defective, but the speech is usually intelligible. Voice quality and inflection are usually normal if amplification is used. Such children require the services of a speech–language pathologist and audiologist, preferential seating in class, and possibly special help from the classroom teacher or a resource person. Preschoolers with this degree of loss are sometimes misdiagnosed as aphasic, brain damaged, mentally retarded, learning disabled, or emotionally disturbed.

Adults with adventitiously acquired hearing loss of this magnitude almost always need amplification. The amount of speech understanding difficulty depends on their unaided word recognition ability. If unaided word recognition is poor, amplification will not restore normal speech understanding.

Hearing Levels of 56 to 70 dB

This degree of loss is considered moderately severe. These individuals do not hear conversational speech unless it is amplified or extremely loud. Children have considerable difficulty in group and classroom discussions even with amplification; the teacher may not be completely understood because of noise levels and reverberation typical of most classrooms. Assistive listening devices should be considered. Language (semantics, syntax and pragmatics) may be limited, and abnormalities of articulation and voice production may be evident. Without good early intervention, speech and language development are usually delayed; early speech is often unintelligible or semi-intelligible. Reading and writing skills may also be affected. With early identification, appropriate amplification, and consistent high-quality intervention, communication skills may be far better than described.

In adults, speech deterioration may occur if the hearing loss has existed without remediation for a long period of time. Amplification is almost always needed.

Hearing Levels of 71 to 90 dB

This is considered a severe hearing loss. These individuals may be able to hear the sound of a very loud voice about one foot from the ear without amplification and may be able to identify some environmental sounds. Amplification is almost always indicated, but the ability to communicate well orally depends on type of loss, configuration of loss, word recognition ability, speechreading ability, and type and amount of remediation. Prelingually deaf children tend to show marked educational retardation unless they have had the benefit of intensive early intervention.

With this degree of hearing loss, speech and English language do not develop spontaneously. Even if amplification is introduced early in life, children need special training for adequate language and speech development. Voice and articulation are usually not normal. Placement in an appropriate quality educational setting as early in life as possible is imperative. Federal law mandates that all school systems must provide appropriate education for children with hearing loss from age 3 through age 21. Many school systems offer parent–infant programs at even younger ages, starting at the time of identification.

The deafened adult needs amplification to function optimally. Without amplification and training to preserve the servo system, deterioration of articulation and voice quality is likely to occur.

Hearing Levels of 90 dB and greater

This is considered a profound loss. There is generally minimal understanding of speech through audition alone even when amplification is used. In prelingually deaf children, severe speech and English language difficulties often exist. Educational problems are common unless effective early intervention (as described in the previous section), including amplification, has occurred.

Deafened adults often demonstrate deterioration of voice quality and articulation. Hearing aids may be useful to provide auditory cues to aid speechreading and awareness of environmental sound and to aid the servo mechanism in monitoring voice level and quality.

CONFIGURATION OF LOSS

The person with a flat configuration has the same degree of hearing loss across the frequency range; all sounds of speech are equally affected. On the other hand, the person with a high-frequency hearing loss and normal or near normal low-frequency hearing is able to hear some aspects of speech quite well and others poorly or not at all. The sound of the voice, the prosodic features of speech such as stress and intonation, and most vowels are usually heard normally; in contrast, much high-frequency consonant information is lost. Therefore, the individual is aware of speech but does not understand it well because it is the consonant sounds that carry speech intelligibility. This ability to "hear but not understand" leads to misdiagnosis in both children and adults. Children may be considered learning disabled, emotionally disturbed, autistic, developmentally handicapped (retarded), willfully disobedient, or simply inattentive. Adults are often accused of not paying attention or "hearing only what they want to hear."

The individual with the rising configuration hears high frequencies more acutely than low frequencies. This is a relatively uncommon hearing loss pattern, but it can create special problems when there is severe loss in the low frequencies and normal hearing in the highs. The individual with this problem hears the consonants well but not the basic sound of the voice or the vowel sounds. Amplification of low frequencies is needed, but it tends to mask the high-frequency consonants. Special amplification is required. Young children with this type of hearing loss often have good voice quality and articulation that is more normal than would be expected for their degree of hearing loss. Such children have been misdiagnosed as having non-organic hearing loss.

AGE OF ONSET

Children who acquire their hearing losses prior to age 5, particularly those who lose their hearing prior to age 2, frequently show far greater educational deficits than children with similar degrees of loss whose hearing problems occurred after the acquisition of English language. This is particularly true of children with severe to profound hearing losses. Academic success is predicated on the normal development of language, which is generally based on the ability to hear the spoken word. Age of onset is probably the primary biological variable affecting English language development in deaf children because the most important period for language acquisition is between birth and five years of age (Bochner, 1982:117–118). The severity of language delay tends to be related to the degree of hearing loss. There is enormous variation in the normalcy of English language development among prelingually deaf children, probably based on the quality and quantity of language input. Nevertheless, the relationship between age of onset and severity of hearing loss on the one hand and language development on the other tends to hold. Deafened and adventitiously hard-of-hearing adults tend to show little language or educational retardation, regardless of degree of loss, because they have had the opportunity to develop language normally. For more complete discussion of the relationship between age of onset, language competence and educational achievement, see Bochner (1982:116–119), Schow and Nerbonne (1989:7–10), Davis and Hardick (1981:174–194), and Newby and Popelka (1985:361–362).

TYPE OF HEARING LOSS

Unilateral Loss

A person with a unilateral hearing loss often experiences sound localization difficulties and problems understanding speech which is presented on the side of the poor ear; these difficulties are increased in the presence of noise. When the normal ear is facing the speaker and noise is not present, the individual generally has little difficulty understanding what is being said. In the presence of noise, however, a person listening with one good ear frequently experiences more difficulty understanding speech than someone with two normal ears. For children with unilateral hearing problems, preferential classroom seating and appropriate assistive listening devices may be indicated.

A unilateral loss, even if severe, usually does not affect speech and language development. If speech and language problems do exist, it is well to search for another cause.

Conductive Loss

With conductive problems, word recognition in quiet and noise is usually normal. The individual has little difficulty understanding speech, provided it is presented at an intensity level sufficiently high to be heard clearly. There is rarely any difficulty tolerating loud sound; hearing aid users with conductive loss often prefer more powerful hearing aids than people with sensorineural loss of the same degree.

A mild acquired conductive loss which is temporary usually does not affect speech and language even if it occurs in early childhood. However, if the loss is congenital, progressive, or persistent, significant speech and language delay may occur. It is widely suspected that there is a link between chronic or recurrent otitis media and delays in speech, language, cognitive development and educational achievement, but current research has not clearly demonstrated a cause–effect relationship. Nevertheless, language screening procedures, home language stimulation programs and even mild gain hearing aids have been suggested for such children. An excellent discussion of this issue can be found in Northern and Downs (1984:4–19).

A conductive loss in an adult usually does not cause deterioration of articulation or voice quality because the normal or near normal bone conduction preserves the servo mechanism. However, adults with conductive impairment may speak in an abnormally soft voice because they hear themselves louder than others hear them.

Sensorineural Loss

The person with a sensorineural loss is far more likely to show decreased word recognition ability than the person with a conductive loss. Word recognition problems tend to become more severe as degree of loss increases, particularly when speech must be understood against competing noise. Although this problem is frequently helped by amplification, normal speech understanding is rarely restored. When the site of lesion is retrocochlear (eighth nerve) or is located in the central auditory pathways, word recognition difficulties are more severe than with a loss of cochlear origin; sometimes there is total lack of understanding. Interestingly, in retrocochlear or central hearing loss there may be normal or near normal sensitivity for pure tones despite the severe deficit in understanding speech.

The problems of the hard-of-hearing adult with sensorineural loss almost always revolve around word recognition difficulties. With or sometimes without amplification, the person may be aware that someone is talking. However, the message is distorted because the auditory system is not capable of accurately receiving or processing all the phonemic information necessary for correct understanding. As a result, the person's responses may be inappropriate, with consequent vocational or social penalties. The child experiencing word recognition difficulties may suffer the same penalties; in addition, the child's incomplete understanding may significantly affect speech and language development and educational achievement.

For further discussion of communicative implications of degree, type, configuration of hearing loss, and age of onset, see Davis and Silverman (1978:88, 271–272, 276–277), Katz (1985:Ch. 39, 40), Newby and Popelka (1985:358–362), Bess and Humes (1990:76, 81), Northern and Downs, (1984: 1–21), and Schow and Nerbonne (1989:5–12, 272–273).

VOICE AND ARTICULATION

Speech production patterns of deaf and hard-of-hearing children vary with the individual, making it difficult to predict voice and articulation characteristics from inspection of the audiogram. Other factors which interact with the hearing loss to affect speech production include:

1. Other problems, such as learning disabilities, which cause delayed speech development.
2. Physiologic problems, such as motor involvement of the speech mechanism (dysarthria) or cleft palate. Certain misarticulations may be caused by these problems rather than a co-existing hearing loss.
3. Speech models available to the child. A child of deaf parents may learn voice and articulation patterns characteristic of the "deaf speech" of the parents. This is more likely to occur when the child is not exposed to other speech models.
4. Extent to which visual cues are used. A child with a mild to moderate hearing loss who is visually alert may compensate for the distorted speech information received through audition by using visual speech cues.
5. Extent to which amplification allows the child to receive the prosodic and phonemic features of speech clearly. This depends on type and degree of hearing loss, age at which hearing aids were fitted, and how well the hearing aids are used.
6. Age of onset of hearing loss. Hearing loss incurred after the normal development of speech may cause some deterioration in the speech; however, speech tends to be more intelligible than that of prelingually deaf or hard-of-hearing children.

Despite the many variables that affect the speech of deaf children, there is a relationship between speech intelligibility, the severity of the hearing loss, and the degree to which an auditory–verbal feedback loop can be established. Certain generalizations can be made related to degree of hearing loss.

Effects of Mild to Moderate Hearing Loss on Speech

Although most children with mild to moderate hearing loss produce intelligible speech, many show misarticulations similar to those of normal-hearing children with developmental disorders of articulation. Vowel articulation, voice quality, and suprasegmental features are generally comparable to those of normal-hearing peers. Sounds characterized by low intensity, high frequency, and short duration are most commonly affected. Primary speech errors (Schow and Nerbonne, 1989:206–208) include the following:

1. Omission of final consonants
2. Omission or distortion of blends and affricates
3. Omission of voiced consonants, particularly fricatives

Effects of Severe to Profound Hearing Loss on Speech

Speech errors found in deaf children may be divided into errors of coordination of respiration and phonation and errors of articulation. Although these problems are dichotomized for purposes of discussion, they generally interact to negatively affect speech intelligibility. Although deaf speakers vary tremendously in their intelligibility and speech error patterns, the following problems are characteristic of "deaf speech."

Errors of Respiration/Phonation One of the most serious impediments to speech intelligibility that occurs in deaf speakers is the failure to coordinate breathing and speaking. Deaf speakers may attempt to speak while inhaling, take a breath in the middle of a word or phrase, or pause inappropriately during connected speech. The consequent abnormal phrasing results in impaired intelligibility of the message. Because of poor breath control, rate is often slower than normal; stress and intonation changes may be limited or deviant; some deaf speakers stress all syllables, while others use differential stress patterns which are incorrect.

Voice quality of deaf speakers has been described as dull, monotonous, harsh, breathy, nasal, and strained. Abnormally high pitch, restricted use of pitch changes, and frequent pitch breaks during connected speech have been reported. Loudness of the voices of some deaf speakers is poorly controlled, resulting in too loud or too soft voice production or in variable intensity patterns not related to the meaning or emotional content of the utterance. Voice quality and suprasegmental problems are caused by poor coordination of respiration and phonation and by increased laryngeal tension.

Errors of articulation Deaf children often produce vowels which are not easily distinguishable from each other; the tongue assumes a neutral position in the mouth and moves only slightly as different vowels are attempted. In addition, some deaf children tend to prolong vowels. Consonant production is characterized by many errors, such as:

1. Omission or misarticulation of final consonants more frequently than initial consonants.
2. Inappropriate voicing of unvoiced consonants and vice versa.
3. Consonants which are hypernasal or are accompanied by nasal emission.
4. Omission of consonants from blends.
5. Insertion of neutral vowels between abutting consonants (e.g., balack instead of black) or after words ending in plosives (e.g., capa instead of cap).

Effect of Adventitious Hearing Loss on Speech

The adult who has a mild to moderate hearing loss, minimal word recognition difficulty, and uses a hearing aid well will probably have few speech problems as a result of hearing loss. With greater degree of hearing loss and word recognition difficulty, speech often shows gradual deterioration, although some individuals maintain clear unaffected speech for long periods of time. Vowels are generally most resistant to deterioration because they are primarily low-frequency, high-intensity, and long-duration phonemes. Voiceless consonants as a group tend to show the greatest frequency of misarticulation.

Voice quality and prosodic features (stress, intonation, phrasing, and juncture) tend to remain normal as long as low-frequency sensitivity remains near normal. However, the greater the loss in the low frequencies, the greater the effects on suprasegmental features. Individuals with severe sensorineural loss tend to speak too loudly because of difficulty hearing themselves speak. Because of difficulty monitoring voice pitch, speech production may be monotonous or characterized by inappropriate changes in pitch. Amplification and/or speech conservation procedures may help to prevent or remediate such problems.

For a more complete discussion of speech re-

lated to hearing loss, see Cozad (1974:Chs. 5 and 6), Davis and Hardick (1981:194–200), Schow and Nerbonne (1989:204–228), Ling (1976:Ch. 2), and Sims et al. (1982:Chs. 5 and 10).

WHO NEEDS A HEARING AID?

Any individual with a hearing loss that impairs communication in any way, and who is motivated to try hearing aids, is a potential candidate. The person with the borderline loss may find a mild gain hearing aid very useful, either on a full-time or part-time basis if vocational or educational needs demand precise hearing of soft speech or speech at a distance. The person with the unilateral loss may find a CROS hearing aid very useful to resolve a localization problem or difficulty understanding speech when it is presented on the side of the poor ear. For further discussion of the CROS hearing aid, see Harford and Dodds (1966), Newby and Popelka (1985:367–369), Hodgson (1986: 191–202), and Pollack (1988:304–315).

People with profound losses often use high gain behind-the-ear hearing aids or occasionally body-worn hearing aids. Even though a hearing aid may not permit a profoundly deaf person to understand speech auditorily, it can facilitate speechreading, improve voice control and allow perception of environmental sounds.

The person with a conductive or mixed loss is usually a better candidate for amplification than the person with a sensorineural loss because of better word recognition ability. However, conductive losses or conductive components of mixed losses are frequently medically correctable; therefore, the vast majority of successful hearing aid users are people with sensorineural losses. Modern hearing aids generally contain far less distortion than hearing aids of the past and can also be obtained with special features, such as directional microphones, compression circuits, telecoils, and direct audio input for use with assistive listening devices. Modern hearing aids allow successful fitting of a much wider range of hearing problems, including severe word recognition and tolerance difficulties. Earmold modifications and internal adjustment of frequency response can make hearing aids usable for people with high-frequency hearing loss and normal and near normal low-frequency sensitivity. Each person's suitability for amplification must be individually evaluated based on degree of loss, configuration of loss, word recognition, tolerance for loud sound, amount of communication difficulty, and motivation to use amplification. For further discussion of hearing aids and earmolds, see Davis and Silverman (1978:Chs. 10 and 11), Bess and Humes (1990:185–189), Pollack (1988:Chs. 4, 5, 6, and 8), Hodgson (1986:Chs. 4, 7, 8, and 9), Ling and Ling (1978:Ch. 6), and Katz (1985:936–939).

Although anyone with a hearing loss who is motivated to try amplification is a candidate for trial use of hearing aids, the prognosis for successful use is better for some than for others. Generally, the prognosis is most favorable when the hearing loss is moderate or moderately severe (40 to 60 dB HL), flat in configuration, has some air–bone gap, is characterized by normal or near normal word recognition in quiet and noise, and includes normal tolerance for loud sound. The poorest risk is the individual with extremely poor word recognition ability and a severe tolerance problem. In all cases, however, the individual's motivation, expectations of benefits of amplification, and understanding of its limitations are important factors in determining the success of hearing aid use.

WHICH EAR TO FIT?

Following is a series of guidelines to help the audiologist determine the proper ear in which to place the hearing aid. If the two ears are similar, binaural amplification should be considered. Some audiologists consider a client a candidate for binaural amplification if both ears can benefit from hearing aids, even though degree, type, or configuration of hearing loss may be different. Binaural amplification can sometimes provide advantages in localization of sound, ability to hear regardless of which ear is in the direct path of the sound, and ability to understand speech in the presence of noise. Young deaf children are almost always fitted with two hearing aids unless there is good reason not to fit one ear. If binaural amplification is tried on an adult, the client should have the option of returning one hearing aid after a trial period if he or she is dissatisfied.

If the individual is to be fitted with monaural amplification, the following criteria should be used to select the proper ear:

1. Fit the ear with the best word recognition in quiet or noise. This is a primary consideration because in most cases a hearing aid will not improve word recognition at PB Max.

2. Fit the ear with the best tolerance for loud speech. This criterion is important because the hearing aid delivers speech to the ear at high intensity levels. Lack of adequate tolerance for amplification often results in non-use of the hearing aid.

3. An ear with a conductive component is preferred for amplification because it generally has reasonably good word recognition and high tolerance for loud speech.

4. If the better ear has a loss of less than 40 dB HL, all other things being equal, fit the poorer ear. The better ear, unaided, provides considerable useful hearing. If the loss in the better ear is moderately severe, severe, or profound, fit the better ear.

5. Fit the ear with the flattest pure tone configuration.

6. If one ear has chronic drainage, fit the opposite ear.

7. If the ears are comparable in all respects, consider fitting the ear that is not used for the telephone. Obviously, if neither ear can be used successfully with the telephone, this factor is irrelevant. If the client drives a car, consider fitting the ear closest to the passenger. Not only does this strategy facilitate conversation, it also keeps the aided ear away from the window and road noise.

If, in spite of these guidelines, there is doubt as to which ear should be fitted, hearing aids should be tried in each ear individually to determine under which condition the client functions best.

COCHLEAR IMPLANTS

During recent years increasing numbers of deaf children and adults have been fitted with cochlear implants. A cochlear implant is a device which sends speech (and other sounds) picked up by a head-worn microphone to a processor which then transmits the processed speech to an array of electrodes implanted along the basilar membrane in the cochlea. The electrodes stimulate eighth nerve fibers arrayed along the basilar membrane, bypassing badly damaged hair cells. All cochlear implants today are multichannel. For a more complete description of cochlear implants, see Patrick and Clark (1991:3S), Owens and Kessler (1989:Chs. 1 and 2), Cooper (1991:Chs. 1–4), and *Cochlear Implant Devices for the Profoundly Hearing Impaired* (Health Technology Assessment Reports, 1986).

Although there are no legal candidacy requirements for cochlear implants, most implant teams follow similar criteria. Most adult implantees have been postlingually deafened, although some highly motivated oral prelingually deaf individuals have received implants. According to a National Institutes of Health Consensus Development Conference Statement on Cochlear Implants (May 1988), clients should demonstrate no residual hearing (total hearing loss) and no significant benefit from a hearing aid. In addition: motivation must be high; the individual and family must have realistic expectations of the benefits and limitations of an implant; there should be no evidence of mental retardation or psychiatric disorders; and there must be no radiological or medical contraindications to implantation.

Audiological criteria are very important in identifying those deaf people who are good candidates for implantation. According to NIH Consensus Conference recommendations, an acceptable cochlear implant candidate should demonstrate hearing levels in the better ear in excess of 95 dB HL, aided thresholds greater than 60 dB HL, 0 percent correct on open set speech recognition tests, and a lack of significant benefit from lipreading combined with an appropriately fitted hearing aid.

It has been found that a substantial number (approximately one-half) of postlingually deaf adults implanted with multichannel systems have achieved some open set word recognition on sentence or monosyllabic word tests. The range of scores on these tests has been wide (0–60% on word tests and 0–100% for words in sentences). In addition, reports have appeared in the literature that 25% to 50% of these clients are able to understand speech on the telephone to varying degrees. Almost all of these clients have demonstrated improved lipreading abilities and awareness and identification of environmental sound compared to that achieved with conventional hearing aids. Pre-

lingually deafened adults, on the other hand, have generally not shown improvement in open set speech recognition but have reported enhanced lipreading skills. Perhaps because of the lack of sound memory, prelingually deafened adults are not considered to be the best candidates for cochlear implants. Despite encouraging reports, it is not possible to predict for any individual client the degree of improvement in speech understanding that an implant will provide. For a more complete discussion of these issues, see Osberger (1990:38) and Cooper (1991:Chs. 6–10).

Determining cochlear implant candidacy in young profoundly deaf children presents a special challenge because of the difficulty obtaining accurate test results. All cochlear implant teams agree that children considered for implants must be at least two years of age for two reasons: (1) to allow time for sufficient skull growth so that the electrode array will remain seated in the cochlea, and (2) to have reasonable expectations that an accurate audiological evaluation can be performed. Only those children are considered candidates who: (1) demonstrate no response to warble tones in the sound field with appropriate hearing aids, or (2) demonstrate aided responses in the lower frequencies at levels greater than 50–60 dB HL with no response above 1000 Hz (Osberger, 1990:30). In some programs, children evaluated for a cochlear implant must undergo a six-month trial period with either a hearing aid or a tactile device. If satisfactory progress cannot be demonstrated in speech, language or listening behavior after this trial period, the child is accepted in the implant program (Clark et al., 1987). No child at any age is considered for an implant if open set word recognition is possible. Geers and Moog (1989:Ch. 11) describe a battery of speech recognition tests that can be used to evaluate young children.

Other candidacy criteria include the absence of medical contraindications for intracochlear electrode placement, appropriate expectations of the family or child, willingness of the child and family to participate in pre- and post-operative training, and the absence of psychological problems or additional disabilities. Adolescents are actively encouraged to participate in the decision-making process. Some programs require children in the cochlear implant program to be enrolled in educational programs (auditory–oral or total communication) that include an auditory–oral component (Mecklenburg et al., 1991:11S). Staller et al. (1991:46S) reported that children in both types of programs who were matched for age of onset of deafness did not show significant differences in performance with cochlear implants.

Staller et al. (1991:34S–46S) reported significant improvement in all areas of speech perception by 142 children wearing multichannel cochlear implants at least 12 months compared to preoperative performance. All children were able to detect sound at normal conversational levels and showed improved lipreading ability. After three years of training with the implant, more than 60% of the children deafened after age two (postlinguistic), demonstrated some open set word recognition. Far fewer (20%) of the children with deafness acquired before age two (prelinguistic) demonstrated similar levels after three years of training. However, these children had not yet plateaued in their performance and might continue to improve with time and training. Additional data are presented by Geers and Moog (1989:Ch. 11), Boothroyd (1989: Ch. 6), Kessler (1989:Ch. 10), Osberger et al. (1991: 66S), and Somers (1991:322).

Questions

QUESTIONS FOR FIGURE 7-1

Case History Information This young man first became aware of a hearing problem one year ago and reports that it is gradually becoming worse. He is in the tenth grade in school and is having some difficulty academically.

1. What degree of hearing loss is present?
2. What type of hearing loss is present?
3. Would you expect this client to have voice, articulation, or language problems in school?
4.. To what would you attribute this client's academic difficulties?
5. How does the use of visual input (speechreading) affect his ability to understand speech?

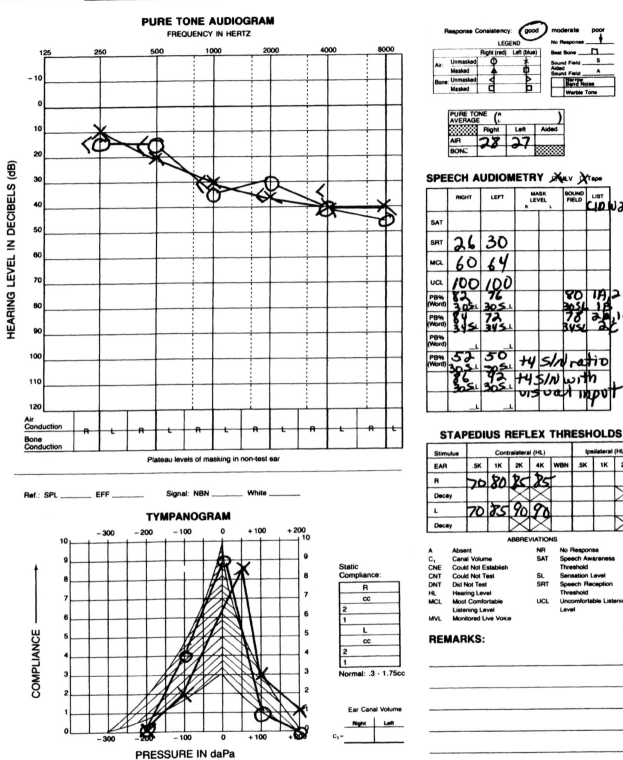

Name: Fig 7-1   Date: XX/XX/XX   Age: 16   Sex: M   Audiologist: HK
AUDIOMETER: GSI-10   ANSI 1969

PURE TONE AUDIOGRAM
FREQUENCY IN HERTZ

Response Consistency: good moderate poor

LEGEND

		Right (red)	Left (blue)
Air:	Unmasked	○	X
	Masked	▲	▢
Bone:	Unmasked	<	>
	Masked	▢	▢

No Response
Best Bone
Sound Field   S
Aided
Sound Field   A
Narrow Band Noise
Warble Tone

PURE TONE AVERAGE	Right	Left	Aided
AIR	28	27	
BONE			

SPEECH AUDIOMETRY MLV Tape

	RIGHT	LEFT	MASK LEVEL R L	SOUND FIELD	LIST
SAT					CID W22
SRT	26	30			
MCL	60	64			
UCL	100	100			
PB% (Word)	82 30SL	76 30SL		80 30SL	1A 2A, 1B
PB% (Word)	84 34SL	72 34SL		78 34SL	2B 1C, 2C,
PB% (Word)					
PB% (Word)	52 30SL	50 30SL		+4 S/N ratio	
PB% (Word)	86 30SL	92 30SL		+4 S/N with visual input	

STAPEDIUS REFLEX THRESHOLDS

Stimulus	Contralateral (HL)					Ipsilateral (HL)		
EAR	.5K	1K	2K	4K	WBN	.5K	1K	2K
R	70	80	85	85				
Decay								
L	70	85	90	90				
Decay								

ABBREVIATIONS

A — Absent
C_1 — Canal Volume
CNE — Could Not Establish
CNT — Could Not Test
DNT — Did Not Test
HL — Hearing Level
MCL — Most Comfortable Listening Level
MVL — Monitored Live Voice
NR — No Response
SAT — Speech Awareness Threshold
SL — Sensation Level
SRT — Speech Reception Threshold
UCL — Uncomfortable Listening Level

Ref.: SPL _____ EFF _____   Signal: NBN _____ White _____

TYMPANOGRAM

Static Compliance:

R	
cc	
2	
1	

L	
cc	
2	
1	

Normal: .3 - 1.75cc

Ear Canal Volume

Right	Left
C_1 —	

PRESSURE IN daPa

REMARKS:

_____
_____
_____
_____

Answers for Figure 7-1

1. This boy has a mild bilateral loss of hearing.
2. The loss in both ears is sensorineural in type.
3. One would not expect this client to have speech or language problems because of late onset and because the degree of loss is mild. However, the hearing loss seems to be progressive and, if it should continue getting worse, speech problems may develop. Another reason speech and language problems would not be probable is that he seems to use visual cues well (note word recognition in noise with speechreading). Frequently, children who use visual cues well can compensate to some degree for the distorted speech input reaching the auditory servo system.
4. This client's academic difficulties are probably attributable to his poor word recognition, particularly in noise. Since the typical classroom is a noisy place, he may be experiencing considerable difficulty understanding his teachers.
5. With auditory input only, his ability to understand speech in the presence of noise is poor. However, when he can see as well as hear the speech, his understanding is within normal limits in the left ear and only slightly reduced in the right. Clearly, this client needs to be helped to use speechreading as much as possible.

QUESTIONS FOR FIGURE 7-2

Case History Information This child was brought to the speech and hearing clinic for a speech and language evaluation. The mother had been aware of an articulation problem for a number of years but thought her child would "outgrow" it. A hearing problem had not been suspected because the child responded consistently when called. Upon being questioned, the mother reported that the little girl did watch carefully when spoken to. The child is repeating kindergarten.

1. How would you describe this child's hearing loss?
2. What type of speech problem would you expect to find?
3. Would you expect to find a language problem?
4. Why do you think the hearing loss went undetected for several years?
5. From your inspection of the word recognition scores, why do you think she is having difficulty in school?
6. Is this child using speechreading?

Name: Fig 7-2   Date: XX/XX/XX Age: 6-10 Sex: F Audiologist: HK

AUDIOMETER: GSI-10   ANSI 1969

PURE TONE AUDIOGRAM
FREQUENCY IN HERTZ

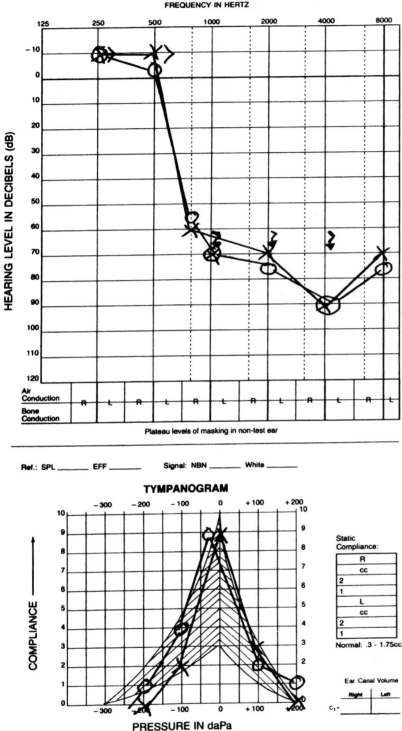

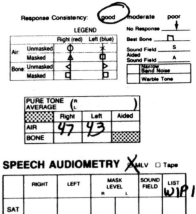

Response Consistency: (good) moderate poor

LEGEND

		Right (red)	Left (blue)
Air:	Unmasked	○	×
	Masked	△	□
Bone:	Unmasked	◁	▷
	Masked	□	▷

No Response ↓
Best Bone ⊓
Sound Field ___ S
Aided
Sound Field ___ A
Narrow Band Noise
Warble Tone

PURE TONE AVERAGE (R: L:)			
	Right	Left	Aided
AIR	47	43	
BONE			

SPEECH AUDIOMETRY ☒ MLV ☐ Tape

	RIGHT	LEFT	MASK LEVEL R	L	SOUND FIELD	LIST
SAT						WIPI
SRT	36	32			30	
MCL	DNT	DNT			DNT	
UCL	100	100			DNT	
PB% (Word)	52 30SL	40 30SL			54 30SL	1,2 3
PB% (Word)	_L	_L			40 50HL	4
PB% (Word)	_L	_L				
PB% (Word)	_L	_L			*76 50HL	
	_L	_L			**20 30SL -S/N=0	
	_L	_L				

STAPEDIUS REFLEX THRESHOLDS

Stimulus	Contralateral (HL)					Ipsilateral (HL)		
EAR	.5K	1K	2K	4K	WBN	.5K	1K	2K
R	70	105	105	NR				
Decay								
L	75	100	105	NR				
Decay								

ABBREVIATIONS

A	Absent	NR	No Response
C₁	Canal Volume	SAT	Speech Awareness
CNE	Could Not Establish		Threshold
CNT	Could Not Test	SL	Sensation Level
DNT	Did Not Test	SRT	Speech Reception
HL	Hearing Level		Threshold
MCL	Most Comfortable	UCL	Uncomfortable Listening
	Listening Level		Level
MVL	Monitored Live Voice		

REMARKS:

*Combined visual & auditory input; **Auditory input in noise.

Air Conduction R L R L R L R L R L R L R L
Bone Conduction

Plateau levels of masking in non-test ear

Ref.: SPL _____ EFF _____   Signal: NBN _____ White _____

TYMPANOGRAM

PRESSURE IN daPa

Static Compliance:

R	
cc	
2	
1	

L	
cc	
2	
1	

Normal: .3 - 1.75cc

Ear Canal Volume

Right	Left
C₁ =	

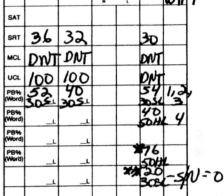

Educational and Communicative Implications of Hearing Loss

329

Answers for Figure 7-2

1. This child has a bilateral, mild to severe sensorineural loss with precipitously falling configurations.

2. Because of the normal low-frequency hearing, one would expect prosodic features to be normal. Misarticulations would probably be restricted to the consonants, particularly voiceless consonants and those consonants not visible on the lips. These expectations were substantiated by speech and language evaluation.

3. Language problems are not uncommon when there is a severe high-frequency hearing loss of early onset. This child's hearing loss may have occurred prelingually, although there is no information in the case history. However, the fact that she is having difficulty in school suggests some degree of language retardation.

4. This girl's hearing loss went undetected for many years because her good hearing sensitivity in the low frequencies allowed her to respond appropriately to many sounds, including some speech. Note that her mother reported that the child responded consistently when called.

5. Monaural word recognition scores indicate very poor speech understanding in both ears. Ability to understand speech at average conversational level (50 dB HL) in quiet and in noise is extremely poor. These scores suggest that in the school situation she is probably having severe difficulty understanding what is being said to her and consequently is responding inappropriately.

6. This child is using visual cues (speechreading). If we compare the word recognition scores obtained at average conversational level with and without speechreading, we can see that the score with visual input is almost double that without visual input.

QUESTIONS FOR FIGURE 7-3

Case History Information This child was referred to the speech and hearing clinic because he is having academic difficulties. He is repeating first grade and is not learning to read.

1. What do you think is this child's greatest expressive communication problem (voice, articulation, vocabulary, etc.)?

2. What do you think are this boy's greatest articulation difficulties?

Name: Fig 7-3   Date: XX/XX/XX Age: 7-2 Sex: M Audiologist: HK
AUDIOMETER: GSI-10   ANSI 1969

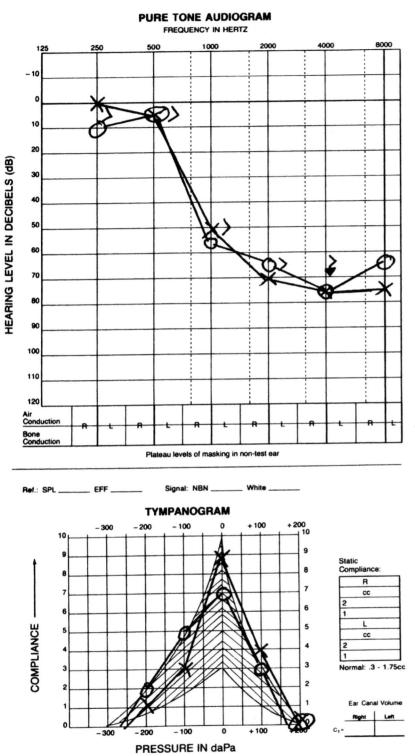

PURE TONE AUDIOGRAM
FREQUENCY IN HERTZ

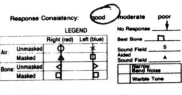

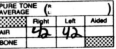

PURE TONE AVERAGE (R / L)			
	Right	Left	Aided
AIR	42	42	
BONE			

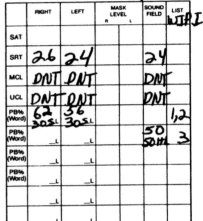

SPEECH AUDIOMETRY ☒MLV ☐ Tape

	RIGHT	LEFT	MASK LEVEL R	MASK LEVEL L	SOUND FIELD	LIST
SAT						WIPI
SRT	26	24			24	
MCL	DNT	DNT			DNT	
UCL	DNT	DNT			DNT	
PB% (Word)	62 30SL	56 30SL				1,2
PB% (Word)	_L	_L			50 50HL	3
PB% (Word)	_L	_L				
PB% (Word)	_L	_L				
	_L	_L				
	_L	_L				

STAPEDIUS REFLEX THRESHOLDS

Stimulus	Contralateral (HL)					Ipsilateral (HL)		
EAR	.5K	1K	2K	4K	WBN	.5K	1K	2K
R	80	100	105	110				
Decay								
L	80	95	105	110				
Decay								

ABBREVIATIONS

A	Absent	NR	No Response
C₁	Canal Volume	SAT	Speech Awareness
CNE	Could Not Establish		Threshold
CNT	Could Not Test	SL	Sensation Level
DNT	Did Not Test	SRT	Speech Reception
HL	Hearing Level		Threshold
MCL	Most Comfortable	UCL	Uncomfortable Listening
	Listening Level		Level
MVL	Monitored Live Voice		

REMARKS:

Ref.: SPL _____ EFF _____   Signal: NBN _____ White _____

TYMPANOGRAM

Static Compliance:

R	
	cc
2	
1	

L	
	cc
2	
1	

Normal: .3 - 1.75cc

Ear Canal Volume

	Right	Left
C₁ =		

PRESSURE IN daPa

Answers for Figure 7-3

1. This boy's greatest expressive communication needs are not in the area of articulation. His greatest needs are in the language area. Although he comes from a family of rather high socioeconomic and educational level and has received many environmental and stimulatory advantages, his expressive vocabulary is below that of a normal-hearing 6-year-old child. In addition to vocabulary problems, this boy also has some syntactic difficulties. His problem with plurals, verb tenses, and proper use of function words may be related to his difficulty hearing high-frequency speech sounds.

2. This boy's articulation problems are primarily in the area of vowel substitutions and inconsistent consonant production.

QUESTIONS FOR FIGURE 7-4

Case History Information This man's hearing loss was discovered during audiometric screening at a health fair. He reported awareness of a hearing loss in his right ear since early childhood.

1. Do you think this man's hearing loss has social or vocational significance?
2. With what communication situations might he have difficulty?

Name: Fig 7-4   **Date:** XX/XX/XX   **Age:** 35   **Sex:** M   **Audiologist:** HK
AUDIOMETER: GSI-10   **ANSI 1969**

PURE TONE AUDIOGRAM
FREQUENCY IN HERTZ

Response Consistency:	good	moderate	poor

LEGEND

		Right (red)	Left (blue)
Air:	Unmasked		
	Masked		
Bone:	Unmasked		
	Masked		

No Response
Best Bone
Sound Field ___ S
Aided
Sound Field ___ A
Narrow Band Noise
Warble Tone

PURE TONE AVERAGE			
	Right	Left	Aided
AIR	35	0	
BONE			

SPEECH AUDIOMETRY ☒ MLV ☐ Tape

	RIGHT	LEFT	MASK LEVEL R	L	SOUND FIELD	LIST
SAT						NU-6
SRT	30	0			0	
MCL	66	DNT			DNT	
UCL	100+	DNT			DNT	
PB% (Word)	98 30 SL	96 30 SL			100 1A 2A, 30SL 2B	
PB% (Word)	L	L			100 50HL 3A	
PB% (Word)	L	L				
PB% (Word)	L	L				
	L	L				
	L	L				

STAPEDIUS REFLEX THRESHOLDS

Stimulus	Contralateral (HL)					Ipsilateral (HL)		
EAR	.5K	1K	2K	4K	WBN	.5K	1K	2K
R	70	80	25	25				
Decay								
L	75	85	90	105				
Decay								

ABBREVIATIONS

A	Absent	NR	No Response
C₁	Canal Volume	SAT	Speech Awareness
CNE	Could Not Establish		Threshold
CNT	Could Not Test	SL	Sensation Level
DNT	Did Not Test	SRT	Speech Reception
HL	Hearing Level		Threshold
MCL	Most Comfortable	UCL	Uncomfortable Listening
	Listening Level		Level
MVL	Monitored Live Voice		

Air Conduction	R	L	R	20-40	R	20-40	R	20-40	R	20-40
Bone Conduction			20-30	20-40		20-40		20-40		

Plateau levels of masking in non-test ear

Ref.: SPL _____ EFF _____   Signal: NBN ✓ White _____

TYMPANOGRAM

PRESSURE IN daPa

Static Compliance:	
R	cc
2	
1	
L	cc
2	
1	

Normal: .3 - 1.75cc

Ear Canal Volume	
Right	Left

C₁ -

REMARKS:

Speech noise was used for word recognition measurement of the right ear. 60dB effective level)

Answers for Figure 7-4

1. In general, this man's mild unilateral sensorineural hearing loss should have very little, if any, social or vocational significance (except as noted in Answer 2 below). Because the left ear is essentially normal, this man should have relatively good receptive communication abilities. Note that all word recognition scores, including those obtained in the poor ear, were well within normal limits.

2. If this man has any social or vocational problem due to his hearing loss, it would be in the areas of localizing the source of sounds, understanding group conversation, and understanding conversation in the presence of noise if the noise is primarily on the left side and important speech signals are on the right. This client did not seem concerned about his inability to localize sound sources and does relatively well in group conversations.

QUESTION FOR FIGURE 7-5

Case History Information This boy has repeated two grades. His teacher reports that he is inattentive and shy in class. He does not seem to understand instructions. He uses very little speech and communicates mostly with gestures. His spoken vocabulary seems far below that of most 8-year-old children.

1. Does this boy's hearing have any relationship to his communicative and educational difficulties?

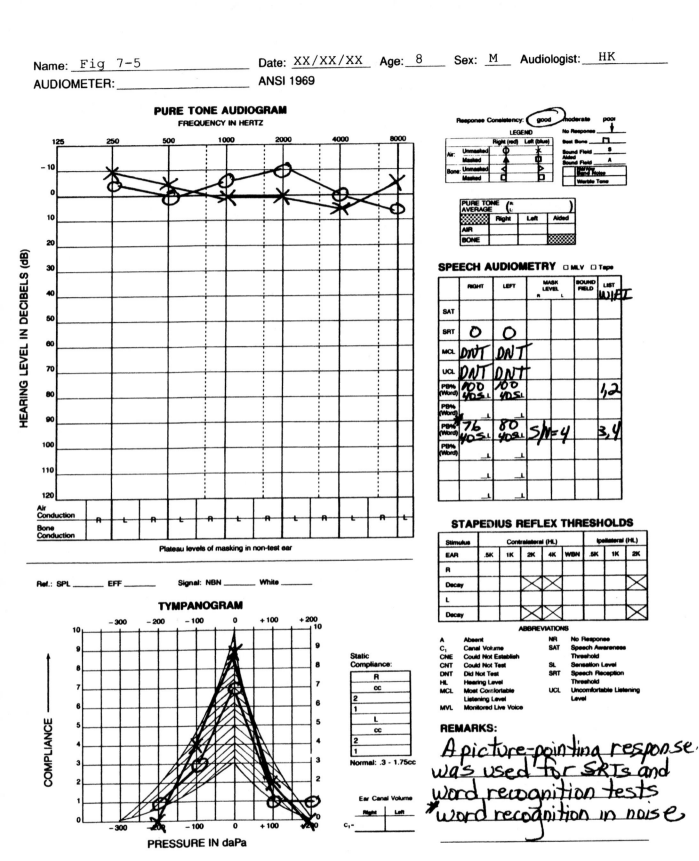

Name: Fig 7-5   Date: XX/XX/XX   Age: 8   Sex: M   Audiologist: HK
AUDIOMETER: _____   ANSI 1969

PURE TONE AUDIOGRAM
FREQUENCY IN HERTZ

Response Consistency: (good) moderate poor

LEGEND

	Right (red)	Left (blue)
Air: Unmasked	O	X
Masked	▲	▢
Bone: Unmasked		>
Masked	▢	▢

No Response
Best Bone
Sound Field S
Aided
Sound Field A
Narrow
Band Noise
Warble Tone

PURE TONE AVERAGE	Right	Left	Aided
AIR			
BONE			

SPEECH AUDIOMETRY ☐ MLV ☐ Tape

	RIGHT	LEFT	MASK LEVEL R L	SOUND FIELD	LIST
SAT					WIPI
SRT	O	O			
MCL	DNT	DNT			
UCL	DNT	DNT			
PB% (Word)	100 40SL	100 40SL			1,2
PB% (Word)					
PB% (Word)	76 40SL	80 40SL	S/N=4		3,4
PB% (Word)					

STAPEDIUS REFLEX THRESHOLDS

Stimulus	Contralateral (HL)					Ipsilateral (HL)		
EAR	.5K	1K	2K	4K	WBN	.5K	1K	2K
R								
Decay		X	X					X
L								
Decay		X	X					X

ABBREVIATIONS

A	Absent	NR	No Response
C₁	Canal Volume	SAT	Speech Awareness
CNE	Could Not Establish		Threshold
CNT	Could Not Test	SL	Sensation Level
DNT	Did Not Test	SRT	Speech Reception
HL	Hearing Level		Threshold
MCL	Most Comfortable	UCL	Uncomfortable Listening
	Listening Level		Level
MVL	Monitored Live Voice		

REMARKS:

A picture-pointing response was used for SRTs and word recognition tests
* word recognition in noise

TYMPANOGRAM

Ref.: SPL _____ EFF _____   Signal: NBN _____ White _____

PRESSURE IN daPa

Static Compliance:

R	
	cc
2	
1	
L	
	cc
2	
1	

Normal: .3 - 1.75cc

Ear Canal Volume

Right	Left
C₁ -	

Answer for Figure 7-5

1. This boy's hearing sensitivity for both pure tones and speech appears to be within normal limits. His word recognition scores in quiet are excellent (100%), and scores obtained in noise are what one would expect for a normal-hearing individual. Since hearing appears to be essentially normal, his lack of normal communication must be due to other factors.

QUESTIONS FOR FIGURE 7-6

Case History Information This girl has had repeated earaches in both the right and left ears. She has missed 25 days of school during the past year due to illness (mostly head colds). She is inattentive and does not follow instructions.

1. What type of hearing loss does this girl have?
2. Is her inattentiveness attributable to her hearing loss?

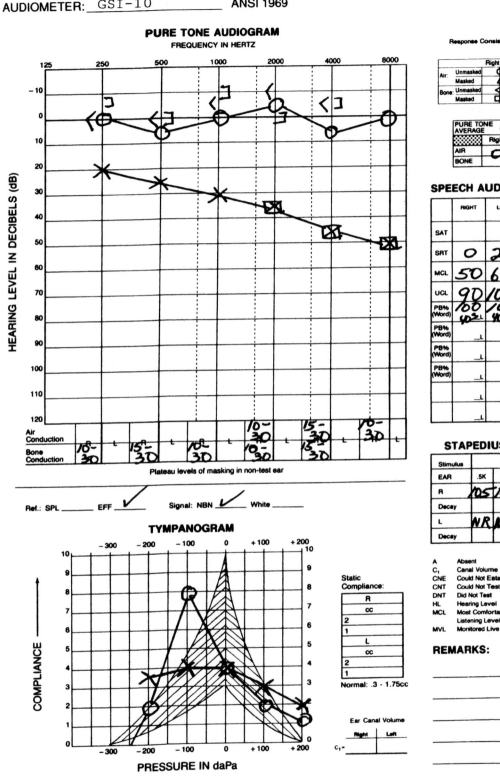

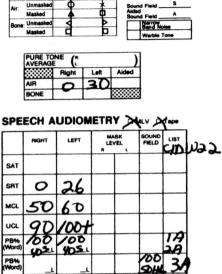

Name: Fig 7-6   **Date:** XX/XX/XX **Age:** 10 **Sex:** F **Audiologist:** HK
AUDIOMETER: GSI-10   **ANSI 1969**

PURE TONE AUDIOGRAM
FREQUENCY IN HERTZ

Response Consistency: (good) moderate poor

LEGEND

		Right (red)	Left (blue)			
Air:	Unmasked	O	X		Best Bone	
	Masked	△	□		Sound Field	S
Bone:	Unmasked	<	>		Aided Sound Field	A
	Masked	□	□		Narrow Band Noise	
					Warble Tone	

No Response

PURE TONE AVERAGE			
	Right	Left	Aided
AIR	O	30	
BONE			

SPEECH AUDIOMETRY MLV tape

	RIGHT	LEFT	MASK LEVEL R L	SOUND FIELD	LIST
SAT					CID W22
SRT	O	26			
MCL	50	60			
UCL	90	100+			
PB% (Word)	100 40SL	100 40SL			1A 2A
PB% (Word)	L	L		100 50HL	3A
PB% (Word)	L	L			
PB% (Word)	L	L			
	L	L			
	L	L			

Air Conduction: 10-30, 15-30, 10-30, 10-30, 15-30, 10-30
Bone Conduction: 10-30, 15-30, 10-30, 10-30, 15-30

Plateau levels of masking in non-test ear

Ref.: SPL _____ EFF ✓   Signal: NBN ✓ White _____

STAPEDIUS REFLEX THRESHOLDS

Stimulus	Contralateral (HL)					Ipsilateral (HL)		
EAR	.5K	1K	2K	4K	WBN	.5K	1K	2K
R	105	105	110	NR				X
Decay			X	X				
L	NR	NR	NR	NR				X
Decay			X	X				X

ABBREVIATIONS

A	Absent	NR	No Response
C₁	Canal Volume	SAT	Speech Awareness
CNE	Could Not Establish		Threshold
CNT	Could Not Test	SL	Sensation Level
DNT	Did Not Test	SRT	Speech Reception
HL	Hearing Level		Threshold
MCL	Most Comfortable	UCL	Uncomfortable Listening
	Listening Level		Level
MVL	Monitored Live Voice		

TYMPANOGRAM

Static Compliance:

R	
	cc
2	
1	

L	
	cc
2	
1	

Normal: .3 - 1.75cc

Ear Canal Volume

Right	Left

C₁ =

REMARKS:

_____

_____

_____

_____

Answers for Figure 7-6

1. The significant air–bone gap, Type B tympanogram, and absent reflexes in the left ear suggest this girl has a mild conductive hearing loss in the left ear and needs medical intervention.

2. In general, a unilateral loss is of relatively little educational significance. However, her hearing loss could be contributing to her educational problems for a number of reasons. First, if the hearing problem is related to a chronic health problem that is causing the girl to miss a considerable amount of school, then the hearing problem is of significance educationally. Second, the history suggests that she has had problems with the right ear as well as the left. Intermittent bilateral hearing loss would be far more detrimental to her ability to follow classroom instruction. Finally, if the child is not seated advantageously in the classroom, with her good ear toward the major source of information, she could have considerable difficulty academically. She needs to be monitored carefully.

QUESTIONS FOR FIGURE 7-7

Case History Information This girl has a history of chronic ear infections with intermittent drainage. She is having difficulty with reading and math skills.

1. What type of loss does this girl have?
2. Is her academic difficulty attributable to the hearing loss?
3. Would you expect to find any speech or language problems?

Name: Fig 7-7   Date: XX/XX/XX   Age: 7   Sex: F   Audiologist: HK

AUDIOMETER: GSI-10   ANSI 1969

PURE TONE AUDIOGRAM
FREQUENCY IN HERTZ

(Audiogram graph: HEARING LEVEL IN DECIBELS (dB) vs frequency 125–8000 Hz)

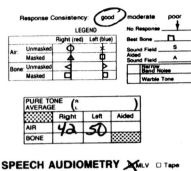

Response Consistency: (good) moderate poor

LEGEND

		Right (red)	Left (blue)
Air:	Unmasked	○	×
	Masked	▲	▢
Bone:	Unmasked	◁	▷
	Masked	▢	▢

No Response ⌐
Best Bone ▢
Sound Field S
Aided
Sound Field A
Narrow Band Noise
Warble Tone

PURE TONE AVERAGE (R / L)

	Right	Left	Aided
AIR	42	50	
BONE			

SPEECH AUDIOMETRY   ☒ MLV   ☐ Tape

PBK-50

	RIGHT	LEFT	MASK LEVEL R	L	SOUND FIELD	LIST
SAT						
SRT	40	44				
MCL	76	80				
UCL	100+	100+				
PB% (Word)	100 40SL	100 40SL	85 dB			1,2
PB% (Word)	⌐	⌐			36 50HL	3
PB% (Word)	⌐	⌐				
PB% (Word)	⌐	⌐				
	⌐	⌐				
	⌐	⌐				

Air Conduction: 60 30 60 55 50 60 45 60 45 60 R L
Bone Conduction: 70 60 70 65 60 70 55 70 55 70

Plateau levels of masking in non-test ear

Ref.: SPL _____ EFF ✓ Signal: NBN ✓ White _____

TYMPANOGRAM

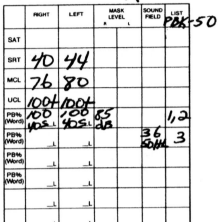

(Tympanogram graph: COMPLIANCE vs PRESSURE IN daPa, −300 to +200)

Static Compliance:

R	cc
2	
1	

L	cc
2	
1	

Normal: .3 – 1.75cc

Ear Canal Volume

Right	Left

C₁ =

STAPEDIUS REFLEX THRESHOLDS

Stimulus	Contralateral (HL)					Ipsilateral (HL)		
EAR	.5K	1K	2K	4K	WBN	.5K	1K	2K
R	NR	NR	NR	NR				
Decay								
L	NR	NR	NR	NR				
Decay								

ABBREVIATIONS

A	Absent	NR	No Response
C₁	Canal Volume	SAT	Speech Awareness
CNE	Could Not Establish		Threshold
CNT	Could Not Test	SL	Sensation Level
DNT	Did Not Test	SRT	Speech Reception
HL	Hearing Level		Threshold
MCL	Most Comfortable	UCL	Uncomfortable Listening
	Listening Level		Level
MVL	Monitored Live Voice		

REMARKS:

_____

_____

_____

_____

Educational and Communicative Implications of Hearing Loss

Answers for Figure 7-7

1. The air–bone gaps, Type B tympanograms, and absent reflexes in both ears suggest a moderate bilateral conductive hearing loss. The audiometric picture is corroborated by her history of ear infections. She should be referred to an otolaryngologist if she is not already being treated.

2. Her difficulty with reading and mathematics may be attributable to her hearing problem, which seems to be constant rather than intermittent. Children with moderate hearing losses frequently have difficulty hearing and understanding speech at average conversational level. Note that her word recognition ability at 50 dB HL, which is average conversational level, is extremely poor even when there is no competing noise. With this word recognition problem, it is not surprising that she is showing learning difficulties. It should be noted that at higher levels of presentation (e.g., 40 dB SL) she had good speech understanding.

3. Some children with moderate bilateral losses show deficits in articulation, voice, and language. A mild acquired conductive loss which is temporary usually does not affect speech and language, but a persistent moderate conductive problem may cause significant speech and language delay. This girl has normal articulation but an unusually soft voice and delayed vocabulary and syntactic development.

QUESTIONS FOR FIGURE 7-8

Case History Information This boy has a congenital hearing impairment in his right ear. He has slightly above average mental ability as measured by the WISC. His voice is too high and his articulation presents many distortions and omissions.

1. What type of hearing loss does this boy have?
2. Why was air conduction in the right ear retested with masking in the left ear?
3. Is this boy's hearing loss of probable etiologic significance to the expressive (voice and articulation) communication problems?

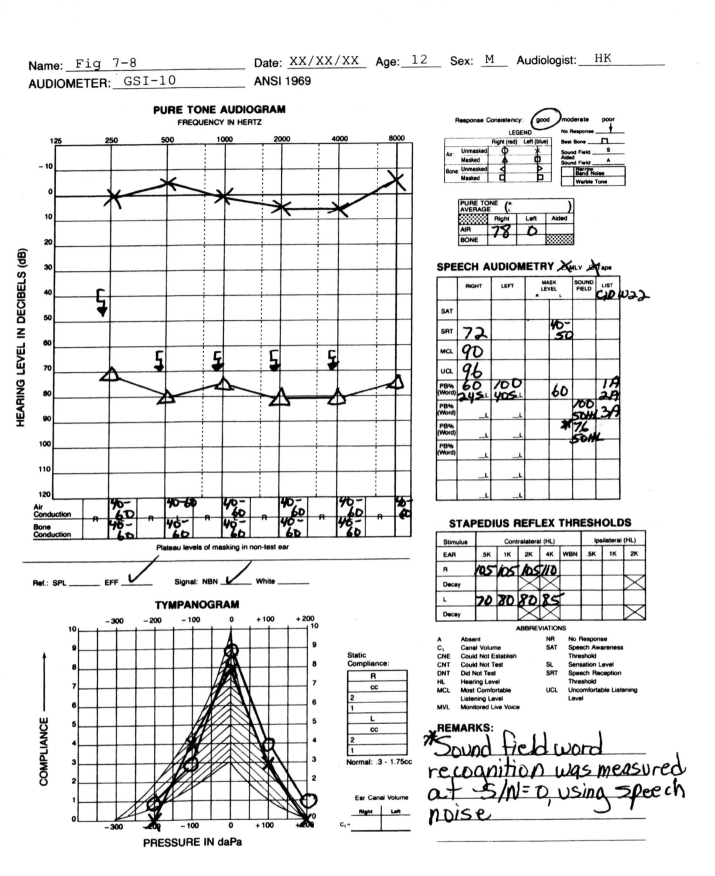

Answers for Figure 7-8

1. This boy has a severe unilateral sensorineural loss in the right ear. There is no air–bone gap.

2. Inspection of the unmasked air conduction threshold in the right ear reveals a curve that is a duplicate of the left ear configuration but at intensities approximately 40–50 dB higher. Such a right ear configuration is known as a shadow curve and suggests that the apparent right ear responses were actually responses of the left ear to tones that were attenuated as a result of crossover of sound from the right. Whenever there is a difference in unmasked thresholds of 40–50 dB between ears, it is necessary to retest the poor ear with masking noise delivered to the good ear (see Chapter 5).

3. A unilateral conductive loss should be of little etiologic importance to this boy's speech difficulties. Only one normal ear is necessary to provide an adequate auditory link in a person's servo mechanism for speech. It should be noted that a unilateral loss may be a factor in language and learning difficulties.

QUESTIONS FOR FIGURE 7-9

Case History Information This girl's hearing loss was first discovered at age nine and has remained stable. Etiology is unknown. She has had difficulty in school and has repeated one grade. Her speech is characterized by consonant substitutions and distortions and her vocabulary is somewhat limited for her chronological age. Her mental ability has been found normal.

1. What type of hearing loss does this girl have?
2. Is there any relationship between her academic difficulties and her hearing loss?
3. Is there any relationship between her speech and language deficits and her hearing loss?

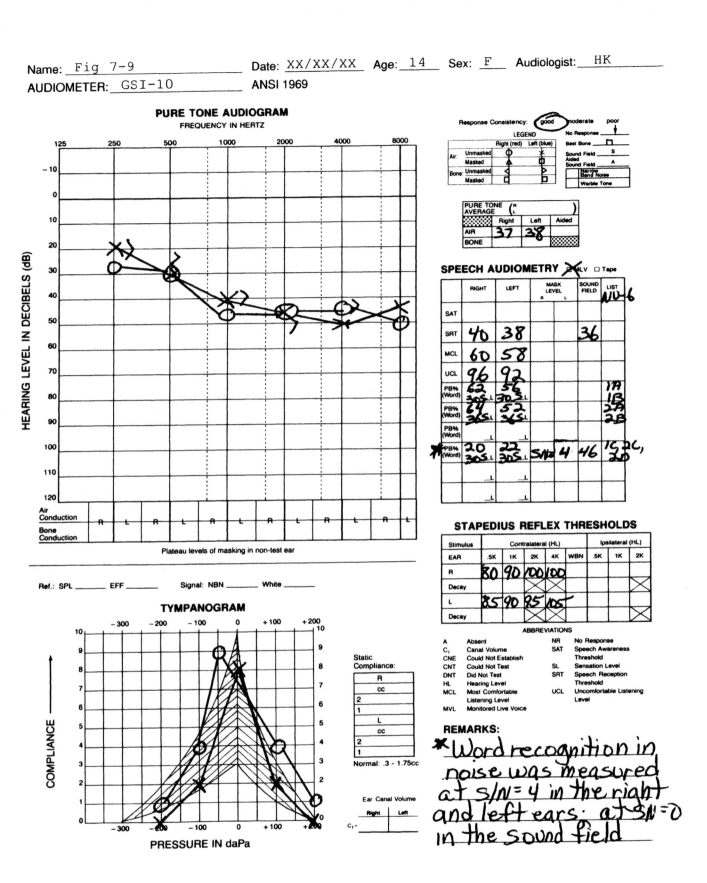

Answers for Figure 7-9

1. This girl has a mild to moderate bilateral sensorineural loss.
2. A hearing loss of this type is frequently related to academic difficulty. Word recognition at average conversational level (50 dB HL) is very poor, and word recognition in noise is poorer still. It is probable that this girl is not understanding a significant portion of classroom instruction. Therefore, it is not surprising that her ability to function adequately in school is impaired.
3. It is not uncommon for speech and language problems to exist with mild to moderate bilateral sensorineural loss. There is frequent difficulty with idiomatic expressions and vocabulary expressing subtleties of meaning. Consonant problems tend to be more common than vowel misarticulations because vowels are primarily low-frequency sounds. In this case, low-frequency sensitivity tends to be better than the high frequencies.

QUESTION FOR FIGURE 7-10

Case History Information This boy's hearing loss was diagnosed as a congenital sensorineural loss of unknown etiology. Articulation testing revealed errors in the production of /t/, /l/, /z/, /s/, and /r/. He scored only 135 items correct on the 176-item Templin-Darley Diagnostic Test.

1. Does this boy have a speech problem that might be related to his hearing loss?

Name: Fig 7-10   Date: XX/XX/XX   Age: 4   Sex: M   Audiologist: HK
AUDIOMETER: GSI-10   ANSI 1969

PURE TONE AUDIOGRAM
FREQUENCY IN HERTZ

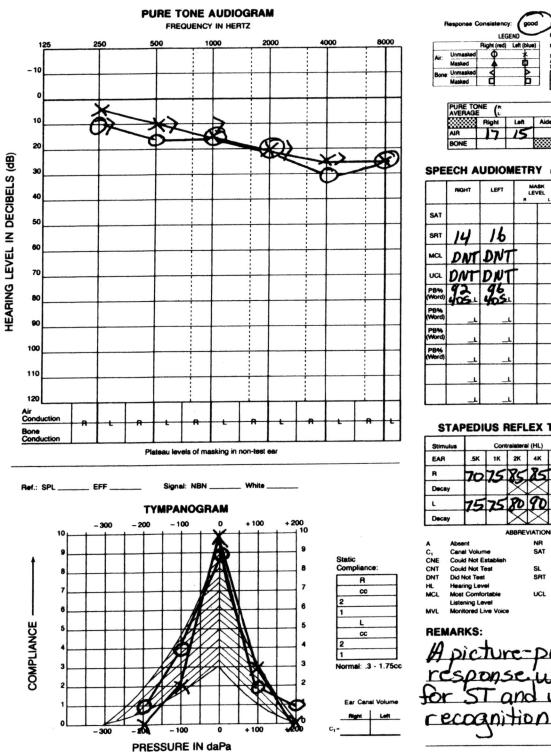

Response Consistency: (good) moderate poor

No Response ↓

LEGEND		
	Right (red)	Left (blue)
Air: Unmasked	◯	✕
Masked	▲	▢
Bone: Unmasked	◁	▷
Masked	▢	▢

Best Bone ▢
Sound Field ___ S
Aided
Sound Field ___ A
Narrow Band Noise
Warble Tone

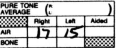

PURE TONE AVERAGE (R: L:)	Right	Left	Aided
AIR	17	15	
BONE			

SPEECH AUDIOMETRY   ☐ MLV   ☐ Tape

	RIGHT	LEFT	MASK LEVEL R	L	SOUND FIELD	LIST WIPI
SAT						
SRT	14	16				
MCL	DNT	DNT				
UCL	DNT	DNT				
PB% (Word)	92 40SL	96 40SL				100 1,2 50AK 3
PB% (Word)	L	L				
PB% (Word)	L	L				
PB% (Word)	L	L				
	L	L				
	L	L				

STAPEDIUS REFLEX THRESHOLDS

Stimulus	Contralateral (HL)					Ipsilateral (HL)		
EAR	.5K	1K	2K	4K	WBN	.5K	1K	2K
R	70	75	85	85	✕			✕
Decay			✕	✕				
L	75	75	80	90	✕			✕
Decay			✕	✕				

ABBREVIATIONS

A	Absent	NR	No Response
C₁	Canal Volume	SAT	Speech Awareness
CNE	Could Not Establish		Threshold
CNT	Could Not Test	SL	Sensation Level
DNT	Did Not Test	SRT	Speech Reception
HL	Hearing Level		Threshold
MCL	Most Comfortable	UCL	Uncomfortable Listening
	Listening Level		Level
MVL	Monitored Live Voice		

REMARKS:

A picture-pointing response was used for ST and word recognition

---

Ref.: SPL _____ EFF _____   Signal: NBN _____ White _____

TYMPANOGRAM

Static Compliance:

R	
	cc
2	
1	

L	
	cc
2	
1	

Normal: .3 - 1.75cc

Ear Canal Volume

	Right	Left
C₁ -		

PRESSURE IN daPa

Answer for Figure 7-10

1. A mild bilateral impairment can be a factor in articulation problems, but this boy does not appear to have a significant articulation problem. It may be that the sounds misarticulated by this child are errors frequently found in the speech of normal-hearing children at age 4 and represent normal development. A score of 135 items correct is slightly above the mean number of items correct for 4½-year-old boys, according to the Templin and Darley norms (1960).

QUESTIONS FOR FIGURE 7-11

Case History Information This boy is repeating first grade because he has had great difficulty learning to read and spell. His speech is normal, but his vocabulary is at the level of a 5-year-old, according to the PPVT. His mental age was found to be within normal limits on the performance scale of the WISC.

1. Does this boy have a significant hearing problem?
2. Can his academic difficulty be attributed to his hearing?

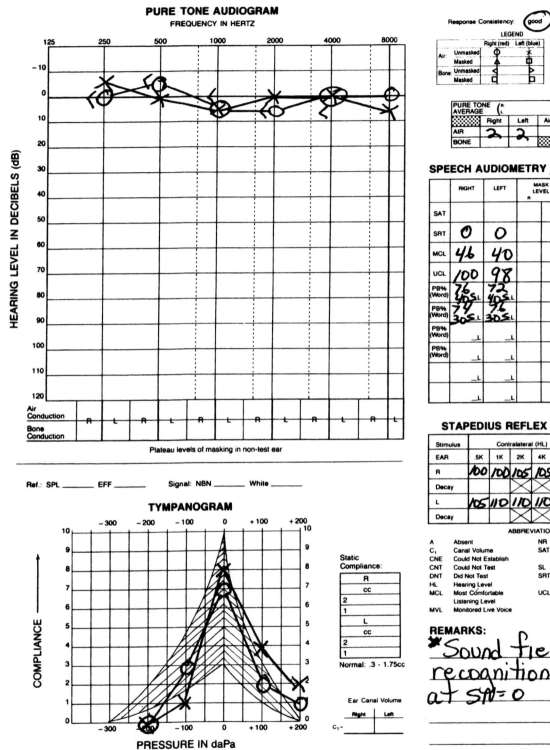

Name: Fig 7-11   Date: XX/XX/XX Age: 7   Sex: M   Audiologist: HK
AUDIOMETER: GSI-10   ANSI 1969

PURE TONE AUDIOGRAM
FREQUENCY IN HERTZ

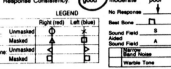

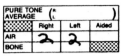

PURE TONE AVERAGE (R, L)			
	Right	Left	Aided
AIR	2	2	
BONE			

SPEECH AUDIOMETRY ☒ MLV ☐ Tape

	RIGHT	LEFT	MASK LEVEL R	L	SOUND FIELD	LIST W2P1
SAT						
SRT	0	0				
MCL	46	40				
UCL	100	98				
PB% (Word)	76 40SL	72 40SL				1,2
PB% (Word)	74 30SL	76 30SL				3,4
PB% (Word)	L	L			78 50HL	1
PB% (Word)	L	L			*20 50HL	2
	L	L				
	L	L				

STAPEDIUS REFLEX THRESHOLDS

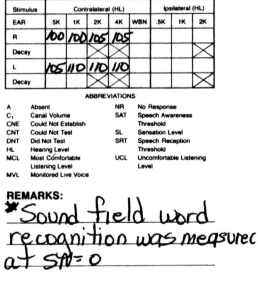

Stimulus	Contralateral (HL)					Ipsilateral (HL)		
EAR	.5K	1K	2K	4K	WBN	.5K	1K	2K
R	100	100	105	105				
Decay								
L	105	110	110	110				
Decay								

ABBREVIATIONS

A	Absent	NR	No Response
C,	Canal Volume	SAT	Speech Awareness
CNE	Could Not Establish		Threshold
CNT	Could Not Test	SL	Sensation Level
DNT	Did Not Test	SRT	Speech Reception
HL	Hearing Level		Threshold
MCL	Most Comfortable	UCL	Uncomfortable Listening
	Listening Level		Level
MVL	Monitored Live Voice		

REMARKS:

*Sound field word recognition was measured at SN = 0

Ref.: SPL _____ EFF _____   Signal: NBN _____ White _____

TYMPANOGRAM

PRESSURE IN daPa

Static Compliance:

R	
	cc
2	
1	

L	
	cc
2	
1	

Normal: .3 - 1.75cc

Ear Canal Volume

Right	Left

$C_1 =$

Answers for Figure 7-11

1. Although this child's pure tone thresholds are well within normal limits, his word recognition is not. Word recognition scores in quiet indicate slight to moderate difficulty understanding speech at comfortable listening levels. His word recognition score at average conversational level in the presence of competing noise indicates that he probably has great difficulty following connected speech. The combination of normal pure tone sensitivity and less than normal speech understanding suggests the presence of a retrocochlear or auditory processing difficulty that should be further evaluated. The possibility of retrocochlear hearing loss is corroborated by the elevated reflex thresholds in the presence of normal pure tone thresholds. This boy should be referred to an otolaryngologist.

2. This boy's reading and spelling difficulties and deficient vocabulary may be attributed at least in part to his speech understanding difficulties. However, other etiologic factors such as amount of language stimulation in the home or visual perceptual difficulties must also be considered.

QUESTIONS FOR FIGURE 7-12

Case History Information This young man has just recuperated from an attack of meningitis which has left him with a profound bilateral sensorineural hearing loss. Before his illness he was considered a superior student in college, and post-testing as measured by the performance scale of the WAIS also suggests superior ability. His speech is free from voice or articulation errors. His language abilities are well within normal limits.

1. In light of the severity of this man's hearing loss, how do you account for his normal speech and language abilities?
2. Would you expect this man to have receptive difficulties?
3. Does he use visual cues?
4. Can this young man benefit from the services of a speech–language pathologist or audiologist? If so, what type(s) of service may be indicated?

Name: Fig 7-12   Date: XX/XX/XX   Age: 21   Sex: M   Audiologist: HK
AUDIOMETER: GSI-10   ANSI 1969

PURE TONE AUDIOGRAM
FREQUENCY IN HERTZ

Air Conduction

Bone Conduction

Plateau levels of masking in non-test ear

Ref.: SPL _____ EFF _____   Signal: NBN _____ White _____

TYMPANOGRAM

PRESSURE IN daPa

Response Consistency: (good) moderate poor

LEGEND

	Right (red)	Left (blue)
Air: Unmasked	O	X
Masked	Δ	□
Bone: Unmasked	<	>
Masked	□	□

No Response
Best Bone
Sound Field — S
Aided Sound Field — A
Narrow Band Noise
Warble Tone

PURE TONE AVERAGE (R: L:)

	Right	Left	Aided
AIR	82	78	
BONE			

SPEECH AUDIOMETRY ☒MLV ☒Tape

CID W22

	RIGHT	LEFT	MASK LEVEL R L	SOUND FIELD	LIST
SAT					
SRT	86	84		80	
MCL	92	94		DNT	
UCL	100+	100+		DNT	
PB% (Word)	50 24 SL	56 26 SL			1A 1B
PB% (Word)	_L	_L			
PB% (Word)	_L	_L			
PB% (Word)	_L	_L			
	_L	_L			

STAPEDIUS REFLEX THRESHOLDS

Stimulus	Contralateral (HL)					Ipsilateral (HL)		
EAR	.5K	1K	2K	4K	WBN	.5K	1K	2K
R	105	110	NR	NR				
Decay			☒	☒				☒
L	110	110	NR	NR				
Decay			☒	☒				☒

ABBREVIATIONS

A   Absent
C₁   Canal Volume
CNE Could Not Establish
CNT Could Not Test
DNT Did Not Test
HL   Hearing Level
MCL Most Comfortable Listening Level
MVL Monitored Live Voice

NR   No Response
SAT Speech Awareness Threshold
SL   Sensation Level
SRT Speech Reception Threshold
UCL Uncomfortable Listening Level

Static Compliance:

R	cc
2	
1	
L	cc
2	
1	

Normal: .3 - 1.75cc

Ear Canal Volume
Right Left
C₁ -

REMARKS:

CID-W22 were presented "face-to-face" without an audiometer with the following results: 0% auditory only (eyes closed) 52% auditory-visual

Answers for Figure 7-12

1. This man's normal speech and language in the presence of a profound sensorineural hearing loss are understandable in light of the relatively short duration of his hearing loss. He developed his present expressive communication abilities with the benefit of normal hearing. His present hearing loss may cause a deterioration in his expressive communication.

2. One would expect this man to have considerable difficulty with receptive communication, particularly if amplification is not used. With his severe loss, he is unable to hear average conversation, which is at a level of 50 dB HL. Even at extremely intense listening levels, such as presentation levels of 74 dB and 76 dB HL, he demonstrates poor word recognition, understanding only approximately half of what he hears.

3. This client does use visual cues to a considerable extent. With auditory input only (eyes closed), he understood none of the words presented in a face-to-face situation at normal conversational level. However, in the same situation, when he was able to look at the speaker as well as listen, he was able to correctly understand 52% of the words.

4. In general, this young man should receive the services of an audiologist and speech–language pathologist for remedial planning, including consideration of amplification, auditory training, speechreading, counseling, and speech conservation to prevent deterioration of speech.

QUESTIONS FOR FIGURE 7-13

Case History Information This girl's profound hearing loss is the result of a viral disease she had at the age of 13 months. She is a graduate of the state school for the deaf and communicates primarily through sign language and fingerspelling.

1. Would you expect this girl to have receptive communication problems as a result of her profound bilateral hearing loss?
2. Would you expect her to have expressive communication problems?
3. Does she use speechreading?

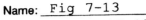

Name: Fig 7-13   Date: XX/XX/XX   Age: 19   Sex: F   Audiologist: HK
AUDIOMETER: GSI-10   ANSI 1969

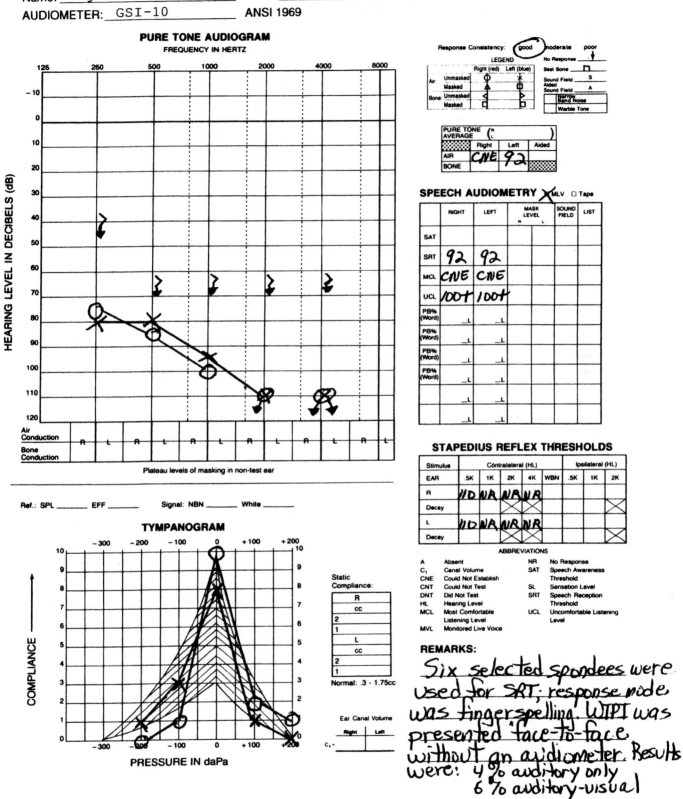

PURE TONE AUDIOGRAM
FREQUENCY IN HERTZ

Response Consistency: (good) moderate poor

LEGEND

		Right (red)	Left (blue)
Air	Unmasked	O	X
	Masked	△	□
Bone	Unmasked	<	>
	Masked	□	□

No Response ↓
Best Bone
Sound Field S
Aided
Sound Field A
Narrow Band Noise
Warble Tone

PURE TONE AVERAGE	(R		)
	Right	Left	Aided
AIR	CNE	92	
BONE			

SPEECH AUDIOMETRY ☒ MLV ☐ Tape

	RIGHT	LEFT	MASK LEVEL R L	SOUND FIELD	LIST
SAT					
SRT	92	92			
MCL	CNE	CNE			
UCL	100+	100+			
PB% (Word)	_L	_L			
PB% (Word)	_L	_L			
PB% (Word)	_L	_L			
PB% (Word)	_L	_L			
	_L	_L			
	_L	_L			

STAPEDIUS REFLEX THRESHOLDS

Stimulus	Contralateral (HL)					Ipsilateral (HL)		
EAR	.5K	1K	2K	4K	WBN	.5K	1K	2K
R	110	NR	NR	NR				
Decay								
L	110	NR	NR	NR				
Decay								

ABBREVIATIONS

A	Absent	NR	No Response
C₁	Canal Volume	SAT	Speech Awareness
CNE	Could Not Establish		Threshold
CNT	Could Not Test	SL	Sensation Level
DNT	Did Not Test	SRT	Speech Reception
HL	Hearing Level		Threshold
MCL	Most Comfortable	UCL	Uncomfortable Listening
	Listening Level		Level
MVL	Monitored Live Voice		

Air Conduction   R L L R L R L R L R L
Bone Conduction

Plateau levels of masking in non-test ear

Ref.: SPL _____ EFF _____   Signal: NBN _____   White _____

TYMPANOGRAM

Static Compliance:

R	
cc	
2	
1	

L	
cc	
2	
1	

Normal: .3 - 1.75cc

Ear Canal Volume

Right	Left

C₁ =

PRESSURE IN daPa

REMARKS:

Six selected spondees were used for SRT; response mode was fingerspelling. WIPI was presented face-to-face without an audiometer. Results were: 4% auditory only 6% auditory-visual

Answers for Figure 7-13

1. In general, one would expect an individual with this degree of hearing loss incurred prelingually to have severe receptive problems. Even with amplification, there is usually minimal understanding of speech, with consequent severe spoken language difficulty and possible educational retardation. Note that in this case, speech reception thresholds could be measured only by using a list of spondees restricted to six words, and word recognition could not be measured. This girl is unable to understand speech even with amplification but can understand English language typical of that of a normal high school senior when it is signed. Her reading ability is that of a 12th-grader. She has been educated through manual communication since age 2.

2. Usually an individual with a profound hearing loss incurred in early childhood shows severe speech and language deficiencies. This girl's use of English in writing is deficient in syntax and idiomatic expressions. However, she seems to be able to express herself adequately to other manually communicating deaf individuals.

3. This girl does not use speechreading to understand speech. Her scores on the WIPI word recognition test were the same regardless of whether or not she was permitted to watch the face of the speaker. Since the "auditory only" condition was below her threshold, the 4% score undoubtedly represented chance responses. The 6% score obtained in the "auditory–visual combined" condition might also represent chance responses.

QUESTIONS FOR FIGURE 7-14

Case History Information This man has been aware of a hearing problem for the past 15 years and reported that it has gradually been getting worse. His voice is now slightly louder than normal and rather monotonous. Several consonants are distorted.

1. Does this man's speech problem appear to be related to his hearing loss?
2. What kind of receptive problems would you expect him to have?

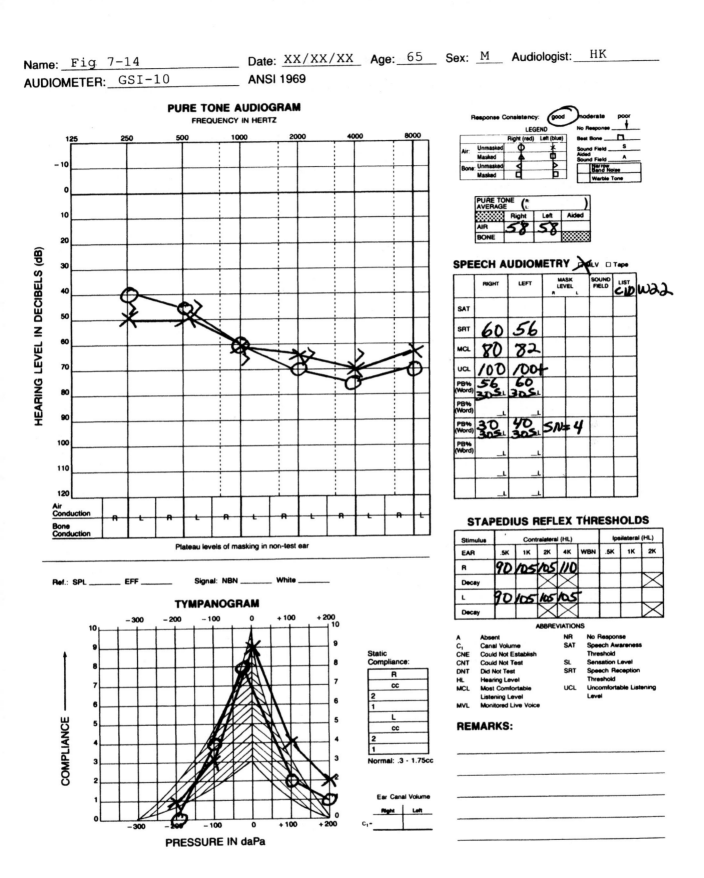

PURE TONE AUDIOGRAM
FREQUENCY IN HERTZ

Name: Fig 7-14   Date: XX/XX/XX   Age: 65   Sex: M   Audiologist: HK
AUDIOMETER: GSI-10   ANSI 1969

Response Consistency: (good) moderate poor

LEGEND

		Right (red)	Left (blue)
Air:	Unmasked	O	X
	Masked	▲	□
Bone:	Unmasked	<	>
	Masked	□	□

Best Bone □
Sound Field S
Aided
Sound Field A
Narrow Band Noise
Warble Tone

PURE TONE AVERAGE (R: / L:)

	Right	Left	Aided
AIR	58	58	
BONE			

SPEECH AUDIOMETRY ☑ MLV ☐ Tape   LIST: CID W22

	RIGHT	LEFT	MASK LEVEL R	L	SOUND FIELD
SAT					
SRT	60	56			
MCL	80	82			
UCL	100	100+			
PB% (Word)	56 30SL	60 30SL			
PB% (Word)	_L_	_L_			
PB% (Word)	30 30SL	40 30SL	SN=4		
PB% (Word)	_L_	_L_			
	_L_	_L_			
	_L_	_L_			

STAPEDIUS REFLEX THRESHOLDS

Stimulus	Contralateral (HL)					Ipsilateral (HL)		
EAR	.5K	1K	2K	4K	WBN	.5K	1K	2K
R	90	105	105	110				
Decay		✕		✕				✕
L	90	105	105	105				
Decay		✕		✕				✕

ABBREVIATIONS

A — Absent
C_1 — Canal Volume
CNE — Could Not Establish
CNT — Could Not Test
DNT — Did Not Test
HL — Hearing Level
MCL — Most Comfortable Listening Level
MVL — Monitored Live Voice
NR — No Response
SAT — Speech Awareness Threshold
SL — Sensation Level
SRT — Speech Reception Threshold
UCL — Uncomfortable Listening Level

REMARKS:

Ref.: SPL _____ EFF _____   Signal: NBN _____ White _____

TYMPANOGRAM

Static Compliance:

R	
cc	
2	
1	

L	
cc	
2	
1	

Normal: .3 - 1.75cc

Ear Canal Volume

	Right	Left
C_1 =		

Answers for Figure 7-14

1. The type of speech difficulties mentioned are the type that one would expect as a result of moderately severe hearing impairment of long duration. The speech difficulties are probably due to a disruption of the auditory servo mechanism.

2. Individuals with this type and degree of hearing loss understand conversational speech only if it is loud, and even then they do not always understand it completely. This man's word recognition scores indicate that even at high intensity levels he has great difficulty understanding speech. Amplification may be of some assistance but will not provide complete remediation of the receptive problem.

QUESTIONS FOR FIGURE 7-15

Case History Information This woman reported difficulty understanding speech in the presence of competing noise or competing speech (group conversation). Her voice is unusually soft.

1. Is her difficulty understanding speech in the presence of a competing signal attributable to her hearing loss?

2. Is her abnormally soft voice due to her hearing loss?

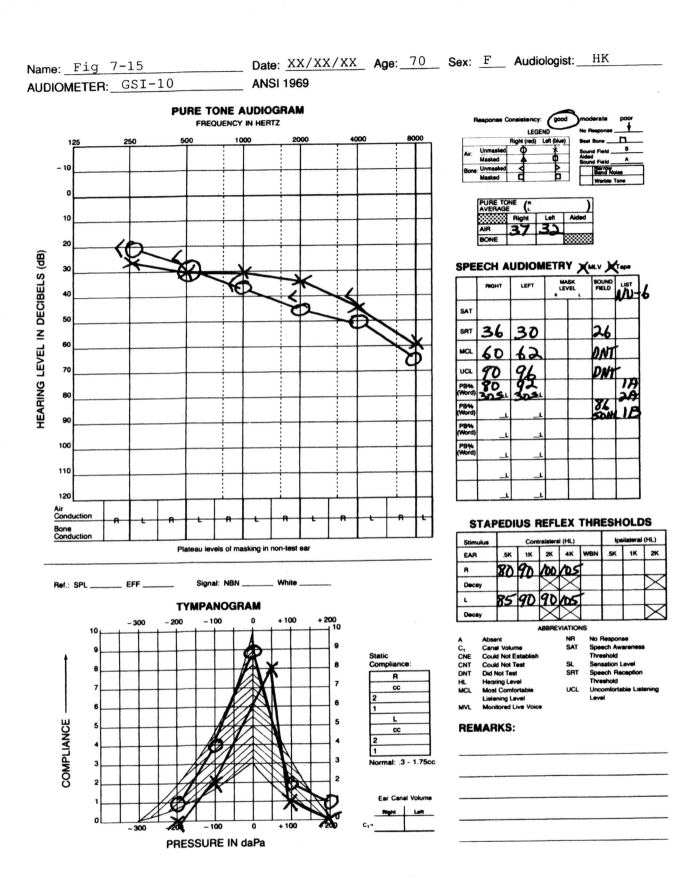

Name: Fig 7-15 **Date:** XX/XX/XX **Age:** 70 **Sex:** F **Audiologist:** HK
AUDIOMETER: GSI-10 **ANSI 1969**

PURE TONE AUDIOGRAM
FREQUENCY IN HERTZ

Response Consistency: (good) moderate poor

LEGEND

	Right (red)	Left (blue)
Air: Unmasked	O	X
Masked	▲	◻
Bone: Unmasked	<	>
Masked	◻	◻

No Response
Best Bone ◻
Sound Field S
Aided
Sound Field A
Narrow Band Noise
Warble Tone

PURE TONE AVERAGE (R L)	Right	Left	Aided
AIR	37	32	
BONE			

SPEECH AUDIOMETRY X MLV X Tape

	RIGHT	LEFT	MASK LEVEL R L	SOUND FIELD	LIST NU-6
SAT					
SRT	36	30		26	
MCL	60	62		DNT	
UCL	90	96		DNT	
PB% (Word)	80 30SL	92 30SL			1A 2A
PB% (Word)	L	L		86 50HL	1B
PB% (Word)	L	L			
PB% (Word)	L	L			
	L	L			
	L	L			

STAPEDIUS REFLEX THRESHOLDS

Stimulus	Contralateral (HL)					Ipsilateral (HL)		
EAR	.5K	1K	2K	4K	WBN	.5K	1K	2K
R	80	90	100	105				X
Decay		X						X
L	85	90	90	105				X
Decay		X						X

ABBREVIATIONS

A	Absent	NR	No Response
C₁	Canal Volume	SAT	Speech Awareness
CNE	Could Not Establish		Threshold
CNT	Could Not Test	SL	Sensation Level
DNT	Did Not Test	SRT	Speech Reception
HL	Hearing Level		Threshold
MCL	Most Comfortable	UCL	Uncomfortable Listening
	Listening Level		Level
MVL	Monitored Live Voice		

REMARKS:

Ref.: SPL _____ EFF _____ Signal: NBN _____ White _____

TYMPANOGRAM
PRESSURE IN daPa

Static Compliance:

R
cc
2
1

L
cc
2
1

Normal: .3 - 1.75cc

Ear Canal Volume

Right	Left
C₁ =	

Educational and Communicative Implications of Hearing Loss

1. This woman has a mild bilateral sensorineural hearing loss not unusual for her age. Her word recognition scores in quiet suggest that she experiences little difficulty understanding conversation in a quiet situation if it is sufficiently loud. However, her word recognition at average conversational level in the presence of competing noise is only 60%, which indicates considerable difficulty. Therefore, her complaint of difficulty understanding speech in the presence of competing noise is consistent with her hearing loss.

2. This woman's abnormally soft voice is probably due to something other than her hearing loss. Her hearing is only mildly impaired in the low frequencies, allowing sufficient auditory feedback to her servo mechanism. Moreover, her hearing loss is sensorineural rather than conductive. If she had a voice deviation related to her hearing loss, it would probably be a loud rather than a soft voice.

QUESTION FOR FIGURE 7-16

Case History Information This man has been aware of intermittent high-frequency tinnitus since his discharge from the service eight years ago. However, he is not aware of any hearing problem.

1. Does this man have a hearing impairment of any social, vocational, or communicative significance?

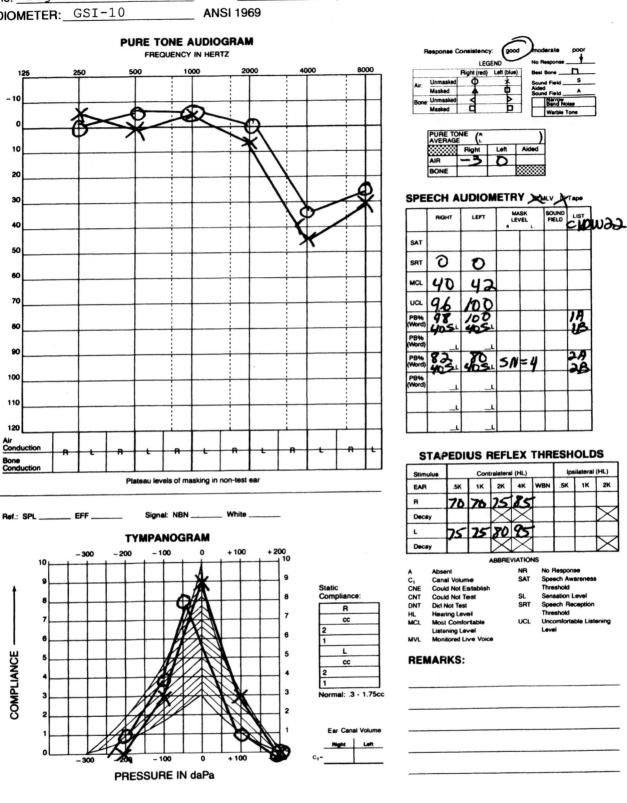

AUDIOMETER: GSI-10   ANSI 1969

PURE TONE AUDIOGRAM
FREQUENCY IN HERTZ

Response Consistency: good moderate poor

LEGEND

	Right (red)	Left (blue)
Air: Unmasked	O	X
Masked	▲	◻
Bone: Unmasked	<	>
Masked	◻	◻

No Response
Best Bone
Sound Field   S
Aided
Sound Field   A
Narrow Band Noise
Warble Tone

PURE TONE AVERAGE (R / L)	Right	Left	Aided
AIR	−3	0	
BONE			

SPEECH AUDIOMETRY   MLV Tape

	RIGHT	LEFT	MASK LEVEL R L	SOUND FIELD	LIST
SAT					C10W22
SRT	0	0			
MCL	40	42			
UCL	96	100			
PB% (Word)	98 40SL	100 40SL			1A 1B
PB% (Word)					
PB% (Word)	82 40SL	80 40SL	SN=4		2A 2B
PB% (Word)					

STAPEDIUS REFLEX THRESHOLDS

Stimulus	Contralateral (HL)					Ipsilateral (HL)		
EAR	.5K	1K	2K	4K	WBN	.5K	1K	2K
R	70	70	75	85				
Decay								
L	75	75	80	95				
Decay								

ABBREVIATIONS

A	Absent	NR	No Response
C₁	Canal Volume	SAT	Speech Awareness
CNE	Could Not Establish		Threshold
CNT	Could Not Test	SL	Sensation Level
DNT	Did Not Test	SRT	Speech Reception
HL	Hearing Level		Threshold
MCL	Most Comfortable	UCL	Uncomfortable Listening
	Listening Level		Level
MVL	Monitored Live Voice		

REMARKS:

Plateau levels of masking in non-test ear

Ref.: SPL _____ EFF _____   Signal: NBN _____ White _____

TYMPANOGRAM

PRESSURE IN daPa

Static Compliance:

R	cc
2	
1	
L	cc
2	
1	

Normal: .3 - 1.75cc

Ear Canal Volume

Right	Left
C₁ -	

Answer for Figure 7-16

1. This man has a mild high-frequency hearing loss. Although some individuals with mild high-frequency hearing losses experience speech understanding problems, especially in noise, this man has good voice recognition scores and is not reporting any particular problems. Note that his scores in the presence of noise are what is expected of a normal-hearing individual (see Chapter 4). He appears to be making good use of his essentially normal hearing for the low and middle frequencies. Case history information suggests that the moderate high-frequency impairment may be noise induced. It is important that the client be careful about further noise exposure, which could cause additional deterioration of hearing.

QUESTIONS FOR FIGURE 7-17

Case History Information This woman has been aware of a hearing problem for ten years. There is a history of otosclerosis in her family. She speaks in an abnormally soft voice.

1. Do you think this woman's abnormally soft voice is related to her hearing problem?
2. Would you expect this client to receive a considerable amount of benefit from a hearing aid?

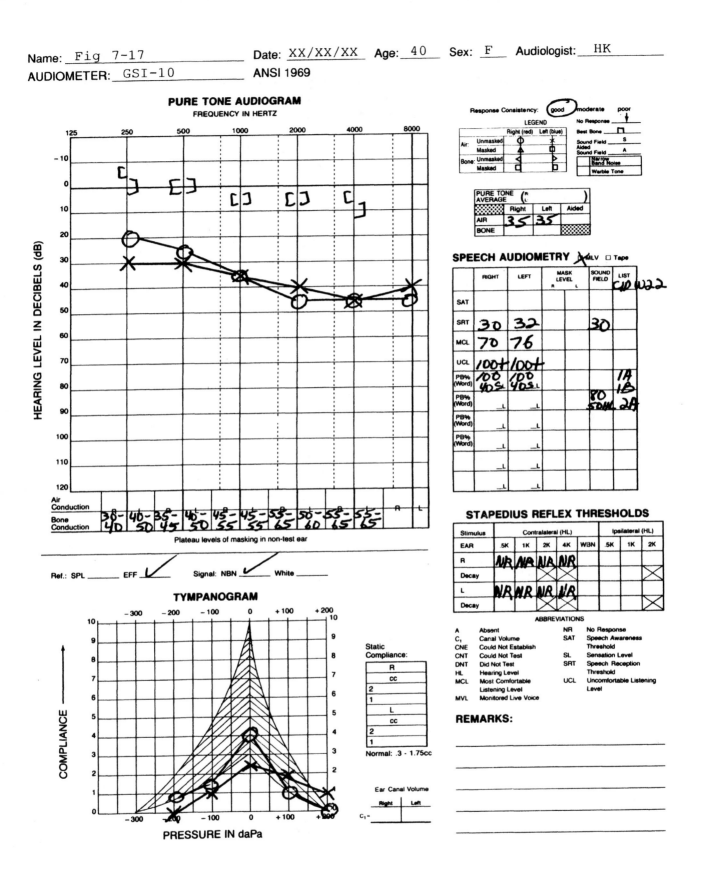

Name: Fig 7-17   Date: XX/XX/XX   Age: 40   Sex: F   Audiologist: HK

AUDIOMETER: GSI-10   ANSI 1969

PURE TONE AUDIOGRAM
FREQUENCY IN HERTZ

Response Consistency: (good) moderate   poor

LEGEND

	Right (red)	Left (blue)
Air: Unmasked	O	X
Masked	△	◻
Bone: Unmasked	<	>
Masked	◻	◻

No Response
Best Bone
Sound Field   S
Aided
Sound Field   A
Narrow Band Noise
Warble Tone

PURE TONE AVERAGE (R / L)

	Right	Left	Aided
AIR	35	35	
BONE			

Plateau levels of masking in non-test ear

Air Conduction										R	L
Bone Conduction	35–40	35–40	45–45	55–50	55–55						
	40–50	45–50	55–55	65–60	65–65						

Ref.: SPL _____ EFF ✓   Signal: NBN ✓   White _____

SPEECH AUDIOMETRY ☑ MLV ☐ Tape

	RIGHT	LEFT	MASK LEVEL R	MASK LEVEL L	SOUND FIELD	LIST
SAT						CID W22
SRT	30	32			30	
MCL	70	76				
UCL	100+	100+				
PB% (Word)	100 40dB	100 40dB				1A
PB% (Word)	⌐	⌐			80 50dB	1B 2A
PB% (Word)	⌐	⌐				
PB% (Word)	⌐	⌐				
	⌐	⌐				
	⌐	⌐				

STAPEDIUS REFLEX THRESHOLDS

Stimulus	Contralateral (HL)					Ipsilateral (HL)		
EAR	.5K	1K	2K	4K	WBN	.5K	1K	2K
R	NR	NR	NR	NR				
Decay								
L	NR	NR	NR	NR				
Decay								

ABBREVIATIONS

A	Absent	NR	No Response
C₁	Canal Volume	SAT	Speech Awareness Threshold
CNE	Could Not Establish		
CNT	Could Not Test	SL	Sensation Level
DNT	Did Not Test	SRT	Speech Reception Threshold
HL	Hearing Level		
MCL	Most Comfortable Listening Level	UCL	Uncomfortable Listening Level
MVL	Monitored Live Voice		

TYMPANOGRAM

Static Compliance:

R	cc
2	
1	

L	cc
2	
1	

Normal: .3 - 1.75cc

Ear Canal Volume

	Right	Left
C₁ =		

PRESSURE IN daPa

REMARKS:

_____
_____
_____
_____
_____

Answers for Figure 7-17

1. A mild to moderate bilateral conductive hearing loss may cause a person to speak with an abnormally soft voice, although such a relationship is not always found. The explanation for a soft voice in the case of a conductive loss is that the normal bone conduction portion of the servo mechanism allows a person to hear his or her own voice as louder than other people's voices. Consequently, the person decreases his voice level to the point where it matches that of others.
2. If this client's hearing cannot be restored medically, there is high probability for considerable benefit from the use of a hearing aid. In general, persons with conductive losses have a more favorable prognosis as hearing aid users than do persons with sensorineural losses.

QUESTIONS FOR FIGURE 7-18

1. Would you expect this man to have a favorable prognosis as a hearing aid user?
2. Which ear would you fit?

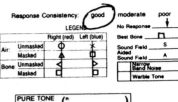

Name: Fig 7-18   Date: XX/XX/XX   Age: 50   Sex: M   Audiologist: HK
AUDIOMETER: GSI-10   ANSI 1969

PURE TONE AUDIOGRAM
FREQUENCY IN HERTZ

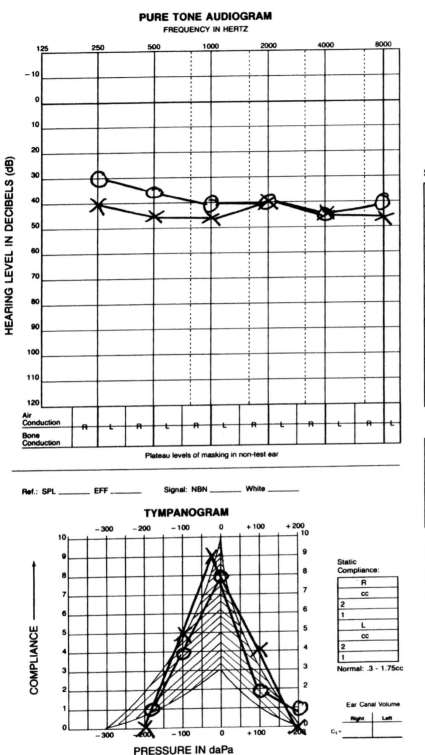

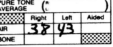

Response Consistency: good moderate poor

LEGEND			
		Right (red)	Left (blue)
Air:	Unmasked	○	×
	Masked	△	▽
Bone:	Unmasked	<	>
	Masked	□	□

No Response
Best Bone
Sound Field   S
Aided
Sound Field   A
Narrow Band Noise
Warble Tone

PURE TONE AVERAGE (R L)	Right	Left	Aided
AIR	38	43	
BONE			

SPEECH AUDIOMETRY ☐ MLV ☐ Tape

	RIGHT	LEFT	MASK LEVEL R L	SOUND FIELD	LIST
SAT					
SRT					
MCL					
UCL					
PB% (Word)	_L_	_L_			
PB% (Word)	_L_	_L_			
PB% (Word)	_L_	_L_			
PB% (Word)	_L_	_L_			
	_L_	_L_			
	_L_	_L_			

STAPEDIUS REFLEX THRESHOLDS

Stimulus	Contralateral (HL)					Ipsilateral (HL)		
EAR	.5K	1K	2K	4K	WBN	.5K	1K	2K
R	70	75	75	80				
Decay			✕	✕		✕	✕	✕
L	75	80	80	80				
Decay			✕	✕		✕	✕	✕

ABBREVIATIONS

A	Absent	NR	No Response
C₁	Canal Volume	SAT	Speech Awareness
CNE	Could Not Establish		Threshold
CNT	Could Not Test	SL	Sensation Level
DNT	Did Not Test	SRT	Speech Reception
HL	Hearing Level		Threshold
MCL	Most Comfortable	UCL	Uncomfortable Listening
	Listening Level		Level
MVL	Monitored Live Voice		

REMARKS:

Ref.: SPL _____ EFF _____   Signal: NBN _____ White _____

TYMPANOGRAM

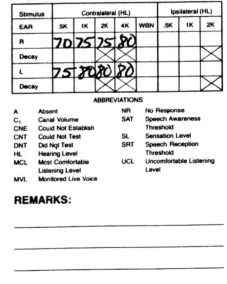

Static Compliance:

R	
	cc
2	
1	

L	
	cc
2	
1	

Normal: .3 - 1.75cc

Ear Canal Volume

	Right	Left
C₁ =		

PRESSURE IN daPa

Answers for Figure 7-18

1. The flat audiometric configuration might suggest a favorable prognosis as a hearing aid user. However, there is insufficient information to make a good judgment. Information concerning the type of loss, the word recognition scores, the presence or absence of tolerance problems, and the motivation of the client is needed.

2. Without information concerning word recognition and tolerance of the two ears, a decision cannot be made about which ear is more suitable for amplification or whether binaural amplification should be considered.

QUESTIONS FOR FIGURE 7-19

Supplementary Information This client is the same one presented in Figure 7-18.
Case History Information This man reported symptoms of dizziness (vertigo), ringing in the ears (tinnitus), and being bothered by loud sounds (possible recruitment). He has been diagnosed by an otologist as having a sensorineural hearing loss and has been referred for trial of hearing aids.

1. Would you expect this man to have a favorable prognosis as a hearing aid user?
2. With which ear should this man attempt to utilize a hearing aid?

Name: Fig 7-19 Date: XX/XX/XX Age: 50 Sex: M Audiologist: HK

AUDIOMETER: GSI-10 ANSI 1969

PURE TONE AUDIOGRAM
FREQUENCY IN HERTZ

HEARING LEVEL IN DECIBELS (dB)

Air Conduction: R L R L R L R L R L R L R L

Bone Conduction

Plateau levels of masking in non-test ear

Ref.: SPL _____ EFF _____ Signal: NBN _____ White _____

TYMPANOGRAM

COMPLIANCE

PRESSURE IN daPa

Static Compliance:

R	
	cc
2	
1	

L	
	cc
2	
1	

Normal: .3 - 1.75cc

Ear Canal Volume

	Right	Left
C₁ =		

Response Consistency: (good) moderate poor

LEGEND

		Right (red)	Left (blue)
Air:	Unmasked	O	X
	Masked	△	◻
Bone:	Unmasked	<	>
	Masked	◻	◻

No Response ↓
Best Bone ◻
Sound Field S
Aided Sound Field A
Narrow Band Noise
Warble Tone

PURE TONE AVERAGE (R L)			
	Right	Left	Aided
AIR	38	43	
BONE			

SPEECH AUDIOMETRY MLV Tape

	RIGHT	LEFT	MASK LEVEL R L	SOUND FIELD	LIST
SAT					CID W22
SRT	40	46		42	
MCL	60	63			
UCL	72	70			
PB% (Word)	68 30SL	52 30SL			1A 2A
PB% (Word)	_L	_L		18 50dB	1B
PB% (Word)	_L	_L			
PB% (Word)	_L	_L			
	_L	_L			
	_L	_L			

STAPEDIUS REFLEX THRESHOLDS

Stimulus	Contralateral (HL)					Ipsilateral (HL)		
EAR	.5K	1K	2K	4K	WBN	.5K	1K	2K
R	70	75	75	80				X
Decay			X					
L	75	80	80	80				X
Decay			X					

ABBREVIATIONS

A	Absent	NR	No Response
C₁	Canal Volume	SAT	Speech Awareness
CNE	Could Not Establish		Threshold
CNT	Could Not Test	SL	Sensation Level
DNT	Did Not Test	SRT	Speech Reception
HL	Hearing Level		Threshold
MCL	Most Comfortable	UCL	Uncomfortable Listening
	Listening Level		Level
MVL	Monitored Live Voice		

REMARKS:

_____
_____
_____
_____
_____

Educational and Communicative Implications of Hearing Loss

Answers for Figure 7-19

1. The low UCLs and consequent narrow dynamic range of 35 dB and 24 dB in the right and left ears, respectively, suggest a poor prognosis as a hearing aid user. The poor word recognition scores at 30 dB SL suggest that even with amplification the man will have some speech understanding problems. The symptoms reported along with the audiometric finding suggest the presence of Ménière's disease (endolymphatic hydrops). Persons with Ménière's disease generally have more difficulty adjusting to hearing aids than those with many other types of sensorineural losses because tinnitus and tolerance problems often complicate a person's ability to use a hearing aid well. Despite the poor prognosis, hearing aids should be tried if the client is motivated to do so.

2. The wider dynamic range in this man's right ear suggests he might better utilize a hearing aid in the right ear than in the left. The differences between word recognition scores could be attributable to chance factors and do not necessarily indicate better understanding in the right ear (see Chapter 4). This client might also consider a trial with binaural amplification.

QUESTIONS FOR FIGURE 7-20

Case History Information This girl has a congenital sensorineural hearing loss. She appears to have essentially normal mental ability but only completed six grades of formal education in a residential school for the deaf. She has never used a wearable hearing aid. Her speech and English language are poor. She is a relatively good speechreader.

1. How would you describe this girl's hearing?
2. How can you explain why the SRT in the left ear is significantly poorer than the pure tone average?
3. Do you feel a personal hearing aid might help this girl?

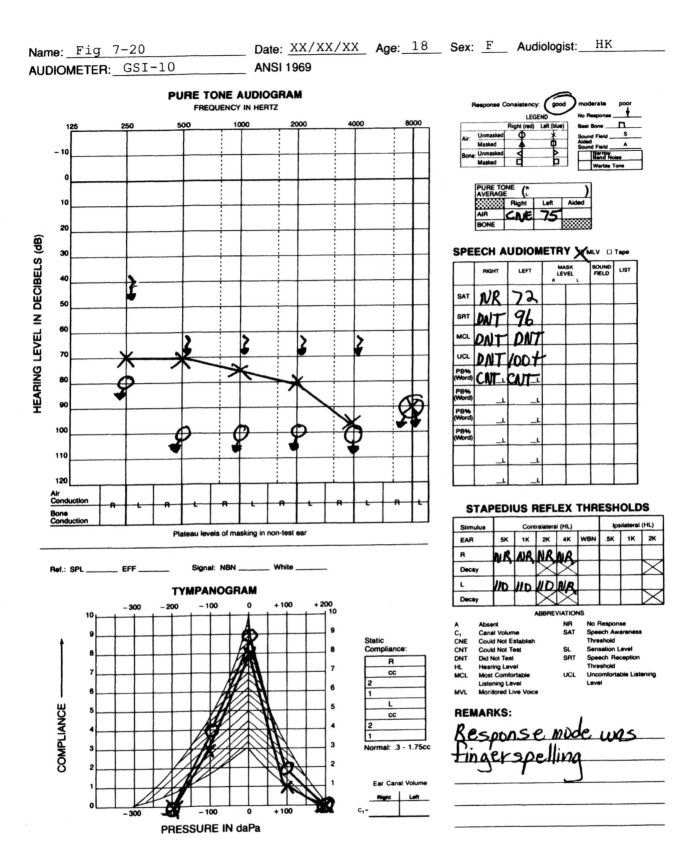

Name: Fig 7-20   Date: XX/XX/XX Age: 18 Sex: F Audiologist: HK
AUDIOMETER: GSI-10   ANSI 1969

PURE TONE AUDIOGRAM
FREQUENCY IN HERTZ

Response Consistency: (good) moderate poor

LEGEND

		Right (red)	Left (blue)
Air:	Unmasked	Φ	×
	Masked	▲	▢
Bone:	Unmasked	◁	▷
	Masked	▢	▢

No Response ↓
Best Bone ▢
Sound Field S
Aided
Sound Field A
Narrow Band Noise
Warble Tone

PURE TONE AVERAGE (R / L)

	Right	Left	Aided
AIR	CNE	75	
BONE			

SPEECH AUDIOMETRY ☒ MLV ☐ Tape

	RIGHT	LEFT	MASK LEVEL R	L	SOUND FIELD	LIST
SAT	NR	72				
SRT	DNT	96				
MCL	DNT	DNT				
UCL	DNT	100+				
PB% (Word)	CNT	CNT				
PB% (Word)	_	_				
PB% (Word)	_	_				
PB% (Word)	_	_				
	_	_				
	_	_				

STAPEDIUS REFLEX THRESHOLDS

Stimulus	Contralateral (HL)					Ipsilateral (HL)		
EAR	.5K	1K	2K	4K	WBN	.5K	1K	2K
R	NR	NR	NR	NR				
Decay								
L	110	110	110	NR				
Decay								

ABBREVIATIONS

A	Absent	NR	No Response
C_1	Canal Volume	SAT	Speech Awareness Threshold
CNE	Could Not Establish		
CNT	Could Not Test	SL	Sensation Level
DNT	Did Not Test	SRT	Speech Reception Threshold
HL	Hearing Level		
MCL	Most Comfortable Listening Level	UCL	Uncomfortable Listening Level
MVL	Monitored Live Voice		

Ref.: SPL _____ EFF _____   Signal: NBN _____ White _____

TYMPANOGRAM

PRESSURE IN daPa

Static Compliance:

R	
	cc
2	
1	

L	
	cc
2	
1	

Normal: .3 - 1.75cc

Ear Canal Volume

	Right	Left
C_1 =		

REMARKS:
Response mode was fingerspelling

Educational and Communicative Implications of Hearing Loss

365

Answers for Figure 7-20

1. This girl has a severe to profound sensorineural hearing loss in the left ear with no responses in the right.

2. This girl's SRT may be depressed because of her general English language retardation or very poor word recognition. It may also be depressed because she does not normally use her hearing in communication. It should be noted that her SAT is in general agreement with her pure tone average. Many times, people with profound congenital hearing losses produce results such as this, where the SAT is in better agreement with the pure tone average than the SRT.

3. This girl may not benefit from a hearing aid in the same way many deaf or hard-of-hearing people would, but she may be able to derive some benefit. The use of amplification in conjunction with auditory training might allow her to recognize environmental sounds and use prosodic features such as stress and inflection to help understand speech. It is also possible that she could learn to interpret auditorally some of the phonemes of speech, particularly the vowels. Even such limited use of a hearing aid would depend upon motivational factors. In all probability, however, she would primarily depend on the visual channel for receptive communication.

QUESTIONS FOR FIGURE 7-21

1. Would you expect this woman to have a favorable prognosis as a hearing aid user?
2. With which ear should she attempt to use a hearing aid?

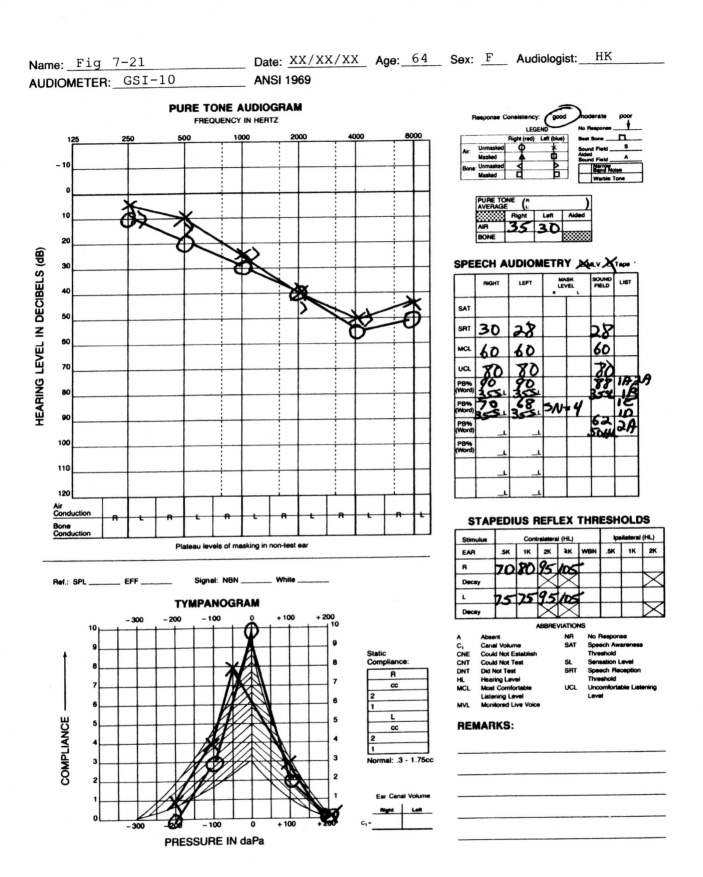

Answers for Figure 7-21

1. Speech audiometry indicates that this woman may receive considerable benefit from a hearing aid. The word recognition scores at 35 dB SL suggest that she has fairly good speech understanding ability if speech is sufficiently loud. Her word recognition scores in competing noise are moderately good. Even though this woman's SRTs may be considered borderline for hearing aid use, many clients with mild hearing losses benefit considerably from properly fitted hearing aids.
2. This woman could probably use a hearing aid equally well in either ear. Since the unaided pure tone and speech audiometry scores, including word recognition in noise, are similar, binaural amplification should be considered.

QUESTIONS FOR FIGURE 7-22

Case History Information This young man was referred by the Division of Vocational Rehabilitation for a hearing aid evaluation. The examining otologist has diagnosed his impairment as sensorineural and has recommended that he be considered for binaural amplification. During the interview the young man expressed no strong feelings about the type of hearing aid he preferred.

1. On what basis do you think the otologist may have recommended binaural hearing aids?
2. Would binaural amplification be advisable for this young man?
3. Which ear do you feel should be fitted?

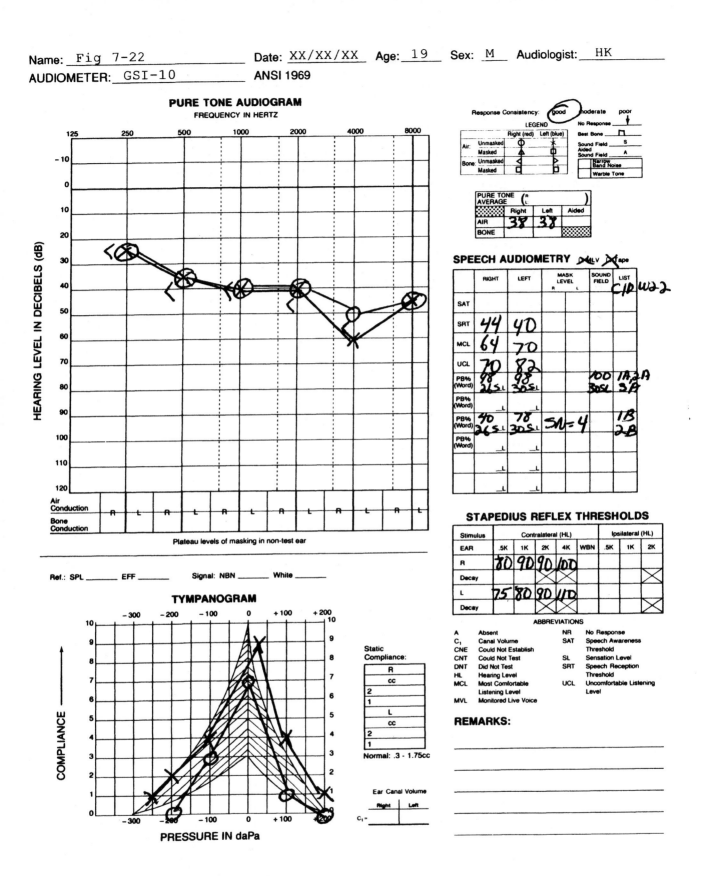

Answers for Figure 7-22

1. Binaural amplification was probably recommended because the pure tone audiogram suggests that hearing in the two ears is very similar.
2. Speech audiometry indicates this man's ears are not functioning as similarly as the pure tone tests would suggest. The UCL in the left ear is significantly higher than the UCL in the right. Although word recognition in quiet is good in both ears, understanding in noise is considerably better in the left ear. Binaural amplification can be tried but might prove to be unsatisfactory.
3. The left ear would be the preferred ear for amplification because of the wider dynamic range and the better speech understanding in noise.

QUESTIONS FOR FIGURE 7-23

1. Would a wearable hearing aid benefit this woman?
2. With which ear should this woman attempt to use a hearing aid?

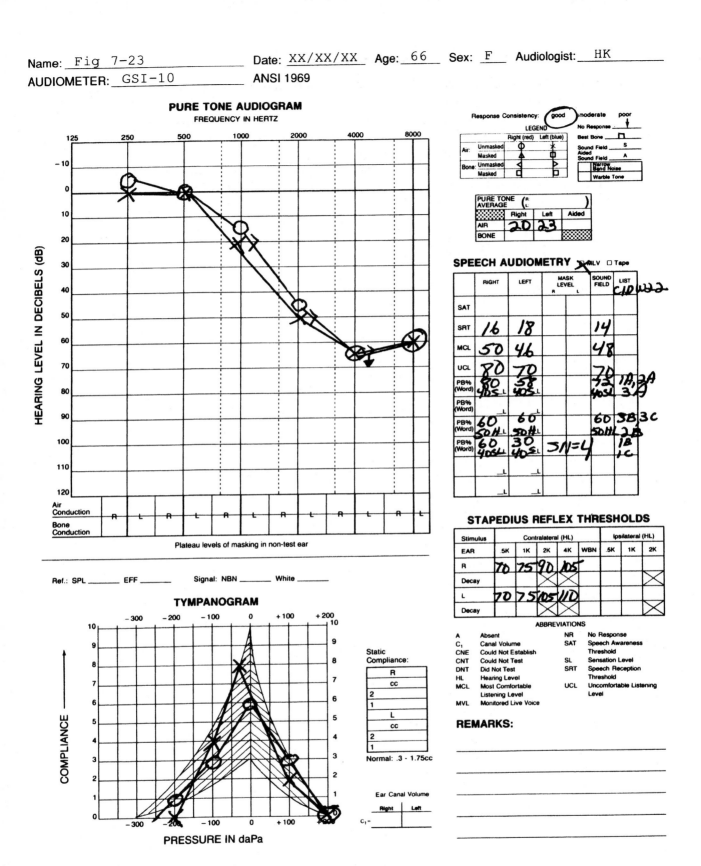

PURE TONE AUDIOGRAM
FREQUENCY IN HERTZ

Name: Fig 7-23   Date: XX/XX/XX   Age: 66   Sex: F   Audiologist: HK
AUDIOMETER: GSI-10   ANSI 1969

Response Consistency: (good) moderate poor

LEGEND

		Right (red)	Left (blue)
Air:	Unmasked	○	×
	Masked	▲	▯
Bone:	Unmasked	◁	▷
	Masked	▭	▯

No Response
Best Bone
Sound Field ___ S
Aided
Sound Field ___ A
Narrow Band Noise
Warble Tone

PURE TONE AVERAGE (R / L)

	Right	Left	Aided
AIR	20	23	
BONE			

SPEECH AUDIOMETRY ☒ MLV ☐ Tape

	RIGHT	LEFT	MASK LEVEL R	L	SOUND FIELD	LIST
SAT						CID W22
SRT	16	18			14	
MCL	50	46			48	
UCL	80	70			70	1A,2A
PB% (Word)	80 40SL	58 40SL			52 40SL	3A
PB% (Word)						
PB% (Word)	60 50HL	60 50HL			60 50HL	3B,3C 2B
PB% (Word)	60 40SL	30 40SL	SN=4			1B 1C

STAPEDIUS REFLEX THRESHOLDS

Stimulus	Contralateral (HL)					Ipsilateral (HL)		
EAR	.5K	1K	2K	4K	WBN	.5K	1K	2K
R	70	75	90	105				
Decay								
L	70	75	105	110				
Decay								

ABBREVIATIONS

A	Absent	NR	No Response
C_1	Canal Volume	SAT	Speech Awareness
CNE	Could Not Establish		Threshold
CNT	Could Not Test	SL	Sensation Level
DNT	Did Not Test	SRT	Speech Reception
HL	Hearing Level		Threshold
MCL	Most Comfortable	UCL	Uncomfortable Listening
	Listening Level		Level
MVL	Monitored Live Voice		

Plateau levels of masking in non-test ear

Ref.: SPL _____ EFF _____   Signal: NBN _____ White _____

TYMPANOGRAM

PRESSURE IN daPa

Static Compliance:

R	
	cc
2	
1	

L	
	cc
2	
1	

Normal: .3 - 1.75cc

Ear Canal Volume

Right	Left

C_1 = _____

REMARKS:

_____

_____

_____

_____

Educational and Communicative Implications of Hearing Loss

Answers for Figure 7-23

1. Word recognition scores at average conversational level (50 dB HL) were 60% in each ear. When the presentation level of the words was increased to 40 dB SL (56 dB and 58 dB HL in the right and left ears, respectively), word recognition improved considerably in the right ear but not in the left. The increase in the right ear score with an increase in presentation level suggests that this woman would be able to benefit from a hearing aid.

2. The higher word recognition scores in quiet and noise and the greater dynamic range for the right ear suggest that this woman would be able to more effectively use an aid in her right ear.

QUESTIONS FOR FIGURE 7-24

1. Would a personal hearing aid benefit this man?
2. Which ear is the better ear?

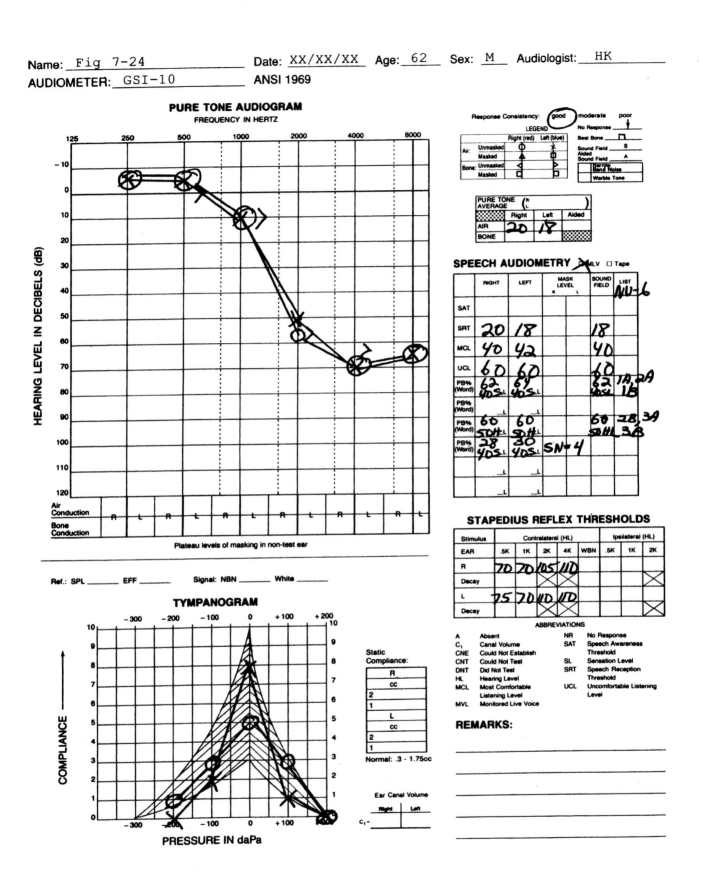

1. The lack of significant increase in the word recognition score with an increase in the presentation level suggests that this man would not benefit from a hearing aid. Note that the client in Figure 7-23 has a similar hearing loss but does show a significant increase in speech understanding with an increase in the presentation level of the words. The low UCLs in both ears and the very poor speech understanding in noise contribute to the poor prognosis for success with amplification. However, before a definite recommendation that this man not consider the purchase of a hearing aid is made, he should be evaluated with several high-frequency response instruments. Assistive listening devices should be considered for specific difficult communication situations such as the theatre or the telephone.

2. All the speech audiometric measures are the same for the two ears. There is no better ear. This man may be able to use binaural amplification or a hearing aid in either ear, if he becomes a hearing aid user.

QUESTIONS FOR FIGURE 7-25

Case History Information This child developed her hearing loss as a result of meningitis six months before the audiological evaluation. Prior to the illness, she had been developing speech and language normally.

1. Is this girl a candidate for amplification?
2. Which ear would you fit?

Name: Fig 7-25   Date: XX/XX/XX   Age: 2-6   Sex: F   Audiologist: BP
AUDIOMETER: GSI-10   ANSI 1969

PURE TONE AUDIOGRAM
FREQUENCY IN HERTZ

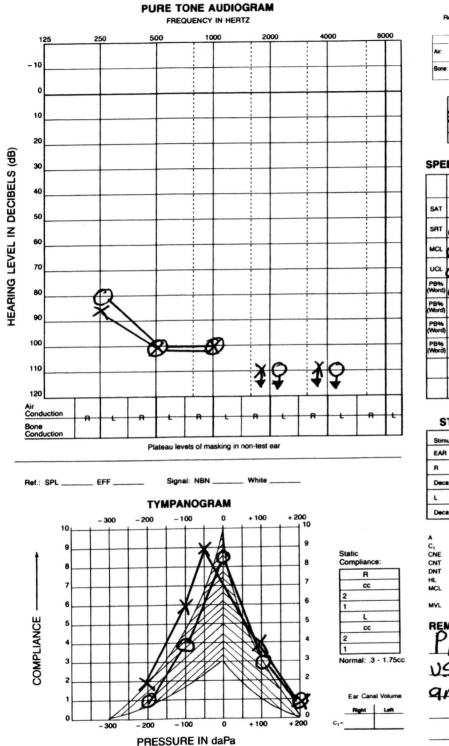

Air
Conduction
Bone
Conduction

Plateau levels of masking in non-test ear

Ref.: SPL _____ EFF _____   Signal: NBN _____ White _____

TYMPANOGRAM

Static
Compliance:

R
cc
2
1

L
cc
2
1

Normal: .3 - 1.75cc

Ear Canal Volume

	Right	Left
C₁=		

PRESSURE IN daPa

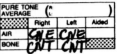

Response Consistency: (good) moderate poor

LEGEND

		Right (red)	Left (blue)
Air:	Unmasked	O	X
	Masked	▲	☐
Bone:	Unmasked	<	>
	Masked	☐	☐

No Response
Best Bone
Sound Field   S
Aided
Sound Field   A
Narrow Band Noise
Warble Tone

PURE TONE AVERAGE	(R: L:)		
	Right	Left	Aided
AIR	CNE	CNE	
BONE	CNT	CNT	

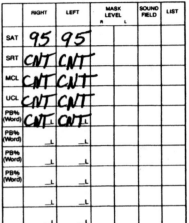

SPEECH AUDIOMETRY ☐ MLV ☐ Tape

	RIGHT	LEFT	MASK LEVEL R	MASK LEVEL L	SOUND FIELD	LIST
SAT	95	95				
SRT	CNT	CNT				
MCL	CNT	CNT				
UCL	CNT	CNT				
PB% (Word)	CNT	CNT				
PB% (Word)						
PB% (Word)						
PB% (Word)						

STAPEDIUS REFLEX THRESHOLDS

Stimulus	Contralateral (HL)					Ipsilateral (HL)		
EAR	.5K	1K	2K	4K	WBN	.5K	1K	2K
R	NR	NR	NR	NR				
Decay								
L	NR	NR	NR	NR				
Decay								

ABBREVIATIONS

A	Absent	NR	No Response
C₁	Canal Volume	SAT	Speech Awareness
CNE	Could Not Establish		Threshold
CNT	Could Not Test	SL	Sensation Level
DNT	Did Not Test	SRT	Speech Reception
HL	Hearing Level		Threshold
MCL	Most Comfortable	UCL	Uncomfortable Listening
	Listening Level		Level
MVL	Monitored Live Voice		

REMARKS:

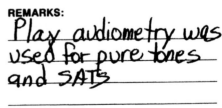

Play audiometry was
used for pure tones
and SATs

Answers for Figure 7-25

1. Even though this girl's audiogram shows minimal residual hearing, she should be fitted with amplification as soon as possible. Prompt fitting of hearing aids may help to prevent deterioration of the speech and language which was present before the illness. Hearing aids may provide awareness of environmental sound and some speech cues to help with her communication, regardless of which communication methodology is used for her education. In addition, she may have more residual hearing than is apparent on the audiogram; recovery of the hearing from the effects of the illness may not be complete.

2. Since the hearing in both ears appears to be similar, she should be fitted with binaural amplification.

QUESTIONS FOR FIGURE 7-26

Case History Information The parents of this child have suspected a hearing problem for approximately one month. Prior to that time, the boy was developing speech and language normally. They have not visited a physician.

1. Is this child a candidate for amplification?
2. Which ear would you fit?

Name: Fig 7-26   Date: XX/XX/XX Age: 2   Sex: M   Audiologist: HK

AUDIOMETER: GSI-10   ANSI 1969

PURE TONE AUDIOGRAM
FREQUENCY IN HERTZ

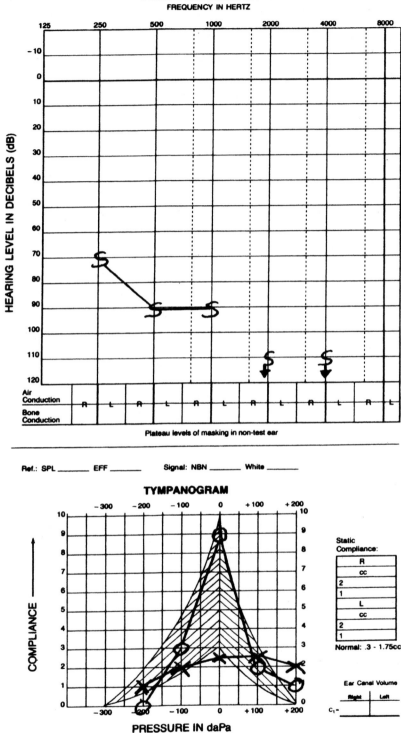

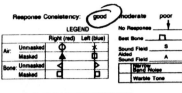

Response Consistency:	(good)	moderate	poor

LEGEND

		Right (red)	Left (blue)
Air	Unmasked	O	X
	Masked	▲	▤
Bone	Unmasked	◁	▷
	Masked	◻	◻

No Response
Best Bone
Sound Field S
Aided
Sound Field A
Narrow Band Noise
Warble Tone

PURE TONE AVERAGE (R: / L:)			
	Right	Left	Aided
AIR			
BONE			

SPEECH AUDIOMETRY ☒ MLV ☐ Tape

	RIGHT	LEFT	MASK LEVEL R	L	SOUND FIELD	LIST
SAT	CNT	CNT			75	
SRT	CNT	CNT				
MCL	CNT	CNT				
UCL	CNT	CNT				
PB% (Word)	CNT	CNT				
PB% (Word)	L	L				
PB% (Word)	L	L				
PB% (Word)	L	L				
	L	L				
	L	L				

STAPEDIUS REFLEX THRESHOLDS

Stimulus	Contralateral (HL)					Ipsilateral (HL)		
EAR	.5K	1K	2K	4K	WBN	.5K	1K	2K
R	NR	NR	NR	NR				
Decay				✕			✕	
L	NR	NR	NR	NR				
Decay				✕			✕	

ABBREVIATIONS

A	Absent	NR	No Response
C₁	Canal Volume	SAT	Speech Awareness
CNE	Could Not Establish		Threshold
CNT	Could Not Test	SL	Sensation Level
DNT	Did Not Test	SRT	Speech Reception
HL	Hearing Level		Threshold
MCL	Most Comfortable	UCL	Uncomfortable Listening
	Listening Level		Level
MVL	Monitored Live Voice		

REMARKS:

COR was used for pure tones and SAT

Ref.: SPL _____ EFF _____   Signal: NBN _____ White _____

TYMPANOGRAM

Static Compliance:

R	
	cc
2	
1	

L	
	cc
2	
1	

Normal: .3 - 1.75cc

Ear Canal Volume

Right	Left
C₁ =	

Plateau levels of masking in non-test ear

Answers for Figure 7-26

1. This child is not a candidate for amplification at present. The tympanogram indicates a middle ear problem, probably otitis media, in the left ear. The child should be referred to an otolaryngologist for evaluation and treatment before anything else is done. It is possible that after medical treatment, there may be only a mild loss in the left ear. Since the sound field scores represent the hearing of the better ear, we have no way of knowing which ear they represent. This boy should receive an audiological evaluation after medical intervention is completed, and at that time decisions concerning amplification should be made.

2. A decision as to which ear to fit cannot be made at this time because of the unresolved medical condition.

QUESTION FOR FIGURE 7-27

Case History Information This client became deaf at age 20 as a result of an automobile accident. She communicates with difficulty, using speechreading and writing; a hearing aid used in the right ear gives her awareness of sound but no speech understanding. She is highly motivated to undergo cochlear implant surgery and participate in follow-up training.

1. Is this client a suitable candidate for a cochlear implant? Why?

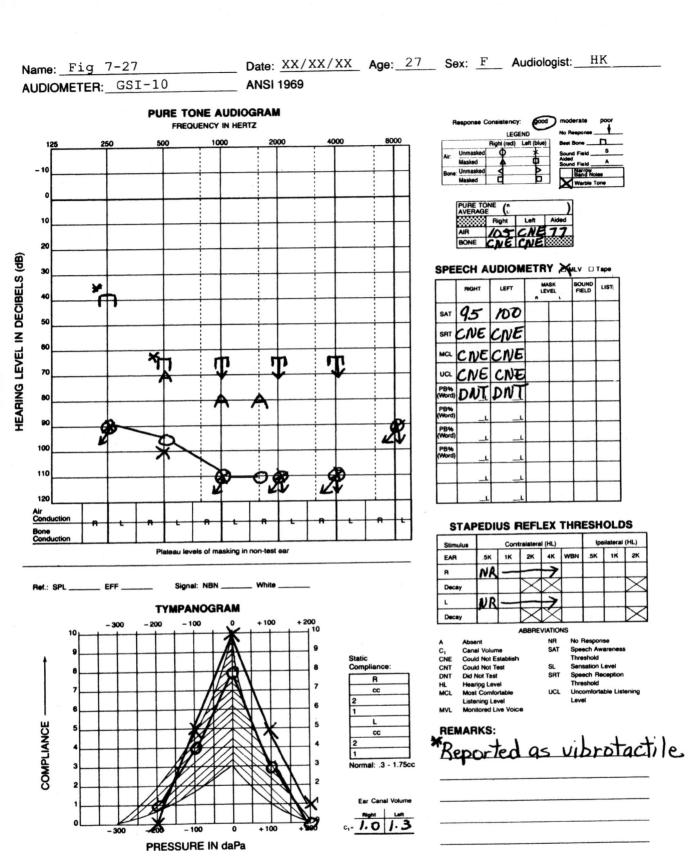

Name: Fig 7-27   Date: XX/XX/XX Age: 27 Sex: F Audiologist: HK
AUDIOMETER: GSI-10   ANSI 1969

PURE TONE AUDIOGRAM
FREQUENCY IN HERTZ

Response Consistency: good moderate poor

LEGEND

		Right (red)	Left (blue)
Air:	Unmasked	O	X
	Masked	▲	☐
Bone:	Unmasked	◁	▷
	Masked	◱	◲

No Response
Best Bone
Sound Field ___ S
Aided
Sound Field ___ A
Narrow Band Noise
Warble Tone

PURE TONE AVERAGE (R / L)

	Right	Left	Aided
AIR	105	CNE	77
BONE	CNE	CNE	

SPEECH AUDIOMETRY ☒MLV ☐Tape

	RIGHT	LEFT	MASK LEVEL R	L	SOUND FIELD	LIST
SAT	95	100				
SRT	CNE	CNE				
MCL	CNE	CNE				
UCL	CNE	CNE				
PB% (Word)	DNT	DNT				
PB% (Word)	_L_	_L_				
PB% (Word)	_L_	_L_				
PB% (Word)	_L_	_L_				
	_L_	_L_				
	_L_	_L_				

Air Conduction
Bone Conduction

Plateau levels of masking in non-test ear

STAPEDIUS REFLEX THRESHOLDS

Stimulus	Contralateral (HL)					Ipsilateral (HL)		
EAR	.5K	1K	2K	4K	WBN	.5K	1K	2K
R	NR →							
Decay								
L	NR →							
Decay								

ABBREVIATIONS

A	Absent	NR	No Response
C₁	Canal Volume	SAT	Speech Awareness
CNE	Could Not Establish		Threshold
CNT	Could Not Test	SL	Sensation Level
DNT	Did Not Test	SRT	Speech Reception
HL	Hearing Level		Threshold
MCL	Most Comfortable	UCL	Uncomfortable Listening
	Listening Level		Level
MVL	Monitored Live Voice		

Ref.: SPL ___ EFF ___   Signal: NBN ___ White ___

TYMPANOGRAM

PRESSURE IN daPa

Static Compliance:

R	
	cc
2	
1	
L	
	cc
2	
1	

Normal: .3 - 1.75cc

Ear Canal Volume

	Right	Left
C₁ -	1.0	1.3

REMARKS:

*Reported as vibrotactile.

Answer for Figure 7-27

1. Based on case history and audiometric information, this client is an excellent candidate for a cochlear implant. First, she is postlingually deaf and has not become part of the deaf community (she does not use sign language). Second, she is highly motivated to undergo implant surgery and follow-up therapy. Third, there are no medical contraindications. Fourth, she meets the audiometric criteria in the following ways:
   a. Pure tone thresholds in the better ear are between 90 and 110 dB HL.
   b. Bone conduction, tympanometry and the absence of acoustic reflexes indicate sensorineural hearing loss.
   c. There is no evidence of speech understanding through audition (SRTs could not be measured).
   d. Aided warble tone thresholds are well below 60 dB.

QUESTION FOR FIGURE 7-28

Case History Information This 3½ year old child has been deaf since recovering from meningitis at 13 months of age. There is no history of middle ear infection or other medical problems. He is enrolled in a total communication preschool program which has a strong auditory–oral component. Although he is learning language at a good pace, he is not using voice. With his hearing aid, he demonstrates awareness of loud environmental sound but not speech. The parents understand the benefits and limitations of cochlear implants and have arranged for follow-up training in the child's preschool program.

1. Is this child a good candidate for a cochlear implant? Why?

Name: Fig 7-28   Date: XX/XX/XX   Age: 3.6   Sex: M   Audiologist: HK
AUDIOMETER: GSI-10   ANSI 1969

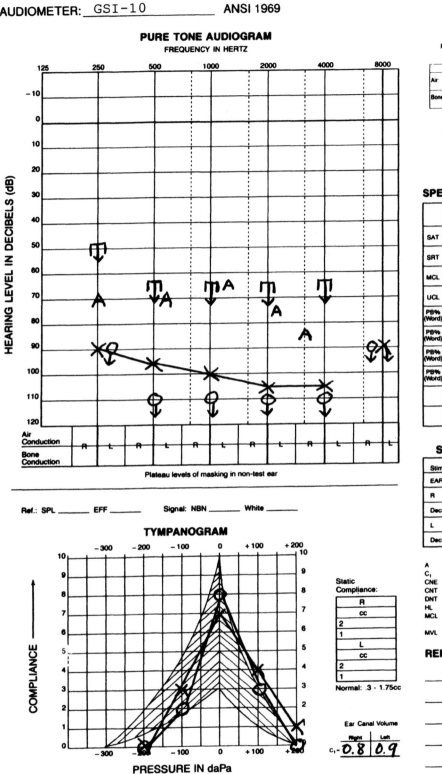

PURE TONE AUDIOGRAM
FREQUENCY IN HERTZ

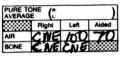

Response Consistency: (good) moderate poor

LEGEND

		Right (red)	Left (blue)	No Response
Air	Unmasked	○	X	Best Bone □
	Masked	▲	▢	Sound Field S
Bone	Unmasked	◁	▷	Aided
	Masked	▢	▢	Sound Field A

Narrow Band Noise
⊠ Warble Tone

PURE TONE AVERAGE (R: / L:)

	Right	Left	Aided
AIR	CNE 100	70	
BONE	CNE	CNE	

SPEECH AUDIOMETRY ⊠MLV ☐ Tape

	RIGHT	LEFT	MASK LEVEL R	L	SOUND FIELD	LIST
SAT	CNE	90				
SRT	CNE	CNE				
MCL	CNE	CNE				
UCL	CNE	CNE				
PB% (Word)	DNT	DNT				
PB% (Word)	L	L				
PB% (Word)	L	L				
PB% (Word)	L	L				
	L	L				
	L	L				

STAPEDIUS REFLEX THRESHOLDS

Stimulus	Contralateral (HL)					Ipsilateral (HL)		
EAR	.5K	1K	2K	4K	WBN	.5K	1K	2K
R	NR →							⊠
Decay		⊠	⊠	⊠				
L	NR →							⊠
Decay		⊠	⊠	⊠				

ABBREVIATIONS

A	Absent	NR	No Response
C₁	Canal Volume	SAT	Speech Awareness
CNE	Could Not Establish		Threshold
CNT	Could Not Test	SL	Sensation Level
DNT	Did Not Test	SRT	Speech Reception
HL	Hearing Level		Threshold
MCL	Most Comfortable	UCL	Uncomfortable Listening
	Listening Level		Level
MVL	Monitored Live Voice		

Ref.: SPL _____ EFF _____   Signal: NBN _____ White _____

TYMPANOGRAM

Static Compliance:

R	
	cc
2	
1	
L	
	cc
2	
1	

Normal: .3 - 1.75cc

Ear Canal Volume

Right	Left
C₁ 0.8	0.9

REMARKS:

_____
_____
_____
_____
_____

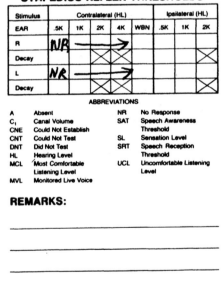

Answer for Figure 7-28

1. This child seems to be an excellent candidate for a cochlear implant. The right ear does not respond to pure tones at any frequency. Although there are pure tone responses in the left ear between 90 and 105 dB at all frequencies, a hearing aid does not allow him to hear speech at average conversational level. There is no evidence of speech understanding through audition. Tympanograms and ear canal volume data indicate normal middle ear function.

    The family has realistic expectations about the benefits and limitations of implantation. The child is already enrolled in a suitable preschool program which will assume responsibility for follow-up training with the cochlear implant.

QUESTION FOR FIGURE 7-29

Case History Information This 8-year-old child was born with a mild to moderate bilateral sensorineural hearing loss of genetic origin. It has been progressive, but thresholds have remained stable for the past three years.

He wears binaural behind-the-ear hearing aids which give him some ability to understand speech, especially when he is able to speechread (see audiogram). Educationally, he is mainstreamed with a sign language interpreter and is functioning academically at age level. The parents are interested in a cochlear implant.

1. Is this child a candidate for cochlear implant? Why?

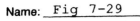

Name: Fig 7-29   Date: XX/XX/XX Age: 8.0 Sex: M Audiologist: HK
AUDIOMETER: GSI-10   ANSI 1969

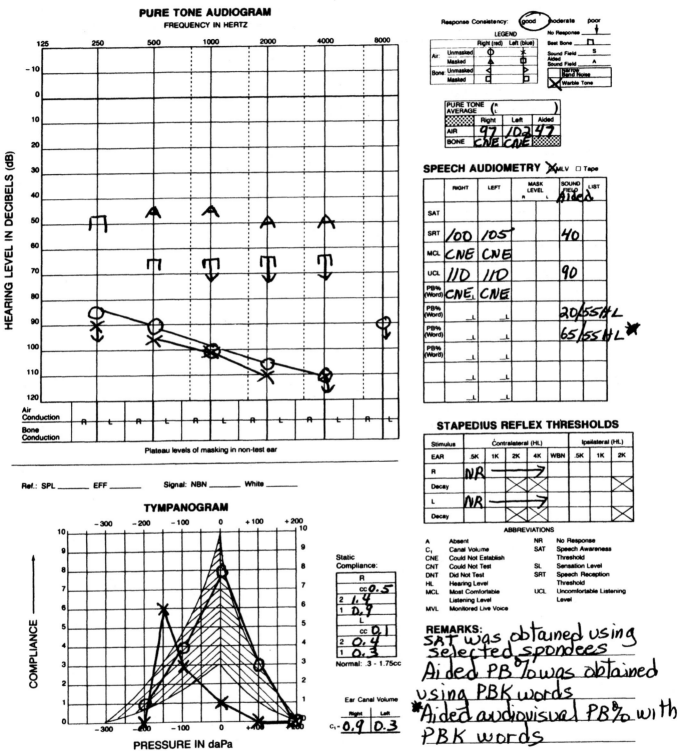

Answer for Figure 7-29

1. This child is not a good candidate for a cochlear implant. Although his pure tone thresholds are in the severe to profound range, he functions too well with binaural amplification to warrant implantation. He is able to hear and understand speech at average conversational level through audition alone, and audiovisually, he is able to understand two-thirds of a list of single-syllable words.

   Furthermore, the left ear tympanogram and static compliance data suggest some middle ear problem in the left ear. It is possible that medical intervention could result in improved hearing and better audiovisual functioning.

   Cochlear implants are indicated only when there is no usable residual hearing. That is not the case with this child.

QUESTION FOR FIGURE 7-30

Case History Information This 16-year-old girl has had a profound bilateral sensorineural hearing loss since birth, due to maternal rubella. Educationally, she has attended total communication day classes in her local public school and is now mainstreamed with a sign language interpreter. She signs fluently and has partially intelligible speech. Her parents want her to have cochlear implant surgery, but she is not interested.

1. Is she a good candidate for a cochlear implant? Why?

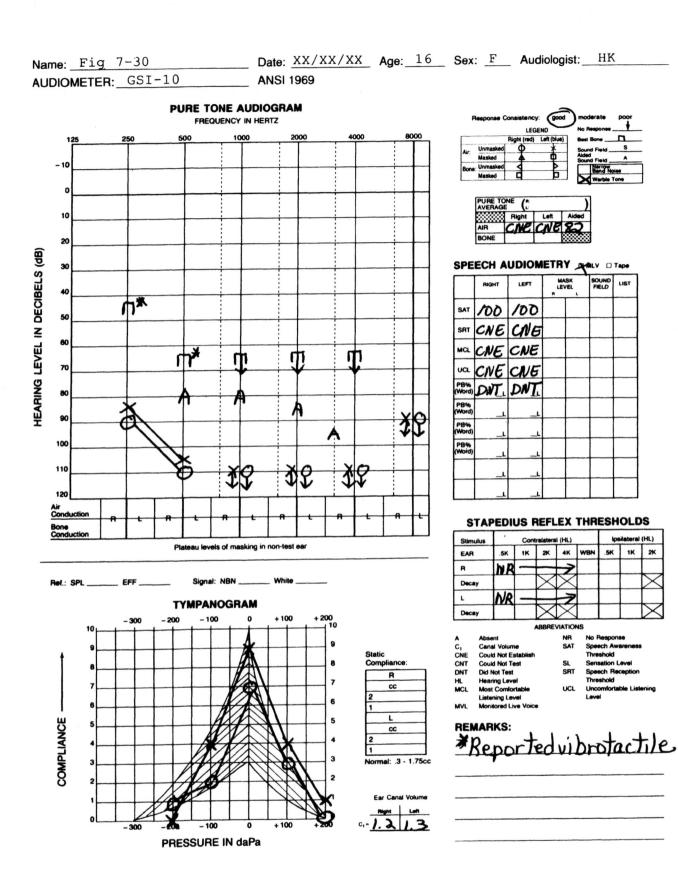

Name: Fig 7-30   Date: XX/XX/XX   Age: 16   Sex: F   Audiologist: HK
AUDIOMETER: GSI-10   ANSI 1969

PURE TONE AUDIOGRAM
FREQUENCY IN HERTZ

HEARING LEVEL IN DECIBELS (dB)

Response Consistency: good moderate poor

LEGEND

		Right (red)	Left (blue)
Air	Unmasked	○	✗
	Masked	△	◻
Bone	Unmasked	<	>
	Masked	◻	◻

No Response
Best Bone
Sound Field S
Aided
Sound Field A
Narrow Band Noise
Warble Tone

PURE TONE AVERAGE (R: L:)	Right	Left	Aided
AIR	CNE	CNE	85
BONE			

SPEECH AUDIOMETRY ☑ MLV ☐ Tape

	RIGHT	LEFT	MASK LEVEL R	L	SOUND FIELD	LIST
SAT	100	100				
SRT	CNE	CNE				
MCL	CNE	CNE				
UCL	CNE	CNE				
PB% (Word)	DNT	DNT				
PB% (Word)						
PB% (Word)						
PB% (Word)						

STAPEDIUS REFLEX THRESHOLDS

Stimulus	Contralateral (HL)					Ipsilateral (HL)		
EAR	.5K	1K	2K	4K	WBN	.5K	1K	2K
R	NR →							
Decay								
L	NR →							
Decay								

ABBREVIATIONS

A	Absent	NR	No Response
C_1	Canal Volume	SAT	Speech Awareness
CNE	Could Not Establish		Threshold
CNT	Could Not Test	SL	Sensation Level
DNT	Did Not Test	SRT	Speech Reception
HL	Hearing Level		Threshold
MCL	Most Comfortable	UCL	Uncomfortable Listening
	Listening Level		Level
MVL	Monitored Live Voice		

Ref.: SPL _____ EFF _____   Signal: NBN _____ White _____

TYMPANOGRAM

PRESSURE IN daPa
COMPLIANCE

Static Compliance:

R	
	cc
2	
1	

L	
	cc
2	
1	

Normal: .3 - 1.75cc

Ear Canal Volume

	Right	Left
C_1=	1.2	1.3

REMARKS:

✳ Reported vibrotactile

Plateau levels of masking in non-test ear

Answer for Figure 7-30

1. This girl is not a good candidate for a cochlear implant, despite the fact that she is suitable audiometrically. She has become a part of the manually communicating deaf community and seems to be comfortable with her deafness. Since she is not motivated to have the surgery, it is questionable how well she will use the implant after surgery. At age 16, she is old enough to make her own decisions concerning mode of communication and cultural identity.

REVIEW AND SEARCH PROJECTS

1. Explain why a child with a moderate sensorineural loss might have a language problem.

2. Explain why a child with a chronic conductive problem might have a language problem.

3. A 3-year-old child who has not yet begun to talk is brought to you for examination. Before you see the child, what possible etiologies can you think of for this child's communication problem?

4. Describe how it is possible for a deaf child to have "communication" and "language" but not have "speech."

5. Briefly describe possible reasons for two children having identical pure tone audiograms to have developed considerably different speech and language abilities.

6. Make a chart illustrating the auditory servo system for speech.

7. Observe the communication of several young children (between 4 and 8 years) with hearing impairments greater than 30 dB in the speech range. What do you notice about their language as compared to normal-hearing children of the same age?

8. List the similarities and differences in verbal communication of a 14-year-old child with a profound hearing loss incurred at the age of one year and that of a 14-year-old whose hearing loss incurred at the age of 12 years.

9. Interview an adult with a hearing problem. What is the person's major problem as a result of the hearing impairment?

10. List several behavioral signs of hearing impairment in children, several behavioral signs of mental retardation, and several behavioral signs common to both problems.

11. Write an account of how you would explain to the parents of the child whose audiogram is shown in Figure 7-2 why their child "hears sometimes but not at other times." The parents have told you that they think the child doesn't pay attention and hears only what she wants to hear.

12. Discuss the differences between personal hearing aids and auditory training units.

13. Cite research supporting and questioning the use of binaural hearing aids.

14. Discuss in order of importance the criteria used in the selection of the appropriate ear for a hearing aid.

15. Discuss the advantages and disadvantages of the behind-the-ear and the in-the-ear hearing aid.

16. Prepare a short presentation that could be given to a group of public school speech–language pathologists, describing compression amplification, directional microphones, and direct auditory input.

17. Prepare a short talk on hearing aid orientation for non-audiologists, including a demonstration on the use of the hearing aid and discussion of common problems.

18. In non-technical terms, explain how the telecoil of a hearing aid works and discuss its benefits.

REFERENCES

Bess, F.H., and Humes, L.E. 1990. *Audiology, The Fundamentals*. Baltimore: Williams & Wilkins.

Bochner, J.H. 1982. English in the deaf population. In D.G. Sims, G.G. Walter, and R.L. Whitehead (Eds.), *Deafness and Communication*. Baltimore: Williams & Wilkins.

Clark, J.G. 1981. Uses and abuses of hearing loss classification. *ASHA* 23:493–500.

Cozad, R.L. 1974. *The Speech Clinician and the Hearing Impaired Child*. Springfield, Ill: Charles C. Thomas.

Davis, J.M., and Hardick, E.J. 1981. *Rehabilitative Audiology for Children and Adults*. New York: J. Wiley & Sons.

Davis, H., and Silverman, S.R. 1978. *Hearing and Deafness*. New York: Holt, Rinehart, and Winston.

Harford, E., and Dodds, E. 1966. The clinical application of CROS. *Archives of Otolaryngology* 83: 455–466.

Hodgson, W.R. (Editor). 1986. *Hearing Aid Assessment and Use in Audiologic Habilitation*. Baltimore: Williams & Wilkins.

Katz, J. (Editor). 1985. *Handbook of Clinical Audiology* Baltimore: Williams & Wilkins.

Ling, D. 1976. *Speech and the Hearing Impaired Child: Theory and Practice*. Washington, D.C.: A.G. Bell Association for the Deaf.

Ling, D., and Ling, A. 1978. *Aural Habilitation*. Washington, D.C.: A.G. Bell Association for the Deaf.

Newby, H.A., and Popelka, G.R. 1985. *Audiology*. Englewood Cliffs, N.J.: Prentice Hall.

Northern, J.L., and Downs, M.P. 1984. *Hearing in Children*. Baltimore: Williams & Wilkins.

Pollack, M. (Editor). 1988. *Amplification for the Hearing Impaired*. Orlando, FL: Grune & Stratton.

Schow, R.L., and Nerbonnne, M.A. 1989. *Inttroduction to Aural Rehabilitation*. Austin: Pro-Ed.

Sims, D.G., Walter, G.G., and Whitehead, R.L. (Editors).

1982. *Deafness and Communication*. Baltimore: Williams & Wilkins.

Templin, M.C., and Darley, F.L. 1960. *The Templin Darley Tests of Articulation*. Iowa City: University of Iowa Bureau of Educational Research and Service.

Chapter 7

Glossary

ABR (auditory brainstem response) an electro-physiological test procedure to evaluate the integrity of the central auditory pathways in the brain stem.

Acoustic mass structures or properties within an acoustic system associated with mass, such as the tympanic membrane and the ossicles.

Acoustic reflex the contraction of the middle ear muscles, primarily the stapedius in humans, in response to an intense acoustic stimulus.

Acoustic reflex decay a diagnostic test for retrocochlear pathology which is positive when the amplitude of the acoustic reflex diminishes by more than one-half its original amplitude in less than 5 seconds under continuous pure tone stimulation.

Acoustic resistance that component of impedance in an acoustic system that is related to friction. Similar to conductance.

Adenoidectomy surgical removal of lymphoid tissue found in the nasopharynx near the opening of the Eustachian tube.

Adhesive otitis media the sequela of chronic middle ear inflammation resulting in the condition of thick, glue-like material in the middle ear. This leads to the development of adhesions or fibrous bands of tissue which firmly fix to the ossicular chain.

Admittance the flow of energy through a system.

Adventitious hearing loss acquired after birth. The term frequently refers to people who became hard-of-hearing or deaf as adults.

Air conduction (AC) pure tones presented to the ear through earphones and transmitted through the outer, middle, and inner ears.

Atelectasis a condition resulting from lack of adequate ventilation of the middle ear, causing severe retraction of the tympanic membrane.

Atrophic tympanic membrane a condition where the eardrum is poorly developed or does not vibrate properly due to damage from disease.

Audiometrically deaf pure tone or speech recognition thresholds greater than 90 dB HL.

Audiometric zero average normal thresholds for a range of frequencies.

Basilar membrane membrane traveling the length of the cochlea on which the hair cells are located.

Bell's Palsy an inflammation of the eighth cranial nerve, characterized by facial paralysis.

Best bone conduction the bone conduction thresholds of the ear with the best bone conduction at each frequency. Unless masking is used, it is possible for the right ear to respond at some frequencies and the left ear at others even though the stimuli are presented to one ear only.

Bone conduction (BC) pure tones presented to the ear through a vibrator placed on the mastoid process behind the ear. Sound bypasses the outer and middle ears, going directly to the inner ear.

Carhart Notch a slight depression in the bone conduction thresholds of patients with otosclerosis, attributable to stapes fixation in the middle ear rather than inner ear problems.

Central hearing loss hearing disorders which occur within the central nervous system (brain stem and temporal lobe cortex).

Central masking a small shift in threshold of the test ear with the introduction of levels of masking noise into the non-test ear that are too low to shift threshold.

Cerumen the dark, bitter-tasting, wax-like substance secreted in the external auditory canal by the ceruminous glands to deter insects and keep the canal skin moist.

Closed message set a test paradigm in which the client is presented with a speech stimulus and has a group of written or pictured options from which to choose.

CNE could not establish.

CNT could not test.

Cochlea the portion of the inner ear housing the end organ of hearing.

Cochlear hearing loss a hearing loss caused by a problem in the inner ear (cochlea).

Cochlear implant amplification system that involves the implantation of an array of electrodes along the basilar membrane of the cochlea. In response to sound, these electrodes stimulate eighth nerve fibers located at the basilar membrane; damaged hair cells are bypassed.

Collapsed canal closure of the ear canal in response to placement of an earphone on the pinna.

Compression a special circuit in a hearing aid which automatically reduces the volume of the hearing aid when sound entering the aid reaches a predetermined level.

Conductance the component of admittance associated with friction. Similar to acoustic resistance.

Conductive loss a hearing loss caused by a problem in the outer or middle ear.

Congenital hearing loss present at birth; may or may not be genetic in origin.

Congenital ossicular fixation a condition, present at birth, where the mobility of the ossicular chain is diminished.

Contralateral reflex stimulation of one ear and recording of the acoustic reflex in the opposite or contralateral ear. Results are reported in terms of the ear stimulated.

CROS hearing aid special type of hearing aid for people with unilateral hearing loss. A microphone is placed on the bad ear to pick up sound on that side of the head; the sound is transmitted via wire or wireless transmission to a mild gain hearing aid on the other ear.

Cross-hearing the ability of a sound to travel from one ear to another by vibrating the bones of the skull.

Culturally deaf people with hearing loss who identify with deaf culture and use American Sign Language as a primary way of communicating.

Deaf hearing loss which is so great that successful processing of auditory information is not possible with or without a hearing aid unless vision is used as a primary communication channel.

Deafened a person, usually an adult, who has been normal hearing or hard of hearing and then becomes deaf.

Decibel a unit which expresses the ratios between two sound pressures. It is used in audiology to express the intensity of a sound.

Diplacusis distortion in the sensation of pitch. A client's two ears may perceive the same frequencies as two different pitches or pure tones may be perceived as noise.

Direct audio input plug-in connection of a microphone or assistive listening device to a hearing aid via a cord and special connector called a "shoe."

Directional microphone a microphone which is more sensitive to sound directly in front than to sound from other directions.

DNT did not test.

Dynamic range the difference in decibels between the client's SRT (or SDT if SRT is not measureable) and UCL. It represents the client's range of usable hearing.

Dysarthria motor involvement of the speech mechanism.

Effective level (effective masking) the softest level of noise required to mask a signal in the same earphone at a given hearing level (HL). On most audiometers, masking noise is calibrated in units of effective masking.

Elastic reactance that component of impedance in an acoustic system that is associated with compliance or springiness.

Equivalent volume a measure expressed in cubic centimeters or milliliters that represents the volume of the ear canal, middle ear or a combination of these two volumes.

Eustachian tube anatomical structure connecting

the nasopharynx to the middle ear. Responsible for equalizing middle ear air pressure and providing for drainage of middle ear mucous secretions.

External auditory meatus the ear canal.

Facial nerve disorder a problem (e.g., facial paralysis) caused by damage to the seventh cranial (facial) nerve.

False negative response failure to respond to a heard sound.

False positive response response in the absence of a stimulus.

Frequency the number of complete oscillations (cycles) a vibrating body completes in a second. In audiology, frequency is described as cycles per second or Hz; the larger the Hz, the higher the frequency. Frequency, in a general way, corresponds to perceived pitch.

Frequency response the amount of amplification a hearing aid or other amplication system provides at each frequency.

Hair cells (of the cochlea) sensory cells containing cilia (hairs) arrayed along the length of the basilar membrane. These cells constitute the end organ of hearing and play a major role in frequency perception.

Hard of hearing sufficient hearing to successfully process linguistic information through aided or unaided audition.

Hearing impaired a generic term including all degrees of hearing loss from mild to profound. Within some segments of the deaf community, the term is synonomous with "hard of hearing".

Hearing level (HL) the number of decibels above average normal threshold for a given signal. The audiometer is calibrated in HL.

Hemotympanum a condition of the middle ear where there is blood in the tympanic cavity.

Hydraulic analog a fluid system that has components or characteristics similar or analogous to another type of system (mechanical) or circuit (electrical).

Hypermobility greater than normal movement. Typically associated with tympanic membrane movement, such as in the case of ossicular discontinuity or monomeric tympanic membrane.

Immittance a generic term that represents energy transfer or the measure of either the opposition to the flow of energy through a system (impedance) or the flow of energy through a system (admittance).

Impedance opposition to the flow of energy through a system.

Impedance matching the ability to equalize impedances of adjoining portions of an electrical circuit or mechanical or hydraulic system.

Inertial opposition the inherent unwillingness of an object or mass to move or be overcome by energy and set into motion.

Insert earphone a small earphone that is inserted into the ear canal rather than placed over the pinna.

Intensity amount of sound energy; the greater the sound energy, the higher the intensity. Intensity, in a general way, corresponds to perceived loudness.

Interaural attenuation the loss of energy to a sound that occurs as it travels from one ear to the other by vibrating the bones of the skull.

Ipsilateral reflex stimulation and recording of the acoustic reflex in the same ear. Results are reported in terms of the ear stimulated.

Juncture the placement of pauses in spoken words or sentences.

Kanamycin an antibiotic medication which is known to be ototoxic. Causes hair cell damage.

Masking the process of placing noise (masker) in the non-test ear to prevent it from participating in the evaluation of the test ear.

Mass reactance that component of impedance in an acoustic system that is associated with mass.

Mastoid process the bony protrusion behind the ear. This is usually the place where the bone conduction vibrator is placed.

Maximum masking the highest level of noise that can be presented to the non-test ear without the noise crossing the skull to shift threshold in the test ear.

Ménière's Syndrome (endolymphatic hydrops) an inner ear disorder characterized by vertigo, tinnitus, and hearing loss. Often the person reports feelings of fullness in the ear.

Middle ear effusion accumulation of fluid in the middle ear.

Minimum effective masking level (also called initial masking) the lowest level of noise (calibrated in effective level) that will mask a pure tone that might appear in the non-test ear because of cross-hearing.

Mixed loss a hearing loss which is partially caused by a problem in the outer or middle ear and by a problem in the inner ear, eighth nerve, or central auditory pathways. It is a combination of conductive and sensorineural problems.

Monomeric tympanic membrane a condition where a portion of the fibrous layer of the tympanic membrane is missing. Usually due to improper healing of the eardrum.

Most comfortable listening level (MCL) the hearing level in decibels (re: audiometric zero) at which the client finds listening most comfortable.

Multichannel (cochlear) implant a cochlear implant system consisting of more than one electrode arrayed along the basilar membrane. The speech processor of the system divides the acoustic components of the speech input to allow different elements of speech to be sent to different electrodes.

Myringotomy surgical opening or incision in the tympanic membrane.

Narrow band noise a noise consisting of a narrow band of frequencies centered around the frequency to be masked.

Neurofibromatosis a genetic condition in which tumors grow on the cranial nerves, particularly the eighth nerve.

Non-organic (functional, psychogenic, malingering, pseudohypacusis, hysterical) deafness hearing loss which is not caused by a physical problem in the auditory system.

NR no response.

Occlusion effect in the absence of conductive hearing loss, an ear which is covered during bone conduction testing will show lowered bone conduction thresholds at 1000 Hz and lower frequencies.

Open message set a test paradigm in which the client is presented with a speech stimulus and does not have written choices or pictures from which to choose. Response choices are almost unlimited.

Organic hearing loss a hearing loss which is caused by a physical problem somewhere in the auditory system.

Ossicular chain the three connected bones of the middle ear: malleus, incus, stapes.

Ossicular discontinuity or disarticulation a condition where there is an interruption in the connections between the ossicles, usually between the incus and stapes.

Otosclerosis a familial disorder in which new bone is deposited in the middle ear, usually around the footplate of the stapes.

Overmasking occurs when the level of masking noise in the non-test ear is too great; it crosses the head to shift threshold in the test ear.

PB Max the highest speech recognition score the client can obtain regardless of presentation level.

Performance-intensity function a graph showing the percentage correct speech recognition as a function of presentation level. Performance-intensity functions can be plotted for word or sentence materials, for individuals or groups.

Peripheral hearing loss hearing disorders occurring outside the central auditory system, in the outer, middle and inner ear or the eighth nerve.

Phonemic features vowel and consonant production.

Phonetically balanced (PB) words lists of 50 single-syllable words used to measure word recognition scores. Each list is supposed to have the same distribution of phonemes as occurs in American connected discourse.

Physical Volume Test a procedure where the volume recorded by the acoustic immittance system indicates a larger equivalent volume than expected of a normal ear canal. This suggests a connection between the ear canal and the middle ear such as is seen with a tympanic membrane perforation or a patent tympanostomy tube.

Plateau a term used in the masking process to indicate that the proper level of masking has been found to eliminate the non-test ear from participating in the evaluation of the test ear. A plateau consists of at least two levels of masking noise at which pure tone or speech scores remain constant.

Post-lingual hearing loss occurred after the development of language.

Pre-lingual hearing loss occurred before the development of language.

Pressure swallow test a measure of Eustachian tube function in the presence of an intact tympanic membrane utilizing the technique of tympanometry as described by Williams (1975).

Prosodic features (suprasegmentals) pitch, intonation, stress, juncture, phrasing, and durational features of speech.

Pure tone average (PTA) the average of the pure tone thresholds obtained at 500, 1000, and 2000 Hz in each ear. It is sometimes called the speech frequency average or the three-frequency average.

Pure tone threshold the softest level a person can hear a tone approximately 50% of the time it is presented. The term refers to both air conduction and bone conduction.

Recruitment a disproportionate increase in loudness sensation with increase in intensity of sound above threshold.

Reflex arc the ipsilateral and contralateral neural pathways which are activated during intense acoustic stimulation. They are mediated in the superior olivary complex of the brainstem. For the ipsilateral pathway, the sensory or afferent neurons of the eighth cranial nerve carry impulses from the cochlea to the ipsilateral ventral cochlear nucleus. Fibers from the ventral cochlear nucleus travel through the trapezoid body of the superior olive to the facial motor nucleus, which sends motor or efferent impulses along the seventh cranial nerve to the ipsilateral stapedius muscle. For the contraleral pathway, the sensory or afferent neurons of the eighth cranial nerve carry impulses from the cochlea to the ipsilateral ventral cochlear nucleus. Fibers from the ventral cochlear nucleus travel to the medial superior olive across to the contralateral facial motor nucleus, which sends motor or efferent impulses along the seventh cranial nerve to the contralateral stapedius muscle.

Response consistency responding correctly whenever sound is presented.

Retrochochlear hearing loss a hearing loss caused by a problem in the eighth nerve or central auditory pathways.

Rollover a word recognition pattern which is suggestive of retrochochlear impairment. After PB Max has been obtained, further intensity increases result in decreased speech recognition scores. This pattern can be clearly seen on a performance-intensity function.

Sensation level (SL) the number of decibels above a person's pure tone or speech threshold.

Sensorineural loss a hearing loss caused by a problem to the inner ear, eighth nerve, or central auditory pathways. Sensory refers to inner ear; neural refers to problems in the eighth nerve or central auditory pathways.

Serous otitis media inflammation of the middle ear characterized by the presence of thin, watery, non-infected secretions.

Shadow curve when thresholds in the two ears differ by 40 dB or more, unmasked thresholds in the poor ear will be spuriously low and will resemble the threshold configuration in the good ear. The responses are actually those of the good ear to high-intensity signals that have crossed the head from the poor ear.

Signal-to-noise (S/N) ratio the difference in decibels between a signal (such as speech) and noise presented to the same ear. When the signal is more intense than the noise, the ratio is positive; when the noise is more intense, the ratio is negative; when signal and noise are equal, the S/N ratio is zero.

Sound field thresholds thresholds obtained to stimuli delivered through loudspeakers rather than earphones. Stimuli may be pure tones, noise, or words.

Sound pressure level (SPL) the pressure or strength of a sound expressed in decibels referenced to 0.0002 dynes/cm^2, 0.0002 microbars, or 20 micropascals.

Speech awareness threshold (SAT) the lowest level of speech in decibels to which the client indicates awareness.

Speech detection threshold (SDT) see speech awareness threshold (SAT).

Speech recognition (speech identification) score (%) measure of speech understanding at suprathreshold levels. It usually involves computing the percentage of correctly identified single-syllable words in a list.

Speech recognition threshold (SRT) the lowest level in decibels at which the client can repeat or otherwise respond correctly to 50% of the speech stimuli presented. This measure is also referred to as speech reception threshold.

Speech spectrum noise white noise filtered to resemble the overall spectrum (frequency and intensity composition) of speech. Like speech, it provides more energy in the low frequencies than in the high frequencies.

Spondee threshold (ST) the speech recognition threshold is usually measured using spondee words (two syllables with equal stress on each syllable). Therefore, the SRT is sometimes called the ST.

Standing wave a standing wave occurs when the wavelength of a tone (which is related to its frequency) is similar to the length of an enclosed space, such as the ear canal; the tone interferes with itself through reflections of sound in such a way that there are areas of sound reinforcement and sound cancellation resulting in sound attenuation and other distortions.

Stapedectomy a middle ear operation designed to improve hearing by removing one of the ossicles (stapes) and replacing it with a prosthesis.

Stapediomyringopexy a condition of the middle ear where the retracted tympanic membrane adheres to the head of the stapes.

Stapedius muscle one of the two middle ear muscles whose tendon is attached to the stapes. Contraction of the stapedius muscle in response to an intense acoustic stimulus forms the basis for the acoustic reflex test.

Stapes fixation normally the stapes (the smallest bone in the ossicular chain) vibrates freely in the oval window. In otosclerosis, bony deposits make the stapes rigid in the oval window so that it is no longer free to vibrate.

Static compliance or static admittance the immittance characteristics of the middle ear system in its resting or static state are assessed by determining the volume of air that has immittance characteristics equivalent to those of the middle ear system. Static admittance is a measure of the amplitude of the tympanogram relative to its minimum or tail value.

Susceptance the component of admittance associated with the relationship between mass and compliance (springiness).

Telecoil a coil of wire in a hearing aid that can pick up speech information in the form of electromagnetic energy rather than acoustic energy. It is also referred to as a t-coil, t-switch, or telephone switch.

Threshold of discomfort (TD) see Uncomfortable listening level.

Tinnitus ringing or other ear or head noises.

Transfer or transformer function the efficient transfer of energy from acoustic form in the ear canal to hydraulic form in the cochlea accomplished by the immittance (impedance) matching characteristics of the middle ear system.

Treacher-Collins syndrome an inherited condition resulting in defects of the eyes, abnormally small jaws and outer ears, and the presence of a conductive hearing loss.

Two-frequency average or Fletcher Average the average of pure tone thresholds of the best two of the three speech frequencies.

Tympanic membrane the eardrum. An anatomic structure located at the medial end of the external auditory meatus. It forms the lateral boundary of the middle ear.

Tympanogram a graph representing the dynamic character of the middle ear system, measured at the tympanic membrane, as a function of artifically changing air pressure in the external ear canal.

Tympanosclerosis a condition of the middle ear in which areas of calcification or plaque form on the tympanic membrane or around the ossicles.

Tympanostomy or tympanotomy tube a small tube surgically inserted into the tympanic membrane to provide a pathway for air to enter the middle ear. Typically utilized in the presence of chronic Eustachian tube dysfunction.

Uncomfortable listening level (UCL) the hearing level in decibels (re: audiometric zero) at which the client reports that sound is uncomfortably loud.

Undermasking occurs when a masking noise presented to the non-test ear is not intense enough to mask a signal that has crossed over from the test ear.

Vertigo the sensation of spinning or that surroundings are spinning.

Von Recklinghausen's Disease also known as neurofibromatosis, which is an inherited condition characterized by multiple tumors of cranial and spinal nerves and of the skin, with subcutaneous pigmentation or cafe au lait spots noted on the skin.

White Noise a noise consisting of a broad band of frequencies with all frequencies having equal energy.

Word recognition score the percentage of words identified correctly on a word recognition test. Phonetically balanced (PB) words are usually used for this test.

Glossary

Index

Disability, and hearing loss, 154
Discrimination. *See* Speech discrimination
Disease and hearing loss. *See Specific types*
Division of Vocational Rehabilitation, 368
DNT (did not test), 4
DR. *See* Dynamic range
Dynamic immittance
    and acoustic reflex, 95–97
    and tympanometry, 90–94
Dynamic range, 155–156
Dysarthria, and hearing loss, 320

E

Ear, nose, and throat exam, and hearing loss, sample
    case, 122–124
Ear canal, 90–94
    collapsed, 286
Eardrum. *See* Tympanic membrane
Education, and hearing loss, 100, 315–388
Effective level, 219
EL. *See* Effective level
Elastic reactance, 87
Electroacoustic admittance meter, 89
Electroacoustic immittance instruments, principles of
    operation, 87–90
Electroacoustic impedance bridge, 89
ENT. *See* Ear, nose, and throat exam
Equipment, audiometric, malfunction, 285
Equivalent volume, 89
Eustachian tube, 98–100
Eustachian tube dysfunction
    and acoustic immittance measurement, 85
    and hearing loss, sample case, 42–44, 112–114, 294–
    296
    and immittance measurement, 9
Eustachian tube test, describing, sample case, 146–148
EV. *See* Equivalent volume
External auditory meatus. *See* Ear canal

F

Facial nerve disorder
    and acoustic immittance measurement, 85
    and acoustic reflex decay, 98
    and hearing loss, 159
    and immittance measurement, 9
False negative response, 3, 284, 285
False positive response, 3, 285
Fingerspelling, 155
Fletcher Average, 8, 155
Fractured skull, and hearing loss, sample case, 132–134

Frequency response, 3–8
Functional deafness, 11–12

G

Goodman Severity Scale, 13
*Guidelines for Screening for Hearing Impairment and
    Middle-Ear Disorders,* 100

H

Hair cells, 323
Hard of hearing, 315–316
    and uncomfortable listening level, 155
Headaches, and hearing loss, sample case, 302–304
Hearing aid, 316, 320. *See also* Amplification; Assistive
    listening device; Cochlear implant
    candidate for, 321–322
    determining need for, sample case, 206–214, 358–364,
    366–374
    and most comfortable listening level, 155
    and noise, 161
    review and research projects concerning, 387
Hearing disorder. *See* Hard of hearing; Hearing
    impaired; Hearing loss; *Specific types*
Hearing impaired, 13, 315–316
Hearing level, 4, 316–318
Hearing loss, 1–8, 8–11, 315. *See also* Birth defects and
    hearing loss; Disease and hearing loss; Hard of
    hearing; Hearing disorder; Hearing impaired
    and acoustic immittance measurement, 85–151
    and age of onset, 318
    and audiometric configuration, 14
    and Barany noise box, 130
    classification, 11–14
    cochlear, 282–283
    and conductive problem, 282
    configuration of, 318
    degree of, 12–13, 315–318
    educational and communicative implications of, 315–
    388
    and heredity, sample case, 68–72, 110–112, 140–142
    interpreting degree of, sample case, 32–36, 294–298,
    326–330
    interpreting type of, sample case, 40–82, 110–112,
    118–120, 226–236, 238–248, 264–270, 290–308,
    326–330, 336–348, 364–366
    non-organic, 284–285
    retrocochlear, 283–284
    review and research projects concerning, 387
    type of, 11–12, 318–319
Hemotympanum, and hearing loss, sample case, 130–132